C/C++

Annotated Archives

ABOUT THE AUTHORS ...

Art Friedman is a member of the C++ compiler team at Hewlett Packard where he has contributed extensively in the areas of exception handling and template instantiation. Art has a BS in physics from the Cooper Union and a MSCS from Stanford University. He has been writing software in C and C++ for over 15 years.

Lars Klander, MCSE, MCSD, MCT is the author or co-author of eight books, including *1001 Visual Basic Programmer's Tips* (Jamsa Press), the winner of the 1997 *Visual Basic Programmer's Journal* Reader's Choice award. A professional network security consultant and Microsoft Certified Trainer, Klander has written and contributed to a wide variety of programming and network security topics, including four books about C/C++ programming, both cross-platform and Windows specific. Klander has been a professional author and trainer for several years and a computer professional for well over 15 years. Early training in Pascal and Fortran led him to C in the early 80s and then onto C++, giving him a depth of both programming knowledge and experience. Currently, he develops and maintains Visual C++ client/server applications for a variety of clients, including Nevada Power Company and several privately held corporations. You can reach him at lklander@lvcablemodem.com.

Mark Michaelis lives in Wheaton, IL. He is a senior software engineer at Real World Technology, which specializes in software for the manufacturing industry. He holds a BA in philosophy from the University of Illinois and has a Masters of Computer Science from the Illinois Institute of Technology. When not bonding with his computer, Mark enjoys traveling the globe. He and his wife recently spent eight months in Africa, working at a children's orphanage in Mozambique. Mark is actively involved with his church, is an enthusiastic amateur musician, and loves the outdoors. As a Microsoft MVP Mark can often be found lurking at the microsoft.public.visual.sourcesafe newsgroups and can be contacted at mark@michaelis.net.

Herb Schildt is a leading authority on C and C++ and a best-selling author whose books have sold more than 2 million copies. His acclaimed C and C++ books include *Teach Yourself C, C++ from the Ground Up, Teach Yourself C++, C++: The Complete Reference, Borland C++: The Complete Reference*, and *C++ Programmer's Reference*, to name a few. Schildt is president of Universal Computing Laboratories, Inc., a software consulting firm in Mahomet, Illinois. He holds a master's degree in computer science from the University of Illinois.

Andrew Gayter is an independent software consultant who lives and works in the United Kingdom. After gaining a degree from Oxford in 1991, he specialized in C++ object oriented programming and started his career writing Geographical Information Systems. He then worked on commercial applications for the Support Services. He is currently working as a COM/DCOM consultant to one of England's largest health insurance companies.

C/C++

Annotated Archives

Art Friedman, Lars Klander,
Mark Michaelis, and Herb Schildt

Osborne **McGraw-Hill**

Berkeley   New York   St. Louis   San Francisco   Auckland   Bogotá
Hamburg   London   Madrid   Mexico City   Milan   Montreal   New Delhi
Panama City   Paris   São Paulo   Singapore   Sydney   Tokyo   Toronto

Osborne/**McGraw-Hill**
2600 Tenth Street
Berkeley, California 94710
U.S.A.

For information on translations or book distributors outside the U.S.A., or to arrange
bulk purchase discounts for sales promotions, premiums, or fund-raisers, please
contact Osborne/**McGraw-Hill** at the above address.

C/C++ Annotated Archives

234567890 DOC DOC 90198765432109

ISBN 0-07-882504-0

Publisher Brandon A. Nordin	**Proofreader** Pamela Vevea
Associate Publisher and **Editor-in-Chief** Scott Rogers	**Indexer** Sheryl Schildt
Acquisitions Editor Wendy Rinaldi	**Computer Designers** Mickey Galicia Roberta Steele
Project Editor Madhu Prasher	**Illustrators** Robert Hansen Brian Wells Beth Young
Contributing Author Andrew Gayter	
Editorial Assistant Monika Faltiss	**Series Design** Roberta Steele Peter Hancik
Technical Editor Herbert Schildt	**Cover Design** Regan Honda
Copy Editor Carol Henry	

Contents at a Glance

V

Contents

Foreword

By Herbert Schildt

This is a book by C/C++ programmers for C/C++ programmers. In its 16 chapters you will find some of the most interesting, intriguing, and useful code available anywhere. The programs and subsystems can be used as-is or as a basis for your own development. Whether you are a relative newcomer to programming or a seasoned pro, I am sure that you will be delighted by this book.

This book came about in a rather curious way. Scott Rogers, the Associate Publisher and Editor-in-Chief at Osborne, had an idea for a series of programming books that came to be called the *Annotated Archives*. These books would bring together lots of practical programs and libraries accompanied by complete, in-depth descriptions of the code, suggestions for enhancements, and usage tips. I immediately recognized that this was a great concept that could be turned into an excellent C/C++ programming book. The only trouble was that my writing schedule was already well into "over-commit" and it was not possible for me to write the entire book on my own. (Because of the speed of change and innovation in programming, demands on my writing schedule are always quite heavy.)

This is when Wendy Rinaldi, my main editor at Osborne, became involved. Putting our heads together we came up with a plan. We decided to bring together several authors, each writing about topics in their own areas of special interest. I would contribute two chapters towards the book and then lend guidance and advice to the others. Using this approach we were able to provide top-notch code in a timely fashion while still producing a cohesive book. I think that you will be pleased with the results.

The book begins with five chapters from Art Friedman that cover several of computing's most fundamental algorithms: sorting, searching, linked lists, binary trees, hashing, sparse arrays, and memory management. Art examines each of these topics in depth and provides some sophisticated and elegant implementations. For the most part, Art designed his code as subsystems, so you can plug them right into your next project. Art even implements a set of routines that support balanced binary trees. If you have ever tried to write such code, you know that it is quite tricky.

Lars Klander contributed several chapters on a variety of popular topics, each of which you will find interesting. For example, Lars covers encryption, file utilities, financial and statistical calculations, and fractals. He even provides the code for a simple Internet browser. So, if you want routines that calculate the regular payments on a loan, compute the standard deviation of a sample, encrypt a file, surf the Web, etc., you'll find them in Lars' chapters.

I provided two chapters. The first contains three versions of a recursive descent parser for numeric expressions such as (10+2) / 3. The parser is quite useful in a variety of situations. My other chapter explores language interpreters. As an example, it combines the parser with an interpreter for a small, BASIC-like language. However, the techniques described there can be adapted to create an interpreter for any type of language you like. If you have ever wanted to design your own computer language, then this chapter is definitely for you!

Mark Michaelis provides one quite intriguing chapter that takes an in-depth look at source code management. He provides routines that parse the tokens from a file, format a file, extract header files, and "colorize" a file. What makes all this the more valuable is that you can adapt his routines for any computer language and you can easily extend them.

Finally, Andrew Gayter contributed a chapter that examines aspects of the STL. If the STL is still new ground for you, then you will find this chapter especially helpful.

One last point: Modern coding style that complies with the ANSI/ISO C++ standard is used throughout this book. Thus, the programs will work with any standard compiler. All code was tested with Microsoft's Visual C++ 6 compiler.

HS
Mahomet, Illinois
1999

Sorting

By Art Friedman

bs.cpp	**qs_basic.cpp**
sort.h	**qs.cpp**
ss.cpp	**ms.cpp**

T he need to sort data into ascending or descending order seems nearly ubiquitous in programming applications. Sorted data is at once more meaningful and easier to navigate. Hence sorting is often seen as a worthwhile investment, especially when it can be done efficiently, and techniques for efficient sorting have been widely studied.

Introduction to Sorting

This chapter presents several well-known techniques for sorting data that resides in memory. Two simple methods, *bubble sort* and *selection sort* are relatively *in*efficient, with average running time proportional to the square of *n*, the number of elements being sorted. These methods are easy to understand and implement reliably. When *n* is small, they're often perfectly adequate.

Two other methods, commonly known as *quick sort* and *merge sort*, are more sophisticated and better behaved for large values of *n*. Their average running time is proportional to $n*lg(n)$. When the number of items being sorted is large, these methods have a significant advantage over the simpler ones. Although the average running time for quick sort is quite good, its worst-case performance is unsatisfactory. Because of this, a second variant is given that greatly reduces the chances of seeing that worst-case behavior in practice. Each of the programs in this chapter sorts data into *ascending* order.

Before getting started, some general comments about the code might be helpful. All of the functions are inline template functions. The reason for using templates is, as usual, to allow these functions to handle a variety of data types. The reason for making them inline is twofold. First, some will be more efficient. Second, declaring them inline makes it easy to incorporate them into a header file if desired. Use of the **inline** keyword is not essential and can easily be dropped.

Each program example is set up as a **.cpp** file that includes the **sort.h** header. This header contains two template functions:

◆ **print<T>(T*, int)** prints the values of an array as a linear sequence.

◆ **swap<T>(T*, int, int)** swaps two elements of an array.

These convenience functions are widely used in the examples. Other than that, **sort.h** has no special significance.

Finally, a word about the use of arrays. An array is perhaps the clearest and simplest way to represent a linear sequence of items. Likewise, an array access of the form **data[n]** is perhaps the clearest way to refer to the *n*th element of the array **data**. For this reason, array indices have been favored instead of pointers. Readers concerned with the potential loss of efficiency may wish to modify some of the array traversals to use pointer arithmetic instead.

Bubble Sort

Bubble sort is extremely simple. To see how it works, visualize an array of five elements standing on end, with element 0 on top and element 4 at the bottom, as shown in Figure 1-1a. Bubble sort scans this array from bottom to top. It compares each array element to the one above it, and if the one above is larger, the two are swapped.

For example, the bottom element (element 4) in Figure 1-1a happens to be the smallest. Bubble sort compares it against the value of element 3 (which is 2), and decides to swap them. Then it compares element 3 against element 2 and swaps them, as well. This process continues until the smallest value in the array has "bubbled" up to the very top. At this point element 0 has the correct value and can be ignored by future scans. The result of this first scan is shown in Figure 1-1b.

Bubble sort then applies the same procedure to the subarray consisting of elements 1 through 4, which guarantees that element 1 has the correct value (in this case, 2). In this manner, bubble sort keeps scanning successively smaller subarrays until none are left. At that point the array has been properly sorted.

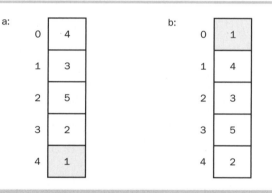

FIGURE 1-1. Bubble sort: The array on the left shows the value 1 in its original position in element 4. The array on the right is the result after "bubbling" this value to its final position in element 0

bs.cpp
sort.h

Code

The file **bs.cpp** contains the code for bubble sort and an example of its usage. Here is **sort.h**, which contains functions used in this and other sort routines in this chapter:

```
#include <iostream>
#include <cassert>
using namespace std;

// File sort.h contains two useful utility functions.


// Swap( ) interchanges the elements in positions
// pos1 and pos2 within array.

template <class T>
inline void swap(T array[], int pos1, int pos2)
{
  T temp;
  temp        = array[pos1];
  array[pos1] = array[pos2];
  array[pos2] = temp;
}


// Print( ) prints out the elements of array
// in a sequence.
template <class T>
inline void print(T array[], int size)
{
  int i;
    for (i=0; i < size; ++i) {
    cout << array[i] << " ";
  }
  cout << endl;
}
```

Here is **bs.cpp**:

```
#include "sort.h"

// File bs.cpp implements bubble_sort( ) template function,
// which sorts the elements of its input array into
// ascending order.  Template type T must support
// operator=( ) and operator<( ).  Copying may be needed
// for initialization.  Operator<<( ) is needed if printing
// is desired.  Array contains the elements to be sorted,
// and size is the number of elements in this array.
```

```cpp
// Sorting is done "in place."  Duplicate elements are
// supported.

template <class T>
inline void bubble_sort(T array[], int size)
{
  int i, j;


  // Upper limit of the outer loop is size-1 rather than
  // size because once all the other elements are in place,
  // the largest has automatically been placed properly.

  for (i=0; i < size-1; ++i) {
    for (j=size-1; j > i; --j ) {
      if (array[j-1] > array[j]) swap(array, j-1, j);
    }
  }
}

int main( )
{
  int array_1[] = {7, 3, 8, 2, 1, 5, 4};
  print(array_1, 7);
  bubble_sort(array_1, 7);
  print(array_1, 7);
  cout << endl;

  int array_2[] = {7, 3, 8, 2, 1, 5, 4, 9, 75, -5};
  print(array_2, 10);
  bubble_sort(array_2, 10);
  print(array_2, 10);
  cout << endl;

  int array_3[] = {1, 2, 3};
  print(array_3, 3);
  bubble_sort(array_3, 3);
  print(array_3, 3);
  cout << endl;

  int array_4[] = {3, 2, 1};
  print(array_4, 3);
  bubble_sort(array_4, 3);
  print(array_4, 3);
  cout << endl;
```

```
    int array_5[] = {3, 2, 1, 3};
    print(array_5, 4);
    bubble_sort(array_5, 4);
    print(array_5, 4);
    cout << endl;

    int array_6[] = {3, 3, 3};
    print(array_6, 3);
    bubble_sort(array_6, 3);
    print(array_6, 3);
    cout << endl;

    return 0;
}
```

Following is the output of **bs.cpp**. Each pair of output lines shows an integer array before and after sorting.

```
7 3 8 2 1 5 4
1 2 3 4 5 7 8

7 3 8 2 1 5 4 9 75 -5
-5 1 2 3 4 5 7 8 9 75

1 2 3
1 2 3

3 2 1
1 2 3

3 2 1 3
1 2 3 3

3 3 3
3 3 3
```

The **bubble_sort(T*, int)** function takes an array parameter along with its size. The entire function consists of an outer loop that controls which subarray is being scanned, and an inner loop that scans a particular subarray and swaps values when necessary. The sort is done in place, and duplicate values are not a problem. Notice that the upper limit of the outer loop is **size-1** rather than **size**. Once all the other elements are known to be in their proper places, the largest element must automatically be in its proper place as well.

The inner **for** loop walks each subarray backwards, opposite to the direction of the outer **for** loop's scan. This can be reversed, with the result that the largest elements "sink" to the bottom rather than the smallest "bubbling" up. The output shows that duplicate values are handled properly.

Selection Sort

Although bubble sort is effective, it does far more work than necessary, even for a simple method. Its most obvious weakness is the number of swaps it performs—instead of moving each element directly to its ultimate home, bubble sort moves elements one cell at a time. *Selection sort* follows a similar overall strategy but addresses this key problem.

When presented with the array in Figure 1-2a, selection sort also scans subarrays looking for the minimum value each time. However, instead of swapping each pair of adjacent values that are out of order, it simply records the index of the minimum value and then performs a *single* swap with the element currently occupying the lowest position. The first scan of Figure1-2a finds that the smallest value, 1, occupies element 4. Once that has been determined, element four and element zero swap values. The result is shown in Figure 1-2b. Selection sort then scans smaller and smaller subarrays in a manner similar to bubble sort.

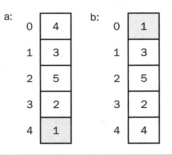

FIGURE 1-2.   Selection sort. The array on the left shows the value 1 in its original position in element 4. The array on the right shows the result after swapping element 0 (i.e. the first array element) with element 4 (the smaller array element)

ss.cpp

Code

File **ss.cpp** contains the code for a selection sort. It produces the same output as **bs.cpp**.

```
#include "sort.h"

// File ss.cpp implements selection_sort( ) template
// function, which sorts the elements of its input
// array into ascending order.  Template type T must
// support operator=( ) and operator<( ).  Copying may
// be needed for initialization.  Operator<<( ) is needed
// if printing is desired.  Array contains the elements
// to be sorted, and size is the number of elements in this
// array.  Sorting is done "in place."  Duplicate elements
// are supported.


// Get_min_index( ) returns the array index corresponding to
// the minimum value of the subarray defined by left and
// right.

template <class T>
inline int get_min_index(T array[], int left, int right)
{
  int min_index = left;
  int i;
```

```
  for (i = left; i <= right; ++i) {
    if (array[i] < array[min_index]) min_index = i;
  }
  return min_index;
}


// Selection_sort( ) works by selecting the proper element for
// each array index, starting at index zero and working its
// way up.

template <class T>
inline void selection_sort(T array[], int size)
{
  int i;
  int min_index;

  // Upper limit of the outer loop is size-1 rather than
  // size because once all the other elements are in place,
  // the largest has automatically been placed properly.

  for (i=0; i < size-1; ++i) {
    min_index = get_min_index(array, i, size-1);
    if (min_index != i) swap(array, i, min_index);
  }
}



int main( )
{
  int array_1[] = {7, 3, 8, 2, 1, 5, 4};
  print(array_1, 7);
  selection_sort(array_1, 7);
  print(array_1, 7);
  cout << endl;

  int array_2[] = {7, 3, 8, 2, 1, 5, 4, 9, 75, -5};
  print(array_2, 10);
  selection_sort(array_2, 10);
  print(array_2, 10);
```

```
    cout << endl;

    int array_3[] = {1, 2, 3};
    print(array_3, 3);
    selection_sort(array_3, 3);
    print(array_3, 3);
    cout << endl;

    int array_4[] = {3, 2, 1};
    print(array_4, 3);
    selection_sort(array_4, 3);
    print(array_4, 3);
    cout << endl;

    int array_5[] = {3, 2, 1, 3};
    print(array_5, 4);
    selection_sort(array_5, 4);
    print(array_5, 4);
    cout << endl;

    int array_6[] = {3, 3, 3};
    print(array_6, 3);
    selection_sort(array_6, 3);
    print(array_6, 3);
    cout << endl;

    return 0;
}
```

ANNOTATIONS

The **ss.cpp** code is similar to that for bubble sort, except for the use of a new function **get_min_index(T*, int, int)**. This function returns the index of the minimum value of the subarray delimited by the function's arguments. The "inner loop" of **selection_sort(T*, int)** is actually a call to this new function.

The call to **swap(T*, int, int)** is made only if the minimum value is not already in place. That way we don't waste time swapping an element with itself. In practice, this strategy may help *or* hurt performance. Clearly, if the input array is already sorted, avoiding these redundant swaps is a good idea. It also helps in situations where the data elements are very large and assigning them is costly. In other situations, the benefit gained may not justify the cost of additional index comparisons.

Basic Quick Sort

Quick sort is fundamentally different from the simple methods considered above. It employs a divide-and-conquer strategy that results in significantly faster execution on the average. It is indeed worthy of its name.

Consider the five-element array shown in Figure 1-3a. Element 0 is shown on the left, and element 4 on the right. The first thing quick sort does is to select a *partition* value from the elements in the array. Any array element at all may be selected as a partition element, but the selection policy has a strong impact on performance. This performance impact will be examined in the following section, which presents an enhanced version of quick sort. For now, we adopt the simple policy of selecting the leftmost array element as the partition element. In our current example, this is element 0, whose value is 3.

The next step is to partition the array into two subarrays, using the partition element value. At the end of this step, the partition value will be in its proper place in the array. All elements to its left (i.e., in the left subarray) will be smaller; all elements to its right will be larger. In this basic version, we do not allow duplicate values.

How is partitioning accomplished? The idea is to set up two pointers—**head** and **tail**—that initially point to the first and last elements of the array. As partitioning proceeds, these pointers move toward each other and eventually meet. At that point, partitioning is complete.

Because partitioning is so central to quick sort, we'll step through the detailed example shown in Figure 1-3. The first step is to compare the tail value (i.e., the value of the element pointed to by **tail**) to the partition value. As long as the tail value is greater than the partition value, we keep moving **tail** to the left; in other words, we decrement it. The result is shown in Figure 1-3b, in which **tail** points to element 2. Next, we do the mirror image of this procedure, using the **head** pointer. We keep moving **head** to the right (by incrementing it) until it points to an element equal to or greater than the partition value. In our current example, this condition is satisfied immediately because element 0 happens to be the partition element. If **head** is still to the left of **tail** (as it is in the current example), we now swap the two values. The result is shown in Figure 1-3c. Because **head** and **tail** have not yet crossed, we continue moving them toward each other as before. The final result is the array in Figure 1-3d. The two pointers have met, and the partition value is in its final position. All values to its left are smaller, and all values to its right are larger. Now that the original array has been partitioned, quick sort calls itself recursively on the left and right subarrays.

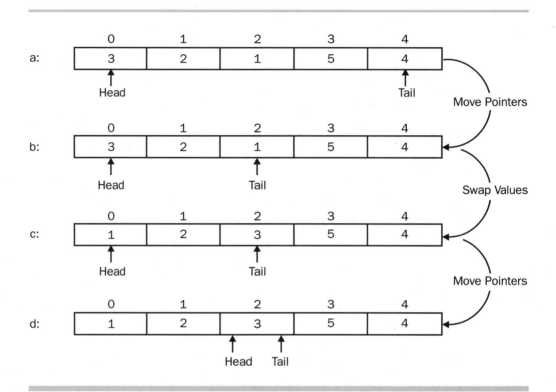

FIGURE 1-3. Quick-sort partitioning (Partition Value is 3)

qs_basic.cpp

Code

Here is file **qs_basic.cpp**:

```
#include "sort.h"

// File qs_basic.cpp implements quick_sort( ) template
// function, which sorts the elements of its input array
// into ascending order.  Template type T must support
// operator=( ) and operator<( ).  Copying may be needed
// for initialization.  Operator<<( ) is needed if printing
// is desired.  Array contains the elements to be
// sorted, and size is the number of elements in this
// array.  Sorting is done "in place."  Duplicate elements
```

```
// are *not* supported.

// Simple version of get_pe( ), just returns first
// array element.
template <class T>
inline int get_pe(T array[], int lower, int upper)
{
  return lower;
}



// Simple version of partition( ), can't handle duplicate
// values.  Partitions the subarray delimited by start and
// end into two smaller subarrays such that all elements in
// the left subarray are smaller than the partition element, and
// all elements in the right subarray are greater.  Hence,
// the partition element itself has been placed in its final
// sorted location.  Returns the array index that now points
// to the partition element.

template <class T>
inline int partition(T array[], int start, int end, int pe_index)
{
  // int k = -1;  // for debugging only.

  // Initialize head and tail to point to the first and
  // last elements of the array.

  T pe = array[pe_index];
  int head = start, tail = end;

  while ( head < tail ) {

    // Decrement tail until we reach an element equal to
    // or smaller than the partition element.
    while ( (array[tail] > pe) ) --tail;
    assert(array[tail] <= pe);

    // Increment head until we reach an element equal to
    // or larger than the partition element.
    while ( (array[head] < pe) ) ++head;
    assert(array[head] >= pe);
```

```
    // Swap head and tail unless they've already crossed.
    if ( head < tail ) swap(array, head, tail);

    // For debugging only.
    // for (k=start; k<=head; ++k) {assert(array[k] <= pe);}
    // for (k=end;   k>=tail; --k) {assert(array[k] >= pe);}
  }

  assert(head == tail);
  assert(array[head] == pe);
  return tail;
}


// Template function qs_helper( ) has primary control of
// the recursion strategy.  After getting the partition
// element, it separates the array into two subarrays
// by calling partition( ).  It then calls itself
// recursively to sort each of these subarrays.

template <class T>
inline void qs_helper(T array[], int head, int tail)
{

  int diff = tail - head;

  // No point trying to sort one element.
  if ( diff < 1 ) return;

  // Special case for 2-eltement array.
  if (diff == 1) {
    if (array[head] > array[tail]) {
      swap(array, head, tail);
      return;
    }
  }

  int pe_index  = get_pe(array, head, tail);

  int mid  = partition(array, head, tail, pe_index);
  assert( (mid >= head) && (mid <= tail) );
```

```
    // The mid'th element now contains the partition value and
    // is in its proper position.  Sort the left and right
    // subarrays.

    qs_helper(array, head,  mid-1);
    qs_helper(array, mid+1, tail);
}


// The interface quick_sort(T array[], int size) is for
// the caller's convenience.  It translates the size
// parameter into a form that's more convenient for
// qs_helper(T array[], int head, int tail), the
// recursive function that does the real work.

template <class T>
inline void quick_sort(T array[], int size)
{
  int head = 0, tail = size-1;
  qs_helper(array, head, tail);
}


int main( )
{
  int array_1[] = {7, 3, 8, 2, 1, 5, 4};
  print(array_1, 7);
  quick_sort(array_1, 7);
  print(array_1, 7);
  cout << endl;

  int array_2[] = {7, 3, 8, 2, 1, 5, 4, 9, 75, -5};
  print(array_2, 10);
  quick_sort(array_2, 10);
  print(array_2, 10);
  cout << endl;

  int array_3[] = {1, 2, 3};
  print(array_3, 3);
  quick_sort(array_3, 3);
  print(array_3, 3);
  cout << endl;
```

```
    int array_4[] = {3, 2, 1};
    print(array_4, 3);
    quick_sort(array_4, 3);
    print(array_4, 3);
    cout << endl;

#if 0
    // Simple version of quick sort does not handle these cases.

    int array_5[] = {3, 2, 1, 3};
    print(array_5, 4);
    quick_sort(array_5, 4);
    print(array_5, 4);
    cout << endl;

    int array_6[] = {3, 3, 3};
    print(array_6, 3);
    quick_sort(array_6, 3);
    print(array_6, 3);
    cout << endl;
#endif
    return 0;
}
```

Here is the output produced by **qs_basic.cpp**. It's identical to the output for bubble sort, except that the two cases involving duplicate values are not shown because this version of quick sort can't handle them.

```
7 3 8 2 1 5 4
1 2 3 4 5 7 8

7 3 8 2 1 5 4 9 75 -5
-5 1 2 3 4 5 7 8 9 75

1 2 3
1 2 3

3 2 1
1 2 3
```

ANNOTATIONS

Function **quick_sort(T*, int)** translates its **size** argument into lower and upper array boundaries and passes them along to **qs_helper(T*, int, int)**, which does the real work. **Qs_helper(T*, int, int)** in turn relies on the two functions **get_pe(T*, int, int)** and **partition(T*, int, int, T)**.

The current version of **get_pe(T*, int, int)** is trivially simple—it just returns its second argument, the index to the leftmost array element. Why dignify this simple operation with a function call? We do it to call attention to the fact that the partition element selection policy can have a critical impact on worst-case performance. Partition element selection is one of quick sort's important building blocks, and separating it in this way facilitates experimentation and tuning. The same can be said for partitioning, which is really the heart of the quick sort algorithm. Examples will be shown in the following section.

PROGRAMMER'S NOTE   *The most natural way to implement quick sort uses recursion, as we've done in our examples. A simple and effective way to reduce the cost of recursion is to use elementary methods for arrays below a certain cutoff size. Note that our version of **qs_helper(T*, int, int)** handles one- and two-element arrays as special cases.*

Enhanced Quick Sort

The worst-case performance for quick sort is, roughly speaking, no better than the performance of the simpler sorting methods. In fact, presenting basic quick sort with an array that's already sorted gives very bad results. Why is this so? The divide-and-conquer strategy depends on roughly halving the problem size with each successive partitioning, and indeed that is what tends to happen on the average. But when our simple partition element selection policy is applied to a sorted array and we choose the leftmost element for the partition element, we clearly do *not* cut the problem in half. In fact, we're left with a subproblem that's nearly the same size as the original.

For the best possible performance, we'd like to choose the median array element as the partition value. But finding the median for each subarray is costly. One way to approximate this result is by choosing the median of the first, last, and middle values for the partition element, and that's exactly what the enhanced version of **get_pe(T*, int, int)** does. This operation has a fixed cost of, at most, three comparisons, and it greatly reduces the odds of worst-case behavior. Another possible approach is to select the partition element randomly.

The other change in this enhanced version is that **partition(T*, int, int, T)** has been upgraded to handle duplicate values. To see an example of why the basic version of quick sort *can't* handle them, consider an array containing the values **[3, 2, 3]**. The partition value is 3, and the partition function of basic quick sort immediately gets stuck in an infinite loop. The enhanced version, however, sorts this array properly.

Code

qs.cpp

Here is file **qs.cpp**. It produces the same output as **bs.cpp**.

```cpp
#include "sort.h"

// File qs.cpp implements quick_sort( ) template function,
// which sorts the elements of its input array into
// ascending order.  Template type T must support
// operator=( ) and operator<( ).  Copying may be needed
// for initialization.  Operator<<( ) is needed if printing
// is desired.  Array contains the elements to be
// sorted, and size is the number of elements in this
// array.  Sorting is done "in place."  Duplicate elements
// are supported.


// This version of get_pe( ) tries to avoid worst case behavior
// by selecting the median of the left, right, and middle
// array values as the partition element.

template <class T>
inline int get_pe(T array[], int lower, int upper)
{
  // Recall that qs_helper does not call get_pe( )
  // for one and two element arrays.  If you modify
  // the code and remove this property, it's probably
  // best to handle these as special cases, e.g.:
  //if ( (upper - lower) < 2 ) return lower;

  assert( (upper - lower) >= 2);

  int mid = (lower + upper) / 2;

  // Simple strategy just tests for each of three possible
  // outcomes.  Requires no more than three comparisons.

  if ( (array[lower] <= array[mid]) ) {
    if (array[mid] <= array[upper]) return mid;
    else if ( array[upper] <= array[lower] ) return lower;
```

```
    else return upper;
  }
  else {
    assert(array[lower] > array[mid]);
    if (array[lower] <= array[upper]) return lower;
    else if ( array[upper] <= array[mid] ) return mid;
    else return upper;
  }
}


// This version of partition handles duplicate values.
// Partitions the subarray delimited by start and end into
// two smaller subarrays such that all elements in the left
// subarray are smaller than the partition element, and all
// elements in the right subarray are greater.  Hence,
// the partition element itself has been placed in its final
// sorted location.  Returns the array index that now points
// to the partition element.

template <class T>
inline int partition(T array[], int start, int end, int pe_index)
{
  // int k = -1;  // for debugging only.

  // Save the partition element value and put the partition element
  // at the extreme right.
  T pe = array[pe_index];
  swap(array, pe_index, end);

  // Initialize head and tail to point to the first and
  // second-to-last elements of the array.
  int head = start, tail = end-1;

  while ( true ) {

    // Increment head until we reach an element equal to
    // or larger than the partition element.
    while ( (array[head] < pe) ) ++head;
    assert(array[head] >= pe);

    // Decrement tail until we reach an element equal to
    // or smaller than the partition element.
```

```
    while ( (array[tail] > pe) && (tail > start) ) --tail;
    assert(array[tail] <= pe);

    // Swap head and tail unless they've already crossed.
    // Forcing the head/tail to increment/decrement following
    // the swap avoids an infinite loop in case they both
    // happen to reference the partition value.
    if ( head >= tail ) break;
    swap(array, head++, tail--);

    // For debugging only.
    // for (k=start; k<=head; ++k) {assert(array[k] <= pe);}
    // for (k=end;   k>=tail; --k) {assert(array[k] >= pe);}
  }
 swap(array, head, end);

  assert(array[head] == pe);
  return head;
}


// Template function qs_helper( ) has primary control of
// the recursion strategy.  After getting the partition
// element, it separates the array into two subarrays
// by calling partition( ).  It then calls itself
// recursively to sort each of these subarrays.

template <class T>
inline void qs_helper(T array[], int head, int tail)
{

  int diff = tail - head;

  // No point trying to sort one element.
  if ( diff < 1 ) return;

  // Special case for 2-element array.
  if (diff == 1) {
    if (array[head] > array[tail]) swap(array, head, tail);
    return;
  }

  int pe_index  = get_pe(array, head, tail);
```

```
  int mid  = partition(array, head, tail, pe_index);
  assert( (mid >= head) && (mid <= tail) );

  // The mid'th element now contains the partition element
  // value and is in its proper position.  Sort the left and right
  // subarrays.

  qs_helper(array, head,  mid-1);
  qs_helper(array, mid+1, tail);
}


// The interface quick_sort(T array[], int size) is
// for the caller's convenience.  It translates
// the size parameter into a form that's more
// convenient for qs_helper(T array[], int head, int tail),
// the recursive function that does the real work.

template <class T>
inline void quick_sort(T array[], int size)
{
  int head = 0, tail = size-1;
  qs_helper(array, head, tail);
}


int main( )
{
  int array_1[] = {7, 3, 8, 2, 1, 5, 4};
  print(array_1, 7);
  quick_sort(array_1, 7);
  print(array_1, 7);
  cout << endl;

  int array_2[] = {7, 3, 8, 2, 1, 5, 4, 9, 75, -5};
  print(array_2, 10);
  quick_sort(array_2, 10);
  print(array_2, 10);
  cout << endl;

  int array_3[] = {1, 2, 3};
  print(array_3, 3);
  quick_sort(array_3, 3);
```

```
int(array_3, 3);
cout << endl;

int array_4[] = {3, 2, 1};
print(array_4, 3);
quick_sort(array_4, 3);
print(array_4, 3);
cout << endl;

int array_5[] = {3, 2, 1, 3};
print(array_5, 4);
quick_sort(array_5, 4);
print(array_5, 4);
cout << endl;

int array_6[] = {3, 3, 3};
print(array_6, 3);
quick_sort(array_6, 3);
print(array_6, 3);
cout << endl;
return 0;
}
```

ANNOTATIONS

As noted, enhanced quick sort is structurally the same as the basic version. It differs only in its implementation of **get_pe(T*, int, int)** and **partition(T*, int, int, int)**. Because its caller handles arrays of size 1 and 2 as special cases, **get_pe(T*, int, int)** assumes that its input array has at least three elements. This assumption is captured in the initial **assert** statement.

The middle array index, **mid**, is calculated as the mean of the arguments **upper** and **lower**. For arrays with an even number of elements, the result is truncated and **mid** takes the smaller of the two possible values. A standard technique for finding the median is to sort the elements and then choose the middle value. Because there are only three elements involved, it's reasonable to do a fixed sequence of comparisons instead and thereby avoid the unnecessary overhead of swapping values. The **get_pe(T*, int, int)** function accomplishes this with either two or three comparisons, depending on the input. Its return value is the array index that corresponds to the partition element value. We return the index instead of the value because **partition(T*, int, int, int)** uses this index to swap the partition element value to a special location. It's essential that the run-time cost of **get_pe(T*, int, int)** *not* increase with the size of the array.

The revisions to **partition(T*, int, int, int)**, though not extensive, change its behavior significantly. Its first action is to swap the partition element with the rightmost element, which will be kept here throughout most of the partitioning process and swapped into its rightful place at the very end. The main **while** loop is now infinite, i.e., the loop termination conditions are tested inside the loop rather than at the beginning.

The loops for incrementing **head** and decrementing **tail** are largely the same. The loop that decrements **tail** now has an additional test to be sure that **tail** doesn't fall off the beginning of the array. This is followed by the loop termination test. The loop terminates whenever **head** and **tail** meet or have crossed. The following statement swaps the elements referenced by **head** and **tail**, and forces them to be incremented/ decremented. This assures that the main loop will terminate even if head and tail both point to partition element values.

Each iteration of the main loop guarantees that no elements to the left of head are larger than the partition element, and that no elements to the right of tail are smaller. After the pointers meet or cross, we swap the rightmost element with **head**. This maintains that condition as well, and also guarantees that the left and right subarrays are separated by at least one partition element. These changes to **partition(T*, int, int, int)** make it capable of handling duplicate values correctly.

Merge Sort

While quick sort's average performance is impressive, we've seen that its worst-case performance is poor. We've also seen how to greatly reduce the odds of worst-case performance.

Merge sort employs a comparable divide-and-conquer strategy with similar average performance, but *without* the problem of poor worst-case performance. Even so, merge sort is not perfect either. Although the other programs in this chapter sort an array *in place*, merge sort requires a second array of equal size for temporary storage. If memory is plentiful and it's important to guarantee against worst-case behavior, merge sort may be a good choice.

Unlike quick sort, merge sort's partitioning scheme is simple. It just cuts the array in half to form two subarrays. No partition element is selected and no subtle pointer crossing scheme is needed. Merge sort then calls itself recursively on each of the two subarrays to sort them. The final step is to merge the two sorted subarrays into one sorted array. This, also, is uncomplicated, but it requires a temporary array to store the results. Notice that the real work is done while unwinding from the call stack.

Code

Here is file **ms.cpp**. It produces the same output as **bs.cpp**.

```cpp
#include "sort.h"

// File ms.cpp implements merge_sort( ) template function,
// which sorts the elements of its input array into
// ascending order.  Template type T must support
// operator=( ) and operator<( ).  Copying may be needed
// for initialization.  Operator<<( ) is needed if printing
// is desired.  Supporting template functions are
// ms_helper( ) and merge( ).  All functions are declared
// inline so they may be used in headers if desired.
// Duplicate elements are supported.


// Merge( ) views array as the concatenation of two subarrays,
// one  consisting of elements start through mid, and the
// other consisting of elements mid+1 through end.   It
// assumes each of these subarrays is sorted and merges them
// into temp_array.  It then copies temp_array back into array.
// Upon return, array has been sorted into ascending order.

template <class T>
inline void merge(T array[], T temp_array[],
         int start, int mid, int end)
{
  int i_temp = 0, i_lower = start, i_upper = mid+1;

  // This loop is live as long as neither subarray
  // is empty.
  while ( (i_lower <= mid) && (i_upper <= end) ) {
    if (array[i_lower] < array[i_upper])
      temp_array[i_temp++] = array[i_lower++];
    else
      temp_array[i_temp++] = array[i_upper++];
  }

  // If either of the subarrays has elements left over, just
  // copy them into temp_array.
  if (i_lower <= mid ) {
    assert(i_upper > end);
```

```
    for (; i_lower <= mid;
      temp_array[i_temp++] = array[i_lower++]) ;
  }
  else {
    assert(i_lower > mid);
    assert(i_upper <= end);
    for (; i_upper <= end;
      temp_array[i_temp++] = array[i_upper++]) ;
  }

  // array size is end - start + 1.
  assert(i_temp == end - start + 1);

  // Now, copy temp_array back into array.
  int i_array = start;
  for (i_temp = 0; i_array <= end;
      array[i_array++] = temp_array[i_temp++]) ;
}


// Ms_helper( ) is the recursive function in charge of
// strategy.  It partitions its input array by simply
// dividing it in half, calls itself recursively to sort
// each half, and then merges the resulting sorted
// subarrays.  The work of sorting is done by merge( )
// while unwinding from the call stack.

template <class T>
inline void ms_helper(T array[], T temp_array[],
            int head, int tail)
{
  // No point trying to sort one element.
  if (head == tail) return;
  assert(tail > head);

  // Find array's mid point.
  int mid = (head + tail) / 2;
  assert( (mid >= head) && mid <= tail);

  // Recursively sort each subarry.
  ms_helper(array, temp_array, head,  mid);
  ms_helper(array, temp_array, mid+1, tail);
```

```
    // Merge the results.
    merge(array, temp_array, head, mid, tail);
}


// The interface merge_sort(T array[], int size) is
// for the caller's convenience.  It translates the size
// parameter into a form that's more convenient for
// ms_helper(T array[], int head, int tail), the
// recursive function that does the real work.  To avoid
// the need to allocate and release temporary arrays for
// each invocation of merge( ), that job is done here once.

template <class T>
inline void merge_sort(T array[], int size)
{
    int head = 0, tail = size-1;
    T *temp_array = new T[size];
    ms_helper(array, temp_array, head, tail);
    delete[] temp_array;
}



// The following program initializes some arrays,
// prints them, sorts them and prints them again.
// Duplicate values are permitted.

int main( )
{
    int array_1[] = {7, 3, 8, 2, 1, 5, 4};
    print(array_1, 7);
    merge_sort(array_1, 7);
    print(array_1, 7);
    cout << endl;

    int array_2[] = {7, 3, 8, 2, 1, 5, 4, 9, 75, -5};
    print(array_2, 10);
    merge_sort(array_2, 10);
    print(array_2, 10);
    cout << endl;

    int array_3[] = {1, 2, 3};
    print(array_3, 3);
```

```
merge_sort(array_3, 3);
 print(array_3, 3);
 cout << endl;

 int array_4[] = {3, 2, 1};
 print(array_4, 3);
 merge_sort(array_4, 3);
 print(array_4, 3);
 cout << endl;

 int array_5[] = {3, 2, 1, 3};
 print(array_5, 4);
 merge_sort(array_5, 4);
 print(array_5, 4);
 cout << endl;

 int array_6[] = {3, 3, 3};
 print(array_6, 3);
 merge_sort(array_6, 3);
 print(array_6, 3);
 cout << endl;

 return 0;
}
```

ANNOTATIONS

The overall structure of this merge sort code is similar to quick sort's. The **merge_sort(T*, int)** function calls **ms_helper(T*, T*, int, int)**, which is the function that controls recursion and merging strategy. In addition to translating its arguments into more convenient form, **merge_sort(T*, int)** allocates a temporary array that will be needed by **merge(T*, T*, int, int, int)**. This is done here because **merge_sort(T*, int)** knows the size of the input array and is able to allocate the temporary storage once at the beginning. Passing this array to the other functions as an argument is a bit clumsy, but it's preferable to the alternative of having **merge(T*, T*, int, int, int)** allocate and de-allocate temporary storage each time the function is called.

The real work horse of this algorithm is **merge(T*, T*, int, int, int)**. It views its first argument, **array**, as two subarrays whose boundaries are delimited by the arguments **start**, **mid**, and **end**. It assumes that each of these subarrays is already sorted and merges them into **temp_array** by walking up both of them in parallel, and at each step choosing the smaller of the two elements to copy into **temp_array**. This is implemented in the initial **while** loop.

Notice that separate array indices are maintained for each of the three arrays of interest. Index **i_lower** points to the current element of the lower, or left subarray. Index **i_upper** does the same for the upper, or right subarray. Index **i_temp** tracks the current element of **temp_array**, which is used for temporary storage during the merging process. Each of these indices traverses its array in ascending order. **i_lower** [**i_upper**] is incremented only when the current element of the left [right] subarray is selected for copying. **i_temp** is incremented no matter which subarray is selected.

When the elements of either subarray have been used up, there's no need to do further comparisons. The remaining elements of the nonempty subarray are then simply copied into the remaining slots of **temp_array**. **temp_array** now contains all the sorted elements. The final step is to copy them back into **array**.

Linked Lists

By Art Friedman

slist_1.h   dlist_1.h
slist_1.cpp   dlist_1.cpp
slist_2.h   dlist_2.h
slist_2.cpp   dlist_2.cpp

L*inked lists* are among the most fundamental data structures. While nearly all programmers have at least a nodding acquaintance with them, they have a number of subtleties that make them more interesting than one might at first expect. This chapter explores linked lists in some detail and provides examples of their implementation.

The term *container* has come into common usage in the C++ community. A container is a data structure whose main purpose is to contain other objects in a well specified way. One example of a container is the *array*, a structure that is built into the language. Lists are good examples of container *classes*. In this chapter we'll explore some important aspects of container class design, using lists as a model.

Keep in mind that there are a great many ways to implement lists. The code presented here is meant to show some of the possibilities and suggest others. It's intended as a starting point and makes no claim to be "best" in any meaningful sense—you can almost certainly improve it and enhance it to meet your specific needs. But you won't have to start with a blank page.

Introduction to Linked Lists

Linked lists are simple data structures that are commonly used as building blocks for stacks, queues, hash tables, and a host of other things. There are few programmers, if any, who haven't encountered linked lists in one form or another. Abstractly, a linked list represents a sequence of objects or values, as does an array. However, unlike an array, a linked list has no fixed size—it can grow or shrink as needed. This flexibility is essential when the number of objects in the list is unknown until runtime.

Figure 2-1 shows what a singly linked list looks like in memory. Each element of the list consists of two separate items: the actual data you're storing and a pointer to the next list element, if any. An element is allocated from memory only when needed, and hooked up to the rest of the list with pointers. When a list element is no longer needed, its memory is released. In exchange for this added flexibility, access to members of the list is a bit more complex than for arrays, and there's more memory overhead. This is often a reasonable trade-off.

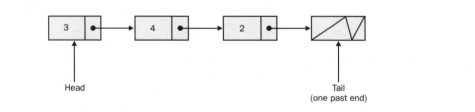

FIGURE 2-1. Memory layout for a singly linked list containing the numbers 3, 4, and 2

Despite the simplicity of the linked list structure, there are many choices to be made when implementing one. Here are some of them:

◆ What type or types of object does the list contain?

◆ How can we tell when the list is empty?

◆ How will errors, such as trying to remove an object from an empty list, be reported?

◆ What operations are needed?

◆ How often do we need to add or remove elements from the middle of the list?

◆ Do we need to traverse the list in both directions or only one?

◆ Do we need to know the number of objects in the list at any given time? If so, should we keep track or just count them when necessary?

This section demonstrates a sequence of linked list examples in C++, along with suggestions as to how they might be extended. The first examples are simple, and each subsequent one adds a new feature that addresses some problem or limitation of its predecessor.

In terms of complexity and sophistication, these examples are far simpler than the Standard Template Library (STL) implementation of lists. Most C++ programmers have ready access to the heavy-duty machinery provided by STL. This chapter's examples are intended to provide some lighter-weight alternatives.

Implementing Lists in C: Note that lists are often implemented in C. To write C versions of the first two examples in this chapter, you can essentially pull the member functions outside the classes, change the word **class** to **struct**; you'll also need to eliminate other C++ keywords such as **private**. In this chapter C++ was used instead because it allows lists to be written as abstract data types—it's possible to provide the needed interface without exposing too much of the underlying implementation. Data structures designed in this way are likely to be far more robust.

List Templates: Finally, C++ allows us to write *templates*, so that any list we implement may be used for a large variety of underlying data types, not just the one we had in mind when designing the list.

PROGRAMMER'S NOTE *Before we get underway, be aware that the linked list examples presented here make extensive use of private nested classes, friend classes, and so on. There's a very good reason for this: It gives the user adequate control but prevents user code from relying too much on implementation details. The potential problem with this approach, however, is that, at this writing, there's still some variation in the way C++ compilers interpret access rules. As a result, your particular compiler may not accept the code exactly as written. If this happens, you can work around the problem by selectively changing some of the private declarations to be public instead. But try to avoid doing this if possible.*

Singly Linked Lists

As shown in Figure 2-1, the elements of a singly linked list have just one pointer to the next element. This means the list can only be traversed in one direction, starting at the head and following the "next" pointers toward the tail. Finding an element with a particular value takes time proportional to the length of the list, because each element must be examined until the desired one is found. Operations such as deletions are limited, as you'll see in the examples. On the positive side, these lists are uncomplicated so it's very efficient to add or remove elements at the head. These simple data structures are ideal for implementing a stack.

All the lists in this chapter have an extra node that's one link beyond the true end of the list. This "one past the end" node imitates STL containers, which define "one past the end" iterators in a similar way. The presence of this node, permanently referenced by the "tail" pointer, makes it very easy to test the list for emptiness. It also allows some fast operations on the back end of the list.

Simple Singly Linked List

The first example, which we'll call **slist_1**, is the simplest. Class **Single_list** implements a list of integers. Note that the parameters and return values of the relevant member functions are integers rather than specialized nodes that contain integers.

Code

slist_1.h
slist_1.cpp

The code is organized into two files: **slist_1.h** is the list itself, and **slist_1.cpp** shows an example of its use. First, here is **slist_1.h**.

```cpp
// File slist_1.h
// Simple non-template singly linked list of integers.
#include <cassert>

class Single_list {

private:
  class Single_node {

    // Single_node's only purpose is to support class Single_list.
    // That's why all its members are private and class Single_list
    // is a friend.
```

```cpp
    friend class Single_list;

    // Make a Single_node with a meaningful value.
    Single_node(int node_val) : val(node_val) { }

    // Make an empty Single_node.
    Single_node( ) { }

    ~Single_node( ) { }

    Single_node *next;   // Points to the next Single_node.
    int val;             // The data.
};

  Single_node *head;     // Points to front end of list.
  Single_node *tail;     // Points to a node one past the end of list.

  // Privately declared, and undefined assignment and copy,
  // to suppress these operations.

  Single_list & operator=(const Single_list &);
  Single_list(const Single_list &);

public:

  // Make an empty list.
  Single_list( )  {
    // Empty "one past the end" node.
    head = tail = new Single_node;
    tail->next = 0;
  }

  // Make a list that contains a single element.
  Single_list(int node_val)  {
    // Empty "one past the end" node.
    head = tail = new Single_node;

    tail->next = 0;
    add_front(node_val);
  }

  // Walk the list from head to tail, delete each element.
```

```
~Single_list( )  {

  Single_node *node_to_delete = head;
  for (Single_node *sn = head; sn != tail;) {
    sn = sn->next;
    delete node_to_delete;
    node_to_delete = sn;
  }

  // assert( node_to_delete == tail );
  delete node_to_delete;
}

bool is_empty( ) const {return head == tail;}

// Add a new element to the head of the list.
void add_front(int node_val)  {
  Single_node *node_to_add = new Single_node(node_val);
  node_to_add->next = head;
  head = node_to_add;
}

// Remove an element from the head of the list.
// Note that remove_front( ) releases the memory used
// by the removed element, so it must handle empty
// lists properly.  Otherwise, it could delete a
// Single_node that should not be deleted.

int remove_front( ) {
  if ( is_empty( ) ) throw "tried to remove from an empty list";

  Single_node *node_to_remove = head;
  int return_val = node_to_remove->val;
  head = node_to_remove->next;
  delete node_to_remove;
  return return_val;
}

// Returns true if list contains node_val, false otherwise.
bool find(const int node_val) const {
  for (Single_node *sn = head; sn != tail; sn = sn->next) {
    if (sn->val == node_val) return true;
  }
```

```
    return false;
  }


  // Returns the value of the nth list element.  User must make
  // sure element_num is at least one, and no bigger than the
  // list size.  Enables user to print the list for testing,
  // although not efficiently.

  int get_nth(const int element_num) const {

    if (element_num < 1)     throw "get_nth argument less than one";

    int count = 1;
    for (Single_node *sn = head; sn != tail; sn = sn->next) {
      if (count++ == element_num) return sn->val;
    }

    throw "element_num exceeds list size";
  }

  // Returns the size of the list by counting elements.
  // Inefficient because we assume this is done infrequently
  // for testing, and we'd rather spend extra time here than
  // spend it incrementing a new size variable each time we
  // add or remove an element.

  int size( ) const {
    int count = 0;
    for (Single_node *sn = head; sn != tail; sn = sn->next) ++count;
    return count;
  }

};
```

Here is **slist_1.cpp**.

```
// File slist_1.cpp

extern "C" printf(char *, ...);
#include "slist_1.h"

// Print_slist print all values in a Single_list.
```

```
// Uses Single_list member functions size( ) and
// get_nth(int).  This implementation is inefficient
// because get_nth(int) walks the entire list preceding
// the nth element each time it's called.  This is
// addressed in later examples.
//

void print_slist(const Single_list & sl)  {

  int list_size = sl.size( );

  if (list_size == 0)
    printf("empty list\n");
  else {
    int elt = 1;
    while ( elt <= list_size ) {
      printf("%d ", sl.get_nth(elt++) );
    }
    printf("\n");
  }
}



// The following main program gives some simple examples of how
// slist_1 is used.

Single_list my_list;     // Create an empty Single_list.

int main( )
{

  // Add some values to the front.
  for ( int val = 0; val < 5; ++val ) {
    my_list.add_front(val);
    print_slist(my_list);
  }


  // Now remove them one at a time.  To empty the
  // list, we don't need to know its length.
  while ( ! my_list.is_empty( ) ) {
    print_slist(my_list);
    my_list.remove_front( );
  }
```

```
    return 0;


}
```

The **slist_1** program gives the following output. Each line of output shows the current contents of **my_list**, as it grows and then shrinks.

```
0
1 0
2 1 0
3 2 1 0
4 3 2 1 0
4 3 2 1 0
3 2 1 0
2 1 0
1 0
0
```

ANNOTATIONS

Class **Single_list** uses a specialized node for linking integer values together. Exposing the structure of this node would provide greater control (and complexity) for the user. It would also restrict us from changing the implementation of **Single_list** in the future.

For this first example we prefer simplicity and robustness. Therefore, the specialized link nodes are implemented as a private nested class called **Single_list::Single_node**. Users of **Single_list** are spared the necessity of knowing the structure—or even the existence of **Single_list::Single_node**, for that matter—and can focus instead on the integers they wish to manipulate. The other private members of **Single_list** (**head** and **tail**) point to nodes representing the head and tail of the list. Note that the tail node is really "one past the end" of the list.

Single_list has two constructors. The default constructor makes an empty list, and **Single_list(int)** makes a list that contains one element. The destructor just walks the list and deletes each **Single_node**.

The member functions **is_empty( )** and **find(const int)** both return **bool** values. The **is_empty( )** function returns true whenever **head** and **tail** point to the same node; that is, whenever the only node in the list is the "one past the end" tail node.

The name **find** is slightly misleading in this simple example, because it doesn't return a location that can be used later. Instead, it just tells you whether its parameter is currently a member of the list. The **find(int)** function walks through the list sequentially until it either finds a node with the requested value (returns **true**) or reaches the end (returns **false**). Later in this chapter, the template version of **class**

Double_list shows a version of **find** that returns an iterator, and thus removes this limitation. That technique can be applied to **Single_list**, as well.

The important work is done by **add_front(int)** and **remove_front( )**. The **add_front(int)** function creates a new list element and adds it to the front of the list. The memory for this element is dynamically allocated using the **new** operator. Let's examine this short function line by line.

```
// Add a new element to the head of the list.

void add_front(int node_val)  {
  Single_node *node_to_add = new Single_node(node_val);
  node_to_add->next = head;
  head = node_to_add;
}
```

On the first line, we see that it takes an **int** parameter and returns **void**, because there's no other useful information to return. However, an application might benefit from a return value to report errors. For example, it's possible for the **new** operator to fail if the system runs out of dynamic memory. The next line allocates the **Single_node** that will contain the new integer value. That value is initialized by the **Single_node(int)** constructor that appears in the **new** expression. The third line initializes the new node's **next** pointer by making it point to the current head of the list. Finally in the fourth line, we make **head** point to the new node. Getting this "pointer surgery" right can be tricky. Having tested code available in the form of a member function helps prevent the occurrence of a broad category of defects.

Remove_front( ) does the opposite of **add_front(int)**: It removes the first element from the list and releases that element's memory.

PROGRAMMER'S NOTE   *In the **Remove_front( )** function, we must handle errors—because trying to remove an element from an empty list is a fairly common mistake and the results could be disastrous. In particular, we must be sure not to delete a node that shouldn't be deleted; this can cause memory corruption that doesn't show up until later in the program. Errors of this kind are very hard to debug.*

Single_list is a ready-made stack if you think of **add_front(int)** as a "push" operation and **remove_front( )** as a "pop."

File **slist_1.cpp** shows how to use **class Single_list** in a working program. First, notice that the user has to implement the **print_slist( )** function. It may be reasonable to omit a printing function from the class itself if it's only used occasionally for debugging. In this case, the user-implemented function, though inefficient, is adequate. (Later examples in this chapter provide **print( )** member functions for convenience and efficiency.) The **main( )** program creates an empty list, adds a few elements, and then removes them until the list is again empty. **Print_list( )** shows the result after each change.

Singly Linked List Template

This second example, **slist_2**, significantly extends the capability of the simple linked list. These are the major differences:

◆ The **slist_2** example is a *template*. This means it can be used to make lists of many different kinds of objects, not just integers. To illustrate this point, our code example shows a list of **float** values. There are some restrictions on the kinds of objects our list template can handle, but most of the types we care about turn out to be acceptable.

◆ The **slist_2** example implements what we'll call an *enumerator*. Each list we create has a "current" element, which we can access or operate on by calling member functions designed for the task. This provides greater flexibility and efficiency without exposing the internals to the user.

◆ The **next** field of the tail node is pressed into service by making it point to the last list element. Recall that in **slist_1**, this field is always null. This simple change makes it possible to write a new member function, **add_rear(int)**, that efficiently appends a value to the end of the list. Having the ability to add elements to the rear and remove them from the front means we can use **slist_2** to implement a queue.

◆ A **print( )** member function is supplied.

PROGRAMMER'S NOTE *We still don't have the ability to efficiently remove the last element. To do that, we'd have to maintain a pointer to the second-to-last element, so we could make its **next** field point to **tail**. It's possible to do this by redefining **tail** so that it has two pointer fields, rather than a pointer field and an (unused) data field. We choose instead to take the simpler approach. Doubly linked lists, described later in this chapter, have a structure that better supports efficient insertions and deletions at any location.*

Code

slist_2.h
slist_2.cpp

The code is organized into two files. The **slist_2.h** file is the list itself, and **slist_2.cpp** shows an example of its use. Here is **slist_2.h**.

```
// File slist_2.h
// Singly linked list template.
//
// Major extension to slist_1: Enumerator.
//
// Incremental extensions to slist_1:  add_rear(T) and print( ).
```

```
//
// Type T must define operator==( ) to support find(T),
// and operator<<( ) to support print( ).
//

#include <cassert>
#include <iostream>
using namespace std;

template <class T>
class Single_list {

private:
  class Single_node {

    friend class Single_list<T>;

    // Make a Single_node with a meaningful value.
    Single_node(T node_val) : val(node_val) { }

    // Make an empty Single_node.
    Single_node( ) { }

    ~Single_node( ) { }

    // Print the value.
    void print_val( ) const {cout << val << " ";}

    Single_node *next;   // Points to the next Single_node.
    T val;               // The data.
  };

  Single_node *head;     // Points to front end of list.
  Single_node *tail;     // Points to a node one past the end of list.
  Single_node *current;  // Points to current node. Supports
enumeration.

  // Privately declared, and undefined assignment and copy,
  // to suppress these operations.

  Single_list & operator=(const Single_list &);
  Single_list(const Single_list &);
```

```cpp
    // Utility function called by Single_node(T), add_front(T),
    // and add_rear(T).

    void add_to_empty(T node_val) {
      Single_node *node_to_add = new Single_node(node_val);
      node_to_add->next = head;
      head = node_to_add;
      tail->next = head;
      current = head;
    }

public:

    // Make an empty list.
    Single_list( ) {
      head = tail = new Single_node;
      tail->next = 0;
      current = tail;
    }

    // Make a list that contains a single element.
    Single_list(T node_val) {
      head = tail = new Single_node;
      tail->next = 0;
      add_to_empty(node_val);
    }

    // Walk the list from head to tail, delete each element.
    ~Single_list( )  {

      Single_node *node_to_delete = head;
      for (Single_node *sn = head; sn != tail;) {
        sn = sn->next;
        delete node_to_delete;
        node_to_delete = sn;
      }

      // assert( node_to_delete == tail );
      delete node_to_delete;
    }
    bool is_empty( ) const {return head == tail;}
```

```
// Add a new element to the head of the list.
// Note special handling for empty lists because
// tail->next is 0, and therefore tail->next->next
// is meaningless.

void add_front(T node_val)  {
  if ( is_empty( ) )
    add_to_empty(node_val);
  else {
    Single_node *node_to_add = new Single_node(node_val);
    node_to_add->next = head;
    head = node_to_add;
  }
}


// Add a new element to the rear of the list.
// Note special handling for empty lists because
// tail->next is 0, and therefore tail->next->next
// is meaningless.

void add_rear(T node_val)  {
  if ( is_empty( ) )
    add_to_empty(node_val);
  else {
    Single_node *node_to_add = new Single_node(node_val);
    node_to_add->next = tail;
    tail->next->next  = node_to_add;
    tail->next        = node_to_add;
  }
}


// Remove an element from the head of the list.
// Note that remove_front( ) releases the memory used
// by the removed element, so it must handle empty
// lists properly.  Otherwise, it could delete a
// Single_node that should not be deleted.

T remove_front( ) {
  if ( is_empty( ) ) throw "tried to remove from an empty list";
```

```
    Single_node *node_to_remove = head;
    T return_val = node_to_remove->val;
    head = node_to_remove->next;

    // Except for constructors, and adding to an empty list,
    // this is the only place current changes as a side effect.
    if (current == node_to_remove) current = node_to_remove->next;

    delete node_to_remove;
    return return_val;
}


// Returns true if list contains node_val, false otherwise.
bool find(T node_val) const {
    for ( Single_node *sn = head; sn != tail; sn = sn->next ) {
        if ( sn->val == node_val ) return true;
    }
    return false;
}


// Returns the value of the nth list element.  User must make
// sure element_num is at least one, and no bigger than the
// list size.

T get_nth(const int element_num) const {

    if ( element_num < 1 ) throw "get_nth argument less than one";

    int count = 1;
    for ( Single_node *sn = head; sn != tail; sn = sn->next ) {
        if ( count++ == element_num ) return sn->val;
    }

    throw "element_num exceeds list size";
}

// Returns the size of the list by counting elements.
// Inefficient because we assume this is done infrequently
// for testing, and we'd rather spend extra time here than
// spend it incrementing a new size variable each time we
// add or remove an element.
```

```cpp
int size( ) const {
  if ( is_empty( ) ) return 0;
  int count = 0;
 for ( Single_node *sn = head; sn != tail; sn = sn->next ) ++count;
  return count;
}



// Prints out list more conveniently and efficiently than
// possible with slist_1.
void print( ) const {
  for ( Single_node *sn = head; sn != tail; sn = sn->next ) {
    sn->print_val( );
  }
  cout << endl;
}


//
// Functions to support enumeration start here
//

void reset_current( ) { current = head; }

bool increment_current( ) {
  if ( current != tail )  {
    current = current->next;
    return true;
  }
  return false;
}

// Calling get_current when current == tail is undefined.
// User must check.
T get_current( ) const  { return current->val; }

bool current_is_tail( ) const { return current == tail; }

// Note that current remains unchanged.
bool insert_after_current( const T node_val )  {
  if ( current_is_tail( ) ) return false;
```

```
    Single_node *node_to_add = new Single_node(node_val);
    node_to_add->next = current->next;
    current->next = node_to_add;
  }

};
```

Here is **slist_2.cpp**.

```
// File slist_2.cpp
#include "slist_2.h"

// The following main program gives some simple examples of how
// slist_2 is used, with a type parameter of float.

Single_list<float> my_list;  // Create an empty Single_list

int main()
{

  // Add some values to the front.

  float f = 0.0;
  for ( int val = 0; val < 5; ++val ) {
    my_list.add_front(f);
    my_list.add_rear(f);
    my_list.print( );
    f += 0.1F;
  }

  // Print the list, with reasonable efficiency, using
  // enumerator functions.

  my_list.reset_current( );
  while ( ! my_list.current_is_tail( ) )  {
    cout << my_list.get_current( ) << " ";
    my_list.increment_current( );
  }
  cout << endl;

  // Now remove them one at a time.  To empty the
  // list, we don't need to know its length.
```

```
while ( ! my_list.is_empty( ) ) {
  my_list.remove_front( );
  my_list.print( );
}

return 0;
}
```

The output from **slist_2** is shown just below. Each line of output shows the current contents of **my_list**, as it grows and then shrinks. When building the list up, we add two elements before each call to **print( )**. When cutting it back down, we print after each element is removed. The full-sized list is printed twice—once using **print( )**, and once using enumerator functions.

```
0  0
0.1 0 0 0.1
0.2 0.1 0 0 0.1 0.2
0.3 0.2 0.1 0 0 0.1 0.2 0.3
0.4 0.3 0.2 0.1 0 0 0.1 0.2 0.3 0.4
0.4 0.3 0.2 0.1 0 0 0.1 0.2 0.3 0.4
0.3 0.2 0.1 0 0 0.1 0.2 0.3 0.4
0.2 0.1 0 0 0.1 0.2 0.3 0.4
0.1 0 0 0.1 0.2 0.3 0.4
0 0 0.1 0.2 0.3 0.4
0 0.1 0.2 0.3 0.4
0.1 0.2 0.3 0.4
0.2 0.3 0.4
0.3 0.4
0.4
```

ANNOTATIONS

Like **slist_1**, the code for **slist_2** is organized into two files. We'll focus here on the differences between **slist_1** and **slist_2**.

The very first line of the template definition is

```
template <class T>
```

This means we can make a list of items of "arbitrary" type **T**—"arbitrary" because there are some restrictions. Generally speaking, the author of a template has to make some assumptions about the operators supported by the type arguments passed in by the user. It's important to pay close attention to these assumptions and make sure they're reasonable and clearly spelled out.

In **slist_2**, the **find(T)** member function relies on **operator==( )**, so type **T** must support it. Similarly, **print( )** assumes that type **T** supports **operator<<( )**. There are no other restrictions. But note that if you modify **slist_2**, you may need to add some restrictions of your own. For example, if you decide to add a **sort( )** member function, type **T** will have to support a comparison function, such as **operator<( )**.

Enumeration support is provided by a private data member, **current**, of type **Single_list::Single_node ***, and several new member functions:

◆ **reset_current( )** makes **current** point to the head of the list.

◆ **increment_current( )** makes **current** point to the "next" element in the list, if there is one. In that case it returns **true**. If **current** is already pointing to **tail** (one past the end), **increment_current( )** makes no change and returns **false**.

◆ **get_current( )** returns the value of the **current** element. This value is undefined when **current** points to **tail**, and the caller is responsible for checking this condition. The function **current_is_tail( )** is provided for just that purpose. It returns **true** unless **current** points to **tail**.

◆ **insert_after_current(const T)** inserts a new node after **current** unless **current** points to **tail**. In that case, it returns **false**. Note that **insert_after_current(const T)** leaves **current** itself unchanged.

There is no function here called **decrement_current( )** because it makes little sense to walk backward through a singly linked list. The "backward" pointers just don't exist. (Such a function would be essential, however, if enumeration support is desired for a *doubly* linked list. We don't provide an example of this, but it's not hard to see how it can be done. The last example in this chapter allows the user to walk backwards, but not using an enumerator. It relies instead on a more powerful model.)

As noted earlier in this section, the new member function **add_rear(T)** makes **slist_2** capable of implementing a queue. Because tail's **next** pointer refers to the last element of the list, we can perform this operation efficiently, without traversing the entire list. This convention required slight implementation changes in the constructor **single_list(T)** and in **add_front(T)**. These functions, as well as **add_rear(T)**, must handle the empty list as a special case, as explained in the source comments. To ease maintenance, this special handling is encapsulated in a new private member function, **add_to_empty(T)**.

Doubly Linked Lists

Doubly linked lists allow us to move efficiently in *both* directions. List elements can be added or removed from either end, making it possible to support constructs that are more general such as *deques*. It also becomes practical to support various splicing operations among lists.

Rather than provide more functions that do "pointer surgery," we'll concentrate on basic operations in the first example, and then show how to implement a simple *iterator* in the second, more advanced, example. Iterators are used extensively in the Standard Template Library (STL), and it's well worth learning something about how they're implemented.

Figure 2-2 shows what a doubly linked list looks like in memory.

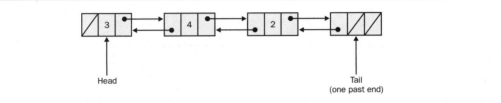

FIGURE 2-2.   Memory layout for a doubly linked list containing the numbers 3, 4, and 2

Simple Doubly Linked List

The first example, **dlist_1**, is similar to **slist_1** and **slist_2** in many respects. We'll use those singly linked list examples as our point of departure here, and focus on the properties of **dlist_1** that make it different.

The most important difference concerns the nested class **Double_node**, which is the counterpart to **Single_node** in **slist_1**. In addition to the **next** pointer, **Double_node** contains a **prev** pointer. This is what makes it a doubly linked list. Any member function that modifies the list must maintain **prev**.

dlist_1.h
dlist_1.cpp

Code

The code is organized into two files: **dlist_1.h** is the list itself, and **dlist_1.cpp** shows an example of its use. Here is **dlist_1.h**.

```
// File dlist_1.h
// Simple non-template doubly linked list of integers.

#include <iostream>
#include <cassert>
using namespace std;

class Double_list {

private:
  class Double_node {
```

```
    // Double_node's only purpose is to support class Double_list.
    // That's why all its members are private and class Double_list
    // is a friend.

    friend class Double_list;

    // Make a Double_node with a meaningful value.
    Double_node(int node_val) : val(node_val) { }

    // Make an empty Double_node.
    Double_node( ) { }

    ~Double_node( ) { }

    // Print the value.
    void print_val( ) const { cout << val << " "; }

    Double_node *next; // Points to front end of list.
    Double_node *prev; // Points to a node one past the end of list.
    int val;           // The data.
  };

  Double_node *head;   // Points to front end of list
  Double_node *tail;   // Points to a node one past the end of list.

  // Privately declared, and undefined assignment and copy,
  // to suppress these operations.

  Double_list & operator=(const Double_list &);
  Double_list(const Double_list &);


public:

  // Make an empty list.
  Double_list( ) {
    // Empty "one past the end" node.
    head = tail = new Double_node;
    tail->next = 0;
    tail->prev = 0;
  }
```

```cpp
  // Make a list that contains a single element.
  Double_list(int node_val) {
    // Empty "one past the end" node.
    head = tail = new Double_node;
    tail->next = 0;
    tail->prev = 0;
    add_front(node_val);
  }

  // Walk the list from head to tail, delete each element.
  ~Double_list( )   {

    Double_node *node_to_delete = head;
    for (Double_node *sn = head; sn != tail;) {
      sn = sn->next;
      delete node_to_delete;
      node_to_delete = sn;
    }

    // assert( node_to_delete == tail );
    delete node_to_delete;
  }

  bool is_empty( ) const {return head == tail;}

  // Add a new element to the head of the list.
  void add_front(int node_val)  {
    Double_node *node_to_add = new Double_node(node_val);
    node_to_add->next = head;
    node_to_add->prev = 0;
    head->prev = node_to_add;
    head = node_to_add;
  }

  void add_rear(int node_val)   {
    if ( is_empty( ) )
      // The "else" clause not valid for empty list because
tail->prev
      // is null, and therefore tail->prev->next is meaningless.
      add_front(node_val);
    else {
      Double_node *node_to_add = new Double_node(node_val);
```

```
        node_to_add->next = tail;
        node_to_add->prev = tail->prev;
        tail->prev->next = node_to_add;
        tail->prev = node_to_add;
    }
}


// Inserts node_val into the list directly after
// the first occurence of key, if key is already
// in the list.  If key is *not* in the list,
// does nothing and returns false.  Note that
// this function could also be implemented for
// Single_list.

bool insert_after(int node_val, const int key)  {

    for ( Double_node *dn = head; dn != tail; dn = dn->next ) {
        // Is key in the list?
        if ( dn->val == key ) {
            // Yes! n now points to it.  Make a new Double_node
            // for node_val and insert it following key.

            Double_node *node_to_add = new Double_node(node_val);
            node_to_add->prev = dn;
            node_to_add->next = dn->next;
            dn->next->prev    = node_to_add;
            dn->next          = node_to_add;
            return true;
        }
    }

    return false;
}


// Note that remove_front( ) and remove_rear( ) release
// the memory used by the removed element, so they must
// handle empty lists properly.  Otherwise, they could
// delete a Double_node that should not be deleted.

int remove_front( ) {
    if ( is_empty( ) ) throw "tried to remove from an empty list";
```

```
    Double_node *node_to_remove = head;
    int return_val = node_to_remove->val;
    head = node_to_remove->next;
    head->prev = 0;
    delete node_to_remove;
    return return_val;
}

int remove_rear( ) {
  if ( is_empty( ) ) throw "tried to remove from an empty list";

  Double_node *node_to_remove = tail->prev;

  if ( node_to_remove->prev == 0 ) {
    //Only one item left, call remove_front( ).
    return remove_front( );
  }
  else {
    int return_val = node_to_remove->val;
    node_to_remove->prev->next = tail;
    tail->prev = node_to_remove->prev;
    delete node_to_remove;
    return return_val;
  }
}

// Removes first occurrence of node_val from the list.
// If not in list, returns false.

bool remove_val(int node_val)  {

  for ( Double_node *dn = head; dn != tail; dn = dn->next ) {
    // Is node_val in the list?
    if ( dn->val == node_val ) {
      // Yes! n now points to it.  Remove it.
      dn->prev->next = dn->next;
      dn->next->prev = dn->prev;
      delete dn;
      return true;
    }
  }
```

```
    return false;
  }

  // Returns true when node_val is in list, false otherwise.
  bool find(int node_val) const {
    for ( Double_node *dn = head; dn != tail; dn = dn->next ) {
      if ( dn->val == node_val ) return true;
    }
    return false;
  }

  // Returns the value of the nth list element.  User must make
  // sure element_num is at least one, and no bigger than the
  // list size.

  int get_nth(const int element_num) const {

    if ( element_num < 1 )    throw "get_nth argument less than one";

    int count = 1;
    for ( Double_node *dn = head; dn != tail; dn = dn->next ) {
      if ( count++ == element_num ) return dn->val;
    }

    throw "element_num exceeds list size";
  }

  // Returns the size of the list by counting elements.
  // Inefficient because we assume this is done infrequently
  // for testing, and we'd rather spend extra time here than
  // spend it incrementing a new size variable each time we
  // add or remove an element.

  int size( ) const {
    int count = 0;
    for ( Double_node *dn = head; dn != tail; dn = dn->next )
++count;
    return count;
  }

  // Prints out list.
  void print( ) const {
```

```
    for ( Double_node *dn = head; dn != tail; dn = dn->next ) {
      dn->print_val( );
    }
    cout << endl;
  }

};
```

Here is **dlist_1.cpp**.

```cpp
// File dlist_1.cpp

#include "dlist_1.h"

// The following main program gives some simple examples of how
// dlist_1 is used.

Double_list my_list;        // Create an empty Double_list.

int main()
{

  // Add some values to the front.
  for ( int val = 0; val < 5; ++val ) {
    my_list.add_front(val);
    my_list.add_rear(val);
    my_list.print( );
  }

  // Insert the value -999 after the first list node
  // whose value is 3.
  my_list.insert_after(-999, 3);
  my_list.print( );(-999, 3);

  // Remove the first node whose value is 3.
  my_list.remove_val(3);
  my_list.print( );(-999, 3);

  // Now remove them one at a time.  To empty the
  // list, we don't need to know its length.
  while ( ! my_list.is_empty( ) ) {
    my_list.remove_front( );
    my_list.print( );
```

```
    }

    return 0;
}
```

The output from the **dlist_1** program is shown just below. Each line of output gives the current contents of **my_list**, as it grows and then shrinks. When building the list up, we add two elements before each call to **print( )**. When cutting it back down, we print after each element is removed.

```
0 0
1 0 0 1
2 1 0 0 1 2
3 2 1 0 0 1 2 3
4 3 2 1 0 0 1 2 3 4
4 3 -999 2 1 0 0 1 2 3 4
4 -999 2 1 0 0 1 2 3 4
-999 2 1 0 0 1 2 3 4
2 1 0 0 1 2 3 4
1 0 0 1 2 3 4
0 0 1 2 3 4
0 1 2 3 4
1 2 3 4
2 3 4
3 4
4
```

ANNOTATIONS

There are several new member functions in this doubly linked list example. The most important of these is **remove_rear( )**, because it makes **dlist_1** capable of implementing a double-ended queue, or deque.

The function **insert_after(int, const int)** inserts a new node into the list directly after the first occurrence of an existing node with specified value. The function **remove_val(int)** removes the first occurrence of a node with the specified value.

Doubly Linked List Template

In **dlist_1**, the functions **insert_after(int, const int)**, **remove_val(int)**, and **find(int)** have limited use, because lists often contain multiple nodes with the same value. If the first occurrence is not the one you care about, these functions don't help you.

So why include them in **dlist_1** at all? They're there because they help illustrate an important design choice. The function **insert_after(int, const int)**, for example, would be far more useful if it could insert a new value after a particular *node* that the user has identified. We would therefore need to give the user a way to access and manipulate the nodes themselves. However, doing that directly would expose implementation details that are best hidden.

The **slist_2** program demonstrated one way to deal with this problem: using an enumerator. Here, **dlist_2** shows a different approach using an iterator. The iterator will be a handle for a **Double_node**. This means it will allow users to access and manipulate a **Double_node** in specific ways, without knowing the details of its implementation. As much as possible, we'd like it to have the look and feel of a pointer. (Iterator design is a rich and complex subject, and we are setting aside its many issues in the interest of clarity and simplicity for this discussion.)

Code

dlist_2.h
dlist_2.cpp

The code for this doubly linked list template is organized into two files: **dlist_2.h** is the list itself, and **dlist_2.cpp** shows an example of its use. Here is **dlist_2.h**.

```
// File dlist_2.h
// Doubly linked list template.  Functions find( ), remove_front( ),
// and remove_rear( ) return a sentinel value to report errors.
// Iterator errors are still reported with exceptions.

#include <iostream>
#include <cassert>
using namespace std;

template <class T>
class Double_list {

public:

    // Forward declaration needed here.
    class  iterator;
    friend class iterator;

private:

  class Double_node;
  friend class Double_node;
```

```
class Double_node {

public:

   friend class Double_list;
   friend class iterator;

   // Make a Single_node with a meaningful value.
   Double_node(T node_val) : val(node_val) { }

   // Make an empty Single_node.
   Double_node( ) { }

   ~Double_node( ) { }

   // Print the node value.  Requires type T to overload
   // operator<<( ).
   void print_val( ) { cout << val << " "; }

   Double_node *next;    // Points to the next Single_node.
   Double_node *prev;    // Points to the previous Single_node.
   T val;                // The data.
};

public:

   class iterator {
     // This class is a "handle" or pseudo pointer for
     // Double_node's.
     //
     // Operators:

     // ++ makes the iterator point to the next Double_node.
     // Undefined if iterator is already one past the end.

     // -- makes the iterator point to the previous Double_node.
     // Undefined if iterator already points to the head.

     // == means two iterators reference the same Double_node.

     // != is the negation of ==.
```

```
      // * returns the node_val in the Double_node.

      friend class Double_list<T>;

  public:

      // Null constructor.
      iterator( ) : the_node(0) { }

      // Make an iterator using a Double_node.
      iterator(Double_node * dn) : the_node(dn) { }

      // Copy constructor needed to support the use of iterator
      // as argument or return value.  Copies the_node.
      iterator(const iterator & it) : the_node(it.the_node) { }

      iterator& operator=(const iterator& it) {
        the_node = it.the_node;
        return *this;
      }

      bool operator==(const iterator& it) const {
        return (the_node == it.the_node);
      }

      bool operator!=(const iterator& it) const {
        return !(it == *this);
      }

      iterator& operator++( ) {

        if ( the_node == 0 )
          throw "incremented an empty iterator";
        if ( the_node->next == 0 )
          throw "tried to increment too far past the end";

        the_node = the_node->next;
        return *this;
      }

      iterator& operator--( ) {
        if ( the_node == 0 )
          throw "decremented an empty iterator";
```

```
        if ( the_node->prev == 0 )
            throw "tried to decrement past the beginning";

        the_node = the_node->prev;
        return *this;
    }

    T& operator*( ) const {
      if ( the_node == 0 )
        throw "tried to dereference an empty iterator";
      return the_node->val;
    }

  private:
    Double_node * the_node;

  };

private:
  Double_node *head;      // Points to front end of list
  Double_node *tail;      // Points to a node one past the end of list.

  // Privately declared, and undefined assignment and copy,
  // to suppress these operations.

  Double_list & operator=(const Double_list &);
  Double_list(const Double_list &);

  iterator head_iterator;
  iterator tail_iterator;

public:
  // Make an empty list.
  Double_list( ) {
    head = tail = new Double_node;
    tail->next = 0;
    tail->prev = 0;

    // These must be initialized *after* head and tail, so it
    // can't be done in Double_list's initialization list.
    head_iterator = iterator(head);
    tail_iterator = iterator(tail);
  }
```

```
// Make a list that contains a single element.
Double_list(T node_val) {
  head = tail = new Double_node;
  tail->next = 0;
  tail->prev = 0;

  // add_front( ) will also have to adjust these.
  head_iterator = iterator(head);
  tail_iterator = iterator(tail);
  add_front(node_val);
}

// Walk the list from head to tail, delete each element.
~Double_list( )  {

  Double_node *node_to_delete = head;
  for (Double_node *sn = head; sn != tail;) {
    sn = sn->next;
    delete node_to_delete;
    node_to_delete = sn;
  }

  // assert( node_to_delete == tail );
  delete node_to_delete;
}

bool is_empty( ) {return head == tail;}

iterator front( ) { return head_iterator; }
iterator rear( )  { return tail_iterator; }

void add_front(T node_val)  {
  Double_node *node_to_add = new Double_node(node_val);
  node_to_add->next = head;
  node_to_add->prev = 0;
  head->prev = node_to_add;
  head = node_to_add;
  head_iterator = iterator(head);
}

// Add a new element to the head of the list.
```

```
void add_rear(T node_val) {
  if ( is_empty( ) )
    // The "else" clause not valid for empty list because
tail->prev
    // is null, and therefore tail->prev->next is meaningless.
    add_front(node_val);
  else {
    Double_node *node_to_add = new Double_node(node_val);
    node_to_add->next = tail;
    node_to_add->prev = tail->prev;
    tail->prev->next = node_to_add;
    tail->prev = node_to_add;
    tail_iterator = iterator(tail);
  }
}



// Inserts node_val into the list directly after the iterator
// key_i.  If key_i is *not* in the list, returns false.

bool insert_after(T node_val, const iterator & key_i) {

  for ( Double_node *dn = head; dn != tail; dn = dn->next ) {
    // Is key in the list?
    if ( dn == key_i.the_node ) {
      // Yes! n now points to it.  Make a new Double_node
      // for node_val and insert it following key.

      Double_node *node_to_add = new Double_node(node_val);
      node_to_add->prev = dn;
      node_to_add->next = dn->next;
      dn->next->prev    = node_to_add;
      dn->next          = node_to_add;
      return true;
    }
  }

  return false;
}



// Remove an element from the head of the list.
```

```
// Note that remove_front and remove_rear release the
// memory used by the removed element, so they must
// handle empty lists properly.  Otherwise, they could
// delete a Double_node that should not be deleted.

T remove_front( ) {
  if ( is_empty( ) ) throw "tried to remove from an empty list";

  Double_node *node_to_remove = head;
  T return_val = node_to_remove->val;
  head = node_to_remove->next;
  head->prev = 0;
  head_iterator = iterator(head);
  delete node_to_remove;
  return return_val;
}

T remove_rear( ) {
  if ( is_empty( ) ) throw "tried to remove from an empty list";

  Double_node *node_to_remove = tail->prev;

  if (node_to_remove->prev == 0) {
    //Only one item left, call remove_front( ).
    return remove_front( );
  }
  else {
    T return_val = node_to_remove->val;
    node_to_remove->prev->next = tail;
    tail->prev = node_to_remove->prev;
    delete node_to_remove;
    return return_val;
  }
}

// Removes node referenced by key_i.
// If not in list, returns false.

bool remove_it(iterator & key_i)  {

  for ( Double_node *dn = head; dn != tail; dn = dn->next ) {
    // Is node_val in the list?
```

```
      if ( dn == key_i.the_node ) {
        // Yes! n now points to it.  Remove it.
        dn->prev->next = dn->next;
        dn->next->prev = dn->prev;
        delete dn;
        key_i.the_node = 0;
        return true;
      }
    }

  return false;
}


// Find( ) returns the first iterator that references node_val.
// If node_val is not on the list, returns tail_iterator.
// class T needs a valid operator==( ) for this to work.

iterator find(T node_val) const {
  for ( Double_node *dn = head; dn != tail; dn = dn->next ) {
    if ( dn->val == node_val ) return iterator(dn);
  }
  return tail_iterator;
}


// Returns an iterator that references the nth list element.
// Returns tail_iterator if element_num is less than one
// or greater than the number of list elements.

iterator get_nth(const int element_num) const {

  if ( element_num < 1 )  return tail_iterator;

  int count = 1;
  for ( Double_node *dn = head; dn != tail; dn = dn->next ) {
    if ( count++ == element_num ) return iterator(dn);
  }

  // element_num is too big.
  return tail_iterator;
}
```

```
  // Returns the size of the list by counting elements.
  // Inefficient because we assume this is done infrequently
  // for testing, and we'd rather spend extra time here than
  // spend it incrementing a new size variable each time we
  // add or remove an element.

  int size( ) const {
    int count = 0;
    for ( Double_node *dn = head; dn != tail; dn = dn->next )
++count;
    return count;
  }


  // Print the list.
  void print( ) const {
    for ( Double_node *dn = head; dn != tail; dn = dn->next ) {
      dn->print_val( );
    }
    cout << endl;
  }

};
```

Here is **dlist_2.cpp**.

```
// File dlist_2.cpp

#include "dlist_2.h"

// The following main program gives some examples
// of iterator usage.

Double_list<int> the_list;        // empty list

int main()
{
  int ret  = 0;
  Double_list<int>::iterator list_iter;

  // Add some values to the front.

  for (int j = 0; j < 5; ++j) {
```

```
    the_list.add_front(j);
}


// Print
the_list.print( );

// Print again, just as efficiently, using iterators
for ( list_iter = the_list.front( ) ;
      list_iter != the_list.rear( ) ;
      ++list_iter )    {

  cout << *list_iter << " ";
}
cout << endl;

// Now, use iterators to print it backwards.
for ( list_iter = the_list.rear( ) ;
      list_iter != the_list.front( )
      ; )          {

  --list_iter;
  cout << *list_iter << " ";
}
cout << endl;

return 0;
}
```

The **dlist_2** program produces the following output:
```
4 3 2 1 0
4 3 2 1 0
0 1 2 3 4
```

ANNOTATIONS

The iterator is implemented as a public nested class called **Double_list::iterator**. Because it's public, **iterator** objects can be defined by users. And because it's nested, the type name of an **iterator** is qualified by the name of the class it supports. This reduces the likelihood of naming conflicts.

The **iterator** must know about some of **Double_list**'s private data members, and therefore **Double_list** must nominate **iterator** as a friend. Similarly, **iterator** nominates **Double_list** as a friend. Note the required forward declarations.

In addition to the standard head and tail pointers, this version of **Double_list** defines **head_iterator** and **tail_iterator**, which reference the head and tail (again, one past the end) respectively.

Now, let's look at the inside of **Double_list::iterator**. It's only (private) data member is defined as follows:

```
Double_node * the_node;
```

This is precisely what **iterator** is intended to hide. The operators defined for **iterator** provide users with a controlled way to manipulate this node. We define these operators to behave as follows:

Operators for iterator	Function
operator=( )	Gives **the_node** the same value as **the_node** in right-hand side of the assignment.
operator==( )	Returns **true** if the two **iterator**s reference the same node. Some may prefer an implementation that compares the iterator addresses rather than node addresses, and this would be more efficient if frequent comparisons are required.
operator!=( )	Is the negation of **operator==( )**.
operator++( )	Makes **iterator** point to the next node in the list.
operator—( )	Makes **iterator** point to the previous node in the list.
operator*( )	Returns the **node_val** in **Double_node**, rather than the node itself.

A copy constructor is defined in order to support the use of iterators as function parameters and return values.

Now that we have an iterator, let's look at the access and modification functions. This is where we expect to see the payoff. This version of **find(T)** returns an **iterator** instead of a **bool**, as does **get_nth(const int)**. Once the iterator is in hand, the user can pass it back to other member functions, access the data, and walk forward and backward through the list.

The revised **insert_after(T, const iterator &)** and **remove_it(iterator &)** functions take iterator parameters. The user can now operate on the list in any reasonable way, and the implementation details remain safely hidden.

Binary Trees

By Art Friedman

bt.h   avl.h
bt.cpp   avl.cpp

T he focus of this chapter is the *binary search tree,* which is an elegant way to organize ordered data in a way that supports efficient searching. Binary trees are useful in a wide range of situations. For example, a parser may use a binary tree to represent expressions composed of binary operators. An inventory program might use a binary tree to store part information.

This chapter explores the advantages of binary trees and shows how some of their problems can be overcome. As always, remember that there are many possible implementations. The ones in this chapter serve only as examples.

Introduction to Binary Trees

Trees and binary trees are a notch more complex than lists. Lists are usually represented as one dimensional, but trees are more naturally represented in more than one dimension.

As shown in Figure 3-1, trees are typically drawn upside-down, with the root at the top. The individual memory cells that make up a tree are called its *nodes.* The links pointing downward from a given node connect the node to its *children.* Naturally enough, any node that has children is considered their *parent.* The family tree analogy also makes use of terms such as *grandparent, ancestor,* and *descendant,* with the obvious meanings. A node with no children is called a *leaf.* Although a node may have more than one child, it cannot have more than one parent. A data structure in which any node has more than one parent is not considered a tree. The root node is the only node with no parent.

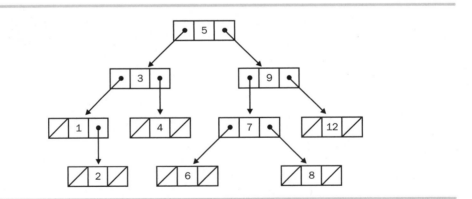

FIGURE 3-1.   Binary search tree's memory layout

The term "binary tree" is both descriptive and misleading. At first glance, it's easy to assume that a binary tree is just a particular kind of tree, but this is not so.

Though related to trees in interesting ways, binary trees are considered a different species altogether. In an ordinary tree, any given node may have an arbitrary number of children. In a binary tree, each node must have zero, one, or two children. The child that appears on the left in a tree drawing is called the *left child*. The one appearing on the right is called the *right child*. Note that although we informally use the term "tree" in this chapter, we're really talking about binary trees.

There are three standard procedures for visiting each node of a binary tree, commonly known as *pre-order*, *in-order*, and *post-order* traversal. Their definitions are recursive.

◆ To traverse a tree in pre-order, you first visit the root node, then traverse the left subtree in pre-order, and finally traverse the right subtree in pre-order.

◆ An in-order traversal first traverses the left subtree in in-order. Next it visits the root node, and finally it traverses the right subtree in in-order.

◆ Post-order traversal follows a similar scheme. First it traverses the left subtree in post-order, and then the right subtree. It visits the root node last.

In our examples, these traversal schemes are the basis of various printing functions. For the functions that print the tree as a linear sequence of values, the term "visit" simply means "print the value of". Our destructors make use of post-order traversal to guarantee that no node is deleted until both of its children have already been deleted. The term "visit" in this context means "delete".

The earlier Figure 3-1 shows what a simple binary search tree looks like in memory. Each node consists of three separate items: the actual data we're storing, a pointer to the left child, and a pointer to the right child. Our implementations will define additional fields as a matter of convenience, but these are the essential ones. Although array-based implementations are possible, we'll follow the more common practice of using dynamically allocated memory instead. We'll implement our binary trees as C++ templates. The caveats given in Chapter 2 about private nested classes apply here too.

Binary Search Trees

What distinguishes a binary *search* tree from any other binary tree? The data stored in a binary search tree must define an ordering relation, such as "less than". Integers provide the simplest example of data that can be ordered, and we'll refer to them extensively. The essential property of a binary search tree is that for any given node, all nodes to its left (that is, its left child and all descendants of its left child) contain values that are less than the value of the node itself. Likewise, all nodes to the right of a given node contain values that are greater. The trees we consider here do not allow duplicate values, so we don't need to decide where to put nodes of equal value.

Consider, for example, the node in Figure 3-1 whose value is 9. All nodes to its left have a value smaller than 9, and all nodes to its right have a value greater than 9. This is often referred to as the *binary search tree property.* Every operation we perform on a binary search tree must preserve this basic property.

What advantage is offered by binary search trees? An example will illustrate. Suppose we want to determine whether the tree in Figure 3-1 contains the value 7. We start at the root and notice that its value is 5. This tells us we can ignore the entire left subtree because the value we want is greater than 5. If the tree is more or less equally balanced, this eliminates roughly half the data in one simple operation—a significant benefit, especially if the tree is large. Repeating the same procedure on the right child, we notice that 7 is less than 9 and examine the left child. This node does indeed contain the value 7, so we're done. On average, the number of comparisons required to locate an item in a binary search tree (or determine that it's not in the tree) is proportional to the log (base 2) of the number of nodes in the tree. As we'll see, there can be a considerable difference between average and worst-case behavior.

Besides searching, we'll want to be able to add and delete elements. Adding elements is straightforward for a simple tree, but deleting them is tricky. As discussed in the section on balanced binary search trees, both adding and deleting are harder for balanced trees. We'll also implement functions that return the nth smallest item in the tree, and print out the tree elements in various useful ways.

Simple Binary Search Tree Template

The first example, template class **Binary_tree,** shows a simple binary search tree. Note that the parameters and return values of the public member functions are of the template parameter type **T**, rather than specialized nodes.

bt.h
bt.cpp

Code

The code is organized into two files. **Bt.h** is the tree itself, and **bt.cpp** shows an example of its use. Here is **bt.h:**

```
#include <iostream>
#include <cassert>
using namespace std;




////////////////////////////////////////////////////////////////////
//
// File bt.h.
```

```
// Simple Binary_tree class template.  Implements a binary search
// tree with no balancing.  Duplicate values not permitted.  Type T
// must support copying, and the following operators:
//
//    operator=( );
//    operator<<( );
//    operator==( );
//    operator!=( );
//    operator<( );
//
// Public member functions:
//
//    Binary_tree( );                          Make empty tree.
//    Binary_tree(const T root_val );          Make tree with one elt.
//    ~Binary_tree( );                         Release dynamic memory.
//
//    bool add( const T insert_value );        Add an element.
//    void remove( T value );                  Remove an element.
//    T get_nth(const int element_num) const;  Value of the nth elt.
//                                             Based on sorted order.
//
//    int size( ) const;                       Number of elements.
//    bool find( T find_value );               True if tree contains
//                                             find_value.
//
//    void print ( int level = 0 ) const;      Print tree sideways.
//
//    void print_pre_order( ) const;           Print as a linear list.
//    void print_in_order( ) const;            Print as a linear list.
//    void print_post_order( ) const;          Print as a linear list.
//
// Implementation Notes:
//
//    Nodes contain a nodecount field to ease implementation of
//    get_nth.  They also contain parent links.  Recursive functions
//    are noted.
//
//
/////////////////////////////////////////////////////////////////////


template <class T>
class Binary_tree {
```

```cpp
private:

  struct Tree_node {

    friend class Binary_tree;

    T val;                       // The data being stored in the tree.
    Tree_node *left_child;
    Tree_node *right_child;
    Tree_node *parent;
    int       nodecount;         // Number of nodes in subtree rooted at
// this node, including the node itself.

    Tree_node( );
    Tree_node( const T node_val ) : val(node_val) { }
    ~Tree_node( ) { }

    // Isa_right_child( ) and isa_left_child( ) return true if the
    // node making the call is the right/left child of its parent
    // and false otherwise.  Return false for root node.
    bool isa_right_child( ) const {
      if ( (parent == 0) || ( parent->right_child != this) )
        return false;
      else
        return true;
    }

    bool isa_left_child( ) const {
      if ( (parent == 0) || ( parent->left_child != this) )
        return false;
      else
        return true;
    }

    // Print( ) prints tree sideways on the page, root at the left.
    // "Backwards" recursive inorder traversal (i.e., right to left)
    // -- otherwise we'd print the mirror image.  Nodecount shown in
    // parentheses.  Null children are printed as "@".

    void print ( const int level = 0 ) const {

      // Initializing to this instead of root makes it possible
      // to print subtrees as well as the entire tree.
```

```
    const Tree_node *tn = this;

    if ( tn != 0 ) tn->right_child->print( level + 1 );

    for (int spaces = 0; spaces < level; ++spaces)
      cout << "   ";

    if ( tn != 0 )
      cout << tn->val << '(' << tn->nodecount << ')' << endl;
    else
      cout << "@" << endl;

    if ( tn != 0 ) tn->left_child->print( level + 1 );

  }

};  // End of Tree_node declaration.


private:

// Binary_tree private data members:

  Tree_node *root;
  Tree_node *zero_node;  // const in usage, provides return
                // value for find_node(const T).

// Binary_tree private member functions:

  //Disallow copy and assignment.

  Binary_tree(const Binary_tree &);
  Binary_tree & operator=( const Binary_tree & );

  // Make a root node, initialize val to root_val,
  // children to null, nodecount to one.
  void make_new_root( const T root_val ) {
    root = new Tree_node(root_val);
    root->left_child  = 0;
    root->right_child = 0;
    root->parent      = 0;
    root->nodecount   = 1;
  }
```

```
// Find_node(T find_value) goes out of its way to return a
// reference to a pointer, to simplify the implementation of
// remove(T).

Tree_node * & find_node( T find_value ) {
  Tree_node *tn = root;
  while ( (tn != 0) && (tn->val != find_value) )  {
    if ( find_value < tn->val )
      tn = tn->left_child;
    else
      tn = tn->right_child;
  }

  // Instead of just returning tn, we do the following slightly
  // complicated dance to be sure we return a *reference* within
  // the tree to the node we're looking for.

  if ( tn == 0 )
    // Find_value is not in the tree.
    return zero_node;
  else if ( tn->isa_left_child( ) )
    // Tn is the left child of its parent.
    return tn->parent->left_child;
  else if ( tn->isa_right_child( ) )
    // Tn is the right child of its parent.
    return tn->parent->right_child;
  else if ( tn == root )
    // No parents, special case.
    return root;
  // Should not reach this point.  Returns a garbage value,
  // to avoid compile time warning.
  assert(false);
  return zero_node;
}


// Insert_node( const T, Tree_node * ) adds a new value to the
// appropriate leaf if it's not already in the tree.  Returns a
// pointer to the new node if one was created, zero otherwise.
// Non-recursive.  Increment nodecount for each node we traverse.
// Do this *after* we insert the node, just in case it turns out to
// be a duplicate, and we decide not to insert it after all.
```

```
Tree_node *
insert_node( const T insert_value, Tree_node * start_node = 0 )
{

  if ( root == 0 )  {
    // Special case for empty tree.
    make_new_root( insert_value );
    return root;
  }


  if ( start_node == 0 ) start_node = root;

  Tree_node *tn = start_node;

  while ( (tn != 0) && (tn->val != insert_value) ) {

    if ( insert_value < tn->val )  {
      // Look at left child.
      if ( tn->left_child == 0 )  {

        // Insert new value as the left child of tn.
        attach_node( tn, tn->left_child, insert_value );

        // Add 1 to the nodecount for tn and all its ancestors.
        adjust_nodecount_to_root(tn, 1);

        return tn->left_child;
      }
      else {
        tn = tn->left_child;
      }
    }
    else {
      // Look at right child.
      if ( tn->right_child == 0 )  {

        // Insert new value as the right child of tn.
        attach_node( tn, tn->right_child, insert_value );

        // Add 1 to the nodecount for tn and all its ancestors.
        adjust_nodecount_to_root(tn, 1);
```

```
        return tn->right_child;
      }
      else {
        tn = tn->right_child;
      }
    }
  }

  // Insert_value is already in the tree.
  assert ( tn != 0 );
  return 0;
}

// Attach_node( Tree_node *, Tree_node * &, T ) is a helper
// function for insert_node( const T insert_value, Tree_node * ).

void attach_node( Tree_node * new_parent,
                  Tree_node * & new_child, T insert_value ) {

  // Insert new value as the left child of tn.
  new_child = new Tree_node( insert_value );
  new_child->left_child  = 0;
  new_child->right_child = 0;
  new_child->parent      = new_parent;
  new_child->nodecount   = 1;
}

// Adjust_nodecount_to_root( Tree_node *, int ) adds incr to the
// nodecount field of tn and all its ancestors including root.
// Note that root's parent link is zero.

void adjust_nodecount_to_root( Tree_node * tn, int incr ) {
  while ( tn != 0 ) {
    tn->nodecount += incr;
    tn = tn->parent;
  }
}

// Get_nth_node( Tree_node *, const int ) returns the node
// corresponding to the nth sorted (or inorder) value in the tree.
// Recursive.  Depends on nodecount field being correctly set.
```

```
Tree_node * get_nth_node(Tree_node * tn, const int nth) const {

  // Special handling for empty root.
  if ( tn == 0 ) return 0;

  //  Remember the nodecount of tn's left child.
  int lc_count
     = (tn->left_child != 0) ? tn->left_child->nodecount : 0 ;

  if ( (lc_count + 1) == nth ) {
    // We're done, because tn itself is the nth value.
    return tn;
  }
  else if ( lc_count >= nth ) {
    // Look for nth in left child
    return get_nth_node(tn->left_child, nth);
  }
  else  {
    // Look for (nth - lc_count - 1) in right child
    return get_nth_node(tn->right_child, nth - lc_count -1);
  }
}


// Cleanup ( Tree_node * ) deletes all Tree_nodes in post-order
// traversal.  Does the real work for ~Binary_tree( ).

void cleanup (Tree_node *tn) {

  // Special handling for empty root.
  if ( tn == 0 ) return;

  if ( tn->left_child != 0 ) {
    cleanup(tn->left_child);
    tn->left_child = 0;
  }
  if ( tn->right_child != 0 ) {
    cleanup(tn->right_child);
    tn->right_child = 0;
  }
  delete tn;
}
```

```
// Print_pre( const Tree_node * ) recursively prints tree values
// for the subtree rooted at tn in pre-order.

void print_pre(const Tree_node * tn) const {

  // Special handling for empty root.
  if ( tn == 0 ) return;

  cout << tn->val << "  ";
  if ( tn->left_child != 0 ) {
    print_pre( tn->left_child );
  }
  if ( tn->right_child != 0 ) {
    print_pre( tn->right_child );
  }
}

// Print_in( const Tree_node * ) recursively prints tree values for
// the subtree rooted at tn in in-order (or sorted order).

void print_in(const Tree_node * tn)  const {

  // Special handling for empty root.
  if ( tn == 0 ) return;

  if ( tn->left_child != 0 ) {
    print_in( tn->left_child );
  }
  cout << tn->val << "  ";
  if ( tn->right_child != 0 ) {
    print_in( tn->right_child );
  }
}

// Print_post( const Tree_node * ) recursively prints tree values
// for the subtree rooted at tn in post-order.

void print_post(const Tree_node * tn) const {

  // Special handling for empty root.
  if ( tn == 0 ) return;
```

```
    if ( tn->left_child != 0 ) {
      print_post( tn->left_child );
    }
    if ( tn->right_child != 0 ) {
      print_post( tn->right_child );
    }
    cout << tn->val << "  ";
  }

// End of Binary_tree private member functions:


public:

// Binary_tree public member functions:

  Binary_tree( ) : zero_node(0) { root = 0; }

  Binary_tree(const T root_val ) : zero_node(0) {
    make_new_root( root_val );
  }


  // Release memory for each Tree_node, in a post-order traversal.
  // Private member cleanup( Tree_node * ) does the work.

  ~Binary_tree( ) {
    cleanup( root );
  }

  // Add( const T ) adds a value to the tree if it's not already
  // there.  Returns true if insert_value was actually added.
  // Private member function insert_node(T) does the real work.

  bool add( const T insert_value ) {
    Tree_node *ret = insert_node(insert_value);
    if (ret) return true;
    else     return false;
  }


  // Remove( T ) removes the node containing value from the tree.
  // This function is the hardest to implement cleanly because
```

```
// the node being deleted may have two children.  These children
// need to be re-attached to the tree, but the node being deleted
// has only one parent, so some surgery is required.  This
// operation is handled in a way that preserves the binary tree
// property and does *not* increase the height of the tree.
// Defining node_to_remove as a reference to a pointer makes
// remove( T ) less complicated than it would otherwise be.

void remove( T value ) {

  Tree_node * & node_to_remove = find_node( value );

  Tree_node * predecessor = 0;
  Tree_node * temp = 0;

  if ( node_to_remove == zero_node ) return;
  assert( node_to_remove->val == value );


  // Handle easy cases first, where node_to_remove has at most one
  // child.

  if ( node_to_remove->left_child == 0 ) {

    // Node_to_remove has no left child.
    temp = node_to_remove;

    if ( node_to_remove->right_child != 0 )  {
      // Node_to_remove does have a right child.
      node_to_remove->right_child->parent = node_to_remove->parent;
    }

    // Replace node_to_remove with its right child.  Ok if the
    // right child is null.  After this statement, the variable
    // node_to_remove no longer references the node we are
    // removing.  But temp still does.
    node_to_remove = node_to_remove->right_child;

    // Node_to_remove's right child now occupies node_to_remove's
    // former position in the tree.  It's nodecount hasn't changed.
    // But the nodecount of its parent and all other ancestors must
    // decrease by one to account for the removed node.
    adjust_nodecount_to_root(temp->parent, -1);
```

```
    // Free the memory of the node that's just been removed from
    // the tree.
    delete temp;

    return;
}
else if ( node_to_remove->right_child == 0 ) {

    // Node_to_remove has no right child.
    temp = node_to_remove;

    // We know the left child is not zero, because we're in
    // the "else clause".  Hence, no need to check this condition
    // before executing the following statement.
    node_to_remove->left_child->parent = node_to_remove->parent;

    // See "if clause" comments above.
    node_to_remove = node_to_remove->left_child;
    adjust_nodecount_to_root(temp->parent, -1);
    delete temp;
    return;
}

// If we reach this point, we know that node_to_remove has
// two children.  Find its immediate predecessor, ie, the
// rightmost descendant of its left child.

predecessor = node_to_remove->left_child;
while ( predecessor->right_child != 0 )
  predecessor = predecessor->right_child;

// Replace the value of node_to_remove with the value of its
// predecessor.
node_to_remove->val = predecessor->val;

// Now that predecessor's value has been moved upward in the
// tree, we must attach predecessor's left child to predecessor's
// parent.  It will become the right child of predecessor's
// parent.  Recall that predecessor has no right child because of
// the way we've defined it.
```

```
  Tree_node * pp = predecessor->parent;
   if ( pp == node_to_remove ) {
     // Special case where predecessor is node_to_remove's left
     // child (i.e., it has no right child).
     pp->left_child = predecessor->left_child;
     if ( predecessor->left_child != 0 )
       predecessor->left_child->parent = pp;
   }
   else if ( predecessor->left_child != 0 ) {
     // Predecessor has a left child, and we must be sure not
     // to leave this child dangling.  Make it the right child
     // of predecessor's parent.
     pp->right_child = predecessor->left_child;
     predecessor->left_child->parent = pp;
   }
   else {
     // Predecessor's left child is zero, so there's nothing for
     // its parent's right_child field to point to.
     assert( pp->right_child == predecessor );
     pp->right_child = 0;
   }

   // Now update the nodecount for predecessor->parent and
   // all its ancestors.  Root's parent link is null.

   adjust_nodecount_to_root(pp, -1);

   // Predecessor's value has been moved to another node, and its
   // children, if any, have been re-attached to predecessor's
   // parent.  We no longer need the memory that originally
   // contained predecessor.
   delete predecessor;
}


// Get_nth( const int ) returns the nth value in the tree, based on
// sorted order.

T get_nth(const int element_num) const {
  Tree_node * tn = get_nth_node(root, element_num);
  return tn->val;
}
```

```cpp
// Size( ) returns the number of nodes in the tree.
int size( ) const { return root ? root->nodecount : 0; }

// Find( T ) returns true if find_value is in the tree,
// false otherwise.
bool find( T find_value ) {
  Tree_node *tn = find_node( find_value );

  if ( tn != 0 )
    return true;
  else
    return false;
}


// Print( ) does a backwards in-order traversal, and prints tree
// "sideways" on the page.

void print ( ) const {
  cout << "\n" << "=====================================" << "\n"
       << endl;

  // The following is a call to Binary_tree::Tree_node::print( ),
  // *not* a recursive call to Binary_tree::print( ).
  root->print( );
}

// The following functions print the elements linearly in pre-
// order, in-order, and post-order, respectively.  Print_inorder( )
// is equivalent to sorting.  These public functions take no
// parameters, but call private recursive functions, taking
// Tree_node * parameters, to do the work.
void print_pre_order( ) const {
  print_pre(root);
  cout << endl;
}

void print_in_order( ) const {
  print_in(root);
```

```
      cout << endl;
  }

  void print_post_order( ) const {
    print_post(root);
    cout << endl;
  }

};
```

After populating a binary search tree with ten elements, **bt.cpp** prints the tree sideways for inspection, with the root node on the left of the page. For each element, it prints the value followed by the **nodecount** field. The **nodecount** field is printed in parentheses. The character **"@"** denotes a null child pointer. Following the full tree, its values are printed out in several linear orders. After showing the initial tree, a leaf node and the root node are deleted, and each resulting tree is printed. Notice that each node's left child is printed below it and to its right. The right child is printed above it, aligned with the left child.

```
// File bt.cpp:  Usage examples for bt.h

#include "bt.h"

// Create a binary search tree containing integers.
// The root node contains the value seven.
Binary_tree<int> my_bt( 7 );

// Populate my_bt with integer values.
void populate( ) {
  my_bt.add( 5 );
  my_bt.add( 9 );
  my_bt.add( 6 );
  my_bt.add( 4 );
  my_bt.add( 11 );
  my_bt.add( 8 );
  my_bt.add( 2 );
  my_bt.add( 10 );
  my_bt.add( 19 );
}

int main( )
{
  populate( );
```

```
// Print full tree
my_bt.print ( );

// Print my_bt in various linear orders.
cout << endl;
cout << "Pre-order:  " ;
my_bt.print_pre_order ( );

cout << "Post-order: " ;
my_bt.print_post_order ( );

cout << "In-order:   " ;
my_bt.print_in_order ( );

cout << "In-order, using get_nth( int ):" << endl;;
cout << "           " ;
int i;
for (i = 1; i <= my_bt.size( ); ++i) {
  cout << my_bt.get_nth(i) << "   ";
}
cout << endl;
cout << endl;

// Remove some values and the print full tree again.

my_bt.remove ( 2 );
cout << "==================================" << endl;
cout << " removed 2" ;

my_bt.print ( );

my_bt.remove ( 7 );
cout << "==================================" << endl;
cout << " removed 7" ;

my_bt.print ( );

return 0;
}
```

Following is the output of **bt.cpp**:

```
====================================
                @
        19(1)
                @
      11(3)
                @
        10(1)
                @
   9(5)
            @
       8(1)
            @
7(10)
            @
       6(1)
            @
   5(4)
            @
       4(2)
                @
        2(1)
                @

Pre-order:  7  5  4  2  6  9  8  11  10  19
Post-order: 2  4  6  5  8  10  19  11  9  7
In-order:   2  4  5  6  7  8  9  10  11  19
In-order, using get_nth( int ):
            2  4  5  6  7  8  9  10  11  19


====================================
 removed 2
====================================

                @
        19(1)
                @
      11(3)
                @
        10(1)
                @
   9(5)
            @
       8(1)
```

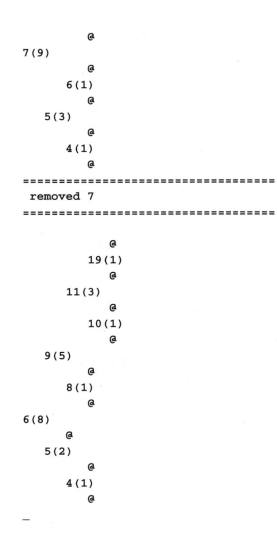

```
            @
    7(9)
              @
        6(1)
              @
      5(3)
              @
        4(1)
              @
==================================
 removed 7
==================================
                @
          19(1)
                @
        11(3)
                @
            10(1)
                @
        9(5)
              @
          8(1)
                @
  6(8)
          @
      5(2)
              @
        4(1)
              @

  —
```

ANNOTATIONS

As shown in the comment block for template class **Binary_tree**, the template parameter type **T** must define a number of operators. Although this implementation requires all of the listed operators to be defined, the ones that are essential to *any* implementation of a binary search tree are **operator==( )** and **operator<( )**. Without these relational operators, it wouldn't even make sense to think about organizing objects of type **T** in binary search tree.

   Binary_tree defines a private nested class, **Tree_node**, to represent the internal structure of the binary tree. Following the same approach taken for linked lists, this structure is kept hidden from the user. Let's look briefly at **Tree_node**'s internal structure.

The field **val** contains the data being stored in the node. **Left_child** and **right_child** are pointers to the node's left and right children. A value of 0 for either of these fields means there is no corresponding child. These are the essential fields for a binary tree.

We define two fields in addition to these, largely for convenience. The **parent** field points to the node's parent. The **nodecount** field contains the number of nodes in the subtree rooted at the node—that is, it tells us the number of nodes this subtree comprises. The existence of **nodecount** makes it possible to implement the member function **Binary_tree::get_nth(const int)** efficiently. Note that these two "convenience" fields come at a cost. Aside from requiring more memory, they must be updated each time the tree is modified. Whether or not this is a good trade-off depends on your intended application.

Tree_node's member functions are **isa_right_child( )**, **isa_left_child( )**, and **print( )**. The first two return **true** if the node is the right (left) child of its parent, and **false** otherwise. **Print( )** prints out the subtree rooted at the node "sideways" on the page. This function is largely for debugging.

Binary_tree has a number of public and private member functions, but only two private data members. The private data member **root** is just a pointer to the root node of the tree. **Zero_node** is a pointer to a **Tree_node** whose only purpose is to assist in the implementation of the private member function **find_node(const T)**, discussed shortly. We're now ready to elaborate on **Binary_tree**'s public and private member functions.

Binary_tree has two public constructors. The default constructor makes an empty tree, and **Binary_tree(const T)** makes a tree that contains one element of type **T**. The destructor deletes each **Tree_node** based on a post-order traversal. Post-order traversal guarantees that no node is deleted until its children have already been deleted.

PROGRAMMER'S NOTE   *For simplicity, we have decided not to support copying and assignment. Therefore, a copy constructor and assignment operator are declared as private members and not defined. This allows the compiler to report an error if you inadvertently try to perform these operations. Should you need to support these operations, you will need to make them public and write the appropriate definitions.*

The public member function **add(const T)** allocates a new **Tree_node** containing the value passed in by the user, and attaches it to the tree as a leaf. The real work is done by the private member function **insert_node(const T)**, which in turn relies on three other private member functions, **make_new_root(const T)**, **attach_node (Tree_node *, Tree_node *, T)**, and **adjust_nodecount_to_root(Tree_node *, int)**.

The **insert_node(const T)** function in effect tries to look up the new value by traversing the tree in the manner described in the section that introduces binary search trees. The function compares the new value to the value held by the root node. If they're equal, nothing needs to be done because our trees do not allow duplicate values. If the new value is greater, **insert_node(const T)** shifts its attention to the root's right child. Otherwise, it looks at the root's left child. This process is repeated for the selected child until either the value is found in the tree (in which case nothing more is done), or the node that is the current focus of attention is empty. This happens when we look at, say, the **left_child** field of a node and find that its value is 0. At this point, we attach the new node as the left child. **Attach_node (Tree_node *, Tree_node *, T)** does that job by allocating a new **Tree_node**, initializing its fields, and doing the simple pointer surgery needed to attach it to the tree.

We're not quite finished, because adding this new node has made it necessary to adjust the **node_count** fields of each its ancestors. **Adjust_nodecount_to_root (Tree_node *, int)** does this for us by walking backward from the new node to the root, incrementing the node count of each node it encounters along the way. The **Tree_node::parent** field makes this very easy to do. **Make_new_root(const T)** handles the special case where the tree is initially empty.

Remove(T) is the function most difficult to implement and to understand. To see why this is so, let's look at the simple cases first. If the node to be removed happens to be a leaf, all we need to do is release its memory, set its parent's left or right child pointer to 0, and decrement the **node_count** fields in each of its ancestors. When the node being removed has a single child, the problem is not much harder. Instead of zeroing out the parent's child pointer, we make it point to the child of the child being removed.

Remove(T) handles these special cases first. It starts by having the private member function **find_node(T)** return *by reference* a pointer to the node being removed. The pointer is returned by reference because **remove(T)** can easily modify the field in the parent node that points to the node being removed. Aside from that special feature, **find_node(T)** is no different from the search procedures previously described.

PROGRAMMER'S NOTE *The function **find_node(T)** has two points that are worth mentioning. Both of these are consequences of the fact that the function returns a reference to a pointer to a **Tree_node**. First, **find_node(T)** needs a pointer to refer to, even when returning a "zero" pointer. This is the only reason we bother to define the private member **zero_node**. Secondly, instead of just returning the node it has found, **find_node(T)** goes out of its way to return a reference to the appropriate child pointer of the node's parent. Would it be more efficient to maintain a separate pointer to the node's parent as we descend the tree? As is the case for most performance issues, the somewhat frustrating answer to this question is "It depends." The approach taken by **find_node(T)** is expensive, but its cost does not increase with the depth of the tree. The cost of maintaining a separate parent pointer does. If performance is important for your application, it might be worth the effort to write a benchmark program to determine the "break even" tree depth.*

What happens when we need to remove a node that has *two* children? Both of these children need to be re-attached to the tree, yet only one attachment point is being freed up. Note also that any rearrangement of nodes we might perform must preserve the binary search tree property. The basic approach we adopt is to leave *in place* the node to be removed, but change its *value* to the value of its immediate predecessor. The immediate predecessor happens to be a node with at most one child, so we can perform "tree surgery" on *it* more easily than on the node we want to remove.

How do we know that the immediate predecessor of a node with two children has, at most, one child? The immediate predecessor is the node with the highest value in the left subtree. We find it by moving from the node to be removed to its left subtree, and then repeatedly moving to the right subtree until we can go no farther. The node we reach by this procedure has no right child. Choosing the immediate predecessor to replace the node being removed also preserves the binary search tree property.

PROGRAMMER'S NOTE *When the node to be removed has two children, **remove(T)** could just as well replace this node with its immediate successor instead of its immediate predecessor. The exclusive choice of predecessor may cause the tree to become unbalanced if **remove(T)** is called frequently and no balancing scheme is in place. If this is a concern, you may wish to modify **remove(T)** so that each call alternately chooses the predecessor and the successor as the replacement node.*

The function **get_nth(int)** returns the nth smallest element of the tree. **Size( )** returns the number of elements in the tree. The **nodecount** field in each node allows these functions to be efficient. If **get_nth(int)** is not needed, or its efficiency is not considered important, the **nodecount** field and all the machinery for keeping it up to date can be eliminated. The **print( )** member function prints the nodes of the tree along with node counts, with the root on the left of the page and its children fanning out to the right. This "sideways" representation is easy to do and very useful for debugging.

The recursive functions **print_pre_order( )**, **print_in_order( )**, and **print_post_order( )** each print the elements of the list as a linear sequence and are standard traversal algorithms for binary trees. **Print_pre_order( )** prints the value of a given node *before* printing any of its descendants. Descendants to the left are printed before descendants to the right. **Print_post_order( )** does the opposite, printing the value of a given node *after* printing its left- and right-hand descendants. **Print_in_order( )** prints a node's left descendants first, then the node itself, and finally its right descendants. For a binary search tree, **print_in_order( )** prints the elements of the tree in ascending order. **Find(const T)** returns **true** if its parameter is found in the tree, and **false** otherwise.

A worthwhile extension to **bt.h** would be a set of iterators, similar to the iterator defined for linked lists in Chapter 2. As they do for lists, iterators could provide an elegant way to give the user greater control over nodes without exposing their internal structure. Defining iterators for pre-order, post-order, and in-order traversal would render the three corresponding print routines unnecessary. A typical implementation would employ a stack. Chapter 15 provides an example of a binary tree in-order iterator that does not require a stack.

Balanced Binary Search Trees

Suppose we wish to set up a binary search tree that contains the integers 1 through 7. Figure 3-2 shows two possible ways to do this. Figure 3-2a is the "ideal" binary tree for this set of values. Because it's nicely balanced, we can find any element with no more than three comparisons. On the other hand, even though Figure 3-2b has all the properties of a binary search tree, it's so lopsided that its access time is the same as for a linear list. We would have to visit each element in this tree to find the value 7.

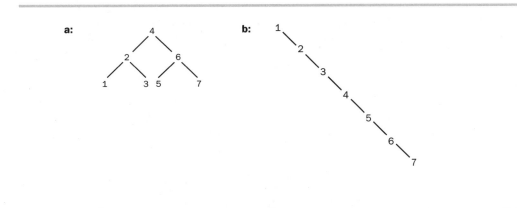

FIGURE 3-2. Balanced and unbalanced binary search trees

What determines whether a simple binary search tree is well balanced? It depends entirely on the order in which the elements are entered. Entering them in strict ascending or descending order gives the worst possible result. Unfortunately, unbalanced trees are not rare enough to ignore.

Despite the simplicity of this underlying concept, balanced trees are surprisingly hard to implement. Because efficiency motivates us to consider balanced trees to begin with, it's pointless to design a solution that forces us to re-structure the entire tree every time an element is added or removed (unless we expect to build the tree once, never modify it, and access it *many* times).

There are a number of approaches to tree balancing. Here we implement a *height-balanced* tree. Height-balanced trees are commonly known as *avl* trees, a term derived from the names of their original developers, Adel'son-Vel'skii and Landis. The central idea is to keep the tree *approximately* balanced by requiring each node to satisfy the following condition: The height of its left subtree cannot differ from the height of its right subtree by more than 1. This requirement results in several implementation features that are not needed for simple binary trees.

Each node needs a new field to store its *balance factor*, which is the height of its right subtree minus the height of its left subtree. The legal values for a balance factor are –1, 0, and +1. Any other value indicates that the node is out of balance. Because the simple approach to adding or deleting elements may make the tree unbalanced, the member functions **add(T)** and **remove(T)** must have additional code to bring an unbalanced tree back into balance. To do this, they will rely on new private member functions **rotate_left(Tree_node *&)** and **rotate_right(Tree_node *&)**.

A *rotation* is a technique for rearranging nodes in a binary tree in a way that preserves the binary tree property. The use of rotations to rebalance subtrees is covered in detail in the source code comments. In order to understand these comments, it's essential to understand rotations themselves. Figure 3-3a shows a simple binary tree with integer values. Figure 3-3b shows what this tree looks like after the node containing 6 is rotated to the right. Figure 3-3c shows the result of rotating the same node (in Figure 3-3b) to the left. These are examples of *single* rotations. Notice that the binary tree property is preserved.

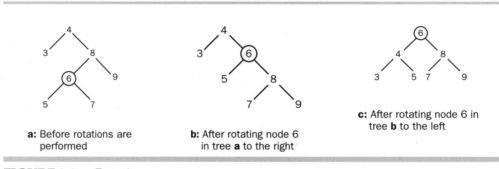

a: Before rotations are performed

b: After rotating node 6 in tree **a** to the right

c: After rotating node 6 in tree **b** to the left

FIGURE 3-3.   Rotations

A *double* rotation is accomplished by rotating a node first to the right and then to the left, *or* first to the left and then to the right. The two single rotations performed on the node containing 6 are equivalent to a double rotation.

The following code implements a balanced binary tree class. It is built upon the preceding binary tree class in this chapter, but adds the necessary mechanisms to keep the tree balanced.

Code

The code is organized into two files. **Avl.h** is the list itself, and **avl.cpp** shows an example of its use. Here is **avl.h**.

```cpp
#include <iostream>
#include <cassert>
using namespace std;

////////////////////////////////////////////////////////////////////////
//
// File avl.h.
// Avl_tree class template.  Implements a binary search tree with
// height balancing.  Local balancing is performed by add( T ) and
// remove ( T ) to maintain balance.  Duplicate values not permitted.
// Type T must support copying, and the following operators:
//
//   operator=( );
//   operator<<( );
//   operator==( );
//   operator!=( );
//   operator<( );
//
// Public member functions:
//
//   Avl_tree( );                      Make an empty tree.
//   Avl_tree(T root_val );            Make a with one element.
//   ~Avl_tree( );                     Release memory for each node.
//
//   bool add( T insert_value );               Add an element.
//   void remove( T value );                   Remove an element.
//   T get_nth(const int element_num) const;   Value of the nth elt.
//                                             Order defined as sorted
//                                             order of the elements.
//
```

```
//    int size( ) const;                    Number of elements.
//    bool find( T find_value );            True if find_value is
//                                          in the tree.
//
//    void print ( int level = 0 ) const;   Print sideways.
//
//    void print_pre_order( ) const;        Print as linear list.
//    void print_in_order( ) const;         Print as linear list.
//    void print_post_order( ) const;       Print as linear list.
//
// Implementation Notes:
//
//    Nodes contain a nodecount field to ease implementation of
//    get_nth.  They also contain parent links.  Recursive functions
//    are noted.
//
//
/////////////////////////////////////////////////////////////////////


template <class T>
class Avl_tree {

private:

  struct Tree_node {

    friend class Avl_tree;

    T val;                      // The data being stored in the tree.
    Tree_node *left_child;
    Tree_node *right_child;
    Tree_node *parent;
    int       bal;              // Balance factor =
                                //     (height right subtree)
                                //   - (height left subtree)
    int       nodecount;        // Number of nodes in subtree rooted
                                // at this node, including the node
                                // itself.

    Tree_node( );
    Tree_node( const T node_val ) : val(node_val) { }
    ~Tree_node( ) { }
```

```
// Isa_right_child( ) and isa_left_child( ) return true if the
// node making the call is the right/left child of its parent
// and false otherwise.  Return false for root node.

bool isa_right_child( ) const {
  if ( (parent == 0) || ( parent->right_child != this) )
    return false;
  else
    return true;
}

bool isa_left_child( ) const {
  if ( (parent == 0) || ( parent->left_child != this) )
    return false;
  else
    return true;
}

bool isa_leaf( ) const {
  return ( (right_child == 0) && (left_child == 0) );
}
// Print( ) prints tree sideways on the page, root at the left.
// "Backwards" recursive inorder traversal (i.e., right to left)
// -- otherwise we'd print the mirror image.  Nodecount/bal shown
// in parentheses.  Null children are printed as "@".

void print ( const int level = 0 ) const {

// Initializing to this instead of root makes it possible
  // to print subtrees as well as the entire tree.
  const Tree_node *tn = this;

  if ( tn != 0 ) tn->right_child->print( level + 1 );

  for (int spaces = 0; spaces < level; ++spaces)
    cout << "        ";

  if ( tn != 0 )
    cout << tn->val << '(' << tn->nodecount << '/' << bal << ')'
         << endl;
  else
    cout << "@" << endl;
```

```
        if ( tn != 0 ) tn->left_child->print( level + 1 );

    }

  };   // End of Tree_node declaration.


private:

// Avl_tree private data members:

  Tree_node *root;
  Tree_node *zero_node;   // const in usage, provides return
                // value for find_node(T).

// Avl_tree private member functions:

  //Dissallow copy and assignment.

  Avl_tree(const Avl_tree &);
  Avl_tree & operator=( const Avl_tree & );

  // Make a root node, initialize val to root_val,
  // children to null, bal to zero, nodecount to one.
  void make_new_root( const T root_val ) {
    root = new Tree_node(root_val);
    root->left_child  = 0;
    root->right_child = 0;
    root->parent      = 0;
    root->bal         = 0;
    root->nodecount   = 1;
  }


  // Find_node(T find_value) goes out of its way to return a
  // reference to a pointer, to simplify the implemenatation of
  // remove(T).

  Tree_node * & find_node( T find_value ) {
    Tree_node *tn = root;
    while ( (tn != 0) && (tn->val != find_value) )  {
      if ( find_value < tn->val )
```

```
        tn = tn->left_child;
      else
        tn = tn->right_child;
  }

  // Instead of just returning tn, we do the following slightly
  // complicated dance to be sure we return a *reference* within
  // the tree to the node we're looking for.

  if ( tn == 0 )
    // Find_value is not in the tree.
    return zero_node;
  else if ( tn->isa_left_child( ) )
    // Tn is the left child of its parent.
    return tn->parent->left_child;
  else if ( tn->isa_right_child( ) )
    // Tn is the right child of its parent.
    return tn->parent->right_child;
  else if ( tn == root )
    // No parents, special case.
    return root;

  // Should not reach this point.  Returns a garbage value,
  // to avoid compile time warning.
  assert(false);
  return zero_node;
}


// Insert_node( const T, Tree_node * ) adds a new value to the
// appropriate leaf if it's not already in the tree.  Returns a
// pointer to the new node if one was created, zero otherwise.
// Non-recursive.  Increment nodecount for each node we traverse.
// Do this *after* we insert the node, just in case it turns out to
// be a duplicate, and we decide not to insert it after all.

Tree_node * insert_node
( const T insert_value, Tree_node * start_node = 0 )
{

  if ( root == 0 )  {
    // Special case for empty tree.
    make_new_root( insert_value );
```

```
      return root;
}

if ( start_node == 0 ) start_node = root;

Tree_node *tn = start_node;

while ( (tn != 0) && (tn->val != insert_value) ) {

  if ( insert_value < tn->val )  {
    // Look at left child.
    if ( tn->left_child == 0 )  {

      // Insert new value as the left child of tn.
      attach_node( tn, tn->left_child, insert_value );

      // Adjust nodecounts and balance factors for all ancestors.
      // If an ancestor is found whose new balance factor is +2
      // or -2, the tree needs to be re-balanced at that point
      // with an appropriate sequence of rotations.  Note that
      // this only needs to be done once.  After the unbalanced
      // node is balanced, its ancestors are known to be
      // balanced as well.

      adjust_for_add( tn->left_child );
      return tn->left_child;
    }
    else {
      tn = tn->left_child;
    }
  }
  else {
    // Look at right child.
    if ( tn->right_child == 0 )  {

      // Insert new value as the right child of tn.
      attach_node( tn, tn->right_child, insert_value );

      adjust_for_add( tn->right_child );
      return tn->right_child;
    }
    else {
      tn = tn->right_child;
```

```
        }
      }
    }

    // Insert_value is already in the tree.
    assert ( tn != 0 );
    return 0;
}


// Attach_node( Tree_node *, Tree_node * &, T ) is a helper
// function for insert_node( const T insert_value, Tree_node * ).

void attach_node( Tree_node * new_parent,
                  Tree_node * & new_child, T insert_value ) {

    // Insert new value as the left child of tn.
    new_child = new Tree_node( insert_value );
    new_child->left_child  = 0;
    new_child->right_child = 0;
    new_child->parent      = new_parent;
    new_child->nodecount   = 1;
    new_child->bal         = 0;
}


// Adjust_nodecount_to_root( Tree_node *, int ) adds incr to the
// nodecount field of tn and all its ancestors including root.
// Note that root's parent link is zero.

void adjust_nodecount_to_root( Tree_node * tn, int incr ) {
    while ( tn != 0 ) {
        tn->nodecount += incr;
        tn = tn->parent;
    }
}


// Adjust_for_add( Tree_node *, Tree_node * ) makes changes in
// balance factors and nodecount for a newly added node and its
// ancestors.  Rotations are performed as needed.  Once we find
// node that's out of balance (i.e., its balance factor is 2 or
// -2), and rebalance its subtree, we can stop because the
```

```
// rebalancing technique preserves the original height of this
// subtree.

void adjust_for_add( Tree_node * new_child ) {

  // New_parent may be root, but new_child can't be.
  assert( new_child != root );
  bool rotate_flag = false;
  bool bal_was_changed = false;

  Tree_node * new_parent      = new_child->parent;
  Tree_node * new_grandparent = new_parent->parent;

  // The parent of a newly inserted node can't be brought out of
  // balance by the insertion.  Its *grandparent* is the first
  // node that can be brought out of balance.  So we handle the
  // first "iteration" outside the loop, and then initialize
  // the three-level ancestry for the loop itself.

  ++(new_parent->nodecount);

  if ( new_child->isa_right_child( ) ) {
    // New_parent was balanced and had no right child.  So the
    // height of its left subtree must be zero or one.
    ++(new_parent->bal);
    bal_was_changed = true;
  }
  else {
    // New_child must be a left child because it can't be root.
    --(new_parent->bal);
    bal_was_changed = true;
  }

  assert ( (new_parent->bal > -2) && (new_parent->bal < 2) );

  while ( new_grandparent != 0 ) {

    // In the loop, we assume new_child and new_parent are up to
    // date.  We update new_grandparent.  First, bring
    // new_grandparent's nodecount and balance factor up to date.

    ++(new_grandparent->nodecount);
```

```
if ( new_parent->isa_right_child( ) ) {
  // If new_parent's new balance factor is 1 or -1, and it has
  // changed, it must have been zero beforehand.  Hence, the
  // height of the subtree rooted at new_parent has increased
  // by one.  Thus, the height of new_grandparent's right
  // subtree has increased by one.  On the other hand, if
  // new_parent->bal has just become zero, it must have
  // previously been 1 or -1, so the new node just evened out
  // the subtree rooted at new_parent, and its height (and
  // hence the balance factor for new_grandparent) are
  // unchanged.
  if ( new_parent->bal != 0 && bal_was_changed )
    // Leave bal_was_changed alone.  We want it to continue
    // being true for the next iteration.
    ++(new_grandparent->bal);
  else
    // No change was made to new_grandparent->bal, so we want
    // bal_was_changed to be false for the next iteration.
    bal_was_changed = false;
}
else if ( new_parent->isa_left_child( ) ) {
  // Above comments apply here too, except that now we
  // decrement new_grandparent->bal because we're looking at
  // its left subtree.
  if ( new_parent->bal != 0 && bal_was_changed )
    --(new_grandparent->bal);
  else
    bal_was_changed = false;
}

if ( (new_grandparent->bal < -1)
  || (new_grandparent->bal > 1) ) {
  rotate_flag = true;
  break;
}

// Take one step up the tree.
new_child       = new_parent;
new_parent      = new_grandparent;
new_grandparent = new_grandparent->parent;
}


if ( rotate_flag ) {
```

```
// New_grandparent is out of balance, so we must rebalance it
// by performing one or two rotations.  Although there are four
// cases, two are mirror images.  Remember that we've only
// adjusted nodecount up to the node that was out of balance.
// When we're done with rotations, update the rest of them
// between that point and root.

// Some balance factor adjustments depend on new_child's
// original balance factor, so record it here before we
// start rotating.
int new_child_orig_bal = new_child->bal;

// Easy case (only one rotation) and its mirror image first
if ( new_parent->isa_left_child( )
  && new_child->isa_left_child( ) ) {

  // Rotate new_parent to the right about new_grandparent.

  // Pass new_grandparent by reference.
  if ( new_grandparent->isa_left_child( ) )
    rotate_right( new_grandparent->parent->left_child );
  else if ( new_grandparent->isa_right_child( ) )
    rotate_right( new_grandparent->parent->right_child );
  else {
    assert( new_grandparent == root );
    rotate_right( root );
  }

  // Adjust balance factors and nodecounts starting at
  // new_parent->parent which is now different from
  // new_grandparent as a result of the above rotation.
  new_parent->bal = 0;
  new_parent->right_child->bal = 0;
  adjust_nodecount_to_root( new_parent->parent, 1 );
}
else if ( new_parent->isa_right_child( )
      && new_child->isa_right_child( ) ) {

  // Rotate new_parent to the left about new_grandparent

  // Pass new_grandparent by reference.
  if ( new_grandparent->isa_left_child( ) )
    rotate_left( new_grandparent->parent->left_child );
```

```
   else if ( new_grandparent->isa_right_child( ) )
     rotate_left( new_grandparent->parent->right_child );
   else {
     assert( new_grandparent == root );
     rotate_left( root );
   }

   // Adjust balance factors and nodecounts.
   new_parent->bal = 0;
   new_parent->left_child->bal = 0;
   adjust_nodecount_to_root( new_parent->parent, 1 );
}

// Now the harder cases that require two rotations.
else if ( new_parent->isa_left_child( )
      && new_child->isa_right_child( ) )
{
   // Rotate new_child.  Pass new_parent by reference.
   // We already know that new_parent is a left child,
   // so no need to test.
   rotate_left( new_grandparent->left_child );

   // Pass rotated new_child by reference.  This time we do have
   // to test, because the child has been rotated, and previous
   // assertions may not hold.  Since new_child has moved up one
   // notch, we need to test new_grandparent instead of
   // new_parent.
   if ( new_grandparent->isa_left_child( ) )
     rotate_right( new_grandparent->parent->left_child );
   else if ( new_grandparent->isa_right_child( ) )
     rotate_right( new_grandparent->parent->right_child );
   else {
     assert( new_grandparent == root );
     rotate_right( root );
   }

   // New_grandparent is now the right child of the newly
   // rebalanced subtree.  Adjust balance factors and nodecounts
   // starting with the parent of this subtree.
   new_grandparent->parent->bal = 0;

   // Other adjustments depend on new_child's original balance
   // factor.
```

```
      if (new_child_orig_bal == 0) {
        new_grandparent->bal = 0;
        new_grandparent->parent->left_child->bal = 0;
      }
      else if (new_child_orig_bal == -1) {
        new_grandparent->bal = 1;
        new_grandparent->parent->left_child->bal = 0;
      }
      else if (new_child_orig_bal == 1) {
        new_grandparent->bal = 0;
        new_grandparent->parent->left_child->bal = -1;
      }

      adjust_nodecount_to_root
          ( new_grandparent->parent->parent , 1 );
  }

  else if ( new_parent->isa_right_child( )
          && new_child->isa_left_child( ) ) {

      // Rotate new_child.  Pass new_parent by reference.
      // We already know that new_parent is a right child,
      // so no need to test.
      rotate_right( new_grandparent->right_child );

      // Pass rotated new_child by reference.  This time we do have
      // to test, because the child has been rotated, and previous
      // assertions may not hold.  Since new_child has moved up one
      // notch, we need to test new_grandparent instead of
      // new_parent.
      if ( new_grandparent->isa_left_child( ) )
        rotate_left( new_grandparent->parent->left_child );
      else if ( new_grandparent->isa_right_child( ) )
        rotate_left( new_grandparent->parent->right_child );
      else {
        assert( new_grandparent == root );
        rotate_left( root );
      }

      // New_grandparent is now the left child of the newly
      // rebalanced subtree.  Adjust balance factors and nodecounts
      // starting with the parent of this subtree.
      new_grandparent->parent->bal = 0;
```

```
      // Other adjustments depend on new_child's original balance
      // factor.
      if (new_child_orig_bal == 0) {
        new_grandparent->bal = 0;
        new_grandparent->parent->right_child->bal = 0;
      }
      else if (new_child_orig_bal == -1) {
        new_grandparent->bal = 0;
        new_grandparent->parent->right_child->bal = 1;
      }
      else if (new_child_orig_bal == 1) {
        new_grandparent->bal = -1;
        new_grandparent->parent->right_child->bal = 0;
      }

      adjust_nodecount_to_root
          ( new_grandparent->parent->parent , 1 );
    }
  }


}

// Get_nth_node( Tree_node *, const int ) returns the node
// corresponding to the nth sorted (or inorder) value in the tree.
// Recursive.  Depends on nodecount field being correctly set.

Tree_node * get_nth_node(Tree_node * tn, const int nth) const {

  // Special handling for empty root.
  if ( tn == 0 ) return 0;

  //  Remember the nodecount of tn's left child.
  int lc_count
      = (tn->left_child != 0) ? tn->left_child->nodecount : 0 ;

  if ( (lc_count + 1) == nth ) {
    // We're done, because tn itself is the nth value.
    return tn;
  }
  else if ( lc_count >= nth ) {
    // Look for nth in left child
    return get_nth_node(tn->left_child, nth);
```

```
    }
    else  {
      // Look for (nth - lc_count - 1) in right child
      return get_nth_node(tn->right_child, nth - lc_count -1);
    }
}

// The rotate functions are static because they don't need
// a "this" pointer.  Note that the parameter is a reference
// to a Tree_node pointer.

static void rotate_right(Tree_node * & node) {
  Tree_node *tn = node->left_child;

  node->left_child   = tn->right_child;
  if (tn->right_child) tn->right_child->parent = node;

  tn->right_child = node;
  tn->parent      = node->parent;
  node->parent    = tn;

  // Update nodecount just before updating node.
  // They must be done in this order, ie, starting
  // with the lower node.

  int leftcount  = node->left_child ?
            node->left_child->nodecount : 0;
  int rightcount = node->right_child ?
            node->right_child->nodecount : 0;

  node->nodecount = leftcount + rightcount + 1;

  leftcount  = tn->left_child ?
               tn->left_child->nodecount : 0;
  rightcount = tn->right_child ?
          tn->right_child->nodecount : 0;

  tn->nodecount   = leftcount + rightcount + 1;

node            = tn;
  }

  static void rotate_left(Tree_node * & node) {
```

```
    Tree_node *tn = node->right_child;

    node->right_child = tn->left_child;
    if (tn->left_child) tn->left_child->parent = node;

    tn->left_child = node;
    tn->parent     = node->parent;
    node->parent   = tn;

    // Update nodecount just before updating node.
    // They must be done in this order, ie, starting
    // with the lower node.

    int leftcount  = node->left_child ?
                     node->left_child->nodecount : 0;
    int rightcount = node->right_child ?
                     node->right_child->nodecount : 0;

    node->nodecount = leftcount + rightcount + 1;

    leftcount  = tn->left_child ?
               tn->left_child->nodecount : 0;
    rightcount = tn->right_child ?
           tn->right_child->nodecount : 0;

    tn->nodecount  = leftcount + rightcount + 1;

    node           = tn;
}

// Cleanup ( Tree_node * ) deletes all Tree_nodes in post-order
// traversal.  Does the real work for ~Avl_tree( ).

void cleanup (Tree_node *tn) {

    // Special handling for empty root.
    if ( tn == 0 ) return;

    if ( tn->left_child != 0 ) {
        cleanup(tn->left_child);
        tn->left_child = 0;
    }
    if ( tn->right_child != 0 ) {
```

```
      cleanup(tn->right_child);
      tn->right_child = 0;
    }
    delete tn;
}


// Print_pre( const Tree_node * ) recursively prints tree values
// for the subtree rooted at tn in pre-order.

void print_pre(const Tree_node * tn) const {

    // Special handling for empty root.
    if ( tn == 0 ) return;

    cout << tn->val << "   ";
    if ( tn->left_child != 0 ) {
      print_pre( tn->left_child );
    }
    if ( tn->right_child != 0 ) {
      print_pre( tn->right_child );
    }
}

// Print_in( const Tree_node * ) recursively prints tree values for
// the subtree rooted at tn in in-order (or sorted order).

void print_in(const Tree_node * tn)  const {

    // Special handling for empty root.
    if ( tn == 0 ) return;

    if ( tn->left_child != 0 ) {
      print_in( tn->left_child );
    }
    cout << tn->val << "   ";
    if ( tn->right_child != 0 ) {
      print_in( tn->right_child );
    }
}

// Print_post( const Tree_node * ) recursively prints tree values
// for the subtree rooted at tn in post-order.
```

```
  void print_post(const Tree_node * tn) const {

    // Special handling for empty root.
    if ( tn == 0 ) return;

    if ( tn->left_child != 0 ) {
      print_post( tn->left_child );
    }
    if ( tn->right_child != 0 ) {
      print_post( tn->right_child );
    }
    cout << tn->val << "   ";
  }

// End of Avl_tree private member functions:


public:

// Avl_tree public member functions:

  Avl_tree( ) : zero_node(0) { root = 0; }

  Avl_tree(const T root_val ) : zero_node(0) {
    make_new_root( root_val );
  }


  // Release memory for each Tree_node, in a post-order traversal.
  // Private member cleanup( Tree_node * ) does the work.

  ~Avl_tree( ) {
    cleanup( root );
  }

  // Add( const T ) adds a value to the tree if it's not already
  // there.  Returns true if insert_value was actually added.
  // Private member function insert_node(T) does the real work.

  bool add( const T insert_value ) {
    Tree_node *ret = insert_node(insert_value);
```

```
    if (ret) return true;
    else      return false;
}
// Remove( T ) removes the node containing value from the tree.
// This function is the hardest to implement cleanly because
// the node being deleted may have two children.  These children
// need to be re-attached to the tree, but the node being deleted
// has only one parent, so some surgery is required.  This
// operation is handled in a way that preserves the binary tree
// property and does *not* increase the height of the tree.
// Defining node_to_remove as a reference to a pointer makes
// remove( T ) less complicated than it would otherwise be.

void remove( T value ) {

  Tree_node * & node_to_remove = find_node( value );

  Tree_node * predecessor = 0;
  Tree_node * temp = 0;
  int delta_balance = 0;

  if ( node_to_remove == zero_node ) return;
  assert( node_to_remove->val == value );

  // Handle easy cases first, where node_to_remove has at most one
  // child.

  if ( node_to_remove->left_child == 0 ) {

    // Node_to_remove has no left child.
    temp = node_to_remove;

    // Adjust the parent's nodecount and bal fields
    // before we start splicing.  Otherwise, the
    // isa functions get confused.
    if (temp->parent) {
      --(temp->parent->nodecount);
      if (temp->isa_left_child( )) {
        ++(temp->parent->bal);
        delta_balance = 1;
      }
      else if (temp->isa_right_child( )) {
        --(temp->parent->bal);
```

```
          delta_balance = -1;
      }
  }

  if ( node_to_remove->right_child != 0 )  {
    // Node_to_remove does have a right child.
    node_to_remove->right_child->parent = node_to_remove->parent;
  }

  // Replace node_to_remove with its right child.  Ok if the
  // right child is null.  After this statement, the variable
  // node_to_remove no longer references the node we are
  // removing.  But temp still does.
  node_to_remove = node_to_remove->right_child;

  // Node_to_remove's right child now occupies node_to_remove's
  // former position in the tree.  It's nodecount hasn't changed.
  // But the nodecount of its parent and all other ancestors must
  // decrease by one to account for the removed node.  We'll
  // adjust the parent's nodecount and bal fields right here,
  // and rely on adjust_for_remove( ) to handle this for nodes
  // from the parent and root.

  // Free the memory of the node that's just been removed from
  // the tree after adjusting.
  adjust_for_remove(temp->parent, delta_balance);
  delete temp;

  return;
}
else if ( node_to_remove->right_child == 0 ) {

  // Node_to_remove has no right child.
  temp = node_to_remove;

  if (temp->parent) {
    --(temp->parent->nodecount);
    if (temp->isa_left_child( )) {
      ++(temp->parent->bal);
      delta_balance = 1;
    }
    else if (temp->isa_right_child( )) {
      --(temp->parent->bal);
```

```
        delta_balance = -1;
      }
  }

  // We know the left child is not zero, because we're in
  // the "else clause".  Hence, no need to check this condition
  // before executing the following statement.
  node_to_remove->left_child->parent = node_to_remove->parent;

  // See "if clause" comments above.
  node_to_remove = node_to_remove->left_child;
  adjust_for_remove(temp->parent, delta_balance);
  delete temp;

  return;
}

// If we reach this point, we know that node_to_remove has
// two children.  Find its immediate predecessor, ie, the
// rightmost descendant of its left child.

predecessor = node_to_remove->left_child;
while ( predecessor->right_child != 0 )
  predecessor = predecessor->right_child;

// Replace the value of node_to_remove with the value of its
// predecessor.
node_to_remove->val = predecessor->val;

// Now that predecessor's value has been moved upward in the
// tree, we must attach predecessor's left child to predecessor's
// parent.  It will become the right child of predecessor's
// parent.  Recall that predecessor has no right child because of
// the way we've defined it.

Tree_node * pp = predecessor->parent;

if ( pp == node_to_remove ) {
  // Special case where predecessor is node_to_remove's left
  // child (i.e., it has no right child).
  pp->left_child = predecessor->left_child;
  ++(pp->bal);
  delta_balance = 1;
```

```
      if ( predecessor->left_child != 0 )
        predecessor->left_child->parent = pp;
    }
    else if ( predecessor->left_child != 0 ) {
      // Predecessor has a left child, and we must be sure not
      // to leave this child dangling.  Make it the right child
      // of predecessor's parent.
      pp->right_child = predecessor->left_child;
      predecessor->left_child->parent = pp;
      --(pp->bal);
      delta_balance = -1;
    }
    else {
      // Predecessor's left child is zero, so there's nothing for
      // its parent's right_child field to point to.
      assert( pp->right_child == predecessor );
      pp->right_child = 0;
      --(pp->bal);
      delta_balance = -1;
    }

    // Now update the nodecount for predecessor->parent and
    // all its ancestors.  Root's parent link is null.  The
    // second argument to adjust_for_remove is 1, because
    // that's the *absolute value* of the change to pp's
    // balance factor for each of the adjustments made above.

    --(pp->nodecount);
    adjust_for_remove(pp, delta_balance);

    // Predecessor's value has been moved to another node, and its
    // children, if any, have been re-attached to predecessor's
    // parent.  We no longer need the memory that originally
    // contained predecessor.
    delete predecessor;
}

// Walk backwards from start_node to root, adjusting
// the nodecount and bal fields for each node along the
// way, starting with start_node's parent.  Rotations
// are performed when a node becomes out of balance.
// Delta_balance is the amount by which start_node's bal field
```

```
    // has changed just prior to the call.  Recall that root's
    // parent is zero.

  void adjust_for_remove( Tree_node * start_node, int delta_balance )
{

    Tree_node * tn    = start_node;
    int tn_bal_orig  = tn->bal;

    if ( (tn->bal == -2) || (tn->bal == 2) )
      tn = rotate_for_remove (tn, delta_balance);

    delta_balance = tn_bal_orig - tn->bal;
    int absdelta = (delta_balance > 0) ? delta_balance :
-delta_balance;
    Tree_node * tnp  = tn->parent;

    while ( tnp != 0 ) {
      // Bring tnp's bal and nodecount fields up to date.
      // If tnp is out of balance, perform proper rotations.
      // Rotate functions have been modified to update these
      // fields as well.
      // Update nodecount
      --(tnp->nodecount);

      // Update balance factor.  Tn itself is already up to
      // date, and we know how its balance factor has changed.
      // If tn is a right child and its current balance factor
      // is zero, then we decrement tnp's balance factor by the
      // absolute value of the change in tn's balance factor.
      // If tn is a left child and its current balance factor
      // is zero, we increment tnp's balance factor by that
      // amount.  Note that unless tn's balance factor has
      // changed to *zero*, tnp's balance factor remains
      // unchanged.  If tnp's balance factor remains unchanged,
      // then so do the balance factors of all its ancestors.
      // From that point on we can stop checking balance
      // factors and simply decrement nodecounts.

      // Note that we need to remember the value of tnp->bal
      // in case rotations are needed, so we can figure out the
      // new value of absdelta for the next iteration.
```

```
    assert(tn != root);
    if ( tn->bal == 0 ) {
      if ( tn->isa_right_child( )) {
        - -(tnp->bal);
        delta_balance = -1;
      }
      else  {
        ++(tnp->bal);
        delta_balance = 1;
      }
    }
    else {
      adjust_nodecount_to_root( tnp->parent, -1 );
      return;
    }


    // Move one step up the tree for the next iteration.
    if ( (tnp->bal > -2) && (tnp->bal < 2) )  {
      tn  = tnp;
      tnp = tn->parent;
      continue;
    }

    // The hard part is done by this call.
    tn = rotate_for_remove (tnp, delta_balance);
    tnp = tn->parent;
  }

}

Tree_node * rotate_for_remove( Tree_node * tn, int delta_balance )
{
    // Now comes the hard part.  If, tnp has become
    // unbalanced, we must re-balance the tree using
    // rotations.

    Tree_node * resume_iteration = 0;
    Tree_node * tnp = tn->parent;

    //if ( tn->isa_left_child( ) ) {
    if ( delta_balance > 0 ) {
      // Tn lost a left descendant.
```

```
// Remember how to reach tn's current right child, because
// for the first case, after rotation, that will be the
// node from which to continue walking up the tree.  For the
// second case, this node's left child will be the point of
// departure.
resume_iteration = tn->right_child;

if ( (tn->bal == 2) &&
     ( (tn->right_child->bal == 1) ||
       (tn->right_child->bal == 0) )
   ) {

  // Adjust balance factors to proper post-rotation values.
  if (tn->right_child->bal == 1) {
    tn->bal = 0;
    tn->right_child->bal = 0;
  }
  else {
    assert(tn->right_child->bal == 0);
    tn->bal = 1;
    tn->right_child->bal = -1;
  }


  // Single Rotation.
  // Complicated dance to pass tnp by reference.
  if ( tn->isa_left_child( ) )
    rotate_left(tn->parent->left_child);
  else if ( tn->isa_right_child( ) )
    rotate_left(tn->parent->right_child);
  else {
    assert(tn == root);
    rotate_left(root);
  }

  return resume_iteration;
}
else if ( (tn->bal == 2) &&
  (tn->right_child->bal == -1) ) {

  // Adjust balance factors to proper post-rotation values.
  if (tn->right_child->left_child->bal == 1) {
    tn->bal = -1;
```

```
          tn->right_child->bal = 0;
          tn->right_child->left_child->bal = 0;
        }
        else if (tn->right_child->left_child->bal == -1) {
          tn->bal = 0;
          tn->right_child->bal = 1;
          tn->right_child->left_child->bal = 0;
        }
        else {
          assert (tn->right_child->left_child->bal == 0);
          tn->bal = 0;
          tn->right_child->bal = 0;
          tn->right_child->left_child->bal = 0;
        }
        // Double Rotation.
        resume_iteration = resume_iteration->left_child;

        // First rotation.
        rotate_right(tn->right_child);

        // Second rotation.
        // Complicated dance to pass tnp by reference.
        if ( tn->isa_left_child( ) )
          rotate_left(tn->parent->left_child);
        else if ( tn->isa_right_child( ) )
          rotate_left(tn->parent->right_child);
        else {
          assert(tn == root);
          rotate_left(root);
        }

        return resume_iteration;
      }
  }
  // else if ( tn->isa_right_child( ) ) {
  else {
    assert ( delta_balance < 0 );
    // Mirror images of above.
    // Tn has lost a right descendant.

    // Remember how to reach tn's current left child, because
    // for the first case, after rotation, that will be the
```

```
      // node from which to continue walking up the tree.  For the
      // second case, this node's right child will be the point of
      // departure.
      resume_iteration = tn->left_child;

  if ( (tn->bal == -2) &&
        ( (tn->left_child->bal == -1) ||
          (tn->left_child->bal == 0) )
      ) {

      // Adjust balance factors to proper post-rotation values.
      if (tn->left_child->bal == -1) {
        tn->bal = 0;
        tn->left_child->bal = 0;
      }
      else {
        assert(tn->right_child->bal == 0);
        tn->bal = -1;
        tn->left_child->bal = 1;
      }

      // Single Rotation.
      // Complicated dance to pass tnp by reference.
      if ( tn->isa_left_child( ) )
        rotate_right(tn->parent->left_child);
      else if ( tn->isa_right_child( ) )
        rotate_right(tn->parent->right_child);
      else {
        assert(tn == root);
        rotate_right(root);
      }

      return resume_iteration;
  }
  else if ( (tn->bal == -2) &&
      (tn->left_child->bal == 1) ) {

      // Adjust balance factors to proper post-rotation values.
      if (tn->left_child->right_child->bal == -1) {
        tn->bal = 1;
        tn->left_child->bal = 0;
        tn->left_child->left_child->bal = 0;
      }
```

```
        else if (tn->left_child->right_child->bal == 1) {
          tn->bal = 0;
          tn->left_child->bal = -1;
          tn->left_child->right_child->bal = 0;
        }
        else {
          assert(tn->left_child->right_child->bal == 0);
          tn->bal = 0;
          tn->left_child->bal = 0;
          tn->left_child->right_child->bal = 0;
        }

        // Double Rotation.
        resume_iteration = resume_iteration->right_child;

        // First rotation.
        rotate_left(tn->left_child);

        // Second rotation.
        // Complicated dance to pass tnp by reference.
        if ( tn->isa_left_child( ) )
          rotate_right(tnp->parent->left_child);
        else if ( tn->isa_right_child( ) )
          rotate_right(tnp->parent->right_child);
        else {
          assert(tn == root);
          rotate_right(root);
        }

        return resume_iteration;
      }
    }

    // Should not reach this point.  Returns a garbage value,
    // to avoid compile time warning.
    assert(false);
    return zero_node;
}

// Get_nth( const int ) returns the nth value in the tree, based on
// sorted order.

T get_nth(const int element_num) const {
```

```
      Tree_node * tn = get_nth_node(root, element_num);
      return tn->val;
  }

  // Size( ) returns the number of nodes in the tree.
  int size( ) const { return root ? root->nodecount : 0; }

  // Find( const T ) returns true if find_value is in the tree,
  // false otherwise.
  bool find( T find_value ) {
    Tree_node *tn = find_node( find_value );

    if ( tn != 0 )
      return true;
    else
      return false;
  }


  // Print( ) does a backwards in-order traversal, and prints the
  // tree "sideways" on the page.

  void print ( ) const {
    cout << "\n" << "======================================" << "\n"
         << endl;

    // The following is a call to Avl_tree::Tree_node::print( ),
    // *not* a recursive call to Avl_tree::print( ).
    root->print( );
  }

  // The following functions print the elements linearly in pre-
  // order, in-order, and post-order, respectively.  Print_inorder( )
  // is equivalent to sorting.  These public functions take no
  // parameters, but call private recursive functions, taking
  // Tree_node * parameters, to do the work.

  void print_pre_order( ) const {
    print_pre(root);
    cout << endl;
  }

  void print_in_order( ) const {
```

```
    print_in(root);
    cout << endl;
  }

  void print_post_order( ) const {
    print_post(root);
    cout << endl;
  }

};
```

Avl.cpp populates a binary search tree with the integers 1 through 7, in sorted order. In an ordinary search tree, this would result in the lopsided tree shown in Figure 3-2b. However, the tree-balancing techniques in **avl.h** generate the tree shown in Figure 3-2a instead. Then the elements 1, 2, and 3 are removed. Again, while a simple removal algorithm would leave the resulting tree unbalanced, the one in **avl.h** keeps it balanced. Balance factors are printed in parentheses to the right of the node count.

```
// File avl.cpp:  Usage examples for avl.h

#include "avl.h"

// Create a balanced binary search tree containing integers.
// The tree is initially empty.
Avl_tree<int> my_avlt;

// Populate my_avlt with integer values.  Enter these
// integers in sorted order, which is the worst possible
// sequence for an ordinary binary search tree.
void populate( ) {
  my_avlt.add( 1 );
  my_avlt.add( 2 );
  my_avlt.add( 3 );
  my_avlt.add( 4 );
  my_avlt.add( 5 );
  my_avlt.add( 6 );
  my_avlt.add( 7 );
}

int main( )
{
  populate( );
```

```
// Print full tree.  It should be well balanced despite
// populate( )'s attempt to make it lopsided.
my_avlt.print ( );

// Remove nodes only from the left subtree, another futile
// attempt to make the tree lopsided.
my_avlt.remove ( 1 );
my_avlt.remove ( 2 );
my_avlt.remove ( 3 );

// Print full tree once more.
my_avlt.print ( );

return 0;
}
```

Here is the output of **avl.cpp:**

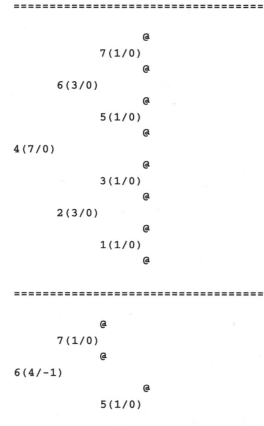

```
====================================

                        @
            7(1/0)
                        @
        6(3/0)
                        @
            5(1/0)
                        @
4(7/0)
                        @
            3(1/0)
                        @
        2(3/0)
                        @
            1(1/0)
                        @

====================================

                        @
            7(1/0)
                        @
6(4/-1)
                        @
            5(1/0)
```

```
                        @
    4(2/1)
                  @


    —
```

ANNOTATIONS

Avl.h's organization closely parallels that of **bt.h**. In addition to the functions provided by **bt.h**, we have the private static members **rotate_left(Tree_node *&)** and **rotate_right(Tree_node *&)**. These utility functions implement the rotation operations described above. They're called by **adjust_for_add(Tree_node *)** and **adjust_for_remove(Tree_node *)**.

PROGRAMMER'S NOTE   *There is no explicit function to implement a double rotation in one step. For simplicity here, double rotations are instead implemented by composing single rotations. Dedicated functions for the two kinds of double rotations would result in improved performance by reducing the number of calls and the number of assignments needed to restructure the tree.*

Add(T) and **remove(T)** were modified only slightly. They now call **adjust_for_add (Tree_node *)** and **adjust_for_remove(Tree_node *)** to rebalance the tree. These two adjustment routines do the major work of tree balancing. Their basic strategy is to walk backward in the tree from the point of change toward the root, adjusting balance factors and performing rotations along the way. **Adjust_for_add(Tree_node *)** only needs to walk back until it finds its first out-of-balance node. At this point it performs an adjustment and then updates the node counts of ancestors, but no further restructuring is required. **Adjust_for_remove(Tree_node *)** doesn't have this luxury, however. It must perform adjustments all the way back to root. Following is a summary of the adjustment functions; more details are provided in the source code comments.

Adjust_for_add(Tree_node *) has two basic parts. The first part walks up the tree from the newly inserted node, and makes fairly straightforward adjustments to the node count and balance factors of each node it visits. The initial code and **while** loop attend to this task. The flag **bal_was_changed** keeps track of whether the balance factor of the new node's parent changed as a result of the insertion. This information helps to determine what adjustments need to be made for the grandparent's balance factor. As we walk up the tree, **bal_was_changed** refers to nodes that are successively higher up.

Aside from doing this work, the initial **while** loop keeps checking to see whether a rotation is needed. The boolean variable **rotate_flag**, whose initial value is **false**, helps with this task. Once we discover a node whose balance factor becomes +2 or –2, we know that a rotation is required, and set the value of this flag to **true**. This discovery also means that we can stop checking balance factors after the rotation is performed. That's why we break out of the loop after setting this flag.

The second part of **adjust_for_add(Tree_node *)** figures out what kind of rotation to perform, performs the rotation, and does the final adjustment of balance factors. (The code in this section is lengthy and somewhat repetitive. It essentially sorts out the various subtree configurations and makes the adjustment appropriate to each. Once you realize that half of these cases are mirror images of the other half, the code becomes much easier to follow.) The final task is to adjust any remaining node counts between the current node and root. This has to be done even though we're finished with balance factors. The final call to **adjust_nodecount_to_root (Tree_node *, int)** accomplishes this task.

Adjust_for_remove(Tree_node *, int) differs in structure from **adjust_for_add (Tree_node *)**. Instead of breaking out of the main loop when the need for a rotation is discovered, **adjust_for_remove(Tree_node *, int)** remains inside the loop. However, it is still possible to break out of this loop before walking all the way up the tree. If we ever find a node whose balance factor stays the same, we can be sure the balance factors of its ancestors also stay the same. The simple (but not obvious) test for this condition is spelled out in detail in the source code comments.

Note that the lengthy case analysis to decide what kind of rotation to perform has been broken out into a separate function, **rotate_for_remove(Tree_node *, int)**. This was done because that analysis occurs in two different places in **adjust_for_remove (Tree_node *, int)**. The **rotate_for_remove(Tree_node *, int)** function also returns a **Tree_node ***, which points to the node its caller should use for the next iteration. This further simplifies the structure of **adjust_for_remove(Tree_node *, int)**. Finally, note that half of the cases in **rotate_for_remove(Tree_node *, int)** are mirror images of the other half.

Be aware that maximum efficiency was not the goal of this implementation. The adjustment functions try to achieve clarity by explicitly considering the various cases that arise in tree balancing. Their efficiency can certainly be improved.

Hash Tables and Sparse Arrays

By Art Friedman

hash_1.h	1d.h
hash_1.cpp	1d.cpp
hash_2.h	2d.h
hash_2.cpp	2d.cpp

T his chapter examines two interesting areas of programming: hash tables and sparse arrays. Their ability to optimize access to certain types of data makes them quite useful in a variety of situations. While each is simple in concept, both raise some intriguing programming challenges.

Introduction to Hash Tables and Sparse Arrays

The term *search*, roughly speaking, refers to any technique whose basic strategy is to look up a record by comparing a known key value to the keys of each element in a data structure. When a matching key is found, the record may be retrieved. The binary search trees in Chapter 3 support efficient searching for ordered data by limiting the number of key comparisons that are needed.

By contrast, records stored in an array whose index corresponds to the key can be looked up very quickly, and with no need to compare keys. Given a key (that is, an array index), the size of the stored records, and the array's starting address, we compute the address of the desired record with just one multiplication and one addition. With these advantages, why don't we just forget about searching and use arrays exclusively? A simple (and somewhat contrived) example will answer this question.

Suppose we want to store records with key values of 3, 10,000,000, and 60,000,000. Storing these three records in an array indexed by key value requires an array of 60 million elements, nearly all of which would be empty. Clearly, this is a bad idea. Virtually any search technique would handle this contrived situation better.

Naturally, the problem gets more interesting when we need to store a significant number of records. Instead of three records, suppose we need to store a half million, and that the key values for these records still range from 1 to 60,000,000. Our hypothetical array of 60 million elements would still be about 99% empty—but now we have to look at alternatives more carefully. We can't just wave our hands at the task of searching a half million records. Hash tables and sparse arrays try to resolve this conflict with a compromise. Both of these techniques combine index manipulation with search. Hash tables emphasize index computation as much as possible; sparse arrays rely more heavily on search.

Hash Table Design

Hash tables often consist of a fixed-size array of the elements to be stored, or pointers to these elements. Rather than using the key value as a direct index into this array, we compute the index with a *hash function* that takes the key value as a parameter. The hash function guarantees that the index it returns will be within the fixed range of the array. It also attempts to compute indexes in a way that assigns a different one to each key value.

Ideally, a hash function would never return the same index for two different key values. In practice, this ideal is very difficult (often impossible) to achieve. When a hash function returns the same index for two or more different keys, these keys are said to *collide*. Each key wants to occupy the same position in the table, but there's only room for one. There are two critical features that distinguish good hash functions from bad ones. One of them is speed—hash functions must be very fast. The other feature is the ability to distribute indexes evenly over the array, thereby avoiding collisions.

Realistically, a hash table implementation must assume that collisions will occur. The way collisions are handled is an important aspect of hash table design. The hash table examples in this chapter manage collisions by *chaining*. This means each element that hashes to a particular index is added to a linked list of elements that hash to the same index. These elements are not forced into any particular order, and the key associated with each element is stored along with it.

When looking up a particular key, we first use the hash function to compute the array index and then search the corresponding linked list for the element with the matching key. Storing the key along with the data allows us to accept duplicate data elements, but the key values themselves must be unique. Hash tables do not capture ordering relationships such as "less than," and it makes no sense to look up the "predecessor" of some given value. Likewise, there's no reason to write an iterator for a hash table. Figure 4-1 shows what this kind of hash table looks like in memory.

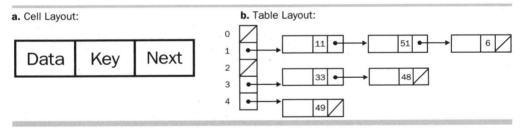

a. Cell Layout:

b. Table Layout:

FIGURE 4-1. Hash table memory layout

Designing a *generic* hash table is tricky. To understand why, consider a straightforward approach that requires the type being hashed to provide a **hash( )** member function that returns an appropriate integer value. The most obvious drawback to this approach is that **hash( )** is not a built-in operator. Hence a "generic" hash table designed in this fashion could not handle built-in types such as **int** and **char**. Also, how is **hash( )** supposed to know the legal range of integers it may return? Generally speaking, if a contained object needs to know a great deal about the implementation of its container, the container is not well designed for generic use.

Rather than grapple further with these design issues, we'll provide some examples that are *not* truly generic but are still widely applicable. Each of our two hash tables will be based on a specific key type and will provide its own hash function. This is a reasonable approach because hash tables are often specially tuned. In all likelihood, you'll want to tailor these tables to meet your own special needs.

Simple Hash Table with Integer Keys

Our first example uses **int** keys. When adding an object to the table, you must explicitly associate a unique integer key with the object being added. At first glance it may seem like a bad idea to force this task onto the user. Might the user need to maintain a *second* table to ensure that keys are unique? The answer is no, because we've defined **add(const T&, int)** to return **false** if the key is a duplicate, and **true** otherwise.

In some situations, integer keys provide a very simple and natural representation. A debugger, for example, must be able to look up a symbol name given its address, or a line of source code given its line number. In this case, the developer doesn't need to do anything special to generate keys or ensure their uniqueness.

Code

hash_1.h
hash_1.cpp

The code is organized into files **hash_1.h** and **hash_1.cpp**. Here is file **hash_1.h**:

```
/////////////////////////////////////////////////////////////
//
// File hash_1.h
// Simple hash table template using integer keys.  In
// the constructor, the user must specify a
// distinguished object of type T to serve as the
// "not found" value returned by find(int) when it
// tries to look up an element that's not in the
// table.  The user also specifies the size of the
// array used to implement the table.  The number of
// table entries has no predetermined limit.
// Add(const T &, int) checks for duplicate keys
// and refuses to add them to the table.  Duplicate
// *data* is permitted, however.
//
// T must support copying.  Support for operator<<( )
// is required for printing.
//
```

```
/
/////////////////////////////////////////////////////

#include <iostream>
using namespace std;

template<class T>
class Hash_table {

private:

  // Private struct cell stores data and keys internally.

  struct cell {
    const T& data;
    int key;
    cell * next;
    cell(const T& cell_data, int cell_key,
         cell * cell_next = 0)
      : data(cell_data), key(cell_key), next(cell_next) { }
  };

  // Table is the internal array.  Each element points
  // to a (possibly empty) list of cells.

  cell **table;
  unsigned int table_size;

  // T_notfound is a distinguished value of type T passed
  // to the constructor by the user.  When find(int) returns
  // this value, it signifies that the key the user tried
  // to look up is not in the table.

  T T_notfound;

  // Hash(int) computes the simplest possible hash function.
  // This may or may not be suitable for your needs.  Hash
  // functions should be as simple (and fast) as possible
  // while still meeting their basic requirements.

  unsigned int hash(int key) {
    return unsigned(key % table_size);
  }
```

```cpp
  // Find_cell( ) returns a pointer to the cell
  // containing key.  Returns zero when key is
  // not found.

  cell * find_cell(int key) {
    unsigned int slot = hash(key);
    for (cell *cp = table[slot]; cp != 0; cp = cp->next) {
      if (cp->key == key) return cp;
    }
    return cp;
  }


  // Assignment and copying not supported.
  Hash_table(const Hash_table &);
  Hash_table & operator=(const Hash_table &);

public:

  // Constructor allocates table and initializes
  // T_notfound.

  Hash_table(unsigned int size, const T& notfound)
    : table_size(size), T_notfound(notfound)
  {
    table = new cell*[table_size];
    for (int i = 0; i < size; table[i++] = 0);
  }



  // Destructor deletes each cell, then deletes
  // table itself.

  ~Hash_table( )
  {
    for (int i = 0; i < table_size; i++) {
      cell *cp, *cp_next;

      if ((cp = table[i]) == 0) continue;
      else cp_next = cp->next;

      // Table[i] is non-empty.
      while (true) {
```

```
      delete cp;
      if (cp_next == 0) break;
      cp = cp_next;
      cp_next = cp_next->next;
    }
  }
  delete [] table;
}


// Add an item to the table unless its key is
// already in the table.  The call to find_cell(int)
// is convenient and facilitates maintenance, but
// duplicates the call to hash(int).  If adding
// elements must be highly efficient, looking up
// the key should be hand coded here instead.
// Elements are added at the front of the list to
// avoid traversals.  If it's important to add
// them to the tail instead, the slightly more
// costly scheme of maintaining a tail pointer
// would work well too.  Returns true if element
// was added successfully, false otherwise.

bool add(const T& item, int key) {

  if (find_cell(key) != 0) return false;

  unsigned int slot = hash(key);
  if (table[slot] == 0)
    table[slot] = new cell(item, key);
  else {
    table[slot] = new cell(item, key, table[slot]);
  }
  return true;
}


// Remove table entry based on key.  Need to
// maintain a pointer to the previous element
// for deletions because list is singly linked.

void remove(int key) {
  unsigned int slot = hash(key);
```

```
    cell * cp_prev = table[slot];
    if (cp_prev == 0) return;

    // Special case for first item.
    if (cp_prev->key == key) {
      table[slot] = cp_prev->next;
      delete cp_prev;
      return;
    }

    for (cell * cp = cp_prev->next;
         cp != 0;
         cp_prev = cp_prev->next, cp = cp->next)
    {
      if (cp->key == key) {
        cp_prev->next = cp->next;
        delete cp;
        return;
      }
    }
}


// Returns the element corresponding to key.  If
// this element is not in the table, return the
// distinguished value T_notfound, supplied by the
// user.

const T& find(int key) {
  cell * cp = find_cell(key);
  return (cp ? cp->data : T_notfound);
}


// Print( ) function for debugging.  Practical only for
// small tables.

void print( ) {
  cout << endl;
  cout << "slot #" << endl << "------" << endl;
  for (unsigned int index = 0; index < table_size; ++index) {
    // Print a row of the table.
    cout << index << ":          ";
```

```
      for (cell *cp = table[index]; cp != 0; cp = cp->next) {
        cout << '[' << cp->data << ',' << cp->key << "] ";
      }
      cout << endl;
    }
    cout << endl;
  }
};
```

Here is file **hash_1.cpp**:

```
#include "hash_1.h"

// Create a hash table of strings with a five-slot array,
// and using the empty string as the distinguished object.
// Hash_1.h uses integers for keys.

Hash_table<char *> my_hash(5,"");

int main( )
{
  // Add some values.
  my_hash.add("abc", 99);
  my_hash.add("abc", 100);  // duplicate data is ok.
  my_hash.add("def", 100);  // duplicate key ignored.
  my_hash.add("ghi", 101);

  // Print the table.
  my_hash.print( ) ;

  // Look up some values based on their keys.
  cout << "my_hash.find(99):  " << my_hash.find(99)  << endl;
  cout << "my_hash.find(100): " << my_hash.find(100) << endl;
  cout << "my_hash.find(101): " << my_hash.find(101) << endl;
  cout << "my_hash.find(66):  " << my_hash.find(66)  << endl;

  // Remove some values based on their keys.
  my_hash.remove(99);
  my_hash.remove(100);
  my_hash.remove(101);
  my_hash.remove(5);  // key ignored -- not in table.

  // Add 25 identical values, each with a different key.
```

```
for (int i = 0; i < 25; ++i) {
  my_hash.add("xyz", i);
}

// Print the table again.
my_hash.print( ) ;

return 0;
}
```

Here is the output of **hash_1.cpp**:

```
slot #
------
0:          [abc,100]
1:          [ghi,101]
2:
3:
4:          [abc,99]

my_hash.find(99):   abc
my_hash.find(100):  abc
my_hash.find(101):  ghi
my_hash.find(66):

slot #
------
0:          [xyz,20] [xyz,15] [xyz,10] [xyz,5] [xyz,0]
1:          [xyz,21] [xyz,16] [xyz,11] [xyz,6] [xyz,1]
2:          [xyz,22] [xyz,17] [xyz,12] [xyz,7] [xyz,2]
3:          [xyz,23] [xyz,18] [xyz,13] [xyz,8] [xyz,3]
4:          [xyz,24] [xyz,19] [xyz,14] [xyz,9] [xyz,4]
```

ANNOTATIONS

The **template <class T> Hash_table** takes a type parameter **T** that must support copying. If you want to print small tables for tuning or debugging purposes, type **T** must also define **operator<<( )**.

Hash_table contains a private nested struct called **cell**, which is the type used for chaining values together. Each **cell** contains an object of type **T**, the integer key associated with this object, and a pointer to the next **cell**. The private data member **table** is defined as a **cell****. This allows it to be used as an array of **cell *** without requiring us to specify the size of this array in advance. Each array slot is the head of a linked list of **cell**s. As a result, **Hash_table** can hold an arbitrary number of elements even though the array size is fixed. **Table_size** represents the size of the array. The user specifies this size by passing it to **Hash_table(int, const T&),** which allocates the array of **cell *** and initializes each one to 0. Private data member **T_notfound** is a distinguished value of type **T**, also specified by the user via the constructor.

Find(int) is a public member function that returns an object of type **T** given its key. This function returns **T_notfound** when its key argument is not in the table. It relies on the private member function **find_cell(int)** to do most of its work.

Add(const T&, int) checks to see whether its key argument is already in the table. If so, the function simply returns **false**. Otherwise, it calls the private member function **hash(int)** to determine the correct array slot for the key, initializes a new cell, adds it to the head of the linked list, and returns **true**.

PROGRAMMER'S NOTE   *It's convenient for **Add(const T&, int)** to rely on **find_cell(int)** to determine whether **key** is a duplicate. Note, however, that this results in an extra call to **hash(int)**. This extra overhead isn't really necessary, and if **add(const T&, int)**'s performance is critical, it should check for duplicates without calling **find_cell(int)**.*

Remove(int) finds the cell that matches its key argument and removes the cell. If no such cell is found, nothing is done. Note that **remove(int)** must re-initialize the array slot to 0 if it removes the last remaining element of the slot's linked list. The code treats this as a special case. The destructor **~Hash_table( )** deletes each cell in **table** and then deletes **table** itself. **Print( )** prints the table out for debugging purposes and is only useful for small tables. Note that assignment and copying are not supported.

Before we finish our examination of **hash_1.h**, the **hash(int)** function deserves a closer look. This function just returns the remainder after dividing its argument by **table_size**. It is the simplest possible function that works, and it therefore meets our speed requirement. But does **hash(int)** distribute hash values evenly over the range of table slots? As you've probably guessed, this depends on the keys themselves. If the keys are randomly distributed, this function is as good as any other. But circumstances often conspire against a random distribution of keys.

For example, on many systems, addresses are likely to be multiples of four. If such addresses are used as keys and **table_size** is a multiple of four, most of the slots will remain empty—clearly a bad result. If you're aware of these circumstances, you can compensate by having **hash(int)** shift its argument 2 bits to the right before computing the remainder. On the other hand, there may be other hidden factors that defeat random behavior. Generally speaking, selecting a prime number for **table_size** helps minimize these factors. In the example given, if **table_size** were 5 instead of 4, none of the array slots would be excluded from participating. It might even be reasonable to revise **Hash_table(int, const T&)** to use the smallest prime number equal to or greater than its first argument, to determine the table size. Testing and refining the hash function and table size is a definite win for almost any hash table.

Hash Table with char *Keys

Our second example uses **char** * keys. When adding an object to the table, you must explicitly associate a unique **char** * key with the object being added. Any application that uses a symbol table would probably find this helpful. Generally speaking, a symbol table provides a way to look up information about a symbol, such as its address, given its string representation. A hash table using **char** * keys is a natural way to accomplish this.

An additional feature of this hash table is an array whose size increases automatically as values are added. Whenever the average list length grows beyond five, the array size is doubled. Again, it may be more effective to select the smallest prime number equal to or greater than double the old array size. The value 5 for the maximum average list length was chosen arbitrarily, and may be adjusted for maximum performance. Or a completely different heuristic may be used instead.

This implementation of a hash table assumes that the **char** * keys will remain stable—that is, the pointers will continue to point to the same unmodified strings throughout the table's lifetime. If there's any doubt about this assumption, the table should be modified to make a private copy of each key string, and delete this copy when the entry is removed or the table is destroyed. Suggestions for such modifications appear in the source code comments.

Code

hash_2.h
hash_2.cpp

Files **hash_2.h** and **hash_2.cpp** contain the code for the hash table with **char** * keys. Here is **hash_2.h**:

```
//////////////////////////////////////////////////////////
//
// File hash_2.h
// Simple hash table template using char * keys.  In
// the constructor, the user must specify a
// distinguished object of type T to serve as the
// "not found" value returned by the find(char *) member
// when it tries to look up an element that's not in
// the table.  The user also specifies the size of the
// array used to implement the table.  The number of
// table entries has no pre-determined limit.
// Add(const T &, char *) checks for duplicate keys
// and refuses to add them to the table.  Duplicate
// *data* is permitted.
//
```

```
/ T must support copying.  Support for operator<<( )
// is required for printing.
//
//
/////////////////////////////////////////////////////

#include <string>
#include <iostream>
using namespace std;

template<class T>
class Hash_table {

private:

  // Private struct cell stores data and keys internally.

  struct cell {
    const T& data;
    char * key;
    cell * next;
    cell(const T& cell_data, char * cell_key,
    cell * cell_next = 0)
      : data(cell_data), key(cell_key), next(cell_next) { }
  };

  // Table is the internal array.  Each element points
  // a (possibly empty) list of cells.

  cell **table;
  unsigned int table_size;
  unsigned int n_entries;

  // T_notfound is a distinguished value of type T passed
  // to the constructor by the user.  When find(char *) returns
  // this value, it signifies that the key the user tried
  // to look up is not in the table.

  T T_notfound;

  // Hash(char *) computes a simple hash function.

  unsigned int hash(char* key) {
```

```
  unsigned int return_value = 0;
  for (char * cp = key; *cp != 0; ++cp) {
    return_value += *cp;
  }
  return unsigned(return_value % table_size);
}


// Find_cell( ) returns a pointer to the cell
// containing key.  Returns zero when key is
// found.  Does string compares rather than
// pointer comparisons.

cell * find_cell(char * key) {
  unsigned int slot = hash(key);
  for (cell *cp = table[slot]; cp != 0; cp = cp->next) {
    if (strcmp(cp->key, key) == 0) return cp;
  }
  return cp;
}


// Assignment and copying not supported.
Hash_table( const Hash_table & );
Hash_table & operator=( const Hash_table & );

void destroy_table(cell ** dead_table,
        unsigned int dead_table_size)
{
  for (int i = 0; i < dead_table_size; i++) {
    cell *cp, *cp_next;

    if ( (cp = dead_table[i]) == 0) continue;
    else cp_next = cp->next;

    // Dead_table[i] is non-empty.
    while (true) {
      delete cp;
      if (cp_next == 0) break;
      cp = cp_next;
      cp_next = cp_next->next;
    }
  }
  delete [] dead_table;
}
```

```
void expand_table( )
{
  // First, set up a temporary pointer to the old (existing)
  // table.

  cell ** old_table = table;
  unsigned int old_table_size = table_size;

  // Set up the new table.

  table_size *= 2;
  n_entries = 0;
  table = new cell*[table_size];

  for (int i = 0; i < table_size; table[i++] = 0);

  // Add each of the old entries to the new table.
  // Traversal similar to destroy_table( ).

  for (int j = 0; j < old_table_size; j++) {
    cell *cp, *cp_next;

    if ( (cp = old_table[j]) == 0) continue;
    else cp_next = cp->next;

    // Old_table[j] is non-empty.
    while (true) {
      add(cp->data, cp->key);
      if (cp_next == 0) break;
      cp = cp_next;
      cp_next = cp_next->next;
    }
  }

  // Finally, destroy the old table.  For
  // greater efficiency, these deletions
  // can be done "by hand" in the preceding loop
  // instead.
  destroy_table(old_table, old_table_size);
}
```

```
public:

  // Constructor allocates table and initializes
  // T_notfound.

  Hash_table( unsigned int size, const T& notfound)
    : table_size(size), T_notfound(notfound), n_entries(0)
  {
    table = new cell*[table_size];
    for (int i = 0; i < size; table[i++] = 0);
  }



  // Destructor deletes each cell, then deletes
  // table itself.

  ~Hash_table( ) { destroy_table(table, table_size ); }



  // Add an item to the table unless it's key is
  // already in the table.  The call to find_cell(char *)
  // is convenient and facilitates maintenance, but
  // duplicates the call to hash(char *).  If adding
  // elements must be highly efficient, looking up
  // the key should be hand coded here instead.
  // Elements are added at the front of the list to
  // avoid traversals.  If it's important to add
  // them to the tail instead, the slightly more
  // costly scheme of maintaining a tail pointer
  // would work well too.  Returns true if element
  // was added successfully, false otherwise.
  // Note that key strings are not copied.  We
  // rely on the assumption that these char pointers
  // will continue to point to the same data throughout
  // the life of the hash table.

  bool add(const T& item, char * key) {

    if ( find_cell(key) != 0 ) return false;

    // Check to see whether the averge length of each
    // list exceeds five.  If so, allocate a new table
    // with twice as many slots, and destroy the old one.
```

```
    if ( (n_entries / table_size) >= 5 ) expand_table( );


    // The new cell is initialized with the address of
    // the key string.  If there's any doubt about these
    // pointers remaining stable (i.e., continuing to point
    // to the same string), a private copy of the string
    // should made first.  If this is done, a ~cell( )
    // destructor should be written to delete these copied
    // strings.

    unsigned int slot = hash(key);
    if (table[slot] == 0)
      table[slot] = new cell(item, key);
    else {
      table[slot] = new cell(item, key, table[slot]);
    }
    ++n_entries;
    return true;
}


// Remove table entry based on key.  Need to
// maintain a pointer to the previous element
// for deletions because list is singly linked.

void remove(char * key) {
  unsigned int slot = hash(key);
  cell * cp_prev = table[slot];
  if ( cp_prev == 0 ) return;

  // Special case for first item.
  if (strcmp(cp_prev->key, key) == 0) {
    table[slot] = cp_prev->next;
    delete cp_prev;
    --n_entries;
    return;
  }

  for (cell * cp = cp_prev->next;
       cp != 0;
       cp_prev = cp_prev->next, cp = cp->next)
  {
```

```cpp
        if (strcmp(cp->key, key) == 0) {
          cp_prev->next = cp->next;
          delete cp;
          --n_entries;
          return;
        }
      }
    }


    // Returns the element corresponding to key.  If
    // this element is not in the table, return the
    // distinguished value T_notfound, supplied by the
    // user.

    const T& find(char * key) {
      cell * cp = find_cell(key);
      return (cp ? cp->data : T_notfound);
    }


    // Print( ) function for debugging.  Practical only for
    // small tables.

    void print( ) {
      cout << endl;
      cout << "slot #" << endl << "------" << endl;
      for (unsigned int index = 0; index < table_size; ++index) {
        // Print a row of the table.
        cout << index << ":             ";
        for ( cell *cp = table[index]; cp != 0; cp = cp->next ) {
          cout << '[' << cp->data << ',' << cp->key << "] ";
        }
        cout << endl;
      }
      cout << endl;
    }
};
```

Here is **hash_2.cpp**:

```cpp
#include "hash_2.h"

// Create a one-slot hash table of integers with
// char * keys, and a distinguished value of -1.
// The number of slots increases automatically as
// more elements are added to the table.

Hash_table<int> my_hash(1,-1);

int main( )
{
  my_hash.add(1, "a");
  my_hash.add(1, "b");
  my_hash.add(1, "c");
  my_hash.add(1, "d");
  my_hash.add(1, "e");

  my_hash.print( ) ;

  my_hash.add(1, "f");

  my_hash.print( ) ;

  my_hash.add(1, "g");
  my_hash.add(1, "h");
  my_hash.add(1, "i");
  my_hash.add(1, "j");
  my_hash.add(1, "k");

  my_hash.print( ) ;

  my_hash.add(1, "l");
  my_hash.add(1, "m");
  my_hash.add(1, "n");
  my_hash.add(1, "o");
  my_hash.add(1, "p");
  my_hash.add(1, "q");
  my_hash.add(1, "r");
  my_hash.add(1, "s");
  my_hash.add(1, "t");
  my_hash.add(1, "u");
  my_hash.add(1, "v");
```

```
my_hash.add(1, "w");
my_hash.add(1, "x");
my_hash.add(1, "y");
my_hash.add(1, "z");

my_hash.print( ) ;

return 0;
}
```

The **hash_2.cpp** program creates a hash table whose initial array size is 1. This is a *terrible* choice of array size. We use it here only to show how the array size grows automatically as elements are added to the table. Here is the output for **hash_2.cpp**:

```
slot #
- - - - - -
0:          [1,e] [1,d] [1,c] [1,b] [1,a]


slot #
- - - - - -
0:          [1,f] [1,b] [1,d]
1:          [1,a] [1,c] [1,e]


slot #
- - - - - -
0:          [1,d] [1,h]
1:          [1,e] [1,a] [1,i]
2:          [1,b] [1,f] [1,j]
3:          [1,k] [1,c] [1,g]


slot #
- - - - - -
0:          [1,x] [1,h] [1,p]
1:          [1,y] [1,i] [1,a] [1,q]
2:          [1,z] [1,j] [1,b] [1,r]
3:          [1,c] [1,k] [1,s]
4:          [1,d] [1,l] [1,t]
5:          [1,u] [1,e] [1,m]
```

```
6:          [1,v] [1,f] [1,n]
7:          [1,w] [1,g] [1,o]
```

ANNOTATIONS

There are two notable differences between **hash_2.h** and **hash_1.h**. First, the hash function has been changed to accommodate a new key type. Besides the obvious change in parameter type from **int** to **char ***, the computation is now based on the characters in the key string. The hash function in **hash_2.h** simply treats each character in the string as an integer and adds up their values. It then divides this sum by **table_size** and returns the remainder.

Once again, this meets our requirement for simplicity but may require further tuning. For example, the strings "abc", "acb", "bac", "bca", "cab", and "cba" each hash to the same slot because ordering makes no difference when adding up the values of the characters. If the key strings tend to have the same length and the same characters in different orders, this hash function would be a poor choice. One way to alleviate this kind of problem might be to negate or complement alternate characters before adding their values to the sum. This would introduce at least some dependence on ordering.

The second major difference between this chapter's examples is that in **hash_2.h** the array size automatically increases as entries are added to the table. Although there's nothing magical about the way this is done, it's worth noting that the code has been slightly reorganized as a result. In particular, we've introduced two new private member functions: **expand_table( )** and **destroy_table(cell **, unsigned int)**. The **add(const T&, char *)** and **~Hash( )** functions have been modified to call these new functions. The new private data member **n_entries** keeps track of how many entries (not slots) the table contains at any given time. This helps us determine when to expand the table.

Expand_table( ) does just what you would expect. After initializing the local variables **old_table** and **old_table_size** to values corresponding to the current (and soon to be obsolete) table, the function allocates a new table twice the size. It then traverses the old table and enters each of its elements into the new table by calling **add(const T&, char *)**. Finally, it calls **destroy_table(cell **, unsigned int)**, passing **old_table** and **old_table_size** as arguments.

PROGRAMMER'S NOTE
*As noted in the source comments, it would be less convenient but more efficient to delete each **cell** "on the fly," while traversing the loop that adds the existing elements to the new table. This would make it unnecessary to call **destroy_table(cell **, int)**, which performs a similar redundant traversal. The code in **destroy_table(cell **, int)** was stolen from ~Hash( ) and broken out as a separate function because **~Hash( )** is no longer the only function that needs to destroy a table.*

Sparse Array Design

Some problems, notably those involving matrices, rely on the indexing mechanism provided by arrays. Some of these applications use very large arrays, most of whose elements are 0, or some other default value. For applications of this type, it often pays to avoid the overhead of storing, say, thousands of 0's. Sparse arrays are objects that behave like arrays but don't explicitly allocate space for elements containing the default value.

Figure 4-2 shows the memory layout for a one-dimensional sparse array of integers. Each cell in this structure has three fields: the column number, the data itself, and a pointer that references the next element to the right. The header element at the very left has a column number of –1, and contains no data. The first data element, element 0, contains the value 4. The second element, element 1, is not shown at all. Hence, *element 1 is considered to have the default value.* The third element, element 2, has the value 12.

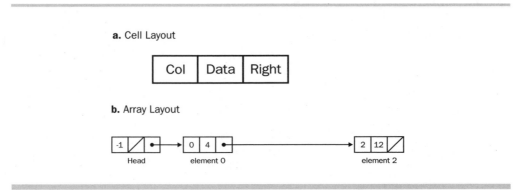

a. Cell Layout

b. Array Layout

FIGURE 4-2.   One-dimensional sparse array

Figure 4-3 shows a two-dimensional sparse array of integers. This is a straightforward generalization of the one-dimensional array, but note that each cell is a member of two lists and has a row number as well as a column number. Although the two-dimensional version is more complex, it's also more useful because the reduction in storage requirements tends to be greater. In a sense, the most important parts of sparse arrays are the holes—the elements that are not explicitly stored.

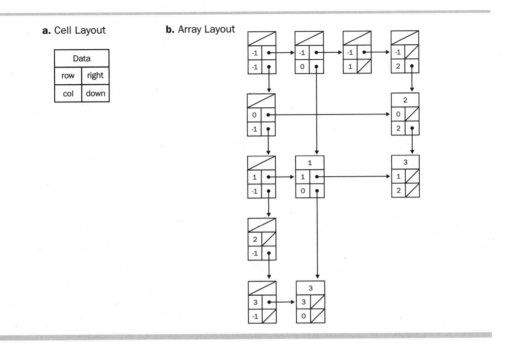

a. Cell Layout   **b.** Array Layout

FIGURE 4-3. Two-dimensional sparse array containing four non-default elements

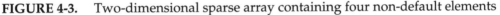

When designing a data structure called a *sparse array*, it's natural to think in terms of overloading **operator[]( )**, and this is indeed how our one-dimensional array is implemented. As we'll see, this approach has certain drawbacks. We'll try to address those with our two dimensional array, which does *not* use **operator[]( )**.

One-Dimensional Sparse Array

Our one-dimensional sparse array is implemented as a linked list. It has no fixed size and grows as elements are added. Because **operator[]( )** is used for both read and write access, its code must handle both of these cases properly, *without knowing* which one applies. The minimum legal index is 0, and range checking is performed to assure that no negative indexes are accepted.

1d.h
1d.cpp

Code

The one-dimensional sparse array code is organized into two files, **1d.h** and **1d.cpp**. Here is **1d.h**:

```cpp
// One dimensional sparse array with variable
// dimension.  We view it as a "horizontal"
// array.  Type T must support copying.  If printing
// is desired, it must also support operator<<( ).

#include <iostream>
using namespace std;

template <class T>
class One_d_sa {

private:
  struct cell {

    // First constructor does not specify data.
    cell(int col_arg, cell * right_arg)
      : col(col_arg), right(right_arg) { }

    // Second constructor specifies data.
    cell(int col_arg, T data_arg, cell * right_arg)
      : col(col_arg), data(data_arg), right(right_arg) { }

    int    col;
    cell * right;
    T      data;

    void print( ) {
      cout << "[" << col << ", " << data << "] ";
    }
  };


  T    default_value;
  cell head;
public:
```

```
One_d_sa(const T & dv)
  : default_value(dv), head(-1, 0) { }

// Because we have no way to tell when operator[](int) is
// being used for access or for modification, the same code
// must handle both cases.  This forces us to add a default
// element to column k, whenever column k is accessed.
// Whenever we access an element that isn't already there,
// we create a new cell for that element, and initialize it
// to the default value.

T& operator[](int col) {

  // Make sure col is non-negative.
  if (col < 0) throw "column out of range";

  // Scan for element col.  If not found,
  // return default value.

  cell * cp_prev = &head;
  cell * cp      = head.right;

  while (true) {
    if ((cp == 0) || (cp->col > col)) {

      // Add a new cell between cp_prev and cp
      // with default value, and return this value.

      cp_prev->right = new cell(col, default_value, cp);
      return cp_prev->right->data;
    }
    else if (cp->col == col) return cp->data;

    cp_prev = cp;
    cp = cp->right;
  }
}

void print( ) {
  cell *cp = head.right;
  cout << endl;
```

```
    while (cp != 0) {
     cp->print( );
      cp = cp->right;
     }
    cout << endl;
   }

};
```

Here is **1d.cpp**:

```
// Horizontal array with variable dimension.

#include "1d.h"

// Create a one dimensional sparse array of integers
// with default value -1.

One_d_sa<int> my_1d(-1);

// Accessing element three causes this element to be
// created with default value -1.
int i = my_1d[3];

int main( )
{
  my_1d.print( );

  my_1d[3] = 5;
  my_1d.print( );

  my_1d[5] = 7;
  my_1d.print( );

  try {
    my_1d[-1];
  }
  catch (const char * msg) {
    cout << msg << endl;
  }
```

```
    return 0;
}
```

The **1d.cpp** code produces following output:
```
[3, -1]

[3, 5]

[3, 5] [5, 7]
column out of range
```

ANNOTATIONS

The array is called **template<class T> One_d_sa**. The private nested **struct cell** defines the storage for each element explicitly stored in the array. Its fields are **col**, which indicates the column number of the element; **right**, which points the cell immediately to the right; and **data**, which holds the actual value being stored. **One_d_sa**'s private data members are **default_value** and **head**. **Default_value** is a value of type **T** passed in by the user as an argument to **One_d_sa(const T&)**. Any element that's not explicitly stored in the array is assumed to have this value. Type **T** must support copying. If printing is desired, **T** must also support **operator<<( )**. The member function **print( )** is provided as a convenience for debugging.

The heart of this implementation is **operator[](int)**, which provides read and write access to the array. As mentioned before, the main problem in implementing this function is that it *doesn't know* whether it's being invoked for read access or write access. To see why this matters, suppose we could distinguish between read- and write-access calls. A read-access call would have very little to do. If it found the requested cell, the function would return a reference to the cell's data field. Otherwise, it would simply return the default value.

What about a call that requires write access? If the requested cell is found, the function would behave just like the read-access call and return a reference to the cell's data field. But if the requested cell is *not* found, the function must create a new cell; otherwise there's no place to write *to*. We solve this problem by assuming that *every* call requires write access. Whenever a nonexistent cell is referenced, a new cell is created with the proper column number and initialized to the default value.

Two-Dimensional Sparse Array

Although the two-dimensional sparse array is not a great conceptual leap from the one-dimensional case, it is also true that the **operator[]( )** implementation does not generalize well. For one thing, the inability to distinguish between read and write access is a source of inefficiency. Each time we try to read a nonexistent cell, we must create a new cell that contains the default value. If this happens often enough, the whole purpose of a sparse array is defeated. This problem is likely to be more severe for two-dimensional arrays.

A second obstacle is that **operator[]( )** is only permitted to take one argument. This would force us to implement the two-dimensional case as an array of arrays. This approach seems reasonable, but we immediately hit a snag when we try to define the default type. We want the two-dimensional array to have a default value of type **T,** just like the one-dimensional case. However, using our simple one-dimensional implementation as a model, the default type for an array of arrays would be *an array.*

Rather than seek a clever solution to these problems, we have abandoned **operator[]( )** for the two-dimensional case and replaced it with two member functions: one each for read and write access. This allows the careful user to avoid creating new cells unnecessarily. Other users, who prefer not to exercise this sort of care, can use the write access function exclusively.

For simplicity, our two-dimensional array has fixed dimensions, which are established by the user. We create a row of column headers "on top" of row 0 and a column of row headers "to the left" of column 0. This layout was shown earlier in Figure 4-3. It would not be hard to modify this approach to allow variable dimensions. Another potential improvement would be to avoid creating a column(row) header until a cell is actually inserted into a particular column(row).

Code

2d.h
2d.cpp

The code is organized into two files, **2d.h** and **2d.cpp**. Here is file **2d.h**:

```cpp
// Two dimensional array with fixed dimensions
// and range checking.  Type T must support copying.
// If printing is desired, it must also support
// operator<<( ).

#include <cassert>
#include <iostream>
using namespace std;

template <class T>
class Two_d_sa {

private:

  struct cell {
```

```
      // First constructor does not specify data.
      cell(int row_arg, int col_arg,
          cell * right_arg, cell * down_arg)
        : row(row_arg), col(col_arg),
          right(right_arg), down(down_arg) { }


      // Second constructor specifies data.
      cell(int row_arg, int col_arg, T data_arg,
          cell * right_arg, cell * down_arg)
        : row(row_arg), col(col_arg), data(data_arg),
          right(right_arg), down(down_arg) { }

      int   row;
      int   col;
      cell * right;
      cell * down;
      T      data;

      void print( ) {
        cout << "[(" << row << "," << col << ")" << data << "] ";
      }
  };
  n_rows;
  int  n_cols;
  T     default_value;
  cell head;

public:

  // Constructor sets up headers for rows and columns.
  Two_d_sa(int rows, int cols, const T & dv)
    : n_rows(rows), n_cols(cols), default_value(dv),
    head(-1, -1, 0, 0)
  {
    int i;
    cell * cp;

    // Set up column headers.
    for (i = 0, cp = &head; i < cols; ++i) {
      cp->right = new cell(-1, i, 0, 0);
      cp = cp->right;
    }
```

```
    // Set up row headers.
    for (i = 0, cp = &head; i < rows; ++i) {
      cp->down = new cell(i, -1, 0, 0);
      cp = cp->down;
    }
}


// We use two different functions for read and
// write access because we want their behavior
// to differ.

// R_access(int, int) looks for a cell whose row and
// col fields match its row and col arguments.  If it
// finds one, it returns a const reference to that
// cell's data field.  Otherwise, it returns a const
// reference to the default value.  No modifications
// to the array are performed or permitted.

const T& r_access(int row, int col) const {

  // Scan for element (row,col).  If not found,
  // return default value.

  // First, check for proper range.
  if ((row < 0) || (row >= n_rows))  throw "row out of range";
  if ((col < 0) || (col >= n_cols))  throw "col out of range";

  // Find the proper row.
  int i;
  const cell * cp;

  for (i = -1, cp = &head; i < row; ++i)
    cp = cp->down;
  assert(cp->row == row);

  // Now, look for cell with matching column.
  cp = cp->right;
  while (true) {
    if ((cp == 0) || (cp->col > col))  return default_value;
    if (cp->col == col) return cp->data;
    cp = cp->right;
  }
}
```

```
// W_access(int, int) looks for a cell whose row and col
// fields match its row and col arguments.  If it
// finds one, it returns a [non const] reference to that
// cell's data field.  Otherwise, it creates the new
// cell, gives it the default value, and returns a
// [non const] reference to its data field.

T& w_access(int row, int col) {

  // Scan for element (row,col).  If not found,
  // return default value.

  // First, check for proper range.
  if ((row < 0) || (row >= n_rows))  throw "row out of range";
  if ((col < 0) || (col >= n_cols))  throw "col out of range";

  // Find the proper row and col headers.
  int i;
  cell * row_p;
  cell * col_p;

  for (i = -1, row_p = &head; i < row; ++i)
    row_p = row_p->down;
  assert(row_p->row == row);

  for (i = -1, col_p = &head; i < col; ++i)
    col_p = col_p->right;
  assert(col_p->col == col);

  // Now, look for cell with matching column.
  // Keep a trailing pointer, row_p_prev, in case
  // an insertion is necessary.

  cell * row_p_prev = row_p;
  cell * col_p_prev = col_p;

  row_p = row_p->right;
  col_p = col_p->down;

  while (true) {
    if ((row_p == 0) || (row_p->col > col)) {
```

```
        // At this point we have enough info to attach a
        // new cell to its row.  But we still need to do
        // some searching before we can hook it up to its
        // column.

      while (true) {
        if ((col_p == 0) || (col_p->row > row)) {

            // Add a new cell between row_p_prev and row_p,
            // and between col_p_prev and col_p, with
            // default value, and return this value.

          row_p_prev->right =
            new cell(row, col, default_value, row_p, col_p);
          col_p_prev->down  = row_p_prev->right;
          return row_p_prev->right->data;
        }
        assert(col_p->row != row);
        col_p_prev = col_p;
        col_p = col_p->right;
      }
    }
    else if (row_p->col == col) return row_p->data;

    row_p_prev = row_p;
    row_p = row_p->right;
  }

}

// Print the array row by row.
void print( ) {

  cell *row_p = head.down;
  while (row_p != 0) {

    // Print the row.
    cell * col_p = row_p->right;
    bool linefeed = (col_p ? 1 : 0);

    while (col_p != 0) {
      col_p->print( );
      col_p = col_p->right;
    }
```

```
      if (linefeed) cout << endl;
      row_p = row_p->down;
    }
    cout << endl;


  }

};
```

Here is file **2d.cpp**:

```
#include "2d.h"

// Create a Two dimensional sparse array of
// integers with three rows, five columns,
// and a default value of -1.

Two_d_sa<int> my_2d(3, 5, -1);

int main( )
{
  my_2d.print( );
  my_2d.w_access(2,3) = -7;
  cout << my_2d.r_access(2,3) << endl;;
  my_2d.print( );
  cout << my_2d.r_access(0,1) << endl;;

  my_2d.w_access(2,4) = -5;
  my_2d.print( );

  my_2d.w_access(2,1) = -4;
  my_2d.print( );

  my_2d.w_access(2,0) = -4;
  my_2d.print( );

  my_2d.w_access(0,1) = -8;
  my_2d.w_access(1,3) = -9;
  my_2d.print( );

  int i, j;
  for (i = 0; i < 3; ++i)
    for (j = 0; j < 5; ++j)
```

```
    my_2d.w_access(i,j) = i+j;

my_2d.print( );

try {
  my_2d.r_access(3,5);
}
catch (const char * msg) {
  cout << msg << endl;
}

return 0;
}
```

File **2d.cpp** produces following output:

```
-7
[(2,3)-7]

-1

[(2,3)-7] [(2,4)-5]

[(2,1)-4] [(2,3)-7] [(2,4)-5]

[(2,0)-4] [(2,1)-4] [(2,3)-7] [(2,4)-5]

[(0,1)-8]

[(1,3)-9]

[(2,0)-4] [(2,1)-4] [(2,3)-7] [(2,4)-5]

[(0,0)0] [(0,1)1] [(0,2)2] [(0,3)3] [(0,4)4]

[(1,0)1] [(1,1)2] [(1,2)3] [(1,3)4] [(1,4)5]

[(2,0)2] [(2,1)3] [(2,2)4] [(2,3)5] [(2,4)6]

    row out of range
```

ANNOTATIONS

The changes of note in **2d.cpp** concern **struct cell** and the access functions. Because each cell is now a member of two lists and has a row number as well as a column number, **struct cell** has two additional fields. **Row** represents the row number, and **down** points to the cell immediately below. The constructor **Two_d_sa(int, int, const T&)** now takes two integers that specify the fixed array dimensions, in addition to the default value.

The access functions are **r_access(int, int)** and **w_access(int, int)**. Each takes a row and column number for arguments. The read-access function, **r_access(int, int)**, returns a **const T&**. After performing a range check, the function walks through the list of row headers until it finds the one specified by the **row** argument. It then scans the row from left to right, looking for a cell that matches the **col** argument. If the function reaches a cell whose **col** field is greater than the **col** argument, or reaches the end of the list, it returns the default value.

W_access(int, int) returns a **T&** and follows a similar strategy. However, when this write-access function discovers that the cell it wants does not exist, it creates one, initializes it to the default value, and inserts it in the proper place. Because this location is found by scanning the appropriate row, **w_access(int, int)** has enough information to insert the new cell into its row as soon as it discovers the need to do so. The function also needs to insert the new cell into its column, however. It does this by scanning the column pointers and, finally, the proper column in a manner that mimics the row scan. The purpose of the inner **while** loop, which is absent from **r_access(int, int)**, is to perform this column scan.

Some users will wish to minimize the number of header cells created and allow variable dimensions. These changes can be made by modifying **Two_d_sa(int, int, const T&)** and the two access functions. The modified constructor would have only one parameter (**const T&**) and, instead of creating all the row and column headers, would only create the header cell at row −1 and column −1. The modified access functions, instead of scanning the header cells by counting, would look for a row or column equal to or greater than the desired row or column. If necessary, a new header cell would be created. This approach would mimic the way we currently scan rows and create new data cells when they're needed.

The **print( )** member function now prints the row and column numbers of each cell, in parentheses and followed by the data value. Printing is provided for illustration and debugging only.

Memory
Management

By Art Friedman

mm_globalnew.cpp   mm_list.h
mm_array.h   mm_list.cpp
mm_array.cpp

A ny language that supports dynamic memory allocation must come to terms with a fundamental issue—whose responsibility should it be? Not surprisingly, there's a wide range of opinion on this subject.

According to one point of view, programmers should never have to bother allocating and de-allocating dynamic memory for their applications. This activity should be kept strictly "under the hood" because it rarely has any direct relevance to the application. The opposite point of view holds that direct programmatic control over memory allocation is essential for run-time efficiency. In real-time applications where response time may be critical, any "behind the scenes" run-time activity may be unacceptable.

Memory Management for C and C++

In keeping with their emphasis on run-time efficiency, C and C++ make the programmer responsible for dynamic memory allocation. In C, programmers most often use the library functions **malloc(size_t)** and **free(void *)** to allocate and de-allocate memory. The corresponding C++ operators are **new** and **delete**.

These two operators typically come in four flavors, which vary according to whether they handle single objects or arrays, and whether or not they throw the **bad_alloc** exception when memory is exhausted. The versions of these operators that handle arrays are called **new[ ]** and **delete[ ]**. C++ implementations of **new** and **delete** often rely on **malloc(size_t)** and **free(void *)** to do the real work. Nonetheless, any memory allocated by **new** (or **new[ ]**) can only be de-allocated using **delete** (or **delete[ ]**).

The fact that **malloc(size_t)** and **free(void *)** are implemented as library functions means that a C programmer can replace these functions with homegrown versions. Hence, in addition to controlling the allocation of dynamic memory within the program, the programmer can actually reimplement the allocator itself. A C++ programmer can exercise similar control by overloading the global **new** and **delete** operators. Note that, in most cases, this is a *bad idea* and a very dangerous thing to do. However, in some carefully selected situations it can be very useful. This is explained more fully in the following section.

In addition to giving the programmer control over the global memory allocator, C++ supports *selective* replacement of the **new** and **delete** operators. By overloading these operators for a particular class, the programmer can write a specialized allocator for objects of that class only. A specialized allocator, because of its limited scope, is less likely to behave in unanticipated ways and hence is less dangerous than a homegrown global allocator. Two of the three programming examples in this chapter demonstrate techniques for writing a specialized memory allocator.

> **PROGRAMMER'S NOTE** *It's usually a bad idea to write specialized allocators for every class in sight. The purpose of writing a specialized allocator is to improve a program's run-time performance and/or memory usage. This is best done by carefully selecting the object types that are most actively allocated and de-allocated.*

Overloading the Global New Operator

As mentioned, overloading the global **new** and **delete** operators—or overriding **malloc(size_t)** and **free(void *)**—is usually unwise. Writing a general-purpose memory allocator from scratch is very challenging. Not only must the allocator be efficient, it must be extremely robust. Memory allocation bugs are hard enough to diagnose even when the allocator itself is defect free! Given these strict requirements, when does it make sense to replace the global allocator?

Two common situations call for replacing the global memory allocator. Sometimes, though not often, a better allocator becomes available, perhaps in the commercial marketplace. Far from being "homegrown," these allocators tend to be carefully designed, thoroughly tested, industrial-strength products. It's nice to be able to try one of them by just plugging it into your program.

Secondly, a hard-to-diagnose memory allocation bug may call for replacing the global memory allocator. Typically, these bugs result from misusing the allocator and are not associated with the allocator itself. For example, the programmer may apply the **delete** operator to an address that has already been deleted. Commercial allocators exist that are specially instrumented to help detect programmer errors at run-time. Once the errors are found and corrected, the standard allocator is plugged back in.

Using the overloading mechanism of C++, programmers can write instrumented versions of **new** and **delete** on their own. Sometimes a crudely instrumented allocator can be very helpful in diagnosing run-time defects. The short program described here demonstrates how this may be done.

Code

The code resides in a single file, **mm_globalnew.cpp**:

mm_globalnew.cpp

```
// Program that demonstrates how to overload global new( )
// and delete( ) operators.  Note that this is usually
// a *bad* idea, and very dangerous.  One situation where
// it makes sense is when linking to a commercially available
// memory manager specially designed for debugging memory
// allocation errors.  Alternatively, some crude debugging
// can be done with simple print statements.
```

```cpp
#include <new>
#include <cstdlib>
#include <cstdio>
using namespace std;

void * operator new(size_t s) throw(bad_alloc)
{

  printf ("Global new: ");

  // Try to allocate the memory using malloc.
  void * allocated_memory = malloc(s);

  // Determine the current new_handler, if any.
  // The second call restores the new_handler
  // value that was zeroed out by the first call.
  new_handler nh = set_new_handler(0);
  if (nh != 0) set_new_handler(nh);

  while (allocated_memory == 0) {
    if (nh != 0) (*nh)( );
    else throw bad_alloc( );
    allocated_memory = malloc(s);
  }

  // Code for crude memory allocation debugging.
  printf("Allocated %d bytes of memory at address 0x%x\n",
      s, allocated_memory);

  return allocated_memory;
}


void operator delete(void * vp) throw( )
{
  printf("Global delete: ");
  if (vp !=0 ) free(vp);
  printf("Deleted memory at address 0x%x\n", vp);
}

int main( )
{
```

```
int * int_pointer = new int;
 printf ("&int_pointer == 0x%x\n", &int_pointer);
 delete int_pointer;


 return 0;
}
```

Here is sample output from the preceding program:

```
Global new: Allocated 64 bytes of memory at address 0x400035d8
Global new: Allocated 64 bytes of memory at address 0x40003620
Global new: Allocated 64 bytes of memory at address 0x40003668
Global new: Allocated 64 bytes of memory at address 0x400036b0
Global new: Allocated 4 bytes of memory at address 0x400035a8
&int_pointer == 0x7b03a548
Global delete: Deleted memory at address 0x400035a8
```

ANNOTATIONS

The **mm_globalnew.cpp** program demonstrates how **new** and **delete** can be implemented in terms of **malloc(size_t)** and **free(void *)**.

We implement the **new** operator by defining the function **operator new(size_t)**. The version we define here throws the **bad_alloc** exception when memory becomes exhausted. Our **operator new(size_t)** does no real memory management other than to call **malloc(size_t)** and return the pointer that **malloc(size_t)** returns. Its purpose is to handle errors correctly and provide a C++ interface.

After the initial call to **malloc(size_t)**, we prepare for the error-checking loop by looking up the current **new_handler**. This function pointer, which we access using the local variable **nh**, contains the address of a function to be called in case memory becomes exhausted. The **new_handler** function may be user specified, and may be null. The call to **set_new_handler(new_handler)** establishes its argument as the current **new_handler** and returns the address of the previous **new_handler**. Our purpose in calling **set_new_handler(new_handler)** here is to record its return value. That's why we call it a second time to restore the original **new_handler**.

The error-checking loop relies on **malloc(size_t)**'s return value to decide whether it needs to call **malloc(size_t)** again. If **malloc(size_t)** returns a nonzero value, we simply return this value. Otherwise, if there's a current **new_handler**, we call it. The hope is that the **new_handler** will somehow arrange for **malloc(size_t)** to have more heap memory at its disposal. Therefore, we try calling **malloc(size_t)** again. Notice that this loop is very optimistic about the **new_handler**'s ability to obtain more heap memory. If a **new_handler** has been defined, it *gets called repeatedly* until **malloc(size_t)** has enough heap space available to return a nonzero value. If this doesn't happen eventually, **operator new(size_t)** loops indefinitely. If a

new_handler has *not* been defined, we just throw a **bad_alloc** exception. This gives functions higher on the stack a chance to catch that exception and either recover or exit gracefully.

The **operator delete(void *)** function is much simpler. It just passes its argument along to **free(void *)** as long as the argument has a nonzero value. No exceptions are thrown.

Note that our **new** and **delete** operators generate some printed output. It should be clear that this is not intended for production use. The output's purpose here is twofold. First, it allows us to write a small test program to prove that these operators are actually being called at run-time. Second, printed output can be used as a crude form of instrumentation for detecting memory allocation defects at run-time. For example, by scanning the printed output of these operators, it would be easy to detect the common error of deleting an address twice, without having re-allocated it between the deletions.

The output of our test program will vary from system to system. For example, the output shown earlier may be surprising to some because it consists of seven lines. A quick inspection of the test program might lead you to expect only the last three lines. What happened here? In C++, global constructors, which may be associated with user code or system libraries, are executed before the main program. On this particular system, global constructors made four calls to **operator new(size_t)**. These "surprise" calls further illustrate the difficulty of anticipating all possible uses of the global **new** and **delete** operators.

Simple Array-Based Allocator

Although general-purpose memory allocators are hard to write, a specialized allocator can be fairly straightforward. It can also be very fast at run-time. The C++ language allows you to overload the **new** and **delete** operators *for a particular class*. This can sometimes result in a significant improvement in run-time speed and/or memory usage. The two remaining examples in this chapter demonstrate a memory allocator for *fixed size objects*. The restriction to fixed size leads to a huge simplification of the programming task.

To see why this is so, consider some of the problems a general-purpose allocator must solve. To begin with, the available free blocks may have various sizes. Clearly, the allocator must find a block that's at least as large as the object the user has requested. One way to do this is to search the free blocks sequentially, stopping as soon as a large enough block is found. This is known as a "first fit" strategy. Other common strategies are "worst fit," which tends to reduce fragmentation, and "best fit," which tends to increase fragmentation but reduce the total amount of wasted space. Evaluating the trade-offs among these and other strategies is no easy task. Another issue is that of coalescing adjacent free blocks. For example, two adjacent

8-byte blocks may be used to satisfy a 16-byte request if the 8-byte blocks are first coalesced into a single block.

An allocator for fixed-size objects does not face these problems. Each fixed-size chunk of memory is equivalent to every other chunk, and we needn't bother with general-purpose allocation strategies such as "best fit," "worst fit," and "first fit." Nor do we need to worry about coalescing adjacent free blocks. An important consequence of the fixed-size constraint is that we no longer need to search for a block with just the right properties. Instead, we just grab the first free block that's available.

The technique developed in this section assumes that the pool of available memory is a fixed-size array of fixed-size objects. The fixed sizes are determined at compile time. A parallel array of **bool**, which we call **is_reserved**, keeps track of the elements that are reserved (that is, the ones currently being used). Once every element of the fixed array has been allocated, we're "out of heap memory" until the program releases some by calling **delete**. These restrictions may be appropriate for embedded systems applications in which the amount of available memory is strictly limited. Even more memory can be saved if the array of **bool** is replaced by a bit vector.

The approach taken here depends on alignment rules and may require modification for other compilers or systems. Why are we concerned with these problems at all? After all, we could simply define an array of **Special_class** objects (**Special_class** is the name we've chosen for the class whose objects we plan to allocate) as our memory pool, and let the compiler work out the details for us as usual. We've backed away from this idea, however, because C++ automatically runs the default constructor for each object in a newly created array. This is exactly what we *don't* want to do because the memory we set aside for our special memory pool needs to be "raw." (The embedded source code comments address this issue in detail.) An alternate approach is described in the final example of this chapter.

Another limitation concerns classes that may be derived from **Special_class**. If a derived class has additional data elements, our special **new** operator will miscalculate its size. Therefore, if any class derived from **Special_class** is to be allocated dynamically, it must have the same size as **Special_class**.

Code

mm_array.h
mm_array.cpp

Files **mm_array.h** and **mm_array.cpp** contain the code for our array-based allocator. File **main_array.cpp** contains an example of its usage. Here is file **mm_array.h**:

```
#include <new>
#include <cstdlib>
#include <cstdio>
using namespace std;
```

```
class Special_class {
  int  int_data;  // actual data content of this class.
  char ch_data;   // actual data content of this class.

public:
  Special_class ( ) { /*Initialize the object*/ }

  void * operator new(size_t s) throw(bad_alloc);
  void   operator delete(void * vp, size_t s);
};
```

Here is file **mm_array.cpp**:

```
// Implementation of specialized new and delete operators
// for class Special_class.  The "static" keyword is used
// liberally to make definitions private to this
// translation unit.

#include "mm_array.h"
#include <cassert>

// Number of fixed size elements in the array.
static const int num_elts = 512;

// Amount of memory allocated for each element in the array.
// It's tricky to get this right without knowing the compiler's
// alignment policy for classes.  We assume that the basic
// type long has the most restrictive alignment, and allocate
// space equivalent to an integer number of long's to contain
// a single element.  Usually this means there's some extra
// unused space for each element.  This rule of thumb may not
// work correctly for all systems.

static const int elt_size =
  (sizeof(Special_class) % sizeof(long)) == 0
  ? sizeof(Special_class)
  : (sizeof(Special_class) / sizeof(long)) * sizeof(long)
      + sizeof(long);

// Fixed array of fixed size memory chunks.  Each chunk
// is properly aligned and contains sufficient space for
```

```
// Special_class object.
//
// This type is implemented as a union in order to force
// the alignment of the first element to be as restrictive
// as possible, and therefore able to contain any kind of
// data.  The basic type "long" tends to have the most
// restrictive alignment and was therefore chosen for this
// purpose.  This is not guaranteed to work on all systems.
//
// The union is anonymous in order to keep it private and
// avoid name pollution.

static union {
  // Imitate the memory footprint of the hypothetical
  // declaration Special_class array[num_elts];
  // Assumes that long has the most restrictive alignment
  // and that sizeof(unsigned char) == 1.
  long dummy;
  unsigned char raw[num_elts * elt_size];
} sc_memory;

// Initially false.
static bool is_reserved[num_elts];


// Perform a simple linear search of is_reserved to find
// the index of the first available memory element.  Then
// return the address of that element.  When memory is exhausted,
// throws bad_alloc exception.  New_handler is not invoked.

void * Special_class::operator new(size_t s)  throw(bad_alloc)
{
  int new_elt = -1;
  for (int elt = 0; elt < num_elts; ++elt) {
    if (is_reserved[elt] == false) {
      new_elt = elt;
      break;
    }
  }

  if (new_elt == -1) throw bad_alloc( );
```

```
  printf
    ("Special_class::new allocated %d bytes at address 0x%x\n",
    s, &(sc_memory.raw[new_elt * elt_size]) );

  // Assert that each element begins on a "long" boundary.
  assert(
    ( (unsigned int)(&(sc_memory.raw[new_elt * elt_size]))
        %
      sizeof(long)
    )   == 0
  );

  is_reserved[new_elt] = true;
  return &(sc_memory.raw[new_elt * elt_size]);
}


// Set the appropriate is_reserved element to false.
void Special_class::operator delete(void * vp, size_t s)
{
  // Calculate the is_reserved index.
  int index =
    ((unsigned char *)vp - &sc_memory.raw[0]) / elt_size;
  is_reserved[index] = false;

  printf
    ("Special_class::delete released %d bytes at address 0x%x\n",
    s, vp);

}
```

Here is **main_array.cpp**:

```
#include "mm_array.h"

Special_class sc;

int main( )
{
  Special_class * scp_0 = new Special_class;
  Special_class * scp_1 = new Special_class;
  Special_class * scp_2 = new Special_class;

  delete scp_1;
```

```
    delete scp_0;
    delete scp_2;

    return 0;
}
```

The **main_array.cpp** code produces the following output:

```
Special_class::new allocated 8 bytes at address 0x400014b8
Special_class::new allocated 8 bytes at address 0x400014c0
Special_class::new allocated 8 bytes at address 0x400014c8
Special_class::delete released 8 bytes at address 0x400014c0
Special_class::delete released 8 bytes at address 0x400014b8
Special_class::delete released 8 bytes at address 0x400014c8
```

ANNOTATIONS

File **mm_array.h** contains the definition of **Special_class**. The **operator new(size_t)** and **operator delete(void *, size_t)** declarations are the only modifications needed for the class definition. File **mm_array.cpp** includes file **mm_array.h** and contains the **new** and **delete** implementations.

An effort was made to keep file-scope constants and variables private to this translation unit. This resulted in the use of an anonymous union and the **static** keyword. The constant **num_elts** is the number of fixed-size memory chunks we plan to make available. This number was arbitrarily chosen to be 512. Any other positive value would also work. The constant **elt_size** is the number of bytes we must allocate for each object. Note that we tend to overestimate this quantity so we can be sure to start each element on a **long** boundary. The anonymous union **sc_memory** contains the raw memory we plan to make available to **new** and **delete** for allocation.

The array of fixed-size memory chunks is called **sc_memory**, which is an anonymous union. We make this type anonymous (that is, nameless) as a way to keep it "secret" from other translation units. This is a good precaution, even though it's unlikely that a .cpp file will be included by another source file.

Why is **sc_memory** a union instead of a **struct** or **class**? We want the array **raw** to have the strictest possible alignment. On many systems, the **long** basic type has this strict alignment. Therefore, declaring both of these types in the same union forces **raw** to have the strictest possible alignment. A different basic type may be needed to achieve this result on some systems. The name given to the **long** member is **dummy**, to emphasize the fact that it has no use other than to force the alignment we want.

The **is_reserved** array contains **bool** values that are initially **false**. A value of **false** in the *n*th element of this array indicates that the *n*th element of the **sc_memory** array is *not* reserved; in other words, this element is available for allocation. A value of **true** indicates that the *n*th element has already been allocated by a prior call to **Special_class::operator new(size_t)** and is currently unavailable for allocation.

The function **Special_class::operator new(size_t)** is straightforward. Based on a sequential search of **is_reserved**, it determines the index, *n*, of the first element that's available. If no such index exists, the function throws the **bad_alloc** exception; otherwise it returns the address of **sc_memory**'s nth element.

Function **Special_class:operator delete(void *, size_t)** is even simpler. Based on the value of its **void *** argument and the known starting address of **sc_memory**, this function calculates the array index, n, of the element being deleted. It then sets the nth element of **is_reserved** to **false**, which makes the corresponding element of **sc_memory** available for allocation once again.

The print statements in these functions are for demonstration and debugging purposes only. They should be commented out of any production code. Notice that both of these functions ignore their **size_t** arguments because the size of the memory chunk being allocated or de-allocated is always the same.

The file **main_array.cpp** shows some simple usage examples. Note that the deletion order for the variables **scp_0, scp_1, and scp_2** is slightly different from their allocation order.

Simple List-Based Allocator

The array-based allocator of the preceding section has two very desirable characteristics: simplicity and speed. Its major drawback is its lack of flexibility. The number of memory chunks available for run-time allocation is determined at compile time. Although this may correspond to the real-world constraints of embedded systems, most other applications require a more flexible policy.

The allocator shown in this section achieves the desired flexibility by building up the memory pool itself at run-time, using the global **::new** operator. The redesigned memory pool looks more like a linked list than an array. Each cell in this list is just a **struct** that consists of a **Special_class** and a pointer to the next cell. Because this design lets the compiler handle all the alignment and size calculations, the default constructor for **Special_class** must be defined to be null, because we don't want to invoke a real constructor each time we allocate a new cell for the memory pool.

At this point, the alert reader may be wondering whether this technique is any better than using the default **::new** operator. After all, what's to be gained by building up a linked list of memory cells if we have to call **::new** to get those cells in the first place? The short answer is "plenty"!

To begin with, once a cell has been allocated by **::new** and added to the memory pool, our specialized allocator can use this cell again and again through any number of rapid allocation/de-allocation cycles. In addition, there's absolutely no reason for **::new** to allocate these cells one at a time. Whenever **Special_class::operator new(size_t)** runs out of available cells in its memory pool, it can ask **::new** to supply a large number of new ones all at once. In fact, when we ask **::new** for more cells, we actually request a large array of them. Once we have this array, we make it look like a linked list by making each cell point to its successor within the array.

What are the drawbacks of this list-based approach? The major disadvantage is that once **::new** adds an array of cells to the specialized memory pool, those cells can never be returned to the heap by **::delete**. When **::new** allocates a fresh array of memory cells, they are all contiguous and empty. If we were to call **::delete** to return these cells to the heap, **::delete** would have to return *all* of them. The problem is that, between the calls to **::new** and **::delete**, there may be any number of calls to **Special_class::operator new(size_t)** and **Special_class::operator delete(void *, size_t)**. This typically results in some cells within the array being free and some being reserved. We would want each of these cells to be free before calling **::delete**, but there's no way to assure this condition. As a result, from the perspective of **::new**, the number of cells allocated for **Special_class** objects grows steadily as the program runs, until it reaches its "high-water mark" (or a somewhat greater number because of leftover cells in the last array to be allocated). In many situations, this trade-off is reasonable.

A second drawback to the list-based approach is carried over from the array-based allocator. Classes derived from **Special_class** must be exactly the same size as **Special_class**. This restriction can be overcome by making two changes.

The first one is to define a virtual destructor for **Special_class**. It's perfectly fine if this destructor does nothing, as long as it's defined. For reasons that will not be explained here, defining a virtual destructor guarantees that the **size_t** arguments passed to **Special_class**'s **new** and **delete** operators will be accurate under all circumstances. This hasn't mattered until now, because so far we've managed to ignore the **size_t** arguments entirely.

The second change is that we must now keep as many linked lists as there are sizes of derived classes, instead of keeping a single linked list of fixed size cells. One way to do this is to define **avail** as an array of pointers rather than as a pointer. A parallel array could be defined that specifies the size of the memory cells in the linked list corresponding to each index.

Code

mm_list.h
mm_list.cpp

Files **mm_list.h** and **mm_list.cpp** contain the code. File **main_list.cpp** contains an example of its usage. Here is **mm_list.h**:

```
#include <new>
#include <cstdlib>
#include <cstdio>
using namespace std;


class Special_class {

private:
  int data;  // data content of this class.


public:
```

```
  // Make sure default constructor does nothing.
  Special_class( ) { }
  Special_class(int i) : data(i) { }

  void * operator new(size_t s) throw(bad_alloc);
  void   operator delete(void * vp, size_t s);
};
```

Here is **mm_list.cpp**:

```
// Implementation of specialized new and delete operators
// for class Special_class.  The "static" keyword is used
// liberally to make definitions private to this
// translation unit.

#include "mm_list.h"

// The following struct is used to build linked lists of
// Special_class memory chunks.

struct Special_class_mem_cell {
  Special_class             memory_chunk;
  Special_class_mem_cell * next;
};

// Number of fixed size elements in the array.
static const int num_elts            = 512;

// Pointer to linked list of available memory chunks.
static Special_class_mem_cell * avail = 0;


void * Special_class::operator new(size_t s) throw(bad_alloc)
{
  // Allocate a new array of Special_class_mem_cells
  // when needed, using ::new.

  if (avail == 0) {
    // ::new throws bad_alloc if memory becomes
    // exhausted.
    avail = ::new Special_class_mem_cell[num_elts];
```

```cpp
    for(int i = 0; i < num_elts-1; ++i) {
      avail[i].next = &(avail[i+1]);
    }
    avail[num_elts-1].next = 0;
  }


  // Detatch the first available Special_class_mem_cell
  // and return its address.

  Special_class_mem_cell * ret_cell = avail;
  avail = avail->next;

  // Not really necessary to zero out the next field.
  // May help distinguish allocated cells from free
  // cells if memory allocation errors arise.
  ret_cell->next = 0;

  printf
    ("Special_class::new allocated %d bytes at address 0x%x\n",
    s, &(ret_cell->memory_chunk));

  return &(ret_cell->memory_chunk);
}

void Special_class::operator delete(void * vp, size_t s)
{
  // Attach Special_class_mem_cell to head of the avail list.
  ((Special_class_mem_cell *)vp)->next = avail;
  avail =  ((Special_class_mem_cell *)vp);

  printf
    ("Special_class::delete released %d bytes at address 0x%x\n",
    s, vp);
}
```

Here is **main_list.cpp**:

```cpp
#include "mm_list.h"

Special_class sc;

int main( )
{
  Special_class * scp_0 = new Special_class;
  Special_class * scp_1 = new Special_class;
```

```
Special_class * scp_2 = new Special_class;

delete scp_1;
delete scp_0;
delete scp_2;

return 0;
}
```

Sample output from **main_list.cpp** looks like this:

```
Special_class::new allocated 4 bytes at address 0x40003768
Special_class::new allocated 4 bytes at address 0x40003770
Special_class::new allocated 4 bytes at address 0x40003778
Special_class::delete released 4 bytes at address 0x40003770
Special_class::delete released 4 bytes at address 0x40003768
Special_class::delete released 4 bytes at address 0x40003778
```

ANNOTATIONS

File **mm_list.h** is quite similar to its array-based counterpart. The only significant difference is that it defines (and *must* define) a default constructor **Special_class::Special_class( )** which does nothing. A second constructor, **Special_class::Special_class(int)**, is also defined and does some useful initialization.

File **mm_list.cpp** includes the header file **mm_list.h** and implements **Special_class::operator new(size_t)** and **Special_class::operator delete(void , size_t)**. The definition of **struct Special_class_mem_cell** is at file scope, so that it's visible to both **Special_class::operator new(size_t)** and **Special_class::operator delete(void *, size_t)**. We can't guarantee that this type name will remain invisible to other translation units, but it's unlikely that any other source file will include **mm_list.cpp**. Unfortunately, it's not impossible for another source file to define a different class with the same name.

Num_elts specifies the number of cells in a single array. Zero or more arrays of cells may be allocated during any program run. The file-scope variable **avail** is defined as a **Special_class_mem_cell ***, and points to a linked list of these cells. The initial value of this pointer is zero.

The first thing **Special_class::operator new(size_t)** does is check the **avail** pointer. If **avail** is zero, there are currently no cells in the memory pool. More must be allocated before the memory request can be satisfied. In this case, **::new** is asked to allocate a 512-element array of **Special_class_mem_cell**s. Note that **::new** may throw a **bad_alloc** exception if its memory becomes exhausted. Each of these cells is then made to point to the subsequent cell in the array. This makes the array look like a linked list. Now that we're sure there are some free cells on the list, we simply detach the first one and return the address of its **memory_chunk** field.

As before, **Special_class::operator delete(void *, size_t)** is the simpler of the two functions. It just assumes that the address passed as its first argument corresponds to a **Special_class_mem_cell**, and attaches that cell to the free list pointed to be **avail**.

As usual, the print statements are just for demonstration and debugging purposes.

PROGRAMMER'S NOTE *The actual size of the arrays **Special_class_mem_cell[num_elts]** may have a significant impact on run-time performance. For example, if the array size happens to be one byte larger than the system page size, performance may suffer as a result of page thrashing. It's usually well worth the effort to tune run-time performance by adjusting **num_elts** based on the characteristics of your particular system and application.*

Working with Files and Directories

By Lars Klander

filter.cpp

tabspace.cpp

walkdirs (Visual C++)

doshex.cpp

winhex (Visual C++)

ne of the most important tasks for any programmer is manipulation of the files and directories used by the computer to structure and manage information stored on disk drives. C/C++ provides a broad set of tools for working with files. Furthermore, the computer's operating system will also expose functions—through the Application Programming Interface (API)—that you can use to manipulate and manage files and directories.

In this chapter, we will focus mostly on the manipulation of the various stream classes that C++ supports. Little of the code we will look at will be computer- or operating-system specific, instead using C++'s high-level management classes. The most notable exception to this is the **walkdirs.cpp** program presented in the middle of the chapter, which uses Windows-based directory services to recursively access and display information about all the files in a tree.

Search and Replace Text File

The first program in the chapter, the **filter.cpp** program, is a command-line search-and-replace utility, which lets you search a text file and replace all instances of a particular word with another word.

filter.cpp

Code

Here is the code for the **filter.cpp** program, a simple command-line filtering utility.

```cpp
#include <cstdlib>
#include <iostream>
#include <fstream>
using namespace std;

int main(int argc, char *argv[])
{
  char buffer[1];
  int i;
  long currentpos;
  bool match = false;

  if (argc != 5) {
    cout << "Usage: filter [search string] [replace string]" <<
        "[infile] [outfile]" << endl;
    return 1;
  }
```

```
string searchstring = argv[1];
string replacestring = argv[2];
string infilename = argv[3];
string outfilename = argv[4];

ifstream input(infilename.c_str(), ios::in);
if (input.fail()) {
  cout << "Unable to open input file!" << endl;
  return 1;
}

ofstream output(outfilename.c_str(), ios::out | ios::trunc);
if (output.fail()) {
  cout << "Unable to open output file!" << endl;
  return 1;
}

while (!input.eof()) {
  currentpos = input.tellg();
  input.read(buffer, sizeof(buffer));
  if (buffer[0] == searchstring[0]) {
    match = true;
    i = 1;
    while (i < searchstring.length() && match) {
      input.read(buffer, sizeof(buffer));
      if (buffer[0] != searchstring[i]) {
        input.seekg(currentpos);
        input.read(buffer, sizeof(buffer));
        match = false;
      }
      else
        i++;
    }
  }
  if (match) {
    output.write(replacestring.c_str(), replacestring.length());
    match = false;
  }
  else
    output.write(buffer, sizeof(buffer));
}
```

```
  input.close();
  output.close();
  ifstream display(outfilename.c_str(), ios::in);

  while (!display.eof()) {
    display.read(buffer, sizeof(buffer));
    if (display.good())
      cout << buffer[0];
  }
  display.close();
  return 0;
}
```

ANNOTATIONS

Most of what is happening within **filter.cpp** is relatively easy to understand. The program's usefulness is its efficiency in managing incoming and outgoing files. The headers at the top of the file are what you might expect: headers to support the **iostream** class and the **fstream** class—not surprising, since we are managing both screen output and text files.

```
#include <cstdlib>
#include <iostream>
#include <fstream>
using namespace std;
```

All of the processing performed by the program occurs within the **main( )** function—although you could easily separate the processing code out and place it within its own function. Note that **main( )** takes command-line parameters in this application. It also uses a small (one-character) buffer when reading from the file; a counter variable (**i**); a variable corresponding to the file pointer's current location (**currentpos**); and a Boolean variable that keeps track of whether the word read from the file matches the user-specified search phrase. Here is **main( )**:

```
int main(int argc, char *argv[])
{
  char buffer[1];
  int i;
  long currentpos;
  bool match = false;
```

The first conditional within the application checks to make sure the user has entered the correct number of parameters. If not, the function exits the program and provides parameter information to the user:

```
if (argc != 5) {
cout << "Usage: filter [search string] [replace string] " <<
    "[infile] [outfile]" << endl;
  return 1;
}
```

Next, the program code declares four string variables that it will use to maintain the parameter information provided by the user. Each of these variables is of the **string** type defined by the standard template library:

```
string searchstring = argv[1];
string replacestring = argv[2];
string infilename = argv[3];
string outfilename = argv[4];
```

Next, the program code uses the input filename provided by the user and opens an incoming file stream of type **ifstream**. Though not strictly necessary, the second parameter to the constructor—**ios::in**—simply tells the compiler to construct the object as an incoming file stream. This parameter is the default; however, it can be combined with other values to give you additional control over the use of the input stream. The **if** statement simply checks to make sure that the program opened the file safely, checking the return value of the **fail( )** member function to ensure that a good stream was obtained. If one was not, the program alerts the user and exits, as shown here:

```
ifstream input(infilename.c_str(), ios::in);
if (input.fail()) {
  cout << "Unable to open input file!" << endl;
  return 1;
}
```

Similar processing is performed to open the variable **output** and connect it to an outbound file stream, although the parameters are slightly different in this case. The **ios::out** parameter is the default. In addition, however, the program code truncates the output file automatically if it currently has contents, using the **ios::trunc** constant. Again, after creating the object, the program makes sure it was able to successfully construct the object, as shown here:

```
ofstream output(outfilename.c_str(), ios::out | ios::trunc);
  if (output.fail()) {
    cout << "Unable to open output file!" << endl;
    return 1;
  }
```

After both the streams are opened successfully, the program enters a **while** loop, which repeats until the input stream's **eof( )** member function indicates that the program has reached the end of the file. Within the **while** loop is where the program actually searches the source file and copies its contents to the output file. The first statement within the loop sets the **currentpos** variable equal to the file pointer's current position within the file, a necessary step because we will be reading ahead in the file whenever we try to match the search phrase. Here's the **while** loop:

```
while (!input.eof()) {
    currentpos = input.tellg();
```

After retrieving the file pointer, the program uses the **read( )** method to read a single character from the file. This method accepts a **char** array as its first parameter, and a value corresponding to the size of the array as its second parameter. Then the program compares the character it has read from the file to the first character from the search string. If they match, the program code executes the then clause of the **if** statement (discussed momentarily):

```
input.read(buffer, sizeof(buffer));
if (buffer[0] == searchstring[0]) {
```

So, the program only executes the code within the then clause if the first letter of the search string matches the character read in from the file. Within this loop, then, the program has to read out as many characters as the search string contains within the file, dropping back out of the loop and copying single characters if any of the characters doesn't match. So, to perform this processing, we use a counter variable (**i**), and a **while** loop that watches the length of the search string and the value of the **boolean** variable **match**, stopping its execution when **i** exceeds the string's length or **match** becomes **false**:

```
match = true;
i = 1;
while (i < searchstring.length() && match) {
```

Within the **while** loop, processing is much as you might expect. The program reads one character out from the file at a time, then checks that character against its corresponding character within the search string. If the characters match, the program code increments the counter variable **i**. If the characters don't match, then it becomes necessary to perform some sleight-of-hand to return the file to its precomparison state.

Returning to the previous state is crucial because you want to make sure you resume reading from the file at the point where you started checking for a match. Otherwise, not only will your search algorithm not work correctly, the resulting file will be missing letters, words, or even whole phrases. The code within the then clause of the **if** statement performs this "reset" processing, as you will see next:

```
input.read(buffer, sizeof(buffer));
if (buffer[0] != searchstring[i]) {
```

Remember from earlier in the chapter that we used the **tellg( )** function to retrieve the current file pointer at the top of the loop iteration. At this point, the file pointer has been advanced some (unknown) distance beyond where we want it to be. The most efficient means of resuming the correct position is to use the **seekg( )** function, passing the **currentpos** variable in as its parameter. Next, the program reads a single character from the file—returning it to the state it was in immediately before entering the matching loop. Finally, the program code sets the **match** variable to **false**, which results in the **while** loop falling through immediately:

```
        input.seekg(currentpos);
        input.read(buffer, sizeof(buffer));
        match = false;
      }
      else
        i++;
    }
  }
```

After the program exits the **while** loop, it's necessary to check and see whether the loop exited because of a successful match or an unsuccessful match. The program does this by checking the value of the **match** variable and responding appropriately. If **match** is **true**, the program writes out the entire replacement string to the output file and sets **match** to **false**, as shown here:

```
  if (match) {
      output.write(replacestring.c_str(), replacestring.length());
      match = false;
  }
```

On the other hand, if there was no match, the program simply writes the single character within the **buffer** array. It is important to note, by the way, that the program *doesn't* reset the file pointer in the event of a successful match. In fact, the outer loop will resume reading at the first character after the search text (in the input file), and will of course start writing at the first character after the replacement text in the output file as shown here:

```
  else
      output.write(buffer, sizeof(buffer));
  }
```

After the outer loop—which reads through the entire input file—completes its processing, the program code cleans up the **input** and **output** variables, closing the streams they are connected to. Then, for the purpose of clarity, the program opens a new **ifstream** object, which it will use to display the newly created file on the screen:

```
  input.close();
  output.close();
  ifstream display(outfilename.c_str(), ios::in);
```

Next the program creates and allocates the new variable (there should be a success test here, in your production-level programs). Afterward, the program simply iterates one character at a time through the output file, sending each character to the **cout** stream, provided it's a recognizable character. Here is the code for these steps:

```
while (!display.eof()) {
  display.read(buffer, sizeof(buffer));
  if (display.good())
    cout << buffer[0];
}
```

After the output loop ends, the program code closes the stream and exits the program successfully:

```
display.close();
return 0;
}
```

When you run this program with the **infile.txt** file contained on this book's companion CD-ROM, you will receive output similar to the following:

```
C:\> filter this TEST infile.txt outfile.txt
Four score and seven years ago, our fathers brought forth upon TEST
continent, a new nation, conceived in liberty, and dedicated to the
proposition that all men are created equal.

Now we are engaged in a great civil war, testing whether that nation,
or any nation so conceived and so dedicated, can long endure. We are
met on a great battlefield of that war. We have come to dedicate a
portion of that field, as a final resting place for those who here
gave their lives that that nation might live. It is altogether
fitting and proper that we should do TEST.

But, in a larger sense, we cannot dedicate -- we cannot consecrate --
we cannot hallow -- TEST ground. The brave men, living and dead, who
struggled here, have consecrated it, far above our poor power to add
or detract. The world will little note, nor long remember what we say
here, but it can never forget what they did here. It is for us the
living, rather, to be dedicated here to the unfinished work which
they who fought here have thus far so nobly advanced. It is rather
for us to be here dedicated to the great task remaining before us --
that from these honored dead we take increased devotion to that cause
for which they gave the last full measure of devotion -- that we here
highly resolve that these dead shall not have died in vain -- that
TEST nation, under God, shall have a new birth of freedom -- and that
government of the people, by the people, for the people, shall not
perish from the earth.
```

As you can see, the program simply replaces each instance of *this* with the word *TEST*, and then displays the output to the screen. You can, of course, replace an entire phrase—just make sure that you enclose the search-and/or-replace strings with double quotes, as shown here:

```
C:\> filter "for the people" "at no cost to the people" infile.txt
outfile.txt
```

The only problem with this **filter.cpp** program is that it doesn't process control characters—such as tabs—correctly. One of the best uses for a filter program is in managing source code files that come from various editors—some use tabs and some use spaces. The following section examines the program **tabspace.cpp**, which uses logic similar to that of the filter program to let the user replace tabs with spaces within a text document, and vice versa. We'll take a look at the code, and then study the differences between the two programs.

Code

Here is the code for the **tabspace.cpp** program.

tabspace.cpp

```cpp
#include <cstdlib>
#include <iostream>
#include <fstream>
using namespace std;

int main(int argc, char *argv[])
{
  char buffer[1];
  int i;
  long currentpos;
  bool match = false;

  if (argc != 5) {
    cout << "Usage: tabspace [infile] [outfile] [-s|-t]" <<
        "[numspaces]" << endl;
    cout << "Use -s to replace spaces with tabs, " <<
        << "and -t to replace tabs with spaces." << endl;
    return 1;
  }

  string infilename = argv[1];
  string outfilename = argv[2];
  string switchtype = argv[3];
  string searchstring, replacestring;
  int numspaces = atoi(argv[4]);
```

```
if ((switchtype[1] != 's') && (switchtype[1] != 't')){
  cout << "Switch must be either -s or -t!" << endl;
  return 1;
}

ifstream input(infilename.c_str(), ios::in);
if (input.fail()) {
  cout << "Unable to open input file!" << endl;
  return 1;
}

ofstream output(outfilename.c_str(), ios::out | ios::trunc);
if (output.fail()) {
  cout << "Unable to open output file!" << endl;
  input.close();
  return 1;
}

if (switchtype[1] == 's'){
  for (i = 0; i < numspaces; i++)
    searchstring += " ";
  replacestring = "\t";
}
else {
  searchstring = "\t";
  for (i = 0; i < numspaces; i++)
    replacestring += " ";
}

while (!input.eof()) {
  currentpos = input.tellg();
  input.read(buffer, sizeof(buffer));
  if (buffer[0] == searchstring[0]) {
    match = true;
    i = 1;
    while (i < searchstring.length() && match) {
      input.read(buffer, sizeof(buffer));
      if (buffer[0] != searchstring[i]) {
        input.seekg(currentpos);
        input.read(buffer, sizeof(buffer));
        match = false;
      }
```

```
        else
            i++;
        }
    }
    if (match) {
        output.write(replacestring.c_str(), replacestring.length());
        match = false;
    }
    else
        output.write(buffer, sizeof(buffer));
}
input.close();
output.close();
ifstream display(outfilename.c_str(), ios::in);

while (!display.eof()) {
    display.read(buffer, sizeof(buffer));
    if (display.good())
        cout << buffer[0];
}
display.close();
return 0;
}
```

ANNOTATIONS

Much like the **filter.cpp** program, most of what is happening within the **tabspace.cpp** program should be relatively evident. The usefulness of the program lies in its efficiency in managing incoming and outgoing files and in the easy specification of conversion characteristics for tabs and spaces. As in the filter program, the headers for **tabspace.cpp** support the **iostream** class and the **fstream** class, since again we are managing both screen output and text files.

```
#include <cstdlib>
#include <iostream>
#include <fstream>
using namespace std;
```

All of the processing performed by **tabspace.cpp** occurs within the **main( )** function—although you could easily separate the processing code out and place it within its own function. Note that **main( )** takes command-line parameters in this application. It also uses a small (one-character) buffer when reading from the file; a counter variable (**i**); a variable corresponding to the file pointer's current location (**currentpos**), and a Boolean variable that keeps track of whether the word read from the file matches the user-specified search phrase. Here are the declarations within **main( )**:

```
int main(int argc, char *argv[])
{
  char buffer[1];
  int i;
  long currentpos;
  bool match = false;
```

The first conditional within the application checks to make sure the user has entered the correct number of parameters. If not, the function exits the program and provides parameter information to the user. These parameters are in a slightly different sequence than they were in the first program, and they have different meanings. The **infile** and **outfile** parameters are the same, but the third parameter is a *switch*. And the fourth parameter will correspond to the number of spaces to be either replaced with a tab, or put in place of a tab.

```
  if (argc != 5) {
    cout << "Usage: tabspace [infile] [outfile] [-s|-t]" <<
        "[numspaces]" << endl;
    cout << "Use -s to replace spaces with tabs, "
        << "and -t to replace tabs with spaces." << endl;
    return 1;
  }
```

Next, the program declares five string variables that it will use to maintain the parameter information provided by the user. Each of these variables is of the **string** type defined by the Standard Template Library. The program also declares the integer variable **numspaces**, converting the command-line value entered (as a string) to a numeric value, using the **atoi( )** function:

```
  string infilename = argv[1];
  string outfilename = argv[2];
  string switchtype = argv[3];
  string searchstring, replacestring;
  int numspaces = atoi(argv[4]);
```

After putting the command-line information into variables it can process, the program checks the value of the **switchtype** string, making sure that the user entered a valid switch. If the user did not, the program displays a warning and exits processing immediately. Here is that code:

```
  if ((switchtype[1] != 's') && (switchtype[1] != 't')){
    cout << "Switch must be either -s or -t!" << endl;
    return 1;
  }
```

Next, the program uses the input filename provided by the user and opens an incoming file stream, of type **ifstream**. The **if** statement simply checks to make sure that the program opened the file safely, checking the return value of the **fail( )** member function to ensure that a good stream was obtained. If one was not, the program alerts the user and exits, as shown here:

```
ifstream input(infilename.c_str(), ios::in);
if (input.fail()) {
  cout << "Unable to open input file!" << endl;
  return 1;
}
```

Similar processing is performed to open the variable **output** and connect it to an outbound file stream, although the parameters are slightly different in this case. Again, after creating the object, the program makes sure it was able to successfully construct the file object. If not, the program also cleans up the **input** variable, as shown here:

```
ofstream output(outfilename.c_str(), ios::out | ios::trunc);
if (output.fail()) {
  cout << "Unable to open output file!" << endl;
  input.close();
  return 1;
}
```

After both the streams are opened successfully, the program must then determine what it is searching for and replacing. If the incoming switch is **–s**, the program will search for spaces and replace them with tabs. The number of spaces to search for corresponds to the fourth parameter at the command-line (which we assigned to **numspaces**), and so we use a loop to concatenate the spaces onto the **searchstring** variable. Then, we assign the C-specified **"\t"** tab escape sequence to the **replacestring** variable. These variables will be used by the program during its processing of the file:

```
if (switchtype[1] == 's'){
  for (i = 0; i < numspaces; i++)
    searchstring += " ";
  replacestring = "\t";
}
```

On the other hand, if the user selects the **–t** switch, the opposite assignment occurs—the spaces are placed in the **replacestring**, and the tab is placed in the search string, as shown here:

```
else {
  searchstring = "\t";
  for (i = 0; i < numspaces; i++)
    replacestring += " ";
}
```

After determining what the replacement strings will be, the program enters a **while** loop that will repeat until the input stream's **eof( )** member function indicates that the program has reached the end of the file. Within the **while** loop is where the program actually searches the source file and copies its contents to the output file. The first statement within the loop sets the **currentpos** variable equal to the file pointer's current position within the file, a necessary step because we will be reading ahead in the file whenever we try to match the search phrase. Here is the **while** loop:

```
while (!input.eof()) {
   currentpos = input.tellg();
```

After retrieving the file pointer, the program uses the **read( )** method to read a single character from the file. The **read** method accepts a **char** array as its first parameter, and a value corresponding to the size of the array as its second parameter. After reading in the character from the file, the program compares that character to the first character from the search string. If they match, the program code executes the then clause of the **if** statement, which we will discuss momentarily:

```
input.read(buffer, sizeof(buffer));
if (buffer[0] == searchstring[0]) {
```

So, the program only executes the code within the then clause if the first letter of the search string matches the character read in from the file. Within this loop, then, the program has to read as many characters as the search string contains within the file, dropping back out of the loop and copying single characters if any of the characters doesn't match. So, to perform this processing, we use a counter variable (**i**), and a **while** loop that watches the length of the search string and the value of the **boolean** variable **match**, stopping its execution when **i** exceeds the string's length or **match** becomes **false**.

```
match = true;
i = 1;
while (i < searchstring.length() && match) {
```

Within the **while** loop, processing is much as you might expect. The program reads one character out from the file at a time, then checks that character against its corresponding character within the search string. If the characters match, the code increments the counter variable **i**. If the characters don't match, then it becomes necessary to perform some sleight-of-hand to return the file to its precomparison state.

Returning to the previous state is crucial because you want to make sure you begin reading from the file again at the point where you started checking for a match. Otherwise, not only will your search algorithm not work correctly, the resulting file will be missing letters, words, or even whole phrases. This "reset" processing is performed by the program code within the then clause of the **if** statement, as you will see next:

```
input.read(buffer, sizeof(buffer));
if (buffer[0] != searchstring[i]) {
```

Remember from earlier in the chapter that we used the **tellg( )** function to retrieve the current file pointer at the top of the loop iteration. At this point, the file pointer has been advanced some (unknown) distance beyond where we want it to be. The most efficient means to return it to the correct position is to use the **seekg( )** function, passing the **currentpos** variable as its parameter. Next, the program reads a single character from the file—returning it to the state it was in immediately before entering the matching loop. Finally, the **match** variable is set to **false**, which results in the **while** loop falling through immediately:

```
    input.seekg(currentpos);
    input.read(buffer, sizeof(buffer));
    match = false;
  }
  else
     i++;
  }
}
```

After the program exits the **while** loop, it's necessary to check and see whether the loop exited because of a successful match or an unsuccessful match. The program does this by checking the value of the **match** variable and responding appropriately. If **match** is **true**, the program writes the entire replacement string to the output file, and sets **match** to **false**, as shown here:

```
if (match) {
  output.write(replacestring.c_str(), replacestring.length());
  match = false;
}
```

On the other hand, if there was no match, the program simply writes the single character within the **buffer** array. It is important to note, by the way, that the program *doesn't* reset the file pointer in the event of a successful match. In fact, the outer loop will resume reading at the first character after the search text (in the input file), and will of course start writing at the first character after the replacement text in the output file as follows:

```
else
    output.write(buffer, sizeof(buffer));
}
```

After the outer loop—which reads through the entire input file—completes its processing, the program code cleans up the **input** and **output** variables, closing the streams they are connected to. Then, for the purpose of clarity, the program opens a new **ifstream** object, which it will use to display the newly-created file on the screen:

```
input.close();
output.close();
ifstream display(outfilename.c_str(), ios::in);
```

Next the program creates and allocates the new variable (as with **filter.cpp**, there should be a success test here, in your production-level programs). Afterward, the program simply iterates one character at a time through the output file, sending each character to the **cout** stream, provided it's a recognizable character. Here is the code for these steps:

```
while (!display.eof()) {
    display.read(buffer, sizeof(buffer));
    if (display.good())
      cout << buffer[0];
}
```

After the output loop ends, the program code closes the stream and exits the program successfully.

```
 display.close();
  return 0;
}
```

You can see the effects of this program by running it against the **tabspace.cpp** source code on the companion CD-ROM. Make sure, however, that you then load the file into a word processor (such as Microsoft Word), or into some other program that displays an indicator of tabs. This lets you see the difference between the spaces native to the file and the tabs with which you replaced them. You can then change the file's contents back, and view the display of the newly created file as well.

Working with the File System

Often, in today's complex applications, working with files alone isn't sufficient— you have to be able to work with the file system that maintains the files. Although C++ provides certain high-level structures to help you in working with file systems, most of them are subsumed by interfaces exposed—that is, made available—by the operating system API the programmer will uses. The Windows development environment is a perfect example of this: The Win32 API provides over 200 functions for interaction with and management of information stored on a Windows drive.

Clearly, all these functions are too extensive to describe here—you are better off consulting a Win32 API reference manual. Instead, we will focus on a single application that you will likely find useful for navigating the operating system. This application, **WalkDirs,** recursively searches through all the files in a directory tree.

Code

walkdirs.cpp

The core of the WalkDirs project is found within the **walkdirs.cpp** program file.

```
#include <windows.h>
#include <windowsx.h>
#include <tchar.h>
#include <cstdlib>
#include <cstdio>
#include <string>
#include "Resource.H"

using namespace std;

static BOOL IsChildDir (WIN32_FIND_DATA *lpFindData)
 {
    return((((lpFindData->dwFileAttributes &
        FILE_ATTRIBUTE_DIRECTORY) != 0) &&
        (lstrcmp(lpFindData->cFileName, _TEXT(".")) !=0) &&
        (lstrcmp(lpFindData->cFileName, _TEXT("..")) != 0));
 }

static BOOL FindNextChildDir (HANDLE hFindFile,
    WIN32_FIND_DATA *lpFindData)
{
  BOOL fFound = FALSE;

  do {
    fFound = FindNextFile(hFindFile, lpFindData);
  } while (fFound && !IsChildDir(lpFindData));
  return(fFound);
}

static HANDLE FindFirstChildDir (LPTSTR szPath,
    WIN32_FIND_DATA *lpFindData)
{
  BOOL fFound;
  HANDLE hFindFile = FindFirstFile(szPath, lpFindData);
```

```
  if (hFindFile != INVALID_HANDLE_VALUE) {
     fFound = IsChildDir(lpFindData);
     if (!fFound)
       fFound = FindNextChildDir(hFindFile, lpFindData);
     if (!fFound) {
       FindClose(hFindFile);
       hFindFile = INVALID_HANDLE_VALUE;
     }
  }
  return (hFindFile);
}


// Data Used by WalkDirRecurse
typedef struct {
  HWND hwndTreeLB;
  int nDepth;
  BOOL fRecurse;
  TCHAR szBuf[1000];
  int nIndent;
  BOOL fOk;
  BOOL fIsDir;
  WIN32_FIND_DATA FindData;
} WALKDIRDATA, *LPWALKDIRDATA;

static void WalkDirRecurse (LPWALKDIRDATA pDW)
{
  HANDLE hFind;

  pDW->nDepth++;
  pDW->nIndent = 3 * pDW->nDepth;
  _stprintf(pDW->szBuf, _TEXT("%*s"), pDW->nIndent, _TEXT(""));
  GetCurrentDirectory(chDIMOF(pDW->szBuf) - pDW->nIndent,
      &pDW->szBuf[pDW->nIndent]);
  ListBox_AddString(pDW->hwndTreeLB, pDW->szBuf);
  hFind = FindFirstFile(_TEXT("*.*"), &pDW->FindData);
  pDW->fOk = (hFind != INVALID_HANDLE_VALUE);
  while (pDW->fOk) {
    pDW->fIsDir = pDW->FindData.dwFileAttributes &
      FILE_ATTRIBUTE_DIRECTORY;
    if (!pDW->fIsDir || (!pDW->fRecurse &&
      IsChildDir(&pDW->FindData))) {
      _stprintf(pDW->szBuf,
      pDW->fIsDir ? _TEXT("%*s[%s]") : _TEXT("%*s%s"),
```

```
          pDW->nIndent, _TEXT(""), pDW->FindData.cFileName);
        ListBox_AddString(pDW->hwndTreeLB, pDW->szBuf);
      }
      pDW->fOk = FindNextFile(hFind, &pDW->FindData);
    }
    if (hFind != INVALID_HANDLE_VALUE)
      FindClose(hFind);
    if (pDW->fRecurse) {
      hFind = FindFirstChildDir(_TEXT("*.*"), &pDW->FindData);
      pDW->fOk = (hFind != INVALID_HANDLE_VALUE);
      while (pDW->fOk) {
        if (SetCurrentDirectory(pDW->FindData.cFileName)) {
          WalkDirRecurse(pDW);
          SetCurrentDirectory(_TEXT(".."));
        }
        pDW->fOk = FindNextChildDir(hFind, &pDW->FindData);
      }
      if (hFind != INVALID_HANDLE_VALUE)
        FindClose(hFind);
    }
    pDW->nDepth--;
}

void WalkDir (HWND hwndTreeLB, LPCTSTR pszRootPath, BOOL fRecurse)
{
    static char szCurrDir[_MAX_DIR];
    WALKDIRDATA DW;

    ListBox_ResetContent(hwndTreeLB);
    GetCurrentDirectory(chDIMOF(szCurrDir), szCurrDir);
    SetCurrentDirectory(pszRootPath);
    WD.nDepth = -1;
    WD.hwndTreeLB = hwndTreeLB;
    WD.fRecurse = fRecurse;
    WalkDirRecurse(&DW);
    SetCurrentDirectory(szCurrDir);
}

BOOL Dlg_OnInitDialog (HWND hwnd, HWND hwndFocus, LPARAM lParam)
{
    RECT rc;
```

```
  WalkDir(GetDlgItem(hwnd, IDC_TREE), _TEXT("\\"), TRUE);
  GetClientRect(hwnd, &rc);
  SetWindowPos(GetDlgItem(hwnd, IDC_TREE), NULL, 0, 0,
      rc.right, rc.bottom, SWP_NOZORDER);
  return(TRUE);
}


void Dlg_OnSize (HWND hwnd, UINT state, int cx, int cy)
{
  SetWindowPos(GetDlgItem(hwnd, IDC_TREE), NULL, 0, 0,
      cx, cy, SWP_NOZORDER);
}


void Dlg_OnCommand (HWND hwnd, int id, HWND hwndCtl, UINT CodeNotify)
{
  switch (id) {
    case IDCANCEL:
      EndDialog(hwnd, id);
      break;

    case IDOK:
      WalkDir(GetDlgItem(hwnd, IDC_TREE), _TEXT("\\"), TRUE);
      break;
  }
}


BOOL CALLBACK Dlg_Proc (HWND hwnd, UINT uMsg,
    WPARAM wParam, LPARAM lParam)
{
  switch (uMsg) {
    chHANDLE_DLGMSG(hwnd, WM_INITDIALOG, Dlg_OnInitDialog);
    chHANDLE_DLGMSG(hwnd, WM_SIZE, Dlg_OnSize);
    chHANDLE_DLGMSG(hwnd, WM_COMMAND, Dlg_OnCommand);
  }
  return(FALSE);
}


int WINAPI WinMain(HINSTANCE hinstExe, HINSTANCE hinstPrev,
    LPSTR pszCmdLine, int nCmdShow)
{
```

```
   DialogBox(hinstExe, MAKEINTRESOURCE(IDD_WALKDIR), NULL, Dlg_Proc);
   return(0);
}
```

ANNOTATIONS

The **walkdirs.cpp** program, together with the other files in the WalkDirs project, defines a recursive program that cycles through the entirety of a hard drive (or through an entire tree on the hard drive, depending on where you tell the program to start). All of the headers used by the file are pretty straightforward.

```
#include <windows.h>
#include <windowsx.h>
#include <tchar.h>
#include <cstdlib>
#include <cstdio>
#include <string>
#include "Resource.H"

using namespace std;
```

The first function defined within the file is the **IsChildDir( )** function, which accepts a structure of type **WIN32_FIND_DATA** and returns a Boolean value indicating whether or not the current item is a child directory. The **WIN32_FIND_DATA** structure is an important one to keep in mind when working with the operating system from Windows, and is explained in detail after the code:

```
static BOOL IsChildDir (WIN32_FIND_DATA *lpFindData)
{
   return(((lpFindData->dwFileAttributes &
      FILE_ATTRIBUTE_DIRECTORY) != 0) &&
      (lstrcmp(lpFindData->cFileName, _TEXT(".")) !=0) &&
      (lstrcmp(lpFindData->cFileName, _TEXT("..")) != 0));
}
```

As you can see, the **return** statement checks the **dwFileAttributes** member to determine whether the current item is a directory. It also checks to make sure that the directory is not a *"."* or *".."* directory as defined by the operating system. If the current item meets all these criteria, **IsChildDir( )** returns **true**; otherwise, the function returns **false**.

The **WIN32_FIND_DATA** structure describes a file found by the Win32 API functions **FindFirstFile( )**, **FindFirstFileEx( )**, and **FindNextFile( )**. The structure contains 10 members, as shown in the following prototype:

```
typedef struct _WIN32_FIND_DATA {
  DWORD dwFileAttributes;
  FILETIME ftCreationTime;
  FILETIME ftLastAccessTime;
  FILETIME ftLastWriteTime;
  DWORD nFileSizeHigh;
  DWORD nFileSizeLow;
  DWORD dwReserved0;
  DWORD dwReserved1;
  TCHAR cFileName[ MAX_PATH ];
  TCHAR cAlternateFileName[ 14 ];
} WIN32_FIND_DATA;
```

Table 6-1 discusses the members of the **WIN32_FIND_DATA** structure in more detail.

Member	Description
dwFileAttributes	Specifies the file attributes of the file object. File attributes describe how the file can be accessed, whether it is a file or directory, and so on. This member can be one or more of the values detailed in Table 6-2.
ftCreationTime	Contains a **FILETIME** structure (a 64-bit value representing the number of 100-nanosecond intervals since January 1, 1601) that specifies the time the file was originally created by the operating system. The **FILETIME** structure contains two **DWORD**s, which the **Find** functions will set to 0 if the file system containing the file does not support this time member.
ftLastAccessTime	This member contains a **FILETIME** structure that specifies the time the file was last accessed by a user. As for **ftCreationTime**, both structure members contain 0 if the file system does not support this time information.
ftLastWriteTime	This member contains a **FILETIME** structure which specifies the time that the file was last written to by a user or process. As for **ftCreationTime** and **ftLastAccessTime**, both structure members contain 0 if the file system does not support this time information.
nFileSizeHigh	File size is stored within the operating system in two **DWORD** values, which when added together using the equation **(nFileSizeHigh * MAXDWORD) + nFileSizeLow** yields the file's total size. (**MAXDWORD** is generally equal to $2^{32}-1$.) This element specifies the high-order value of the file size; this value is 0 unless the file size is greater than **MAXDWORD**.

TABLE 6-1.   WIN32_FIND_DATA Members

Member	Description
nFileSizeLow	Specifies the low-order **DWORD** value of the file size. This two-**DWORD** structure allows for file sizes into the terabytes (not a maximum you will frequently encounter).
dwReserved0, dwReserved1	Reserved for future use by Microsoft.
cFileName	A null-terminated string that contains the long name of the file. Its length is always less than **MAX_PATH**, a system constant generally set to either 255 or 260.
cAlternateFileName	A null-terminated string that contains the alternate name for the file. This filename is in the classic 8.3 format (*filename.ext*). Use this value when you are unsure about whether every function or system accessing the file supports long filenames.

TABLE 6-1. WIN32_FIND_DATA Members (continued)

As indicated in Table 6-1, the **dwFileAttributes** member can have one or a combination of constant values providing information about the file itself. Table 6-2 lists these constants and their descriptions.

Constant	Description
FILE_ATTRIBUTE_ARCHIVE	Applications use this value to mark files for backup or removal. Each time you change a file, Windows marks the archive bit. Each time a backup program backs up the file, the program turns off the archive bit.
FILE_ATTRIBUTE_COMPRESSED	For a file, this means all of the data in the file is compressed—that is, the file is a ZIP file or has a similar compression format. For a directory, this means compression is the default for newly created files and subdirectories (that is, either the operating system or a third-party tool compresses new files and subdirectories as they are created).
FILE_ATTRIBUTE_DIRECTORY	The file object corresponds to a directory or folder—that is, it is a logical operating-system object that stores no data of its own, but rather serves as an organizational tool for other data.

TABLE 6-2. Constant Values for **dwFileAttributes**

Constant	Description
FILE_ATTRIBUTE_HIDDEN	The file is hidden, meaning it is not included in an ordinary directory listing. This attribute is commonly used with system files, helper files, or other files that the application developer wants to hide from casual observation.
FILE_ATTRIBUTE_NORMAL	The file is a normal, read/writeable, nonhidden, nonsystem file. In short, this value means that the file has no other attributes set and is therefore valid only if used alone.
FILE_ATTRIBUTE_OFFLINE	The data of the file is not immediately available for access. Indicates that the file data has been physically moved to offline storage. This particular attribute is very rarely used, except in certain networking environments.
FILE_ATTRIBUTE_READONLY	The file is read-only. Applications can read the file but cannot write to it or delete it. An application needing to write to or delete the file must either first clear the read-only bit, or save the file under a different filename.
FILE_ATTRIBUTE_SYSTEM	The file is part of the operating system (for instance, dynamic link libraries) or is used exclusively by the operating system (for instance, the operating system kernel). In general, modifying system files is a very bad idea because this may cause Windows to work incorrectly or even not boot up.
FILE_ATTRIBUTE_TEMPORARY	The file is being used for temporary storage. This attribute is assigned to files when they are created using the **tmpfile( )** function, or any of the Windows temporary file functions such as **tmpnam( )** and **_tempnam( )**. Temporary files created by an application are not persistent—they should be erased by the creating application on exit.

TABLE 6-2. Constant Values for **dwFileAttributes** (continued)

PROGRAMMER'S NOTE *If a file has a long filename, the complete name appears in the **cFileName** field. The API will then return the classic (8.3 format), truncated version of the name within the **cAlternateFileName** field. If the operating system does not support long filenames, or if the file in question does not use a long filename, the **cAlternateFileName** member is empty and **cFileName** contains the 8.3 name. As an alternative, you can use the API **GetShortPathName( )** function, which returns a formatted, 12-character string, to find the 8.3 format version of a filename.*

So far, you've seen the **IsChildDir( )** function, which checks to determine whether a specific instance of a **WIN32_FIND_DATA** object corresponds to a child directory. This function is used primarily by the **FindNextChildDir( )** function, which searches a directory for the next child directory within the tree. **FindNextChildDir( )** accepts a handle to a file and a **WIN32_FIND_DATA** object.

```
static BOOL FindNextChildDir (HANDLE hFindFile,
    WIN32_FIND_DATA *lpFindData)
{
  BOOL fFound = FALSE;
```

FindNextChildDir( ) also declares a **Boolean** variable that it uses to look for the next child directory. Within the function, the program uses a **do** loop that iterates each time the next file in the tree is not a child directory. To perform the search, the program code uses the **FindNextFile( )** function, explained in the next section. If the search finds no file, the loop will also exit, returning **false** to the calling function. But if the search finds a child directory, the function will return **true** to the calling function:

```
do {
    fFound = FindNextFile(hFindFile, lpFindData);
  } while (fFound && !IsChildDir(lpFindData));
  return(fFound);
}
```

The **FindNextFile( )** function continues the search after an initiating call to a **FindFirstFile( )** or **FindFirstFileEx( )** function. The first parameter is the handle returned by the initial call; the second parameter, a **WIN32_FIND_DATA** object.

The function that calls the **FindNextChildDir( )** function is the **FindFirstChildDir( )** function, which does exactly what its name indicates. It accepts a string variable corresponding to the path in which to begin the search, and a **WIN32_FIND_DATA** object. Here is **FindFirstChildDir( )**:

```
static HANDLE FindFirstChildDir (LPTSTR szPath,
    WIN32_FIND_DATA *lpFindData)
{
  BOOL fFound;
  HANDLE hFindFile = FindFirstFile(szPath, lpFindData);
```

The call to **FindFirstFile( )** returns a value to the **hFindFile** handle, which the program will subsequently use for all other file searches. This value will be either a valid handle, or **INVALID_HANDLE_VALUE**, indicating that no valid file was found. If the return value is **INVALID_HANDLE_VALUE**, the function will immediately exit and return; otherwise, the program code looks at the returned file to determine whether or not it is a child directory.

```
if (hFindFile != INVALID_HANDLE_VALUE) {
    fFound = IsChildDir(lpFindData);
```

If the returned file is a child directory, the function also falls through. Otherwise, the program code tries to access additional values in the directory to search, calling the **FindNextChildDir( )** function discussed previously:

```
if (!fFound)
    fFound = FindNextChildDir(hFindFile, lpFindData);
```

If the call to **FindNextChildDir( )** is not successful, the program code closes the handle to the find operation, returns **INVALID_HANDLE_VALUE**, and exits its processing, as shown here:

```
if (!fFound) {
    FindClose(hFindFile);
    hFindFile = INVALID_HANDLE_VALUE;
    }
  }
  return (hFindFile);
}
```

The next section of the source code defines a structure used by the recursing search functions. It could just as easily be defined at the top of this file (or in a header); however, for the clarity of the chapter, we moved the definition farther down in the source code file to give you the opportunity to consider some of the lower-level activity before moving into the structure.

```
typedef struct {
  HWND hwndTreeLB;
  int nDepth;
  BOOL fRecurse;
  TCHAR szBuf[1000];
  int nIndent;
  BOOL fOk;
  BOOL fIsDir;
  WIN32_FIND_DATA FindData;
} WALKDIRDATA, *LPWALKDIRDATA;
```

This structure maintains information used by the recursing functions to maintain information about the current state of the program's processing. Table 6-3 describes the members of the **WALKDIRDATA** structure.

The next two functions are the center of the processing for the program. The **WalkDir( )** function performs the walking, while the **WalkDirRecurse( )** function performs the recursive processing necessary to move down through the trees.

WalkDirRecurse( ) travels the directory structure and fills a ListBox control with filenames. If **pDW–>fRecurse** is set, the function will also list any child directories

Member	Description
hwndTreeLB	A handle to the output ListBox where the program displays file information.
nDepth	Indicates the nesting depth of the current file—that is, how far down in the tree the file is located.
fRecurse	Set this member to **true** to list subdirectories.
szBuf[1000]	Output formatting buffer that holds the string describing the file.
nIndent	Indentation character count—used for clarity in the display of the tree.
fOk	Loop control flag value.
fIsDir	Loop control flag value.
FindData	A **WIN32_FIND_DATA** object that contains file information.

TABLE 6-3. WALKDIRDATA Members

by recursively calling itself. The function accepts a pointer to a **WALKDIRDATA** structure. It also defines a **HANDLE** to maintain the reference to the file being searched for.

```
static void WalkDirRecurse (LPWALKDIRDATA pDW)
{
  HANDLE hFind;
```

Each time the function is called, it increases the count within the **nDepth** variable (because the code has reached a new level in the tree) and also increases the **nIndent** value to reflect the amount to indent the output. It then formats the **szBuf** member with the number of indented spaces.

```
  pDW->nDepth++;
  pDW->nIndent = 3 * pDW->nDepth;
  _stprintf(pDW->szBuf, _TEXT("%*s"), pDW->nIndent, _TEXT(""));
```

Next, the program code calls the **GetCurrentDirectory( )** API function, which returns the current directory and places it within the **szBuf** member, starting at the **nIndent** position in the character array. Finally, the function adds the contents of **szBuf** to the list box referenced by the **hwndTreeLB** handle:

```
  GetCurrentDirectory(chDIMOF(pDW->szBuf) - pDW->nIndent,
      &pDW->szBuf[pDW->nIndent]);
  ListBox_AddString(pDW->hwndTreeLB, pDW->szBuf);
```

After all this initial processing, the program calls the **FindFirstFile( )** function, passing in a wildcard string as the file to find. You can, of course, modify the program so that it calls the functions with a filename specified by the user. For the sake of the example, however, we're just returning all the values. **FindFirstFile( )** then sets the **fOk** member to **true** or **false**, depending on whether the function returned a valid file handle or the **INVALID_HANDLE_VALUE** constant. If **fOk** is **true**, the program then enters a **while** loop, where it stays as long as **fOk** remains true.

```
hFind = FindFirstFile(_TEXT("*.*"), &pDW->FindData);
pDW->fOk = (hFind != INVALID_HANDLE_VALUE);
while (pDW->fOk) {
```

Inside the loop, the first statement executed uses the **dwFileAttributes** member to determine whether the current file is a directory or not, assigning the result to the **fIsDir** member. It then checks **fIsDir**, as well as **fRecurse** and the return value from **IsChildDir( )**, to determine whether it should output the file to the text box or not. If the file is not a directory, or recursion is disabled, the program code outputs the file to the list box.

```
pDW->fIsDir = pDW->FindData.dwFileAttributes &
    FILE_ATTRIBUTE_DIRECTORY;
if (!pDW->fIsDir || (!pDW->fRecurse &&
    IsChildDir(&pDW->FindData))) {
  _stprintf(pDW->szBuf,
  pDW->fIsDir ? _TEXT("%*s[%s]") : _TEXT("%*s%s"),
  pDW->nIndent, _TEXT(""), pDW->FindData.cFileName);
  ListBox_AddString(pDW->hwndTreeLB, pDW->szBuf);
}
```

After the **if** statement, the program code calls **FindNextFile( )** to search for the next file:

```
pDW->fOk = FindNextFile(hFind, &pDW->FindData);
}
```

After falling out of the loop, the program closes the handle if it is a valid handle. Then the program looks to see if recursion is turned on. If so, the **FindFirstChildDir( )** function is called to look for child directories to search:

```
if (hFind != INVALID_HANDLE_VALUE)
  FindClose(hFind);
if (pDW->fRecurse) {
  hFind = FindFirstChildDir(_TEXT("*.*"), &pDW->FindData);
```

The program then again assigns a Boolean value corresponding to the search's success, to the **fOk** variable. If the search is successful, the program enters another **while** loop:

```
pDW->fOk = (hFind != INVALID_HANDLE_VALUE);
while (pDW->fOk) {
```

However, the processing within this loop is a little different from what you have seen previously—it tries to set the current directory to the child directory name. If it's successful, it then recurses itself. Similarly, the ending condition falls within the same **if** block. The ending condition, as you might expect, sets the current directory one level higher in the tree:

```
if (SetCurrentDirectory(pDW->FindData.cFileName)) {
    WalkDirRecurse(pDW);
    SetCurrentDirectory(_TEXT(".."));
  }
```

Then (after recursing however many times are necessary, and coming back up in the tree) the program looks for the next child directory. If one is found, the program code loops again, repeating its processing:

```
pDW->fOk = FindNextChildDir(hFind, &pDW->FindData);
}
```

On the back end of the function, we again check to make sure there is a valid handle value in **hFind**, and if it's there we call **FindClose( )**. Note that if you call **FindClose( )** without **hFind** containing a valid handle, the program will fail. (You could also use a **try..catch** block for this check.)

```
if (hFind != INVALID_HANDLE_VALUE)
    FindClose(hFind);
}
```

Finally, before exiting the function—which the program does only when it has iterated all the files in a "dead-end" of the tree—the program decreases the count within the **nDepth** variable, since we are going back up one level in the tree:

```
 pDW->nDepth--;
}
```

The **WalkDir( )** function is the starting case for the **WalkDirRecurse( )** function—it sets the starting condition, sets the starting directory, and then makes the initial call to **WalkDirRecurse( )**. The **WalkDir( )** function is also what the program will return to after the recursing function traverses all the possible paths.

WalkDir( ) accepts a handle to the list box, a string corresponding to the root search path, and a Boolean value representing whether or not the function should recurse during its search. The function also declares a static variable of size **_MAX_DIR**, defined by the **windows.h** header file as 260 characters. Finally, **WalkDir( )** declares the instance of **WALKDIRDATA** used by the rest of the program:

```
void WalkDir (HWND hwndTreeLB, LPCTSTR pszRootPath, BOOL fRecurse)
{
```

```
static char szCurrDir[_MAX_DIR];
WALKDIRDATA WD;
```

Next, the **WalkDir( )** function performs its preparatory work. It clears the list box and then obtains the current directory from the operating system. This directory is stored away in the **szCurrDir** array for cleanup when the program finishes. Then **WalkDir( )** sets the current directory to the **pszRootPath** value:

```
ListBox_ResetContent(hwndTreeLB);
GetCurrentDirectory(chDIMOF(szCurrDir), szCurrDir);
SetCurrentDirectory(pszRootPath);
```

Next, the code initializes some of the members of the **WD** object. **nDepth** is initialized to –1 (so it will be 0 on the first iteration of **WalkDirRecurse( )**). The **hwndTreeLB** member is set to point at the list box. Finally, the code sets the **fRecurse** member to the value it received as a parameter:

```
WD.nDepth = -1;
WD.hwndTreeLB = hwndTreeLB;
WD.fRecurse = fRecurse;
```

After setting up the initial values, the code calls the **WalkDirRecurse( )** function, passing in the **WD** object. The program will perform all its execution within **WalkDirRecurse( )**. When it returns to **WalkDir( )**, the code within **WalkDir( )** will again call the **SetCurrentDirectory( )** function to return the operating system to whatever directory it was in before the program started its search:

```
WalkDirRecurse(&WD);
SetCurrentDirectory(szCurrDir);
}
```

The **OnInitDialog( )** function is called by the framework when the program displays the dialog box defined within the resource file. This function's primary job is to call the **WalkDir( )** function, passing it a handle to the list box that the dialog box contains.

```
BOOL Dlg_OnInitDialog (HWND hwnd, HWND hwndFocus, LPARAM lParam)
{
  RECT rc;

  WalkDir(GetDlgItem(hwnd, IDC_TREE), _TEXT("\\"), TRUE);
  GetClientRect(hwnd, &rc);
  SetWindowPos(GetDlgItem(hwnd, IDC_TREE), NULL, 0, 0,
      rc.right, rc.bottom, SWP_NOZORDER);
  return(TRUE);
}
```

The **OnSize( )** event is called whenever the user resizes the dialog box. The job for **OnSize( )** is to redraw the list box and all its contents, in the event they are moved or hidden:

```
void Dlg_OnSize (HWND hwnd, UINT state, int cx, int cy)
{
  SetWindowPos(GetDlgItem(hwnd, IDC_TREE), NULL, 0, 0,
      cx, cy, SWP_NOZORDER);
}
```

The **OnCommand( )** function handles messages sent to the dialog box. There are only two messages we are concerned with handling in this application—one that closes the dialog box (**ID_CANCEL**) and one that reruns the search program (**ID_OK**). Both are processed within a single switch statement:

```
void Dlg_OnCommand (HWND hwnd, int id, HWND hwndCtl, UINT CodeNotify)
{
  switch (id) {
    case ID_CANCEL:
      EndDialog(hwnd, id);
      break;
```

When **ID_CANCEL** is received, the program code closes the dialog box with a call to **EndDialog( )**, which also results in the closing of the program.

When **ID_OK** is received, the program calls the **WalkDir( )** function, passing in information about its processing.

```
    case ID_OK:
      WalkDir(GetDlgItem(hwnd, IDC_TREE), _TEXT("\\"), TRUE);
      break;
  }
}
```

The **Dlg_Proc( )** callback function receives messages from the operating system. It then uses the macros defined within the **CmnHdr** file to process the messages:

```
BOOL CALLBACK Dlg_Proc (HWND hwnd, UINT uMsg,
    WPARAM wParam, LPARAM lParam)
{
  switch (uMsg) {
    chHANDLE_DLGMSG(hwnd, WM_INITDIALOG, Dlg_OnInitDialog);
    chHANDLE_DLGMSG(hwnd, WM_SIZE, Dlg_OnSize);
    chHANDLE_DLGMSG(hwnd, WM_COMMAND, Dlg_OnCommand);
  }
  return(FALSE);
}
```

Finally, the **WinMain( )** function, which does nothing more than create the dialog box and exit the program with a success return code when the dialog box closes, is shown here:

```
int WINAPI WinMain(HINSTANCE hinstExe, HINSTANCE hinstPrev,
    LPSTR pszCmdLine, int nCmdShow)
{
  DialogBox(hinstExe, MAKEINTRESOURCE(IDD_WALKDIR), NULL, Dlg_Proc);
  return(0);
 }
```

The **WalkDirs** program is a useful example of manipulating the operating system. You are unlikely to need it within your programs, but in this usage it does show you how to access the operating system, both returning and setting information about directories and files.

PROGRAMMER'S NOTE   *The **WalkDirs** program may not execute correctly under Windows NT, because it makes no allowance for the Windows NT security model. You will need to make minor changes to the program for it to execute correctly under Windows NT in such cases.*

The last program that we will consider within this chapter, coming up in the next section, actually has two implementations on the CD-ROM—one for console output and one for Windows output. However, the logic in both programs is identical, so we will examine only the console-based program.

Viewing File Contents

One of the most useful utilities for many programmers and power users is one that lets them see (and often edit) the contents of a file in hexadecimal. A hex editor is beyond the scope of what we are doing in this book, but writing a program to read files and display their contents in hex is both simple and useful. The **doshex.cpp** and the **winhex** programs both perform this task; however, the **doshex.cpp** program uses streams directly, so we will review its contents.

Code

Following is the code for the **doshex.cpp** program.

doshex.cpp

```
#include <iostream>
#include <fstream>
#include <iomanip>
#define numcols 18

using namespace std;

int main(int argc, char *argv[])
{
```

```cpp
int counter = 0, j = 0, i = 0;
char text[numcols];

if (argc != 2) {
  cout << "Usage for DOSHEX:  doshex <filename>" << endl;
  return 1;
}

ifstream incoming(argv[1], ios::in | ios::binary);
if (!incoming) {
  cout << "Cannot open file for display!" << endl;
  return 1;
}

cout.setf(ios::uppercase);
while (!incoming.eof()) {
  for (i = 0; (i < numcols && !incoming.eof()); i++)
    incoming.get(text[i]);

  if (i < numcols)
    i--;

  for (j = 0; j < i; j++)
    cout << setw(3) << hex << (int) text[j];
  for (; j < numcols; j++)
    cout << "   ";

  cout << "\t";
  for (j = 0; j < i; j++)
    if ((isprint(text[j])))
      cout << text[j];
    else
      cout << ".";
  cout << endl;

  if (++counter == 24) {
    counter = 0;
    cout << "Press Enter/Return to Continue...";
    cin.get();
    cout << endl;
  }
}
incoming.close();
return 0;
}
```

ANNOTATIONS

The **doshex.cpp** program takes the tools we have used previously—reading characters one at time from a file—and uses them in a slightly different manner, generating screen output that corresponds to both hexadecimal and text values for the file's contents. Since we are using streams, however, in this case the presence of the **iostream** and **fstream** headers is necessary. We also have to include the **iomanip** header because we will be calling some inline stream-operator functions. Finally, the code defines the **numcols** constant, which it uses to control the number of columns displayed in the viewer. We employed a constant here so that you can easily change the program's method for displaying information depending on your console's screen resolution.

```
#include <iostream>
#include <fstream>
#include <iomanip>
#define numcols 18

using namespace std;
```

The processing for the program occurs entirely within **main( )**. The function accepts command-line parameters—a necessity, since we need to specify what the program is going to process. Once in the function, we declare some integer counter variables, and a **char** array that will hold the text output for each line. Here are the declarations for **main( )**:

```
int main(int argc, char *argv[])
{
  int counter = 0, j = 0, i = 0;
  char text[numcols];
```

Next, we check to make sure that the user has entered a filename, and nothing else, when invoking the program. If the user has invoked the program incorrectly, it displays a message describing its usage and what parameters it accepts:

```
if (argc != 2) {
  cout << "Usage for DOSHEX:  doshex <filename>" << endl;
  return 1;
}
```

If the user has invoked the program correctly, the program declares and initializes the **incoming** variable, of type **ifstream**. Note that we specify that the program should read from the file as binary—a necessary step to make sure that we are retrieving actual values from the file, rather than interpreted values. Again, if the program cannot open the file, it displays a message to that effect and exits.

```
ifstream incoming(argv[1], ios::in | ios::binary);
if (!incoming) {
  cout << "Cannot open file for display!" << endl;
```

```
    return 1;
}
```

After all this, we enter the read loop, where the program cycles through the entirety of the file, reading it a block at a time. Within the **while** loop, the program immediately enters a **for** loop, which reads in a number of characters equal to the **numcols** constant set earlier—unless the **eof** marker is reached, in which case the code falls out of the **for** loop immediately. Within the interior loop, the program uses the **get( )** function to read in the values from the file one byte at a time.

```
while (!incoming.eof()) {
    for (i = 0; (i < numcols && !incoming.eof()); i++)
        incoming.get(text[i]);
```

After exiting the **for** loop, the program checks to determine whether it exited because of reaching **numcols** or the **eof**. If it reached the end-of-file, the program decrements the counter variable by one (so the program doesn't try to display the **eof** marker).

```
    if (i < numcols)
        i--;
```

Within the next interior loop, the program displays the hex values for the bytes it just read in. The **setw( )** operator specifies the width for printing the number (in this case, three spaces). The **hex** operator specifies that the output should appear in hexadecimal form, as opposed to decimal or octal. Finally, the program casts the byte in the array to an integer and displays it:

```
    for (j = 0; j < i; j++)
        cout << setw(3) << hex << (int) text[j];
```

After the program exits the loop, it uses a second loop to add filler spaces, to ensure that the textual data on the right side of the output is always properly positioned in the column, even for the last line in the file:

```
    for (; j < numcols; j++)
        cout << "   ";
```

After adding the spaces (if necessary), the program sends a tab to the output and enters a third loop. This loop prints the textual values of the items in the array, so that the user can view the hex and textual values side-by-side:

```
    cout << "\t";
    for (j = 0; j < i; j++)
```

Within the loop, the **isprint( )** function checks the array item's value to make sure it is a valid, printable character—if it isn't, the program prints a period (.) instead :

```
        if ((isprint(text[j])))
            cout << text[j];
```

```
    else
      cout << ".";
```

After finishing the output of the textual values, the program sends a CRLF pair to the output; it also checks the value of the **counter** variable, which corresponds to the number of lines displayed. If the **counter** variable equals 24, the program displays a prompt to the user to press any key, so that the information doesn't scroll off screen:

```
      cout << endl;

      if (++counter == 24) {
        cout << "Press Enter/Return to Continue...";
        cin.get();
        counter = 0;
```

After the user presses a key, the code resets **counter** to 0, so the program can display another 24 lines before halting. After all the file's contents have been displayed, the program closes the file and exits with a successful return code.

```
        cout << endl;
      }
    }
    incoming.close();
    return 0;
}
```

When you execute the **doshex.cpp** program against the **doshex.cpp** source code file, your screen will display output similar to the following:

```
23 69 6E 63 6C 75 64 65 20 3C 69 6F 73 74 72 65 61 6D      #include <iostream
3E  D  A 23 69 6E 63 6C 75 64 65 20 3C 66 73 74 72 65      >..#include <fstre
61 6D 3E  D  A 2F 2F 23 69 6E 63 6C 75 64 65 20 3C 63      am>..//#include <c
74 79 70 65 3E  D  A 23 69 6E 63 6C 75 64 65 20 3C 69      type>..#include <i
6F 6D 61 6E 69 70 3E  D  A 23 69 6E 63 6C 75 64 65 20      omanip>..#include
3C 63 73 74 64 69 6F 3E  D  A 23 64 65 66 69 6E 65 20      <cstdio>..#define
6E 75 6D 63 6F 6C 73 20 31 36  D  A  D  A 75 73 69 6E      numcols 16....usin
67 20 6E 61 6D 65 73 70 61 63 65 20 73 74 64 3B  D  A      g namespace std;..
 D  A 69 6E 74 20 6D 61 69 6E 28 69 6E 74 20 61 72 67      ..int main(int arg
63 2C 20 63 68 61 72 20 2A 61 72 67 76 5B 5D 29 20  D      c, char *argv[]) .
 A 7B  D  A 20 20 69 6E 74 20 63 6F 75 6E 74 65 72 20      .{..  int counter
3D 20 30 2C 20 6A 20 3D 20 30 3B  D  A 20 20 63 68 61      = 0, j = 0;..  cha
72 20 74 65 78 74 5B 6E 75 6D 63 6F 6C 73 5D 3B  D  A      r text[numcols];..
 D  A 20 20 69 66 20 28 61 72 67 63 20 21 3D 20 32 29      ..  if (argc != 2)
20 7B  D  A 20 20 20 20 20 63 6F 75 74 20 3C 3C 20 22 55   {..    cout << "U
```

```
73 61 67 65 20 66 6F 72 20 44 4F 53 48 45 58 3A 20 20        sage for DOSHEX:
64 6F 73 68 65 78 20 3C 66 69 6C 65 6E 61 6D 65 3E 22        doshex <filename>"
20 3C 3C 20 65 6E 64 6C 3B  D  A 20 20 20 20 20 72 65 74         << endl;..    ret
75 72 6E 20 31 3B  D  A 20 20 7D  D  A  D  A 20 20 69        urn 1;..  }.... i
66 73 74 72 65 61 6D 20 69 6E 63 6F 6D 69 6E 67 28 61        fstream incoming(a
72 67 76 5B 31 5D 2C 20 69 6F 73 3A 3A 69 6E 20 7C 20        rgv[1], ios::in |
69 6F 73 3A 3A 62 69 6E 61 72 79 29 3B  D  A 20 20 69        ios::binary);..  i
66 20 28 21 69 6E 63 6F 6D 69 6E 67 29 20 7B  D  A 20        f (!incoming) {..
20 20 20 63 6F 75 74 20 3C 3C 20 22 43 61 6E 6E 6F 74            cout << "Cannot
```

Press Enter/Return to Continue...

```
20 6F 70 65 6E 20 66 69 6C 65 20 66 6F 72 20 64 69 73        open file for dis
70 6C 61 79 21 22 20 3C 3C 20 65 6E 64 6C 3B  D  A 20        play!" << endl;..
20 20 20 72 65 74 75 72 6E 20 31 3B  D  A 20 20 7D  D            return 1;..  }.
 A  D  A 20 20 63 6F 75 74 2E 73 65 74 66 28 69 6F 73        ...  cout.setf(ios
3A 3A 75 70 70 65 72 63 61 73 65 29 3B  D  A 20 20 77        ::uppercase);..  w
68 69 6C 65 20 28 21 69 6E 63 6F 6D 69 6E 67 2E 65 6F        hile (!incoming.eo
66 28 29 29 20 7B  D  A 20 20 20 20 66 6F 72 20 28 69        f()) {..    for (i
6E 74 20 69 20 3D 20 30 3B 20 28 69 20 3C 20 6E 75 6D        nt i = 0; (i < num
63 6F 6C 73 20 26 26 20 21 69 6E 63 6F 6D 69 6E 67 2E        cols && !incoming.
65 6F 66 28 29 29 3B 20 69 2B 2B 29  D  A 20 20 20 20        eof()); i++)..
20 20 69 6E 63 6F 6D 69 6E 67 2E 67 65 74 28 74 65 78          incoming.get(tex
74 5B 69 5D 29 3B  D  A  D  A 20 20 20 20 69 66 20 28        t[i]);....    if (
69 20 3C 20 6E 75 6D 63 6F 6C 73 29  D  A 20 20 20 20        i < numcols)..
20 20 69 2D 2D 3B  D  A 20 20 20 20 66 6F 72 20        i--;....    for
28 6A 20 3D 20 30 3B 20 6A 20 3C 20 69 3B 20 6A 2B 2B        (j = 0; j < i; j++
29  D  A 20 20 20 20 20 20 63 6F 75 74 20 3C 3C 20 68        )..      cout << h
65 78 20 3C 3C 20 73 65 74 77 28 33 29 20 3C 3C 20 28        ex << setw(3) << (
69 6E 74 29 20 74 65 78 74 5B 6A 5D 3B  D  A 20 20 20        int) text[j];..
20 66 6F 72 20 28 3B 20 6A 20 3C 20 6E 75 6D 63 6F 6C        for (; j < numcol
73 3B 20 6A 2B 2B 29  D  A 20 20 20 20 20 20 63 6F 75        s; j++)..      cou
74 20 3C 3C 20 22 20 20 20 22 3B  D  A  D  A 20 20 20 20        t << "   ";....
63 6F 75 74 20 3C 3C 20 22 5C 74 22 3B  D  A 20 20 20        cout << "\t";..
20 66 6F 72 20 28 6A 20 3D 20 30 3B 20 6A 20 3C 20 69        for (j = 0; j < i
3B 20 6A 2B 2B 29  D  A 20 20 20 20 20 20 69 66 20 28        ; j++)..      if (
```

Press Enter/Return to Continue...

```
28 69 73 70 72 69 6E 74 28 74 65 78 74 5B 6A 5D 29 29        (isprint(text[j]))
29  D  A 20 20 20 20 20 20 20 20 20 63 6F 75 74 20 3C 3C        )..        cout <<
20 74 65 78 74 5B 6A 5D 3B  D  A 20 20 20 20 20 20 65        text[j];..      e
6C 73 65  D  A 20 20 20 20 20 20 20 20 20 63 6F 75 74 20        lse..        cout
```

```
3C 3C 20 22 2E 22 3B  D  A 20 20 20 20 63 6F 75 74 20      << ".";..       cout
3C 3C 20 65 6E 64 6C 3B  D  A  D  A 20 20 20 20 69 66       << endl;....      if
20 28 2B 2B 63 6F 75 6E 74 65 72 20 3D 3D 20 6E 75 6D       (++counter == num
63 6F 6C 73 29 20 7B  D  A 20 20 20 20 20 20 20 63 6F 75    cols) {..       cou
6E 74 65 72 20 3D 20 30 3B  D  A 20 20 20 20 20 20 63       nter = 0;..       c
6F 75 74 20 3C 3C 20 22 50 72 65 73 73 20 45 6E 74 65       out << "Press Ente
72 2F 52 65 74 75 72 6E 20 74 6F 20 43 6F 6E 74 69 6E       r/Return to Contin
75 65 2E 2E 2E 22 3B  D  A 20 20 20 20 20 20 63 69 6E       ue...";..       cin
2E 67 65 74 28 29 3B  D  A 20 20 20 20 20 20 63 6F 75       .get();..       cou
74 20 3C 3C 20 65 6E 64 6C 3B  D  A 20 20 20 20 7D  D       t << endl;..    }.
 A 20 20 7D  D  A 20 20 69 6E 63 6F 6D 69 6E 67 2E 63      . }..  incoming.c
6C 6F 73 65 28 29 3B  D  A 20 20 72 65 74 75 72 6E 20       lose();..  return
30 3B  D  A 7D                                              0;..}
```

The Windows version generates similar output, placing it within a window instead of sending it to the console, meaning you can scroll back and forth through the output. When you run the Windows version of the hex viewer against a source code file, you will receive output similar to that shown in Figure 6-1.

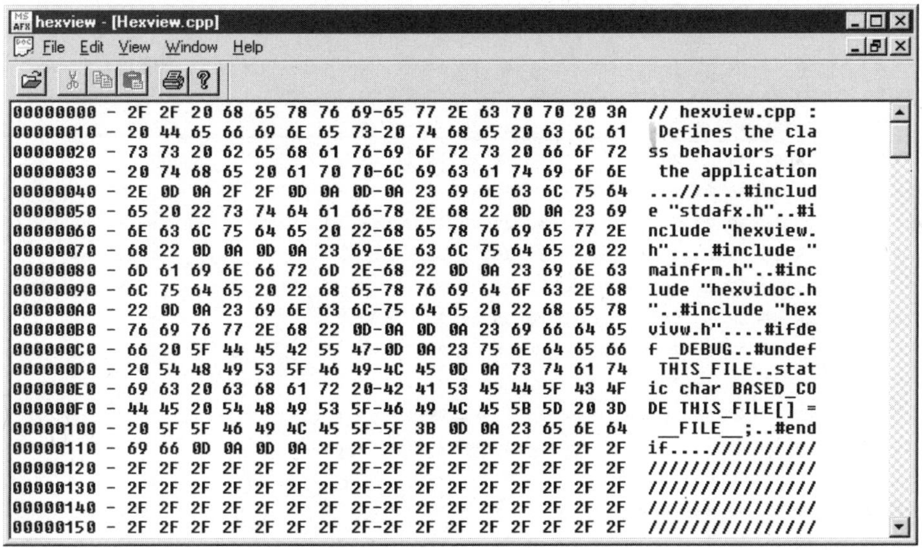

FIGURE 6-1. The output of the Windows-based hex viewer for files

Encryption Fundamentals

By Lars Klander

simple1.cpp	CryptoNotes
SimpXOR.cpp	CCryptoDoc

ompanies today are storing more and more information on computers. Every day, both companies and individuals transmit more digital information over the Internet and through other communication channels, such as corporate intranets and wireless transmissions. As this trend continues, protecting that information becomes more important. To protect information from the casual observer and from the dedicated hacker, most companies and computer users turn to *encryption*.

Historically, to protect information, encryption systems have used two encryption *keys*, one key at the sending end and one key at the receiving end of the transmission. In these *cryptosystems*, keys were maintained in code books, with both parties having exactly the same copy of the code book. In other words, at some point one party had to send the code book (containing the keys) to the other party.

The mathematical processing power of today's computers has changed the way people use encryption. The introduction of *public-key cryptosystems* has let computer users encrypt documents and other data to send to other users, without sharing both keys in advance, or sending a book of keys, or any other similar limitations of old-fashioned cryptosystems. Instead, with a public-key cryptosystem, users can post their public keys anywhere, and other users can use those public keys to encrypt documents. The user who has the public key's corresponding private key, then, is the only party who can decode the message encrypted with the public key.

In this chapter, you will explore the basic concepts of encryption. From the programmer's perspective there are two basic types of encryption—*stream* encryption and *block* encryption. You will see three programs in this chapter. The first implements a very simple encryption model; it's breakable with a pencil and paper. The second program implements a slightly more secure encryption model, useful for situations where you simply want to dissuade people from looking at data—a model which, nevertheless, can be broken quickly with a computer. Finally, you will see a more common implementation of cryptographic programming: the use of a third-party key structure, which handles the actual mathematics of the encryption for you but which provides a convenient means of adding strong encryption to your programs. Although the third model is built specifically for use with Win32 platforms, there are UNIX and Macintosh third-party libraries that provide similar encryption tools.

This chapter does not discuss mathematical specifics of encryption models, or even implementation specifics of copyrighted encryption models like the Digital Signature Standard. You'll find many other books out there offering discussions of those mathematics. Here we focus on how you can apply encryption within your own programs.

A Better Understanding of Encryption

Suppose you want to send a confidential message to your cousin over the Internet. In other words, you do not want anyone who might intercept the message to be able

to read it. To protect the message you send, you will *encrypt* or *encipher* the message. You do this by using a complicated scheme to change the letters within the message, with the goal of rendering it unreadable to anyone except your cousin. While such a goal is conceptually not possible—anyone with the knowledge, the time, and the processing power can potentially break a code—there are certain levels beyond which something can be reasonably expected to be secure.

You will give your cousin a cryptographic key to unscramble the message and make it legible. In a conventional *single-key* cryptosystem, you will share the cryptographic key with your cousin *before* you use it to encrypt the message (you may send it in another e-mail, mail a copy of it, and so on). For example, a simple single-key cryptosystem might shift each letter in the message forward three letters in the alphabet, with the space character immediately following the letter Z. For instance, the word DOG becomes GRJ. Figure 7-1 shows a one-line document encrypted with the single-key cryptosystem.

```
T H I S   I S   A   S I M P L E   C R Y P T O S Y S T E M
W K L V C L V C D C V L P S O H C F U A S W R V W A W H P
```

FIGURE 7-1.   A line of text encrypted with a simple cryptosystem

Your cousin will receive the encrypted message and shift all the letters back three letters in the alphabet to decrypt it, which will convert GRJ back to DOG. Figure 7-2 shows the key for the single-key encryption system you use to send the message to your cousin.

A	B	C	D	E	F	G	H	I	J	K	L	M	N	O	P	Q	R	S	T	U	V	W	X	Y	Z	-
D	E	F	G	H	I	J	K	L	M	N	O	P	Q	R	S	T	U	V	W	X	Y	Z	-	A	B	C

FIGURE 7-2.   The decryption key for a simple single-key cryptosystem

Code

Let's consider a simple program, **simple1.cpp**, which implements a similar cryptographic model to what you have already seen on a string entered by the user.

```cpp
#include <string>
#include <cstdio>
#include <iostream>
#include <fstream>
using namespace std;

char *strencrypt(char *source)
{
  char *original = source;

  while (*source) {
    *source = *source + 3;
    source++;
  }
  return(original);
}

char *strdecrypt(char *source)
{
  char *original = source;

  while (*source) {
    *source = *source - 3;
    source++;
  }
  return(original);
}

int main()
{
  char linein[81], converted[81];
  int encryptdecrypt = 1;
```

```
int i;
ifstream in, inclear;

cout << "Enter 1 to encrypt, 2 to decrypt: ";
cin >> encryptdecrypt;
if (encryptdecrypt == 1)
  in.open("test-enc.txt");
else
  in.open("test-dec.txt");
if(!in) {
  cout << "Cannot open file." << endl;
  return (1);
}

while (!in.eof()) {
  for (i=0; i < 80 && !in.eof(); i++)
    in.get(linein[i]);
  linein[i] = NULL;
  if (encryptdecrypt == 1)
    strcpy(converted, strencrypt(linein));
  else
    strcpy(converted, strdecrypt(linein));
  cout << converted << endl;
}

in.close();

cout << endl << endl;
if (encryptdecrypt == 1)
  inclear.open("test-enc.txt");
else
  inclear.open("test-dec.txt");
if(!inclear) {
  cout << "Cannot open file." << endl;
  return (1);
}
```

```
while (!inclear.eof()) {
  for (i=0; i < 80 && !inclear.eof(); i++)
    inclear.get(linein[i]);
  linein[i] = NULL;
  cout << linein << endl;
}

inclear.close();
return 0;
}
```

ANNOTATIONS

The first function in the code is the **strencrypt( )** function, which returns the pointer to the beginning of a **char** array. The code for the function looks like this:

```
char *strencrypt(char *source)
{
  char *original = source;

  while (*source) {
    *source = *source + 3;
    source++;
  }
  return(original);
}
```

The processing performed by **strencrypt( )** is pretty simple. It first declares a local variable, **original**, which it points to the beginning of the **char** array passed in by the calling function. Then the function loops through the **source** pointer, adding 3 to the ASCII value of each character in the array. When the pointer reaches a **NULL** value, the loop ends, and the function returns a pointer to the beginning of the new, now-encrypted array.

The **strdecrypt( )** function performs much the same processing as the **strencrypt( )** function, as you can see in the following code:

```
char *strdecrypt(char *source)
{
  char *original = source;

  while (*source) {
    *source = *source - 3;
    source++;
```

```
    }
    return(original);
}
```

Again, the function declares a local variable to point to the beginning of the incoming array. It also loops through the array, this time reducing the ASCII value by 3 (and therefore returning it to its original value). When the function completes, it returns the pointer to the beginning of the character array.

The **main( )** function in the program simply reads in a text file from the hard drive, encrypts the file, and displays the encrypted file on the screen. This function uses the C++ **iostream** and **fstream** libraries to perform its tasks, as shown here:

```
int main()
{
    char linein[81], converted[81];
    int encryptdecrypt = 1;
    int i;
    ifstream in, inclear;

    cout << "Enter 1 to encrypt, 2 to decrypt: ";
    cin >> encryptdecrypt;
    if (encryptdecrypt == 1)
        in.open("test-enc.txt");
    else
        in.open("test-dec.txt");
```

The **main( )** function declares the variables it will use for reading and writing the character arrays, the stream variables used to manage the files, and some miscellaneous variables used for processing. It then prompts the user to enter a value specifying whether to encrypt or decrypt. If the user chooses to encrypt, the function will encrypt the file and display the encrypted text; otherwise, it will decrypt the file and display the decrypted text.

```
    if(!in) {
        cout << "Cannot open file." << endl;
        return (1);
    }
```

This **if** statement is just good programming procedure—making sure that the program was successfully able to open the file before it tries to process the file. If the program is not successfully opened, the function will exit without performing any further processing. If it opens the file okay, the program then enters a **while** loop to process the file, as shown here:

```
    while (!in.eof()) {
        for (i=0; i < 80 && !in.eof(); i++)
```

```
      in.get(linein[i]);
    linein[i] = NULL;
    if (encryptdecrypt == 1)
      strcpy(converted, strencrypt(linein));
    else
      strcpy(converted, strdecrypt(linein));
    cout << converted << endl;
  }
```

As constructed, the program simply reads in a line (80 characters) of the file at a time, within the inner **for** loop. After it reads in a line, it encrypts or decrypts the line (depending on the user's prior selection), copies the encrypted text into the **converted** array, and prints out the text to the default display device. The program then loops back through the **while** loop until it reaches the end of the file. Then it closes the file and reopens it for unmodified output, as shown here:

```
  in.close();

  cout << endl << endl;
  if (encryptdecrypt == 1)
    inclear.open("test-enc.txt");
  else
    inclear.open("test-dec.txt");
  if(!inclear) {
    cout << "Cannot open file." << endl;
    return (1);
  }

  while (!inclear.eof()) {
    for (i=0; i < 80 && !inclear.eof(); i++)
      inclear.get(linein[i]);
    linein[i] = NULL;
    cout << linein << endl;
  }
```

This portion of the program performs the same processing as the earlier loop, except it simply outputs the file, rather than performing any processing on it. The program does this so you can more easily see the relationship between the modified and the unmodified file.

Finally, the program closes up the open file handle and exits, as shown in the following code:

```
  inclear.close();
  return 0;
}
```

When you execute the simple1.cpp program, the output is pretty much what you might expect—a series of letters and symbols that don't seem to correspond with anything, as shown here:

```
Enter 1 to encrypt, 2 to decrypt: 1
Wklv#lv#d#whvw#ri#wkh#hqfu|swlrq#v|vwhp1#Wklv#whvw#xvhv#d#vlpsoh#urwd
wlrq#ydoxh#
wr#hqfu|sw#wkh#wh{w1#\rx#zloo#vhh#pruh#dgydqfhg#hqfu|swlrq#odwhu00wkh
#pdmru#lvv
xh#zlwk#d#urwdwlrq#olnh#wklv#lv#lw#ohqgv#lwvhoi#wr#fudfnlqj1


This is a test of the encryption system. This test uses a simple
rotation value
to encrypt the text. You will see more advanced encryption later--the
major iss
ue with a rotation like this is it lends itself to cracking.
C:\>
```

As you can see, encrypting the text in the file generates the required output: an altered form of the input array. However, this is clearly not much of an encryption program—it falls somewhere around the level of the decoder rings you used to find in cereal boxes.

In addition to its limitation of requiring a known key value, the **simple1.cpp** program is not a strong encryption technique because it is remarkably simple to break—in fact, most people could break the code by simply looking at it. Some of the encryption models that you will examine later in this chapter go to great lengths to make code cryptographically strong—that is, very difficult to break.

Strengthening the Encryption

Most cryptographically strong solutions use *block encryption,* performing extremely complex mathematical functions to do the encryption. Block encryption performs its processing on a minimum "block" of data—generally, somewhere between 128 and 512 bytes. If you have to encrypt less than a full block, you fill the rest of the block with junk (which your decryption algorithm must then remove) so that you can do the encryption. In general, you should use block encryption with datasets that are several times the size of each block. For example, if your encryption algorithm uses 512-byte blocks, you shouldn't encrypt anything smaller than 2K with that algorithm.

Often, however, your programs will simply need to encrypt information in a relatively strong manner. A more important consideration might be speed—strong block encryption has a tendency to take an extended period of time to perform. A useful solution in such a case is *stream encryption,* which encrypts bytes as they come

into the processor (or before being sent down a pipe, socket, or other communication device). Stream encryption can work on as little as one byte at a time. Stream encryption techniques, then, will work well on small amounts of data, perform adequately for most commercial applications, and have a significantly smaller memory footprint than similar block-encryption solutions.

In a recent issue of *C/C++ User's Journal*, William Ward presented an excellent C++ program that implements a relatively strong stream encryption process. While we will not revisit that level of encryption here, we will use the same basic encryption technique (**XOR**ing) that Ward uses in his program. The difference comes in how the **XOR** value is generated. After you consider the next program, **SimpXOR.cpp**, and the technique it uses to mask data, you will learn briefly what is necessary to make it a more secure encryption tool—that is, something more akin to Ward's implementation. Once you've worked through the next section, we'll examine a common implementation of block encryption within your program code—one where you use someone else's encryption algorithms and simply call functions that implement those algorithms to perform your processing.

A Slightly More Complex Encryption Algorithm

The **SimpXOR.cpp** program uses the most basic technique of encryption—a technique which, in fact, forms the basis of all computer encryption. The difference between this technique and true, strong encryption lies in the creation of the key. In the **SimpXOR.cpp** program, the key is a simple sequence of values that repeats every 255 characters. A good encryption key, in general, should not repeat itself any less than about every 263-1—and even that encryption key is breakable. That is why most modern-day encryption processes use large keys (as large as 4,096 bits) to encrypt blocks, rather than using individual characters or sequences of characters.

The **SimpXOR.cpp** program simply creates a repeating string of characters by cycling through each character in the ASCII character set, **XOR**ing each character in the string to be encrypted with the next character in the key string. If the total number of characters to be encrypted exceeds the length of the key string, the key string will repeat at its beginning each time the encryption routine reaches the end of the string. When decrypting the file, you simply **XOR** it against the key string again.

PROGRAMMER'S NOTE *Please note that this **XOR** method of encryption, which will deter only the most casual of observers, should not be used when protecting the data is a serious concern. In such cases, you should either use a pseudorandom number generator in conjunction with a shift register, or some other proven technique to encrypt the data. There are quite a few techniques which, in the hands of anyone willing to spend a little time and effort, will quickly break encryption of the style presented in this program. Nevertheless, it is still worthwhile to examine the technique so that you can understand its applications.*

SimpXOR.cpp

Code

Here is the code for the **SimpXOR.cpp** program.

```cpp
#include <iostream>
#include <fstream>
#include <string>
using namespace std;

void XOR_Char(unsigned char & Target, unsigned char & CryptVal) {
  Target = (Target ^ CryptVal);
  return;
}

void SampleFile  (const string & SourceName, const string &
TargetName) {
  char InChar  = 'A';
  int CryptChar = 0;

  ifstream Source(SourceName.c_str(),
    ios::in | ios::out | ios::binary);
  ofstream Target(TargetName.c_str(),
    ios::in | ios::out | ios::binary);

  while (EOF != (InChar = Source.peek())) {
    Source.read(& InChar, sizeof(InChar));
    XOR_Char((unsigned char &) InChar, (unsigned char &) CryptChar);
    Target.write(& InChar, sizeof(InChar));
    if (++CryptChar == 255)
      CryptChar = 0;
  }
  Source.close();
  Target.close();
  return;
}

void SampleString (string & Target) {
  int  Position = 0;
  int  Length = 0;
  int CryptChar = 255;

  Length = Target.length();
  for (Position = 0; Position < Length; Position++) {
```

```
      XOR_Char ((unsigned char &) Target[Position],
          (unsigned char &) CryptChar);
      if (--CryptChar == 0)
        CryptChar = 255;
    }
  return;
}

int main() {
  bool Success = true;
  int  Return_Code = 0;

  string  Target_String("C/C++ Annotated Archives");

  cout << "Original String: " << endl;
  cout << Target_String << endl;
  SampleString(Target_String);
  cout << "Encrypted String: " << endl;
  cout << Target_String << endl;

  SampleString(Target_String);
  cout << "Decrypted String: " << endl;
  cout << Target_String << endl;

  string Source_Name("c:\\gbaddr.txt");
  string Target_Name("c:\\engbaddr.txt");

  char Character;
  cout << "Before encryption (gbaddr.txt):" << endl;
  ifstream Source_File (Source_Name.c_str(),
      ios::in | ios::binary);
  if (Source_File.fail()) {
    cout << "Unable to open source file!" << endl;
    return 1;
  }
  while (EOF != (Character = Source_File.peek())) {
    Source_File.read(& Character, sizeof(Character));
    cout << Character;
  }
  Source_File.close();
  cout << endl;
```

```
/* Encrypt the contents of the Source file and save
   them to the target file. */
SampleFile(Source_Name, Target_Name);

// Display the contents of the Encrypted file.
Character = 'A';
cout << "After encryption (engbaddr.txt):" << endl;
ifstream EncFile (Target_Name.c_str(),
    ios::in | ios::binary);
if (EncFile.fail()) {
  cout << "Unable to open encrypted file!" << endl;
  return 1;
}
while (EOF != (Character = EncFile.peek())) {
  EncFile.read(& Character, sizeof(Character));
  cout << Character;
}
EncFile.close();
cout << endl;

// Decrypt the target file to a third file.
string Dec_Target_Name("c:\\decbaddr.txt");
SampleFile(Target_Name, Dec_Target_Name);

// Display the decrypted contents
Character = 'A';
cout << "After decryption (decbaddr.txt):" << endl;
ifstream DecFile (Dec_Target_Name.c_str(),
    ios::in | ios::binary);
if (DecFile.fail()) {
  cout << "Unable to open decrypted file!" << endl;
  return 1;
}
while (EOF != (Character = DecFile.peek())) {
  DecFile.read(& Character, sizeof(Character));
  cout << Character;
}
DecFile.close();
cout << endl;
return 0;
}
```

ANNOTATIONS

The **XOR_Char( )** routine performs the real encryption work for the program. As it is the first function in the program, we will examine it first:

```
#include <iostream>
#include <fstream>
#include <string>
using namespace std;

void XOR_Char(unsigned char & Target, unsigned char & CryptVal) {
  Target = (Target ^ CryptVal);
  return;
}
```

The **XOR_Char( )** function accepts two unsigned character values: the character to transform, and the value to transform it with. **XOR_Char( )** then transforms the character and returns the newly transformed character within the function's first parameter, **Target**. This step—**XOR**ing the cryptographic value with the value to transform—is the root of all computer-based cryptography. It is also, conceptually, the mathematical root method of all cryptography.

Note, as well, that we talk about *transforming*, rather than *encrypting*, the character. This is an important difference. **XOR**ing the character initially encrypts it, but **XOR**ing it again decrypts it—presuming that the **XOR** value is the same in both cases. It is also important to note that, in any encryption program that you might design, you will have this step at some location. The primary difference between the simple encryption program shown here and an encryption program that provides true, strong encryption is in the algorithm used by the program for the generation of that key value.

Here's what that means, conceptually: In this application, the key value is a simple cycling value: 1, 2, 3, 4, …255, 1, 2, and so on. For any cryptographer, breaking the key value under these circumstances is a piece of cake—they will begin to see repetition in the code quite quickly, because the key repeats every 255 characters. Given a document of 10,000 characters or so, a good cryptographer could break this key in minutes.

But it's not the method that's flawed; it's simply the implementation. If you changed the way you generated the cryptographic key—that is, made it cycle in some known way, but a way that didn't repeat itself in any easily predictable sequence without knowledge of the key—you would have a highly secure program. The limitation here is not in the **XOR**ing method—it's in the fact that the key repeats itself so quickly and so often. But create the **XOR** byte using a method that did not repeat values with any regularity, and you could easily make the program much more secure.

Visualizing this might be easier if you again consider the sequence of values in the cryptographic key:

```
1, 2, 3, 4, 5, 6, 7, ...
```

In other words, every time a byte in the string is encrypted with the value 3, the byte before it is encrypted with 2, and the byte after it is encrypted with 4, and so on.

Now consider the following sequence:

```
2, 3, 7, 22, 128, 3, 1, 255, ...
```

In this case, there is not an easily-predictable way to figure out what the values to either side of the 3 are. Optimally, a good encryption algorithm would *never repeat itself* in the encryption of any given file. That is what we mean by saying the method isn't flawed, but rather the implementation.

The rest of the program is pretty straightforward. Each of the two functions simply processes the string of values, passing one at a time to the **XOR_Char( )** function. The following code implements the **SampleFile( )** function:

```
void SampleFile (const string & SourceName,
    const string & TargetName) {
  char InChar = 'A';
  int CryptChar = 0;

  ifstream Source(SourceName.c_str(),
      ios::in | ios::out | ios::binary);
  ofstream Target(TargetName.c_str(),
      ios::in | ios::out | ios::binary);
```

The function accepts as its sole parameters the name of the source file and the name of the file in which to save the transformed values. It then declares a couple local variables—one in which to store the characters read from the file, and one to contain the cycling cryptographic value. After that, **SampleFile( )** opens the two files referenced by the parameters, accessing one for input and one for output.

```
  while (EOF != (InChar = Source.peek())) {
    Source.read(& InChar, sizeof(InChar));
    XOR_Char((unsigned char &) InChar, (unsigned char &) CryptChar);
    Target.write(& InChar, sizeof(InChar));
    if (++CryptChar == 255)
      CryptChar = 0;
  }
```

Next, the program code simply loops through the source file, making sure the next character isn't the end of file. If it isn't, the program reads that character in, passes it to the **XOR_Char( )** function, and writes the newly transformed character out to the target file. Each time through the loop, it also increments the **CryptChar** value by 1, resetting the value to 0 when it reaches 255—the weak point of the encrypting process, as discussed earlier in the chapter.

```
 Source.close();
 Target.close();
 return;
}
```

After **SampleFile( )** finishes processing the entire file, the function cleans up after itself and exits. This implementation returns no value. In a real-world application, however, you would want to test and make sure the program successfully opened both the source and target files, and returned an error code if it didn't or a success code if everything worked as planned.

The **SampleString( )** function performs almost identically to the **SampleFile( )** function. However, instead of reading until it reaches the end of the string, **SampleString( )** first uses the standard C++ string library's **length( )** method to determine how many characters are in the string, before it begins. It also writes the encrypted value back into the same string that it received originally—a technique that you will likely want to avoid in your applications. The following code implements the **SampleFile( )** function:

```
void SampleString (string & Target) {
  int Position = 0;
  int Length = 0;
  int CryptChar = 255;

  Length = Target.length();
  for (Position = 0; Position < Length; Position++) {
    XOR_Char ((unsigned char &) Target[Position],
        (unsigned char &) CryptChar);
    if (--CryptChar == 0)
      CryptChar = 255;
  }
  return;
}
```

Note again that the function simply cycles through the values sequentially for the cryptographic character (although this function counts downwards instead of upwards, just for a change). Of course, in a real-world implementation, you would likely want this function to return some success value, and you would definitely want the function to generate the **CryptChar** value in a different manner.

The code in the **main( )** function doesn't really do much beyond calling the two transforming functions and displaying output of current values. It processes a simple string first, as shown here:

```
int main() {
  int  Return_Code = 0;

  string  Target_String("C/C++ Annotated Archives");
```

```
cout << "Original String: " << endl;
cout << Target_String << endl;
SampleString(Target_String);
cout << "Encrypted String: " << endl;
cout << Target_String << endl;

SampleString(Target_String);
cout << "Decrypted String: " << endl;
cout << Target_String << endl;
```

Notice how the code invokes the **SampleString( )** function twice—once to
encrypt the text within the string, which it then displays; and again to decrypt the
text, which it also displays. As you will see in the program output, the original value
and the post-decryption value are identical.

This next block of code defines a pair of strings for the files on the disk—one for
the plain-text file, and one for the destination cipher-text file. It then opens the
source file and outputs its contents to the screen, one character at a time.

```
string Source_Name("c:\\gbaddr.txt");
string Target_Name("c:\\engbaddr.txt");

char Character;
cout << "Before encryption (gbaddr.txt):" << endl;
ifstream Source_File (Source_Name.c_str(),
    ios::in | ios::binary);
if (Source_File.fail()) {
  cout << "Unable to open source file!" << endl;
  return 1;
}
while (EOF != (Character = Source_File.peek())) {
  Source_File.read(& Character, sizeof(Character));
  cout << Character;
}
Source_File.close();
cout << endl;
```

Notice that the program reads the file in as binary. This is really unnecessary for
this particular text file, because it is known to be text, but it *is* necessary when
processing the actual encrypted file.

CAUTION *When using any encryption algorithm with files, always treat the files as binary files—even if they
are known text files. The transformation process can, and often does, create '\0' characters in the
output file. Functions expecting null-terminated strings or explicit end-of-line and end-of-file
characters will not perform correctly when working with the files, if you open them as text files.*

In fact, if you change the program code to simply check for an end-of-file marker, the program will often halt the reading of the file early—or, worse, keep reading beyond the file's end.

Again, you will see in the next file read that the program reads the encrypted file in as a binary file and processes each character individually:

```
SampleFile(Source_Name, Target_Name);


Character = 'A';
cout << "After encryption (engbaddr.txt):" << endl;
ifstream EncFile (Target_Name.c_str(),
    ios::in | ios::binary);
if (EncFile.fail()) {
  cout << "Unable to open encrypted file!" << endl;
  return 1;
}
while (EOF != (Character = EncFile.peek())) {
  EncFile.read(& Character, sizeof(Character));
  cout << Character;
}
EncFile.close();
cout << endl;
```

This code performs the same processing as the code shown in the earlier program does—it simply reads the encrypted file and outputs each character, instead of the original file. The **while** loop reads the decrypted file and outputs each character.

When you execute the compiled **SimpXOR.cpp** program, it will generate the following output. (The output of the source file is not reprinted here, for space considerations.)

```
Original String:
C/C++ Annotated Archives
Encrypted String:
C.A(/%Giff~jxhj/Qcq{}csd
Decrypted String:
C/C++ Annotated Archives
Before encryption (gbaddr.txt):
Four score and seven years ago…
After encryption (engbaddr.txt):
Fnwq$vehzl*jbi.|ugw}4lsvjj:z{r2?OTP_BDROM[Y
N_AZWYF_RZDCP_OKSS-K((1c'*(3!'/%8an.p?7$t;7#164w|>11__
__F_I___"_  ]R___V_""__"
___ õí£ðíã§øûåûãþçûùþü³àý÷ã¸øö÷¼ðûñ<<Unicode:
```

```
80>>ÀÐÆ„ÆÔÂÉÝÏÏŒÈßÚÑÝœ"¹¿øØÏ™ÍÞœÙÍÚà
¤¬¤¥¢££è ¤ë-í©½₁°¦ó·¼ ¾´ù-º®ñþ«…'—ŠŠ‚Æ<<Unicode: 90>><<Unicode:
80>>Œ ƒ%ӂÎ·˜<<Unicode: 90>><<Unicode: 86>>Óš",—ÖÛ" Þao
{#jdrngg*xc-m'~rwzbpr7yw~;or>{EEK@EQCC_ IJBB@^V_VZQCE]__lY"_M%a/&0e))
h(j,>(/;p33' 9311<6?|28 _ __D___FI=L____Q "__V__Y--__"-ôä¢â¤õéõü
àåå¬âè¯äùóç´ó
```
After decryption (decbaddr.txt):

Four score and seven years ago, our fathers brought forth upon this
continent, a new nation, conceived in liberty, and dedicated to the
proposition that all men are created equal.

Now we are engaged in a great civil war, testing whether that nation,
or any nation so conceived and so dedicated, can long endure. We are
met on a great battlefield of that war. We have come to dedicate a
portion of that field, as a final resting place for those who here
gave their lives that that nation might live. It is altogether
fitting and proper that we should do this.

But, in a larger sense, we cannot dedicate -- we cannot consecrate --
we cannot hallow -- this ground. The brave men, living and dead, who
struggled here, have consecrated it, far above our poor power to add
or detract. The world will little note, nor long remember what we say
here, but it can never forget what they did here. It is for us the
living, rather, to be dedicated here to the unfinished work which
they who fought here have thus far so nobly advanced. It is rather
for us to be here dedicated to the great task remaining before us --
that from these honored dead we take increased devotion to that cause
for which they gave the last full measure of devotion -- that we here
highly resolve that these dead shall not have died in vain -- that
this nation, under God, shall have a new birth of freedom -- and that
government of the people, by the people, for the people, shall not
perish from the earth.

Although the encrypted string and the encrypted file are not easily decodable to the naked eye (as you can see from their appearance in the program's output), they are still quite breakable with a program similar to that used to generate the output. Again, adding greater complexity to the method used to generate the cryptographic key value will help make this encryption technique less vulnerable.

In the next section, we will consider some of the limitations of single-key cryptosystems, as well as your alternatives to overcome those limitations. You will also learn a more common method of accessing cryptographic algorithms: using an interface to access someone else's proven-secure algorithm.

The Limitations of Conventional Single-Key Cryptosystems

In conventional single-key cryptosystems, both the transmitter and the receiver use a *single key* (the same key) for both encryption and decryption. Thus, the transmitter and receiver must initially exchange a key through secure channels so that both parties have the key available before they send or receive encrypted messages over unsecure channels. Figure 7-3 shows a typical exchange using a single-key cryptosystem like those you have already seen in this chapter.

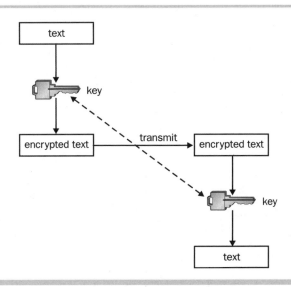

FIGURE 7-3.   A single-key cryptosystem requires that both parties have a copy of the key

What are the limitations of this system?

◆   The primary flaw when you use single-key cryptosystems on the Internet is that they require both parties to know the key before each transmission.

◆   In addition, because you will want only the recipient to have the ability to decrypt your transmissions, you must create different single keys for each individual, group, and business to which you transmit. Clearly, you will have to maintain an inconveniently large number of single keys.

◆ If you use a secure channel for exchanging the key itself, you could simply transmit the data along the same secure channel (which defeats the purpose of cryptography). Most people, however, do not have access to a secure channel and therefore must transmit the data along an unsecure channel.

Modern-day cryptographic transmissions use a new type of cryptography, called a public-key cryptosystem, to avoid the issues that surround single-key cryptosystems.

Public-Key Cryptosystems

A *public-key cryptosystem* requires two related, complementary keys. You can freely distribute one key, the public key, to your friends, business associates, and even your competitors. You will maintain the second key, the *private key*, in a secure location (on your computer) and never release it to anyone. The private key unlocks the encryption that the public key creates, as shown in Figure 7-4.

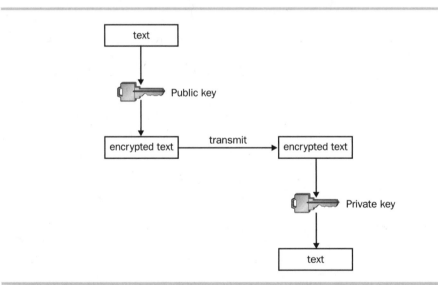

FIGURE 7-4. The basic model of the public-key cryptosystem

With a public-key cryptosystem, your cousin can publish his or her public key anywhere on the Internet, or send it to you within an unencrypted e-mail. You can

then encrypt a message using the public key. Only your cousin will be able to decrypt this message—not even you, the sender (and encrypter) can decrypt the message. When your cousin wants to send a message back to you, your cousin will encrypt that message using your public key. Only you will be able to decrypt that message.

The public-key protocol effectively eliminates the need for the secure channels required by conventional single-key cryptosystems. Two groups of individuals—Rivest, Shamir, and Adleman; and Diffie and Hellman—designed the fundamental algorithms governing cryptography within a public-key cryptosystem. You will learn more about the Rivest, Shamir, and Adleman (RSA) implementation in later sections in this chapter, because it is one of the underlying protocols that you can easily use from the Windows Encryption API.

Digital Signatures

Public-key encryption programs make extensive use of *message authentication,* a method that message recipients can use to verify a message's originator and validity. The message authentication process is relatively straightforward. The sender must use the sender's secret key to encrypt a unique value corresponding to the message's contents, thereby *signing* the message. The secret key creates a *digital signature* on the message, which the recipient (or anyone else, for that matter) can check by using the sender's public key to decrypt the digital signature.

With the process of digital signing, the message recipient can prove that the sender is indeed the true originator of the message. Because only the private-key holder can create a digital signature decryptable by the public key, the digital signature guarantees the identity of the message sender. In addition, a digital signature processes the file and creates a unique number representative of the file's contents, date, time, and so on. Therefore, when the digital signature is verified, it proves that no one has modified the file during or after the transmission.

The Digital Signature's Construction

Signing programs generate the digital signature value through a two-step process. The receiving program uses a similar process to verify the signature. First, the signing program passes the text or code to sign through a mathematical function called a *hash.* The hash function creates a unique value from the bytes that constitute the file. Moreover, the hash function computes the value such that you cannot derive the file from the hash value. Figure 7-5 shows how a hash function receives incoming values and yields a unique result.

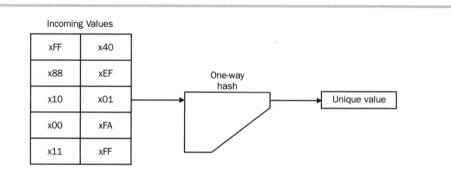

FIGURE 7-5. The hash function derives a unique value from a series of other values

After creating the hash value, the signing program encrypts the hash value using the file encryptor's (user's) private key. Finally, the signing program writes a signed version of the file, which typically includes information about the signing program, and indicators of where a signed file begins and ends. Figure 7-6 is a simple model of how a program digitally signs a document.

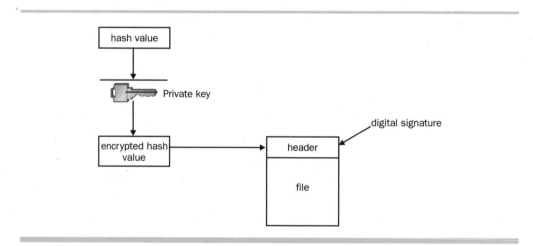

FIGURE 7-6. The program attaches the signature to the file after encrypting the hash value

To verify the signature, the file's receiver first runs software to decrypt the signature's hash value using the sender's public key. After the software program

decrypts the hash value, the program stores the hash value in a temporary location. Figure 7-7 shows how the decryption program gets the file's encrypted hash value and converts it back to a usable value.

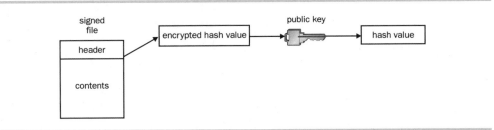

FIGURE 7-7.   The receiving program first retrieves and decrypts the hash value

The receiver's software program then parses the file through the same hash the sender originally used to create the hash value. The receiver's software program next checks the computed hash value against the decrypted hash value. If the values are the same, the receiver's software program informs the user that the signature is accurate and the message is, therefore, authentic. Figure 7-8 shows how the receiver's software program computes its own hash value and compares it with the decrypted hash value.

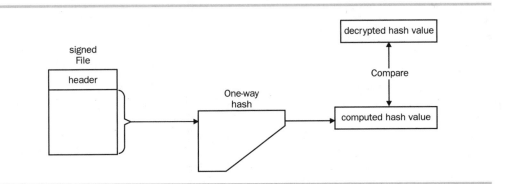

FIGURE 7-8.   The receiving program computes its own hash value and compares it with the decrypted hash value

CAUTION   *Digital signatures are **not** the same thing as electronic signatures. As you have learned, digital signatures help to identify message creators and senders. In an electronic message, a digital signature carries the same weight as a handwritten signature in printed correspondence. Unlike handwritten signatures, however, **digital signatures are virtually impossible to forge**. Digital signatures are dynamic—each is unique to the message it signs. The data in the message itself, plus the private key the sender uses to encrypt the message, are themselves mathematical components in the signature's construction. Electronic signatures, on the other hand, are simply a copy of a handwritten signature (like that on a fax, or the package-signing keyboard used by UPS). Be careful not to confuse the two.*

The Rivest, Shamir, and Adleman (RSA) Algorithm

It's important for you to understand that even though you will most frequently use public-key cryptography to encrypt textual messages, the computer accomplishes public-key cryptography by applying a set of mathematical actions to the data. Programmers collectively refer to this set of mathematical operations as an *encryption algorithm*. One of the most successful and important algorithms in public-key cryptographic systems is the *RSA Algorithm*. Earlier versions of Pretty Good Privacy (one of the most well known encryption programs), as well as many other types of encrypted transmissions and encryption programs, used the RSA Algorithm.

When you consider encryption, you must differentiate between an algorithm, which is a mathematical construct, and a program such as **CryptoNotes** (which you will see at work later in this chapter) that applies the algorithm to accomplish a task. In other words, an algorithm is like a hammer: Without a hand (a program such as **CryptoNotes**) to swing the hammer, the hammer is useless.

Three mathematicians at the Massachusetts Institute of Technology (MIT) created the RSA Algorithm. The RSA Algorithm randomly generates a very large prime number (the public key). The algorithm uses the public key to derive another very large prime number (the private key) through some relatively complex mathematical functions. A later section in this chapter explains the mathematics in detail. Users then employ the keys to encrypt documents that two or more individuals send between themselves, and to decrypt documents after addressees receive them.

Properties of the RSA Algorithm

The four foundation properties for the RSA Algorithm, as defined by Rivest, Shamir, and Adleman, are as follows:

1. Deciphering a message's enciphered form yields the original message. Conceptually, you could write that equation as shown here:

   `D(E(M))=M`

   In this equation, **D** represents the deciphering action, **E** represents the enciphering action, and **M** represents the actual message.

2. **E** and **D** are relatively easy to compute.

3. Publicly revealing **E** does not reveal any easy way to compute **D**. Therefore, only the user holding the value **D** can decrypt a message encrypted with **E**.

4. Deciphering a message **M**, and then enciphering the message, results in **M**. In other words, the converse of the previously shown function holds true, as shown here:

   `E(D(M))=M`

As Rivest, Shamir, and Adleman point out, if someone transmitting data used a procedure that satisfies Property 3, another user trying to decipher the message would have to try all the possible keys until the would-be decoder found a key that fulfills the requirement **E(M)=D**. This evaluation is relatively simple when the encrypting numbers are 10 or even 20 digits in length. However, historic RSA encryption schemes used a number up to 512 bits for both the public key (**E**) and the private key (**D**)—a number that has 154 digits in a decimal representation. In addition, both **E** and **D** numbers are very large prime numbers. To process those numbers would take extraordinary computing power—in fact, to date no one has been able to break a 512-bit key using a brute-force attack (that is, trying all possible keys until the program finds a match). More recently, programs have begun using keys as long as 4,096 bits.

A function that satisfies Properties 1 through 3 of the RSA Algorithm list is known as a *trap-door one-way function* because, as you have learned, you can easily compute the function in one direction but not in the other. The term *trap-door* means you can easily compute the inverse functions after you know certain private (trap-door) information.

The RSA Algorithm Itself

The RSA Algorithm is a relatively simple concept. The process is similar to what the previous section details, with the implementing program doing certain additional processing to ensure that it encrypts the file correctly. The encryption key, represented as **E**, includes an associated constant **n**. The constant **n** represents an encrypted

block's length limit (that is, the number of data bytes a single encrypted block can contain). The encryption occurs in three steps, as follows:

1. The program that implements the RSA Algorithm converts the textual message into a representative integer between 0 and (**n**–1). The method used to convert the text to an integer varies from program to program. The program will break large messages (large enough that an integer smaller than n–1 cannot adequately represent the messages) into a number of blocks, with each block represented by its own integer less than **n**–1.

2. The program encrypts the message by raising each of the integer values to the Eth power (in other words, block^E). The program then performs modulo arithmetic (a specific type of arithmetic that maintains only the remainder from a division operation) on the resulting value, dividing the value by **n** and saving the remainder as the encrypted message. The encrypted message is now cyphertext document **C**. The word *cyphertext* refers to text that results from a cipher—in other words, encrypted text.

3. To decrypt cyphertext document **C**, the message receiver raises the message to the Dth power and then performs modulo division on the result using **n**. The resulting series of values represent the blocks within the decrypted file. The program then converts the blocks back to text using the same method it used originally to convert the text.

The user makes the encryption key **(E,n)** public and keeps the decryption key **(D,n)** private.

The RSA Algorithm's Math

You have learned the fundamental steps performed by the RSA Algorithm. However, there is more complexity to the algorithm than is described by the three simplified steps outlined in the preceding section. The RSA Algorithm's math is as follows:

1. Find two very large prime numbers, **p** and **q**.

2. Find the value **n** (the *public modulus*) such that **n = p * q**. In a 256-bit cryptosystem, **n** is a number 300 digits or more in length.

3. Choose E (the *public exponent*), so that **E < n**, and E is relatively prime to **(p - 1) * (q - 1)**. *Relatively prime* means that **E** is a number that shares no common factors (except 1) with **(p - 1) * (q - 1)**.

4. Compute D (the *private exponent*) so that **ED = 1 mod ((p - 1) * (q - 1))**.

The public key is **(E,n)** while the private key is **(D,n)**. The user should never reveal the values **p** and **q**, and preferably should destroy them. Most public-key software packages will maintain **p** and **q** to accelerate internal operations, but the software maintains **p** and **q** within an encrypted file and does not let anyone (even the user) access the values directly.

For more discussion about the RSA Algorithm math, visit the RSA Corporation's Web site at http://www.rsa.com.

PROGRAMMER'S NOTE   *When you work with the CryptoAPI, the RSA encryption provider (the RSA Cryptographic Service Provider) handles the RSA encryption algorithm's underlying mathematics for you. Using the CryptoAPI makes it possible to use the same function to encrypt a buffer with any cryptographic provider—it is the provider's responsibility to ensure that it accepts your function calls.*

Hash Values

As you have learned, a hash function (in cryptography) is a mathematical function that creates a unique value from the bytes of a given input—a string, a file, or some other type of binary data. Moreover, a hash function computes the value such that you cannot derive the original information from the hash function.

You can consider the hash value a unique number that represents the incoming data stream's exact contents. Each time you pass the same stream of data (for example, a file) through the hash, the hash will always return the same hash value.

The Windows Encryption API

Because many computer users are using encryption, Microsoft integrated cryptographic support into the Windows NT 4.0 operating system; it is also built into the Internet Explorer browser and into Windows 95 (OEM Service Release 2) and 98. Microsoft's *Cryptographic Application Programming Interface (CryptoAPI)* is a set of functions that you can use from within your Visual C++, Visual Basic, or other languages to provide encryption and decryption services to your programs' users.

The CryptoAPI programming interface enables you to add cryptographic functions to your programs. It uses the Windows Open Services Architecture (WOSA) to provide three basic sets of functions:

◆   Certificate functions

◆   Simplified cryptographic functions

◆   Base cryptographic functions

Figure 7-9 shows the model you will use to implement these functions.

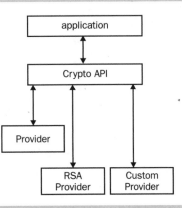

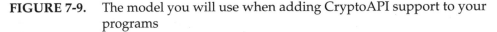

FIGURE 7-9.   The model you will use when adding CryptoAPI support to your
programs

The *simplified cryptographic functions* include high-level functions for creating and
using keys and for encrypting and decrypting information. The *certificate functions*
provide the means to extract, store, and verify the digital signature certificates that
transmitters can enclose with documents, as well as the means to enumerate the
certificates previously saved to a machine. At a lower level are the *base cryptographic
functions.* Your programs should avoid calling the base cryptographic functions, to
prevent conflicts resulting from Cryptographic Service Providers (CSPs) that you
have uninstalled, another program's required use of a particular CSP, and so on.
CSPs are discussed in the upcoming section.

The CryptoAPI supports multiple cryptographic providers. For example, you might
use RSA encryption with some information, and digitally sign other information with
the Digital Signature Standard (DSS). Table 7-1 lists the Cryptographic Service Providers
(CSPs) and their associated types of encryption.

The CryptoAPI uses *key databases* to maintain password information. When you
are creating an encrypted application, be sure to first create the necessary key
databases. The best way to ensure that your application has a key database to work
with is to check for the existence of the database each time the application runs, and
then create and initialize a new key database if one does not already exist.

Cryptographic Service Providers *(CSPs)*

A typical CSP is comprised of a DLL and a signature file that the CryptoAPI uses to
periodically verify the integrity and identity of the users accessing that provider.
Sometimes a CSP may implement some of its functionality in hardware, to prevent
tampering or to improve performance. Put another way, a CSP is a server able to

Cryptographic Service Provider	Encryption	Signature
PROV_RSA_FULL	RC2, RC4	RSA
PROV_RSA_SIG	n/a	RSA
PROV_DSS	n/a	DSS
PROV_FORTEZZA	SkipJack	DSS
PROV_SSL	RSA	RSA
PROV_MS_EXCHANGE	CAST	RSA

TABLE 7-1.   Cryptographic Service Providers

perform a standard set of tasks invoked by the system through the CryptoAPI functions. An application should not assume that a CSP has capabilities exceeding the known standard. A CSP is just a removable plug-in module. The role played by a CSP makes it very similar to Windows drivers that implement print or graphic functions. Once you have registered the CSP, you may start using it without changing anything at the application level.

To ensure privacy, all the data a CSP manipulates (especially keys) is returned to the caller as opaque handles and remains inaccessible at the application level. Moreover, programs cannot affect the way the data is actually encoded. A program must limit itself to passing in the data and specifying the encryption type required. A provider can always return a type that explains what it can do and how. Different providers may use identical algorithms but must adopt different logic for padding and different key sizes.

Bundled with the CryptoAPI SDK is a default CSP called the Microsoft RSA Base Provider, implemented in **rsabase.dll**. It's a **PROV_RSA_FULL** type provider supporting the RSA public-key algorithm for both key exchange and signatures. (The key is 512 bits long.) The RSA Base Provider also uses RC2 and RC4 cipher algorithms for encryption with a 40-bit key. Applications should not rely on these lengths for a particular implementation, however, because CSPs can be swapped in without the application's knowledge.

Each CSP is associated with a database of key containers that stores all the private and public keys for the users accessing that computer. Each container has a unique name that is the key to the CryptoAPI programming world. Without this key database, all CryptoAPI functions will fail. The database typically has a default key container with the logon name of each user. A particular application, however, may create a custom key container and key pairs during installation, assigning them the application's own name. Since the type of the provider affects the behavior of the cryptographic functions, two connected applications should use the same CSP, or

at least CSPs with a common subset of functions. Figure 7-10 shows a simplified model of a key database.

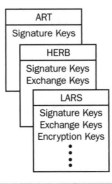

FIGURE 7-10. A simplified model of the CryptoAPI key database

The CryptoAPI Programming Model

Before adding public-key cryptography to real-world applications, you must become familiar with terms such as *context, session keys, exchange keys,* and *signature keys.*

A *context* represents an established session between CryptoAPI and the client application. To begin, you need to acquire a context. In doing so, you pass in the name of the key container you need and the name of the provider to which you want to connect. The handle you obtain must be used in all subsequent calls to the CryptoAPI routines.

A *session key* comes into play when it's time to encrypt or decrypt data. Session keys are volatile objects whose actual bytes never leave the CSP for reasons of privacy and security. The session key determines how a file is encrypted and must be inserted in a ciphered file to allow decryption. If you need to bring a session key out of the CSP for exchange or storage purposes, you will use *key blobs.* A key blob is a binary chunk of data and may be considered an encrypted and exportable version of the key itself. (Blob stands for Binary Large Object.)

The safekeeping mechanism is completed with *exchange keys.* They are pairs of keys (one public and one private) that take care of encrypting the session keys inside the key blobs and handling the digital signatures. A session key is created dynamically from the information stored in the user's key container. Once you have a session key, you are ready to make the calls that will scramble the bytes of the file.

Bear in mind that supporting cryptography in your applications doesn't require that you're familiar with the details of the RSA, Data Encryption Standard (DES), or

any other commonly used algorithm, or with subtle concepts such as public and private keys.

Using the Cryptographic API's Basic Functions

When you want to use the CryptoAPI, you must apply the basic CryptoAPI functions within your programs—which will let you perform the three basic activity types—encryption, hashing, and digitally signing—previously discussed in this chapter.

The CryptoAPI's designers divided its functions into four principal areas: CSPs, keys, hash objects, and signatures. Within an encryption application, you will typically call the **CryptAcquireContext( )** function before any other; it lets you select or access a Cryptographic Service Provider. The **wincrypt.h** header declares the **CryptAcquireContext( )** function as shown in the following prototype:

```
BOOL WINAPI CryptAcquireContext (HCRYPTPROV *phProv,
    LCTSTR pszContainer, LPCTSTR pszProvider,
    DWORD dwProvType, DWORD dwFlags)
```

This function returns a 32-bit long value, which indicates to the remaining CryptoAPI functions that **CryptAcquireContext( )** has established a working cryptography session. You may specify a particular CSP and key container through the **pszContainer** and **pszProvider** parameters.

After you have obtained a handle to the successful session, you can invoke the functions listed in Table 7-2 to perform encryption activities within your programs.

CryptoAPI Function	Description
CryptAcquireContext( )	Returns a handle to the key container in a Cryptographic Service Provider (CSP).
CryptCreateHash( )	Creates a hash object (a numeric interpretation of a value).
CryptDecrypt( )	Uses a decryption key to decrypt a buffer's contents.
CryptDeriveKey( )	Derives an encryption key from a hash object. Generally, you will hash a password or other specific string, create a hash object, and then derive the key from that object.
CryptDestroyHash( )	Destroys a hash object created with **CryptCreateHash( )**.
CryptDestroyKey( )	Destroys a key, whether imported with **CryptImportKey( )** or created with **CryptDeriveKey( )**.

TABLE 7-2.   The CryptoAPI Functions

CryptoAPI Function	Description
CryptEncrypt( )	Uses an encryption key to encrypt a buffer's contents.
CryptExportKey( )	Returns a key blob from a key. A **key_blob** is an encrypted copy of a key that you can transmit to a key's receiver. Generally, you will use a key blob to encrypt a single key and send it along with a single-key encrypted document.
CryptGenKey( )	Generates random keys to use with the CSP.
CryptGetHashParam( )	Retrieves data p reviously associated with a hash object.
CryptGetKeyParam( )	Retrieves data previously associated with a key.
CryptGetProvParam( )	Retrieves data previously associated with a CSP.
CryptGetUserKey( )	Returns the handle to a signature or previously defined key (as opposed to a key that you derive from a hash object).
CryptHashData( )	Hashes a data stream.
CryptImportKey( )	Extracts the key from a key blob.
CryptReleaseContext( )	Releases the handle to the key container.
CryptSetProvParam( )	Customizes a CSP's operations.
CryptSetProvider( )	Sets the default CSP.
CryptSignHash( )	Uses an encryption key to digitally sign a data stream. (You will learn more about digital signatures in later sections of this chapter.)
CryptVerifySignature( )	Verifies a hash object's digital signature.

TABLE 7-2. The CryptoAPI Functions (continued)

Each function applies the CryptoAPI in a manner consistent with the function's name. For example, to export a key is a two-step process. The first step retrieves the user's public key from the CSP using **CryptGetUserKey( )**. After your program has retrieved the public-key handle, you can call **CryptExportKey( )** to get a key blob (binary large object). You can then transmit the key blob to another user, who will use the **CryptImportKey( )** function to retrieve the key from the key blob.

The returned **HCRYPTPROV** handle is proof that a working session was established between the application and the CSP. You may specify a particular CSP

to which you want to connect, as well as the key container you want to access. You do this through the **pszProvider** and **pszContainer** arguments. You may restrict your query by indicating what type the provider should be. The function first tries to locate a provider with the given name and characteristics. If it's successful, the function will then search for a **pszContainer** key container in that CSP. The **dwFlags** parameter lets you create a new key container or delete an existing one. The handle obtained should be released via **CryptReleaseContext( )**.

The following code fragment, for example, shows a common set of steps for acquiring a context within your application:

```
HCRYPTPROV hProv = NULL;
CryptAcquireContext(&hProv, NULL, NULL, PROV_RSA_FULL, 0);
```

This call, in which both **pszContainer** and **pszProvider** are set to **NULL**, will connect your application to the default RSA provider and the default key container. The function **CryptSetProvider( )** lets you change this default, but Microsoft generally recommends against doing so.

None of the functions dealing with CSPs (except for **CryptAcquireContext( )**) should be used at the application level; they must be called only from within system-level and administrative tools. **CryptAcquireContext( )** gives you a handle to an encryption provider. You can then use this handle to create or derive keys.

There are two methods for generating session keys: using a random seed through **CryptGenKey( )** or using a hash method with **CryptDeriveKey( )**. **CryptGenKey( )** requires four parameters, as shown in the following prototype:

```
BOOL CryptGenKey(HCRYPTPROV hProv, ALG_ID algid,
    DWORD dwFlags, HCRYPTKEY* phKey);
```

The first parameter is a handle to the selected CSP, and the last is a buffer that will contain a valid key handle. The **algid** argument specifies a value identifying the algorithm to be used for creating the key. The algorithms available depend upon the provider's capabilities. The Microsoft RSA Base Provider offers two possible choices: **CALG_RC4** and **CALG_RC2**. The key may or may not be exportable.

As mentioned earlier, a session key is a volatile object unless you assign it the **CRYPT_EXPORTABLE** attribute. This flag allows the key to originate a key blob, which is nothing more than a nonvolatile and encrypted version of the key. Often a key blob is attached to a message or file.

The two-step process for exporting a key involves another special object, the *exchange key*. The first step consists of asking the CSP for the user's public key with a call to the **CryptGetUserKey( )** function. Once you've got an exchange key handle, you're ready to get a key blob. The following code fragment performs both steps and yields a key blob within the **pBuf** variable:

```
HCRYPTKEY hXKey = NULL;
LPBYTE pBuf = NULL;
```

```
CryptGetUserKey(hProv, AT_KEYEXCHANGE, &hXKey);
CryptExportKey(hKey, hXKey, SIMPLEBLOB, 0, NULL, &dwSize);
pBuf = (LPBYTE) malloc(dwSize)
CryptExportKey(hKey, hXKey, SIMPLEBLOB, 0, pBuf, &dwSize);
```

The function **CryptExportKey( )** returns the key blob, which is stored in the **pBuf** buffer. When **pBuf** is **NULL**, the same function will instead return the amount of required memory. To decode a key blob and finally decipher the document, the destination user calls **CryptImportKey( )**, passing in the key blob and receiving an **HCRYPTKEY** handle.

A session key may also be generated through hashing. You just need to provide a stream of data to work on, and you get back a previously initialized hash object. The functions involved are **CryptCreateHash( )**, whose purpose is creating a hash object; **CryptHashData( )**, which hashes in the given data; and **CryptDeriveKey( )**, which generates an **HCRYPTKEY** handle from the hash object. You might use them in conjunction as shown in the following code fragment:

```
CryptCreateHash(hProv, CALG_MD5, 0, 0, &hHash);
CryptHashData(hHash, szData, lstrlen(szData));
CryptDeriveKey(hProv, CALG_RC4, hHash, 0, &hKey);
```

The **szData** parameter represents the string whose content is hashed using an MD5 hash algorithm. Typically, **szData** will be a password. All the objects created have destructors that must be called when finished.

Adding Digital Signatures with CryptoAPI

If you want to add a digital signature to your document, you will use the CryptoAPI hash functions. To sign and verify documents, you should create a hash object, hash the content (exactly as described previously for passwords), and call **CryptSignHash( )**. The following code fragment creates the hash, hashes the passed-in data, and then generates a signature, again within the **pBuf** variable:

```
CryptCreateHash(hProv, CALG_MD5, 0, 0, &hHash);
CryptHashData(hHash, szDocContent, sizeOfDoc);
CryptSignHash(hHash, AT_SIGNATURE, szDesc, 0, NULL, &dwSize);
pBuf = (LPBYTE) malloc(dwSize)
CryptSignHash(hHash, AT_SIGNATURE, szDesc, 0, pBuf, &dwSize);
```

In this example, **pBuf** contains the signature information that will typically end up in a separate file, and **szDesc** is a description string. Both concur with the authentication process governed by **CryptVerifySignature( )**. In addition, the **CryptSignHash( )** function requires a hashed version of the source file and the public signature key used to sign the file. This key is returned by **CryptGetUserKey( )** with the **AT_SIGNATURE** flag.

Adding CryptoAPI Support to Your MFC Programs

Clearly, the CryptoAPI provides powerful support for encryption. It quickly simplifies the adding of encryption support to your applications. For example, the companion CD-ROM contains a sample program called **CryptoNotes**. The application uses an MFC AppWizard-generated skeleton.

The core of **CryptoNotes** is inside its **CCryptoDoc** document class. **CCryptoDoc** is derived from **CDocument** and overrides two methods, **OnOpenDocument( )** and **OnSaveDocument( )**.

CDocument implements two methods (**OnOpenDocument( )** and **OnSaveDocument( )**) that are invoked after a user chooses a file to open or to save. Figure 7-11 shows how the **CCryptoDoc** class modifies the standard behavior of these methods.

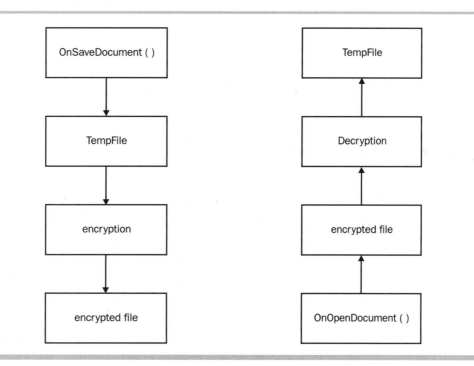

FIGURE 7-11.   The open and save processes performed by the CCryptoDoc document class

Clicking on the Open button in the application's toolbar and selecting an existing filename results in a call to **OnOpenDocument( )** with the specified filename as an

argument (the same happens for Save and Save As commands). All of the crucial processing for the **CryptoNotes** application occurs within the **CCryptoDoc** class, and that is the code we will consider here. However, because of space limitations and the prohibitive size of the class, we will consider only two implementations within the class—**OnSaveDocument( )** and **EncryptFile( )**.

▎PROGRAMMER'S NOTE   *Because of how the **<wincrypt.h>** header file is constructed in Visual C++ 6.0, you will be unable to compile the program correctly if you are not running Windows NT 4.0, without modification to the header file. The simplest adjustment to make in that situation is to comment out the operating system conditional test in the third line of the file. Make sure to comment out the **#endif** at the end of the file that closes that test.*

Code for the CCryptoDoc Class

CryptoNotes
CCryptoDoc
Here is the code for the **CCryptoDoc** class's **OnSaveDocument( )** and **EncryptFile( )** functions.

```cpp
// CryptoDoc.cpp : implementation of the CCryptoDoc class
#include "stdafx.h"
#include "CryptoDoc.h"
#include "PswdDlg.h"

#define TEMP    _T("c:\\temp.ctx")

BOOL CCryptoDoc::OnSaveDocument(LPCTSTR lpszPathName)
{
  // local data
  TCHAR szPswd[PSWD_MAXSIZE];
  BOOL b, bPswd;

  if(!m_bCryptoEnabled)
    return CDocument::OnSaveDocument(lpszPathName);

  CDocument::OnSaveDocument(TEMP);
  bPswd = GetPassword(lpszPathName, szPswd);
  b = EncryptFile(TEMP, lpszPathName,
      (bPswd ?szPswd :NULL));
  DeleteFile(TEMP);
  return b;
}


BOOL CCryptoDoc::EncryptFile(LPCTSTR szSource, LPCTSTR szTarget,
    LPCTSTR szPswd)
```

```
{
  // local data
  HCRYPTPROV hProv = NULL;
  HCRYPTKEY hKey = NULL, hXchgKey = NULL;
  HCRYPTHASH hHash = NULL;
  PBYTE pbKeyBlob = NULL, pbBuffer = NULL;
  DWORD dwKeyBlobLen, dwNumOfBytes, dwBlockLen = 1000;
  BOOL bResult = FALSE, bOkay = FALSE, bEof = FALSE;

  HFILE hSource = _lopen(szSource, OF_READ);
  if(hSource == HFILE_ERROR)
    return FALSE;

  HFILE hTarget = _lcreat(szTarget, 0);
  if(hTarget == HFILE_ERROR)
    goto exit;

  bOkay = CryptAcquireContext(&hProv, NULL, NULL,
      PROV_RSA_FULL, 0);
  if(!bOkay)
    goto exit;

  if(szPswd == NULL) {
    bOkay = CryptGenKey(hProv, ENCRYPT_ALGORITHM,
        CRYPT_EXPORTABLE, &hKey);
    if(!bOkay)
      goto exit;

    bOkay = CryptGetUserKey(hProv, AT_KEYEXCHANGE, &hXchgKey);
    if(!bOkay)
      goto exit;

    bOkay = CryptExportKey(hKey, hXchgKey, SIMPLEBLOB, 0,
        NULL, &dwKeyBlobLen);
    if(!bOkay)
      goto exit;

    pbKeyBlob = (PBYTE) malloc(dwKeyBlobLen);
    if(pbKeyBlob == NULL)
      goto exit;

    bOkay = CryptExportKey(hKey, hXchgKey, SIMPLEBLOB,
        0, pbKeyBlob, &dwKeyBlobLen);
    if(!bOkay)
```

```
      goto exit;

    CryptDestroyKey(hXchgKey);
    hXchgKey = NULL;

    INT iFileID = CTX_RANDOM_KEY;
    _hwrite(hTarget, (LPCSTR)&iFileID, sizeof(INT));

    dwNumOfBytes = _hwrite(hTarget, (LPCSTR)&dwKeyBlobLen,
        sizeof(DWORD));
    if(dwNumOfBytes != sizeof(DWORD))
      goto exit;

    // write the key blob itself
    dwNumOfBytes = _hwrite(hTarget, (LPCSTR)pbKeyBlob,
        dwKeyBlobLen);
    if(dwNumOfBytes != dwKeyBlobLen)
      goto exit;
}
else {
  bOkay = CryptCreateHash(hProv, CALG_MD5, 0, 0, &hHash);
  if(!bOkay)
    goto exit;

  bOkay = CryptHashData(hHash, (PBYTE) szPswd,
      lstrlen(szPswd), 0);
  if(!bOkay)
    goto exit;

  bOkay = CryptDeriveKey(hProv, ENCRYPT_ALGORITHM, hHash,
      0, &hKey);
  if(!bOkay)
    goto exit;

  CryptDestroyHash(hHash);
  hHash = NULL;
  INT iFileID = CTX_HASH_KEY;
  INT iPswdLen = lstrlen(szPswd);
  TCHAR szBuf[PSWD_MAXSIZE];
  lstrcpy(szBuf, szPswd);
  _hwrite(hTarget, (LPCSTR)&iFileID, sizeof(INT));
  _hwrite(hTarget, (LPCSTR)&iPswdLen, sizeof(INT));
  for(int i = 0; i < iPswdLen; i++)
    szBuf[i] = 255-szBuf[i];
```

```
    _hwrite(hTarget, szBuf, iPswdLen);
  }

  pbBuffer = (PBYTE) malloc(dwBlockLen);
  if(pbBuffer == NULL)
    goto exit;

  do {
    dwNumOfBytes = _hread(hSource, pbBuffer, dwBlockLen);
    if(dwNumOfBytes == HFILE_ERROR)
      goto exit;
    bEof = (dwNumOfBytes < dwBlockLen);
    bOkay = CryptEncrypt(hKey, NULL, bEof, 0, pbBuffer,
        &dwNumOfBytes, dwBlockLen);
    if(!bOkay)
      goto exit;
    DWORD dwWritten = _hwrite(hTarget, (LPCSTR)pbBuffer,
        dwNumOfBytes);
    if(dwWritten == HFILE_ERROR)
      goto exit;
  } while(!bEof);

  bResult = TRUE;

  // cleanup: files, keys and provider
exit:
  if(hSource)
    _lclose(hSource);
  if(hTarget)
    _lclose(hTarget);
  if(pbKeyBlob)
    free(pbKeyBlob);
  if(pbBuffer)
    free(pbBuffer);
  if(hKey)
    CryptDestroyKey(hKey);
  if(hXchgKey)
    CryptDestroyKey(hXchgKey);
  if(hHash)
    CryptDestroyHash(hHash);
  if(hProv)
    CryptReleaseContext(hProv, 0);
  return bResult;
}
```

ANNOTATIONS

Here are the annotations for the two described functions within the **CCryptoDoc** class; we'll start with **OnSaveDocument( )**.

```
BOOL CCryptoDoc::OnSaveDocument(LPCTSTR lpszPathName)
{
    TCHAR szPswd[PSWD_MAXSIZE];
    BOOL b, bPswd;

    if(!m_bCryptoEnabled)
        return CDocument::OnSaveDocument(lpszPathName);
```

The **OnSaveDocument( )** function accepts as its parameter a string indicating the path to the file. It then declares some local variables that it will use, and checks to see if cryptography has been enabled. If not, the program code exits the save document function immediately.

```
    CDocument::OnSaveDocument(TEMP);
    bPswd = GetPassword(lpszPathName, szPswd);
    b = EncryptFile(TEMP, lpszPathName, (bPswd ?szPswd :NULL));
    DeleteFile(TEMP);
    return b;
}
```

The program code then uses the **TEMP** constant to create a temporary file. If the user has specified that the file is to be saved with a password, the program obtains that password. It then passes all that information to the **EncryptFile( )** function, which generates the encrypted file. **OnSaveDocument( )** wraps up its processing by deleting the temporary file and returning to the program.

The **EncryptFile( )** function accepts as its parameters the source file, the target file, and an optional password. If a password is specified, it is used to generate the encryption key—otherwise the key is provided to the program by **CryptGenKey( )**.

Of course, an encrypted file must be decryptable, so you need to save the key somewhere. This is where the concept of a key blob finally comes into play. Once you determine the key, you make it exportable and store the key blob and its size at the beginning of the target file. With the Microsoft RSA Base Provider, the length of a key blob is 76 bytes. To make things easier, **CryptoNotes** simply adds a small header to .ctx files to denote whether they are encrypted with a password. The first four bytes are just a file ID (a **LONG** value) with so-called "magic" values.

If you save with a password, **EncryptFile( )** will create a hash object, encrypt the data, and then flush it to disk. Although it is necessary to make a random key persistent, in theory there is no need to store the password with the file data. A password is just a word—cryptic though it might be—and can be transmitted or remembered. A key, on the other hand, is just a sequence of bits, which is much

more difficult to keep in mind. For simplicity in the file format, the password is encrypted with a trivial **NOT** operator rather than with the CryptoAPI.

The member function **GetPassword( )** just examines the given file, returning the password, if any. **DecryptFile( )** loads the data from the source file. If a .ctx file is password-encrypted, then you need to check the password before decryption occurs. If you try to decipher with the wrong hash data, you'll simply obtain a pile of meaningless characters.

Let's take a look at the **EncryptFile( )** function. The header and local variables are shown here:

```
BOOL CCryptoDoc::EncryptFile(LPCTSTR szSource, LPCTSTR szTarget,
    LPCTSTR szPswd)
{
  HCRYPTPROV hProv = NULL;
  HCRYPTKEY hKey = NULL, hXchgKey = NULL;
  HCRYPTHASH hHash = NULL;
  PBYTE pbKeyBlob = NULL, pbBuffer = NULL;
  DWORD dwKeyBlobLen, dwNumOfBytes, dwBlockLen = 1000;
  BOOL bResult = FALSE, bOkay = FALSE, bEof = FALSE;
```

The function accepts parameters that reflect the name of the file to encrypt, the new name to save it with, and the password for the file, if the user selects one. The next few lines declare handles for the various cryptographic components, and then the last few lines define variables to hold encryption information and success values.

These next statements open two files: The source file contains the unencrypted text; the target file will hold the encrypted text. If either step fails, the function exits immediately.

```
HFILE hSource = _lopen(szSource, OF_READ);
if(hSource == HFILE_ERROR)
  return FALSE;
HFILE hTarget = _lcreat(szTarget, 0);
if(hTarget == HFILE_ERROR)
  goto exit;
```

Next, the program acquires a context to the RSA provider. The context is placed within the **hProv** handle, and the success value is placed within the **bOkay** local variable. If the context is not acquired successfully, the program exits.

```
bOkay = CryptAcquireContext(&hProv, NULL, NULL,
    PROV_RSA_FULL, 0);
if(!bOkay)
  goto exit;
```

The first **if** statement checks to see whether the user chose a password with which to save the file. If so, the routine falls through to the **else**, where the cryptographic

key is generated based on the password. If the user did not choose a password, the program simply creates a key at random based on the RSA algorithm.

```
if(szPswd == NULL) {
    bOkay = CryptGenKey(hProv, ENCRYPT_ALGORITHM,
        CRYPT_EXPORTABLE, &hKey);
    if(!bOkay)
      goto exit;
```

In these next few statements, the program creates a user key from the base key, and then determines how much space will be necessary to export that key into a key blob (remember, a "blob" is a Binary Large Object). Again, if any step is not successful, the program falls through to the function's exit routine.

```
    bOkay = CryptGetUserKey(hProv, AT_KEYEXCHANGE, &hXchgKey);
    if(!bOkay)
      goto exit;

    bOkay = CryptExportKey(hKey, hXchgKey, SIMPLEBLOB, 0,
        NULL, &dwKeyBlobLen);
    if(!bOkay)
      goto exit;
```

After determining the necessary size requirement in the previous call to **CryptExportKey( )**, the program allocates the space into the **pbKeyBlob** local variable and then exports the key blob into that variable.

```
pbKeyBlob = (PBYTE) malloc(dwKeyBlobLen);
    if(pbKeyBlob == NULL)
      goto exit;

    bOkay = CryptExportKey(hKey, hXchgKey, SIMPLEBLOB,
        0, pbKeyBlob, &dwKeyBlobLen);
    if(!bOkay)
      goto exit;
```

The program code next destroys the key it created to generate the user key and the key blob.

```
    CryptDestroyKey(hXchgKey);
    hXchgKey = NULL;
```

After all these steps are performed, the program is ready to encrypt and save the file.

The **CTX_RANDOM_KEY** constant indicates to the program that the key was generated at random—that is, without a password—so that, when the program reads the file back in, it knows whether to prompt the user for a password or use a non-password-based key blob. The program then writes the constant and the key blob's size to the beginning of the file.

```
INT iFileID = CTX_RANDOM_KEY;
_hwrite(hTarget, (LPCSTR)&iFileID, sizeof(INT));

dwNumOfBytes = _hwrite(hTarget, (LPCSTR)&dwKeyBlobLen,
    sizeof(DWORD));
if(dwNumOfBytes != sizeof(DWORD))
  goto exit;
```

After writing the constant and the key blob's size, the program writes the key blob itself to the file. It then falls through to the end of the function, where the actual writing of the encrypted text will be performed.

```
dwNumOfBytes = _hwrite(hTarget, (LPCSTR)pbKeyBlob,
    dwKeyBlobLen);
if(dwNumOfBytes != dwKeyBlobLen)
  goto exit;
}
```

As you saw earlier, if the user does enter a password, the program handles the encryption slightly differently. The **else** clause begins by creating a one-way hash into which it will hash the password. (Remember, a hash is a function that extracts a unique value from an entry.) The function to create a hash is shown here:

```
else {
  bOkay = CryptCreateHash(hProv, CALG_MD5, 0, 0, &hHash);
  if(!bOkay)
    goto exit;

  bOkay = CryptHashData(hHash, (PBYTE) szPswd,
      lstrlen(szPswd), 0);
  if(!bOkay)
    goto exit;
```

After creating the hash, the program uses the **CryptHashData( )** function to hash the password and store the result within the **hHash** handle. As with every other step in this function, failure causes the function to exit immediately.

```
  bOkay = CryptDeriveKey(hProv, ENCRYPT_ALGORITHM, hHash,
      0, &hKey);
 if(!bOkay)
   goto exit;
```

Unlike the **if** clause that you saw just above, the program here uses the **hHash** handle to create the key that it will use to encrypt the text—the **CryptDeriveKey( )** function derives a key from the hash value referenced by the handle.

```
  CryptDestroyHash(hHash);
  hHash = NULL;
  INT iFileID = CTX_HASH_KEY;
```

```
INT iPswdLen = lstrlen(szPswd);
TCHAR szBuf[PSWD_MAXSIZE];
lstrcpy(szBuf, szPswd);
_hwrite(hTarget, (LPCSTR)&iFileID, sizeof(INT));
_hwrite(hTarget, (LPCSTR)&iPswdLen, sizeof(INT));
```

Once again, the program does some cleanup, destroying the hash—it is no longer needed because the key has been derived. The program then uses the constant **CTX_HASH_KEY** to indicate to the program, when the **OnOpenDocument( )** function reads the file back in, that the key used to encrypt the text in the file was hashed from a password. After writing the constant, the output code writes an indicator into the file so that the program knows how many characters to read back in as the password.

```
for(int i = 0; i < iPswdLen; i++)
   szBuf[i] = 255-szBuf[i];
_hwrite(hTarget, szBuf, iPswdLen);
}
```

The **for** loop simply writes the password backwards into the file—it inverts the password within a 255 character string and writes the string into the file. Because the password in this example is saved as cleartext (for simplicity), writing the password in backwards and leading it with a bunch of garbage makes breaking the password more difficult. The program then falls through to the routine that actually writes the encrypted text to the file.

Next, the code allocates a buffer of 1,000 characters (the value of **dwBlockLen**), which it will then use to read and encrypt the file in groups. You can increase or decrease this buffer size as you want, but 1,000 is a relatively efficient number.

```
pbBuffer = (PBYTE) malloc(dwBlockLen);
if(pbBuffer == NULL)
   goto exit;
```

This next loop's actions are pretty straightforward—it reads the block in from the file, then uses the **CryptEncrypt( )** function to encrypt the file. It then writes out the now-encrypted block to the target file. At each step along the way, the program code checks for errors to ensure that nothing has gone wrong unexpectedly.

```
do {
    dwNumOfBytes = _hread(hSource, pbBuffer, dwBlockLen);
    if(dwNumOfBytes == HFILE_ERROR)
      goto exit;
    bEof = (dwNumOfBytes < dwBlockLen);
    bOkay = CryptEncrypt(hKey, NULL, bEof, 0, pbBuffer,
       &dwNumOfBytes, dwBlockLen);
    if(!bOkay)
      goto exit;
```

```
    DWORD dwWritten = _hwrite(hTarget, (LPCSTR)pbBuffer,
        dwNumOfBytes);
    if(dwWritten == HFILE_ERROR)
      goto exit;
    } while(!bEof);
```

If the program got to this point normally, everything went okay and it is now cleaning up its allocations. If the program got to this point because of a **goto** statement, **bResult** will be **False** and the program will simply clean up after itself before exiting the function.

```
    bResult = TRUE;

exit:
```

The next series of statements should be pretty obvious; each one checks to see whether a handle exists. If it does, the code performs the appropriate processing to clear the handle. In the case of the file handles, the program code closes the handle to the file.

```
    if(hSource)
      _lclose(hSource);
    if(hTarget)
      _lclose(hTarget);
    if(pbKeyBlob)
      free(pbKeyBlob);
    if(pbBuffer)
      free(pbBuffer);
    if(hKey)
      CryptDestroyKey(hKey);
    if(hXchgKey)
      CryptDestroyKey(hXchgKey);
    if(hHash)
      CryptDestroyHash(hHash);
    if(hProv)
      CryptReleaseContext(hProv, 0);
    return bResult;
}
```

When you save the file, the version you see within CryptoNotes will appear in plain text. However, if you use another program (such as Notepad) to view the file, it will look somewhat different. Figure 7-12 shows how a simple text file appears within CryptoNotes and Notepad.

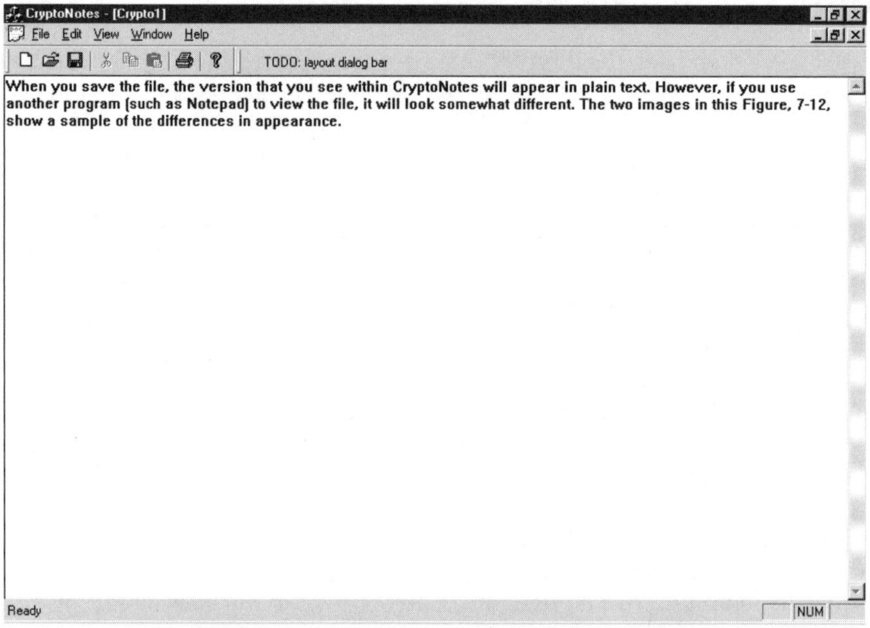

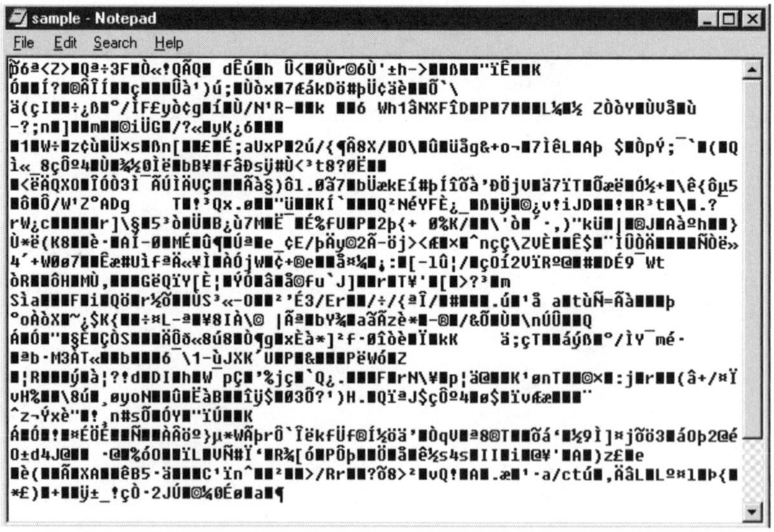

FIGURE 7-12. The encrypted file is unreadable by other programs unless they can process the key

Final Thoughts on CryptoNotes and Encryption

So, you have seen how the **CryptoNotes** program uses the Windows Encryption API to encrypt a file when saving it. The same strategy is behind the opening procedure. Once you select a filename for the saved file, the class flushes the archive to disk using a temporary filename. The actual encryption is performed in a successive step, which creates a valid .ctx file.

The temporary file, although useful, probably seems a bit clunky for actual implementations. Unfortunately, if you want to maintain the high-level interface to the MFC applications, you can't choose a different approach, primarily because of the file-based nature of the MFC serialization.

Aside from the **OnSaveDocument( )** method and **EncryptFile( )** member mentioned previously, the **CCryptoDoc** class exports two public methods called **OnOpenDocument( )** and **OnSaveDocumentWithPswd( )**. Additionally, there are two other protected members, **DecryptFile( )** and **GetPassword( )**.

The **CryptoNotes** program offers the standard MFC menu items plus a Save With Password command and an Options menu with a checked item called Encryption. This lets you enable or disable the cryptographic power of your application simply by calling **CCryptoDoc::EnableEncryption( )**. If this functionality is not active, then the overridden methods just pass the control down to the base class.

So, all this being said, what is the long and short of it? Each solution—stream, block, and public-key-based encryption—has its own benefits and limitations—meaning each is most appropriate and helpful in situations specific to its use. Before making a decision, you should carefully evaluate how you will use encryption in your programs. And don't feel tied to a single method within one program—multiple methods may be most effective for managing various features of the program.

Managing Source Code

By Mark Michaelis

Token.h	CodeMaintCPP.h
Token.cpp	CodeParser.h
Scanner.h	CodeParser.cpp
Scanner.cpp	SCodeMnt.cpp

The management of source code is one of the greatest challenges facing programmers today. As programs become longer and more complex, the need to organize and manage source code increases. In this chapter we will examine three utilities that will help you gain control over your source code. Before beginning, let's examine precisely what we mean by source code management.

In general, *source code management* involves two operations: analysis and manipulation. The analysis of the source code can yield useful information about the program that may not be readily apparent or easily obtained. For example, when files are shared among projects, it is difficult to track which files are dependent on others. A *source-code management utility* can examine a code file and extract a list of the additional files needed by the shared file. A sophisticated *maintenance program* can parse the source code and produce documentation that describes each class, its member variables, and functions.

Source code can be manipulated to conform to standardized styles, or to better display program flow. For example, a particular indentation format can facilitate code sharing among team members. Maintaining structured code amongst team members is extremely difficult and time-consuming because programmers must modify their individual styles. One programmer may insist that the curly bracket following an **if** statement appear on a new line, while another programmer may prefer appending the bracket to the same line as the **if** statement. A *source code formatter* offers a convenient solution to this problem.

In this chapter we design and write a source-code management program that scans code and outputs it to a slightly different format. The program performs three primary commands:

◆ The first command, **/include**, causes the program to scan through a C++ file and list all the filenames that have been included in the file being scanned.

◆ The second command, **/html**, generates a colorized version of the input file in HTML. After parsing the input file, HTML tags surrounding each token are written out to a new stream so that all the token types appear in unique colors within a browser.

◆ The **/ai** command indents the lines of the file according to rules defined for the language.

One of the most powerful features of the last two commands is that they are not limited to the C++ language. Although the modules in this chapter are specifically written to handle C++ code maintenance, they are generic enough to work with many programming languages with little modification.

Code Manager Program Design

Many tasks are shared between compiler front-ends and code maintenance modules. Both receive source code as input, break the code down into tokens, and then output

these tokens in a new format. The compiler output is machine code or p-code. The maintenance program's output depends on the specific task being performed by the module. In some ways, code management programs are like simplified versions of compilers. The management programs, however, lack the complexity of the code generator modules and generally do not have the performance demands commonly associated with compilers. Readers who are familiar with compiler concepts will easily understand the design of the code maintenance programs within this chapter. A basic outline of the code maintenance process is shown in Figure 8-1.

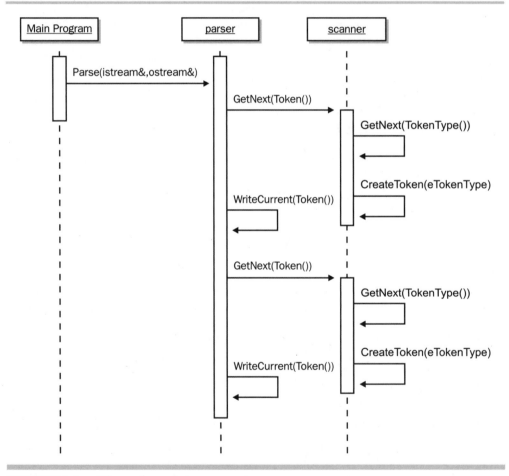

FIGURE 8-1. The code maintenance process

The most basic element of any programming language is called a *token*. Tokens are the smallest recognizable elements of a program; they comprise the building

blocks for creating meaningful statements. Compilers generally do not work with anything smaller than tokens. Comments, constants, identifiers, numbers, punctuation, and string literals are all examples of tokens. It is the job of the *scanner* to read the code, break it down into these basic elements, and return them back to the parser. In the process of breaking the code down, the scanner also identifies the type of token to return.

The *parser* requests successive tokens from the scanner and takes appropriate action before requesting the next token. In Figure 8-1, the action of the parser is to write out the token.

The source-code management utility developed in this chapter is based on three class groups: tokens, scanners, and parsers. Each group consists of a declaration file that defines the classes, and an implementation file that contains the code. We will examine each group separately; each group implements the functionality of the previous group, so they need to be understood in order.

The Token Classes

To facilitate adaptation to individual applications, the token class code has been implemented using one class for each token type. Although this increases the total amount of code, it allows users to adapt classes to their own requirements more easily. This object-oriented approach allows encapsulation of token-type-specific functionality and provides greater flexibility for future development.

Token.h

Code

The following code, file **Token.h,** shows the **CToken** class and all the subclasses that are derived from **CToken**.

```
// Token.h: Defines the different types of token classes
///////////////////////////////////////////////////////////////////

#if !defined(TOKEN_H_INCLUDED)
#define TOKEN_H_INCLUDED


// -------------------------------------------------
// Microsoft Idiosyncrasies.
// -------------------------------------------------
#if _MSC_VER > 1000
// disable warning C4786: symbol greater than 255 character,
// okay to ignore (MSVC)
#pragma warning(disable: 4786)
```

```
#pragma once
#endif // _MSC_VER > 1000


// -----------------------------------------------
// Library include files.
// -----------------------------------------------
#include <istream>
#include <string>
#include <set>
using namespace std;


// -----------------------------------------------
// Typedef declarations
// -----------------------------------------------
typedef set<string> TokenTextList;


// -----------------------------------------------
// Enum declarations
// -----------------------------------------------

// Each token is identified as a specific type.
enum ETokenType{
  // Token type has not been set
  eTokenTypeUnknown = 1,

  // End of file token
  eTokenTypeEOF,

  // End of line token
  eTokenTypeEOL,

  // A tab or space character.  Note that end of lines characters
  // have their own tokens.
  eTokenTypeWhiteSpace,

  // A string token
  eTokenTypeString,

  // A character string ('\n')
  eTokenTypeCharacter,

  // A number token
```

```
    eTokenTypeNumeric,

    // A comment
    eTokenTypeComment,

    // A specialized version of eTokenTypeComment which uses
    // '\n' as the comment end identifier by default.
    eTokenTypeEOLComment,

    // Any set of operations.  Note that operators and punctuation
    // are the same tokens (have the same value).
    eTokenTypePunctuation,
    eTokenTypeOperator = eTokenTypePunctuation,

    // A word token.  Usually this would be a variable or function.
    eTokenTypeWord,

    // Allows the statement to continue onto the next line
    // as if there was no new line.
    eTokenTypeStatementEnd,

    // Indicates that a statement is completed.
    // Note:
    // For some languages such as vb this is
    // a new line so it will never appear. For C++,
    // however, the ';' is used.
    eTokenTypeLineContinuation,

    // None of the above tokens
    eTokenTypeOther,

    // The number of token types. This is the minimum value
    // that can be used when defining a custom token.
    eTokenTypeCount
};

// ------------------------------------------------
// Miscellaneous constants
// ------------------------------------------------
#define EOL_CHARACTER '\n'

// The following characters could possibly appear within a number
// a, b, c, d, e, f are for hex, u is for unsigned, l is for long
// and i is for 64 bit.  e Could also be for exponential.
```

```
#define POSSIBLE_NUMERIC_CHARACTERS "0123456789abcdefxABCDEFXuUlLi."

////////////////////////////////////////////////////////////////
// CToken
////////////////////////////////////////////////////////////////
class CToken  : virtual public string
{

// ------------------------------------------------
// Constructor/Destructor
// ------------------------------------------------
public:
  CToken();
  CToken(int nType);
  virtual ~CToken();

// ------------------------------------------------
// Protected member variables
// ------------------------------------------------
protected:
  // The type of token.  Usually this is of type ETokenType.
  int m_nType;

// ------------------------------------------------
// Member variable access functions
// ------------------------------------------------
public:
  virtual int GetType() const
  {
    return m_nType;
  }

  virtual void SetType(const int m_nTokenType)
  {
    m_nType = m_nTokenType;
  }
  virtual string GetTokenText() const
  {
    return *this;
  }

  virtual void SetTokenText(const string sNewText)
  {
```

```
    this->assign(sNewText);
  }

  virtual void SetTokenText(const char cNewText)
  {
    this->erase() += cNewText;
  }


// -------------------------------------------------
// Helper functions
// -------------------------------------------------
protected:
  // Indicates that the character, c, is alpha or an underscore
  // Note: Visual C++ supports the built in function __iscsymf
  static int isalpha_(const char c)
  {
    return (isalpha(c) || c == '_');
  }


  // Note: Visual C++ supports the built-in function __iscsym
  static int isalnum_(const char c)
  {
    return (isalnum(c) || c == '_');
  }



  // Because istream.eof is only true after
  // looking at the end of file it is necessary
  // to peek before calling istream.eof.  The
  // following functions are sure to return the
  // correct values because they perform
  // the peek.
  static bool IsEOF(istream& input);
  static bool IsNotEOF(istream& input);

  // The following function clears the eof bit on the
  // input stream.  This is necessary when
  // checking the next character and encountering
  // and eof even though we don't want to make
  // any changes to the input stream.
  static void ClearEOF(istream& input);
```

```cpp
public:
  // The following functions check to see if the specified string
  // is what is currently being pointed to by istream's get()
  static bool IsSpecifiedString(
    // The input stream to check
    istream& input,
    // The string being checked
    const string sSearchFor);

  static bool IsSpecifiedString(istream& input,
    const char cSearchFor);

  // Move the istream get pointer to point to the character
  // that appears after sGet.  It is assumed that currently
  // the get pointer points to the beginning of a stream
  // equal to sGet.  If this is not the case false is
  // returned.
  static bool GetSpecifiedString(istream& input,
    const string sGet);
  static bool GetSpecifiedString(istream& input,
    const char cGet);

  // Returns true whether there are any more significant
  // tokens on the line.  Significant tokens are those
  // that are not white space.
  static bool IsOnlyWhiteSpaceLeft(istream& input);
  // Returns true if there are only comments or whitespace
  // tokens left on the line.
  static bool IsOnlyWhiteSpaceOrCommentsLeft(istream& input,
    const char* sBeginCommentIdentifier,
    const char* sEndCommentidentifier,
    const char* sBeginEOLCommentIdentifier);

};

///////////////////////////////////////////////////////////////
// EOFToken
///////////////////////////////////////////////////////////////
class CEOFToken : public CToken
{
// -----------------------------------------------
// Constructor/Destructor
// -----------------------------------------------
```

```cpp
public:
  CEOFToken(istream& input);


// ------------------------------------------------
// Identify functions
// ------------------------------------------------
public:
  static bool IsA(const string);
  static bool IsA(const char c);
  static bool IsA(istream& input);
};



//////////////////////////////////////////////////////////////////////
// CEOLToken
//////////////////////////////////////////////////////////////////////
class CEOLToken : public CToken
{
// ------------------------------------------------
// Constructor/Destructor
// ------------------------------------------------
public:
  CEOLToken(istream& input);
  // Constructs an EOL token without having
  // an input stream;
  CEOLToken();



// ------------------------------------------------
// Identify functions
// ------------------------------------------------
public:
  static bool IsA(const char c);
  static bool IsA(istream& input);
};



//////////////////////////////////////////////////////////////////////
// CWhiteSpaceToken
//////////////////////////////////////////////////////////////////////
class CWhiteSpaceToken : public CToken
{
// ------------------------------------------------
```

```
// Constructor/Destructor
// ------------------------------------------------
public:
  CWhiteSpaceToken(istream& input);


// ------------------------------------------------
// Identify functions
// ------------------------------------------------
public:
  static bool IsA(const char c);
  static bool IsA(const string);
  static bool IsA(istream& input);
};



//////////////////////////////////////////////////////////////////
// CStringToken
//////////////////////////////////////////////////////////////////
class CStringToken : public CToken
{
// ------------------------------------------------
// Constructor/Destructor
// ------------------------------------------------
public:

  // cEscapeCharacter is used to designate the escape character.
  // In C++ for example it would be '\'.  This is needed
  // in order to display the string identifier
  // within a string as in "Elisabeth said, \"Hi!\""
  CStringToken::CStringToken(istream& input,
    const char cStringIdentifier,
    const char cEscapeCharacter);
// ------------------------------------------------
// Protected member variables
// ------------------------------------------------
protected:
  char m_cEscapeCharacter;
  char m_cStringIdentifier;


// ------------------------------------------------
// Member variable access functions
// ------------------------------------------------
public:
```

```cpp
  // Note that these values could be NULL
  const char GetStringIdentifier()
    { return m_cStringIdentifier; }
  const char GetEscapeCharacter()
    { return m_cEscapeCharacter; }


// --------------------------------------------------
// Identify functions
// --------------------------------------------------
public:
  // Checks that the next token on the input stream
  // is a string.  Only the first character is
  // checked.
  static bool IsA(istream& input,
    const char cStringIdentifier,
    const char cEscapeCharacter);
};



//////////////////////////////////////////////////////////////////////////
// CCharacterToken
//////////////////////////////////////////////////////////////////////////
class CCharacterToken : public CStringToken
{
// --------------------------------------------------
// Constructor/Destructor
// --------------------------------------------------
public:

  // cEscapeCharacter is used to designate the escape character.  In
  // C++ for example it would be '\'.  This is needed
  // in order to display the character identifier
  // within a string as in '\''
  CCharacterToken::CCharacterToken(istream& input,
    const char cCharacterIdentifier,
    const char cEscapeCharacter);
  const char GetCharacterIdentifier()
    { return m_cStringIdentifier; }

};
```

```
////////////////////////////////////////////////////////////
// CNumericToken
////////////////////////////////////////////////////////////
class CNumericToken : public CToken
{
// -----------------------------------------------
// Constructor/Destructor
// -----------------------------------------------
public:
  // Note that the text is not checked to be a valid number
  // If something invalid like 0XX was used that
  // would still be considered a number.  Compilers
  // will, however, throw this out.
  CNumericToken::CNumericToken(istream& input);


// -----------------------------------------------
// Protected member variables
// -----------------------------------------------
protected:


// -----------------------------------------------
// Member variable access functions
// -----------------------------------------------
public:


// -----------------------------------------------
// Identify functions
// -----------------------------------------------
public:
  // Checks that the entire string sText is a number
  static bool IsA(const string sText);

  // Checks that the next token on the input stream
  // is a number.  Only the first character is
  // checked.
  static bool IsA(istream& input);
};



////////////////////////////////////////////////////////////
// CCommentToken
////////////////////////////////////////////////////////////
```

```cpp
class CCommentToken : public CToken
{
// --------------------------------------------------
// Constructor/Destructor
// --------------------------------------------------
public:
  CCommentToken(istream& input,
    const string sBeginCommentIdentifier,
    const string sEndCommentIdentifier);


// --------------------------------------------------
// Protected member variables
// --------------------------------------------------
protected:
  string m_sBeginCommentIdentifier;
  string m_sEndCommentIdentifier;


// --------------------------------------------------
// Member variable access functions
// --------------------------------------------------
public:
  const char* GetBeginCommentIdentifier()
    { return m_sBeginCommentIdentifier.c_str(); }
  const char* GetEndCommentIdentifier()
    { return m_sEndCommentIdentifier.c_str(); }
// --------------------------------------------------
// Identify functions
// --------------------------------------------------
public:
  // Returns true if the next token is a comment
  // identified by sBeginCommentIdentifier and
  // sEndCommentIdentifier.
  static bool IsA( istream& input,
    const string sBeginCommentIdentifier,
    const string sEndCommentIdentifier = "",
    // Check that the comment ends before the end of the file.
    const bool bCheckEnd = false);
};


//////////////////////////////////////////////////////////////////////
// CEOLCommentToken
//////////////////////////////////////////////////////////////////////
```

```
class CEOLCommentToken : public CCommentToken
{
// -------------------------------------------------
// Constructor/Destructor
// -------------------------------------------------
public:
  // Note that an end of line closes the
  // token even if there is a LineContinuation
  // character.  LineContinuations within comments,
  // therefore, are ignored.
  CEOLCommentToken(istream& input,
    const char* sBeginCommentIdentifier);


// -------------------------------------------------
// Identify functions
// -------------------------------------------------
public:
  // Checks that a comment is started.  It is assumed
  // that if there is no new line at the end then
  // the eof will signify the end so it is not necessary
  // to look for the end of line.
  static bool IsA( istream& input,
    const char* sBeginCommentIdentifier);
};



/////////////////////////////////////////////////////////////////////
// CPunctuationToken
/////////////////////////////////////////////////////////////////////
// Punctuation tokens are tokens that include
// any punctuation and operator tokens.  It
// should be understood, therefore, that the
// string, ">=" will be considered two
// punctuation tokens.
class CPunctuationToken : public CToken
{
// -------------------------------------------------
// Constructor/Destructor
// -------------------------------------------------
public:
  CPunctuationToken::CPunctuationToken(istream& input);

// -------------------------------------------------
```

```
// Identify functions
// -----------------------------------------------
public:
  // Returns true if the specified character is
  // considered an operator.
  static bool IsA(const char c);

  // Returns true if all characters in the string
  // are punctuation characters
  static bool IsA(const string sText);

  // Checks that the next token on the input stream
  // is an operator.
  static bool IsA(istream& input);
};


///////////////////////////////////////////////////////////////////
// CWordToken
///////////////////////////////////////////////////////////////////
class CWordToken : public CToken
{
// -------------------------------------------------
// Constructor/Destructor
// -------------------------------------------------
public:

  CWordToken::CWordToken(istream& input,
    // Indicates that an underscore, '_', is
    // allowable as the first character
    const bool bAllowPreUnderscore = true,
    const TokenTextList* pReservedWords = NULL);
// -------------------------------------------------
// Protected member variables
// -------------------------------------------------
protected:
  // A pointer to the list of reserved
  // words.
  const TokenTextList* m_pReservedWords;

  // Indicates that IsReservedWord has
  // already been called and m_bReservedWord
  // has therefore been set.  This means that
```

```
  // the next time IsReservedWord is called
  // the collection will not have to be
  // searched.
  bool m_bReserveWordChecked;
  bool m_bReservedWord;


// -----------------------------------------------
// Member variable access functions
// -----------------------------------------------
public:
  bool IsReservedWord();


// -----------------------------------------------
// Identify functions
// -----------------------------------------------
public:
  // Checks that the entire string sText is a word
  static bool IsA(const string sText,
    // Indicates that an underscore, '_', is
    // allowable as the first character
    const bool bAllowPreUnderscore = true);

  // Checks that the next token on the input stream
  // is a word.
  static bool IsA(istream& input,
    // Indicates that an underscore, '_', is
    // allowable as the first character
    const bool bAllowPreUnderscore = true);
};



/////////////////////////////////////////////////////////////////
// CLineContinuationToken
/////////////////////////////////////////////////////////////////
class CLineContinuationToken : public CToken
{
// -----------------------------------------------
// Constructor/Destructor
// -----------------------------------------------
public:
  CLineContinuationToken(istream& input,
    // In order to identify whether the next token is a line
    // continuation token it is necessary to also pass in the
```

```
     // set of characters that identifies a line continuation.
     const char* sLineContinuationIdentifier
     );

// --------------------------------------------------
// Protected member variables
// --------------------------------------------------
protected:
   string m_sLineContinuationIdentifier;

// --------------------------------------------------
// Member variable access functions
// --------------------------------------------------
public:
   const char* GetLineContinuationIdentifier()
     { return m_sLineContinuationIdentifier.c_str(); }

// --------------------------------------------------
// Identify functions
// --------------------------------------------------
public:
   static bool IsA(istream& input,
     const string sLineContinuationIdentifier);

};

///////////////////////////////////////////////////////////////////
// CStatementEndToken
///////////////////////////////////////////////////////////////////
class CStatementEndToken : public CToken
{
// --------------------------------------------------
// Constructor/Destructor
// --------------------------------------------------
public:

   CStatementEndToken(istream& input,
     const char cStatementEndIdentifier);

// --------------------------------------------------
// Protected member variables
// --------------------------------------------------
protected:
```

```
  const char m_cStatementEndIdentifier;

// ------------------------------------------------
// Member variable access functions
// ------------------------------------------------
public:
  const char GetStatementEndIdentifier()
    { return m_cStatementEndIdentifier; }

// ------------------------------------------------
// Identify functions
// ------------------------------------------------
public:
  static bool IsA(const char c, const char
    cStatementEndIdentifier);
  static bool IsA(istream& input, const char
    cStatementEndIdentifier);

};

//////////////////////////////////////////////////////////////////////
// COtherToken
//////////////////////////////////////////////////////////////////////
class COtherToken : public CToken
{
// ------------------------------------------------
// Constructor/Destructor
// ------------------------------------------------
public:

  COtherToken::COtherToken(istream& input);

// ------------------------------------------------
// Identify functions
// ------------------------------------------------
public:
  static bool IsA(istream& input);

};

#endif // !defined(TOKEN_H_INCLUDED)
```

ANNOTATIONS

The **CToken** class is the generic version of a token. **CToken** is a subclass of **std::string**; this allows it to behave in the same manner as a **std::string**, inheriting all **std::string** operators and functions. Figure 8-2 shows the token class hierarchy for **CToken**, **CCommentToken**, **CEOLCommentToken** and **CWhiteSpaceToken**.

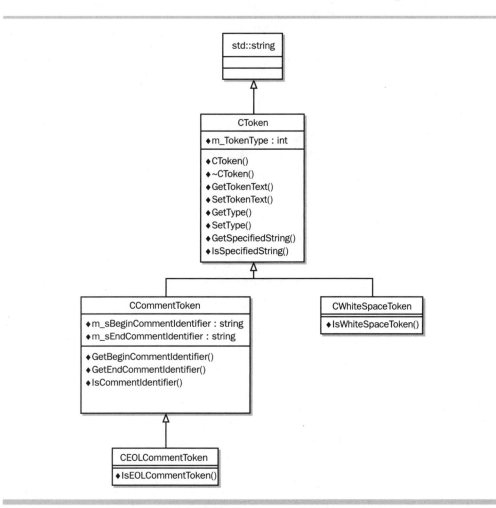

FIGURE 8-2. A sample of the CToken hierarchy

In addition to the three derived classes shown in Figure 8-2, there are several other subclasses of **CToken**. These subclasses are listed in Table 8-1.

Class Name	Class Description
CEOFToken	End of file
CEOLToken	End of line
CWhiteSpaceToken	White space (either a space or a tab character)
CEOLCommentToken	End of line comment
CCommentToken	Inline comment (for example: **/* my comment */**)
CStringToken	String literal (for example: **"this is a string"**)
CCharacterToken	Character literal (for example: **';'**)
CNumericToken	Any numeric value
CPunctuationToken	Punctuation (for example '**{**' and '**.**')
CWordToken	Any string of characters that does not fit any of the other categories defined in this table. Reserved words are a special type of **CWordToken**, but they do not have their own class. Variable and function names are types of **CWordToken** objects.
CLineContinuationToken	This token represents the characters that cause a statement to continue onto the next line (for example: "****")
CStatementEndToken	Signifies the end of the statement. For C++ this would be a semicolon. Other languages may not have such a character. Instead, a linefeed is assumed to indicate the end of the statement.

TABLE 8-1. Token Classes Derived from CToken

Take a look at some of the detail in **Token.h** and you will notice that each method within **CToken** is virtual; this allows any of the subclasses derived from **CToken** to override any of the methods. In addition, **CToken** is not a pure virtual class, so it can be used without ever having to implement one of the derived classes. It can be used to create custom tokens without necessarily creating an entirely new class. This allows the scanner to use the token for any language—even languages that do not use white space to separate the various tokens.

PROGRAMMER'S NOTE *Each token class identifies its objects with a specific **ETokenType** value that is stored in **m_nType**. To create a custom token from **CToken**, assign **m_nType** using **SetType(int m_nTokenType)**. To prevent a custom token from overlapping with existing token types, the custom token should have a type value greater than **eTokenTypeCount**.*

Each token implements two groups of functions:

◆ The **IsA( )** static functions identify the next token to be of the type specified. All tokens that are derived from **CToken** implement an **IsA( )** static function. This enables the scanner to call each token class to aid in identifying what type of token to create and return to the parser. For example, when the scanner checks whether the next token is the end-of-file token, it simply calls **CEOFToken::IsA( )**. This allows specific token functionality to remain local to the token.

◆ The second set of functions are the constructor functions for each token type class. With the exception of **CToken** and **CEOLToken**, no token class can be constructed without an **istream** parameter.

Token.cpp, listed next, shows the implementation of all the token classes.

Code

Token.cpp contains the implementation of the token classes.

Token.cpp

```
// Token.cpp: implementation of all the Token classes class.
///////////////////////////////////////////////////////////////

// ------------------------------------------------
// Local include files.
// ------------------------------------------------
#include "Token.h"


// ------------------------------------------------
// Library include files.
// ------------------------------------------------
#include <istream>
#include <cassert>
#include <string>
#include <vector>
#include <algorithm>


// ------------------------------------------------
// Debug macros
// ------------------------------------------------
#define SAVE_STATE( rdstateIn, rdstate ) int rdstateIn = rdstate
#define VALIDATE_STATE( rdstateIn, rdstate ) \
  assert( rdstateIn == rdstate )
```

```
//////////////////////////////////////////////////////////////////////
// CToken
//////////////////////////////////////////////////////////////////////
CToken::CToken()
  : m_nType(eTokenTypeUnknown)
{
}

CToken::CToken(int nType)
  : m_nType(nType)
{
}

CToken::~CToken()
{

}

bool CToken::IsEOF(istream& input)
{
  SAVE_STATE(rdstateIn, input.rdstate());

  bool bRet;

  // The state of the input flag when entering the function.
  bool bNotEOFIn = (input.eof() != 0);

  // Peek to trigger the eof if we are there
  // but we don't know it yet.
  input.peek();

  bRet = (input.eof() != 0);

  // If input.eof was set by peek
  // then unset it.  We try not to change
  // the input stream inside an IsA function.
  if( bRet && !bNotEOFIn)
    ClearEOF(input);

  // Check that input.eof is the same as
  // when entering the function.
  assert( bNotEOFIn == (input.eof() != 0) );
```

```
   VALIDATE_STATE(rdstateIn, input.rdstate());

   return bRet;
}

bool CToken::IsNotEOF(istream& input)
{
   return !IsEOF(input);
}

void CToken::ClearEOF(istream& input)
{
   // Clear the eof bit by taking it and "&" with the current
   // state to make sure we don't set it when it isn't
   // set and then "^" with current state to clear it if it
   // wasn't cleared.
   input.clear( (ios::eofbit & input.rdstate()) ^ input.rdstate() );
}

bool CToken::IsSpecifiedString(istream& input,
   const string sSearchFor)
{
   SAVE_STATE(rdstateIn, input.rdstate());
   // Iterator for each character removed from stream
   char c;
   bool bRet;
   long nIncomingStreamPosition = input.tellg();

   bRet = IsNotEOF(input);

   //  Move forward in the stream getting
   //  each character that matches
   for (int i = 0; (bRet && (i < sSearchFor.length())
      && IsNotEOF(input) ); i++ )
   {
      c = input.get();
      bRet = ( sSearchFor[i] == c);
   }

   input.seekg(nIncomingStreamPosition, ios::beg );

   // Check that we didn't move the get pointer.
   assert( nIncomingStreamPosition == input.tellg() );
```

```
    VALIDATE_STATE(rdstateIn, input.rdstate());

    return bRet;
}

bool CToken::IsSpecifiedString(istream& input,
 const char cSearchFor)
{
   bool bRet = false;

   SAVE_STATE(rdstateIn, input.rdstate());

   // First check for EOF.  Although bRet will
   // return the same value either way IsNotEOF
   // will not change the state of the input stream
   if( IsNotEOF(input) )
     bRet = (input.peek() == cSearchFor);

   VALIDATE_STATE(rdstateIn, input.rdstate());

   return bRet;
}

bool CToken::GetSpecifiedString(istream& input, const char cGet)
{
   SAVE_STATE(rdstateIn, input.rdstate());

   bool bRet = false;

   if(IsSpecifiedString(input, cGet))
   {
     input.get();
     bRet = true;
   }

   VALIDATE_STATE(rdstateIn, input.rdstate());

   return bRet;
}

bool CToken::GetSpecifiedString(istream& input, const string sGet)
{
```

```
  SAVE_STATE(rdstateIn, input.rdstate());

  long nIncomingStreamPosition = input.tellg();
  bool bRet;

  bRet = IsSpecifiedString(input, sGet);

  if (bRet)
    input.seekg( nIncomingStreamPosition + sGet.length() );

  VALIDATE_STATE(rdstateIn, input.rdstate());

  return bRet;
}

// Verify that there is only white space left on the line.
bool CToken::IsOnlyWhiteSpaceLeft(istream& input)
{
  SAVE_STATE(rdstateIn, input.rdstate());

  // Iterator for each character removed from stream
  char c;
  bool bNotEOF;

  // Save the position of the get pointer so
  // we can return to it
  // when the function completes.
  long nIncomingStreamPosition = input.tellg();

  bool bRet = false;

  while( (bNotEOF = IsNotEOF(input))
    && CWhiteSpaceToken::IsA(c = input.get()) );

  if(bNotEOF)
    // Put back the last character retrieved.
    input.putback(c);

  // After moving past all the white space we now
  // check that the next token is an EOL token.
  bRet = CEOLToken::IsA(input);
```

```
      // Everything checks out move back to the
      // position after the line continuation token
      input.seekg(nIncomingStreamPosition);

      VALIDATE_STATE(rdstateIn, input.rdstate());

      return bRet;
}

// Verifies that only white space or comments are left on
// the remaining part of the current line.
bool CToken::IsOnlyWhiteSpaceOrCommentsLeft(istream& input,
   const char* sBeginCommentIdentifier,
   const char* sEndCommentidentifier,
   const char* sBeginEOLCommentIdentifier)
{
   SAVE_STATE(rdstateIn, input.rdstate());
   bool bRet = true;

   // Save the position of the get pointer so
   // we can return to it
   // when the function completes.
   long nIncomingStreamPosition = input.tellg();

   string();
   while(bRet && IsNotEOF(input) && !CEOLToken::IsA(input))
   {
      if( CWhiteSpaceToken::IsA(input) )
         CWhiteSpaceToken::CWhiteSpaceToken(input);
      else if ( CCommentToken::IsA(input, sBeginCommentIdentifier) )
         CCommentToken::CCommentToken(input,
            sBeginCommentIdentifier, sEndCommentidentifier);
      else if ( CEOLCommentToken::IsA(input,
         sBeginEOLCommentIdentifier) )
         CEOLCommentToken::CEOLCommentToken(input,
            sBeginEOLCommentIdentifier);
      else
         bRet = false;
   }

   // Everything checks out move back to the
   // position after the line continuation token
```

```
  input.seekg(nIncomingStreamPosition);

  assert( nIncomingStreamPosition == input.tellg() );

  VALIDATE_STATE(rdstateIn, input.rdstate());

  return bRet;
}


//////////////////////////////////////////////////////////////////
// EOFToken
//////////////////////////////////////////////////////////////////
CEOFToken::CEOFToken(istream& input)
  // Initialize member variables.
  : CToken(eTokenTypeEOF)
{
  // Iterator for each character removed from stream
  char c;

  // Remove the token from the stream and set
  // m_sTokenText to be the characters removed.
  assert( CEOFToken::IsA(input) );

  // Note that the following get will change the state of
  // the file to fail and eof.
  c = input.get();

  SetTokenText(c);
}

bool CEOFToken::IsA(istream& input)
{
  return CToken::IsEOF(input);
}


//////////////////////////////////////////////////////////////////
// CEOLToken
//////////////////////////////////////////////////////////////////
CEOLToken::CEOLToken()
  // Initialize member variables.
```

```
    : CToken(eTokenTypeEOL)
{
  SetTokenText(EOL_CHARACTER);
}

CEOLToken::CEOLToken(istream& input)
  // Initialize member variables.
  : CToken(eTokenTypeEOL)
{
  // Iterator for each character removed from stream
  char c;

  c = input.get();

  assert( CEOLToken::IsA(c) );

  SetTokenText(c);
}

bool CEOLToken::IsA(const char c)
{
  return ( (c == EOL_CHARACTER) );
}

bool CEOLToken::IsA(istream& input)
{
  return ( IsSpecifiedString(input, EOL_CHARACTER) );
}


///////////////////////////////////////////////////////////////////////
// CWhiteSpaceToken
///////////////////////////////////////////////////////////////////////
CWhiteSpaceToken::CWhiteSpaceToken(istream& input)
  // Initialize member variables.
  : CToken(eTokenTypeWhiteSpace)
{
  SAVE_STATE(rdstateIn, input.rdstate());

  // Iterator for each character removed from stream
  char c;
```

```
  bool bNotEOF;
  string sTokenText;

  // Remove whitespace characters from the stream and set
  // m_sTokenText to be the whitespace characters removed.
  while( (bNotEOF = IsNotEOF(input)) && IsA(c = input.get()))
  {
    sTokenText += c;
  }

  if(bNotEOF)
    // Put back the last character.
    input.putback(c);

  assert( CWhiteSpaceToken::IsA(sTokenText) );

  SetTokenText(sTokenText);

  VALIDATE_STATE(rdstateIn, input.rdstate());
}

bool CWhiteSpaceToken::IsA(const char c)
{
  return( !CEOLToken::IsA(c) &&
      ((isspace(c)!= 0)|| (c==0))
    );
}

bool CWhiteSpaceToken::IsA(const string sText)
{
  bool bRet = !sText.empty();

  string::const_iterator c;

  for(c = sText.begin(); ( bRet && (c != sText.end()) ); c++)
    bRet = IsA(*c);

  return bRet;
}

bool CWhiteSpaceToken::IsA(istream& input)
{
```

```
  if( IsNotEOF(input) )
    return CWhiteSpaceToken::IsA(input.peek());
  else
    return false;
}


///////////////////////////////////////////////////////////////
// CStringToken
///////////////////////////////////////////////////////////////
CStringToken::CStringToken(istream& input,
    const char cStringIdentifier,
    const char cEscapeCharacter)
  // Initialize member variables.
  : CToken(eTokenTypeString),
  m_cStringIdentifier(cStringIdentifier),
  m_cEscapeCharacter(cEscapeCharacter)
{
  SAVE_STATE(rdstateIn, input.rdstate());

  // Iterator for each character removed from stream
  char c;

  bool bStringEnded = false;
  string sTokenText;

  assert(IsSpecifiedString(input, cStringIdentifier));

  GetSpecifiedString(input, cStringIdentifier);

  sTokenText += cStringIdentifier;

  while( IsNotEOF(input) &&
    !(bStringEnded = IsSpecifiedString(input, cStringIdentifier)) )
  {
    c = input.get();
    if ((c == cEscapeCharacter) && IsNotEOF(input))
    {
      sTokenText += c;
      c = input.get();
    }
    sTokenText += c;
  }
```

```cpp
    // It is not guaranteed that the string ended before
    // the end of the file.  If so we add it to the token.
    if ( GetSpecifiedString(input, cStringIdentifier) )
      // Add the StringIdentifier to the string token
      sTokenText += cStringIdentifier;

  SetTokenText(sTokenText);

  VALIDATE_STATE(rdstateIn, input.rdstate());
}

bool CStringToken::IsA(istream& input,
  const char cStringIdentifier,
  const char cEscapeCharacter)
{
  SAVE_STATE(rdstateIn, input.rdstate());

  bool bRet;
  long nIncomingStreamPosition = input.tellg();

  // Check that the next character is a string token
  bRet = IsSpecifiedString(input, cStringIdentifier);

  // Check that the previous character was not an escape character
  // This is necessary because we could currently be looking at
  // a character '\"' for example.
  if(bRet)
  {
    // Move to examine the previous character
    input.seekg(-1, ios::cur);
    bRet = !IsSpecifiedString(input, cEscapeCharacter);
    // Move back to the starting place.
    input.seekg(nIncomingStreamPosition, ios::beg);

    assert(nIncomingStreamPosition == input.tellg());
  }

  VALIDATE_STATE(rdstateIn, input.rdstate());

  return bRet;
}
```

```
/////////////////////////////////////////////////////////////////
// CCharacterToken
/////////////////////////////////////////////////////////////////
CCharacterToken::CCharacterToken(istream& input,
  const char cCharacterIdentifier,
  const char cEscapeCharacter)
  : CStringToken(input, cCharacterIdentifier, cEscapeCharacter)
{
  m_nType = eTokenTypeCharacter;
}



/////////////////////////////////////////////////////////////////
// CNumericToken
/////////////////////////////////////////////////////////////////
CNumericToken::CNumericToken(istream& input)
  : CToken(eTokenTypeNumeric)
{
  SAVE_STATE(rdstateIn, input.rdstate());

  // A string of all the possible characters that
  // could appear within a number.
  static string sPossibleNumericCharacters
    = POSSIBLE_NUMERIC_CHARACTERS;

  // Iterator for each character removed from stream
  char c;
  bool bNotEOF;
  string sTokenText;

  // Continue extracting characters flag.
  bool bCont;

  assert(IsNotEOF(input));

  // Verify that the first character is a digit
  c = input.get();
  assert(isdigit(c) || (c == '.'));

  // Now we are sure we have a number in some form

  bCont = true;
```

```
  while (bCont)
  {
    sTokenText += c;
    bCont = (bNotEOF = IsNotEOF(input));

    bCont =
      // We have not reached the end of the file. AND
      IsNotEOF(input) &&
      (
        // The character is a digit OR
        (isdigit(c = input.get()) != 0) ||
        // The character is a possible numeric character OR
        (sPossibleNumericCharacters.find(c)
          != string::npos) ||
        // The character is '+' or '-' and there are digits after
        ( ((c == '+') || (c == '-'))
          && IsNotEOF(input)
          && (isdigit((input.peek()))!=0)
        )
      );
  }

  if(bNotEOF)
    // Return the last character to the stream
    input.putback(c);

  SetTokenText(sTokenText);

  VALIDATE_STATE(rdstateIn, input.rdstate());
}

// Check that the next character is a digit
// or a period, '.', and then a digit
bool CNumericToken::IsA( istream& input)
{
  SAVE_STATE(rdstateIn, input.rdstate());

  // Iterator for each character removed from stream
  char c;
  bool bRet = false;

  if (IsEOF(input))
```

```
    bRet = false;
  else if( isdigit(input.peek()) != 0 )
    bRet = true;
  else if(input.peek() == '.')
  {
    // look at the next character
    c = input.get();
    if ( IsNotEOF(input) )
      bRet = ( isdigit(input.peek()) != 0 );

    // Return the last character to the stream
    input.putback(c);
  }

  VALIDATE_STATE(rdstateIn, input.rdstate());

  return bRet;
}


//////////////////////////////////////////////////////////////////
// CCommentToken
//////////////////////////////////////////////////////////////////
CCommentToken::CCommentToken(istream& input,
    const string sBeginCommentIdentifier,
    const string sEndCommentIdentifier)
  // Initialize member variables.
  : CToken(eTokenTypeComment),
  m_sBeginCommentIdentifier(sBeginCommentIdentifier),
  m_sEndCommentIdentifier(sEndCommentIdentifier)
{
  SAVE_STATE(rdstateIn, input.rdstate());

  bool bNotEOF;
  string sTokenText;

  assert ( !sBeginCommentIdentifier.empty() );
  assert ( !sEndCommentIdentifier.empty() );

  // verify that the sBeginCommentIdentifier text is next
  // on the stream
  assert( IsSpecifiedString(input, sBeginCommentIdentifier));
```

```
    GetSpecifiedString(input, sBeginCommentIdentifier);

    sTokenText += sBeginCommentIdentifier;

    while( (bNotEOF = IsNotEOF(input))
       && !IsSpecifiedString(input, sEndCommentIdentifier) )
    {
      sTokenText += input.get();
    }

    // It is possible that the comment didn't end before the
    // end of the file.  If, however, this isn't the case
    // then add the EndCommentIdentifier to the token.
    if (bNotEOF)
    {
      assert( IsSpecifiedString(input, sEndCommentIdentifier) );
      GetSpecifiedString(input, sEndCommentIdentifier);
      sTokenText += sEndCommentIdentifier;
    }

    SetTokenText(sTokenText);

    VALIDATE_STATE(rdstateIn, input.rdstate());
}

bool CCommentToken::IsA( istream& input,
    const string sBeginCommentIdentifier,
    const string sEndCommentIdentifier,
    const bool bCheckEnd )
{
  SAVE_STATE(rdstateIn, input.rdstate());

  bool bRet = false;
  long nIncomingStreamPosition;

  assert (!sBeginCommentIdentifier.empty() );

  if (!bCheckEnd || (sEndCommentIdentifier.length() == 0))
    bRet = IsSpecifiedString(input, sBeginCommentIdentifier);
  else
  {
    nIncomingStreamPosition = input.tellg();
```

```
    bRet = GetSpecifiedString(input, sBeginCommentIdentifier);

    if (bRet)
      while(IsNotEOF(input) &&
        !(bRet = IsSpecifiedString(input, sEndCommentIdentifier)) )
      {
        input.get();
      }

    // Return to the starting position on the input stream.
    input.seekg(nIncomingStreamPosition, ios::beg);
  }

  VALIDATE_STATE(rdstateIn, input.rdstate());

  return bRet;
}


///////////////////////////////////////////////////////////////////
// CEOLCommentToken
///////////////////////////////////////////////////////////////////
CEOLCommentToken::CEOLCommentToken(istream& input,
    const char* sBeginCommentIdentifier)
  // Initialize member variables.
  : CCommentToken(input, sBeginCommentIdentifier, "\n")
{
  // The CCommentToken sets the type to ETokenTypeComment
  // so we need to reset it to eTokenTypeEOLComment.
  m_nType = eTokenTypeEOLComment;

  // Remove the '\n' from the end.  With EOLComments
  // the end of line will be included as a new EOL
  // token rather than part of the EOL comment.
  SetTokenText(GetTokenText().substr(0, length()-1));
}

bool CEOLCommentToken::IsA( istream& input,
    const char* sBeginCommentIdentifier)
{
  return CCommentToken::IsA(input, sBeginCommentIdentifier, "\n");
```

```
}

//////////////////////////////////////////////////////////////////
// CPunctuationToken
//////////////////////////////////////////////////////////////////
CPunctuationToken::CPunctuationToken(istream& input)
  // Initialize member variables.
  : CToken(eTokenTypePunctuation)
{
  SAVE_STATE(rdstateIn, input.rdstate());

  // Iterator for each character removed from stream
  char c;

  // Remove the token from the stream and set
  // m_sTokenText to be the character removed.
  if(IsNotEOF(input))
    c = input.get();

  assert( CPunctuationToken::IsA(c) );

  SetTokenText(c);

  VALIDATE_STATE(rdstateIn, input.rdstate());
}

bool CPunctuationToken::IsA(const char c)
{
  return (ispunct(c) != 0);
}

// Verify all characters in the string are punctuation characters.
bool CPunctuationToken::IsA(const string sText)
{
  bool bRet = !sText.empty();
  string::const_iterator c;

  for( c = sText.begin(); ( bRet && (c != sText.end()) ); c++)
    bRet = (CPunctuationToken::IsA(*c));

  return bRet;
```

```
}

// All that needs to be checked in this function
// is the first character.  Even if only the first character
// is valid for a word then the token is a word.
bool CPunctuationToken::IsA(istream& input)
{
  if(IsNotEOF(input))
    return CPunctuationToken::IsA(input.peek());
  else
    return false;
}



/////////////////////////////////////////////////////////////////////
// CWordToken
/////////////////////////////////////////////////////////////////////
// The following CWordToken constructor
// creates a token with all the characters
// that are separated by whitespace.  This
// includes punctuation and operator characters
// In the future the constructor could become more
// specialized.
CWordToken::CWordToken(istream& input,
  const bool bAllowPreUnderscore,
  const TokenTextList* pReservedWords)
  // Initialize member variables.
  : CToken(eTokenTypeWord),
  m_bReserveWordChecked(false),
  m_pReservedWords(pReservedWords)
{
  SAVE_STATE(rdstateIn, input.rdstate());

  // Iterator for each character removed from stream
  char c;
  bool bNotEOF;
  string sTokenText;

  assert(IsNotEOF(input));

  // Get the first character in the word.
  c = input.peek();
```

```
  // Verify that the character is a valid initial
  // word character
  if(bAllowPreUnderscore)
    assert(isalpha_(c));
  else
    assert(isalpha(c));

  // Remove the token from the stream and set
  // m_sTokenText to be the characters removed.
  while ((bNotEOF = IsNotEOF(input))
    && isalnum_(c = input.get()) != 0)
  {
    sTokenText += c;
  }

  if(bNotEOF)
    // Put back the additional character retrieved.
    input.putback(c);

  assert( CWordToken::IsA(sTokenText, bAllowPreUnderscore) );

  SetTokenText(sTokenText);

  VALIDATE_STATE(rdstateIn, input.rdstate());
}

bool CWordToken::IsReservedWord()
{
  if (m_bReserveWordChecked)
    return m_bReservedWord;
  else
    m_pReservedWords->find(GetTokenText());

  m_bReserveWordChecked = true;

  return m_bReservedWord;
}
bool CWordToken::IsA(const string sText,
    const bool bAllowPreUnderscore)
{
  bool bRet = !sText.empty();
```

```
  string::const_iterator c;

  if ( bRet && bAllowPreUnderscore )
    bRet = (isalpha_(sText[0]) != 0);

  for(c = sText.begin(); bRet, c != sText.end(); c++)
    bRet = (isalnum_(*c) != 0);

  return bRet;
}


// All that needs to be checked in this function
// is the first character.  Even if only the first character
// is valid for a word then the token is a word.
bool CWordToken::IsA(istream& input,
  const bool bAllowPreUnderscore )
{
  bool bRet = IsNotEOF(input);
  if(bRet)
  {
  if ( bAllowPreUnderscore )
    bRet = (isalpha_(input.peek()) != 0);
  else
    bRet = (isalnum_(input.peek()) != 0);
  }
  return bRet;
}



//////////////////////////////////////////////////////////////////
// CLineContinuationToken
//////////////////////////////////////////////////////////////////
CLineContinuationToken::CLineContinuationToken(istream& input,
  // In order to identify whether the next token is a line
  // continuation token it is necessary to also pass in the
  // character that identifies a line continuation.
  const char* sLineContinuationIdentifier
  )
  // Initialize member variables.
  : CToken(eTokenTypeLineContinuation),
  m_sLineContinuationIdentifier(sLineContinuationIdentifier)
{
```

```
    SAVE_STATE(rdstateIn, input.rdstate());

  GetSpecifiedString(input, sLineContinuationIdentifier);

  // Verify that there is only white space left on the line.
  assert( IsOnlyWhiteSpaceLeft(input) );

  SetTokenText(sLineContinuationIdentifier);

  VALIDATE_STATE(rdstateIn, input.rdstate());
}


bool CLineContinuationToken::IsA(istream& input,
    const string sLineContinuationIdentifier)
{
  SAVE_STATE(rdstateIn, input.rdstate());
  bool bRet;

  // Save the position of the get pointer so
  // we can return to it
  // when the function completes.
  long nIncomingStreamPosition = input.tellg();

  bRet = GetSpecifiedString(input, sLineContinuationIdentifier);
  bRet = bRet && IsOnlyWhiteSpaceLeft(input);

  input.seekg(nIncomingStreamPosition);

  VALIDATE_STATE(rdstateIn, input.rdstate());

  return bRet;
}


/////////////////////////////////////////////////////////////////////
// CStatementEndToken
/////////////////////////////////////////////////////////////////////
CStatementEndToken::CStatementEndToken(istream& input,
  const char cStatementEndIdentifier)
  // Initialize member variables.
  : CToken(eTokenTypeStatementEnd),
```

```
    m_cStatementEndIdentifier(cStatementEndIdentifier)
{

  // Check that the cStatementEndIdentifier is next on the stream
  assert( IsSpecifiedString(input, cStatementEndIdentifier) );

  // Get cStatementEndIdentifier from the stream;
  GetSpecifiedString(input, cStatementEndIdentifier);

  SetTokenText(cStatementEndIdentifier);
}

bool CStatementEndToken::IsA(const char c,
  const char cStatementEndIdentifier)
{
  return (c == cStatementEndIdentifier);
}

bool CStatementEndToken::IsA(istream& input,
  const char cStatementEndIdentifier)
{
  return IsSpecifiedString(input, cStatementEndIdentifier);
}


//////////////////////////////////////////////////////////////////
// COtherToken
//////////////////////////////////////////////////////////////////
// A token that doesn't fit with any of the
// other tokens.
COtherToken::COtherToken(istream& input)
  // Initialize member variables.
  : CToken(eTokenTypeOther)
{
  SAVE_STATE(rdstateIn, input.rdstate());

  // Iterator for each character removed from stream
  char c;
  bool bNotEOF;

  string sTokenText;
```

```
  // Get the first character in the word.

  // Remove the token from the stream and set
  // m_sTokenText to be the characters removed.
  while ( (bNotEOF = IsNotEOF(input)) && IsA(input))
  {
    c = input.get();
    sTokenText += c;
  }

  if(bNotEOF)
    // Put back the additional character retrieved.
    input.putback(c);

  SetTokenText(sTokenText);

  VALIDATE_STATE(rdstateIn, input.rdstate());
}


// A token that doesn't fit with any of the
// other tokens.  Because many of the functions
// that check for a particular type
// of token also require additional parameters
// these tokens cannot be checked.
bool COtherToken::IsA(istream& input)
{
  SAVE_STATE(rdstateIn, input.rdstate());

  bool bRet;

  if (CEOFToken::IsA(input)
    || CEOLToken::IsA(input)
    || CWhiteSpaceToken::IsA(input)
    )
    bRet = false;
  else
    bRet = true;

  VALIDATE_STATE(rdstateIn, input.rdstate());

  return bRet;
}
```

ANNOTATIONS

To better understand how the token classes work, let us take a look at **CNumericToken** and **CCommentToken**.

The **CNumericToken::IsA(istream& input)** function examines the next two characters that are on the input stream. If the first character is a digit, the function identifies the token as a number and returns **true**. If the first character is a period (**.**), then the function checks to see whether the next character is a digit.

As with most of the **IsA( )** functions, **CNumericToken::IsA( )** does not check that the entire number is valid. For example, the string **"0.9.9ee8.e"** when appearing on the input stream would be considered a number even though the compiler would report an error for this token. In general, the **IsA( )** functions only classify the token type to its closest match. They do not check for certainty that the items are of a particular type. Rigorous error-detection is generally left to the compiler. Although identifying the token type may not make an exact match, the functions are written so that if the **IsA( )** function returned **true** you could successfully instantiate a token of that class. For example, if **CNumerictoken::IsA(istreaminput)** returns true, then **CToken token = CNumericToken::CNumericToken(input)** will successfully create a **CNumericToken**.

Note that all the **IsA( )**functions are static. This allows them to be accessed by other classes without having to instantiate any tokens before necessary.

One of the idiosyncrasies with **istream** is that calling **peek( )** or **get( )** on the last character of the file causes the **istream::eof( )** to return **true**. Unfortunately, however, once you have read the **eof** character, you can no longer traverse to a different position in the file and so **istream::seekg( )** will fail. If the next character to be retrieved from **istream** is an **eof** character, but no function has been called to actually check the character's value, then **istream::eof( )** will return **false**. In effect, this causes a catch-22: to know that you have reached the end of the file, you have to read the **eof** character, but in so doing the file can no longer be traversed.

CToken::IsEOF( ) and its twin, **CToken::IsNotEOF( )**, are designed to implement safe checking for end-of-file. These functions identify when the program is at the end of the file, and resets the **istream::eof** value back to **false** if the end-of-file is encountered. In other words, the **IsEOF( )** function performs a **peek( )** on the input stream. If it triggers an end-of-file, then it resets the **eof** flag and moves the **istream** back to the last character on the stream.

The constructors for the tokens are similar to the **IsA( )** functions, except the constructors assume that the next token is of the type being requested and they proceed to remove the token from the stream. Most of the constructors will assert an error if, for some reason, the token was not of the expected type. Let's examine the details of a token constructor by looking at **CCommentToken::CCommentToken( )**.

Unlike the majority of the other token constructors, **CCommentToken** requires two additional parameters. These two strings identify the beginning and end of a comment. If the token classes were not written to support multiple languages, then these values could just be hard-coded to the values required by C++ ("/*" and "*/"). After verifying that **sBeginCommentIdentifier** is not empty, the function then removes from the **istream** all the characters until the end of the comment is reached.

In order to remove specific characters from the **istream**, the function

`CToken::GetSpecifiedString(istream& input, const string sGet)`

is called. This verifies that the **sGet** is indeed the next set of characters on the stream, and then it moves the **istream**'s next pointer **(istream::tellg( ))** to be the character just past **sGet**.

Now that we have taken a look at the token classes, let's examine the scanner class to see how the token classes are used.

The Scanner Class, CScanner

The **CScanner** class is used to identify which token is next on the **istream**, and then to instantiate this token and pass it back to the parser. The class is implemented as a subclass of **istream**.

Scanner.h

Code

Below is a listing of the declaration for the **CScanner** class.

```
// Scanner.h: interface for the CScanner class.
////////////////////////////////////////////////////////////////

#if !defined(SCANNER_H_INCLUDED)
#define SCANNER_H_INCLUDED


// -----------------------------------------------
// Microsoft Idiosyncrasies.
// -----------------------------------------------
#if _MSC_VER > 1000
// disable warning C4786: symbol greater than 255 character,
// okay to ignore (MSVC)
#pragma warning(disable: 4786)
#pragma once
#endif // _MSC_VER > 1000
```

```cpp
// ------------------------------------------------
// Local include files.
// ------------------------------------------------
#include "token.h"


// ------------------------------------------------
// Library include files.
// ------------------------------------------------
#include <iostream>
#include <fstream>
#include <string>
using namespace std;

class CScanner  : public ifstream
{
// ------------------------------------------------
// Constructor/Destructor
// ------------------------------------------------
public:
  CScanner();
  CScanner(const char* szName);
  virtual ~CScanner();


// ------------------------------------------------
// Protected member variables
// ------------------------------------------------
protected:

  // Tracks a count of each type of token
  // m_TokenCount[eTokenTypeCount] stores the
  // total number of tokens scanned
  int m_TokenCount[eTokenTypeCount+1];

  // Character used to identify a string
  char m_cStringIdentifier;

  // Character used to identify a character
  // string such as in 'c' or '\n'
  char m_cCharacterIdentifier;

  // Escape character used within a string
```

```
    // for example using '\' before a quote
    // character in C++
    char m_cEscapeCharacter;

    // Indicates the beginning of a comment
    string m_sBeginCommentIdentifier;

    // Indicates the end of a comment
    string m_sEndCommentIdentifier;

    // indicates the beginning of an EOL comment
    string m_sEOLCommentIdentifier;

    // Indicates that underscores can be used
    // at the beginning of words.
    bool m_bAllowUnderscore;

    // Indicates a character used to continue
    // a line.
    string m_sLineContinuationIdentifier;

    // Used to identify the end of a statement.
    char m_cStatementEndIdentifier;

    // Stores the languages reserved words.
    TokenTextList m_ReservedWords;

// -----------------------------------------------
// Member variable access functions
// -----------------------------------------------
public:

    // Return the count of the number of tokens processed
    // of a particular type.  GetTokenCount(eTokenTypeCount)
    // returns the total number of tokens processed.
    long GetTokenCount(int nTokenType)
    {
      return m_TokenCount[nTokenType];
    }

    // Reset the token counts
    void Reset()
```

```
{
  for(int i = 0; i < eTokenTypeCount+1; i++)
    m_TokenCount[i] = 0;
  // Initialize the number of lines to be one.
  m_TokenCount[eTokenTypeEOL] = 1;
}


// String related settings
const char GetStringIdentifier()
{
  return m_cStringIdentifier;
}
void SetStringIdentifier( const char cStringIdentifier,
  const char sEscapeCharacter )
{
  m_cStringIdentifier = cStringIdentifier;
  m_cEscapeCharacter = sEscapeCharacter;
}


// Character string related settings
const char GetCharacterIdentifier()
{
  return m_cCharacterIdentifier;
}
void SetCharacterIdentifier( const char cCharacterIdentifier,
  const char sEscapeCharacter )
{
  m_cCharacterIdentifier = cCharacterIdentifier;
  m_cEscapeCharacter = sEscapeCharacter;
}


const char GetEscapeCharacter()
{
  return m_cEscapeCharacter;
}
void SetEscapeCharacter( const char cEscapeCharacter )
{
  m_cEscapeCharacter = cEscapeCharacter;
}


// Comment related settings
const char* GetBeginCommentIdentifier()
```

```
{
  return m_sBeginCommentIdentifier.c_str();
}
const char* GetEndCommentIdentifier()
{
  return m_sEndCommentIdentifier.c_str();
}
void SetCommentIdentifiers(
  const char* sBeginIdentifier, const char* sEndIdentifier)
{
  m_sBeginCommentIdentifier = sBeginIdentifier;
  m_sEndCommentIdentifier = sEndIdentifier;
}

// EOL Comment related settings
const char* GetEOLCommentIdentifier()
{
  return m_sEOLCommentIdentifier.c_str();
}
void SetEOLCommentIdentifier( const char* sEOLCommentIdentifier )
{
  m_sEOLCommentIdentifier = sEOLCommentIdentifier;
}

// Word related settings
bool GetAllowUnderscore()
{
  return m_bAllowUnderscore;
}
void SetAllowUnderscore( const bool bAllowUnderscore )
{
  m_bAllowUnderscore = bAllowUnderscore;
}

// Line continuation
const char* GetLineContinuationIdentifier()
{
  return m_sLineContinuationIdentifier.c_str();
}
void SetLineContinuationIdentifier(const char* nNewIdentifier)
{
```

```
    m_sLineContinuationIdentifier = nNewIdentifier;
  }

  const char GetStatementEndIdentifier()
  {
    return m_cStatementEndIdentifier;
  }
  void SetStatementEndIdentifier(
    const char cStatementEndIdentifier)
  {
    m_cStatementEndIdentifier = cStatementEndIdentifier;
  }

  bool IsReservedWord(const string sTokenText)
  {
    return (m_ReservedWords.find(sTokenText)
      != m_ReservedWords.end());
  }
  TokenTextList* GetReservedWords()
  {
    return &m_ReservedWords;
  }

  bool IsOnlyWhiteSpaceLeft()
  {
    return CToken::IsOnlyWhiteSpaceLeft(*this);
  }

  bool IsOnlyWhiteSpaceOrCommentsLeft()
  {
    return CToken::IsOnlyWhiteSpaceOrCommentsLeft(
      *this, GetBeginCommentIdentifier(),
      GetEndCommentIdentifier(),
      GetEOLCommentIdentifier()
      );
  }

// ------------------------------------------------
// Public functions
// ------------------------------------------------
public:
```

```
   // Identify what type of token is next.
   virtual int PeekTokenType();

   // Return the next token in the input stream
   // If there is not token return false.
   virtual CToken GetToken();

};

#endif // !defined(SCANNER_H_INCLUDED)
```

ANNOTATIONS

The idea behind **CScanner** is to implement the same functionality as in **istream**, but with individual tokens rather than individual characters. Since the main purpose of the scanner class is to retrieve the next token, the most important function of **CScanner** is **GetToken( )**. The parser repeatedly calls **CScanner::GetToken( )** in order to move through the entire file.

What the scanner essentially does is allow the parser to work with individual tokens rather than individual characters. This enables the parser to work with larger blocks of data. Spoken languages work the same way. Although it would be possible to speak in letters, this would be very impractical and extremely inefficient. Instead, letters are combined to form words, which are then interpreted as a whole. Similarly, the scanner combines characters to form "words," which the parser can then interpret.

You can take a look at the **GetNextToken( )** function in the following section, along with the rest of the **CScanner** class implementation.

Code

Here is the implementation code for **CScanner**.

Scanner.cpp

```
// Scanner.cpp: implementation of the CScanner class.
//////////////////////////////////////////////////////////////////////


// ------------------------------------------------
// Local include files.
// ------------------------------------------------
#include "Scanner.h"
```

```
// ------------------------------------------------
// Library include files.
// ------------------------------------------------
#include <cassert>

//////////////////////////////////////////////////////////////////////
// Construction/Destruction
//////////////////////////////////////////////////////////////////////
CScanner::CScanner()
  // Initailize all member variables
  : m_cStringIdentifier('\"'),
    m_cCharacterIdentifier(NULL),
    m_cEscapeCharacter(NULL),
    m_bAllowUnderscore(true),
    m_cStatementEndIdentifier(NULL),
    ifstream()
{
  Reset();
}

CScanner::CScanner(const char* szName)
  // Initailize all member variables
  : m_cStringIdentifier('\"'),
    m_cCharacterIdentifier(NULL),
    m_cEscapeCharacter(NULL),
    m_bAllowUnderscore(true),
    m_cStatementEndIdentifier(NULL),
    ifstream(szName)
{
  Reset();
}

CScanner::~CScanner()
{
}


// Identify the next token on m_input.
// The tokens are checked in the specified
// order because some tokens could be
// misidentified otherwise.  For example,
// if the eTokenTypeOther was checked
// before CWordToken we would never have
```

```
// word tokens.  In addition, checking
// for punctuation before checking
// for a word would not detect a word
// that begins with an underscore (if
// underscores are allowed.)
int CScanner::PeekTokenType()
{
  int nType;

  if ( CWhiteSpaceToken::IsA(*this) )
    return eTokenTypeWhiteSpace;

  else if ( CWordToken::IsA(*this, GetAllowUnderscore()) )
    nType = eTokenTypeWord;

  else if ( CEOLToken::IsA(*this) )
  {
    nType = eTokenTypeEOL;
  }

  else if ( CCommentToken::IsA(*this,
    GetBeginCommentIdentifier(), GetEndCommentIdentifier()) )
  {
    nType = eTokenTypeComment;
  }

  else if ( CEOLCommentToken::IsA(*this,
    GetEOLCommentIdentifier()) )
  {
    nType = eTokenTypeEOLComment;
  }

  else if ( CStringToken::IsA(*this,
    GetStringIdentifier(), GetEscapeCharacter()) )
  {
    nType = eTokenTypeString;
  }

  else if ( CCharacterToken::IsA(*this,
    GetCharacterIdentifier(), GetEscapeCharacter()) )
  {
    nType = eTokenTypeCharacter;
```

```
    }

    else if ( CNumericToken::IsA(*this) )
      nType = eTokenTypeNumeric;

    else if ( CStatementEndToken::IsA(*this,
      GetStatementEndIdentifier()) )
    {
      nType = eTokenTypeStatementEnd;
    }

    else if ( CLineContinuationToken::IsA(*this,
      GetLineContinuationIdentifier()) )
    {
      nType = eTokenTypeLineContinuation;
    }

    else if ( CPunctuationToken::IsA(*this) )
      nType = eTokenTypePunctuation;

    else if ( CEOFToken::IsA(*this) )
      nType = eTokenTypeEOF;

    else
      nType = eTokenTypeOther;

    return nType;
}

// Return the next token that appears
// in m_input.
CToken CScanner::GetToken()
{

    CToken token;
    switch (PeekTokenType())
    {
    case eTokenTypeWhiteSpace:
      token = CWhiteSpaceToken(*this);
      break;
    case eTokenTypeWord:
      token = CWordToken(*this, GetAllowUnderscore(),
```

```
      GetReservedWords());
   break;
case eTokenTypeStatementEnd:
   token =  CStatementEndToken(*this, GetStatementEndIdentifier());
   break;
case eTokenTypePunctuation:
   token =  CPunctuationToken(*this);
   break;
case eTokenTypeEOL:
   token = CEOLToken(*this);
   break;
case eTokenTypeComment:
   token = CCommentToken(*this, GetBeginCommentIdentifier(),
     GetEndCommentIdentifier());
   break;
case eTokenTypeEOLComment:
   token = CEOLCommentToken(*this, GetEOLCommentIdentifier());
   break;
case eTokenTypeString:
   token = CStringToken(*this, GetStringIdentifier(),
     GetEscapeCharacter());
   break;
case eTokenTypeCharacter:
   token = CCharacterToken(*this, GetCharacterIdentifier(),
     GetEscapeCharacter());
   break;
case eTokenTypeNumeric:
   token = CNumericToken(*this);
   break;
case eTokenTypeLineContinuation:
   token = CLineContinuationToken(*this,
     GetLineContinuationIdentifier());
   break;
case eTokenTypeEOF:
   token =  CEOFToken(*this);
   break;
case eTokenTypeOther:
   token = COtherToken(*this);
   break;
default:
   assert(false);
}
```

```
    m_TokenCount[eTokenTypeCount]++;
    m_TokenCount[token.GetType()]++;
    return token;
}
```

ANNOTATIONS

The main task of the scanner is to break the input file down into individual tokens. The scanner identifies what the next token is going to be, instantiates a token of that type, and returns it back to the parser.

With the abundance of static **IsA( )** functions found on each of the token classes, the scanner simply has to ask each token class if the next token is of its type. Complications arise, however, because of the order in which the tokens need to be checked. Ideally, they should be checked in order of frequency, to avoid needless calling of **IsA( )** functions when they usually return **false**. This approach presents a problem because some of the **IsA( )** functions do not check for certain that the next token is of a particular type, so there is a chance that a token could be misidentified. If, for example, the **CPunctuationToken::IsA( )** function were called before calling **CStringToken::IsA( )**, the string might never get identified because the punctuation token would not know that '\"' is a string identifier and not simply another punctuation character. The **CPunctuationToken** constructor would identify the next token as **etokenTypePunctuation**, when instead **CStringToken** should be used. The scanner therefore needs to be sure to identify the various tokens in the correct order.

The **Scanner.cpp** program's **CScanner::PeekTokenType( )** function uses the following order for identifying tokens:

1. **IsWhiteSpaceToken**,

2. **IsWordToken**,

3. **IsEOLToken**,

4. **IsCommentToken**,

5. **IsEOLCommentToken**,

6. **IsStringToken**,

7. **IsNumericToken**,

8. **IsStatementEndToken**,

9. **IsLineContinuationToken**,

10. **IsPunctuationToken**, and

11. **IsEOFToken**.

PROGRAMMER'S NOTE *Although there is some flexibility in changing this order, changes should be made with great care.*

A second important function of the scanner is to keep a list of the language characteristics needed to identify a token. For example, the scanner keeps a list of reserved words and tracks all the string, comment, and other miscellaneous identifiers. Although some defaults are set for these values, it is necessary to explicitly assign the values for each type of language file that is to be scanned. There is a long list of member-variable access functions within **scanner.h**, which allows the language identifiers to be defined. Each of the methods is prefixed with "Set".

Initializing the Scanner for C++

Now that we have completed the token and scanner classes, we can write a simple function to see how they are used. The function is called **GetIncludeFileList( )** and is used to retrieve a list of all the files that have been included in source code being scanned.

Since the parser and scanner are written to handle any language, it is necessary to set them up so that they recognize the characteristics of C++. We use the functions within **CodeMaintCPP.h** to do this. It is within this file that we load the identifiers and reserved words for C++, and define the C++ formatting characteristics. (Further explanation of the formatting definition will be discussed when we look at the **AutoIndent( )** function.)

All the C++ load functions and the **GetIncludeFileList( )** function are included inside **CodeMaintCPP.cpp**. Therefore, **CodeMaintCPP.cpp** contains all the code that is specifically written to handle the C++ language.

Code

Following is the **CodeMaintCPP.h** code, which sets up the scanner for C++.

CodeMaintCPP.h

```
// CodeMaintCPP.h : Defines some C++ specific functions
//
// This file is used to load up the CScanner and
// CCodeParser objects with data specific to C++.
// Additional C++ code maintenance functions are
// also included.
//////////////////////////////////////////////////////////////////////

#if !defined(CODEMAINTCPP_H_INCLUDED)
#define CODEMAINTCPP_H_INCLUDED
```

```
// ------------------------------------------------
// Microsoft Idiosyncrasies.
// ------------------------------------------------
#if _MSC_VER > 1000
// disable warning C4786: symbol greater than 255 character,
// okay to ignore (MSVC)
#pragma warning(disable: 4786)
#pragma once
#endif // _MSC_VER > 1000


// ------------------------------------------------
// Local include files.
// ------------------------------------------------
#include "Scanner.h"
#include "CodeParser.h"
#include "Token.h"


// ------------------------------------------------
// Library include files.
// ------------------------------------------------
#include <set>
#include <string>
#include <cassert>
using namespace std;


// ------------------------------------------------
// C++ Language definitions.
// ------------------------------------------------
#define CPP_LINE_CONTINUATION_CHARACTER "\\"
#define CPP_ALLOW_UNDERSCORE                true
#define CPP_COMMENT_IDENTIFIERS             "/*", "*/"
#define CPP_EOL_COMMENT_IDENTIFIER          "//"
#define CPP_STRING_IDENTIFIER_CHARACTER     '\"'
#define CPP_CHARACTER_IDENTIFIER            '\''
#define CPP_STRING_ESCAPE_CHARACTER         '\\'
#define CPP_STATEMENT_END_CHARACTER         ';'

#define CPP_RESERVE_WORD_COUNT 60
#define CPP_RESERVED_WORDS \
  "auto", "bool", "break", "case", "catch", "char", "class",     \
  "const", "const_cast", "continue", "default", "delete", "do",  \
```

```
   "double", "dynamic_cast", "else", "enum", "explicit", "extern", \
   "false", "float", "for", "friend", "goto", "if", "inline",       \
   "int", "long", "mutable", "namespace", "new", "operator",        \
   "private", "protected", "public", "register",                   \
   "reinterpret_cast", "return", "short", "signed", "sizeof",       \
   "static", "static_cast", "struct", "switch", "template",         \
   "this", "throw", "true", "try", "typedef", "typeid",             \
   "typename", "union", "unsigned", "using", "virtual", "void",     \
   "volatile", "while"


// -----------------------------------------------
// C++ Formating rules.
// -----------------------------------------------
#define CPP_FORMAT_STRINGS_COUNT 10
#define CPP_FORMAT_STRINGS                                          \
   "#", "{", "}", ":", "case", "default", "for",                    \
   "private", "protected", "public"


#define CPP_FORMAT_FLAGS                                            \
   /* "#"          */                                               \
   eIndentIgnore,                                                   \
                                                                    \
   /* "{"          */                                               \
   eIndentAll | eIndentIgnoreStatementEnd | eIndentStatementEnded   \
   | eIndentNewLineBefore | eIndentNewLineAfter,                    \
                                                                    \
   /* "}"          */                                               \
   eIndentStatementEnded | eIndentDecrement                         \
   | eIndentIgnoreStatementEnd | eIndentNewLineBefore,              \
                                                                    \
   /* ":"          */                                               \
   eIndentStatementEnded,                                           \
                                                                    \
   /* "case"       */                                               \
   eIndentDecrement | eIndentAll | eIndentIgnoreStatementEnd,       \
                                                                    \
   /* "default"    */                                               \
   eIndentDecrement | eIndentAll | eIndentIgnoreStatementEnd,       \
                                                                    \
   /* "for"        */                                               \
   eIndentIgnoreNewLineAfter,                                       \
                                                                    \
```

```
  /* "private"   */                                                    \
  eIndentIgnore,                                                       \
                                                                       \
  /* "protected" */                                                    \
  eIndentIgnore,                                                       \
                                                                       \
  /* "public"    */                                                    \
  eIndentIgnore


typedef set<string> FileList;


// ------------------------------------------------
// C++ Loading functions
// ------------------------------------------------

// Load the scanner for C++.
void LoadCPPScanner(CScanner& scanner)
{
  TokenTextList* pReservedWords;
  const nReservedWordElements = CPP_RESERVE_WORD_COUNT;
  char* ReservedWordsArray[nReservedWordElements]
    = {CPP_RESERVED_WORDS};
  int nCount;

  pReservedWords = scanner.GetReservedWords();

  for(nCount = 0; nCount < nReservedWordElements; nCount ++)
  {
    pReservedWords->insert(pReservedWords->end(),
      ReservedWordsArray[nCount] );
  }

  scanner.SetAllowUnderscore(CPP_ALLOW_UNDERSCORE);
  scanner.SetCommentIdentifiers(CPP_COMMENT_IDENTIFIERS);
  scanner.SetEOLCommentIdentifier(CPP_EOL_COMMENT_IDENTIFIER);
  scanner.SetLineContinuationIdentifier(
    CPP_LINE_CONTINUATION_CHARACTER);
  scanner.SetStringIdentifier(CPP_STRING_IDENTIFIER_CHARACTER,
    CPP_STRING_ESCAPE_CHARACTER);
  scanner.SetCharacterIdentifier(CPP_CHARACTER_IDENTIFIER,
```

```
      CPP_STRING_ESCAPE_CHARACTER);
  scanner.SetStatementEndIdentifier(CPP_STATEMENT_END_CHARACTER);


}


// Load the parser for C++
void LoadCPPFormat(CCodeParser& parser)
{
  int nCount;

  FormaterStringCol* pFormatStrings;
  const nFormatStringCount = CPP_FORMAT_STRINGS_COUNT;
  const char* FormatStrings[nFormatStringCount]
    = {CPP_FORMAT_STRINGS};
  const long StringFormatingFlags[] = {CPP_FORMAT_FLAGS};

  pFormatStrings = parser.GetFormatStrings();
  for(nCount = 0; nCount < nFormatStringCount; nCount ++)
  {
    // Add each string and its flgs to the FormatStrings collection
    pFormatStrings->insert(pFormatStrings->end(),
      FormaterStringCol::value_type(
      FormatStrings[nCount],
      StringFormatingFlags[nCount]) );
  }


}




// ------------------------------------------------
// Other C++ specific functions
// ------------------------------------------------


// Return the list of files names included in
// CScanner& input.
bool GetIncludeFileList(CScanner& input, FileList& fileList)
{

  // Return false if the function does not complete
  bool bSuccess = false;
  CToken token;
```

```cpp
string sToken;

token = input.GetToken();
while(token.GetType() != eTokenTypeEOF)
{
  // Search for #include.
  if (token.GetTokenText() == "#")
  {
    // Get the next token
    token = input.GetToken();
    if (token.GetTokenText() == "include")
    {
      // Ignore whitespace and comments.
      do
      {
        token = input.GetToken();
      }
      while ( (token.GetType() == eTokenTypeWhiteSpace)
        || (token.GetType() == eTokenTypeComment) );

      if(token.GetType() == eTokenTypeString)
      {
        // The filename is surrounded by quotes as in
        // #include "CPPParser.h"
        sToken = token.GetTokenText();
        fileList.insert(sToken.substr(
          1, sToken.length()-2) );
      }
      else
      {
        // The filename is surrounded with angled
        // brackets indicating a library file as in
        // #include <map>
        if(token.GetTokenText() == "<")
        {             sToken = "<";
          token = input.GetToken();
          while( (token.GetType() != eTokenTypeEOF)
            && (token != ">"))
          {
            sToken += token;
            token = input.GetToken();
          }
```

```
            if( (token.GetType() == eTokenTypePunctuation)
              && (token.GetTokenText() == ">") )
            {
              sToken += ">";
              fileList.insert(sToken);
            }
            else
              bSuccess = false;
          } // End if (token.GetTokenText() == "<")
        }   // End if (token.GetType() == eTokenTypeString)
      } // End if (token.GetTokenText() == "include")
    } // End if (token.GetTokenText() == "#")

    token = input.GetToken();
  }

  // If we were able to scan to the end of the file then
  // return true.
  if (token.GetType() == eTokenTypeEOF)
  {
    bSuccess = true;
  }

  return bSuccess;
}


// The following function is used to test the auto indent
// function.  It removes all the indentations from a file.
bool Jumbalize(CScanner& input, ostream& output)
{
  assert(input.good() && input.is_open());

  CToken token;
  bool bRet = false;
  bool bPrintEOL = false;
  string sCurrentLine;

  token = input.GetToken();

  while(token.GetType() != eTokenTypeEOF)
  {
```

```
switch( token.GetType() )
{
case eTokenTypeEOLComment:
  bPrintEOL= true;
  sCurrentLine += token;
  break;
case eTokenTypeLineContinuation:
  bPrintEOL= true;
  sCurrentLine += token;
  break;
case eTokenTypeEOL:
  output << sCurrentLine;
  if (bPrintEOL || sCurrentLine.empty()
     || (input.PeekTokenType() == eTokenTypePunctuation)
     || CToken::IsOnlyWhiteSpaceLeft(input) )
  {
    output << token;
  }

  sCurrentLine.erase();
  bPrintEOL = false;
  break;
case eTokenTypeWhiteSpace:
  if(!sCurrentLine.empty())
    sCurrentLine += token;
  break;
case eTokenTypePunctuation:
  if( token.GetTokenText() == "#")
    bPrintEOL= true;
  sCurrentLine += token;
  break;
case eTokenTypeWord:
  if(input.IsReservedWord(token))
    bPrintEOL = true;
  sCurrentLine += token;
  break;

default:
  sCurrentLine += token;
  break;
}
token = input.GetToken();
```

```
    }

    // Write out the last line just in case there is something left.
    output << sCurrentLine;

    // If we were able to scan to the end of the file then
    // return true.
    if (token.GetType() == eTokenTypeEOF)
    {
      bRet = true;
    }

    return bRet;
}

#endif // !defined(CODEMAINTCPP_H_INCLUDED)
```

ANNOTATIONS

CodeMaintCPP.h uses some **#define** directives to set up the string identifiers
for C++, along with the reserved words and other miscellaneous constants.
The **LoadCPPScanner( )** uses these **#define** directives to store the language
characteristics in the scanner. Once the **LoadCPPScanner** has run, the
GetIncludeFileList( ) can be called. **GetIncludeFileList( )** shows a listing
of the filenames that have been included into the input file, as the following
output illustrates:

```
C:\>SCodeMnt SCodeMnt.cpp /include
<assert.h>
<fstream>
<iostream>
<ostream>
<set>
CPPParser.h
CommandLine.h
Scanner.h
stdafx.h

C:\>
```

The **CCPPParser::GetIncludeFileList( )** function is relatively simple. The body of
the function is a **while** loop, within which each token is requested from the scanner
and then processed. The **while** loop ends when the scanner returns a token of type

eTokenTypeEOF. While iterating through, **GetIncludeFileList( )** looks for a token equal to **"#"**. Once this token is found, the function checks that the very next token equals **include**. If this is true, we know that we have found an include file. The function then removes any comments and white space from before the filename so that the next token to be retrieved is the filename.

The file may be listed in two ways: The filename may be enclosed by quotes, as in **"CodeParser.h"** or it could be enclosed by angled brackets as in **<stdio.h>**. Unfortunately, when the filename is included with angle brackets, there are as many as five tokens (**<**, **stdio**, **.** , **h**, and **>**) that make up the filename, so the process of retrieving the name is more complex. Once the filename has been identified, it is added to the **fileList** parameter so that it can be returned to the calling function.

GetIncludeFileList( ) is the only function that is implemented specifically to perform code maintenance on C++ source code. This is why the function has been included in **CodeMaintCPP.h** rather than with the other parser functions found in **CodeParser.cpp**. All the other functions are written generically, so if a different language were loaded into the scanner, the appropriate tokens for this language would be instantiated.

Although **GetIncludeFileList( )** is a simple function, it serves as a good introduction to some of the more complex functions that are coming up in the **CCodeParser** class.

The Parser Class, CCodeParser

The parser class is where the practical code-manipulation functions are implemented. Within this class is where we find the **WriteHTML( )** and **AutoIndent( )** functions.

Code

CodeParser.h

CCodeParser is designed to handle the parsing of source code. The declaration of **CCodeParser** is found in the file **CodeParser.h** as follows:

```
// CodeParser.h: interface for the CCodeParser class.
//
// This class is used to parse programming source code.
// One of its main functions is to format the code based on the
// indentation criteria specified.
```

```
//////////////////////////////////////////////////////////////////

#if !defined(CODEPARSER_H_INCLUDED)
#define CODEPARSER_H_INCLUDED


// -------------------------------------------------
// Microsoft Idiosyncrasies.
// -------------------------------------------------
#if _MSC_VER > 1000
// disable warning C4786: symbol greater than 255 character,
// okay to ignore (MSVC)
#pragma warning(disable: 4786)
#pragma once
#endif // _MSC_VER > 1000



// -------------------------------------------------
// Local include files.
// -------------------------------------------------
#include "token.h"
#include "scanner.h"


// -------------------------------------------------
// Library include files.
// -------------------------------------------------
#include <string>
#include <map>
#include <set>
#include <ostream>
using namespace std;


// -------------------------------------------------
// Miscellaneous Define Stuff
// -------------------------------------------------
#define SUMMARY_HEADER "\n\nSUMMARY INFORMATION\n";

// The defualt string to be used to indent a line.
#define DEFAULT_INDENT_STRING "  "


// -------------------------------------------------
// HTML Constants
// -------------------------------------------------
```

```
#define HTML_HEADER                                                    \
  "<HTML>"                                                             \
  "\n<HEAD>"                                                           \
  "\n<META NAME=\"\" Content=\"Source Code Parser\">"                 \
  "\n<META HTTP-EQUIV=\"Content-Type\"content=\"text/html\">"         \
  "\n<TITLE>"

#define DEFAULT_TITLE "Source Code Colorized"

#define HTML_SUBHEADER                                                 \
  "\n</TITLE>"                                                         \
  "\n</HEAD>\n\n"                                                      \
  "\n<BODY>"                                                           \
  "\n<PRE>\n"

#define HTML_FOOTER                                                    \
  "\n\n</PRE>"                                                         \
  "\n</BODY>"                                                          \
  "\n</HTML>"

#define HTML_TAB "     "

#define HTML_SPACE " "

#define HTML_EOF "<P></P>"

#define HTML_GREATERTHAN "&gt;"

#define HTML_LESSTHAN "&lt;"


// -----------------------------------------------
// Enum declarations
// -----------------------------------------------
// EIndent defines the formating rules for a
// particular string.
enum EIndent
{
  // Does not cause an indent.
  eIndentNone = 0,

  // Indent all the NEXT lines.
```

```
   // (Until an eIndentDecrement token is encountered)
   eIndentAll = 1,

   // Do not indent CURRENT line at all when this token encountered.
   eIndentIgnore = eIndentAll << 1,

   // Do not increase the indent even if the statement on the
   // previous line was not reported as ended.
   eIndentIgnoreStatementEnd = eIndentIgnore << 1,

   // Decrement the indent count for the CURRENT and
   // FOLLOWING lines.
   eIndentDecrement = eIndentIgnoreStatementEnd << 1,

   // Indicates that the text ends a statement or that
   // the statement has ended.
   eIndentStatementEnded = eIndentDecrement << 1,

   // This token extends the statement to the next line.
   // The following line should indent as though the
   // statement on the previous line was not completed.
   eIndentLineContinuation = eIndentStatementEnded << 1,

   // Put this token onto a new line.
   eIndentNewLineBefore = eIndentLineContinuation << 1,

   // Put a new line after this token
   eIndentNewLineAfter = eIndentNewLineBefore << 1,

   // Don't put a new line even if eIndentNewLineAfter is
   // true.  For example, if eIndentNewLineAfter is true
   // for ';'.  Declaring a eIndentIgnoreNewLineAfter
   // for the string "for" will prevent a new line
   // occuring within 'for' statements.
   eIndentIgnoreNewLineAfter = eIndentNewLineAfter << 1
} ;

typedef map<string, long> FormaterStringCol;
typedef map<string, string> FormaterPairCol;
```

```cpp
// ------------------------------------------------
// Class Declaration
// ------------------------------------------------
class CCodeParser
{
// ------------------------------------------------
// Constructor/Destructor
// ------------------------------------------------
public:
  CCodeParser();
  virtual ~CCodeParser();


// ------------------------------------------------
// Protected member variables
// ------------------------------------------------
protected:
    // The scanner used by the parser to retrieve each token
  CScanner* m_pScanner;

    // The colors used for HTML output
    map<int, string> m_Colors;

    // The color of reserved words when displaying HTML
    string m_ColorReservedWord;

    // Stores the format characteristics for the AutoIndent
    // function.  Each entry is a string flag AutoIndent
    // definer.
    FormaterStringCol m_FormaterStrings;

    // The current token being processed.
    CToken m_CurrentToken;

    // The stream to which format sends its output
    ostream* m_pOutput;

    // Indicates that the last line ended with
    // a complete statement.
    int m_nLastStatementEnded;

    // The current line inside the format function.
    string m_sCurrentLine;
```

```cpp
    // Defines the string used for each indent.  For
    // example this could be five spaces or the
    // tab character.
    string m_sIndentText;

    // Indicates the indent level for the current line.
    int m_nCurrentLineIndentLevel;

    // Indicates the indent level for the next line.
    int m_nNextLineIndentLevel;

    // Stores the flags for formating the current line.
    int m_nCurrentFormatFlags;

// ----------------------------------------------
// Member access functions
// ----------------------------------------------
public:
  CScanner* GetScanner()
  {
    return m_pScanner;
  }

  void SetIndentString(const string sIndentText)
  {
    m_sIndentText = sIndentText;
  }
  const string GetIndentString()
  {
    return m_sIndentText;
  }

  FormaterStringCol* GetFormatStrings()
  {
    return &m_FormaterStrings;
  }

  TokenTextList* GetReservedWords()
  {
    return m_pScanner->GetReservedWords();
  }
```

```cpp
// -------------------------------------------------
// Protected functions
// -------------------------------------------------
protected:
  // Print some summary information (lines read etc)
  // about the parsing process.
  void PrintStatistics(ostream& output = cout);
  virtual void PrintStatisticsHeader(ostream& output = cout);

  // Surround the token with appropriate
  // formatting.
  string FormatHTML(const CToken& token);

  // Some characters cannot be written directly
  // to HTML.  GetHTMLToken replaces these
  // characters with their HTML equivalents.
  string GetHTMLToken(const CToken& token);

  // write html header
  WriteHTMLHeader(ostream& output, string sTitle);
  WriteHTMLFooter(ostream& output);


  // AutoIndent functions

  // Process the FormatDefinition for the current
  // token and store the flags.
  // Note that if the eIndentNewLine before token
  // is set then a line will be written to the output
  void SetIndentHandler(const long nIndentFlags);
  // Format the current line including the indentation.
  string GetIndentedLine();
  // Insert the next token onto the current line.  If
  // the token is an EOL token then write it to output.
  void PutIndentedToken();

// -------------------------------------------------
// Public functions
// -------------------------------------------------
public:
  // Reset all the current counters, returning the
  // object to the state it was immediately
  //  after it was created.
```

```
virtual void Reset();

  // Returns the next token from the scanner
  virtual CToken GetNextToken();

  // Copies the input stream onto the output stream
  virtual bool Copy(CScanner& input, ostream& output);

  virtual bool WriteHTML(CScanner& input, ostream& output);
  virtual bool AutoIndent(CScanner& input, ostream& output);
};

#endif // !defined(CODEPARSER_H_INCLUDED)
```

ANNOTATIONS

Although **CCodeParser** is a specialized parser designed to handle programming languages, it is not restricted to any particular programming language. The two main functions of **CCodeParser** are **WriteHTML( )** and **AutoIndent( )**.

WriteHTML( ) generates an HTML version of the source code, surrounding each token with HTML tags that display the token types in their own color. The file can then be displayed in a browser and printed on a color printer.

The second function, **AutoIndent( )**, outputs the file with indents in all the "right" places. When it comes to indenting a file, there are probably more ideas of what is "right" than there are programmers. **AutoIndent( )** uses one approach, but it can easily be modified to use another. The indent rules are stored inside a **FormaterStringCol** collection called **m_FormaterStrings**. **FormaterStringCol** is a typedef for **map<string, long>**. Each **long** value within the **m_FormaterStrings** collection stores the set of flags used to define the indentation when a particular string is encountered. Table 8-2 lists the format flags, which are declared by **enum EIndent**.

PROGRAMMER'S NOTE
*To change the indent rules, retrieve the **m_FormaterStrings** by calling **GetFormatStrings()** and then modify the items within the collection. Using the various **enum** values, OR together the rules you wish to declare for the specified string. For example, if you want a particular string to appear on its own line, then set the **long** value for that string equal to **eIndentNewLineBefore | eIndentNewLineAfter**.*

Enum Name	Enum Description
eIndentNone	Does not cause an indent.
eIndentAll	Indent all the NEXT lines (until an **eIndentDecrement** token is encountered).
eIndentIgnore	Do not indent CURRENT line at all when this token is encountered. (This is used for tokens such as **#include** in C++.)
eIndentIgnoreStatementEnd	Do not increase the indent even if the statement on the previous line was not reported as ended.
eIndentDecrement	Decrement the indent count for the CURRENT and FOLLOWING lines.
eIndentStatementEnded	Indicates that the text ends a statement or that the statement has ended.
eIndentLineContinuation	Extend the statement to the next line. The following line should be indented as though the statement on the previous line was not completed.
eIndentNewLineBefore	Put this token onto a new line.
eIndentNewLineAfter	Put a new line after this token.
eIndentIgnoreNewLineAfter	If this token appears before a token with **eIndentNewLineAfter**, then ignore the **eIndentNewLineAfter** flag (for example, to prevent a linefeed from occurring inside a C++ for statement).

TABLE 8-2. Valid Formatting Flags

Code

CodeParser.cpp

Following is all the code needed to implement the **CCodeParser** class. The file is called **CodeParser.cpp**.

```
// CodeParser.cpp: implementation of the CCodeParser class.
//////////////////////////////////////////////////////////////////////

// -------------------------------------------------
// Local include files.
// -------------------------------------------------
#include "CodeParser.h"
#include "scanner.h"
```

```cpp
// -------------------------------------------------
// Library include files.
// -------------------------------------------------
#include <istream>
#include <ostream>
#include <cassert>
using namespace std;


// -------------------------------------------------
// Construction/Destruction
// -------------------------------------------------
CCodeParser::CCodeParser()
  // Initialize member variables.
  : m_sIndentText(DEFAULT_INDENT_STRING),
  m_nCurrentLineIndentLevel(0),
  m_nNextLineIndentLevel(0),
  m_nLastStatementEnded(1),
  m_nCurrentFormatFlags(eIndentStatementEnded)
{
  // Initialize each tokens color
  m_Colors[eTokenTypeEOF] = "";
  m_Colors[eTokenTypeEOL] = "";
  m_Colors[eTokenTypeWhiteSpace] = "";
  m_Colors[eTokenTypeString] = "DarkMagenta";
  m_Colors[eTokenTypeCharacter] = "Magenta";
  m_Colors[eTokenTypeNumeric] = "BlueViolet";
  m_Colors[eTokenTypeComment] = "Green";
  m_Colors[eTokenTypeEOLComment] = "DarkGreen";
  m_Colors[eTokenTypePunctuation] = "Maroon";
  m_Colors[eTokenTypeWord] = "Black";
  m_Colors[eTokenTypeLineContinuation] = "Crimson";
  m_Colors[eTokenTypeStatementEnd] = "Red";
  m_Colors[eTokenTypeOther] = "Fuchsia";
  m_ColorReservedWord = "Blue";
}


CCodeParser::~CCodeParser()
{

}
```

```cpp
// Reset all the current counters, returning the object to the state
// it was immediately after it was created.
void CCodeParser::Reset()
{
  m_pScanner->Reset();
}


CToken CCodeParser::GetNextToken()
{
  return ( m_pScanner->GetToken() );
}


bool CCodeParser::Copy(CScanner& input, ostream& output)
{
  CToken token;
  bool bRet = false;

  assert(input.good() && input.is_open());

  m_pScanner = &input;

  token = GetNextToken();

  while(token.GetType() != eTokenTypeEOF)
  {
    output << token;
    token = GetNextToken();
  }

  // If we were able to scan to the end of the file then
  // return true.
  if (token.GetType() == eTokenTypeEOF)
  {
    PrintStatistics();
    bRet = true;
  }

  m_pScanner = NULL;

  return bRet;
}
```

```cpp
void CCodeParser::PrintStatisticsHeader(ostream& output)
{
  output <<  SUMMARY_HEADER;
}


// Print summary information.
void CCodeParser::PrintStatistics(ostream& output)
{
  PrintStatisticsHeader(output);

  output << "Total number of whitespace tokens is " <<
    m_pScanner->GetTokenCount(eTokenTypeWhiteSpace) << endl;

  output << "Total number of strings tokens is " <<
    m_pScanner->GetTokenCount(eTokenTypeString) << endl;

  output << "Total number of numeric tokens is " <<
    m_pScanner->GetTokenCount(eTokenTypeNumeric) << endl;

  output << "Total number of comments tokens is " <<
    m_pScanner->GetTokenCount(eTokenTypeComment) +
      m_pScanner->GetTokenCount(eTokenTypeEOLComment) << endl;

  output << "Total number of punctuation tokens is " <<
    m_pScanner->GetTokenCount(eTokenTypePunctuation) << endl;

  output << "Total number of word tokens is " <<
    m_pScanner->GetTokenCount(eTokenTypeWord) << endl;

  output << "Total number of line continuation tokens is " <<
    m_pScanner->GetTokenCount(eTokenTypeLineContinuation) << endl;

  output << "Total number of unidentified tokens is " <<
    m_pScanner->GetTokenCount(eTokenTypeOther) << endl;

  output << "-------------------------------------------------------"
    << endl;
  output << "Total number of statements is " <<
    m_pScanner->GetTokenCount(eTokenTypeEOL) << endl;

  // We assume that even if the istream is 0 bytes it still
  // is considered to have one line.
```

```
  output << "Total number of lines is " <<
    m_pScanner->GetTokenCount(eTokenTypeEOL)+1 << endl;

  output << "Total number of tokens is " <<
    m_pScanner->GetTokenCount(eTokenTypeCount) << endl;

}


// ---------------------------------------------
// HTML Functions
// ---------------------------------------------
// Write the header for the HTML file
CCodeParser::WriteHTMLHeader(ostream& output, string sTitle)
{
  output << HTML_HEADER;
  if(sTitle.empty())
    output << DEFAULT_TITLE;
  else
    output << sTitle;
  output << HTML_SUBHEADER;
}


// Write the footer for the HTML file
CCodeParser::WriteHTMLFooter(ostream& output)
{
  output << "<HR>";
  PrintStatistics(output);
  output << HTML_FOOTER;
}


// Some characters cannot be written directly
// to HTML.  GetHTMLToken replaces these
// characters with their HTML equivalents.
string CCodeParser::GetHTMLToken(const CToken& token)
{
  long nPos;
  string sOutput;

  switch(token.GetType())
  {
  case eTokenTypeEOF:
    sOutput += HTML_EOF;
```

```
    break;
  case eTokenTypeWhiteSpace:
    for( nPos = 0; (nPos < token.GetTokenText().length()); nPos++ )
    {
      if (token.GetTokenText()[nPos] == '\t' )
        sOutput += HTML_TAB;
      else
        sOutput += HTML_SPACE;
    }
    break;

  default:
    sOutput = token;

    // Replace all '>' with HTML_GREATERTHAN
    nPos = sOutput.find('>');
    while(nPos != string::npos)
    {
      sOutput = sOutput.substr(0, nPos) + HTML_GREATERTHAN +
sOutput.substr(nPos+1, sOutput.length());
      nPos = sOutput.find('>', nPos);
    }

    // Replace all '<' with HTML_LESSTHAN
    nPos = sOutput.find('<');
    while(nPos != string::npos)
    {
      sOutput = sOutput.substr(0, nPos) + HTML_LESSTHAN +
sOutput.substr(nPos+1, sOutput.length());
      nPos = sOutput.find('<', nPos);
    }
  }
  return sOutput;
}

// Get the text for each m_CurrentToken when written
// in HTML
string CCodeParser::FormatHTML(const CToken& token)
{
  string sOutput;
  string sColor;
```

```cpp
  if( (token.GetType() == eTokenTypeWord)
      && m_pScanner->IsReservedWord(token.GetTokenText()) )
    sColor = m_ColorReservedWord;
  else
    sColor = m_Colors[token.GetType()];

  switch (token.GetType())
  {
  case eTokenTypeEOF:
  case eTokenTypeWhiteSpace:
    sOutput += GetHTMLToken(token);
    break;
  default:
    if( !m_Colors[token.GetType()].empty() )
    {
      sOutput += "<FONT color=\"";
      sOutput += sColor;
      sOutput += "\" >";
      sOutput += GetHTMLToken(token);
      sOutput += "</FONT>";
    }
    else
      sOutput += token.GetTokenText();
  }

  return sOutput;
}

// Write each m_CurrentToken in HTML to the output file.
bool CCodeParser::WriteHTML(CScanner& input, ostream& output)
{
  // Verify that the input scanner is open.
  assert( input.good() && input.is_open() );

  bool bRet = false;

  m_pScanner = &input;
  m_pOutput = &output;

  WriteHTMLHeader(output, DEFAULT_TITLE);

  m_CurrentToken = GetNextToken();
```

```
  while(m_CurrentToken.GetType() != eTokenTypeEOF)
  {
    output << FormatHTML(m_CurrentToken);
    m_CurrentToken = GetNextToken();
  }

  WriteHTMLFooter(output);

  // If we were able to scan to the end of the file then
  // return true.
  if (m_CurrentToken.GetType() == eTokenTypeEOF)
  {
    bRet = true;
  }

  m_pScanner = NULL;
  m_pOutput = NULL;

  return bRet;
}


// -----------------------------------------------
// AutoIndent Functions
// -----------------------------------------------
// Return the current line indented.
string CCodeParser::GetIndentedLine()
{
  // The return string
  string sOutput;

  // The text that creates the indent
  string sIndentText;

  // If previous line statement did not end
  // and not eIndentIgnoreStatementEnd then
  // indent at least once.
  if(  !(m_nLastStatementEnded)
    && !(m_nCurrentFormatFlags & eIndentIgnoreStatementEnd) )
    sIndentText = m_sIndentText;

  // The entire line has been captured.
```

```
if( m_nCurrentFormatFlags & eIndentIgnore )
{
  if( !(m_nCurrentFormatFlags & eIndentLineContinuation) )
  {
    // The ignore indent flag was set.  Unset it
    m_nCurrentFormatFlags &= ~eIndentIgnore;

    // Assume the previous statement has ended.
    // If there was no continuation character
    // Set this statement as ended.
    m_nCurrentFormatFlags |= eIndentStatementEnded;
  }

}
else
{

  // Indent for each level.
  for(int i=0; (i < m_nCurrentLineIndentLevel); i++)
  {
    sIndentText += m_sIndentText;
  }
}

// Write out the indent.
sOutput += sIndentText;

// Output the current line.
sOutput += m_sCurrentLine;

// Output the current token
sOutput += CEOLToken();

// We are now moving on to setting up the next line.
// The indent level for this line should be set
// to m_nNextLineIndentLevel.
m_nCurrentLineIndentLevel = m_nNextLineIndentLevel;

// Clear out the contents of the line
m_sCurrentLine.erase();

// Save whether or not the previous line ended with a
// complete statement.
```

```
    m_nLastStatementEnded = (
      (m_nCurrentFormatFlags & eIndentStatementEnded)
      && !(m_nCurrentFormatFlags & eIndentLineContinuation) );

    // Unset the eIndentLineContinuation flag
    m_nCurrentFormatFlags &= ~eIndentLineContinuation;

    // Unset the eIndentIgnoreStatementEnd flag
    m_nCurrentFormatFlags &= ~eIndentIgnoreStatementEnd;

    // Unset the eIndentIgnoreNewLineAfter flag
    m_nCurrentFormatFlags &= ~eIndentIgnoreNewLineAfter;

    // Unset the eIndentNewLineAfter flag
    m_nCurrentFormatFlags &= ~eIndentNewLineAfter;

    return sOutput;
}

// Set the indent handler for the current token
void CCodeParser::SetIndentHandler(const long nFormatFlags)
{
    CToken CurrentToken;

    if ( (nFormatFlags & eIndentNewLineBefore)
      && (!m_sCurrentLine.empty()) )
    {
      // This token begins on a new line so
      // force the new line
      m_nCurrentFormatFlags |= eIndentNewLineBefore;
      *m_pOutput << GetIndentedLine();
    }

    // Set the ended bit to false
    m_nCurrentFormatFlags &= ~eIndentStatementEnded;

    if(nFormatFlags & eIndentDecrement)
    {
      m_nCurrentLineIndentLevel--;
      m_nNextLineIndentLevel--;
    }
```

```
    // Bump the indent for the next lines
    if (nFormatFlags & eIndentAll)
      m_nNextLineIndentLevel++;


    // Set indent ignore so that when it is time to indent
    // no indenting will take place
    if (nFormatFlags & eIndentIgnore)
      m_nCurrentFormatFlags |= eIndentIgnore;


    if (nFormatFlags & eIndentLineContinuation)
      m_nCurrentFormatFlags |= eIndentLineContinuation;


    if ( (nFormatFlags & eIndentIgnoreStatementEnd)
      && (m_sCurrentLine.empty()) )
      // Ignore the fact that the previous statement
      // was not complete as long as the
      // current line is empty.
      m_nCurrentFormatFlags |= eIndentIgnoreStatementEnd;


    // Mark the statement as ended after this m_CurrentToken
    if (nFormatFlags & eIndentStatementEnded)
      m_nCurrentFormatFlags |= eIndentStatementEnded;


    // Assign the m_CurrentToken to the current line after checking
    // the format because some of the formatting checks whether
    // the m_sCurrentLine is empty.
    m_sCurrentLine += m_CurrentToken;


    if ( nFormatFlags & eIndentIgnoreNewLineAfter )
      m_nCurrentFormatFlags |= eIndentIgnoreNewLineAfter;


    if ( (nFormatFlags & eIndentNewLineAfter)
      && !(m_nCurrentFormatFlags & eIndentIgnoreNewLineAfter)
      && !m_pScanner->IsOnlyWhiteSpaceLeft() )
    {
      // Force a new line
      m_nCurrentFormatFlags |= eIndentNewLineAfter;
      *m_pOutput << GetIndentedLine();
    }


}
```

```cpp
// Place the current token onto the
// current line.
void CCodeParser::PutIndentedToken()
{
  CToken PreviousToken;
  string sNextLine;
  FormaterStringCol::const_iterator FormatStringIterator;
  FormaterPairCol::const_iterator FormatPairIterator;

  // Build up the line.
  switch(m_CurrentToken.GetType())
  {
  case eTokenTypeEOL:

    // This should not happen.  We should
    // be checking for EOL before getting here.
    assert(false);
    break;
    //-----------------

  case eTokenTypeWhiteSpace:

    if(!m_sCurrentLine.empty())
    {
      // So far the current line is not empty so
      // write the specified white space.
      m_sCurrentLine += m_CurrentToken;
    }
    break;
    //-----------------

  case eTokenTypeComment:
  case eTokenTypeEOLComment:

    m_sCurrentLine += m_CurrentToken;
    break;
    //-----------------

  case eTokenTypeStatementEnd:

    m_nCurrentFormatFlags |= eIndentStatementEnded;
    m_sCurrentLine += m_CurrentToken;
```

```
      // Always place a new line at the end of
      // statement unless a rule specifically
      // says not to.
      if( !(m_nCurrentFormatFlags & eIndentIgnoreNewLineAfter)
        && !m_pScanner->IsOnlyWhiteSpaceOrCommentsLeft() )
      {
        m_nCurrentFormatFlags |= eIndentNewLineAfter;
        *m_pOutput << GetIndentedLine();
      }

      break;
      //-----------------

    case eTokenTypeLineContinuation:

      m_nCurrentFormatFlags |= eIndentLineContinuation;
      m_sCurrentLine += m_CurrentToken;
      break;
      //-----------------

    default:

      // Check if the m_CurrentToken has a format definer.
      FormatStringIterator =
        m_FormaterStrings.find(m_CurrentToken.GetTokenText());

      if(FormatStringIterator != m_FormaterStrings.end())
      {

        // Process FD
        SetIndentHandler(FormatStringIterator->second);

      }
      else
      {
        // Set the ended bit to false
        m_nCurrentFormatFlags &=  ~eIndentStatementEnded;

        m_sCurrentLine += m_CurrentToken;
      }
  }
}
```

```
bool CCodeParser::AutoIndent(CScanner& input, ostream& output)
{
  assert(input.good() && input.is_open());

  m_pScanner = &input;
  m_pOutput = &output;

  bool bSuccess = false;

  m_nLastStatementEnded = 1;

  m_CurrentToken = GetNextToken();

  while(m_CurrentToken.GetType() != eTokenTypeEOF)
  {
    switch(m_CurrentToken.GetType())
    {
    case eTokenTypeEOL:
      // Write out the line.
      *m_pOutput << GetIndentedLine();
      break;

    default:
      // Insert the next token onto the
      // current line.
      PutIndentedToken();
    }   // End switch(m_CurrentToken.GetType())

    m_CurrentToken = GetNextToken();

  } // End while(m_CurrentToken.GetType() != eTokenTypeEOF)

  *m_pOutput << GetIndentedLine();

  // If we were able to scan to the end of the file then
  // return true.
  if (m_CurrentToken.GetType() == eTokenTypeEOF)
```

```
{
    bSuccess = true;
}

PrintStatistics();

m_pScanner = NULL;
m_pOutput = NULL;

return bSuccess;
}
```

ANNOTATIONS

Let's examine in greater detail the two main code-parser functions **WriteHTML( )** and **AutoIndent( )**. Like **GetIncludeFileList( )**, each of these parser functions implements a **while** loop, within which each token is requested from the scanner and then processed. The **while** loop exits when the scanner returns a token of type **eTokenTypeEOF**.

The **while** loop within **WriteHTML( )** is surrounded by the **WriteHTMLHeader( )** and **WriteHTMLFooter( )** functions; these function open and format the new HTML file. Inside the **while** loop, multiple calls are made to **GetToken( )**. As each token is returned, **WriteHTML( )** calls **GetHTML( )** to retrieve the HTML format of the token. **GetHTML( )** is slightly more complicated. **GetHTML( )** encapsulates a switch statement that converts the token into its appropriate HTML version.

Notice that spaces, tabs, and end-of-files cannot be written directly to HTML, so they are converted to their HTML equivalents. Each is defined in the header file **CodeParser.h**:

```
#define HTML_TAB    "     "
#define HTML_SPACE  " "
#define HTML_EOF    "<P></P>"
```

If the token is not of type **eTokenTypeWhitespace** or **eTokenTypeEOF**, then by default the token text is surrounded by a font tag identifying the token's display color. The colors are stored in **m_Colors**, which is declared as **map<int, string>**. This allows additional colors to be added for custom token types that do not yet exist. After creating an HTML file using the **/html** switch, you can view the file within a browser window as shown in Figure 8-3.

```
/* Demo file */
#define HEADER "The punctuation characters " \
   "in order are: "

#include <iostream>
#include <set>

int main( int argc, char **argv )
{
   int i = 0e0;
   std::set<char>::const_iterator pC;
   std::set<char> CharSet;

   while( i <= 255 )
   {
      if (ispunct(i)!=0)
         CharSet.insert((char)i);
      i++;
   }

   // Print out each punctuation character
   // in order
   for(pC = CharSet.begin(); pC != CharSet.end(); pC++)
   {
      /* write out the character */
      std::cout << *pC << std::ends;
   }
   std::cout << std::endl;
   return 0;
}
```

FIGURE 8-3. A browser window displaying the contents output by the /html switch. Each token type appears in a different color

AutoIndent( ) is more complex than any function examined so far because we want the indentation operation to be customizable, without having to modify code within the **AutoIndent( )** function. Instead, changing the strings listed within the **m_FormaterStrings** map will dynamically change how a file is formatted. For example, if you add the string **if** to **m_FormaterStrings** and set the **eIndentNewLineBefore** flag to true for this entry, then whenever a token is returned whose string is **if**, a new line will be inserted into the output stream before the **if** token.

Similar to the previous parser functions we have examined so far, the **AutoIndent( )** function contains a **while** loop that iterates through all the tokens returned from the scanner and processes them. After retrieving each token, the parser sets the **m_CurrentToken** variable and calls the **PutIndentedToken( )** function (as long as the token type is not **eTokenTypeEOL**). **PutIndentedToken( )** inserts the next token onto the current line. If the token is of type **eTokenTypeEOL**, then the current line is padded with the indentation string and written to the output stream.

The **PutIndentedToken( )** function comprises a large **switch** statement, which appropriately handles each token based on its type. If the token is not explicitly

handled by any of the **case** statements, then it falls through to the default section of the **switch** statement. Once in this section of the code, a token will be checked against the list of format strings. If the token is found, it will be processed by the **SetIndentHander( )** function. This function sets the **m_CurrentFormatFlags** variable for the next line and increments or decrements the indentation level. **PutIndentedToken( )** is also used to force a new line after each statement and to remove any white space from the beginning of lines (because it will be added back when **GetIndentedLine( )** is called).

Finally, once all the tokens for the current line have been processed, the **case eTokenTypeEOL:** will be encountered inside **AutoIndent( )**. From here, the **GetIndentedLine( )** function will be called so that the entire line can be formatted and indented before being written to the output.

The following two listings show a file before and after autoindentation. Notice that in the first listing there are no indentations, and some lines contain two statements.

Original File

```
/* Demo file */
#include <iostream>
#include <set>

int main( int argc, char **argv )
{int i = 0e0;
std::set<char>::const_iterator pC;
std::set<char> CharSet;

while( i <= 255 )
{if (ispunct(i)!=0)
CharSet.insert((char)i);
i++;}

// Print out each punctuation character
// in order
for(pC = CharSet.begin(); pC != CharSet.end(); pC++)
{ /* write out the character */
std::cout << *pC << std::ends;}std::cout << std::endl;return 0;
}
```

Output File Produced by Autoindentation

```
/* Demo file */
#include <iostream>
#include <set>

int main( int argc, char **argv )
```

```
{
  int i = 0e0;
  std::set<char>::const_iterator pC;
  std::set<char> CharSet;

  while( i <= 255 )
  {
    if (ispunct(i)!=0)
      CharSet.insert((char)i);
    i++;
  }

  // Print out each punctuation character
  // in order
  for(pC = CharSet.begin(); pC != CharSet.end(); pC++)
  {
    /* write out the character */
    std::cout << *pC << std::ends;
  }
  std::cout << std::endl;
  return 0;
}
```

Now that **AutoIndent( )**'s basic structure is understood, we can examine more closely the formatting flags used for C++. In **CodeMaintCPP.h** we saw the **LoadCPPFormat( )** function. Let's look at the details of setting up the C++ formatting. Table 8-3 lists the strings for which formatting is specified.

Format String	Assigned enum Flags
"#"	eIndentIgnore
"{"	eIndentAll | eIndentIgnoreStatementEnd | eIndentStatementEnded | eIndentNewLineBefore | eIndentNewLineAfter
"}"	eIndentStatementEnded | eIndentDecrement | eIndentIgnoreStatementEnd | eIndentNewLineBefore
":"	eIndentStatmentEnded
"case", "default"	eIndentDecrement | eIndentAll
"for"	eIndentIgnoreNewLineAfter
"private" "protected" "public"	eIndentIgnore

TABLE 8-3.   Format Strings for C++

Table 8-4 presents the explanations for each string and the flags assigned.

String	Flags Assigned

"#"	The character used to define precompile items such as **#define** and **#endif**. These lines always start in the first column so they should not be indented at all. The indent flag, therefore, is set to **eIndentIgnore**.
	
	```// Library include files```
	```#include <iostream>```

"{"	Used to start a block of code.
	eIndentNewLineBefore combined with **eIndentNewLineAfter** cause the bracket to appear on its own line.
	eIndentIgnoreStatementEnd causes the line starting with this bracket to not indent even if the previous line did not end. The bracket could be placed following a **while** statement, for example, where the line containing the **while** statement does not end in a semicolon.
	eIndentIgnoreStatementEnd allows the bracket to appear directly below the beginning of the **while** statement.
	eIndentStatementEnded causes the line ending with a bracket to be considered a complete statement.
	
	```while (token.GetType() != eTokenTypeEOF)```
	``` {```
	``` cout << token;```
	``` token = scanner.GetNextToken();```
	``` }```

"}"	Decrements the current line and all the following lines because of the **eIndentDecrement** flag. This returns the indent level to the level before the opening bracket appeared. **eIndentNewLineBefore** causes the close bracket to start on a new line. Note that the **eIndentNewLineAfter** flag was not set. This would cause closing comments or a semicolon on the same line to be shifted to the following line. **eIndentIgnoreStatementEnd** was used so that even if the previous line did not end, the bracket would not be indented. This is needed when the bracket is used in an **enum** declaration because there are not semicolons to indicate that a statement ended within the **enum**. The last flag, **eIndentStatementEnded**, is used so that the line following the close bracket is not indented.

TABLE 8-4. Format Strings and Flags

String	Flags Assigned

"}"	Consider the following fragment:
	
	``
	enum EType
	    {
	    eInteger,
	        eFloat,
	        eDouble
	    }
	    while(bNotFinished)
	    {
	    bNotFinished = GetNext();
	    }
	``
	
	Note in the above code that **eFloat** is indented one more than **eInteger**. This is because the **eInteger** line does not end with a semicolon and yet there is no character to assign the **eIndentIgnoreStatementEnd** flag to. Of course, you can alter this behavior. A second caveat concerns array definition and assignment. Because arrays are assigned using brackets as well, the array will appear on its own line.
	
	``
	int array[] =
	{
	  1,2,3,4
	}
	``

":"	**eIndentStatementEnded** is used so that the statement following a case or default will not be indented.

"case"
"default"
	eIndentDecrement and **eIndentAll** cause the case and default lines to appear at the same level as the **switch** statement.
	
	``
	void myfunc()
	{
	  switch (token.GetType())
	  {
	  case eTokenTypeEOF:
	    sOutput += HTML_EOF;
	    break;
	  default:
	    sOutput += token;
	  }
	}
	``

TABLE 8-4. Format Strings and Flags *(continued)*

String	Flags Assigned

"for"	**eIndentIgnoreNewLineAfter** is set to prevent a new line from occurring even if a statement end is encountered on the same line. This is necessary because **for** statements include two semicolons, which are end-of-statement characters.
	
	``cpp
	void MyFunc(int repeat)
	{
	  int i
	  for(i = 0; i < repeat; i ++)
	  {
	    cout << "-";
	  }
	}
	``
	One caveat with the **for** statement: If the original **for** statement carries over to two lines, then each part of the autoindented **for** statement will also appear on its own line.
	
	``cpp
	void MyFunc(int repeat)
	{
	  int i
	  for(i = 0;
	    i < repeat;
	  i ++)
	  {
	    cout << "-";
	  }
	}
	``

"private"
"public"
"protected"
	Lines containing these tokens are placed flush against the margin in the same manner as **#define** and **#include**. They therefore have the **eIndentIgnore** flag.
	
	``cpp
	class MyClass
	{
	public:
	  MyClass();
	  ~MyClass();
	protected:
	  bool bInitialized;
	}
	``

TABLE 8-4. Format Strings and Flags *(continued)*

With an understanding of how the C++ formatter is defined, you can define formatters for other languages as well.

The Main Program

The following **main( )** shows how the various code-management utilities can be used. It instantiates a parser and a scanner object and then calls each of the functions we have discussed in this chapter, depending on which command-line switches are specified.

Code

SCodeMnt.cpp

The main program can be found in **SCodeMnt.cpp**, which is listed here.

```
// SCodeMnt.cpp
// Defines the entry point for the console application.
///////////////////////////////////////////////////////////////////////


// -------------------------------------------------
// Microsoft Idiosyncrasies.
// -------------------------------------------------
#if _MSC_VER > 1000
// disable warning C4786: symbol greater than 255 character,
// okay to ignore (MSVC)
#pragma warning(disable: 4786)
#endif // _MSC_VER > 1000


// -------------------------------------------------
// Local include files.
// -------------------------------------------------
#include "CodeParser.h"
#include "CodeMaintCPP.h"
#include "Scanner.h"


// -------------------------------------------------
// Library include files.
// -------------------------------------------------
#include <iostream>
#include <ostream>
#include <set>
```

```
#include <string>
#include <vector>
using namespace std;

// -----------------------------------------------
// Miscellaneous constants
// -----------------------------------------------
#define HELPTEXT                                                      \
  "Identifies which files are included in the specified file.\n"  \
  "\n"                                                                \
  "ScodeMnt.exe SourceCode [Output] {[/?] | [/j] | [/ai] | [/c] " \
  ""                "| [/html]}\n\n"                                  \
  ""                                                                  \
  "SourceCode        "                                                \
  "Identifies the file in which to look for the include files.\n" \
  ""                                                                  \
  "Output            "                                                \
  "Specifies the name of the output file. Defaults to stdout.\n"  \
  ""                                                                  \
  "/?                "                                                \
  "Shows this help screen.\n"                                         \
  ""                                                                  \
  "/j                "                                                \
  "Removes the indents from a file.  Used for testing the\n"      \
  "               [/format] switch.\n"                               \
  ""                                                                  \
  "/ai               "                                                \
  "Automatically indents each line in SourceCode.\n"                 \
  ""                                                                  \
  "/c                "                                                \
  "Copies SourceCode to OutputFile.  Used for testing the\n"      \
  "               tokenizing code.\n"                                \
  ""                                                                  \
  "/html             "                                                \
  "Writes SourceCode out to OutputFile using HTML so\n"              \
  "               that each type of token appears in a"              \
  ""               "different color.\n"                              \
  ""                                                                  \
  "/include        Lists all the included files found "             \
  ""               "in SourceCode.\n"                                \
  "\n"                                                                \
  ""                                                                  \
```

```
   "NOTES:         The command line is case sensitive. \n"      \
   "               If OutputFile is left blank all output "     \
   ""              "will be sent to stdout.\n"                  \
   "               The InputFile and OutputFile can be the same."

#define NO_INCLUDE_FILES "No include files found."

// Command Switches
#define SWITCH_HELP         "?"
#define SWITCH_AUTOINDENT   "ai"
#define SWITCH_INCLUDE      "include"
#define SWITCH_HTML         "html"
#define SWITCH_COPY         "c"
#define SWITCH_JUMBALIZE    "j"

#define SWITCH_CHARACTERS "/-"

#define BACKUP_FILE_EXTENSION ".bak"

// -----------------------------------------------
// Error messages
// -----------------------------------------------
#define ERR_FILE_NOT_EXIST "ERROR:  " \
  "The file '%s' does not exist or is in use."
#define ERR_UNEXPECTED_ERROR "ERROR:  " \
  "An unexpected error occurred."
#define ERR_FILE_NOT_OPENED "ERROR:  " \
  "The file '%s' could not be opened for output."
#define ERR_PARAMETERS_INCORRECT "ERROR:  " \
  "The program parameters are invalid."


// -----------------------------------------------
// Typedef Declarations
// -----------------------------------------------
// Type used to store the collection
// of arguments
typedef vector<string> ArgumentCol;
// Type used to store the collection
// of command line switches.
typedef set<string> SwitchCol;
```

```
// ------------------------------------------------
// Function Declarations
// ------------------------------------------------
// Save Command Line so we can retrieve each
// parameter later.
void SaveCommandLine(
  // The number of parameters on the command line
  const int argc,
  // The parameters that appear on the command line
  char* argv[],
  // The collection of arguments
  ArgumentCol& arguments,
  // The collection of switches on the command line
  SwitchCol& switches);

// Prints the HELPTEXT to stdout.
void PrintHelp();


// ------------------------------------------------
// main
// ------------------------------------------------
int main(int argc, char* argv[])
{
  // ---------------
  // Declarations
  // ---------------
  // The input file stream
  CScanner SourceCode;

  // The destination output file
  ofstream OutputFile;

  // The output stream used by all the
  // codemaintenance functions.
  ostream* pOutputStream;

  // The C++ parser object
  CCodeParser parser;

  // Stores the list of include files.
  FileList files;
```

```
// Indicates all is well so continue processing
bool bRet = false;

// Used to output an error message
char sErrorMsg[255];

// Collection of arguments
ArgumentCol arguments;

// Collection of Switches
SwitchCol switches;

// ---------------
// Begin Processing
// ---------------
// Save the command line information.
SaveCommandLine(argc, argv, arguments, switches);


// Check that the filename was given.
// The first argument is the name of the
// program being executed (SCodeMnt.exe)
// so it is ignored.
if (arguments.size() > 1)
{

  // Check if the input name is the same as the output name
  // If so back it up and scan the backup file.
  if( (arguments.size() >= 2) && (arguments[1] == arguments[2]) )
  {
    // Change the input filename and move
    // the input file to this new name.
    arguments[1]+= BACKUP_FILE_EXTENSION;

    // Remove the last backup file
    // No warning will be issued
    remove(arguments[1].c_str());

    // Rename the input file to the backup file
    rename(arguments[2].c_str(), arguments[1].c_str());
  }
```

```cpp
    // Set the scanner to scan the filename on the command line.
    // Attempt to open the input file. If this fails the file
    // was not able to be opened or does not exist.

    SourceCode.open(arguments[1].c_str());
    if ( !(SourceCode.good() && SourceCode.is_open()) )
    {
      // The input file could not be opened.
      sprintf(sErrorMsg, ERR_FILE_NOT_EXIST, arguments[1].c_str());
      cerr << sErrorMsg << endl << endl;
      bRet = false;
    }
    else
      bRet = true;
}
else if ( switches.find(SWITCH_HELP)!=switches.end() )
{
  PrintHelp();
  bRet = false;
}
else if (arguments.size() <= 1)
{
  cerr << ERR_PARAMETERS_INCORRECT << endl << endl;

  // The input file was not specified.  Print out the help text.
  PrintHelp();

  bRet = false;
}


// If everything is still go
if(bRet)
{
  try
  {
    // Load scanner with C++ definition
    LoadCPPScanner(SourceCode);

    // Check if an ouput filename is specified
    if(arguments.size() > 2)
    {
```

```
            // delete the file if it exists already.
            // Note that no warning is issued
            remove(arguments[2].c_str());

            // Open up the ouput stream
            OutputFile.open(arguments[2].c_str());

            // Check that the open worked
            if ( !(OutputFile.good() && OutputFile.is_open()) )
            {
              // Open failed! Send output to stdout.
              pOutputStream = &cout;

              // Print out an error message
              sprintf(sErrorMsg, ERR_FILE_NOT_OPENED,
                arguments[2].c_str());

              // Output the error message
              cerr << sErrorMsg << endl << endl;
            }
            else
              pOutputStream = &OutputFile;
        }
        else // Output filename not specified. Use stdout.
          pOutputStream = &cout;


        // ---------------
        // Include command
        // ---------------
        // Handle the include command
        if( switches.find(SWITCH_INCLUDE)!=switches.end() )
        {
          GetIncludeFileList(SourceCode, files);
          FileList::const_iterator i;
          if (files.empty())
            *pOutputStream << NO_INCLUDE_FILES << endl;
          else
          {
            for(i = files.begin(); i != files.end(); i++)
            {
              *pOutputStream << *i << endl;
```

```
      }
    }  // end if (files.empty())
  } // end if ( switches.find(SWITCH_INCLUDE)!=switches.end() )


  // --------------
  // Copy command
  // --------------
  // copy the file
  else if( switches.find(SWITCH_COPY)!=switches.end() )
    bRet = parser.Copy(SourceCode, *pOutputStream);


  // --------------
  // Jumbalize command
  // --------------
  // Mix up the code removing excess whitespace.
  else if( switches.find(SWITCH_JUMBALIZE)!=switches.end() )
    bRet = Jumbalize(SourceCode, *pOutputStream);


  // --------------
  // AutoIndent command
  // --------------
  // Appropriately format the code indenting it in
  // all the 'right' places.
  else if( switches.find(SWITCH_AUTOINDENT)!=switches.end() )
  {
    LoadCPPFormat(parser);
    bRet = parser.AutoIndent(SourceCode, *pOutputStream);
  }


  // --------------
  // HTML command
  // --------------
  // Write an html version of the file.
  else if( switches.find(SWITCH_HTML)!=switches.end() )
    bRet = parser.WriteHTML(SourceCode, *pOutputStream);

  // Switch is "/?" or invalid or no switch specified.
  else
  {
    PrintHelp();
    bRet = false;
  }
```

```
    }
    catch(...)
    {
      // Report an unexpected error
      cerr << ERR_UNEXPECTED_ERROR << endl << endl;
      // No matter what we must be sure to close the file
      bRet = false;
    }
  }
  // end if (bRet)

  if (SourceCode.is_open())
    SourceCode.close();
  if (OutputFile.is_open())
    OutputFile.close();

  return bRet;
}


void SaveCommandLine(
  // The number of parameters on the command line
  const int argc,
  // The parameters that appear on the command line
  char* argv[],
  // The collection of arguments
  ArgumentCol& arguments,
  // The collection of switches on the command line
  SwitchCol& switches)
{
  for(int i = 0; i < argc; i++)
  {
    if (strchr(SWITCH_CHARACTERS, argv[i][0])!=NULL)
      // The first character is a switch character.
      // Add this argument to the set of switches.
      switches.insert(argv[i]+1);
    else
      // This must be an argument because it is not
      // prefixed with a switch character
      arguments.push_back(argv[i]);
  }
```

```
    return;
}


// Print the commandline help text.
void PrintHelp()
{
    std::cout << HELPTEXT << std::endl;
}
```

ANNOTATIONS

To start, **main( )** calls **SaveCommandLine( )** to save the command parameters
so it can examine them later. After this, it conditionally attempts to open up the
input file. After establishing that no errors have been made on the command
line, the program loads the scanner with the C++ language definition, by calling
LoadCPPScanner( ). Upon return from **LoadCPPScanner( )**, a quick check is made
to decide where to send the output. At this point the command the user selected
is executed.

Notice that all the parsing code is surrounded by a **try catch** block. This traps any
file input/output errors.

Prior to **main( )** ending, all the open files are closed.

Compiling SCodeMnt.exe

Now that you have seen all of the modules, it's time to see how to put them
together. In general, compile and link the files **SCodeMnt.cpp**, **Token.cpp**,
Scanner.cpp, and **CodeParser.cpp**. For example, if you are using Visual C++, then
the following command line will compile and link the code mantanaince program:

```
CL -GX SCodeMnt.cpp Token.cpp Scanner.cpp CodeParser.cpp
```

To build from within the Visual C++ IDE, simply load the **SCodeMnt.dsw** project
workspace and rebuild the entire project. A make file, called **SCodeMnt.mak**, is also
available.

Running SCodeMnt.exe

From the command line, you can enter

```
SCodeMnt /?
```

to print a list of the command parameters of the program. The syntax for executing the program is as follows:

```
INCLUDE SourceCode [OutputFile] {[/?] | [/j] | [/ai] | [/c] | [/html]}
```

Parameter	Definition
SourceCode	Specifies the input file.
OutputFile	Specifies the name of the output file. Defaults to **stdout**.
/?	Shows this help screen.
/j	Removes the indents from a file. Used for testing the [**/format**] switch.
/ai	Automatically indents each line in *SourceCode*.
/c	Copies *SourceCode* to *OutputFile*. Used for testing the tokenizing code.
/html	Writes *SourceCode* out to *OutputFile* using HTML so that each type of token appears in a different color.
/include	Lists all the included files found in *SourceCode*.

Note that each of the switches is case-sensitive. In addition, if *OutputFile* is left blank, all output will be sent to **stdout**. Finally, you can successfully use the same name for both the input and output files, so that the output writes over the input.

Things to Try

The code maintenance program discussed in this chapter is easily expanded and enhanced. Here are some ideas. Hopefully they will spark some creative thinking about the potential of a source-code parser.

You can colorize or autoindent other languages by defining new load functions similar to **LoadScannerCPP( )** and **LoadFormatCPP( ),** so that additional languages can also be displayed in a browser window or automatically formatted. An even better solution would be to change the program so it can read a language-definition file. Using this method, the language definition could be loaded at run-time and be data driven—rather than having to write code each time you wish to parse a new language.

Another idea would be to try adding a function that creates a file containing each unique token found in a program file. This token file could be used as a custom dictionary by a word processor, for example.

One last suggestion would be to create a cross-reference database that indicates each line where a particular function or variable is used.

C/C++ for Internet Access

By Lars Klander

CSimpBrowseDoc   SimpBrowseView.cpp

Today, it seems everyone is on the Internet—whether it's for business or personal use, even people who know little else about computers are making the effort to "surf the Web." Knowing how to take advantage of Web protocols is an important consideration for you as a developer—particularly if you are developing after-market applications.

The Internet communicates using *protocols*. Some of these protocols are shared among various types of Internet services, while others are unique to specific services. At a lower level, however, all communications across the Internet occur through the use of *sockets*, a two-way communication mechanism. The remainder of this chapter focuses on client-side communications over the socket in concept, and how to access remote objects on a server in specific. To perform the communications, we will write our own, simple browser program—and we'll also take advantage of a third-party browser library to more easily integrate browser services into the application.

Internet Services

Many types of services are in widespread use on IP networks. Examples include FTP, telnet, gopher, the World Wide Web, archie, DNS name service, whois, finger, and many others. The protocols used for these services are defined in the Internet Request For Comment documents, or *RFCs*.

The services themselves are usually available on *well-known* port numbers. For example, to connect to a telnet server on any host on the Internet, you would attempt to connect to Transport Control Protocol (TCP) port 23 on that host machine. Well-known ports that a host recognizes are typically identified in the system's services file. This file is used in UNIX as well as Windows TCP/IP implementations.

Sockets are the foundation of communications on the Internet. You can think of a socket as a two-way communication pipe between two remote systems. In Windows, the Berkeley sockets interface is implemented through the WinSock API, which lets you create and manage sockets. There are some platform-specific differences in socket implementations, but the models in this chapter provide a strong basis for your work with sockets in any environment. The function names may differ slightly from platform to platform, but their purposes will always be similar.

The WinSock API

The Berkeley sockets interface can be used for communicating using connection-oriented protocols such as TCP, as well as connectionless protocols such as UDP. The applicable programming model is the *client-server* model; servers wait for incoming requests, while clients initiate sessions.

Among the implementation differences between WinSock and the UNIX version of Berkeley sockets, perhaps the most significant is that socket descriptors and file descriptors cannot be used interchangeably in WinSock as they can in UNIX. This has a notable effect when porting applications that make an assumption of this equivalence.

Another difference is that the WinSock library requires initialization. Applications that intend to use WinSock functions must first call the **WSAStartup( )** function. When their work with the WinSock library is finished, the applications should call **WSACleanup( )** for proper termination.

The WinSock API also introduces several WinSock-specific functions for performing asynchronous I/O on sockets. This assists in the development of responsive GUI WinSock applications.

WinSock Initialization

You initialize the WinSock library from within your application, with a call to **WSAStartup( )**. The application calling this function provides the address to a **WSADATA** structure, which will hold initialization information.

During the call to **WSAStartup( )**, your application negotiates a version number with the WinSock library. The initialization request fails if there is no overlap between the version number supported by the application and the version number supported by the WinSock library. If an error occurs, **WSAStartup( )** returns a nonzero value. Applications can retrieve extended error information through the function **WSAGetLastError( )**.

A socket is created by a call to the **socket( )** function. Parameters to this function indicate the type of socket, the type of network address, and the protocol being used. For example, the following call creates a TCP socket:

```
socket(AF_INET, SOCK_STREAM, IPPROTO_TCP)
```

To associate a socket with an actual host address and port number, an application typically calls the **bind( )** function. In addition to the socket identifier or *socket descriptor* (which is returned by the **socket( )** call), **bind( )** takes a parameter that is a pointer to a structure describing the socket address. This structure is defined as follows:

```
struct sockaddr {
  u_short sa_family;
  char sa_data[14];
};
```

The **sa_family** member of this structure specifies the type of address. For Internet addresses, this value is set to **AF_INET**. The **sa_data** member contains the actual address.

Applications can easily access the various components of the address by referring to it through a **sockaddr_in** structure (instead of using **sockaddr**). Here is the definition of this structure:

```
struct sockaddr_in {
  short sin_family;
  u_short sin_port;
  struct in_addr sin_addr;
  char sin_zero[8];
};
```

Of these members, **sin_port** is the 16-bit port number, and **sin_addr** is the 32-bit host address.

Name Service

In order to assign meaningful values to the host address field in the **sockaddr_in** structure, your application must first obtain a 32-bit host address. To obtain an address when the symbolic name of a host is known, use the **gethostbyname( )** function.

When calling **gethostbyname( )**, applications pass the symbolic name of the host and receive a pointer to a **HOSTENT** structure in return. The **HOSTENT** structure is defined as follows:

```
struct HOSTENT {
  char FAR *h_name;
  char FAR * FAR * h_aliases;
  short h_addrtype;
  short h_length;
  char FAR * FAR * h_addr_list;
};
```

This structure is necessary because a host name may be associated with several host addresses (the reverse is also true). In most cases, applications just take the first (and often the only) address in **h_addr_list**. To make this easier, the symbol **h_addr** is defined as **h_addr_list[0]**.

PROGRAMMER'S NOTE   *Even though Visual C++ and many other compilers no longer distinguish **NEAR** and **FAR** definitions, the sockets library nevertheless defines the structure in this manner (its original definition), so we have left the definition as is.*

If an application wishes to use a numeric address instead, it can use the **inet_addr( )** function to convert a string containing a numeric address into a 32-bit address value. Once that value has been obtained, you can use the **gethostbyaddr( )** function to return a **HOSTENT** structure for the specified host.

Network Issues with Byte Ordering

When it comes to designing applications that are expected to work on hybrid networks, an issue of particular importance is *byte ordering*. Some system architectures, such as the Motorola 68000 processor family, are *big-endian* (most significant byte comes first). Others, such as the Intel family of processors and DEC CPUs, are *little-endian* (most significant byte comes last).

Internet numbers (for example, host addresses) are always big-endian. To ensure correct conversion between machine-independent Internet numbers and their machine-dependent representation, you can use the following set of functions: **htonl( )**, **htons( )**, **ntohl( )**, and **ntohs( )**. These functions convert short or long integers from network to host format and vice versa. These functions may be implemented as macros, depending on your compiler.

You can also use the Windows Sockets API functions **WSAHtonl( )**, **WSAHtons( )**, **WSANtohl( )**, and **WSANtohs( )**. If you use these Sockets API functions, you can use the **WSAGetLastError( )** function to determine what may have caused an error if you receive one.

Communication Through Sockets

In the case of the connection-oriented TCP protocol, the server application binds to a specific TCP port and then uses the **listen( )** function to indicate willingness to accept incoming connection requests. Immediately after the call to listen, the server calls **accept( )** to wait for incoming connections. When **accept( )** returns, it provides the address of the peer process.

The client, after creating a socket using the **socket( )** call, can immediately initiate a connection using the **connect( )** call. It is not necessary to bind the socket to a specific port using **bind( )** prior to calling **connect( )**.

Once the connection has been successfully initiated, both the client and the server can use the **send( )** call to transmit data and the **recv( )** call to receive data. The semantics of **send( )** and **recv( )** are similar to the semantics of the **read( )** and **write( )** calls for low-level file I/O. Indeed, on UNIX systems it's possible to use the latter pair of functions to perform I/O on sockets.

Unfortunately, as mentioned earlier, this is not possible with WinSock due to the differences between a file descriptor and a socket descriptor. For the same reason, it is not possible to use the **close( )** system call to close a socket from WinSock; applications must use **closesocket( )** when a socket connection is about to be terminated. Either the client or the server can terminate the connection using **closesocket( )**. The **closesocket( )** function will return a value of **SOCKET_ERROR**. You can then use the **WSAGetLastError( )** function to retrieve a value representative of the error.

In the case of the connectionless UDP protocol, the sequence of events is somewhat different; the activities of the client and server application are more symmetrical. In this case, both the client and the server create their respective sockets and bind those to specific port numbers. The server then makes a call to the **recvfrom( )** function, which waits for any incoming data. The client, in turn, uses the **sendto( )** function to send data to a specific address. When this data is received by the server, the **recvfrom( )** call returns, and the server also obtains the address from which the data has been received. The server can then use this address in a subsequent call to **sendto( )**, as it replies to the client.

The Blocking Problem and the select( ) Call

In the simplistic models discussed in the preceding section, both the client and the server use *blocking* calls when waiting for data. A blocking call does not return to the calling function until the requested data becomes available. In other words, the application that makes such a call becomes suspended until the call is completed. This model will suffice in many simple situations, but it is clearly unacceptable for interactive applications. Such an application (for example, a telnet client) cannot simply freeze until data becomes available from the server.

The solution employed by most UNIX TCP/IP applications relies on the **select( )** system call. This call makes it possible to wait on multiple (file or socket) descriptors. This way, a UNIX process can easily wait for data on a socket as well as the standard input, and spring into action whenever data is received on either of them.

Again, things are not this easy with WinSock, however, because socket and file descriptors are not interchangeable. Unfortunately, **select( )** is no exception; it can only wait on multiple socket descriptors, not on a mix of socket and file descriptors. Although it's possible to monitor a socket while polling, this is not a very efficient solution—but Win32's multithreading capability saves the day. A process can easily start additional threads and have a separate thread for each input source. This mechanism works well for both command-line and graphical TCP/IP utilities.

Nevertheless, the WinSock library offers yet another family of functions that assist in writing well-behaved TCP/IP applications without having to resort to multithreaded solution: asynchronous socket calls, discussed in the next section.

Asynchronous Socket Calls

Asynchronous socket calls rely on the Windows message-passing mechanism to communicate socket events to Windows applications. At the center of this mechanism is the **WSAAsyncSelect( )** function call. Through this function, an application can wait for a combination of socket events. Applications may receive

notifications indicating readiness for reading, writing, incoming, and completed connections, and for socket closure. (This same call can also be used for notifications regarding *out-of-band* data, something we have not discussed in this section.) The event notification takes place in the form of a user-defined message that is posted to a window, also defined in the call to **WSAAsyncSelect( )**.

WSAAsyncSelect( ) posts a single message for every event in which the application has expressed interest. Once the message has been posted, no further messages will be posted for the same event until the application implicitly resets the event by calling the appropriate socket library function. For example, if a notification for incoming data is posted, no further such notifications will be posted for the given socket until the application retrieves that data with a call to **recv( )** or **recvfrom( )**.

Other asynchronous socket functions include, for example, asynchronous versions of the standard Berkeley **gethostbyname( )** and **gethostbyaddr( )** calls: **WSAAsyncGetHostByName( )** and **WSAAsyncGetHostByAddr( )**. WinSock applications can also influence the blocking mechanism used in the standard Berkeley-style calls by using the **WSASetBlockingHook( )** function.

Synchronous Operations and Serialization

The purpose of the **CAsyncSocket** class is to provide a low-level interface to the WinSock library. In contrast, the **CSocket** class, which is derived from **CAsyncSocket**, provides somewhat higher-level functionality.

Unlike **CAsyncSocket**, **CSocket** provides blocking. Its member functions do not return until a requested operation has been completed.

PROGRAMMER'S NOTE   *The callback functions **OnConnect( )** and **OnSend( )** are never called for **CSocket** objects.*

One particular use of **CSocket** objects is in conjunction with **CFileSocket** objects to enable the MFC serialization functions to work on sockets. A **CFileSocket** object can be attached to a **CArchive** object and a **CSocket** object; afterwards, you can send and receive data simply using MFC serialization.

The Simple Browser Project

All that being said, and now that we have reviewed some of the basics of working with sockets from Windows, let's move on to the consideration of a simple browser program. Though in some ways it's harder to write than a simple server program is, the browser program is arguably more useful. The following section presents the code for the document and view classes within the simple browser program. After the code, we will review the annotations for these classes.

Code

Because most of the processing for the simple browser program occurs within its document and view objects, we will review only the implementation of the **CSimpBrowseDoc** and **CSimpBrowseView** classes within this chapter. Here is the code for the **CSimpBrowseDoc** class.

```
#include "stdafx.h"
#include "simpbrowse.h"
#include "SimpBrowseDoc.h"
#include "openhttp.h"

#ifdef _DEBUG
#define new DEBUG_NEW
#undef THIS_FILE
static char THIS_FILE[] = __FILE__;
#endif

IMPLEMENT_DYNCREATE(CSimpBrowseDoc, CDocument)
BEGIN_MESSAGE_MAP(CSimpBrowseDoc, CDocument)
  //{{AFX_MSG_MAP(CSimpBrowseDoc)
  ON_COMMAND(ID_FILE_HTTP, OnFileHttp)
  //}}AFX_MSG_MAP
  ON_COMMAND(ID_FILE_SEND_MAIL, OnFileSendMail)
  ON_UPDATE_COMMAND_UI(ID_FILE_SEND_MAIL, OnUpdateFileSendMail)
END_MESSAGE_MAP()

CSimpBrowseDoc::CSimpBrowseDoc() {}
CSimpBrowseDoc::~CSimpBrowseDoc() {}

BOOL CSimpBrowseDoc::OnNewDocument()
{
  if (!CDocument::OnNewDocument())
    return FALSE;

  strcpy (real_file_name, "CANARCH.HTM");
  strcpy (file_name, "CANARCH.HTM");
  OpenHttpFile (real_file_name);
  return TRUE;
}

void CSimpBrowseDoc::Serialize(CArchive& ar)
{
```

```
  if (ar.IsStoring()) {
    // TODO: add storing code here
  }
  else {
    // TODO: add loading code here
  }
}


#ifdef _DEBUG
void CSimpBrowseDoc::AssertValid() const
{
  CDocument::AssertValid();
}


void CSimpBrowseDoc::Dump(CDumpContext& dc) const
{
  CDocument::Dump(dc);
}
#endif //_DEBUG

BOOL CSimpBrowseDoc::OpenHttpFile (LPCTSTR lpszPathName,
    LPCTSTR local_file_name)
{
  strcpy (real_file_name, lpszPathName);

  if (strnicmp (real_file_name, "http://", 7) == 0) {
    internet = InternetOpen ("Browser", INTERNET_OPEN_TYPE_DIRECT,
        NULL, NULL, NULL);

    if (internet) {
      HINTERNET file_handle = InternetOpenUrl
          (internet, real_file_name,
           NULL, 0, INTERNET_FLAG_RAW_DATA, 0);
      if (file_handle) {
        DWORD bytes_read = 0;
        InternetReadFile (file_handle, buffer, 10000, &bytes_read);

        FILE* fp;
        if ((fp = fopen (local_file_name, "wb")) != NULL) {
          fwrite (buffer, bytes_read, 1, fp);
          fclose (fp);
          strcpy (file_name, local_file_name);
        }
```

```
          else
            return FALSE;
        }
        else
          return FALSE;
      }
      else
        return FALSE;
      InternetCloseHandle (internet);
    }
    else {
      if (!CDocument::OnOpenDocument(file_name))
        return FALSE;
      strcpy (file_name, real_file_name);
    }
    return TRUE;
}

void CSimpBrowseDoc::OnFileHttp()
{
  OpenHTTP dialog_box;
  if (dialog_box.DoModal() == IDOK) {
    OpenHttpFile (dialog_box.m_file_name);
    UpdateAllViews (NULL);
  }
}
```

ANNOTATIONS

Within the MFC document/view architecture, it is the document class's responsibility to maintain persistent or semipersistent data. In the simple browser program, the document file maintains information about the opened HTML file, while the view class handles the actual display of the class within the window.

Most of the functions within the **SimpBrowseDoc.cpp** file are straightforward, MFC architecture defaults. Three functions within the file, however, perform custom processing for the management of Internet files—**OnNewDocument( )**, **OpenHTTPFile( )** and **OnFileHTTP( )**. Let's consider the **OnNewDocument( )** implementation first.

Within the MFC framework, **OnNewDocument( )** is called whenever the program creates a new document object. The code within the function simply tells the program to open the **canarch.htm** file (which is contained on the companion CD-ROM) whenever the user opens a new document. This file is similar to the default browser document that appears whenever you open a browser without providing a URL. Within the function, the program first makes sure it is able to successfully open a new document, calling the **OnNewDocument( )** function within the **CDocument** base class, as shown here:

```
BOOL CSimpBrowseDoc::OnNewDocument()
{
  if (!CDocument::OnNewDocument())
    return FALSE;
```

Next, the program copies the name of the local file into the **real_file_name** and **file_name** member variables. It then calls the **OpenHttpFile( )** function, explained just below, to open and display the **canarch.htm** file.

```
  strcpy (real_file_name, "CANARCH.HTM");
  strcpy (file_name, "CANARCH.HTM");
  OpenHttpFile (real_file_name);
  return TRUE;
}
```

Finally, the function returns **TRUE**, letting the program know that the document was constructed and filled correctly.

THE OPENHTTPFILE( ) FUNCTION

Needless to say, the key processing occurs within the **OpenHttpFile( )** function. The function accepts a path name parameter, which it then analyzes to determine whether the name refers to a local file or an Internet file. The determination occurs within the first **if** statement, which uses the C **strnicmp( )** function to determine whether the path contains the **http://** protocol identifier:

```
BOOL CSimpBrowseDoc::OpenHttpFile (LPCTSTR lpszPathName,
    LPCTSTR local_file_name)
{
  strcpy (real_file_name, lpszPathName);

  if (strnicmp (real_file_name, "http://", 7) == 0) {
```

If the path is an Internet address, the program uses the **InternetOpen( )** function, defined by the Win32 API, to open the Internet connection. This function accepts five parameters. The key parameters used here are for the agent name—**SimpBrowse**, which corresponds to our application—and the Internet connection type. The second parameter specifies the connection type, and can be one of three constants:

INTERNET_OPEN_TYPE_DIRECT	Tells the Internet API to resolve all host names locally (the method we use in this program).
INTERNET_OPEN_TYPE_PROXY	Tells the API to pass all resolution requests to a proxy server.
INTERNET_OPEN_TYPE_PRECONFIG	Tells the computer to retrieve the configuration it should use from the Registry entries for the Internet. In Windows, these entries can be set or modified from the Control Panel.

For simplicity's sake, we're opening a direct connection by default in this program. The next two parameters specify information for use in a proxy server environment—the name of the proxy server, and a list of local addresses that the program can bypass the server to access. The last parameter lets you set specific connection flags; the Win32 Internet API reference explains these flags in detail.

```
internet = InternetOpen ("SimpBrowse", INTERNET_OPEN_TYPE_DIRECT,
    NULL, NULL, NULL);
```

So, now, if the filename is an Internet file, we try to open the Internet connection. We use an **if** statement here in the event that traps the processing if, for some reason, the program is unable to open the connection. If the connection is opened successfully, the program code defines an **HINTERNET** handle, and initializes it with a call to the **InternetOpenUrl( )** function.

```
if (internet) {
    HINTERNET file_handle = InternetOpenUrl
        (internet, real_file_name,
        NULL, 0, INTERNET_FLAG_RAW_DATA, 0);
```

The function returns a valid file handle if it successfully opens the file; otherwise, it returns **NULL**. The parameters to this function are explained in detail within the Win32 Internet API reference; for our purposes here, notice the following key points: The first parameter must be a handle to an open Internet session; the second parameter a string containing the fully qualified address name of the URL to open; and the third and fourth parameters deal with headers you want to send to the

server. The fifth parameter tells the API call how to return the data—in this case, we are requesting raw data, rather than formatted data—and the sixth parameter passes context information, useful for handling program-defined callback functions.

After initializing the file handle, we must again check to make sure that we were successful. If so, the program code then begins to read the data in from the file, using the **InternetReadFile( )** API function and reading in a buffer of 10,000 characters, as shown here:

```
if (file_handle) {
    DWORD bytes_read = 0;
    InternetReadFile (file_handle, buffer, 10000, &bytes_read);
```

PROGRAMMER'S NOTE   *For a real, deployment environment, you would probably want to allow for the reading of significantly larger files—although there's little likelihood of a Web page's having more than 10,000 characters unless it contains scripting code.*

Next, we have to create a local, temporary file in which to store the data being retrieved from the Internet. We retrieve and store the file information, then parse and display it later within the view class. Again, for safety, we test the file's successful creation (as a write-only file with binary format) within an **if** statement:

```
FILE* fp;
if ((fp = fopen (local_file_name, "wb")) != NULL) {
```

If the file is created successfully, the program writes all the characters in the buffer into the file and then closes the file. Finally, it copies the file's name into the **file_name** variable, which the program will use elsewhere to parse the file (within the view class):

```
        fwrite (buffer, bytes_read, 1, fp);
        fclose (fp);
        strcpy (file_name, local_file_name);
    }
```

As you saw earlier, the program code will fall through to these internal **else** clauses any time an action against the remote file fails. In such cases, the program will return **FALSE**, indicating it was unable to open the file successfully:

```
    else
        return FALSE;
    }
    else
      return FALSE;
  }
else
  return FALSE;
```

In any event, the program has to close the **HINTERNET** handle before it exits the function, which it does with a call to **InternetCloseHandle( )**, as shown here:

```
InternetCloseHandle (internet);
}
```

PROGRAMMER'S NOTE   *While the code as written uses **if** statements for its error testing, you can, of course, use **try...catch** clauses instead—which will require only slight rewriting of the program code, and will likely perform better in a production environment because of the additional control you will have over the nature of error-handling.*

If you look back through the code, you'll see that the next **else** clause is invoked whenever the program determines that the file is a local file rather than a remote file. In such cases, the program invokes the parent class's **OnOpenDocument( )** function to open the file, again returning **FALSE** if it does not do so successfully. When the file opens, the program code copies the name of the local file into the **file_name** variable:

```
else {
   if (!CDocument::OnOpenDocument(file_name))
      return FALSE;
   strcpy (file_name, real_file_name);
}
return TRUE;
}
```

THE ONFILEHTTP( ) FUNCTION

The **OnFileHttp( )** function is invoked whenever the user selects the File menu's Open option from the program's main window. The function displays a dialog box with the **IDD_HTTP_FILE** resource identifier (for which the **OpenHTTP** class is a wrapper). The dialog box simply displays a text box within which the user can enter the URL to open, as well as OK and Cancel buttons, as shown in Figure 9-1.

For simplicity, we open the dialog as a modal dialog box, as shown here:

```
void CSimpBrowseDoc::OnFileHttp()
{
  OpenHTTP dialog_box;
  if (dialog_box.DoModal() == IDOK) {
```

If the user clicks OK, the program looks for the URL that the user entered within the text box. The program code passes the value of the **m_file_name** string to the **OpenHttpFile( )** function, which opens and reads the file, as you saw previously. It

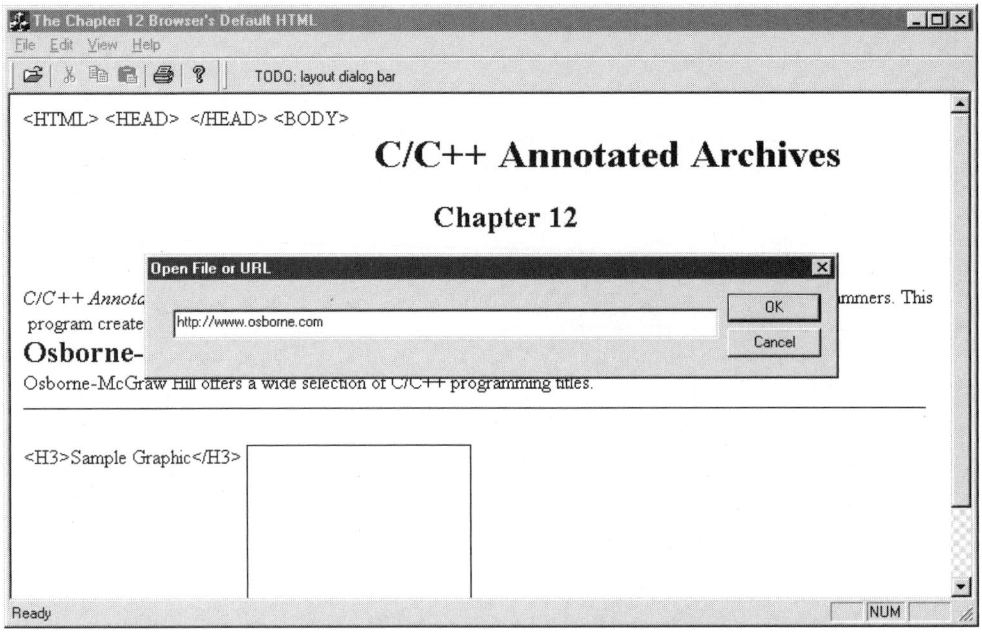

FIGURE 9-1. The dialog box within which the user enters the URL to open

then invokes the **UpdateAllViews( )** function, which forces the views of the document to repaint themselves. (You'll see more about what happens during the repainting later in this chapter.)

```
OpenHttpFile (dialog_box.m_file_name);
UpdateAllViews (NULL);
}
}
```

So, as you have seen, the document maintains information about the currently opened file; and it contains the code to retrieve the user-requested file, either from the Internet or from the local computer. The display of the file, however, is handled within **SimpBrowseView.cpp**. This file contains all the painting code for the view, as well as the parsing code for the handling of the HTML file. The following sections present the code for the file, followed by annotations about each of the custom functions within the file.

Code

SimpBrowseView.cpp

```cpp
// SimpBrowseView.cpp : implementation of the CSimpBrowseView class
//

#include "stdafx.h"
#include "SimpBrowse.h"
#include "SimpBrowseDoc.h"
#include "SimpBrowseView.h"

#ifdef _DEBUG
#define new DEBUG_NEW
#undef THIS_FILE
static char THIS_FILE[] = __FILE__;
#endif

IMPLEMENT_DYNCREATE(CSimpBrowseView, CScrollView)
BEGIN_MESSAGE_MAP(CSimpBrowseView, CScrollView)
  //{{AFX_MSG_MAP(CSimpBrowseView)
  ON_WM_MOUSEMOVE()
  ON_WM_LBUTTONDOWN()
  //}}AFX_MSG_MAP
  // Standard printing commands
  ON_COMMAND(ID_FILE_PRINT, CScrollView::OnFilePrint)
  ON_COMMAND(ID_FILE_PRINT_DIRECT, CScrollView::OnFilePrint)
  ON_COMMAND(ID_FILE_PRINT_PREVIEW, CScrollView::OnFilePrintPreview)
END_MESSAGE_MAP()

CSimpBrowseView::CSimpBrowseView()
{
  frame_window = NULL;
  printing_document = FALSE;
  for (int i = 0; i < MAX_HREFS; i++)
    href [i].clicked = FALSE;
}


CSimpBrowseView::~CSimpBrowseView() {}

BOOL CSimpBrowseView::PreCreateWindow(CREATESTRUCT& cs)
{
  return CScrollView::PreCreateWindow(cs);
}
```

```
void CSimpBrowseView::OnDraw(CDC* pDC)
{
  CSimpBrowseDoc* pDoc = GetDocument();
  ASSERT_VALID(pDoc);

  parser (pDoc, pDC);
}

void CSimpBrowseView::OnInitialUpdate()
{
  CScrollView::OnInitialUpdate();
  CSize sizeTotal;
  // TODO: calculate the total size of this view
  sizeTotal.cx = sizeTotal.cy = 100;
  SetScrollSizes(MM_TEXT, sizeTotal);
}

BOOL CSimpBrowseView::OnPreparePrinting(CPrintInfo* pInfo)
{
  // default preparation
  return DoPreparePrinting(pInfo);
}

void CSimpBrowseView::OnBeginPrinting(CDC* /*pDC*/,
    CPrintInfo* /*pInfo*/)
{
  printing_document = TRUE;
}

void CSimpBrowseView::OnEndPrinting(CDC* /*pDC*/,
    CPrintInfo* /*pInfo*/)
{
  printing_document = FALSE;
}

#ifdef _DEBUG
void CSimpBrowseView::AssertValid() const
{
  CScrollView::AssertValid();
}

void CSimpBrowseView::Dump(CDumpContext& dc) const
{
```

```
    CScrollView::Dump(dc);
}

CSimpBrowseDoc* CSimpBrowseView::GetDocument()
// non-debug version is inline
{
  ASSERT(m_pDocument->IsKindOf(RUNTIME_CLASS(CSimpBrowseDoc)));
  return (CSimpBrowseDoc*)m_pDocument;
}
#endif //_DEBUG

void CSimpBrowseView::parser(CSimpBrowseDoc* pDoc, CDC* pDC)
{
  dc = pDC;

  if (!printing_document) {
    CWnd* window = dc->GetWindow();
    RECT rect;
    window->GetClientRect (&rect);
    frame_window = window->GetParentFrame();
    width = (int) rect.right;
    height = (int) rect.bottom;
  }
  COLORREF old_color = dc->SetTextColor(RGB(0,0,0));
  current_font = new CFont;
  current_font->CreatePointFont (120, "Times New Roman");
  x_begin = X_BEGIN;
  y_begin = Y_BEGIN;
  y_increment = Y_INCREMENT;
  x = x_begin;
  y = y_begin;
  y_top = y_begin;
  y_bottom = y_top + y_increment;
  href_index = 0;
  parse(pDoc->file_name);
  dc->SetTextColor (old_color);
  CSize x (width, y+30);
  SetScrollSizes (MM_TEXT, x);
}

void CSimpBrowseView::parse(char* filename)
{
```

```
FILE* fp;
if ((fp = fopen(filename, "r")) == NULL) {
  string.Format ("Unable to open <%s>", filename);
  dc->TextOut (0, 0, string);
  return;
}
title = FALSE;
center = FALSE;
int done = 0;
while (!done) {
  done = get_tag (fp, tag);
  if (done)
    break;
  if (stricmp (tag, "TITLE") == 0) {
    title = TRUE;
    string.Empty();
  }
  else if (stricmp (tag, "/TITLE") == 0) {
    title = FALSE;
    if (frame_window)
      frame_window->SetWindowText (string);
    string.Empty();
  }
  else if (stricmp (tag, "HR") == 0) {
    y += y_increment + y_increment/2;
    dc->MoveTo (x_begin, y);
    dc->LineTo (width - X_BEGIN*2, y);
    x = x_begin;
    y += y_increment - y_increment/2;
    y_top = y;
    y_bottom = y_top + y_increment;
  }
  else if (stricmp (tag, "BR") == 0 || stricmp (tag, "P") == 0) {
    print_string();
    string.Empty();
  }
  else if (stricmp (tag, "CENTER") == 0) {
    center = TRUE;
    string.Empty();
  }
  else if (stricmp (tag, "/CENTER") == 0) {
    center = FALSE;
    x = (width - (dc->GetTextExtent (string)).cx) / 2;
```

```
    print_characters (string);
    x = x_begin;
    y += y_increment;
    y_top = y;
    y_bottom = y_top + y_increment;
}
else if (stricmp (tag, "B") == 0) {
  bold_on ();
}
else if (stricmp (tag, "/B") == 0) {
  bold_off ();
}
else if (stricmp (tag, "I") == 0) {
  italic_on ();
}
else if (stricmp (tag, "/I") == 0) {
  italic_off ();
}
else if (stricmp (tag, "U") == 0) {
  underline_on ();
}
else if (stricmp (tag, "/U") == 0) {
  underline_off ();
}
else if (strnicmp (tag, "A ", 2) == 0) {
  href_on();
}
else if (stricmp (tag, "/A") == 0) {
  href_off();
}
else if (stricmp (tag, "PRE") == 0) {
  preformatted_on ();
}
else if (stricmp (tag, "/PRE") == 0) {
  preformatted_off ();
}
else if (stricmp (tag, "UL") == 0) {
  unordered_list_on ();
}
else if (stricmp (tag, "/UL") == 0) {
  unordered_list_off ();
}
else if (stricmp (tag, "OL") == 0) {
  ordered_list_on ();
```

```
      }
      else if (stricmp (tag, "/OL") == 0) {
        ordered_list_off ();
      }
      else if (stricmp (tag, "LI") == 0) {
        insert_list_item();
      }
      else if (strnicmp (tag, "IMG ", 4) == 0) {
        display_image();
      }
      else if (stricmp (tag, "H1") == 0) {
        set_head1();
      }
      else if (stricmp (tag, "H2") == 0) {
        set_head2();
      }
      else if (stricmp (tag, "/H1") == 0 ||
          stricmp (tag, "/H2") == 0) {
        set_normal();
      }
      else {
        print_characters ("<");
        print_characters (tag);
        print_characters (">");
      }
      tag [0] = '\0';
  }
  fclose(fp);
}

int CSimpBrowseView::get_tag(FILE* fp, char* tag)
{
  int c;

  while ((c = fgetc(fp)) != EOF) {
    if (c == '<') {
      int i = 0;
      while ((c = fgetc(fp)) != '>') {
        if (i < TAG_LENGTH)
          tag[i++] = c;
      }
      tag[i] = '\0';
      return(0);
    }
```

```
    else
      process_info(c);
  }

  if (c == EOF)
    return(1);
  else
    return(0);
}

void CSimpBrowseView::process_info (int c)
{
  if (c == '\n') {
    if (center) {
      print_string();
      return;
    }
    else if (x != x_begin)
      c = ' ';
    else
      return;
  }

  if (title || center) {
    string += c;
    return;
  }
  print_character (c);
}

void CSimpBrowseView::print_characters(CString characters)
{
  int length = characters.GetLength();
  for (int i = 0; i < length; i++)
    print_character (characters.GetAt (i));
}

void CSimpBrowseView::print_character(char c)
{
  char s[2];
  s[0] = c;
  s[1] = '\0';
```

```
   CString character(s);
   CFont* old_font = dc->SelectObject (current_font);
   dc->TextOut (x, y, character);
   x += (dc->GetTextExtent(character)).cx;
   dc->SelectObject (old_font);
   if (x > (width-X_BEGIN*2)) {
     x = x_begin;
     y += y_increment;
     y_top = y;
     y_bottom = y_top + y_increment;
   }
}

void CSimpBrowseView::bold_on()
{
   LOGFONT lf;
   current_font->GetLogFont (&lf);
   lf.lfWeight = 700;
   delete current_font;
   current_font = new CFont;
   current_font->CreateFontIndirect (&lf);
}

void CSimpBrowseView::bold_off()
{
   LOGFONT lf;
   current_font->GetLogFont (&lf);
   lf.lfWeight = 400;
   delete current_font;
   current_font = new CFont;
   current_font->CreateFontIndirect (&lf);
}

void CSimpBrowseView::italic_on()
{
   LOGFONT lf;
   current_font->GetLogFont (&lf);
   lf.lfItalic = TRUE;
   delete current_font;
   current_font = new CFont;
   current_font->CreateFontIndirect (&lf);
}
```

```
void CSimpBrowseView::italic_off()
{
  LOGFONT lf;
  current_font->GetLogFont (&lf);
  lf.lfItalic = FALSE;
  delete current_font;
  current_font = new CFont;
  current_font->CreateFontIndirect (&lf);
}

void CSimpBrowseView::underline_on()
{
  LOGFONT lf;
  current_font->GetLogFont (&lf);
  lf.lfUnderline = TRUE;
  delete current_font;
  current_font = new CFont;
  current_font->CreateFontIndirect (&lf);
}

void CSimpBrowseView::underline_off()
{
  LOGFONT lf;
  current_font->GetLogFont (&lf);
  lf.lfUnderline = FALSE;
  delete current_font;
  current_font = new CFont;
  current_font->CreateFontIndirect (&lf);
}

void CSimpBrowseView::href_on()
{
  underline_on ();
  if (href [href_index].clicked)
    dc->SetTextColor (RGB (255, 0, 0));
  else
    dc->SetTextColor (RGB (0, 0, 255));
  char* p1 = strchr (tag, '"') + 1;
  char* p2 = strchr (p1, '"');
  int length = (int) (p2 - p1);
  href [href_index].rect.left = x;
```

```
    href [href_index].rect.top   = y;
    href [href_index].ref.Format ("%*.*s", length, length, p1);
}

void CSimpBrowseView::href_off()
{
  underline_off ();
  dc->SetTextColor (RGB (0, 0, 0));
  href [href_index].rect.right  = x;
  href [href_index].rect.bottom = y + 20;
  if (href_index < MAX_HREFS-1)
    href_index++;
}

void CSimpBrowseView::preformatted_on()
{
  delete current_font;
  current_font = new CFont;
  current_font->CreatePointFont (100, "Courier New");
}

void CSimpBrowseView::preformatted_off()
{
  delete current_font;
  current_font = new CFont;
  current_font->CreatePointFont (120, "Times New Roman");
}

void CSimpBrowseView::unordered_list_on()
{
  ordered_list = FALSE;
  x_begin = X_BEGIN + 40;
  x = x_begin;
  if (string.GetLength() > 0) {
    print_string();
    string.Empty();
  }
  print_string();
}

void CSimpBrowseView::unordered_list_off()
{
  x_begin = X_BEGIN;
  print_string();
```

```
  string.Empty();
  print_string();
}

void CSimpBrowseView::ordered_list_on()
{
  ordered_list = TRUE;
  list_item = 0;
  x_begin = X_BEGIN + 40;
  x = x_begin;
  if (string.GetLength() > 0) {
    print_string();
    string.Empty();
  }
  print_string();
}

void CSimpBrowseView::ordered_list_off()
{
  ordered_list = FALSE;
  x_begin = X_BEGIN;
  print_string();
  string.Empty();
  print_string();
}

void CSimpBrowseView::insert_list_item()
{
  print_string();
  string.Empty();
  if (ordered_list) {
    list_item++;
    CString characters;
    characters.Format ("%d.", list_item);
    x -= 20;
    print_characters (characters);
  }
  else {
    CBrush brush (RGB (0, 0, 0));
    CBrush* old_brush = dc->SelectObject (&brush);
    dc->Ellipse (x-10, y+6, x-4, y+12);
    dc->SelectObject (old_brush);
  }
```

```
  x = x_begin;
}

void CSimpBrowseView::display_image()
{
  char* p1 = strchr (tag, '"') + 1;
  char* p2 = strchr (p1, '"');
  int length = (int) (p2 - p1);
  char filename[100];
  strncpy (filename, p1, length);
  filename [length] = '\0';
  WORD image_width, image_height;
  FILE* fp;
  if ((fp = fopen (filename, "r")) != NULL) {
    fseek (fp, 6L, SEEK_SET);
    fread (&image_width, 2, 1, fp);
    fread (&image_height, 2, 1, fp);
    fclose (fp);
  }
  else {
    char old_file_name [100];
    char old_real_file_name [100];
    char image_file [100];
    CSimpBrowseDoc* pDoc = GetDocument();
    strcpy(old_real_file_name, pDoc->real_file_name);
    strcpy(old_file_name, pDoc->file_name);
    if (strnicmp (filename, "http://", 7) == 0)
      strcpy(image_file, filename);
    else {
      strcpy(image_file, old_real_file_name);
      strcat(image_file, filename);
    }
    if (pDoc->OpenHttpFile (image_file, "IMAGE.FIL") &&
        (fp = fopen ("IMAGE.FIL", "r")) != NULL) {
      fseek (fp, 6L, SEEK_SET);
      fread (&image_width, 2, 1, fp);
      fread (&image_height, 2, 1, fp);
      fclose (fp);
      if (image_width > 1000 || image_height > 1000) {
        image_width = 100;
        image_height = 100;
      }
    }
```

```
   else {
     image_width = 100;
     image_height = 100;
   }
   strcpy(pDoc->real_file_name, old_real_file_name);
   strcpy(pDoc->file_name, old_file_name);
 }
 y = y_top;
 dc->MoveTo (x, y);
 dc->LineTo (x + image_width - 1, y);
 dc->LineTo (x + image_width - 1, y + image_height - 1);
 dc->LineTo (x, y + image_height - 1);
 dc->LineTo (x, y);
 y_top = y;
 y_bottom = y_top + image_height;
 x += image_width;
 y = y + image_height - y_increment;
}

void CSimpBrowseView::set_head1()
{
  delete current_font;
  current_font = new CFont;
  current_font->CreatePointFont (240, "Times New Roman");
  bold_on ();
  if (x != x_begin) {
    y += y_increment;
    x = x_begin;
    y_top = y;
    y_bottom = y_top + y_increment;
  }
  y_increment = Y_INCREMENT_H1;
}

void CSimpBrowseView::set_head2()
{
  delete current_font;
  current_font = new CFont;
  current_font->CreatePointFont (180, "Times New Roman");
  bold_on ();
  if (x != x_begin) {
    y += y_increment;
    x = x_begin;
```

```
    y_top = y;
    y_bottom = y_top + y_increment;
  }
  y_increment = Y_INCREMENT_H2;
}

void CSimpBrowseView::set_normal()
{
  print_string();
  delete current_font;
  current_font = new CFont;
  current_font->CreatePointFont (120, "Times New Roman");
  bold_off ();
  if (x != x_begin) {
    y += y_increment;
    x = x_begin;
    y_top = y;
    y_bottom = y_top + y_increment;
  }
  y_increment = Y_INCREMENT;
}

void CSimpBrowseView::print_string()
{
  if (center)
    x = (width - (dc->GetTextExtent (string)).cx) / 2;
  print_characters (string);
  string.Empty();
  x = x_begin;
  y += y_increment;
  y_top = y;
  y_bottom = y_top + y_increment;
}

void CSimpBrowseView::OnMouseMove(UINT nFlags, CPoint point)
{
  if (frame_window) {
    CClientDC dc(this);
    OnPrepareDC(&dc);
    dc.DPtoLP(&point);
    BOOL message_not_set = TRUE;
```

```
      for (int i = 0; i < href_index; i++) {
        if (point.x >= href [i].rect.left &&
            point.x <= href [i].rect.right &&
            point.y >= href [i].rect.top  &&
            point.y <= href [i].rect.bottom) {
          frame_window->SetMessageText (href [i].ref);
          message_not_set = FALSE;
          break;
        }
      }
      if (message_not_set)
        frame_window->SetMessageText ("");
    }
    CScrollView::OnMouseMove(nFlags, point);
}

void CSimpBrowseView::OnLButtonDown(UINT nFlags, CPoint point)
{
    CClientDC dc(this);
    OnPrepareDC(&dc);
    dc.DPtoLP(&point);

    for (int i = 0; i < href_index; i++) {
      if (point.x >= href [i].rect.left &&
          point.x <= href [i].rect.right &&
          point.y >= href [i].rect.top  &&
          point.y <= href [i].rect.bottom) {
        href [i].clicked = TRUE;
        CSimpBrowseDoc* pDoc = GetDocument();
        if (strnicmp (href [i].ref, "http://", 7) == 0)
          pDoc->OpenHttpFile (href [i].ref);
        else if (strnicmp (pDoc->real_file_name, "http://", 7) == 0) {
          strcat (pDoc->real_file_name, href [i].ref);
          pDoc->OpenHttpFile (pDoc->real_file_name);
        }
        else {
          strcpy (pDoc->real_file_name, href [i].ref);
          pDoc->OpenHttpFile (pDoc->real_file_name);
        }
        RedrawWindow();
        break;
      }
    }
}
```

ANNOTATIONS

Needless to say, there is quite a bit happening within the view class—the parsing and display of the HTML file being not so much a complex bit of programming as it is tedious. The browser program shown here—even at over 1500 lines of code—is an extremely simple implementation; indeed, it doesn't even display graphics, but only placeholder boxes for the graphics.

The program doesn't display graphics because most graphics on the Web are in Graphics Interchange Format (GIF) or Joint Photographic Experts Group (JPEG) format. Neither format is supported natively by Windows—so you actually need to convert the graphics to bitmaps. Such conversion is not terribly complex, and there is substantial source code out there on the Net that details the compression standards and how to convert them, but these programs are large. The shortest converter set that we were able to find in the public domain is another 3200 lines of code. However, the stub is there—you can easily add the code yourself, should you want to.

So, let's look at the code within the view file. We'll start with the constructor for the **CSimpBrowseView** class, where we set a couple of member variables equal to **NULL** and **FALSE**, respectively.

```
CSimpBrowseView::CSimpBrowseView()
{
  frame_window = NULL;
  printing_document = FALSE;
```

Next, we iterate through our array of **href_struct** structures. This structure contains information about the hyperlinks within the document, and is defined within the **CSimpBrowseView.h** file as shown here:

```
struct href_struct {
  CRect rect;
  BOOL clicked;
  CString ref;
} href[MAX_HREFS];
```

As you can see, the structure contains a **rect** structure, which will hold information about the hyperlink's position on the screen; a **clicked** variable, which the program will use to set the color of the hyperlink; and a **CString**, which will contain the URL referenced by the hyperlink. When iterating through the array, we set the **clicked** value to **False** for items in the array (the default):

```
  for (int i = 0; i < MAX_HREFS; i++)
    href [i].clicked = FALSE;
}
```

The next function of importance within the file is the **OnDraw( )** function, which controls the painting of information on the view. The first two statements are defaults, retrieving a pointer to the document object:

```
void CSimpBrowseView::OnDraw(CDC* pDC)
{
  CSimpBrowseDoc* pDoc = GetDocument();
  ASSERT_VALID(pDoc);
```

The last statement calls the **parser( )** function, passing it the reference to the document and to the device context. As you will see later, the program code within the **parser( )** function actually parses the HTML file, isolating and processing the tags within the file and changing the information displayed in the window appropriately.

```
  parser (pDoc, pDC);
}
```

Remember, the **OnDraw( )** function is called any time the user changes the view, resizes the window, and so on. It's important to reparse the file each time this occurs, primarily because of the need to maintain accurate information within the **rect** structure associated with each hyperlink.

The next function, **OnInitialUpdate( )**, lets us determine the total size of the view, sets it up, and tells the scroll bars what their sizes should be:

```
void CSimpBrowseView::OnInitialUpdate()
{
  CScrollView::OnInitialUpdate();
  CSize sizeTotal;
  sizeTotal.cx = sizeTotal.cy = 100;
  SetScrollSizes(MM_TEXT, sizeTotal);
}
```

Within both the **OnBeginPrinting( )** and **OnEndPrinting( )** functions, shown next, the program code merely manages the contents of the **printing_document** member variable—setting it to True when the user starts to print, and resetting it to False when the program finishes the output.

```
void CSimpBrowseView::OnBeginPrinting(CDC* /*pDC*/,
    CPrintInfo* /*pInfo*/)
{
  printing_document = TRUE;
}

void CSimpBrowseView::OnEndPrinting(CDC* /*pDC*/,
    CPrintInfo* /*pInfo*/)
{
  printing_document = FALSE;
}
```

THE PARSER( ) AND PARSE( ) FUNCTIONS

The next important function to consider is the **parser( )** function, which gets the window size, sets the font, and calls the **parse( )** function. First, the code makes sure the user is not currently printing the document and, if not, determines the size of the window. The **GetWindow( )** function is invoked first, and the reference to the window is placed within the **window** local variable:

```
void CSimpBrowseView::parser(CSimpBrowseDoc* pDoc, CDC* pDC)
{
  dc = pDC;
  if (!printing_document) {
    CWnd* window = dc->GetWindow();
```

Next, the program creates a **RECT** structure and gets the client rectangle inside the window, placing the returned values into the structure. Finally, it gets the handle to the frame window, placing that within the **frame_window** member variable of the class:

```
    RECT rect;
    window->GetClientRect (&rect);
    frame_window = window->GetParentFrame();
```

Once all the information is obtained, the program sets the **width** and **height** values equal to the width and height of the client rectangle, storing them within the variables for easier access later:

```
    width = (int) rect.right;
    height = (int) rect.bottom;
  }
```

Next, the program code stores the current pen color within the **old_color** structure, and creates the **current_font** object to store information about the current display font. The program will use this information later to return the display to its state upon entry to the **parser( )** function:

```
  COLORREF old_color = dc->SetTextColor(RGB(0,0,0));
  current_font = new CFont;
  current_font->CreatePointFont (120, "Times New Roman");
```

Now we set some member variables equal to constants defined within the header file. We use variables here because values such as the increments will change later, depending on the size of the text we are rendering:

```
  x_begin = X_BEGIN;
  y_begin = Y_BEGIN;
  y_increment = Y_INCREMENT;
```

Next, we set some other member variables that we will use to display information equal to their beginning values. And finally, we set the **href_index** value, which will refer to the current hyperlink within the hyperlink array; we set it to 0 so it starts at the beginning of the array:

```
x = x_begin;
y = y_begin;
y_top = y_begin;
y_bottom = y_top + y_increment;
href_index = 0;
```

Once this is all done and the setup is complete, the program calls the **parse( )** function, passing in the filename from the document object:

```
parse(pDoc->file_name);
```

After **parse( )** returns, the file is displayed—so we just need to do some cleanup. The program resets the pen color for text, then creates a new **CSize** object corresponding to the current size of the document. It then uses the object to set the scroll bars correctly.

```
dc->SetTextColor (old_color);
CSize x (width, y+30);
SetScrollSizes (MM_TEXT, x);
}
```

After **parser( )** returns, the screen is displayed (or the file is printed). However, the code that actually parses and displays the file is contained within the **parse( )** function. The **parse( )** function opens the file and iterates through all the tags in the file, displaying text, placeholders, and formatting as it goes. Once the file completes its processing, the screen display is fully drawn for the page in question. The **parse( )** function begins by opening the local, temporary file, whose name it receives as the **filename** parameter:

```
void CSimpBrowseView::parse(char* filename)
{
  FILE* fp;
  if ((fp = fopen(filename, "r")) == NULL) {
    string.Format ("Unable to open <%s>", filename);
    dc->TextOut (0, 0, string);
    return;
  }
```

As usual, we have put in a quick test to make sure the file opens correctly, displaying a warning to the user in the event of failure and exiting the function. If the file opens correctly, however, we can move on to its parsing and display.

We start off by setting the **title** and **center** variables, which we will use to maintain specific formatting information, to **FALSE**. Finally, we initialize the variable **done**, which indicates that we have finished parsing, to 0; then we enter a **while** loop that repeats until **done** is **TRUE**.

```
title = FALSE;
center = FALSE;
int done = 0;
while (!done) {
```

Within the loop, the first step is to call the **get_tag( )** function. This function reads through the file, looking for a tag (which is considered to be anything enclosed within < and >). If **get_tag( )** finds a tag, it returns 0, or 1 if it doesn't.

```
done = get_tag (fp, tag);
if (done)
  break;
```

When the function returns, **tag** contains the string value representing the characters within the < and >. Within the **get_tag( )** function, by the way, the program outputs every character it encounters which *isn't* a <. When the program does return the **tag** value, the program simply uses a series of **if** and **else if** statements to determine what the tag indicates. The first **if** statement checks to see if the value corresponds to **TITLE**, in which case the code sets the **title** variable to **TRUE** and clears the **string** variable. This processing is relatively consistent throughout the rest of the function:

```
if (stricmp (tag, "TITLE") == 0) {
  title = TRUE;
  string.Empty();
}
```

If the tag isn't **TITLE**, the program next checks to see if it is **/TITLE**. If so, the program code sets the **title** variable to False, and sets the window text of the **frame_window** object (the parent window of the page display) to the string value contained between the **TITLE** and **/TITLE** tags. Afterward, the code again clears the contents of the **string** variable:

```
else if (stricmp (tag, "/TITLE") == 0) {
  title = FALSE;
  if (frame_window)
    frame_window->SetWindowText (string);
  string.Empty();
}
```

The next tag the code checks for is the **HR** tag, which indicates that the program should draw a horizontal rule (line) in the display. If the code encounters this tag, it uses the **MoveTo( )** and **LineTo( )** member functions of the **CDC** device context class to draw the rule:

```
else if (stricmp (tag, "HR") == 0) {
    y += y_increment + y_increment/2;
    dc->MoveTo (x_begin, y);
    dc->LineTo (width - X_BEGIN*2, y);
    x = x_begin;
    y += y_increment - y_increment/2;
    y_top = y;
    y_bottom = y_top + y_increment;
}
```

On the other hand, the **BR** tag indicates a simple line-break, as does the **P** tag. If the program code encounters either tag, it displays the current text, followed by a line break, and clears the **string** variable:

```
else if (stricmp (tag, "BR") == 0 || stricmp (tag, "P") == 0) {
    print_string();
    string.Empty();
}
```

Next, we test for the **CENTER** tag. If it's there, we set the **center** variable to **TRUE** and get ready to receive the text that will be centered:

```
else if (stricmp (tag, "CENTER") == 0) {
    center = TRUE;
    string.Empty();
}
```

As you might expect, we next determine if the tag is the closing center tag (**/CENTER**). If so, we perform some processing to place the string within the horizontal center of the screen. The program first uses the **GetTextExtent( )** function to find the total width of the string. This is divided by two to find out how far back from the horizontal center of the screen the function should start drawing the text:

```
else if (stricmp (tag, "/CENTER") == 0) {
    center = FALSE;
    x = (width - (dc->GetTextExtent (string)).cx) / 2;
```

After setting the **x** value to the correct horizontal starting position, the code prints out the string's contents. It also resets some information about the current **x** and **y** position for the next line of the HTML file:

```
    print_characters (string);
    x = x_begin;
    y += y_increment;
```

```
   y_top = y;
   y_bottom = y_top + y_increment;
}
```

Next, we check to see whether the incoming tag indicates that the bold attribute is to be turned on or off, calling a member function that you will examine later to respond appropriately:

```
else if (stricmp (tag, "B") == 0) {
   bold_on ();
}
else if (stricmp (tag, "/B") == 0) {
   bold_off ();
}
```

Similarly, if the program code indicates that italic should be turned on or off, the program will process that within the following **else if** statements and call the appropriate servicing function:

```
else if (stricmp (tag, "I") == 0) {
   italic_on ();
}
else if (stricmp (tag, "/I") == 0) {
   italic_off ();
}
```

Finally, the last of the formatting tags handled by the program are for turning the underlining attribute on or off on the text in the document. The program includes two helper functions for this, which are invoked by the following **else if** statements:

```
else if (stricmp (tag, "U") == 0) {
   underline_on ();
}
else if (stricmp (tag, "/U") == 0) {
   underline_off ();
}
```

The next tag to process is the **A** tag, which indicates that subsequent text refers to a hyperlink. If the code encounters the **A** tag, it will call the **href_on( )** function.

```
else if (strnicmp (tag, "A ", 2) == 0) {
   href_on ();
}
```

In the next **else if** clause (when we receive the closing tag), the program calls the **href_off( )** function to end the tag display.

```
else if (stricmp (tag, "/A") == 0) {
   href_off();
}
```

The next tag pair we check for is for preformatted text, and again we call a pair of helper functions to perform the appropriate processing:

```
else if (stricmp (tag, "PRE") == 0) {
  preformatted_on ();
}
else if (stricmp (tag, "/PRE") == 0) {
  preformatted_off ();
}
```

The **UL** tag indicates the start of a bulleted list (with each item in the list preceded by an **LI** tag); the **/UL** tag indicates the end of the list. Similarly, the **OL** and **/OL** tags indicate the start and end of a numbered list (again, with each item in the list preceded by an LI tag):

```
else if (stricmp (tag, "UL") == 0) {
  unordered_list_on ();
}
else if (stricmp (tag, "/UL") == 0) {
  unordered_list_off ();
}
else if (stricmp (tag, "OL") == 0) {
  ordered_list_on ();
}
else if (stricmp (tag, "/OL") == 0) {
  ordered_list_off ();
}
```

All the processing for the list items occurs within the **insert_list_item( )** function, which you will learn more about later. The next clause invokes the function:

```
else if (stricmp (tag, "LI") == 0) {
  insert_list_item();
}
```

The next **else if** checks the tag to see if it refers to an image file. If it does, the program code invokes the **display_image( )** helper function, as shown here:

```
else if (strnicmp (tag, "IMG", 4) == 0) {
  display_image();
}
```

Similarly, the next **else if** clause checks the tag to see if it indicates that the text should be formatted in the **H1** (header level one) style. If so, the program code calls the **set_head1( )** helper function, explained later:

```
else if (stricmp (tag, "H1") == 0) {
  set_head1();
}
```

The next-to-last case that the program code tests for is to see if the page formatting tag indicates the text should be formatted in the **H2** (header level two) style. If so, the program code calls the **set_head2( )** helper function, explained later:

```
else if (stricmp (tag, "H2") == 0) {
   set_head2();
}
```

The last **else if** clause tries to determine if the tag turns off either heading level one or heading level two formatting. If so, the program returns the text formatting to the normal style by calling the **set_normal( )** function:

```
else if (stricmp (tag, "/H1") == 0 ||
     stricmp (tag, "/H2") == 0) {
   set_normal();
}
```

Clearly, the program code as written doesn't process all of the possible tag values—but we still want to display those values for the user, so they know what they *aren't* seeing. We do that within the last **else if,** which generically captures all tags and displays their contents, as shown here:

```
else {
   print_characters ("<");
   print_characters (tag);
   print_characters (">");
}
tag [0] = '\0';
}
```

Once we've read all the contents in the file, we go ahead and close the file and exit the function, with the entire contents of the file displayed on the screen.

```
fclose(fp);
}
```

THE GET_TAG( ) AND PROCESS_INFO( ) FUNCTIONS

The next function, whose processing you saw in the discussion of the **parse( )** function, searches through the file, pulling tags. The **get_tag( )** function searches for a < character; when it finds one, it saves all characters to the **tag** parameter until a > is found, which signifies the end of the tag.

PROGRAMMER'S NOTE   *The get_tag( ) function does not check for quotes ("), so any '<' character found inside quotes is also regarded as the beginning of a real tag.*

The **get_tag( )** function accepts as its parameters a pointer to the file, and the **char** array in which to return the tag. Within the function, the program declares the **char** variable, which it uses to read the next byte from the file:

```
int CSimpBrowseView::get_tag(FILE* fp, char* tag)
{
  int char;
```

The **while** loop iterates until the code reaches the end of the file (although the program code will exit the loop and the function whenever it finds an entire tag). Within the loop, we check the value of the **char** variable and make sure it isn't a < (left bracket). If it is, we start to read the tag:

```
while ((char = fgetc(fp)) != EOF) {
   if (char == '<') {
     int i = 0;
     while ((char = fgetc(fp)) != '>') {
       if (i < TAG_LENGTH)
         tag[i++] = char;
     }
```

The tag cannot be any longer than the constant **TAG_LENGTH**, and each character within the tag is stored in sequence within the **tag** parameter. The code then adds a terminating **NULL** character at the end of the string and exits the function.

```
     tag[i] = '\0';
     return(0);
   }
```

If the character is not a tag indicator, the program code calls the **process_info( )** function with the character as its parameter:

```
   else
     process_info(char);
}
```

Outside the **while** loop, the program code returns 1 if the end of the file has been reached, or 0 if the program exited the loop for some other reason:

```
if (char == EOF)
  return(1);
else
  return(0);
}
```

The **process_info( )** function, as indicated previously, processes non-tag information. The function receives the information one character at a time from the **get_tag( )** function, and processes the character in one of several ways, depending on the current output format. The first thing the code does is check to see if the character is a carriage return:

```
void CSimpBrowseView::process_info (int c)
{
  if (c == '\n') {
```

If it's not, then the code checks to see if text centering is turned on. If it is, the program immediately prints the **string** member:

```
    if (center) {
      print_string();
      return;
    }
```

Next, we check to see if **x** is not equal to **x_begin**, in which case we set the character to a space. Otherwise, we simply return to the calling function:

```
    else if (x != x_begin)
      c = ' ';
    else
      return;
  }
```

If the character is not a carriage return, the program code then checks to see if either the **title** or the **center** member is set to **True**. If either one is True, the program adds the character to the **string** variable and outputs nothing:

```
  if (title || center) {
    string += c;
    return;
  }
```

If the character has passed all the previous tests, the program simply calls the **print_character( )** function, which outputs the character to the screen using the current formatting settings:

```
  print_character (c);
}
```

THE PRINT_CHARACTERS( ) AND PRINT_CHARACTER( ) FUNCTIONS

The **print_characters( )** function uses the **print_character( )** function to print all the characters in a string, one at a time:

```
void CSimpBrowseView::print_characters(CString characters)
{
  int length = characters.GetLength();
  for (int i = 0; i < length; i++)
    print_character (characters.GetAt (i));
}
```

As indicated before, the program calls the **print_character( )** function to print each character passed as an argument, and increments the x-coordinate and (if necessary) the y-coordinate. The function accepts a single parameter (the character), which it places within the first element of the **s** array:

```
void CSimpBrowseView::print_character(char c)
{
  char s[2];
  s[0] = c;
  s[1] = '\0';
```

Next, the program constructs a **CString** object with the character and the terminator, and makes sure the font is set to the **current_font** font setting:

```
CString character(s);
CFont* old_font = dc->SelectObject (current_font);
```

After setting the font, the code uses the **TextOut( )** member function to print the text. It then adds the width of the character to the horizontal increment value, and returns to the old font:

```
dc->TextOut (x, y, character);
x += (dc->GetTextExtent(character)).cx;
dc->SelectObject (old_font);
```

If the character is at the end of the line, the program sets the x-coordinate back to the beginning of the line and increments the y-coordinate by the height specified within the **y_increment** value:

```
if (x > (width-X_BEGIN*2)) {
  x = x_begin;
  y += y_increment;
  y_top = y;
  y_bottom = y_top + y_increment;
  }
}
```

THE BOLDING, ITALICIZING, AND UNDERLINING FUNCTIONS

The next several functions are the member functions called from within the **parse( )** function to change the formatting of the program's output. The first of the member functions is the **bold_on( )** function, which turns on the bold font. It does this by increasing the font's weight value, creating a new font with the **CreateFontIndirect( )** function after increasing the weight:

```
void CSimpBrowseView::bold_on()
{
```

```
  LOGFONT lf;
  current_font->GetLogFont (&lf);
  lf.lfWeight = 700;
  delete current_font;
  current_font = new CFont;
  current_font->CreateFontIndirect (&lf);
}
```

The **bold_off( )** function performs similar processing, setting the font's weight back to 400, as shown here:

```
void CSimpBrowseView::bold_off()
{
  LOGFONT lf;
  current_font->GetLogFont (&lf);
  lf.lfWeight = 400;
  delete current_font;
  current_font = new CFont;
  current_font->CreateFontIndirect (&lf);
}
```

As you might expect, the **italic_on( )** function turns on the italic attribute for the current font—no matter its size or color. The function does this by setting the **lfItalic** member to **TRUE** and creating a new font, as shown in the following code:

```
void CSimpBrowseView::italic_on()
{
  LOGFONT lf;
  current_font->GetLogFont (&lf);
  lf.lfItalic = TRUE;
  delete current_font;
  current_font = new CFont;
  current_font->CreateFontIndirect (&lf);
}
```

Similarly, the **italic_off( )** function sets the **lfItalic** member to **FALSE**, and then again creates a new font.

Note that, in every one of these functions, we delete the **current_font** member and create it anew with the new definition:

```
void CSimpBrowseView::italic_off()
{
  LOGFONT lf;
  current_font->GetLogFont (&lf);
  lf.lfItalic = FALSE;
```

```
    delete current_font;
    current_font = new CFont;
    current_font->CreateFontIndirect (&lf);
}
```

Like the **bold_on( )** and **italic_on( )** functions shown previously, the **underline_on( )** function sets a member of a **LOGFONT** structure. In this case, we set the **lfUnderline** member to **TRUE,** and re-create the font with all the other characteristics as they were without the underlining on:

```
void CSimpBrowseView::underline_on()
{
    LOGFONT lf;
    current_font->GetLogFont (&lf);
    lf.lfUnderline = TRUE;
    delete current_font;
    current_font = new CFont;
    current_font->CreateFontIndirect (&lf);
}
```

Again, the **underline_off( )** function turns off the underlining by setting the appropriate member to **FALSE**:

```
void CSimpBrowseView::underline_off()
{
    LOGFONT lf;
    current_font->GetLogFont (&lf);
    lf.lfUnderline = FALSE;
    delete current_font;
    current_font = new CFont;
    current_font->CreateFontIndirect (&lf);
}
```

THE HREF_ON( ) AND HREF_OFF( ) FUNCTIONS

As you saw earlier in the chapter, when the program code encounters an A tag, it draws the following text as a hyperlink. The program code uses the **href_on( )** function to perform its initial processing of the hyperlink information, and the **href_off( )** function to finish its processing. Most browsers display hyperlinks as underlined text, so the first thing the **href_on( )** function's code does is turn on the underlining:

```
void CSimpBrowseView::href_on()
{
    underline_on ();
```

Next, the code checks to see if the hyperlink has been clicked—if so, the hyperlink display is set to red; otherwise, the code sets it to blue:

```
if (href [href_index].clicked)
   dc->SetTextColor (RGB (255, 0, 0));
else
   dc->SetTextColor (RGB (0, 0, 255));
```

Now this is where it gets a little tricky. At this point, the program knows the upper-left point in the rectangle that surrounds the hyperlink, but it doesn't yet know where the bottom-right point is. So, within this **if** clause, we set the left-top corner for the tag, knowing that we won't know the bottom-right until we reach the end of the hyperlink:

```
char* p1 = strchr (tag, '"') + 1;
char* p2 = strchr (p1, '"');
int length = (int) (p2 - p1);

href [href_index].rect.left = x;
href [href_index].rect.top  = y;
href [href_index].ref.Format ("%*.*s", length, length, p1);
}
```

We also don't yet know the entirety of the reference, so we format the reference as an empty string until we do know its entirety—which happens in the **href_off( )** function. In the function (called when we receive the closing tag), the program turns off the underlining and resets the text color to black. We also put the bottom corner information into the **href** structure, and increment the index value by one (provided it is still less than the total number of allowable hyperlinks).

The **href_off( )** function turns off the underlining and resets the text color to black. We also put the bottom corner information into the **href** structure, and increment the index value by one (provided it is still less than the total number of allowable hyperlinks):

```
void CSimpBrowseView::href_off()
{
   underline_off ();
   dc->SetTextColor (RGB (0, 0, 0));
   href [href_index].rect.right  = x;
   href [href_index].rect.bottom = y + 20;

   if (href_index < MAX_HREFS-1)
      href_index++;
}
```

THE PREFORMATTED_ON( ) AND PREFORMATTED_OFF( ) FUNCTIONS

The **preformattted_on( )** function performs slightly different processing from that done by the other "on/off" functions we've discussed. Rather than simply changing an attribute of the current font type, it creates a whole new font using the Courier New definition, with a point size of 100 (slightly smaller than regular text in the page):

```
void CSimpBrowseView::preformatted_on()
{
  delete current_font;
  current_font = new CFont;
  current_font->CreatePointFont (100, "Courier New");
}
```

The **preformatted_off( )** function resets the font back to the default size. Thus, if for some odd reason, someone embedded a **PRE** tag inside of an **H1** tag, text after the **/PRE** tag would appear in the normal font, not the **H1** font:

```
void CSimpBrowseView::preformatted_off()
{
  delete current_font;
  current_font = new CFont;
  current_font->CreatePointFont (120, "Times New Roman");
}
```

THE LIST PROCESSING FUNCTIONS

There are five functions within the program whose purpose is to help in the management of lists—two unordered list functions, two ordered list functions, and a list item insertion function. The first one we will look at handles the creation of an unordered list (the **UL** tag). It starts off by setting the **ordered_list** member to **FALSE**, and then moves the beginning point for text 40 points to the right (giving it enough room to draw the bullet point):

```
void CSimpBrowseView::unordered_list_on()
{
  ordered_list = FALSE;
  x_begin = X_BEGIN + 40;
  x = x_begin;
```

Next, the program code checks to see whether the **string** member contains a value; if so, it prints it out and empties the string:

```
  if (string.GetLength() > 0) {
    print_string();
    string.Empty();
  }
```

Otherwise, the code simply prints the string and leaves it alone (generating a carriage return before the list):

```
 print_string();
}
```

Once we are done displaying the bulleted list, the program has to set the left column back to its default value, which it does within the **unordered_list_off( )** function:

```
void CSimpBrowseView::unordered_list_off()
{
   x_begin = X_BEGIN;
```

The program code also outputs any text held in the **string** variable and clears its contents:

```
   print_string();
   string.Empty();
   print_string();
}
```

The **ordered_list_on( )** function performs much the same processing as the **unordered_list_on( )** function. The major difference is that the **ordered_list** variable is set to **TRUE** within this function:

```
void CSimpBrowseView::ordered_list_on()
{
   ordered_list = TRUE;
   list_item = 0;
   x_begin = X_BEGIN + 40;
   x = x_begin;
```

Again, the function clears anything in the **string** variable out, starting the list on a new line:

```
   if (string.GetLength() > 0) {
     print_string();
     string.Empty();
   }
   print_string();
}
```

Just like the **unordered_list_off( )** function, the **ordered_list_off( )** function simply sets the **ordered_list( )** variable to **False**, resets the leftmost column on the page, and prints out any contents remaining within the **string** variable:

```
void CSimpBrowseView::ordered_list_off()
{
   ordered_list = FALSE;
   x_begin = X_BEGIN;
```

```
   print_string();
   string.Empty();
   print_string();
}
```

As you saw, the **LI** tag may indicate an item in either a numbered or a bulleted list. We have to allow for that in the tag's processing, which we do using the **ordered_list** member variable. If its value is **True**, we know it's a numbered list—meaning we have to place a number at the beginning of the list item. The insertion of list items is handled by the **insert_list_item( )** function:

```
void CSimpBrowseView::insert_list_item()
{
   print_string();
   string.Empty();
   if (ordered_list) {
```

Once inside the **if** statement, we first increment the **list_item** member variable, then format the number in the list, move the x-coordinate to the left, and print the number:

```
      list_item++;
      CString characters;
      characters.Format ("%d.", list_item);
      x -= 20;
      print_characters (characters);
   }
```

On the other hand, if the list is a bulleted list, we need to draw a bullet on the screen—which we do with the **Ellipse( )** member function, drawing a small circle to the left of the text item:.

```
   else {
      CBrush brush (RGB (0, 0, 0));
      CBrush* old_brush = dc->SelectObject (&brush);
      dc->Ellipse (x-10, y+6, x-4, y+12);
      dc->SelectObject (old_brush);
   }
```

In any event, after drawing the circle or the number, the program resets the **x** value to the point where it should draw the text:

```
   x = x_begin;
}
```

THE DISPLAY_IMAGE( ) FUNCTION

As noted earlier, we don't actually draw images in this implementation—instead, we draw a box indicating that an image belongs there. To draw the correctly sized box, we have to access the actual file, which we find by placing the filename within the **filename** variable:

```
void CSimpBrowseView::display_image()
{
  char* p1 = strchr (tag, '"') + 1;
  char* p2 = strchr (p1, '"');
  int length = (int) (p2 - p1);
  char filename[100];
  strncpy (filename, p1, length);
  filename [length] = '\0';
  WORD image_width, image_height;
```

The browser begins by retrieving the file whose name is stored within the tag, trying to pull it first from the local drive:

```
FILE* fp;
if ((fp = fopen (filename, "r")) != NULL) {
```

If successful, the program gets the dimensions of the image. The program assumes that every image uses the GIF format (an assumption you need to eliminate if you actually add support for graphics to the program). GIF stores the image's pixel width and height as two bytes each, starting at the sixth byte in the file. The program stores width and height of the image within the aptly named **image_width** and **image_height** variables:

```
    fseek (fp, 6L, SEEK_SET);
    fread (&image_width, 2, 1, fp);
    fread (&image_height, 2, 1, fp);
    fclose (fp);
}
```

If the program cannot find the file on the local drive, it then goes out and tries to pull the file from the Internet, using the reference to the image contained within the tag:

```
else {
    char old_file_name [100];
    char old_real_file_name [100];
    char image_file [100];
```

First the program gets a reference to the document and then copies the name of the parent HTML document into a pair of temporary arrays. This is a necessary step because we will be opening and copying the file down to the local machine from the remote machine using the **OpenHttpFile( )** member function.

```
CSimpBrowseDoc* pDoc = GetDocument();
strcpy(old_real_file_name, pDoc->real_file_name);
strcpy(old_file_name, pDoc->file_name);
```

Next, the program code looks at the filename and ensures that it starts with the HTTP protocol reference—making the reference an absolute reference. If the filename does start appropriately, the program simply copies the fully qualified path name into the **image_file** variable. If the filename doesn't contain the HTTP protocol reference, the code assumes the reference is a relative reference, and copies the address of the parent document into the **image_file** variable and concatenates the relative reference onto its end:

```
if (strnicmp (filename, "http://", 7) == 0)
  strcpy(image_file, filename);
else {
  strcpy(image_file, old_real_file_name);
  strcat(image_file, filename);
}
```

Next, the program code retrieves the file and ensures that it can successfully open the file locally. If it can, the width and height information is again retrieved from the file:

```
if (pDoc->OpenHttpFile (image_file, "IMAGE.FIL") &&
    (fp = fopen ("IMAGE.FIL", "r")) != NULL) {
  fseek (fp, 6L, SEEK_SET);
  fread (&image_width, 2, 1, fp);
  fread (&image_height, 2, 1, fp);
  fclose (fp);
```

Next, to simplify the display of the page, we make sure the image is smaller than a certain maximum size (1000 pixels in either direction); if it is, we use its actual size to draw the figure. Otherwise, we use a size of 100 x 100 to draw the figure:

```
if (image_width > 1000 || image_height > 1000) {
  image_width = 100;
  image_height = 100;
}
}
```

Alternatively, if the program is unable to open the file for any reason, we also set the dimensions of the placeholder graphic to 100 x 100:

```
else {
    image_width = 100;
    image_height = 100;
}
```

After pulling the information, the program places the HTML filename back into the member variables in the document class:

```
strcpy(pDoc->real_file_name, old_real_file_name);
strcpy(pDoc->file_name, old_file_name);
}
```

Now that we have the dimensions of the box to draw, we can go ahead and draw the box with the **MoveTo( )** and **LineTo( )** functions, as shown here:

```
y = y_top;
dc->MoveTo (x, y);
dc->LineTo (x + image_width - 1, y);
dc->LineTo (x + image_width - 1, y + image_height - 1);
dc->LineTo (x, y + image_height - 1);
dc->LineTo (x, y);
```

Next, we do some clean-up with the x- and y-coordinates in the display document:

```
y_top = y;
y_bottom = y_top + image_height;
x += image_width;
y = y + image_height - y_increment;
}
```

TURNING HEADERS ON AND OFF

The next three helper functions process formatting commands that specify the turning off and on of header-sized type. The first function, **set_head1( )**, is called by the program when it encounters the **H1** formatting tag, which specifies a larger, boldfaced text size. If the tag is found, we first clear out the **current_font** variable, creating a new font for the larger size and turning on boldfacing:

```
void CSimpBrowseView::set_head1()
{
    delete current_font;
    current_font = new CFont;
    current_font->CreatePointFont (240, "Times New Roman");
    bold_on ();
```

We also check to make sure the text is at the beginning of the line. If it isn't, we drop down to the next line to start the drawing of new, larger text:

```
if (x != x_begin) {
  y += y_increment;
  x = x_begin;
  y_top = y;
  y_bottom = y_top + y_increment;
}
```

We also have to set the amount to increment, in order to be consistent with the larger header style. This is accomplished with the **Y_INCREMENT_H1** constant, as shown here:

```
 y_increment = Y_INCREMENT_H1;
}
```

The program performs similar processing if it encounters the **H2** tag, only using a smaller font and the **Y_INCREMENT_H2** constant. In such cases, the program invokes the **set_head2( )** function:

```
void CSimpBrowseView::set_head2()
{
  delete current_font;
  current_font = new CFont;
  current_font->CreatePointFont (180, "Times New Roman");
  bold_on ();
  if (x != x_begin) {
    y += y_increment;
    x = x_begin;
    y_top = y;
    y_bottom = y_top + y_increment;
  }
  y_increment = Y_INCREMENT_H2;
}
```

When the code encounters the closing tag for either the **H1** or **H2** style, it resets the output to the default type size. In such cases, the program calls the **set_normal( )** function. Within the function, the program code first prints out all the text received so far (in the larger font size), as shown here:

```
void CSimpBrowseView::set_normal()
{
  print_string();
```

Then it performs processing similar to what you saw before, returning the font size to the default size, and turning off the boldfacing:

```
delete current_font;
current_font = new CFont;
current_font->CreatePointFont (120, "Times New Roman");
bold_off ();
```

Again, we can't change point size in the middle of a line, so the code sends the equivalent of a carriage return, moving to the beginning of the following line and resetting the **y_increment** to the constant corresponding to the default font size:

```
if (x != x_begin) {
  y += y_increment;
  x = x_begin;
  y_top = y;
  y_bottom = y_top + y_increment;
}
y_increment = Y_INCREMENT;
}
```

THE PRINT_STRING( ) FUNCTION

The **print_string( )** function, as you have seen throughout the preceding discussion, displays the contents of the current string. The first test within the function is of the **center** variable. If it is **TRUE**, the program code sets the x-coordinate appropriately, offsetting it half the string's width from the center of the window:

```
void CSimpBrowseView::print_string()
{
  if (center)
    x = (width - (dc->GetTextExtent (string)).cx) / 2;
```

In any event, the program code calls the **print_characters( )** function, which prints out all the characters within the string, one at a time, and then clears the string:

```
print_characters (string);
string.Empty();
```

After printing the string, the program generates a carriage return by setting the x-coordinate to the leftmost column position. It increments the y-coordinate to move the output line down to the next line on the display:

```
x = x_begin;
y += y_increment;
y_top = y;
y_bottom = y_top + y_increment;
}
```

THE OVERLOADED VIEW CLASS FUNCTIONS

There are two overloaded functions within the view class to consider—**OnMouseMove( )** and **OnLMouseButtonDown( )**. To display a link's reference when the user moves the mouse over a link, we have to overload the **OnMouseMove( )** function. Windows calls this function each time the user moves the mouse, passing the mouse cursor's x- and y-coordinates to the function as parameters:

```
void CSimpBrowseView::OnMouseMove(UINT nFlags, CPoint point)
{
```

The program first checks to make sure that a frame window exists, and if so creates a device context to the client window:

```
if (frame_window) {
    CClientDC dc(this);
    OnPrepareDC(&dc);
    dc.DPtoLP(&point);
```

Then the code iterates through the array of **href**s, checking each of the hyperlinks displayed within the document. If the user's mouse is over any of those hyperlinks, the program uses the **SetMessageText( )** function to display the hyperlink's reference in the frame window:

```
    BOOL message_not_set = TRUE;
    for (int i = 0; i < href_index; i++) {
        if (point.x >= href [i].rect.left &&
            point.x <= href [i].rect.right &&
            point.y >= href [i].rect.top  &&
            point.y <= href [i].rect.bottom) {
          frame_window->SetMessageText (href [i].ref);
          message_not_set = FALSE;
```

After it finds a matching hyperlink, the loop exits, since the user will never be over more than one hyperlink at once.

```
          break;
        }
    }
```

If the user is not over a hyperlink, the program code sets the text displayed within the window to nothing (""), so that the user doesn't keep seeing reference information even when the mouse is no longer over a hyperlink.

```
    if (message_not_set)
        frame_window->SetMessageText ("");
}
```

Finally, the function invokes the function from which it derives, so that function can perform its processing:

```
CScrollView::OnMouseMove(nFlags, point);
}
```

Just as the **OnMouseMove( )** function has to check and see if the user is over a hyperlink, the **OnLMouseButtonDown( )** function checks to see if the user has clicked on a hyperlink. Windows calls the **OnLMouseButtonDown( )** function each time the user clicks the left mouse button (again, like **OnMouseMove( )**), passing the mouse cursor's x- and y-coordinates to the function as parameters:

```
void CSimpBrowseView::OnLButtonDown(UINT nFlags, CPoint point)
{
  CClientDC dc(this);
  OnPrepareDC(&dc);
  dc.DPtoLP(&point);
```

After creating a device context for local use, the program again checks to see if the user has clicked on a hyperlink. If so, in this case the code performs slightly more complex processing. First, it sets the **clicked** member to **TRUE**:

```
for (int i = 0; i < href_index; i++) {
   if (point.x >= href [i].rect.left &&
       point.x <= href [i].rect.right &&
       point.y >= href [i].rect.top  &&
       point.y <= href [i].rect.bottom) {
     href [i].clicked = TRUE;
```

Next, it opens a reference to the document class. Then the code checks to see whether the URL referenced by the hyperlink is absolute or relative. If it's absolute, the code invokes the **OpenHttpFile( )** function with the reference string as its parameter:

```
        CSimpBrowseDoc* pDoc = GetDocument();
        if (strnicmp (href [i].ref, "http://", 7) == 0)
          pDoc->OpenHttpFile (href [i].ref);
```

If the URL is relative and the current document has a valid **http://** address, the program concatenates the relative URL to the current address and calls **OpenHttpFile( )** with the constructed address:

```
        else if (strnicmp (pDoc->real_file_name, "http://", 7) == 0) {
          strcat (pDoc->real_file_name, href [i].ref);
          pDoc->OpenHttpFile (pDoc->real_file_name);
        }
```

If the current page is a local file, the code treats the new page as a local file, too, and simply goes out and opens it:

```
else {
  strcpy (pDoc->real_file_name, href [i].ref);
  pDoc->OpenHttpFile (pDoc->real_file_name);
}
```

RedrawWindow( ) is called next, which invalidates the window and forces **parser( )** to process the new file:

```
    RedrawWindow();
    break;
  }
 }
}
```

This simple browser program works well enough, processing pure-text HTML files quite handily. Figure 9-2 shows the browser after opening the default local file. Figure 9-3, on the other hand, shows the browser after opening an Osborne/McGraw-Hill Web page.

Needless to say, writing a browser is no simple matter—for Netscape Communicator, for example, the source code alone is over 12MB. The implementation shown in this chapter is useful, but if you are using Visual C++ for

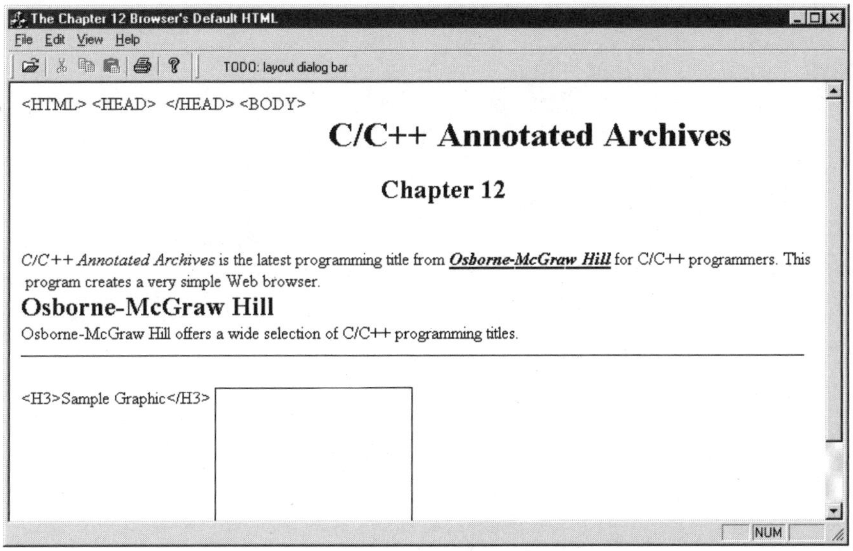

FIGURE 9-2. The simple browser after opening the default local file

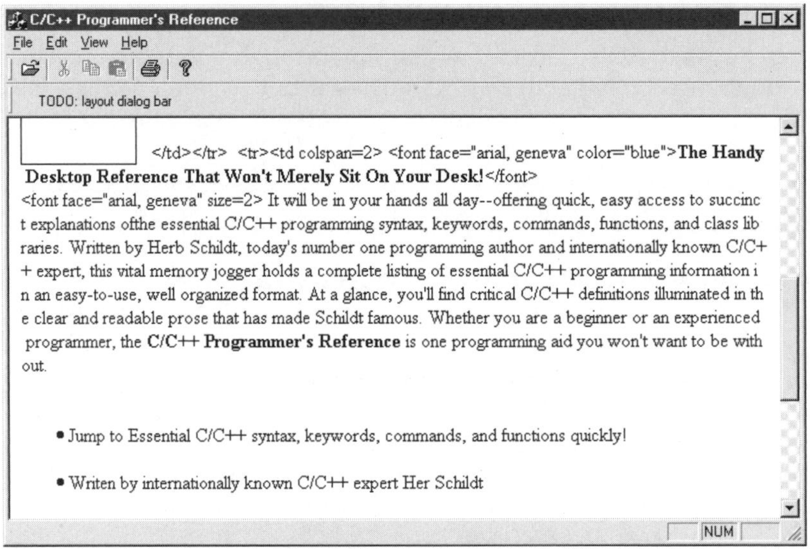

FIGURE 9-3.   The simple browser displaying a Web page

development, and you know that your users will all have Internet Explorer (as in an intranet environment), you can use the **CHtmlView** class to implement browser functionality within your applications much more simply. The following section briefly discusses this technique.

Using the New CHtmlView Internet Class

By adding the Microsoft Web Browser control to your applications, you can easily provide users with the ability to browse sites on the World Wide Web, or folders and files on a local or networked file system. It's easy to create a Web application with the Browser control because there are relatively few steps to creating such an application, especially when you compare it with the effort required to write your own, full-featured browser—an effort that you've already had a taste of.

For most applications today, support for the World Wide Web model and implementation is a requirement for end-users. Adding Internet support to your applications can take a variety of forms, but adding browser support is arguably the most common. In the next sections, you will learn more about the Internet Browser control, examine Visual C++ 6.0 support for Web browsing, and see what you can do to more effectively manage the control.

The Web Browser Control

The Web Browser control supports browsing through point-and-click hyperlinking, and through direct navigation to URLs. The control even maintains a history list that lets you browse forward and backward through previously browsed sites, folders, and documents.

Applications can also use the Web Browser control as an Active Document container to host other active documents. In other words, richly formatted documents (such as Word documents and Excel spreadsheets) can be opened and edited in place from within the Web Browser control.

As if the Web Browser weren't enough, Microsoft also offers an MFC class that encapsulates the control so that it is even easier to use. The **CHtmlView** class gives your applications easy access to the Web Browser control's functionality within the context of MFC's document-view architecture.

The Web Browser ActiveX control (and therefore the **CHtmlView** class) is available only to programs running under Windows 95, Windows 98, and Windows NT versions 3.51 or later in which the user has installed Internet Explorer 4.0 (or later).

Some **CHtmlView** member functions apply to the Internet Explorer application only. These functions will succeed on the Web Browser control, but they will have no visible effect. These functions are **GetAddressBar( )**, **GetFullName( )**, **GetStatusBar( )**, **SetAddressBar( )**, **SetFullScreen( )**, **SetMenuBar( )**, **SetStatusBar( )**, and **SetToolBar( )**.

Creating a Project That Uses CHtmlView

The task of creating an application based on the **CHtmlView** class has the simplicity that you have probably come to expect from simple document-view architecture programs. You should create an application framework that supports either the single-document or multiple-document framework.

Most of the options, including those that determine whether you have a toolbar and whether you allow print and print preview, do not affect the program's ability to use the **CHtmlView** class in any way. You can set these options however you need to for the rest of your application, and it will support the Web Browser control (and **CHtmlView**) with no problem, no matter what these options are.

The only important thing that you must remember to do is adjust the **CView** base class option presented in the AppWizard's last dialog box; change it to be a **CHtmlView** base class. Alternatively, of course, you can always add the **CHtmlView**-derived class as an additional view within your application. (Generally, this additional view will also use a separate document from the rest of the application, particularly if the Web support is separate and distinct from the rest of the application.)

After you create the **CHtmlView**-based project, you can compile and run it without further changes. The default URL will point to the Visual C++ home page on the Microsoft Web site at http://www.microsoft.com/visualc, as shown in Figure 9-4.

FIGURE 9-4.   The Microsoft Web page automatically comes up when the
CHtmlView-based project first runs

You can easily change the starting URL by editing the **OnInitialUpdate( )**
function. For instance, if you want the application to start at
http://www.osborne.com, you would change the **OnInitialUpdate( )** function as
follows:

```
void CSampleHTMLView::OnInitialUpdate()
{
  CHtmlView::OnInitialUpdate();
  Navigate2(_T("http://www.osborne.com"), NULL, NULL;
}
```

Navigating Through CHtmlViews

When a program that is based on **CHtmlView** runs, users can navigate for
themselves by clicking the mouse on the HTML hyperlinks displayed by the
program. Enabling this functionality requires no code from you—the underlying
Web Browser control handles all the necessary processing. However, you will often
need the capability to navigate to various URLs, and to control the browser's
destination from code.

The most notable example of this type of processing is letting users browse
forward and backward through a history list—for instance, if they're at a given Web
page they may want to back up to the Web page they were viewing just before that.

Most browsers have Back and Forward buttons to support this type of navigation, and Internet Explorer is no exception. The Web Browser control does not, however, automatically display icons (like Internet Explorer's) to let the user do this.

An icon-based user interface, with additional icons on the toolbar, probably lets users move backwards and forwards most easily. Additionally, you will likely want to position menu items (with shortcuts) in your program for the user to access.

Within the handlers for those menu and toolbar items, you might want to call a **Back( )** function within the view class to go backward, as shown here:

```
void CSampleHtmlView::Back()
{
  GoBack();
}
```

Similarly, you will probably want to implement a **Forward( )** function, also within the view class, as shown here:

```
void CSampleHtmlView::Forward()
{
  GoForward();
}
```

The other important functions exposed by the Web Browser control that you will want to make available to users include the **Stop( )**, **Refresh( )**, **GoHome( )**, and **GoSearch( )** functions.

◆ **Stop( )** tells the Web Browser control to stop loading the current Web page's contents.

◆ **Refresh( )** tells the Web Browser control to re-retrieve the current page's contents from the target Web server, refreshing the display within the browser when it completes the retrieval.

◆ If users want to go their home page, you can use the **GoHome( )** function. The home page is retrieved from the Registry preferences, which are set by Internet Explorer.

◆ **GoSearch( )** takes users to their default search page (once again, this is with Internet Explorer).

There are two functions exposed by the Web Browser control that you can employ to take users directly to a new URL. The **Navigate( )** and **Navigate2( )** functions perform this processing. The only difference between the two functions is in the type of URL that they expect. **Navigate( )** expects a relative URL (although it can process absolute URLs), whereas **Navigate2( )** expects and can process only absolute URLs. For example, the user might be viewing a Web page located at

http://www.osborne.com/index.html

and wants to move to

> http://www.osborne.com/archives/index.html

The new URL is simply one level deeper in the server's subdirectory hierarchy. The following code will perform the task quite sufficiently:

```
Navigate("archives/index.html");
```

Note, however, that the following code will not work (and will throw an exception), because the **Navigate2( )** function can only process absolute URLs:

```
Navigate2("archives/index.html");
```

If you wanted to use **Navigate2( )**, you would have to append the entire server and directory path onto the navigation call, as shown here:

```
Navigate("http://www.osborne.com/archives/index.html");
```

One important point about both the navigation functions deserves mention here. In both functions, you can omit the **http://** protocol preface from the URL you pass to the function. The Web Browser control presumes that all connections will use the HTTP protocol, and therefore parses the URL and (if the protocol name is not at the URL's beginning) automatically adds the protocol name to the URL for you.

Using the CHtmlView Class to Write a Simple Browser Program

Taking what you have learned in the preceding sections and using it together with the **CHtmlView** class to write a simple, single-document interface program will be a generally straightforward process. You'll find an implementation of the MFCBrowse program on the companion CD-ROM. The code is almost all MFC-default, so there is no real benefit to presenting it here.

To create a simple browser, all you need to do is

- ◆ Create an application based on the **CHtmlView** class
- ◆ Provide implementations of the functions defined in the sections of this chapter
- ◆ Provide menus and toolbars for the user to access

The only tool that you must provide is a way to enter URLs for the user to jump directly to, regardless of the contents of the history file.

In the MFCBrowse program, the **OnNavigateGoto( )** function creates a modal dialog box (from a dialog template) that displays a single text field into which the user can enter a URL. The implementation for the **OnNavigateGoto( )** function is as shown here:

```
void CMFCBrowseView::OnNavigateGoto()
 {
```

```
    CNewUrl NewURL;
    if (NewURL.DoModal() == IDOK)
        Navigate2(NewURL.m_strNewUrl, 0, 0, 0);
}
```

The **CNewUrl** class is derived from **CDialog** and corresponds to the dialog box, which should be evident from the code itself.

Tweaking a Browser to Look at Search Results

Implementation of a multiple-document interface version of the browser is just as simple—requiring only that you use a **CMultiDocTemplate** object and perform the other various housekeeping steps necessary to create MDI views.

Also of value, however, is to create an MDI application to show off some of the possible uses you might have for **CHtmlView** within your own applications. On the companion CD-ROM you'll find the MultiSearch program, which takes advantage of **CHtmlView** to provide the user with helpful information. The program itself is intended to help a user look through the results of a search done by a search engine.

When the program first runs, it displays four child windows within the main frame. Three are blank, and the fourth points to http://www.yahoo.com, a common search engine. (You can, of course, make it point to whatever you want from within the program code.)

Each link clicked on within the search engine window will cause the requested URL to display in one of the other windows. The program will send to each of the three windows in order, meaning that the fourth URL will be sent to the first window.

To perform this processing, the program overrides the **CHtmlView:: OnBeforeNavigate2( )** function. This function looks at a **Navigate2( )** request before it executes. In the MultiSearch program, the application intercepts the request and sends it to one of the other windows, where the requested URL is displayed.

Search engines request URLs to display their results. These URLs always have HTML arguments preceded by a ?. The **OnBeforeNavigate2( )** function takes advantage of this by checking the URL to see if it is a search engine request. If it is, the function passes it on without doing anything to it. If the URL is a normal URL, however, then the function intercepts it, sends a **Navigate2( )** command within the target display window, and sets the *pbCancel member to **true**, which tells the framework not to execute the **Navigate2( )** command within the search window. Figure 9-5 shows the MultiSearch application after a search for C++ and the selection of several Web pages.

FIGURE 9-5. The MultiSearch application displaying a search window and three result windows

Performing Financial Calculations

By Lars Klander

sld.cpp

syd.cpp

ddb.cpp

fv.cpp

fvseries.cpp

fvs2.cpp

pv.cpp

pvseries.cpp

loan.cpp

retire.cpp

Everyone knows that the computer's biggest strength is performing calculations. In fact, at some level, everything a computer does is focused on performing a calculation. Even so, many books about C/C++ ignore some of the important calculations that you might need to include within your applications. Although the standard C/C++ libraries include a series of functions to help you compute values such as tangents and cosines, the libraries aren't much help when it comes to performing nonscientific calculations. In this chapter and the next, you will look at some custom functions that you can use to perform financial and statistical calculations within your programs.

For clarity, this chapter is divided into two general categories:

◆ **Computing depreciation of assets.** This is an important technique for accounting programs.

◆ **Computing information about annuities.** Although the chapter refers to annuities in general, there are two basic types of annuities—one for which money is paid to you, and one for which money is paid to someone else. In general, an annuity for which you pay money to someone else is considered a loan.

The programs in this chapter are all relatively straightforward—in fact, most of the discussion will be about the computations performed within the actual computing functions themselves, and how those computations relate to real-world use.

Computing Depreciation

Depreciation is a means of determining the value of an asset at a given point in time after the asset has been purchased.

In the world of accounting, computing the depreciation of an asset is one of the accountant's most important tasks. The depreciation method for a given asset will have consequences for the company's balance sheet and taxes owed. It may even affect the company's stock price, depending on whether the company is publicly traded or not, and the significance of the company assets as a function of its balance sheet. Depreciation is generally used only on "hard" assets—for example, computers, die-stampers, and so on.

You will see three types of depreciation at work in this chapter: *straight-line depreciation, sum-of-the-years digits depreciation*, and *double-declining balance depreciation*.

Straight-Line Depreciation

Probably the best way to understand depreciation is to consider a simple straight-line depreciation example.

Suppose your company bought a server cluster, which cost you $10,000. For computers, accountants generally depreciate the asset over a period of either three or five years. For a computer purchase of this type, using straight-line depreciation the accountant would generally depreciate the asset over five years. Because computers are generally worthless after a certain period of time, this asset would probably be depreciated to a value of $0 (as opposed to a car, which might be depreciated to one-third of its original value after five years).

Given these circumstances, Table 10-1 shows the value of the asset after each year of its effective lifetime.

As you can see, the straight-line depreciation model simply divides the difference between the purchase price and the salvage value by the number of years over which you are depreciating the asset. If you instead depreciated the asset over ten years, the asset depicted in Table 10-1 would depreciate at the value of $1,000 per year.

The function for straight-line depreciation, then, can be written as shown here:

Depreciation Amount = (Purchase Price – Salvage Value) / Number of Years

Once you know the Depreciation Amount, you can compute the current value of the asset with the following formula:

Current Value = Purchase Price – (Depreciation Amount * Number of Years)

Thus you can compute the straight-line depreciation of an asset if you know its Purchase Price, its worth at the end of the depreciation term (Salvage Value), and the Number of Years over which you intend to depreciate it.

Purchase Price	Salvage Value	Current Year	Current Value
$10,000	$0	1	$8,000
$10,000	$0	2	$6,000
$10,000	$0	3	$4,000
$10,000	$0	4	$2,000
$10,000	$0	5	$0

TABLE 10-1. A Simple Straight-Line Depreciation Example

PROGRAMMER'S NOTE   *Accountants do not arbitrarily decide how they want to depreciate an asset. In general, they use an agreed-upon number of years for the depreciation of that asset. That number of years may be specified by the Internal Revenue Service, the Association of Certified Public Accountants, or some other recognized body. If your program that performs depreciation is for public use, you should obtain the appropriate table and ensure that your depreciation calculation uses the correct value for the equipment type.*

sld.cpp

Code for Program Using Straight-Line Depreciation

The following program, **sld.cpp**, uses the formula that you have just seen to compute the straight-line depreciation of an asset.

```cpp
#include <iostream>
using namespace std;

double sld(double cost, double salvage, int lifetime)
{
  return (cost - salvage) / lifetime;
}

int main()
{
  double cost, salvage, deprecval;
  int lifetime;
  int i;

  cout << "Enter the original cost of the asset: ";
  cin >> cost;

  cout << "Enter the salvage value of the asset: ";
  cin >> salvage;

  cout << "Enter the lifetime in years of the asset (integer): ";
  cin >> lifetime;

  deprecval = sld(cost, salvage, lifetime);
  cout << "The straight-line depreciation of the asset is: " <<
      deprecval << " dollars per year." << endl;

  for (i=1; i < lifetime + 1; i++) {
    cout << "The value of the asset after year " << i;
```

```
    cout << " is: " << cost - (i * deprecval) << endl;
  }

  return 0;
}
```

ANNOTATIONS

Let's look a little more closely at the code—particularly the code within the **sld( )**
function.

```
double sld(double cost, double salvage, int lifetime)
{
  return (cost - salvage) / lifetime;
}
```

As you can see, the **sld( )** function accepts three incoming parameters—the
initial cost of the asset, the salvage value of the asset, and the lifetime over which
to depreciate the asset. In turn, the function returns a **double** value to the calling
location. The **sld( )** function returns the amount to depreciate per year. The **return**
statement returns the value specified by the equation you saw earlier in this
section—the purchase price of the asset minus the salvage value of the asset, divided
by the number of years of depreciation for the asset.

The **sld.cpp** program accepts user input for these three values (cost, salvage, and
lifetime), and then calls the **sld( )** function to compute the depreciation per year. It
then uses the **for** loop at the end of the **main( )** function to display the value of the
asset over each year of its depreciation, as shown here:

```
deprecval = sld(cost, salvage, lifetime);
cout << "The straight-line depreciation of the asset is: " <<
    deprecval << " dollars per year." << endl;

for (i=1; i < lifetime + 1; i++) {
  cout << "The value of the asset after year " << i;
  cout << " is: " << cost - (i * deprecval) << endl;
}
```

Because the program code uses the depreciation value within the loop, the
program code first assigns the return value from the **sld( )** function to a local
variable. (This costs some memory overhead, but it reduces the function-calling
overhead for the function by eliminating the invariant code.)

When you run the **sld.cpp** program as written, you will generate output similar
to the following. Notice that the entries for this sample correspond to the values in
Table 10-1.

```
Enter the original cost of the asset: 10000
Enter the salvage value of the asset: 0
Enter the lifetime in years of the asset (integer): 5
The straight-line depreciation of the asset is: 2000 dollars per
year.
The value of the asset after year 1 is: 8000
The value of the asset after year 2 is: 6000
The value of the asset after year 3 is: 4000
The value of the asset after year 4 is: 2000
The value of the asset after year 5 is: 0
```

Depending on your application, you might implement the **sld( )** function differently. For example, if you wanted to compute the current value of the asset at a specific point in time, you might write the function as shown here:

```
double sld(double cost, double salvage, int lifetime,
    int currentyear)
{
  double deprecval;

  deprecval = (cost - salvage) / lifetime
  return (cost - (salvage * currentyear));
}
```

In this case, you are simply folding the second part of the depreciation computation—determining the asset's current value—into the function that computes the amount of depreciation per year.

Sum-of-Years Digits Depreciation

Although straight-line depreciation is the simplest of the depreciation methods, it is also the least used in business—specifically because of its simplicity. In fact, very few items depreciate on a straight line. For example, it is often said that a car depreciates 20% the minute you drive it off the lot. By the same token, however, most cars have value long beyond the fifth year of their lifetime. Clearly, automobile assets do not depreciate at a constant value.

The second customary method of depreciation is the *sum-of-the-years digits* depreciation of an asset. This depreciation method is front-loaded, meaning that the asset depreciates more quickly in the early years of its lifetime and more slowly in the later years of its lifetime. To see how this works, consider again the example of the $10,000 server that you want to depreciate over five years. Using sum-of-years digits depreciation, the asset will depreciate as shown in Table 10-2.

Purchase Price	Salvage Value	Current Year	Current Value
$10,000	$0	1	$6,666.66
$10,000	$0	2	$4,000.00
$10,000	$0	3	$2,000.00
$10,000	$0	4	$666.67
$10,000	$0	5	$0.00

TABLE 10-2.   The Sum-of-the-Years Digits Depreciation for an Asset

As you can see from the table, the asset still has a value of $0 at the end of the fifth year. However, the asset depreciates faster at the beginning of its lifetime than it does at the end—depreciating a full 1/3 of its value in the first year, and only 1/15 of its value in the fifth year. It's easier yet to see the impact that such a computation will have on an asset if you consider the ten-year depreciation shown in Table 10-3.

As you can see, the asset loses almost half its value by the end of the third year, and by the halfway point of the asset's lifetime, it loses nearly three-quarters of its value. In general, for assets such as computers, sum-of-the-years digits depreciation provides a more accurate value for the asset.

Purchase Price	Salvage Value	Current Year	Current Value
$10,000	$0	1	$8,181.81
$10,000	$0	2	$6,545.44
$10,000	$0	3	$5,090.89
$10,000	$0	4	$3,818.16
$10,000	$0	5	$2,727.25
$10,000	$0	6	$1,818.15
$10,000	$0	7	$1,090.87
$10,000	$0	8	$545.41
$10,000	$0	9	$181.77
$10,000	$0	10	$0.00

TABLE 10-3.   Sum-of-the-Years Digits Depreciation Over 10 Years

Computing sum-of-the-years digits depreciation is only slightly more complex than computing the straight-line depreciation of an asset. Again, the easiest way to visualize the formula is in two parts. The depreciation for any given year can be computed as shown here:

(Lifetime Remaining / Sum of the Years) * (Cost – Salvage)

The Lifetime Remaining value corresponds to the number of years left between the computing year and the end of the asset's useful life. For example, say you're depreciating over ten years. If you're computing for year 2, the number of years remaining between the computing year and the end of the asset's useful life is
`(10 - 2 = 8)`

The Sum of the Years value corresponds to the sum of the number of years. In other words, if you are depreciating over five years, the Sum of the Years value equals
`(1 + 2 + 3 + 4 + 5 = 15)`

An easier way to compute the Sum of the Years value is shown here:

((Lifetime * (Lifetime + 1)) / 2)

To use the five-year example again, this computation works out as
`((5 * (6)) / 2 = 15)`
However, using this equation in your program is simpler than writing some type of recursing **sum( )** function that adds up the values in order.

After you compute the depreciation for any given year, you compute the value of the asset after that depreciation, as shown here:

Original Cost – Σ(Depreciation(1)..Depreciation(N))

In this case, the total depreciation is the Original Cost of the asset, minus each year's depreciation through the current year. In other words, if the asset is in its third year of depreciation, the depreciated value of the asset is equal to the following value:

Original Cost – (Depreciation(1) + Depreciation(2) + Depreciation(3))

Therefore, just as with straight-line depreciation, you can compute the depreciation of an asset at any point during its lifetime, as long as you know the Original Cost, the Salvage Value, and the Number of Years over which to depreciate the asset. To compute the current value of an asset at any point over its lifetime, you must also know where you are in the asset's depreciation cycle.

syd.cpp

Code for Program Using Sum-of-the-Years Digits Depreciation

The **syd.cpp** program on the companion CD-ROM uses the sum-of-the-years digits depreciation formulas to compute depreciation.

```cpp
#include <iostream>
#include <cmath>
using namespace std;

double syd(double cost, double salvage, double lifetime,
    int deprecyear)
{
  double multiplier, sumyears, valuetodeprec;

  valuetodeprec = cost - salvage;
  sumyears = lifetime * ((lifetime + 1) / 2);
  multiplier = (lifetime - (deprecyear-1)) / sumyears;
  return multiplier * valuetodeprec;
}

double roundtohundreds(double roundvalue)
{
  roundvalue = ceil(roundvalue * 100);
  return roundvalue / 100;
}

int main()
{
  double cost, salvage, deprecval, currentval, lifetime;
  int i;

  cout << "Enter the original cost of the asset: ";
  cin >> cost;

  cout << "Enter the salvage value of the asset: ";
  cin >> salvage;
```

```
cout << "Enter the lifetime in years of the asset (integer): ";
cin >> lifetime;

cout << "The sum-of-the years' digits depreciation of "
    << "the asset is as follows:" << endl;

currentval = cost;
for (i=1; i < lifetime + 1; i++) {
  deprecval = syd(cost, salvage, lifetime, i);
  currentval = currentval - deprecval;
  cout << "The depreciation for year " << i << " is: " <<
      roundtohundreds(deprecval) << endl;
  cout << "The value of the asset after year " << i;
  cout << " is: " << roundtohundreds(currentval) << endl;
}
return 0;
}
```

ANNOTATIONS

Let's look at the code a little more closely. This program adds another function, **roundtohundreds( )**. In addition, the depreciation is processed differently from the **sld.cpp** program you saw earlier. The biggest difference, however, is in the function that computes the depreciation—called **syd( )** in the **syd.cpp** program, and shown here:

```
double syd(double cost, double salvage, double lifetime,
    int deprecyear)
{
  double multiplier, sumyears, valuetodeprec;

  valuetodeprec = cost - salvage;
  sumyears = lifetime * ((lifetime + 1) / 2);
  multiplier = (lifetime - (deprecyear-1)) / sumyears;
  return multiplier * valuetodeprec;
}
```

As you can see, the **syd( )** function has a major difference in the parameters it accepts—the **lifetime** parameter in this function must be a **double**, rather than the **int** that it was in the first program. This constraint exists because of the calculation to compute the **sumyears** value. If **lifetime** were not a **double**, C/C++ would automatically truncate the result in the **sumyears** variable to a whole number (because of precision issues)—which would throw your depreciation values off significantly. You could also cast the value.

PROGRAMMER'S NOTE *To see the impact of precision on the computation, you can change the **lifetime** parameter to an **int** (make sure you change it in **main( )** as well). The calculation will actually depreciate the asset value into the negatives.*

In any event, the program code in the **syd( )** function also uses some local variables—mostly for clarity. (Although the entire computation could occur within the **return** statement, it would be confusing.) The first computation determines the total amount to depreciate, and places that value within the **valuetodeprec** local variable. The second computation performs the sum-of-the-years digits computation you saw earlier and places the result within a **double**, aptly named **sumyears**. The third computation determines the current fraction to depreciate, and the **return** statement multiplies that fraction by the total amount to depreciate. The function returns the current year's depreciation.

Within the **syd.cpp** program, a **for** loop is used to display the depreciation at every year. You could, however, change the **syd( )** function to return the value after depreciation for the current year, using code similar to the following:

```
double syd(double cost, double salvage, double lifetime,
    int deprecyear)
{
  double multiplier, sumyears, valuetodeprec, currentvalue;

  valuetodeprec = cost - salvage;
  sumyears = lifetime * ((lifetime + 1) / 2);
  currentvalue = cost;
  for (int i=0; i < deprecyear; i++) {
    multiplier = (lifetime - (i)) / sumyears;
    currentvalue = currentvalue - (multiplier * valuetodeprec);
  }
  return currentvalue;
}
```

Such a change would return the current value of the asset at the end of the depreciation year specified.

The second function within the program does some rounding, with the goal of simplifying output. In general, you wouldn't use a function such as this to round, because over time it will introduce depreciation errors into the formula (ranging anywhere from a few pennies to thousands of dollars, depending on the value of the asset). You should instead simply apply the rounding to the output, as is done in the **syd.cpp** program. The following code implements the **roundtohundreds( )** function:

```
double roundtohundreds(double roundvalue)
{
  roundvalue = ceil(roundvalue * 100);
  return roundvalue / 100;
}
```

The **roundtohundreds( )** function multiplies the incoming **double** value by 100, rounds it to the nearest whole value, and then returns that integer divided by 100. The function uses the C/C++ standard math library's **ceil( )** function to perform the rounding.

The **main( )** function within the program performs essentially the same processing as it did within the **sld.cpp** program. The biggest difference here in **syd.cpp** is the **for** loop's role of computing the depreciation over each year and depreciating the value correctly, as shown here:

```
currentval = cost;
for (i=1; i < lifetime + 1; i++) {
  deprecval = syd(cost, salvage, lifetime, i);
  currentval = currentval - deprecval;
  cout << "The depreciation for year " << i << " is: " <<
      roundtohundreds(deprecval) << endl;
  cout << "The value of the asset after year " << i;
  cout << " is: " << roundtohundreds(currentval) << endl;
}
```

Before entering the loop, the program simply sets the **currentval** value to the original cost of the asset. The **currentval** value is then adjusted each time through the loop, deducting the current depreciation amount for the asset from **currentval**. When you run the program, using the depreciation values from Table 10-3 ($10,000 initial cost, $0 salvage value, 10-year depreciation), the program will generate the following output:

```
Enter the original cost of the asset: 10000
Enter the salvage value of the asset: 0
Enter the lifetime in years of the asset (integer): 10
The sum-of-the years' digits depreciation of the asset is as follows:
The depreciation for year 1 is: 1818.19
The value of the asset after year 1 is: 8181.82
The depreciation for year 2 is: 1636.37
The value of the asset after year 2 is: 6545.46
The depreciation for year 3 is: 1454.55
The value of the asset after year 3 is: 5090.91
The depreciation for year 4 is: 1272.73
The value of the asset after year 4 is: 3818.19
The depreciation for year 5 is: 1090.91
The value of the asset after year 5 is: 2727.28
The depreciation for year 6 is: 909.1
The value of the asset after year 6 is: 1818.19
The depreciation for year 7 is: 727.28
The value of the asset after year 7 is: 1090.91
The depreciation for year 8 is: 545.46
The value of the asset after year 8 is: 545.46
```

```
The depreciation for year 9 is: 363.64
The value of the asset after year 9 is: 181.82
The depreciation for year 10 is: 181.82
The value of the asset after year 10 is: 0.01
```

PROGRAMMER'S NOTE   *As you can see, the rounding function, though useful for formatting, will occasionally result in an apparent error. Notice the output for the last year, which should be $0.00. The error is only in the output, however—the values themselves are correct; the operations are simply smaller than pennies.*

Using Double-Declining Balance Depreciation

So far, you have seen two types of depreciation at work—straight-line depreciation and sum-of-the-years digits depreciation. The third type you will commonly encounter is double-declining balance depreciation. This method is implemented in two ways: one for "pure" accounting purposes, and one for tax purposes. However, because the "pure" accounting method never depreciates the asset value entirely to the salvage value, this chapter focuses on the tax method of using double-declining balance depreciation. The annotations for the program code will explain how you can change the function to support "pure" double-declining balance depreciation, as well.

Like sum-of-the-years digits depreciation, double-declining balance depreciation computes an asset's depreciation at an accelerated rate—the highest depreciation occurs in the first period, and the depreciation in any subsequent period will always be lower than it was in the previous period.

The tax-approved implementation of the double-declining balance method actually uses two separate sets of equations to compute the depreciation. Generally speaking, the asset depreciates annually during the first half of its lifetime at twice the rate of straight-line depreciation; however, the depreciation amount is always computed based on the current value of the asset. In the second half of the asset's lifetime, it depreciates in a straight-line manner based on the number of years remaining in its lifetime.

The easiest way to visualize double-declining balance depreciation is to consider again the $10,000 computer system, depreciated over ten years and worth nothing at the end. In a straight-line depreciation, the system would depreciate at 10% per year for each year. In the double-declining balance method, the system will depreciate at 20% of its current value for the first five years. In other words, it will depreciate $2,000 in its first year ($10,000 * 20% = $2,000), leaving its current value at $8,000. In the second year, the asset will depreciate $1,600 ($8,000 * 20% = $1,600), resulting in a year-end value of $6,400. This depreciation model will continue until the end of the fifth year.

At the end of the fifth year, the computation method switches to straight-line, at the rate of 20% per year (full depreciation of the remaining value over five years equals 100% divided by five). The resulting depreciation set for this example appears in Table 10-4.

Compare Tables 10-3 and 10-4, and you'll see that the double-declining balance method depreciates faster than the sum-of-the-years digits method for the first two years, then depreciates more slowly thereafter. Also, you will notice that the asset depreciates at the rate of $655.36 for every year after the fifth year in the double-depreciating balance method.

Needless to say, the computations of the current depreciation in the double-declining balance method tend to be a bit more complex, because each year's depreciation during the first half of the asset's lifetime depends on the asset's value at the beginning of the year. The formula for the depreciation of the current year is as follows:

Current Depreciation = (Starting Asset Value − Salvage) * (2 / Lifetime)

Note that you divide 2 by the Lifetime value, since you are doubling the straight-line depreciation amount.

From a programming perspective, the processing your code will perform is most simply shown in the following formula, where n is the current depreciation year:

Current Depreciation(n) = (Ending Value(n − 1) − Salvage) * (2 / Lifetime)

Purchase Price	Salvage Value	Current Year	Current Value
$10,000	$0	1	$8,000.00
$10,000	$0	2	$6,400.00
$10,000	$0	3	$5,120.00
$10,000	$0	4	$4,096.00
$10,000	$0	5	$3,276.80
$10,000	$0	6	$2,621.24
$10,000	$0	7	$1,966.08
$10,000	$0	8	$1,310.72
$10,000	$0	9	$655.36
$10,000	$0	10	$0.00

TABLE 10-4.   Sum-of-the-Years Digits Depreciation Over Ten Years

In such case, the following constraint must be true at the beginning of the series:

Current Depreciation(1) = (Purchase Cost – Salvage) * (2 / Lifetime)

Conceptually, then, the formula for asset value at the end of any given year is:

Ending Value(n) = Ending Value(n – 1) – Current Depreciation(n)

Depending on your implementation, it's pretty clear that this computation might be a good candidate for recursion. However, in the **ddb.cpp** program, the computation is implemented inside a **for** loop for simplicity.

Before you continue, remember that the formula you have just considered only applies to the first half of the depreciation period. (In the **ddb.cpp** implementation, halves are rounded up—meaning this formula is used in the first three years of a five-year asset lifetime.) You will use standard straight-line depreciation for the remaining years of the asset's lifetime. In other words, after the halfway point of the asset's lifetime, you should use the following formula to compute the remaining depreciation:

Depreciation = (Current Value – Salvage Value) / (Lifetime – Remaining Years)

In the **ddb.cpp** program, the program code actually calls the **sld( )** function that you saw earlier to compute the depreciation for the remainder of the term. Now that you have a good understanding of how to apply and use the double-declining balance method, take a look at the **ddb.cpp** program code (presented in the following section), which implements this depreciation method.

PROGRAMMER'S NOTE *The double-declining balance method is the method most commonly used by accountants for depreciating assets, so understanding its use is arguably more important than mastering the other two methods.*

ddb.cpp

Code for Program Using Double-Declining Balance Depreciation

Here is the code for the **ddb.cpp** program:

```
// double-declining balance depreciation
#include <iostream>
#include <cmath>
using namespace std;

double sld(double cost, double salvage, int lifetime)
{
```

```
    return (cost - salvage) / lifetime;
}

double roundtohundreds(double roundvalue)
{
  roundvalue = ceil(roundvalue * 100);
  return roundvalue / 100;
}

double ddb(double cost, double salvage, double lifetime,
    int deprecyear)
{
  double multiplier, currentdeprec, valuetodeprec, currentvalue;
  int breakpoint, i;

  if (ceil((lifetime / 2) + 0.5) > ceil((lifetime / 2) - 0.5))
    breakpoint = ceil((lifetime / 2) + 0.5);
  else
    breakpoint = ceil((lifetime / 2) - 0.5);

  multiplier = 2 / lifetime;

  currentvalue = cost;
  valuetodeprec = currentvalue - salvage;
  if (deprecyear < breakpoint)
    breakpoint = deprecyear;
  for (i = 1; i < breakpoint + 1; i++) {
    valuetodeprec = currentvalue - salvage;
    currentdeprec = valuetodeprec * multiplier;
    cout << "Current depreciation for year " << i << " is: "
        << currentdeprec << endl;
    currentvalue = currentvalue - currentdeprec;
    cout << "End-of-year depreciated value is: " <<
        currentvalue << endl;
  }
  if (deprecyear > breakpoint) {
    currentdeprec = sld(currentvalue, salvage,
        (lifetime - breakpoint));
    for (i=breakpoint + 1; i < deprecyear + 1; i++) {
      cout << "Current depreciation for year " << i << " is: "
          << currentdeprec << endl;
      currentvalue = currentvalue - currentdeprec;
```

```
        cout << "End-of-year depreciated value is: " <<
           roundtohundreds(currentvalue) << endl;
     }
   }
   return currentvalue;
}

int main()
{
  double cost, salvage, currentval, lifetime;
  int currentyear;

  cout << "Enter the original cost of the asset: ";
  cin >> cost;

  cout << "Enter the salvage value of the asset: ";
  cin >> salvage;

  cout << "Enter the lifetime in years of the asset (integer): ";
  cin >> lifetime;

  cout << "Enter the year through which to compute depreciation: ";
  cin >> currentyear;

  cout << "The double-declining balance depreciation "
       << "of the asset is as follows:"
       << endl;

  currentval = ddb(cost, salvage, lifetime, currentyear);
  return 0;
}
```

ANNOTATIONS

At the very least, the use of the **ddb( )** function in **ddb.cpp** demands some explanation. You've already studied the **sld( )** function and the **roundtohundreds( )** function. The **main( )** function does not do any particularly special processing; simply obtaining the values from the user and then placing the current value of the asset in the **currentval** variable. (Note that in this simple implementation, this value gets no further use.)

Let's look closely, then, at the **ddb( )** function's processing that is most interesting (and probably most likely to confuse).

```
double ddb(double cost, double salvage, double lifetime,
    int deprecyear)
{
  double multiplier, currentdeprec, valuetodeprec, currentvalue;
  int breakpoint, i;
```

As with the other depreciation functions you have seen, the **ddb( )** function accepts the purchase cost, salvage value, lifetime, and the year for which you want the depreciated value. The function also declares some local variables that it uses for its math, and defines the **breakpoint** value, which will correspond to the halfway point in the depreciation:

```
 if (ceil((lifetime / 2) + 0.5) > ceil((lifetime / 2) - 0.5))
     breakpoint = ceil((lifetime / 2) + 0.5);
 else
     breakpoint = ceil((lifetime / 2) - 0.5);
```

This **if** statement tests to see whether the number of years to depreciate is odd or even. If even, the code sets the **breakpoint** variable to the halfway value (for example, 3 if the number of years is 6). If odd, the code sets the **breakpoint** variable to the first year after the halfway value, meaning that it will again contain 3 if the number of years is 5.

The **multiplier** value contains the percentage to depreciate—remember, this is double-declining depreciation, so the multiplier value is twice what it would be in a straight-line depreciation. The **currentvalue** variable contains the asset value (which is the purchase price at this point), and the **valuetodeprec** variable contains the amount to depreciate. Here is that code:

```
  multiplier = 2 / lifetime;
  currentvalue = cost;
  valuetodeprec = currentvalue - salvage;
```

The next **if** statement:

```
if (deprecyear < breakpoint)
    breakpoint = deprecyear;
```

checks to see whether the year for which to return the depreciated value is before or after the depreciation's halfway point. If before, it sets the **breakpoint** value as equal to the depreciation year. This technique simplifies the loops for depreciation and avoids a lot of repeated code.

The first **for** loop, shown just below, counts either to the halfway point or the depreciation year (whichever is less) and applies the scaled depreciation to the value through that point. When the loop ends, the **currentvalue** variable contains the depreciated value of the asset through either the depreciation year or the breakpoint.

```
for (i = 1; i < breakpoint + 1; i++) {
    valuetodeprec = currentvalue - salvage;
    currentdeprec = valuetodeprec * multiplier;
```

```
       cout << "Current depreciation for year " << i << " is: "
           << currentdeprec << endl;
       currentvalue = currentvalue - currentdeprec;
       cout << "End-of-year depreciated value is: " <<
           currentvalue << endl;
   }
```

The next **if** statement:

```
if (deprecyear > breakpoint) {
```

serves two purposes—if the depreciation year falls before the breakpoint, the code makes sure the function does not depreciate the value any further. The same control is effected if the depreciation year is exactly on the breakpoint. If the depreciation year falls past the halfway point, the code then executes the straight-line depreciation function once for each year remaining until the depreciation year (or the end of the asset's lifetime, if the depreciation year you enter is equal to the asset's lifetime).

This **for** loop performs the straight-line depreciation on the current-year value until the ending year is reached:

```
   currentdeprec = sld(currentvalue, salvage,
       (lifetime - breakpoint));
   for (i=breakpoint + 1; i < deprecyear + 1; i++) {
     cout << "Current depreciation for year " << i << " is: "
         << currentdeprec << endl;
     currentvalue = currentvalue - currentdeprec;
     cout << "End-of-year depreciated value is: " <<
         roundtohundreds(currentvalue) << endl;
   }
 }  return currentvalue;
}
```

When you execute this program, and enter 10 for the year to depreciate through (which corresponds to the asset's lifetime), the program code will generate the following output:

```
Enter the original cost of the asset: 10000
Enter the salvage value of the asset: 0
Enter the lifetime in years of the asset (integer): 10
Enter the year through which to compute depreciation: 10
The double-declining balance depreciation of the asset is as follows:
Current depreciation for year 1 is: 2000
End-of-year depreciated value is: 8000
Current depreciation for year 2 is: 1600
End-of-year depreciated value is: 6400
Current depreciation for year 3 is: 1280
End-of-year depreciated value is: 5120
Current depreciation for year 4 is: 1024
```

```
End-of-year depreciated value is: 4096
Current depreciation for year 5 is: 819.2
End-of-year depreciated value is: 3276.8
Current depreciation for year 6 is: 655.36
End-of-year depreciated value is: 2621.44
Current depreciation for year 7 is: 655.36
End-of-year depreciated value is: 1966.08
Current depreciation for year 8 is: 655.36
End-of-year depreciated value is: 1310.72
Current depreciation for year 9 is: 655.36
End-of-year depreciated value is: 655.36
Current depreciation for year 10 is: 655.36
End-of-year depreciated value is: 0
```

Financial Functions for Handling Annuities

So far in this chapter, you have focused on how to handle the depreciation of an asset over time. You studied three different possible methods, and the functions that you need to implement to use those methods. Thankfully, however, assets do not always decline—in fact, in many cases, their value increase. In the best of all worlds, assets will increase while liabilities decrease.

Throughout the rest of this chapter, you will learn about *annuities*, and how you can use them to analyze financial information—the current value of an investment portfolio, the payments made on a loan, and so on. Computing annuity values is often more complex than working with depreciation—but for most of us, the results of working with annuities are much more pleasant. Moreover, you will probably use annuity computations far more often than you will use depreciation computations—because annuity calculations have many different applications.

Some Definitions. As you consider annuities, you'll encounter certain terms again and again. Following are discussions of the most common and ubiquitous terms; others will be explained as they come up in the subsequent sections.

◆ **Interest Rate:** Annuities include a built-in concept of the interest paid on, or due on, the principal of the annuity. Interest rates, in most cases, will be somewhere between 2.9% (for cars) and 14%–16% (for high-performing mutual funds). In general, when you compute an annuity, you presume a fixed interest rate and build the annuity analysis around that rate.

◆ **Payments:** Although you can compute annuities based on a single initial contribution that remains static for the life of the annuity, you will more commonly be making regular payments into the annuity (or making payments against a loan, if you are computing a loan). Payments are crucial considerations for annuity computations; in the following sections you will

evaluate situations calling for no payments, and situations calling for regular payments.

◆ **Future Value:** The future value of an annuity is its value at maturity—that is, its worth when the lifetime of the annuity expires.

Computing the future value is the basis for most financial computations, and so the first program that you'll examine in this section explains computation of the future value of a single payment into an annuity.

Computing the Future Value Based on a Single Payment

There are two primary considerations to be addressed when computing the future value of an annuity: the annuity's value at the beginning of the period, and whether regular contributions are made to the annuity over its lifetime. The simplest case to consider is an annuity for which you set a present value, and to which you make no further contributions over time.

The best example of this type of investment structure is probably the conversion of a 401(k) or other retirement plan into some type of fixed-interest retirement plan, where you deposit all the money at the beginning of the plan period and leave the funds untouched until retirement.

Let's again use a table to visualize the way an annuity of this type will work. Table 10-5 shows the value of the annuity at the end of each of the first seven years.

As you can see, by the end of the seventh year the annuity has nearly doubled. This is known as the *Rule of Seven*, which specifies that, every seven years, an annuity should double its value (or nearly double, as in this case). The Rule of Seven is a common concern for financial planners when working with annuities. If a

Value at Beginning of Year	Interest Rate	Value at End of Year
(Initial deposit) $10,000.00	10%	$11,000.00
$11,000.00	10%	$12,100.00
$12,100.00	10%	$13,310.00
$13,310.00	10%	$14,641.00
$14,641.00	10%	$16,105.10
$16,105.10	10%	$17,715.61
$17,715.61	10%	$19,487.17

TABLE 10-5. The Annuity's Value Over the First Seven Years of Its Lifetime.

computed annuity value does not achieve returns on a close order to the Rule of Seven, then the annuity is probably not a good investment.

So, as you can see, the annuity compounds its interest every year—meaning that the amount of interest increases as the interest itself accrues interest from the previous year. The **fv.cpp** program performs this series of calculations and informs you of the future value of an annuity at its maturity.

There are several ways to compute interest in this manner; in this program we use a simple mathematical equation. Think of the current value of an annuity in the terms shown by the following equation (where n is the current year):

$$value(n) = value(n - 1) * (1 + rate)$$

As with other functions you have seen, this seems like a good candidate for recursion, with the ending condition being as follows:

$$value(1) = Present\ Value * (1 + rate)$$

However, as you probably know, recursion is not necessarily the most effective way to perform this type of calculation. In fact, when you consider the current value as being the result of the series of previous values, you'll be able to see that you can simplify the equation to reflect the current value, as shown here:

$$value(n) = Present\ Value * (1 + rate)^n$$

This equation is the one that the **fv.cpp** program will use.

Code for Computing Future Value Based on a Single Payment

fv.cpp

Here is the code for the **fv.cpp** program.

```cpp
// future value of single payment
#include <iostream>
#include <cmath>
using namespace std;

double fv(double pv, double numyears, double rate)
{
   return pv * pow((1 + rate), numyears);
}


double roundtohundreds(double roundvalue)
{
```

```
    roundvalue = ceil(roundvalue * 100);
    return roundvalue / 100;
}

int main()
{
    double presentvalue, interest, lifetime;

    cout << "Enter the present value of the annuity: ";
    cin >> presentvalue;

    cout << "Enter the fixed interest rate for the annuity ""
        << (in the form 0.xx for xx%): ";
    cin >> interest;

    cout << "Enter the lifetime in years of the annuity (integer): ";
    cin >> lifetime;

    cout << "The value of the annuity at maturation is: " <<
        roundtohundreds(fv(presentvalue, lifetime, interest)) << endl;
    return 0;
}
```

ANNOTATIONS

The **fv.cpp** program is relatively straightforward—you simply retrieve the annuity's start information from the user, then compute the future value of the annuity. We'll take a closer look at several things in the implementation—the first of which is the **fv( )** function, shown here:

```
double fv(double pv, double numyears, double rate)
{
    return pv * pow((1 + rate), numyears);
}
```

The **fv( )** function accepts the present value of the annuity (the initial contribution), the number of years in the annuity's lifetime, and the fixed interest rate for the annuity. As you can see, the function simply returns the result of the equation that you saw earlier as the function's value. The equation uses the C/C++ math library's standard **pow( )** function to compute the value of $(1 + rate)^n$. The first parameter to the **pow( )** function is the value to raise to a power, and the second parameter is the power to which to raise the value.

You have already studied the **roundtohundreds( )** function, including some of the traps that you must be concerned with when using the function. In the **pv.cpp** program, you don't have to worry about those traps, because the program only uses the **roundtohundreds( )** function to display the annuity value—it never actually changes the value.

```
cout << "The value of the annuity at maturation is: " <<
     roundtohundreds(fv(presentvalue, lifetime, interest)) << endl;
```

As you can see, the **main( )** function only takes in some input, then computes the future value and displays it on the screen. The following listing shows sample output of the **fv.cpp** program:

```
Enter the present value of the annuity: 10000
Enter the fixed interest rate for the annuity
(in the form 0.xx for fxx%): .10
Enter the lifetime in years of the annuity (integer): 20
The value of the annuity at maturation is: 67275
```

Computing the Future Value of a Series of Payments

Now that you have seen the simple computation necessary to determine the future value of a single deposit into an annuity, making the leap to determining the value of a series of payments should not be difficult.

Obviously, if you make a single deposit today, it will be worth more at the end of 20 years than if you make small deposits over time. In fact, if you deposit $500 a year for 20 years into the 10% annuity that you worked with in the preceding section, the annuity will only be worth $28,637.50 at the end of its term.

In contrast, most of us are more likely to make payments into an annuity over time. Computing the value of an annuity with payments made over time, then, is an important task. In fact, for IRA and similar contributions, understanding the

Years of Contributions	Ending Value
20	$114,550.00
30	$328,988.00
40	$885,185.00

TABLE 10-6.   Annuity Values After Various Lifetimes

implications of annuity becomes even more valuable. Consider Table 10-6, which shows the value of an IRA after $2,000 contributions are made for 40 years (starting at age 25), 30 years (starting at age 35), and 20 years (starting at age 45). Computations in this table are based on a fixed 10% interest rate.

Notice that the difference in value is much greater than the $40,000 disparity you might expect (20 years * $2,000). In fact, as you can see, the 40-year annuity is worth almost eight times as much as the 20-year annuity—which meets the Rule of Seven requirement that the value should double three times—or 2^3, which equals 8.

The computations for the value of an annuity after a given period of time with regular payments are consistent with the computation for the value of an annuity from a fixed starting payment. You could write the value of the annuity at the end of a given year as shown here:

$$\text{value}(n) = (\text{value}(n-1) * (1 + \text{rate})) + \text{Contribution}$$

Again here, as with the calculation based on a single payment, recursion might be an acceptable option, with the ending condition being the end of the first year of the annuity's existence. The value at that point would be

$$\text{value}(1) = (\text{Contribution} * (1 + \text{rate})) + \text{Contribution}$$

However, as indicated earlier, recursion is not necessarily the most efficient option for calculations of this nature—in part because this series can easily be converted to a single equation that you can use to compute the value of the annuity at any year-ending point, as shown here:

$$\text{Ending Value} = \text{Contribution} * ((((1 + \text{rate})^n) - 1) / \text{rate})$$

This equation specifies an annuity on which you pay in an initial value, and then make identical contributions at the end of every period (the equation for payments at the beginning of the period is slightly different).

fvseries.cpp

Code for Computing Future Value Based on a Series of Payments

The **fvseries.cpp** program shows how to compute the value of an annuity which is comprised of a series of payments from within a C/C++ program. Here is the code:

```cpp
#include <iostream>
#include <cmath>
using namespace std;

double fvs(double payperperiod, double rate, double lifetime)
```

```
{
  double multiplier;

  multiplier = (pow((1 + rate), lifetime) - 1) / rate;
  return multiplier * payperperiod;
}

double roundtohundreds(double roundvalue)
{
  roundvalue = ceil(roundvalue * 100);
  return roundvalue / 100;
}

int main()
{
  double payment, rate, lifetime;

  cout << "Enter the value per period paid into the annuity: ";
  cin >> payment;

  cout << "Enter the interest rate (in the form 0.xx for xx%): ";
  cin >> rate;

  cout << "Enter the lifetime in years of the annuity (integer): ";
  cin >> lifetime;

  cout << "The value of the annuity at maturation is: ";
  cout << roundtohundreds(fvs(payment, rate, lifetime));
  return 0;
}
```

ANNOTATIONS

As in most of the programs in this chapter, the key processing for **fvseries.cpp** occurs within the computation function—in this case, **fvs( )**. Let's take a closer look.

```
double fvs(double payperperiod, double rate, double lifetime)
{
  double multiplier;
```

```
    multiplier = (pow((1 + rate), lifetime) - 1) / rate;
    return multiplier * payperperiod;
}
```

Like the **fv( )** function that you saw in the preceding section, **fvs( )** accepts three incoming values, two of which it shares with the **fv( )** function—**rate** and **lifetime**. The third parameter, **payperperiod**, is the present value of money paid into the annuity. The **multiplier** variable is used only for clarity—you could just as easily write the entire equation into the **return** statement.

The primary statement is in the function derivation for the **multiplier** (which performs the calculation enclosed within parentheses in the equation that you saw earlier in this section). The function then multiplies that result by the contribution per period (**payperperiod**), to return the value of the annuity at ending.

Like the **fv.cpp** program, the **fvseries.cpp** program simply passes in values to the **fvs( )** function and displays the output, as shown here:

```
Enter the value per period paid into the annuity: 2000
Enter the interest rate (in the form 0.xx for xx%): .10
Enter the lifetime in years of the annuity (integer): 40
The value of the annuity at maturation is: 885185
```

Often, you will find that you must combine the two future-value formulas that you have seen demonstrated in this chapter—computing the value of an annuity based on an initial contribution—with standard monthly contributions thereafter. You can simply concatenate the formulas to do so as follows:

```
double fvs(double pv, double payperperiod, double rate,
    double lifetime)
{
  double multiplier, firsthalf;

  firsthalf = pv * pow((1 + rate), lifetime);
  multiplier = (pow((1 + rate), lifetime) - 1) / rate;
  return ((multiplier * payperperiod) + firsthalf);
}
```

The **fvs2.cpp** program (contained on the companion CD-ROM) uses this logic to generate its output.

So far, you have used information to compute the future value of something based on a set of conditions. Often you will know what you want the ending value to be (say, for example, your desired amount of money for retirement), and you will want to compute what you need to do now, or over time, to reach that goal. The following sections examine how to compute the present value of an annuity to reach a specified future value.

Computing a Single Payment to Reach a Future Value

Just as computing a future value from a single payment is slightly easier than computing a future value from a series of payments, so is computing a current value for a single payment easier than computing one for a series of present-value payments. The first program we will consider, **pv.cpp**, computes the present value required for an annuity based on the user's input of a future value, interest rate, and lifetime of the annuity.

The computation of the present value in such a situation is pretty straightforward, and is based on the equation that we saw previously:

Future Value(n) = Present Value * $(1 + rate)^n$

To obtain the present value, you need to perform some algebraic steps—divide through by future value, divide through by present value, and then invert both sides of the equation. At the end, you have the following equation:

Present Value = Future Value(n) / $(1 + rate)^n$

The **pv.cpp** program uses this function to perform its processing.

Code for Computing a Single Payment to Reach a Future Value

pv.cpp

Here is the code for the **pv.cpp** program.

```cpp
#include <iostream>
#include <cmath>
using namespace std;

double pv(double fv, double rate, double lifetime)
{
  return (fv / (pow((1 + rate), lifetime)));
}

double roundtohundreds(double roundvalue)
{
  roundvalue = ceil(roundvalue * 100);
  return roundvalue / 100;
}
```

```
int main()
{
  double futureval, rate, lifetime;

  cout << "Enter the future value of the annuity (at maturation): ";
  cin >> futureval;

  cout << "Enter the fixed interest rate for the annuity "
      << "(in the form 0.xx for xx%): ";
  cin >> rate;

  cout << "Enter the lifetime in years of the annuity (integer): ";
  cin >> lifetime;

  cout << "The present value of the annuity is: ";
  cout << roundtohundreds(pv(futureval, rate, lifetime));
  return 0;
}
```

ANNOTATIONS

As with the other programs you have seen, the crucial processing here happens within the **pv( )** function. Let's look at the function more closely, as well as the program's output:

```
double pv(double fv, double rate, int lifetime)
{
  return (fv / (pow((1 + rate), lifetime)));
}
```

As you would expect, based on the equation explained just above, the **pv( )** function accepts an incoming future value, interest rate, and annuity term as its parameters. It then applies the equation for Present Value and returns the present value of the annuity as its value.

The program code within the **main( )** function in **pv.cpp** simply accepts a series of inputs from the user, and then generates output showing the present value required to reach the final value. Here is the code to display the sample output:

```
cout << "The present value of the annuity is:";
cout << roundtohundreds(pv(futureval, rate, lifetime));
```

The **roundtohundreds( )** function appears again in this program, to display the result in dollars and cents. You can test the **pv.cpp** program by using the previous

examples—the values for the **fv.cpp** program, in reverse, should yield the $10,000 contribution, as shown here:

```
Enter the future value of the annuity (at maturation): 67275
Enter the fixed interest rate for the annuity
(in the form 0.xx for xx%): .10
Enter the lifetime in years of the annuity (integer): 20
The present value of the annuity is: 10000
```

Computing the Contributions Necessary to Reach a Specified Ending Value

We've mentioned that people are more likely to make a series of contributions over time into an annuity. It is also likely that those people will want to know what they have to put into the annuity each period in order to reach the desired ending value. Just as you did when computing the single present value, you will need to do some algebraic trickery with the initial function in order to determine the present value. Here again is the formula for future value of a series of payments, seen earlier in the section on computing the future value of a series of payments:

Ending Value = Contribution * (((($1 + rate)^n$) −1) / rate)

As before, you must divide through by the ending value and the contribution, and then invert both sides of the equation to determine the formula for present value. The formula for the amount of contribution you must make to an annuity, with a known future value, interest rate, and number of years in its lifetime, is as follows:

contribution = ending value / (((($1 + rate)^n$) −1) / rate)

pvseries.cpp

Code for Computing Series of Payments Toward a Goal

The **pvseries.cpp** program uses this computation to determine the payments you must make to reach a certain goal.

```cpp
#include <iostream>
#include <cmath>
using namespace std;

double pvs(double fv, double rate, double lifetime)
{
  return fv / ((pow((1 + rate), lifetime) - 1) / rate);
}
```

```
double roundtohundreds(double roundvalue)
{
  roundvalue = ceil(roundvalue * 100);
  return roundvalue / 100;
}

int main()
{
  double futurevalue, rate, lifetime;

  cout << "Enter the future value of the annuity: ";
  cin >> futurevalue;

  cout << "Enter the interest rate of the annuity " <<
      " (in the form 0.xx for xx%): ";
  cin >> rate;

  cout << "Enter the lifetime in years of the annuity (integer): ";
  cin >> lifetime;

  cout << "The amount you need to deposit for each period is: " <<
    roundtohundreds(pvs(futurevalue, rate, lifetime)) << endl;
  return 0;
}
```

ANNOTATIONS

The computations for the **pvseries.cpp** program all occur within the **pvs( )** function. Let's take a quick look at that function:

```
double pvs(double fv, double rate, double lifetime)
{
  return fv / ((pow((1 + rate), lifetime) - 1) / rate);
}
```

As discussed earlier in this section, the **pvs( )** function turns the future value function on its head, dividing the future value by the compounded interest rate, yielding the payments that you must make to reach an ending value. It returns that total as its value to the calling location, which is within the **main( )** function, as shown here:

```
  cout << "The amount you need to deposit for each period is: " <<
    roundtohundreds(pvs(futurevalue, rate, lifetime)) << endl;
```

Your old companion, the **roundtohundreds( )** function, converts the present-value figure into dollars and cents for you. You can check the program results by inputting the opposite of values that you have put in previously for the **fvseries.cpp** program. However, it is more interesting to check what you might need to do. For example, suppose that you are currently 25 and you want to retire at 65 with five million dollars. Determining how much you need to put into the fund annually is well within the **pvseries.cpp** program's capabilities, and the output is shown here:

```
Enter the future value of the annuity: 5000000
Enter the interest rate of the annuity
(in the form 0.xx for xx%): .10
Enter the lifetime in years of the annuity (integer): 40
The amount you need to deposit for each period is: 11297.1
```

In other words, you only need to save $11,297.10 each year to reach your goal—not too bad.

In the next section of this chapter, you will study another application of the annuity formulas: the loan calculator.

Writing a Simple Loan Calculator

Throughout this chapter, you have examined annuities as investments—long-term items that grow over time. There is also another kind of annuity to consider: long-term loans. The most common of these long-term loans is a home mortgage. The computation for a home mortgage payment is similar to the computation for an annuity.

In general, when you compute a mortgage payment, you have to determine the total amount of the loan (the loan *principal*); the term of the loan; and the interest rate of the loan. In general, for a mortgage, the user will know the price of the home, and the amount to put down on the home. The **loan.cpp** program requests this information from the user and then generates the payment amount per month, as well as displaying the total amount of the down payment.

Code for Calculating Loan Payments

Here is the code for the **loan.cpp** program:

loan.cpp

```cpp
#include <iostream>
#include <cmath>
using namespace std;
```

```
double payment(double loanamt, double rate, double years)
{
  double months;

  rate = rate / 12.00;
  months = years * 12;
  return loanamt * (rate / (1 - (1 / (pow((1 + rate), months)))));
}

double roundtohundreds(double roundvalue)
{
  roundvalue = ceil(roundvalue * 100);
  return roundvalue / 100;
}

int main()
{
  double purchaseprice, loanamount, percentdown, term, interest;

  cout << "Enter the purchase price of the house: ";
  cin >> purchaseprice;

  cout << "Enter the percent down on the house " <<
      " (in the form 0.xx for xx%): ";
  cin >> percentdown;

  loanamount = purchaseprice - (purchaseprice * percentdown);
  cout << "Enter the interest rate of the mortgage " <<
      " (in the form 0.xx for xx%): ";
  cin >> interest;

  cout << "Enter the length of the mortgage in years: ";
  cin >> term;

  cout << "The amount down will be: " <<
      purchaseprice - loanamount << endl;
  cout << "The payments for the mortgage will be: " <<
    roundtohundreds(payment(loanamount, interest, term)) << endl;
  return 0;
}
```

The key portion of the **loan.cpp** program is the **payment( )** function, which computes the monthly payment for the mortgage. Let's take a closer look at the function:

```
double payment(double loanamt, double rate, double years)
{
  double months;

  rate = rate / 12.00;
  months = years * 12;
  return loanamt * (rate / (1 - (1 / (pow((1 + rate), months)))));
}
```

As you have seen in previous annuities, the **payment( )** function accepts the amount of the loan, the interest rate, and the number of years in the loan. However, because mortgages are computed monthly, the function performs additional processing on the **rate** parameter and the **years** parameter to convert them into monthly figures.

The function divides the **rate** parameter by 12 (to get a monthly interest rate), and then multiplies the **years** parameter (to generate the number of **months** in the loan). Finally, the payment amount is generated and returned as the **payment** value. The payment is computed from the loan amount, and the annuity function that you have seen many times before:

pow((1 + rate), months)

So, when you run the **loan.cpp** program, you will generate the following output:

```
Enter the purchase price of the house: 200000
Enter the percent down on the house  (in the form 0.xx for xx%): .20
Enter the interest rate of the mortgage
(in the form 0.xx for xx%): .075
Enter the length of the mortgage in years: 30
The amount down will be: 40000
The payments for the mortgage will be: 1118.75
```

Putting Together Multiple Computations

As you saw in the last section, applying the functions explained in this chapter to real-life computations is a relatively straightforward process. Before we close on this chapter, let's consider one more common, day-to-day situation that you will likely encounter.

For most people, determining how much money they need to save for retirement is an important consideration. Very few people today expect to live solely on Social Security benefits when they get older. It's a good plan to know how much you will need to have squirreled away.

Computing your desired retirement savings is a function of several variables, the most important of which is how much you plan to take out of the retirement fund monthly after retirement. Additionally, you must estimate how long you plan to be retired, the ongoing interest rate on the money after your retirement, the interest rate during the time you contribute to the fund, and how long you intend to contribute.

Figuring out projected savings per month toward retirement is best determined in two parts, which is how the **retire.cpp** program processes it. First, based on the monthly desired payout, term of retirement, and interest rate, the program computes how much money must be in the account when you retire. To do so, the program uses a variation on the formula that you saw at work in the **loan.cpp** program to compute loan payments. Instead of computing the payments, however, the program uses the information to compute the start value of the annuity. The operative formula is as follows:

$$\text{Start Amount} = \text{Payment} / (\text{rate} / (1 - (1 / (1 + \text{rate})^{\text{months}})))$$

PROGRAMMER'S NOTE   *The computations in this program differ slightly from some of the other computations in this chapter, because the principal amount will decrease on a monthly basis rather than annually.*

Once you know the amount you need to have in the fund at retirement, computing the amount to pay into the fund is a simple Present Value of a series computation, adjusted slightly to allow for monthly contributions. The **retire.cpp** program implements all these computations and displays the amount that you must contribute to the fund monthly.

retire.cpp

Code for Computing Retirement Fund Contributions

Here is the code for the **retire.cpp** program.

```cpp
#include <iostream>
#include <cmath>
using namespace std;

double fpayoutamount(double payment, double rate, double years)
{
    double months;
```

```cpp
    rate = rate / 12.00;
    months = years * 12;
    return payment / (rate / (1 - (1 / (pow((1 + rate), months))))));
}

double pvs(double fv, double rate, double lifetime)
{
    rate = rate / 12.00;
    return fv  / ((pow((1 + rate), lifetime * 12) - 1) / rate);
}

double roundtohundreds(double roundvalue)
{
    roundvalue = ceil(roundvalue * 100);
    return roundvalue / 100;
}

int main()
{
    double stipend, outrate, outlife;
    double valueatretirement;
    double inrate, inlifetime;

    cout << "Enter the amount you want to remove monthly "
        << "from the fund " << endl;
    cout << "after retirement: ";
    cin >> stipend;

    cout << "Enter the annual interest rate of the annuity " <<
        " (in the form 0.xx for xx%): ";
    cin >> outrate;

    cout << "Enter the lifetime in payout years of the "
        << "retirement fund (integer): ";
    cin >> outlife;

    // Compute what the fund must be worth at 0-point
    valueatretirement = fpayoutamount(stipend, outrate, outlife);

    cout << "Enter the annual interest rate during the "
        << "contribution period " << endl;
    cout << "(in the form 0.xx for xx%): ";
    cin >> inrate;
```

```
cout << "Enter the contribution lifetime in years of "
    << "the fund (integer): ";
cin >> inlifetime;

cout << "You must pay the following amount monthly into "
    << "the fund: $";
cout <<
    roundtohundreds(pvs(valueatretirement, inrate, inlifetime));
return 0;
}
```

ANNOTATIONS

Most of the computations in the **retire.cpp** program are pretty straightforward—they don't differ significantly from what you have seen. Let's consider, however, the two computation functions. The first function, **fpayoutamount( )**, computes the amount of the retirement fund at retirement based on the monthly draw, the interest rate, and the length of retirement:

```
double fpayoutamount(double payment, double rate, double years)
{
  double months;

  rate = rate / 12.00;
  months = years * 12;
  return payment / (rate / (1 - (1 / (pow((1 + rate), months)))));
}
```

As you can see, the function here is fundamentally the same as the **payment( )** function in the **loan.cpp** program. The only difference is that you are computing the start amount rather than the payment amount. To do so, you simply divide through the previous equation by the left-hand side, then by the right-hand side, which yields the following:

$$1 \text{ / Start Amount} = (\text{rate} / (1 - (1 / (1 + \text{rate})^{\text{months}}))) \text{ / Payment}$$

You then invert the functions on both sides of the equation, which yields the following:

$$\text{Start Amount} = \text{Payment} / (\text{rate} / (1 - (1 / (1 + \text{rate})^{\text{months}})))$$

The function returns the start amount as its value.

The **pvs( )** function then computes the amount that must be paid into the fund to reach that start amount, based on the length of time you indicated that you would

contribute to the fund and the interest rate during that contribution period. The **pvs( )** function looks like this:

```
double pvs(double fv, double rate, double lifetime)
{
  rate = rate / 12.00;
  return fv  / ((pow((1 + rate), lifetime * 12) - 1) / rate);
}
```

Notice that this one differs slightly from the **pvs( )** function you saw earlier—it adjusts its computation based on a monthly rather than annual contribution.

That's all there is to it—the rest of the program is concerned with getting the actual retirement fund information from the user. When you execute the **retire.cpp** program, the output will look similar to the following:

```
Enter the amount you want to remove monthly from the fund
after retirement: 4000
Enter the annual interest rate of the annuity
(in the form 0.xx for xx%): .08
Enter the lifetime in payout years of the retirement fund
(integer): 20
Enter the annual interest rate during the contribution period
(in the form 0.xx for xx%): .12
Enter the contribution lifetime in years of the fund (integer): 40
You must pay the following amount monthly into the fund: $40.65
```

Performing Statistical Calculations

By Lars Klander

avg.cpp   prob.cpp
moreavg.cpp   reganal.cpp

As discussed in Chapter 10, the computer's greatest strength is in performing calculations. In addition, however, computers are very good at combining and analyzing large amounts of data. One of the disciplines in which you will most often perform such processing is statistics.

In this chapter, we will consider some of the common types of statistical analyses and present some programs that perform the necessary calculations. Statistics present a real programming challenge; they are difficult to process cleanly with a computer. The task of combining many pieces of information and then deriving other information from it often makes statistical work confusing for even the most accomplished programmer. In this chapter we will present only simple statistical programs, taking advantage of functions that perform these calculations for us.

Introduction to Averages

One of the most important fundamental concepts in statistics is the *average*. However, even this simple principle can be confusing to those with no experience in statistics—there are several different types of averages, each of them appropriate to certain situations. In general, *average* refers to the most typical value, or the most expected value, in a collection of numerical data. When you collect data, the results can vary in a number of ways from one observation to another—even when conditions are supposed to be the same. Working with averages lets you make general statements about the nature of the data, even when the data comprises a range of values.

The range of values may vary for several reasons, the most obvious of which is simply the variation in the events themselves. For example, when rolling two six-sided dice, you'd expect that all of the resulting values would fall into the range between 2 and 12. However, making general statements about the average values of a specific series of rolls may result in the range being only between 4 and 9 (for example).

Additionally, in many cases—most commonly, in the social sciences—there will also be measurement and observational error. If you were timing patient responses for a psychology study, for example, you might end up with different values for patient responses because of the minute variations in the timing of how you press a stopwatch.

Finally, some variations are simply normal, such as in natural phenomena. Consider the owner of a vineyard who observes information about the number of grapes per bunch in his vineyard. If the owner wanted to know information about the dispersal of grapes throughout the vineyard, he might look at the first vine in each row of a series of grapes and count the number of bunches on the vine. Then, in looking at 20 rows of grapes, he might find that each vine held between 1 and 6 bunches of grapes. In such a case, determining the average number of grapes may require one of several calculations.

The Arithmetic Mean, the Median, and the Mode

Despite all the possible variations in averages, the most common calculations of average typically are the *arithmetic mean*, the *median*, and the *mode*. Each of these is a little different from the other two, and all of them are the "correct" averages when used in the right contexts. To understand this better, let's consider the vineyard data a little more closely. Table 11-1 shows the raw data itself.

The *arithmetic* mean is the average that most people use. The mean is nothing more than the sum of all values, divided by the number of different values (expressed as *n*). In mathematical notation, the mean is expressed as follows:

```
Mean = Σ 1(x₁…xₙ) / n
```

Vine Number	Number of Bunches
1	5
2	6
3	5
4	5
5	3
6	6
7	5
8	3
9	1
10	4
11	5
12	3
13	1
14	6
15	5
16	2
17	5
18	2
19	3
20	4

TABLE 11-1.   The Basic Grape Data Gathered By the Vineyard Owner

The sum of all 20 values in Table 11-1 is 79, so the mean can be computed as (79 / 20) = 3.95. The mean average for this example is 3.95, though you shouldn't expect to find that vine with 3.95 bunches anywhere—it obviously doesn't exist.

The *median* is another type of average. It is the middle value in the data set—that is, the value where exactly half of the values are above it and half are below it. In the case of our vineyard, there are 20 values. That's an even number, so the median will be midway between two of those values—with ten values above it and ten values below it. In Table 11-1, there are ten values between 0 and 4, and 10 values between 5 and 7. That means the median value will be halfway between 4 and 5, or 4.5. If there were an odd number of data points, then the middle point—the median—would be the actual data point that has an equal number of points above it and below it.

The *mode* is also an average; it is the most frequently occurring value in the data set. If you plot the data in Table 11-1 into a chart, as shown in Figure 11-1, you can see the mode of the data pretty easily. There were more vines with 5 bunches than with any other number, so that's the mode.

Different situations call for different averages. If the data are perfectly symmetrical, then the mean, median, and mode will be the same number. In fact, that's nearly the case for the data we have analyzed so far. If the mean, median, and mode are not the same, then the data won't be symmetrical around the mean—and the difference is a test of that symmetry. In the vineyard bunches, the data is nearly symmetrical, so the mean could be used. However, there are other situations where trying to use the mean as an average would be terribly misleading. For example, if you were considering compensation in a large company, where the CEO made $500 million last year after exercising his stock options, the mean might indicate that everyone in the company made over $1 million last year. However, the reality might be that most employees made only $50,000 last year; in such a case, the median would be more reflective.

After briefly examining the **avg.cpp** program, which takes the data presented in Table 11-1 and performs the three types of average calculations against that data, we will move on to consider a couple of other types of means that you might find yourself calculating in different situations.

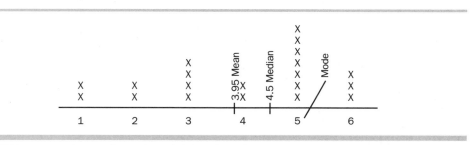

FIGURE 11-1. A simple x-plot of the values for bunches and vines

avg.cpp

Code

Here is the code for the **avg.cpp** program, which computes the three averages we have discussed so far—arithmetic mean, median, and mode—for a series of 20 values.

```cpp
// simple average
#include <iostream>
#include <cmath>
#include <cstdlib>"
#define numvals 20

using namespace std;

int compare_int(int *a, int *b)
{
   if (*a < *b)
     return(-1);
   else if (*a == *b)
     return(0);
   else
     return(1);
}

double median(int valarr[], int numels)
{
  double returnval = 0;
  for (int i=0; (i < numels / 2); i++)
    returnval = valarr[i];
  if (numels % 2)
    returnval = valarr[i];
  else
    returnval = (returnval + valarr[i]) / 2;
  return returnval;
}

double mode(int valarr[], int numels)
{
  int instances = 0, tempinstances = 1, i = 1;
  int tempmode, returnmode = 1;

  tempmode = valarr[0];
  while (i < numels) {
    while (valarr[i] == tempmode) {
```

```
      i++;
      tempinstances++;
    }
    if (tempinstances > instances)
    {
      returnmode = tempmode;
      instances = tempinstances;
    }
    tempinstances = 1;
    tempmode = valarr[i];
    i++;
  }
  return returnmode;
}
double arith_mean(int valarr[], int numels)
{
  double average = 0;

  for (int i=0; i < numels; i++)
    average = average + valarr[i];
  return average / numels;
}

int main()
{
  int values[numvals] = { 5, 6, 5, 5, 3,
                          6, 5, 3, 1, 4,
                          5, 3, 1, 6, 5,
                          2, 5, 2, 3, 4 };
  double average = 0;

  cout << "Defined values:" << endl;
  for (int i=0; i< numvals; i++)
      cout << values[i] << "  ";
  cout << endl;

  cout << "The arithmetic mean of the values: ";
  cout << arith_mean(values, numvals) << endl;

  qsort(values, numvals, sizeof(int),
    (int (*) (const void*, const void*)) compare_int);
  cout << "Sorted values:" << endl;
  for (i=0; i< numvals; i++)
```

```
      cout << values[i] << "   ";
  cout << endl;

  cout << "The median of the values: ";
  cout << median(values, numvals) << endl;

  cout << "The mode of the values: ";
  cout << mode(values, numvals) << endl;
  return 0;
}
```

ANNOTATIONS

Let's look a little more closely at the **avg.cpp** program. The declarations at the top of the program are pretty standard, with the exception of the following:

```
#define numvals 20
```

The only unique declaration at the top of the file is in the creation of the compiler variable **numvals**, which the application uses to track the size of the array. This is a common technique, but is only useful when you know the size of the array at design time.

```
int compare_int(int *a, int *b)
{
   if (*a < *b)
     return(-1);
   else if (*a == *b)
     return(0);
   else
     return(1);
}
```

The standard C library defines the **qsort( )** function, contained within the body of the program and explained later in this chapter. However, **qsort( )** accepts as its last parameter the name of a comparison function, which returns values in accordance with the following specifications:

1. If the first parameter is less than the second parameter, the function returns –1.

2. If the first parameter is equal to the second parameter, the function returns 0.

3. If the first parameter is greater than the second parameter, the function returns 1.

In the **avg.cpp** program, the **compare_int( )** function performs this role for the built-in **qsort( )** function. Note that the comparison function will always return an integer value, though you may pass any of the built-in types to the function. However, make sure that the parameters in the comparison function match the type of parameters you pass into **qsort( ),** and that those types match the type of the array that you are sorting. As discussed earlier in this chapter, the median value is the value that falls right in the middle of the series—that is, the value where exactly half the values in the series are above it and half the values in the series are below. The **median( )** function within the **avg.cpp** program performs this processing on the integer array that the program uses. It accepts as its parameters two values: the reference to the array, and the value indicating the total number of items within the array.

```
double median(int valarr[], int numels)
{
  double returnval = 0;
  for (int i=0; (i < numels / 2); i++)
    returnval = valarr[i];
```

Once within the function, the simple **for** loop divides the number of elements by two (remember, the median is exactly midway in the series of values) and loops through to that middle value, exiting the loop with the **returnval** variable set equal to that last value. Note that the code presumes that the data is in ascending order. If you try to pass unsorted data into this function, your results will be incorrect. After reaching that halfway value, the program code must determine whether there are an odd or even number of entries, which it does in the following **if** statement:

```
  if (numels % 2)
    returnval = valarr[i];
  else
    returnval = (returnval + valarr[i]) / 2;
```

The program code uses the modulo operator—which returns the remainder of an integer division operation—to determine whether the number of elements is odd or even. If it's an odd number, the code sets **returnval** equal to the next value in the array (necessary because the integer division will round down automatically). If the number of elements is even, the code adds the next value in the array to the existing **returnval** and divides the result by two—selecting a value midway between the two central numbers. For the **avg.cpp** program, the code is actually adding the values of **valarr[10]** and **valarr[11]** together and dividing them by two. The program code then returns that value to the calling function with the **return** statement.

```
  return returnval;
}
```

The **mode( )** function is a bit more complex. Although visualizing the mode is pretty straightforward on a graph, as shown in Figure 11-1, computing the mode from a series of values is not quite so easy in C/C++. You have to do a little mathematical trickery to make the whole thing work. If you abstract the purpose of the mode, you might phrase its computation as being something like the following: "Take the sorted list of items and break it up into a series of smaller lists, each of which contains only the same numbers. Then count the number of items in each list, and the list with the most items will be the *mode* of the series."

When you abstract the mode in this fashion, computing it within your C/C++ program actually becomes much simpler. It allows you to visualize the computing code as a pair of loops that, through their iterations, effectively break up the sorted array into a series of smaller arrays.

PROGRAMMER'S NOTE *This abstraction of the mode, and the **mode( )** function within the **avg.cpp** program, will only work if the array is sorted. If **mode( )** does not know whether it will receive a sorted array, the function should sort the array before performing its processing. You may even want to copy the passed-in array to another array and sort that array, depending on your program's needs.*

The **mode( )** function accepts as its parameters two values: the reference to the array, and the value indicating the total number of items within the array. The function then defines a series of local variables, which it uses to maintain information about the number of instances and to set the return value for the function. The declarations are shown here:

```
double mode(int valarr[], int numels)
{
  int instances = 0, tempinstances = 1, i = 1;
  int tempmode, returnmode = 1;
```

The program code next sets the **tempmode** variable equal to the first value in the array, and enters the **while** loop within which it will do its primary processing. The outer **while** loop iterates until the whole array has been processed, as shown here:

```
  tempmode = valarr[0];
  while (i < numels) {
```

Then, inside that outer loop is a second, inner loop which repeats itself for each sequence of values within the list. In other words, if the value in the **valarr[0]** element is 1, the program code will iterate through the inner loop until **valarr[i]** is not equal to 1. Each time through the inner loop, the program code increments the array counter variable **i** and also increments the **tempinstances** variable, which corresponds to the number of instances of that specific value found by the program code. The code for the inner **while** loop looks like this:

```
    while (valarr[i] == tempmode) {
      i++;
      tempinstances++;
    }
```

The code exits the inner loop whenever the value in the array changes. Then it uses an **if** statement to determine whether there were more instances of this value than of any previous values in the array. To do so, the code compares the **tempinstances** and **instances** variables. If the number of instances of the current value is larger than the value currently set within the **instances** variable, the program code within the **if** block sets the **returnmode** variable to the current value and sets the number of instances equal to the total current instances. The implementation of this logic is as shown here:

```
if (tempinstances > instances) {
  returnmode = tempmode;
  instances = tempinstances;
}
```

The comparison described just above is the key part of the mode computation. The remainder of the outer **while** loop simply resets the temporary instances variable and sets the temporary mode variable equal to the current value in the array. After the loop exits, the function returns the value within the **returnmode** variable to the calling function.

```
    tempinstances = 1;
    tempmode = valarr[i];
    i++;
  }
  return returnmode;
}
```

As you saw with Figure 11-1, for the **avg.cpp** program the **mode( )** function will return 5. However, this function will work just as well with a series of 100 values as it does with a series of 20 values, and as such is a useful addition to your library. The nicest thing about the function, arguably, is that it doesn't need to iterate through the array in multiple dimensions—an outer loop covering all the elements and an inner loop repeating that count—a problem that is solved by using a sorted array.

The last function before **main** is the **arith_mean( )** function, which simply accepts the array and the number of elements as parameters, sums the values in the array, and divides by the number of elements, to generate its return values as shown here:

```
double arith_mean(int valarr[], int numels)
{
  double average = 0;

  for (int i=0; i < numels; i++)
    average = average + valarr[i];
  return average / numels;
}
```

This code is probably the simplest for adapting to a situation with a series of **float** or **double** values, because it does not perform comparisons between two values. You could make the **arith_mean( )** function return the average of a series of **double** values simply by changing the function's definition, as shown here:

```
double arith_mean(double valarr[], int numels)
```

In the case of the **avg.cpp** program, we are working solely with integers, which greatly simplifies the process of comparisons. The **main( )** function in the program, as you would expect, simply declares and sets the values for the array and then generates output for the three different types of averages. The first part of the function looks like this:

```
int main()
{
    int values[numvals] = { 5, 6, 5, 5, 3,
                            6, 5, 3, 1, 4,
                            5, 3, 1, 6, 5,
                            2, 5, 2, 3, 4 };

    cout << "Defined values:" << endl;
    for (int i=0; i< numvals; i++)
        cout << values[i] << "  ";
    cout << endl;

    cout << "The arithmetic mean of the values: ";
    cout << arith_mean(values, numvals) << endl;
```

Notice how the program computes the mean before it performs the sort of the values within the array. If fact, you could also compute and display the mode before sorting the array—it's only for the computation of the median that we need to know the values within the array, in order. The **qsort( )** function, as mentioned earlier, performs the sort for us. You must pass the array and the number of elements in the array as the first two parameters to the function; the third parameter corresponds to the size of each element in the array. The final parameter is the generalized declaration of the comparison function, and its name within the program. Here is **qsort( )**:

```
qsort(values, numvals, sizeof(int),
    (int (*) (const void*, const void*)) compare_int);
```

The program then outputs the sorted values in the array and proceeds to display the median and the mode by calling both those functions:

```
cout << "Sorted values:" << endl;
for (i=0; i< numvals; i++)
    cout << values[i] << "  ";
cout << endl;
```

```
    cout << "The median of the values: ";
    cout << median(values, numvals) << endl;

    cout << "The mode of the values: ";
    cout << mode(values, numvals) << endl;
    return 0;
}
```

So, when you put it all together and compile and run the program, it will compute the three basic average types on the data and display that information for you on the screen. The program's output is as follows:

```
Defined values:
5  6  5  5  3  6  5  3  1  4  5  3  1  6  5  2  5  2  3  4
The arithmetic mean of the values: 3.95
Sorted values:
1  1  2  2  3  3  3  3  4  4  5  5  5  5  5  5  5  6  6  6
The median of the values: 4.5
The mode of the values: 5
```

Now that you have had a brief introduction to working with the basics of averages and means, let's move on to consider some other averaging issues.

Other Common Average Computations

In addition to the three basic types of averages discussed so far, there are four other general types of averages that you will often encounter in statistics. These averages return somewhat different values, and in different ways, than what you have evaluated so far. These averages are the *weighted mean, the geometric mean, root mean squares,* and *root sum squares.* Each has its own computation methods, so let's consider them in turn before we look at the program.

Weighted Mean

The *weighted mean* is an average that takes into account the importance of each value to the overall total of the values. For example, consider a university class. In that particular class, the homework counts 25% toward the final grade, the midterm exam counts 20%, quizzes count 15%, and the final exam counts for 40%. A specific student's grades might look something like those shown in Table 11-2.

Evaluation Type	Grade
Homework	84
Midterm	78
Quizzes	72
Final	89

TABLE 11-2. A Student's Grades in a Specific University Course

In such a case, to compute the student's final grade you will need to use the formula for a weighted mean, which is expressed as the following function. Here *w* corresponds to the weight of a particular item and *x* corresponds to the item itself:

```
weighted mean = Σ (w * x) / Σw
```

In other words, multiply each grade by its corresponding weight, and add up all those values. Then, divide the result by the sum of the weights (in this case, 1) and divide by that value.

So for the student's grade calculation, the result is pretty straightforward:

```
grade = (.25 * 84) + (.20 * 78) + (.15 * 72) + (.40 * 89) /
    (.25 + .2 + .15 + .4)
```

which yields a final grade for the student of 83—vastly different than the 80.75 he would have received if we simply took the arithmetic mean.

If the student's grades were more disparate—really good results on the final, for example—the difference between the two means would be even more clear. If the student got 100 on the final exam, the weighted mean would result in a grade of 87.4, while the arithmetic mean would result in a grade of 83.5. Conversely, a major difference in the student's quiz grade wouldn't necessarily affect the weighted mean much, but *would* have significant effect on the arithmetic mean.

Geometric Mean

The *geometric mean* calculation is used a lot when the data in the series is not very symmetrical, particularly in biological studies. To understand the geometric mean better, let's consider a situation where you have $48 dollars to spend, and you spend one-half of your available money each day for 5 days. The data on the amount of money you have, then, would look like Table 11-3.

Day	Amount of available cash
1	$48
2	$24
3	$12
4	$ 6
5	$ 3

TABLE 11-3.   Your Available Cash Over a Given 5-day Period

The arithmetic mean in such a case is

(48 + 24 + 12 + 6 + 3) / 5

which equals 18.6—a value which is not necessarily reflective of much. If you then graph these values onto a standard graph, you will note that the line connecting the tops of the items in the graph is not straight, but rather traces a hyperbola. Figure 11-2 shows the graph of your expenditures.

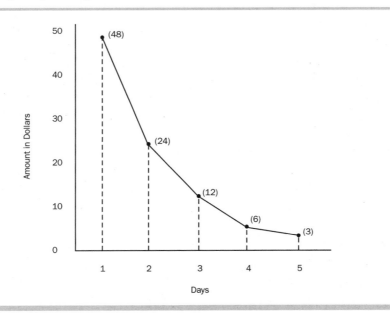

FIGURE 11-2.   The graph of your available money over the 5-day period

On the other hand, if you graphed the same data onto semilog paper, you would find that the line *does* trace a straight line. The difference in the graphs' natures indicates that this calculation might be a good candidate for a geometric mean.

To compute the geometric mean, we need to find the logarithm of each value, add up the logs, and then take the *logarithmic mean*. After determining the logarithmic mean, we will take the antilog of that value, which will be the geometric mean of the function. The *logarithmic mean* (often called simply the *log-mean*) is computed as

$$(\log 48 + \log 24 + \log 12 + \log 6 + \log 3) / 5$$

which corresponds to 1.079. The antilog (or the log-1) of that value is 11.99—which is the geometric mean.

Computing the Root Mean Square and the Root Sum Square

Two other averages are sometimes seen in science and technology (particularly in electronics): the *root mean square* (rms), and the *root sum square* (rss).

The rms value is used extensively in electrical circuits and certain other technologies. For example, the alternating electrical current in your home or business is a sine wave. The "average" of a sine wave is actually always zero, since the positive and negative values are equal but opposite and therefore cancel each other out. In such a case, the root mean square is more meaningful (and therefore more important). In the case of electricity, the root mean square evaluates to 0.707Vp, where Vp corresponds to the peak voltage of the feed. You have to use extended calculus—including, most specifically, integrals—to compute rms values, and such a calculation is somewhat beyond the scope of this book, so we won't consider it here.

We will, however, consider the computation of rss. Root sum squares are used in cases where unrelated data are combined. For example, noise signals in electronic circuits are errors and may come from several different sources. Suppose, then, that we have n independent noise voltage sources (vn_1, vn_2, ...vn_n). When these sources are truly independent, they cannot be combined in a linear manner. Instead, you must combine them using the rss method, which specifies that the result is the square root of the sum of $(vn)^2$ for each item in the series. This method will be clearer to you after we consider it in the context of the program **moreavg.cpp**, detailed in the following sections.

Code

Here is the code for the **moreavg.cpp** program, which computes weighted mean, geometric mean, and root sum squares.

```cpp
#include <iostream>
#include <cmath>
#define numweightvals 4

using namespace std;

double arith_mean(int valarr[], int numels)
{
  double average = 0;

  for (int i=0; i < numels; i++)
    average = average + valarr[i];
  return average / numels;
}

int weight_mean(double weight[], int scores[][4],
    int weights, int rows)
{
  int j = 0;
  double totalscores = 0, totalweights = 0;

  for (int i =0; i < rows; i++) {
    cout << "Weighted grade for Student #: " << (i + 1) << " is: ";
    for (j = 0; j < weights; j++) {
      totalscores = totalscores + (weight[j] * scores[i][j]);
      totalweights = totalweights + weight[j];
    }
    cout << (totalscores / totalweights) << endl;
  }
  return 0;
}

double geo_mean(int values[], int numvals)
{
  double logmean = 0;

  for (int i = 0; i < numvals; i++)
    logmean = logmean + log(values[i]);
  logmean = logmean / numvals;
  return exp(logmean);
```

```
}

double rss(double vals[], int numvals)
{
  double sums = 0;
  for (int i= 0; i < numvals; i++)
    sums = sums + pow(vals[i], 2);
  return pow(sums, .5);
}

int main()
{
  double weightings[numweightvals] = {0.25, 0.20, 0.15, 0.40};
  int weightvals[4][numweightvals] = {{84, 78, 72, 79},
                                      {84, 78, 72, 100},
                                      {84, 78, 45, 79},
                                      {84, 85, 72, 95}};

  double average = 0;

  cout << "Computing Weighted Means: " << endl;
  weight_mean(weightings, weightvals, numweightvals, 4);
  cout << endl;


  int spending[5] = {48, 24, 12, 6, 3};
  cout << "Computing Geometric Mean: " << endl;

  cout << "The arithmetic mean of the values: ";
  cout << arith_mean(spending, 5) << endl;

  cout << "The geometric mean of the values: ";
  cout << geo_mean(spending, 5) << endl;

  double noise[10] = {0.705, 0.387, 0.215, 0.476, 0.121,
                      0.325, 0.888, 0.287, 0.414, 0.542};

  cout << "Computing the root sum square:" << endl;
  cout << "Noise values: " << endl;
  for (int i = 0; i < 10; i ++)
    cout << noise[i] << "   ";
  cout << endl << "The root sum square is: "
       << rss(noise, 10) << endl;
  return 0;
}
```

ANNOTATIONS

Let's look a little more closely at the code, which models almost exactly the computations that we performed earlier in the chapter.

```
double arith_mean(int valarr[], int numels)
{
  double average = 0;

  for (int i=0; i < numels; i++)
    average = average + valarr[i];
  return average / numels;
}
```

The **arith_mean( )** function is exactly the same as the one you saw in the **avg.cpp** program. It is used here in **moreavg.cpp** only to show the differences between the geometric mean and the arithmetic mean. The first new function in this program is the **weight_mean( )** function, which accepts four parameters: an array of weighting values (percentages); a two-dimensional array of scores; an integer corresponding to the number of scores per student; and an integer corresponding to the total number of sets of scores. The program code then declares some local variables, a counter variable and two summary variables.

```
int weight_mean(double weight[], int scores[][4],
    int weights, int rows)
{
  int j = 0;
  double totalscores = 0, totalweights = 0;
```

Next, the program enters the outer loop, which loops through each of the sets of scores, generating a result for each student. The program displays some captioning information and then enters the inner loop. This inner loop performs some addition, adding the **(weight * score)** value that you saw earlier into the **totalscores** variable, and the weights into the **totalweights** value. When the program exits the inner loop, it sends the weighted total divided by the total weight to the output, as you saw in the function definition earlier. Following is the code that performs this processing:

```
  for (int i =0; i < rows; i++) {
    cout << "Weighted grade for Student #: " << (i + 1) << " is: ";
    for (j = 0; j < weights; j++) {
      totalscores = totalscores + (weight[j] * scores[i][j]);
      totalweights = totalweights + weight[j];
    }
    cout << (totalscores / totalweights) << endl;
  }
  return 0;
}
```

The computation of the geometric mean performed by the **geo_mean( )** function is similarly straightforward. As discussed in the section on the geometric mean, you must compute the logarithmic mean first, and then compute the antilog of that value. The **geo_mean( )** function accepts as parameters an array of values and the number of elements in the array. It uses a **for** loop to sum up the logarithm values, as shown here:

```
double geo_mean(int values[], int numvals)
{
  double logmean = 0;

  for (int i = 0; i < numvals; i++)
    logmean = logmean + log(values[i]);
```

Note that the program uses the C math library's **log( )** function to compute the natural logarithm of the values in the array. After exiting the **for** loop, the **logmean** variable will contain the sum of all the logarithmic values. The program then divides that by the total number of elements, yielding the log-mean. Finally, the function's code uses the C math library's **exp( )** function to return the antilog of the log-mean. The code for these steps is shown here:

```
  logmean = logmean / numvals;
  return exp(logmean);
}
```

So, the last function in the program computes the root sum square. As you saw, the root sum square (rss) is uncomplicated: Square every value in the series, add them all up, and take the square root of the result. The **rss( )** function performs just this processing, using the C math library's **pow( )** function. The function accepts two parameters, as usual—the array and the number of elements therein. It then defines a local variable to maintain the summary information.

```
double rss(double vals[], int numvals)
{
  double sums = 0;
```

The **for** loop simply steps through the array, squaring each value in turn and adding it to the **sums** variable. When the loop exits, the function returns the square root of the value stored within the **sums** variable—which it generates using the **pow( )** function with an exponent of one-half.

```
  for (int i= 0; i < numvals; i++)
    sums = sums + pow(vals[i], 2);
  return pow(sums, .5);
}
```

The **main( )** function, just as it was in the **avg.cpp** program, is simply a shell for declaring the arrays and calling the various functions to perform their processing.

The **moreavg.cpp** program declares a few more arrays than the **avg.cpp**, simply because we can't use the same data for all the examples. The **main( )** function begins by declaring the array that contains the score weightings for the weighted mean example, and then declares the two-dimensional array that contains the scores for four students.

```
int main()
{
  double weightings[numweightvals] = {0.25, 0.20, 0.15, 0.40};
  int weightvals[4][numweightvals] = {{84, 78, 72, 79},
                                      {84, 78, 72, 100},
                                      {84, 78, 45, 79},
                                      {84, 85, 72, 95}};
```

Next, the code that generates the weighted mean information is invoked, with a caption before the function's invocation, as shown here:

```
cout << "Computing Weighted Means: " << endl;
weight_mean(weightings, weightvals, numweightvals, 4);
cout << endl;
```

We then move on to considering the geometric mean computation. As mentioned previously, the program displays the arithmetic mean of the values, simply to show the difference between the two values:

```
int spending[5] = {48, 24, 12, 6, 3};
cout << "Computing Geometric Mean: " << endl;
cout << "The arithmetic mean of the values: ";
cout << arith_mean(spending, 5) << endl;
cout << "The geometric mean of the values: ";
cout << geo_mean(spending, 5) << endl;
```

Finally, the code within **main( )** declares a ten-element array to store noise values, all of which are less than 1. It then displays the noise values for the user and computes and displays the root sum square:

```
double noise[10] = {0.705, 0.387, 0.215, 0.476, 0.121,
                    0.325, 0.888, 0.287, 0.414, 0.542};

cout << "Computing the root sum square:" << endl;
cout << "Noise values: " << endl;
for (int i = 0; i < 10; i ++)
  cout << noise[i] << "   ";
cout << endl << "The root sum square is: "
     << rss(noise, 10) << endl;
return 0;
}
```

When you compile and execute the **moreavg.cpp** program, it will generate output on each of these different types of averages. The output looks similar to the following:

```
Computing Weighted Means:
Weighted grade for Student #: 1 is: 79
Weighted grade for Student #: 2 is: 83.2
Weighted grade for Student #: 3 is: 80.45
Weighted grade for Student #: 4 is: 82.0375

Computing Geometric Mean:
The arithmetic mean of the values: 18.6
The geometric mean of the values: 12
Computing the root sum square:
Noise values:
0.705  0.387  0.215  0.476  0.121  0.325  0.888  0.287  0.414  0.542

The root sum square is: 1.54141
```

Considering Probability

Now that we have evaluated the use of averages when examining data, let's move on to the other fundamental area of statistics that we will discuss in this chapter—*probability*. Probability deals in likelihood rather than absolutes. It allows us to anticipate how often to expect certain outcomes in situations where more than one outcome is possible—for example, in the classical examinations of a coin flip or a dice roll. Probability theory is an essential tool in statistical analysis.

Probability problems use the letter P to denote the probability of an expected event occurring, with an argument following the P in parentheses or brackets to indicate what events are being discussed. For example, P(x) means the probability of event x occurring. In flipping coins, you might write **P(heads)** to denote the probability of heads occurring on a flip, or **P(tails)** to mean the opposite case.

The value of P is always a fraction (sometimes written in decimal form) between 0 and 1.

◆ P(x) = 0 means that there is no possibility whatsoever that event x will occur.

◆ P(x) = 1 means that there is no possibility that event x will *not* occur.

◆ P values between 0 and 1 are an indication of the relative likelihood of x occurring. For example, if the likelihood of x occurring is 0.5, that means half the time you can expect x to occur, and half the time x will not occur. It does not predict the absolute outcome of any specific future event, only the likelihood of each possible outcome.

Suppose, for example, that we know that 4.5% of the programmers in the world use DVORAK keyboards. This means 4.5 programmers out of every 100 are using that type of keyboard, which is a proportion of 0.045. What is the probability of randomly meeting a programmer with a DVORAK keyboard among all the possible programmers you could meet? The probability is *P(DVORAK)* = 0.045, or about 1 in 22. Statistically, one out of every 22 programmers you meet will use the DVORAK keyboard.

The probability of this statistic only holds true if two conditions are met: (a) All programmers have an equal chance of meeting you (that is, all the DVORAK-using programmers aren't on the other side of the world); and (b) All possible programmers are in the pool of people you might meet.

Various aspects of probability theory are used to cover two broad classes of events—simple and compound. Simple events cannot be reduced further into more possible events; for example, the flip of a coin can only result in heads or tails, or a rolled six-sided die can only result in 1, 2, 3, 4, 5, or 6. You cannot take the "3" face of a die and dissect it into smaller elements of "threeness"—it always comes up "3" or not at all.

If a simple event can have more than one outcome, and if all possible outcomes are equally likely, then the probability of any one of them occurring in a single fair trial is the proportion the outcome has of all possible outcomes. If there are N different possibilities of event A, and n outcomes are "successes," then the probability of event A—that is P(A), is n/N. The probability of event A is a fraction between 0 and 1. Thus, for the flipping of a coin, there are two possibilities (H or T), so the probability of "calling it" on any one flip is one success over two possibilities, or one-half. This fact is sometimes called the *First Law of Probability*.

Compound events can be decomposed into two or more possible events. For example, the probability that rolling a die will result in either an even number (2, 4, 6) or an odd number (1, 3, 5) is a compound event. The probability of the event is the sum of the probabilities of the individual possibilities. For example, the possibility of rolling an even number can be constructed as follows:

```
P(even) = P(2) + P(4) + P(6)
```

which evaluates out to $1/6 + 1/6 + 1/6$, or one-half.

The Second Law of Probability

If an event can have more than one outcome, and if all possible outcomes are equally likely, then the results will nearly always vary somewhat from the calculated ideal probability. But for a large number of trials, the variation will be smaller if all the events are truly equally likely. In other words, the more times you perform the trial, the more the results will approach the actual probability.

It is a common fallacy to assume that the Law of Large Numbers (the Second Law of Probability) requires the proportion of each possibility to be exact. For example, when dealing with a coin toss, the probability of *P(H)* or *P(T)* to be exactly 0.5000 after 10,000 trials is extremely low; however, the probability that it will be *near* 0.5 is extremely high.

The Third Law of Probability

If something can have more than one outcome, and if all possible outcomes are equally likely, then the probability of alternative results on a single trial will be the sum of their individual probabilities. This is called the Law of Addition. We saw this law in operation in the discussion of compound events previously in this chapter.

As you saw there, if the probability of any one event is 1 in 6, and we are considering three possible events, the probability of any of the three events occurring is 3 in 6, or one-half.

The Fourth Law of Probability

There's one more law of probability to consider, and then we'll move on to the example program. Whenever something can have more than one outcome, and all outcomes are equally likely, then the probability of any particular combination of outcomes on two or more independent trials is the product of their respective probabilities. This is known as the Law of Multiplication.

If each event is truly independent, and the order is not specified, than the probability of either event occurring on a single trial is the sum of their probabilities. This situation is controlled by the addition law. What is the probability, however, of getting a particular combination on two or more successive trials? In other words, what is the probability of throwing a 4 and a 5 on successive rolls of the dice? To compute this probability, you can turn to the Fourth Law of Probability:

`P(A and B) = P(A) * P(B)`

In this example, the result is P(4) * P(5), or 1/6 * 1/6, which equals 1/36. However, that's not the entirety of the consideration. The 4 might be rolled on the first throw, or it might come on the second throw—and vice versa for the 5. The probability of either event occurring is 1/36—meaning that the probability of either event occurring on a single trial is 1/36 + 1/36 = 1/18.

There is much more to probability than what we have discussed here, but this introduction provides a good basis for your understanding of some of the issues concerned. The **prob.cpp** program performs a series of tests using a random number generator to show you how probabilities will approach a limit.

Code

Following is the code for the **prob.cpp** program.

prob.cpp

```cpp
#include <iostream>
#include <cmath>
#include <cstdlib>

using namespace std;

int gen_rand(int numposs)
{
  return ((rand() % numposs) + 1);
}

int out_flips(int heads, int tails, double flips)
{
  cout << endl << "Total Flips: " << flips << endl;
  cout << "Total Heads: " << heads << endl;
  cout << "Total Tails: " << tails << endl;
  cout << "Prob Head: " << heads / flips << endl;
  cout << "Prob Tails: " << tails / flips << endl;
  return 0;
}

int out_rolls(int val[], double rolls)
{
  cout << endl << "Total Rolls: " << rolls << endl;
  cout << "Total 1s: " << val[0] << ";   ";
  cout << "Prob 1s: " << val[0] / rolls << endl;
  cout << "Total 2s: " << val[1] << ";   ";
  cout << "Prob 2s: " << val[1] / rolls << endl;
  cout << "Total 3s: " << val[2] << ";   ";
  cout << "Prob 3s: " << val[2] / rolls << endl;
  cout << "Total 4s: " << val[3] << ";   ";
  cout << "Prob 4s: " << val[3] / rolls << endl;
  cout << "Total 5s: " << val[4] << ";   ";
  cout << "Prob 5s: " << val[4] / rolls << endl;
  cout << "Total 6s: " << val[5] << ";   ";
  cout << "Prob 6s: " << val[5] / rolls << endl;
  return 0;
}
```

```cpp
int main()
{
  int headinstances = 0, tailinstances = 0;
  double totalflips = 0;

  cout << "Coin Flip Probabilities:" << endl;
  for (int i = 0; i < 50; i++) {
    if (gen_rand(2) - 1)
      headinstances++;
    else
      tailinstances++;
    totalflips++;
  }
  out_flips(headinstances, tailinstances, totalflips);

  cout << endl << "Coin Flip Probabilities (Trial 2):" << endl;
  headinstances = 0;
  tailinstances = 0;
  totalflips = 0;
  for (i = 0; i < 500; i++) {
    if (gen_rand(2) - 1)
      headinstances++;
    else
      tailinstances++;
    totalflips++;
  }
  out_flips(headinstances, tailinstances, totalflips);

  cout << endl << "Coin Flip Probabilities (Trial 3):" << endl;
  headinstances = 0;
  tailinstances = 0;
  totalflips = 0;
  for (i = 0; i < 5000; i++) {
    if (gen_rand(2) - 1)
      headinstances++;
    else
      tailinstances++;
    totalflips++;
  }
  out_flips(headinstances, tailinstances, totalflips);

  int val[6] = {0, 0, 0, 0, 0, 0};
  double totalrolls = 0;
```

```
cout << endl << "Die Roll Trials (one-sixth = 0.167)" << endl;
for (i = 0; i < 50; i++) {
  val[(gen_rand(6) - 1)]++;
  totalrolls++;
}
out_rolls(val, totalrolls);

cout << endl << "Die Roll Trial 2 (one-sixth = 0.167)" << endl;
for(i=0; i < 6; i++)
  val[i] = 0;
totalrolls = 0;
for (i = 0; i < 500; i++) {
  val[(gen_rand(6) - 1)]++;
  totalrolls++;
}
out_rolls(val, totalrolls);

cout << endl << "Die Roll Trial 3 (one-sixth = 0.167)" << endl;
for(i=0; i < 6; i++)
  val[i] = 0;
totalrolls = 0;
for (i = 0; i < 5000; i++) {
  val[(gen_rand(6) - 1)]++;
  totalrolls++;
}
out_rolls(val, totalrolls);
return 0;
}
```

ANNOTATIONS

Let's take a closer look at the **prob.cpp** program. The first function of significance is the **gen_rand( )** function, which simply uses a **rand( )** function to return a value in a user-specified range. (Older C/C++ compilers may still support the **randomize( )** function, which lets you specify the range of random values directly against the function.) The **gen_rand( )** function uses modulo arithmetic to reduce the random number to within the range of possible values, and then adds 1 to make it a 1-based number (module arithmetic always results in a 0-based number). The function looks like this:

```
int gen_rand(int numposs)
{
  return ((rand() % numposs) + 1);
}
```

Note that **rand( )** actually generates a number between 0 and **RAND_MAX**, as defined in the C standard library header (**cstdlib**). The use of the modulo division operator is necessary to return the result as a usable value in the range expected by the program.

The next two functions, **out_flips( )** and **out_rolls( )**, simply generate the output for the two different types of probability problems that we have considered here. The first function generates output information on the coin-flips simulation, as shown here:

```
int out_flips(int heads, int tails, double flips)
{
  cout << endl << "Total Flips: " << flips << endl;
  cout << "Total Heads: " << heads << endl;
  cout << "Total Tails: " << tails << endl;
  cout << "Prob Head: " << heads / flips << endl;
  cout << "Prob Tails: " << tails / flips << endl;
  return 0;
}
```

The function **out_flips( )** outputs information on the total number of flips, the number of heads and tails resulting from the flips, and the probability of each occurrence based on the results achieved in the trial. Note that the **flips** parameter is a **double**, which is necessary to prevent the compiler from performing integer division and returning meaningless values to the user. The **out_rolls( )** function performs similar processing, although there are more output lines because of the additional possibilities from the die roll, as shown here:

```
int out_rolls(int val[], double rolls)
{
  cout << endl << "Total Rolls: " << rolls << endl;
  cout << "Total 1s: " << val[0] << ";   ";
  cout << "Prob 1s: " << val[0] / rolls << endl;
  cout << "Total 2s: " << val[1] << ";   ";
  cout << "Prob 2s: " << val[1] / rolls << endl;
  cout << "Total 3s: " << val[2] << ";   ";
  cout << "Prob 3s: " << val[2] / rolls << endl;
  cout << "Total 4s: " << val[3] << ";   ";
  cout << "Prob 4s: " << val[3] / rolls << endl;
  cout << "Total 5s: " << val[4] << ";   ";
  cout << "Prob 5s: " << val[4] / rolls << endl;
  cout << "Total 6s: " << val[5] << ";   ";
  cout << "Prob 6s: " << val[5] / rolls << endl;
  return 0;
}
```

As you can see, **out_rolls( )** accepts the array with the results and the total number of rolls as its parameters. Again, **rolls** is a double to ensure that the program does not perform integer division. The array contains the total results of each type of roll for the trial. The program code prints the number of rolls and the probability on the same line, just to save space on the output.

The **main( )** function, then, really just calls the random numbers and then displays the trial results and probability information. It starts off by declaring information for the coin flips, as shown here:

```
int main()
{
  int headinstances = 0, tailinstances = 0;
  double totalflips = 0;

  cout << "Coin Flip Probabilities:" << endl;
  for (int i = 0; i < 50; i++) {
    if (gen_rand(2) - 1)
      headinstances++;
    else
      tailinstances++;
    totalflips++;
  }
  out_flips(headinstances, tailinstances, totalflips);
```

It then does a short trial of only 50 coin flips. The loop increments the results as appropriate, using an **if** statement to test the result returned by the **gen_rand( )** function. After completing the trial, the program calls the **out_flips( )** function to display the information for the trial. This structure is repeated, differing only in loop size, twice more for the two additional trials. The loop grows to 500 iterations in the second trial, and grows again to 5,000 iterations in the third trial.

After completing the coin-flips trials, the program code moves on to the trials of the die rolls. It uses an array of integers to keep the count of occurrences of each possible value. It also uses the double variable **totalrolls** to keep track of the total number of rolls performed.

```
  int val[6] = {0, 0, 0, 0, 0, 0};
  double totalrolls = 0;

  cout << endl << "Die Roll Trials (one-sixth = 0.167)" << endl;
  for (i = 0; i < 50; i++) {
    val[(gen_rand(6) - 1)]++;
    totalrolls++;
  }
  out_rolls(val, totalrolls);
```

The trial code is much like the code for the coin flip. The header at the top notes what 1/6 is when represented as a decimal—just for clarity, since we have mentioned its being 1/6 throughout this chapter. The program code then enters the **for** loop to simulate the die rolls. However, within the loop, rather than using an **if** statement or a **switch** statement as we did earlier when computing the mode, the program code simply increments the appropriate element in the array based on the return value from the **gen_rand( )** function. Once the loop finishes its processing, it calls the **out_rolls( )** function to display the information from the trial.

```
cout << endl << "Die Roll Trial 2 (one-sixth = 0.167)" << endl;
for(i=0; i < 6; i++)
  val[i] = 0;
totalrolls = 0;
for (i = 0; i < 500; i++) {
  val[(gen_rand(6) - 1)]++;
  totalrolls++;
}
out_rolls(val, totalrolls);

cout << endl << "Die Roll Trial 3 (one-sixth = 0.167)" << endl;
for(i=0; i < 6; i++)
  val[i] = 0;
totalrolls = 0;
for (i = 0; i < 5000; i++) {
  val[(gen_rand(6) - 1)]++;
  totalrolls++;
}
out_rolls(val, totalrolls);
return 0;
}
```

Again, trials 2 and 3 simply repeat the processing performed in trial 1, but 2 and 3 iterate through the cycles more times—500 times in trial 2 and 5,000 times in trial 3. As you will see when you look at the program's output, the goal of the increasing iterations in the trials is to track how the actual percentages approach the probability of the events' occurring.

The output of the **prob.cpp** program clarifies this a little. This output will look similar to the following, differing slightly on your computer because of the randomizations:

```
Coin Flip Probabilities:

Total Flips: 50
Total Heads: 28
Total Tails: 22
Prob Head: 0.56
Prob Tails: 0.44
```

```
Coin Flip Probabilities (Trial 2):

Total Flips: 500
Total Heads: 243
Total Tails: 257
Prob Head: 0.486
Prob Tails: 0.514

Coin Flip Probabilities (Trial 3):

Total Flips: 5000
Total Heads: 2505
Total Tails: 2495
Prob Head: 0.501
Prob Tails: 0.499

Die Roll Trials (one-sixth = 0.167)

Total Rolls: 50
Total 1s: 7;   Prob 1s: 0.14
Total 2s: 1;   Prob 2s: 0.02
Total 3s: 7;   Prob 3s: 0.14
Total 4s: 16;  Prob 4s: 0.32
Total 5s: 10;  Prob 5s: 0.2
Total 6s: 9;   Prob 6s: 0.18

Die Roll Trial 2 (one-sixth = 0.167)
Total Rolls: 500
Total 1s: 90;  Prob 1s: 0.1800
Total 2s: 80;  Prob 2s: 0.1600
Total 3s: 78;  Prob 3s: 0.1560
Total 4s: 87;  Prob 4s: 0.1750
Total 5s: 82;  Prob 5s: 0.1640
Total 6s: 83;  Prob 6s: 0.1660

Die Roll Trial 3 (one-sixth = 0.167)
Total Rolls: 5000
Total 1s: 816;  Prob 1s: 0.1632
Total 2s: 812;  Prob 2s: 0.1624
Total 3s: 817;  Prob 3s: 0.1634
Total 4s: 850;  Prob 4s: 0.17
Total 5s: 856;  Prob 5s: 0.1712
Total 6s: 849;  Prob 6s: 0.1698
```

You can see from the coin-flip trials that the probability rapidly approaches 50% for each event as the trial size gets larger. In fact, by the 5,000-flip trial, the difference in probability between the two possible events is only two one-thousandths. Although the movement is not as pronounced with the die rolls—because of the greater number of possible events—the movement is still clearly there. Eventually, we would expect that each of the probabilities would approach 0.167 over time.

Regression Analysis

Let's examine one last type of statistical analysis: a process known as *regression analysis*. Regression analysis is a way to make general statements about a series or set of specific datums—in other words, it is a means of "regressing" from specific information to more general data.

In statistical surveys, data are often recorded and then plotted on a scatter diagram, such as that shown in Figure 11-3. The horizontal or x-axis is used for the *independent variable*; the vertical or y-axis is used for the *dependent variable*. This is a useful technique for investigating any number of important questions. Often, these questions are relational, such as "Is weight related to height?" and "Do SAT scores really predict college performance?"

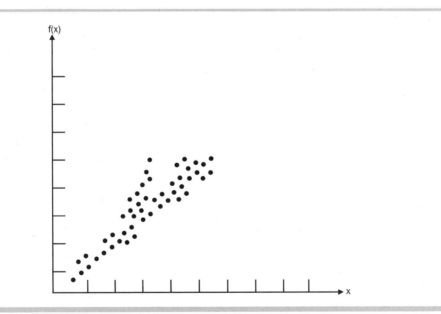

FIGURE 11-3.   A scatter diagram plots data points as f(x) versus x

To understand this better, let's consider an example. Suppose an electrical heating element is immersed in a vessel containing water, and you suspect that the temperature of the water is a function of the electrical current flowing in the heater element. You might plot the electrical current (E) along the x-axis, while plotting the temperature (T) along the y-axis, and label it either T or T = f(E).

When all of the data points are plotted, a pattern may emerge that suggests some relationship. That is, it appears there is some *correlation* between x and f(x). In Figure 11-3, for example, it appears that the values of f(x) increase with increases in the value of x. This fact implies that there is some correlation between x and *f(x)*. Because f(x) increases as x increases, we say there is a positive correlation between x and f(x).

Figure 11-4 shows several different types of correlation that might be found in data sets. A strong positive correlation is found in the data of Figure 11-4a, while approximately the same degree of negative correlation (in other words, f(x) decreases as x increases) is shown in Figure 11-4b. A weak-to-moderate positive correlation exists in the data of Figure 11-4c, indicating either that the connection between them is not strong, or possibly that some measurement error exists or that an uncontrolled variable is influencing the data. When there is no correlation between f(x) and x, then there is little or no evidence of a pattern in the placement of the data points, as shown in Figure 11-4d.

It is tempting to assume that a causal relationship exists between x and f(x) when we see a strong correlation between the data in a scatter chart. Sometimes such an assumption is valid, and sometimes it isn't. When the assumption is valid, we can then construct a *mathematical model* of the relationship between x and f(x) that predicts values of f(x) for the values of x other than those that were actually measured. The strength of the model is revealed in the reliability of that prediction for data outside the measured set. It matters little whether or not a causal relationship exists, *if knowledge of x predicts f(x).* In other words, whether x "causes" f(x) or not is less important for a mathematical model than whether x corresponds to f(x).

Several methods are at your disposal for constructing such a model, but the most common is to calculate a straight line that concisely summarizes the relationship between the two variables. This line is known as the *regression line*, or the *least-squares line*. The assumption made when constructing such a line is that the relationship is linear, and that the y component of each data point is subject to a certain small error Σ (the Greek letter epsilon). In other words, the function can be written as follows:

estimate(y) = $a + bx \pm \Sigma$

That is, the estimated value of y at any point can be described by the line, plus or minus the small margin of error. The goal of the least-squares fit is to minimize the distance between each point in the data set and the selected line. The equation for finding b in the above equation is a little complex but can be described as the sum of $x * y$ minus the sum

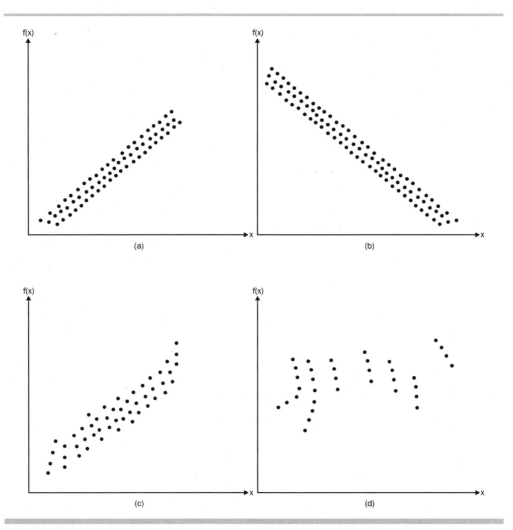

FIGURE 11-4.   Scatter diagrams showing four different types of correlation

of x multiplied by the sum of y. You then divide the result of that computation by the number of terms multiplied by the sum of x squared, minus x squared.

How all this works is shown in the following program, **reganal.cpp**, which lets the user enter a set of x and y values, and then uses the least-squares method to try to derive a line from the entered values. The next section presents the program code and annotations for **reganal.cpp**.

Code

Following is the code for the **reganal.cpp** program.

```cpp
// regression analysis
#include <iostream>
#include <cmath>
#include <cstdlib>
using namespace std;

double arith_mean(double valarr[], int numels)
{
  double average = 0;

  for (int i=0; i < numels; i++)
    average = average + valarr[i];
  return average / numels;
}

int main()
{
  int numvals = 0;
  double xmean, ymean;
  double xmultiplier, constant, sumxbysumy = 0;
  double xbyy = 0, sumx = 0, sumy = 0, sumxsq = 0;
  double x[30], y[30];
  /*double x[] = { 6.6,   9.1, 17.4, 17.9, 12.9, 13.3,
                13.6, 18.1, 29.1, 25.6, 36.5, 35.0,
                30.0, 30.7, 39.3, 47.5, 40.9, 48.5 };
  double y[] = {20.1, 45.0, 67.4, 73.4, 95.9, 98.9,
                103.1, 90.6, 92.7, 114.7, 119.0, 109.8,
                121.8, 117.3, 145.8, 171.6, 174.8, 206.5 };
  */
  cout << "Enter the number of values (integer, less than 30): ";
  cin >> numvals;
  if (numvals == 0 || numvals > 30)
    return 0;

  for (int i = 0; i < numvals; i++) {
    cout << "Enter the " << i << "th X value: ";
    cin >> x[i];
```

```
   cout << "Enter the " << i << "th Y value: ";
   cin >> y[i];
}
xmean = arith_mean(x, numvals);
ymean = arith_mean(y, numvals);
for (i = 0; i < numvals; i ++) {
   xbyy = xbyy + (x[i] * y[i]);
   sumx = sumx + x[i];
   sumy = sumy + y[i];
   sumxsq = sumxsq + (x[i] * x[i]);
}
xmultiplier = ((double) numvals * xbyy) - (sumx * sumy);
xmultiplier = xmultiplier / (((double) numvals * sumxsq)
   - (sumx * sumx));
constant = ymean - (xmultiplier * xmean);

cout << "The mean of the x values: " << xmean << endl;
cout << "The mean of the y values: " << ymean << endl;
cout << "The line's definition: y = " << constant << " + "
     << xmultiplier << "x" << endl;
return 0;
}
```

ANNOTATIONS

The code for the **reganal.cpp** program is pretty straightforward, in general implementing the computations described earlier to reach a least-squares line. The code for the program uses the **arith_mean( )** function from the **avg.cpp** program that you saw earlier, but otherwise does its computation right within the **main( )** function. Since you've already seen the **arith_mean( )** function previously (the only difference being that this one takes a **double** array rather than an **integer** array), we will jump right into the discussion of the **main( )** function.

The function starts off by declaring a bunch of different variables that it will use for its processing. These variables include a value to keep the number of elements in the sample, values for the arithmetic mean of both sample sets, and values necessary for the computation of the line.

```
int main()
{
   int numvals = 0;
   double xmean, ymean;
   double xmultiplier, constant, sumxbysumy = 0;
```

```
double xbyy = 0, sumx = 0, sumy = 0, sumxsq = 0;
double x[30], y[30];
```

As written, the program lets the user enter up to 30 values for *x* and *y* into their sample, which the program can then use to generate the line. If you want to simplify your input, however, the program code also contains two predefined arrays, consisting of 18 values each, that we used when creating and testing this program. The output that you will see later is generated with these 18 values. Those two predefined arrays are as follows:

```
/*double x[] = { 6.6,   9.1, 17.4, 17.9, 12.9, 13.3,
               13.6, 18.1, 29.1, 25.6, 36.5, 35.0,
               30.0, 30.7, 39.3, 47.5, 40.9, 48.5 };
  double y[] = {20.1, 45.0, 67.4, 73.4, 95.9, 98.9,
               103.1, 90.6, 92.7, 114.7, 119.0, 109.8,
               121.8, 117.3, 145.8, 171.6, 174.8, 206.5 };
*/
```

The program code then lets the user enter a number of elements for the arrays, and stores the entry within the **numvals** variable. If the user enters 0 for the number of values, or enters something that the **cin** operation doesn't recognize, the program exits.

```
cout << "Enter the number of values (integer, less than 30): ";
cin >> numvals;
if (numvals == 0 || numvals > 30)
  return 0;
```

The program then enters a simple **for** loop that lets the user enter the **x** and **y** values for each point in the sample, placing each point within the corresponding location in the array.

```
for (int i = 0; i < numvals; i++) {
  cout << "Enter the " << i << "th X value: ";
  cin >> x[i];

  cout << "Enter the " << i << "th Y value: ";
  cin >> y[i];
}
```

After entering the data set, it's time for the program to get down to the performance of the mathematical calculations necessary for computing the line. The first calculations are the generation of the mean for each set, which the program then places into the **xmean** and **ymean** variables:

```
xmean = arith_mean(x, numvals);
ymean = arith_mean(y, numvals);
```

Next, the program enters another **for** loop that loops through the entire data set, generating the values we need for computing the lines. The **xbyy** variable computes the sum of *x* * *y* for the entire set, while the *sumx* and *sumy* variables compute the

sum of the *x* and *y* arrays for the entire set. Finally, the *sumxsq* variable computes the sum of elements in the *x* array squared. The program code to perform all these computations looks like this:

```
for (i = 0; i < numvals; i ++) {
    xbyy = xbyy + (x[i] * y[i]);
    sumx = sumx + x[i];
    sumy = sumy + y[i];
    sumxsq = sumxsq + (x[i] * x[i]);
}
```

The program then uses the values to compute the *x*-multiplier and the constant, as we discussed earlier. The computation of the **xmultiplier** variable could be done in a single line, but for clarity is done in two in this program. The computation of the constant is then the **ymean** minus the **xmultiplier** multiplied by the **xmean**. The computations are shown here:

```
xmultiplier = ((double) numvals * xbyy) - (sumx * sumy);
xmultiplier = xmultiplier / (((double) numvals * sumxsq)
    - (sumx * sumx));
constant = ymean - (xmultiplier * xmean);
```

Next the program displays some values and shows the resulting equation. Three **cout** statements satisfy this task, as shown here, after which the code returns:

```
cout << "The mean of the x values: " << xmean << endl;
cout << "The mean of the y values: " << ymean << endl;
cout << "The line's definition: y = " << constant << " + "
    << xmultiplier << "x" << endl;
return 0;
}
```

This is not the entirety of the regression analysis—unfortunately, it is also necessary to compute a value called the *standard deviation* for both the *x* and *y* values. Using that value and a computation of the values in the series, you can then find a value between 0 and 1 called the *correlation coefficient*. This value represents how closely the line matches the data—with 0 indicating that there really is no relationship, and 1 representing a perfect relationship. In general, this value will never be 0 or 1, but will only approach those two values. Standard deviation, however, is left as a topic for you to pursue on your own. The computation of standard deviation is pretty complex, but you can find the mathematical basis for it in any statistics textbook.

All that being said, when you execute the **reganal.cpp** program using either the predefined array or by manually entering the values it contains, it will generate the following output:

```
Enter the number of values (integer, less than 30): 18
The mean of the x values: 26.2222
The mean of the y values: 109.356
The line's definition: y = 28.3846 + 3.08787x
```

Creating Fractals with Graphics Routines

By Lars Klander

FractalsDoc.cpp

FractalsView.cpp

Most programmers and computer users find complex computer graphics
exciting and intriguing. Although the end-user may simply find computer
graphics interesting, the programmer is often fascinated by graphic images
because of appreciation for the complex programming that creates them. Within the
field of graphics programming, *fractal images* such as the one in Figure 12-1 combine
sophisticated mathematical equations with equally sophisticated programming.

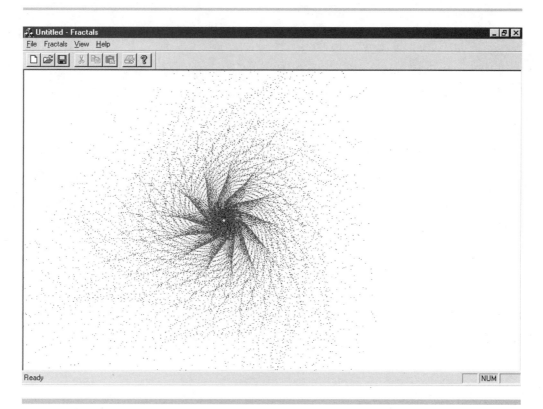

FIGURE 12-1. Complex fractal graphic image

Fractal images can be generated and displayed on any platform that supports
graphics. In this chapter, however, the program code is written to display images
to the Windows GUI for simplicity's sake. As you will see when you look at the
functions more closely later in this chapter, the majority of processing that occurs
within the functions is mathematical. Therefore, to make the drawing functions
work on another platform, the only change you really need to make is to alter the
actual method calls (that currently invoke the Windows GUI classes) themselves.

Introduction to Fractals

In this chapter, you will examine a Visual C++ program that draws colorful images from mathematical equations. The mathematical equations can be simple or complex.

The images you will see in this chapter may look abstract or realistic, just as paintings can have different styles. *Abstract* means the image is dissimilar to scenes in nature. *Realistic* means you can easily recognize the image. For example, an art critic might assign the abstract classification to a painting consisting of a blue circle on a white canvas, even though circles are not abstract, because the painting does not depict a specific object. Likewise, a painting of a sunset would be classified as realistic. The fractal images you will create within this chapter use abstract objects to create images that the user can visualize as "real" objects.

No matter what the style, most fractal images consist of small circles. Similarly, a painting will generally consist of many, many very small, short lines (which the artist generally creates with brush strokes). In this chapter, you will use the Microsoft Foundation Classes (MFC) **CDC** (device context) class's **SetPixelV( )** function to draw the images that make up the fractal. This function lets you set the color of a specific pixel as you desire. You will also use the **CDC** class's **Ellipse( )** function to draw circles on the screen.

If you look closely at a TV screen's image, you will see that it's composed of tiny colored rectangles. When you step back from the TV, you see the complete image. In this chapter, you will use the **SetPixelV( )** and **Ellipse( )** built-in methods to draw tiny colored boxes or larger circles from a math equation. When you step back from the computer screen (in other words, when you see all the boxes and circles as an entire picture rather than distinct boxes and circles), you will see an image called a *fractal*. Before you design the Visual C++ Fractals project, the following short discussion of fractals will help you understand how they work.

Gaston Julia first recorded fractals in the early twentieth century. Julia knew he could calculate one or more values from a math equation, such as Y=X. (Obviously, creating complex images requires significantly more complex equations.) He calculated a large number of X and Y values by hand from a complex math equation, and then drew dots on paper at different positions representing each value. As he drew more dots, an image took shape. The images intrigued Julia and he recorded his work, now known as the *Julia set*.

Benoit Mandelbrot discovered the Julia set in the mid-twentieth century. Mandelbrot thought of using a computer to draw the images. After Mandelbrot drew the images, he named them fractals, saying, "I coined fractal from the Latin adjective *fractus*." *Fractus* means "fragmented" and "irregular." As an example, if you broke a wine glass you would see fragmented and irregular pieces of glass. Mandelbrot recorded his work, too; it's known as the *Mandelbrot set*.

It is important to understand, in the case of both the Julia set and the Mandelbrot set, that the graphics depicted by the functions detailed by the set will be intimately governed by the starting values you assign to the set. For one of the sets in this chapter's

program, the Kam Torus set, the program actually generates random starting values when it draws the set. These random values can ultimately have vastly different results for two drawings from the same basic mathematical function. The Julia and Mandelbrot sets depicted in this chapter are interesting, but you can achieve other, perhaps more interesting results by varying the starting values going into the set.

In the Fractal project, you will calculate values from a math equation, manipulate those values to locate two points and a color value, and draw fractal images from the resulting points and color values. Within a math equation, the values will change as you alter the input. For example, in the sample equation $Y=X$, when X equals 2, then Y equals 2; similarly, when X equals 100, then Y equals 100. To draw an image from a math equation, you will calculate many x and y values, and then draw a circle or line on the computer screen where each x and y value is located.

A Brief Note on Graphs

In the Fractal project, you will use a *graphing method* to determine the position of each point within the fractal image. When your program uses the **SetPixelV( )** or **Ellipse( )** methods to draw a box or circle, Windows interprets the method call and draws each box or circle at a specific position on a graph in the computer screen. A *graph* represents a position with two values, called the *x- and y-coordinates.*

Your computer screen is two-dimensional. If you place your finger on a point on the screen, Windows has an x and y value that marks the spot. The graph represents the top-left corner of your computer screen as an x- and y-coordinate value of (0,0). As Windows moves down the left side of your screen, the y value will increase, and as Windows moves right across the top of your screen, the x value will increase. Figure 12-2 shows a logical model of an x- and y-coordinate system mapped against the Windows display.

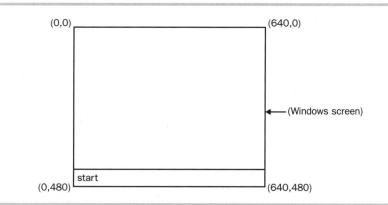

FIGURE 12-2.   Windows uses a graphing coordinates system

Depending on the size of a screen, the bottom-right corner of the screen can have a variety of x and y values. In the Fractals project, the functions are all constructed around a screen size of 640 x 480 pixels. Because your program will calculate thousands of X and Y values per equation, you must make sure that the bottom-right corner of your computer screen is large enough to hold the image position. Manipulating pixels (the individual dots the screen displays that make up the entire screen image) lets your program closely control the drawing of the fractal image.

As you probably know, pixels are small rectangular areas on your computer screen that can be any color. In general, a pixel is about the size of a pinhead; it is the smallest unit of measurement on a TV or computer screen. When you move very close to a TV screen, you can see the small dots or pixels. As you pull back from the TV screen, you can see the image of what's currently being shown. Because each screen—computer or TV—is composed of many pixels, the more pixels a screen display has, the clearer the screen's image will be.

In the Fractals project, you will draw several images of different sizes, from as small as a single pixel to a circle half the screen's size. As you draw the pixel-sized images and the circles, a larger image, composed of thousands of pixel-sized images, will take shape. The program will position each pixel-sized image at a specific x and y position on the graph.

The Fractals project is written in Visual C++, and uses the MFC-based Document/View architecture. Without going into great detail about the Document/View architecture, the following brief overview will help to make the layout of the Fractals project files a bit more understandable.

Overview of MFC Document/View Architecture

At the core of an MFC application are the concepts of a *document object* and a corresponding *view window*. The document object usually represents a file the application has opened. The view window provides a visual presentation of the document's data and accepts user interaction. The relationship between a document and its views is a one-to-many relationship. In other words, a document can have many views, but you can associate a view with only one document.

Within a Visual C++ application, you represent document objects within classes that you derive from the MFC **CDocument** base class. You derive your view window classes from the MFC **CView** class. In this chapter, the Fractals project uses a single document and view class. This type of structure is known as the *single-document interface* (SDI).

SDI applications that you produce using AppWizard use one document and one view type only, and instantiate only one each of the **CDocument** and **CView** classes. Figure 12-3 shows which classes can support a simple SDI application that you implement using MFC objects.

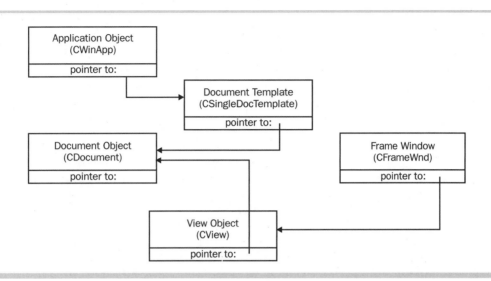

FIGURE 12-3. The model of the relationship between the five base classes for an SDI application

In AppWizard-generated SDI applications, the **CMainFrame** class implements the frame window itself. In such cases, AppWizard will define the **CMainFrame** class for you in the **Mainfrm.h** header file and implement the class in the **MainFrm.cpp** source file. The **CMainFrame** class derives most of its functionality from the **CFrameWnd** class, which is the MFC wrapper class for a simple window. The **CFrameWnd** class itself does not do much in the SDI application. The notable exceptions: If you have added a status bar or dockable toolbars to the application, the **CMainFrame** class will handle the creation and initialization of those objects.

The MFC-provided **CDocument** class provides the basic functionality for your application's document objects. This class's basic functionality includes the ability to create new documents, serialize document data, provide cooperation between a document object and view window, and more. MFC also provides a series of **CDocument**-derived classes that implement functionality specific to certain application types. For example, the **CRecordset** and **CDAORecordset** types serve to simplify the creation of database views. The relationship between documents and views is illustrated in Figure 12-4.

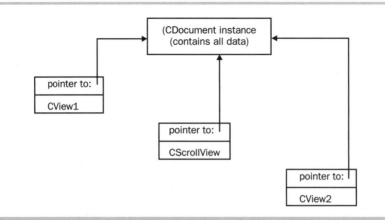

FIGURE 12-4. The one-to-many relationship between a document and its views

For every **CDocument**-derived class that presents a visual interface to the user, there is a **CView**-derived class that provides the interface. The **CView**-derived class provides the visual presentation of the document's data and handles user interaction through the view window.

The view window, in turn, is a child of a frame window. In an SDI application, the view window is a child of the main frame window. In MDI applications, the view window is a child of the MDI child window. A frame window, in turn, may contain several view windows (for example, through the use of splitter windows).

In the Fractals program, we use only a single document and a single view. The document maintains information about what fractal the user has selected to draw. The view does the actual drawing, and contains all the necessary code to compute and draw the points that make up the fractal.

PROGRAMMER'S NOTE   *By the way, it's important to note that the program, as constructed, writes directly to the screen context—meaning that no copy of the image is saved anywhere. If you open another screen over an existing fractal, Windows will erase the fractal. You can sidestep this issue by drawing onto a memory device context, rather than directly into the window, and then copying from memory onto the display. This technique lets you persist the image that the program displays, and only clear it if you choose to do so.*

Because the Fractals program is so large, let's get started with the application. We will discuss the contents of only two of the files in this chapter, as they are the only ones that differ significantly from the AppWizard-generated code. Further, we will discuss only relevant excerpts from the files. Refer to the program code on the CD-ROM for additional information about the program—such as the ID definitions in the resource file that the program uses.

Code

FractalsDoc.cpp As you've learned, the document class maintains the information about the program. In the case of the **CFractalsDoc** class, it simply keeps an integer value representing what fractal the user has selected, and returns that value to the drawing routine in the **CFractalsView** class when it requests it. Here is the code for the **CFractalsDoc** class:

```
#include "stdafx.h"
#include "Fractals.h"
#include "FractalsDoc.h"

#ifdef _DEBUG
#define new DEBUG_NEW
#undef THIS_FILE
static char THIS_FILE[] = __FILE__;
#endif


//////////////////////////////////////////////////////////////////////
////////
// CFractalsDoc

IMPLEMENT_DYNCREATE(CFractalsDoc, CDocument)

BEGIN_MESSAGE_MAP(CFractalsDoc, CDocument)
  //{{AFX_MSG_MAP(CFractalsDoc)
  ON_COMMAND(ID_FRACTALS_KAMTORUS, OnFractalsKamtorus)
  ON_COMMAND(ID_FRACTALS_DUFF, OnFractalsDuff)
  ON_COMMAND(ID_FRACTALS_CLOUDS, OnFractalsClouds)
  ON_COMMAND(ID_FRACTALS_JULIAS, OnFractalsJulias)
  ON_COMMAND(ID_FRACTALS_MANDELBROT, OnFractalsMandelbrot)
  //}}AFX_MSG_MAP
END_MESSAGE_MAP()
```

```
/////////////////////////////////////////////////////////////////////
////////
// CFractalsDoc construction/destruction

CFractalsDoc::CFractalsDoc()
{
  // TODO: add one-time construction code here
  CurrentFractalNum = 0;
}

CFractalsDoc::~CFractalsDoc()
{
}

BOOL CFractalsDoc::OnNewDocument()
{
  if (!CDocument::OnNewDocument())
    return FALSE;

  // TODO: add reinitialization code here
  // (SDI documents will reuse this document)

  return TRUE;
}

/////////////////////////////////////////////////////////////////////
////////
// CFractalsDoc serialization

void CFractalsDoc::Serialize(CArchive& ar)
{
  if (ar.IsStoring())
  {
    // TODO: add storing code here
  }
  else
  {
    // TODO: add loading code here
```

```
  }
}

//////////////////////////////////////////////////////////////////
////////
// CFractalsDoc diagnostics

#ifdef _DEBUG
void CFractalsDoc::AssertValid() const
{
  CDocument::AssertValid();
}

void CFractalsDoc::Dump(CDumpContext& dc) const
{
  CDocument::Dump(dc);
}
#endif //_DEBUG

//////////////////////////////////////////////////////////////////
////////
// CFractalsDoc commands

int CFractalsDoc::GetCurrentFractal()
{
  return CurrentFractalNum;
}

void CFractalsDoc::SetCurrentFractal(int FracNum)
{
  CurrentFractalNum = FracNum;
}

void CFractalsDoc::OnFractalsKamtorus()
{

  SetCurrentFractal(1);
  UpdateAllViews(NULL);
```

```
}

void CFractalsDoc::OnFractalsDuff()
{
  SetCurrentFractal(2);
  UpdateAllViews(NULL);
}

void CFractalsDoc::OnFractalsClouds()
{
  SetCurrentFractal(3);
  UpdateAllViews(NULL);
}

void CFractalsDoc::OnFractalsJulias()
{
  SetCurrentFractal(4);
  UpdateAllViews(NULL);
}

void CFractalsDoc::OnFractalsMandelbrot()
{
  SetCurrentFractal(5);
  UpdateAllViews(NULL);
}

int CFractalsDoc::GetCurrentFractal()
{
  return CurrentFractalNum;
}

void CFractalsDoc::SetCurrentFractal(int FracNum)
{
  CurrentFractalNum = FracNum;
}

void CFractalsDoc::OnFractalsAbstract()
{
```

```
  SetCurrentFractal(3);
  UpdateAllViews(NULL);
}
```

ANNOTATIONS

Let's take a closer look at some of the code in the **CFractalsDoc** class. Several of the functions are repetitive, so we will only consider their generalized functions. The first custom function, exposed as a public method outside the class, is the **GetCurrentFractal( )** function, which returns an integer corresponding to the user-selected fractal.

```
int CFractalsDoc::GetCurrentFractal()
{
  return CurrentFractalNum;
}
```

As you can see, **CurrentFractalNum** is a member variable of the class. In keeping with good design principles, **CurrentFractalNum** is declared as private, and is only accessible outside the class through the interface functions. While **GetCurrentFractal( )** returns the current value, **SetCurrentFractal( )** accepts the value as a parameter and sets the **CurrentFractalNum** variable equal to that value, as shown here:

```
void CFractalsDoc::SetCurrentFractal(int FracNum)
{
  CurrentFractalNum = FracNum;
}
```

All of the other functions in the **CFractalsDoc** class are message map functions. When the user selects a fractal from the Fractals menu within the application, the program maps to one of the defined functions. Each function sets the current fractal number, then calls the MFC **UpdateAllViews( )** function, which forces the program to redraw the view. The **OnFractalsKamtorus( )** function, for example, sets the current fractal to 1 and fires the view update, as shown here:

```
void CFractalsDoc::OnFractalsKamtorus()
{
```

```
  SetCurrentFractal(1);
  UpdateAllViews(NULL);
}
```

The value that the program sets within each of the message handlers is then interpreted within the **CFractalsView** class's **OnDraw( )** function, using a **switch** statement.

The primary processing of the program, then—with respect to the drawing of the fractals, at least—occurs within the **CFractalsView** class. Since that is the center of the program's processing, let's move on to consideration of its components.

Code

FractalsView.cpp

The following code implements the **CFractalsView** class. As with the **CFractalsDoc** class, the code reprinted here is only the custom code added to the file. When you look at the file, you will also find certain definitions and functions placed there by the MFC AppWizard when it creates the application framework.

Here, then, is the code for the **CFractalsView** class:

```
#include "stdafx.h"
#include "Fractals.h"
#include <cstdlib>
#include <cmath>
#include <complex>
#include "FractalsDoc.h"
#include "FractalsView.h"

#ifdef _DEBUG
#define new DEBUG_NEW
#undef THIS_FILE
static char THIS_FILE[] = __FILE__;
#endif

using namespace std;


/////////////////////////////////////////////////////////////////////
////////
// CFractalsView
```

```
MPLEMENT_DYNCREATE(CFractalsView, CView)

BEGIN_MESSAGE_MAP(CFractalsView, CView)
  //{{AFX_MSG_MAP(CFractalsView)
    // NOTE - the ClassWizard will add and remove mapping macros
    // here.
    //     DO NOT EDIT what you see in these blocks of generated code!
  //}}AFX_MSG_MAP
END_MESSAGE_MAP()

/////////////////////////////////////////////////////////////////////
/////////
// CFractalsView construction/destruction

CFractalsView::CFractalsView()
{
  // TODO: add construction code here


}


CFractalsView::~CFractalsView()
{
}


BOOL CFractalsView::PreCreateWindow(CREATESTRUCT& cs)
{
  // TODO: Modify the Window class or styles here by modifying
  //   the CREATESTRUCT cs

  return CView::PreCreateWindow(cs);
}
void DuffDraw (CDC *pDC, double x, double y, int cl)
{
    double i1, j1, c;
    int i, k;
    DWORD Color;
    CPen* pOldPen;
    CPen DrawPen;
    // CBrush* pOldBrush;
    // CBrush DrawBrush;

    Color = RGB(rand() % 255, rand() % 255,rand() % 255);
    DrawPen.CreatePen(PS_SOLID, 4, Color);
```

```
   pOldPen = pDC->SelectObject(&DrawPen);
   // DrawBrush.CreateSolidBrush(Color);
   // pOldBrush = pDC->SelectObject(&DrawBrush);

   i1 = 150.0*x + 320.0;
   j1 = -176.0*y + 240.0;
   k = 7;

   for (i=1;i<=7;i++) {
     c = 0.09*i;
     pDC->Ellipse((int)(i1+c),(int)(i1-c), (int)(j1+c),
         (int)(j1-c));
     // circle ((int)(i1+c),(int)(j1+c),k);
     k--;
   }
   pOldPen = pDC->SelectObject(pOldPen);
//    pOldBrush = pDC->SelectObject(pOldBrush);
   return;
}


void DrawDuff(CDC *pDC)
{
  int k1;
  double a, cl, t, x, y, x1, y1, pi=3.141592653589793, twopi;

  x = 1.0;
  y = 0.0;
  t = 0.0;
  a = 0.3;
  twopi = 2.0*pi;

  for (int loop = 0; loop < 500; loop++) {
    k1++;
    x1 = x + y/twopi;
    y1 = y + (-(x*x*x) + x -0.25*y + a*cos(t))/twopi;
    t = 0.01*(k1 % 628);
    x = x1;
    y = y1;
    if (t > pi)
      cl = 0;
    else
      cl = 7;
```

```
      DuffDraw(pDC, (int) x, (int) y, (int) cl);
  }
}

void DrawKamTorus(CDC *pDC)
{
  int a, c, nx, ny;
  time_t t;
  double an, can, san, can1, san1, e, ax, ay;
  double x, xa, x1, x2, x3, y, y1, y2, y3, rand1, rand2;
  CPen* pOldPen;
  CPen DrawPen;

  DrawPen.CreatePen(PS_SOLID, 1, RGB(rand() % 255, rand()
      % 255,rand() % 255));
  pOldPen = pDC->SelectObject(&DrawPen);

  nx = 320;
  ny = 240;
  ax = 400.0;
  ay = ax;

  c = 1;
  srand((unsigned) time(&t));
  rand1 = rand() % 20000;
  rand2 = rand() % 20000;
  rand1 = 5.0e-5*rand1;
  rand2 = 5.0e-5*rand2;
  an = 10.0*(rand1-rand2);
  can = 0.99*cos(an);
  san = 0.99*sin(an);
  can1 = 1.01*cos(an);
  san1 = 1.01*sin(an);
  x3 = 0.01;
  y3 = 0.01;
  do {
    xa = x3*x3 - y3;
    x2 = x3*can1 + xa*san1;
    y2 = x3*san1 - xa*can1;
    x3 = x2;
    y3 = y2;
    x = x2;
```

```
    y = y2;
    a = 0;
    do {
      xa = x*x - y;
      x1 = x*can + xa*san;
      y1 = x*san - xa*can;
      x = x1;
      y = y1;
      a++;
      pDC->SetPixelV((int)(ax*x+nx) -1, (int)(ay*y+ny) + 1, c);
    }  while ((fabs(x1)<=2.0e3) && (fabs(y1)<=2.0e3) && a <=100);
    e = e + 0.075;
    c = rand() % 32767;
  } while ((fabs(x2) <= 2.0e3) && (fabs(y2) <= 2.0e3));
}


double abs_random(void)
{
  int random_integer, temp_integer;
  double random_double, temp_double;

  random_integer = rand();
  random_double = (double)random_integer / RAND_MAX;
  temp_integer = rand() % 32767;
  temp_double = (double)temp_integer / 1000000000L;
  random_double += temp_double;
  return(random_double);
}

void DrawAbstract(CDC *pDC)
{
  int Raio[5000], Cx[5000], Cy[5000], color, npix, npiy, iopt;
  float Tcor, Cor[5000];
  int xpix, ypix, Cmax, ic, index, dx, dy, Rmax;

  npix = 640;
  npiy = 480;
  Cmax = (rand() % 2000) + 500;
  Rmax = (rand() % 320) + 1;

  for (ic=1; ic<=Cmax; ic++) {
    Cx[ic]   = (int)(npix*abs_random());
```

```
    Cy[ic]   = (int)(npiy*abs_random());
    Raio[ic] = (int)(Rmax*abs_random());
    if (iopt == 1)
      Cor[ic] = (float) (16.0*abs_random() + 15.0);
    else
      Cor[ic] = (float) (256.0*abs_random());
  }
  for (xpix=0; xpix<=(npix-1); xpix++) {
    for (ypix=0; ypix<=(npiy-1); ypix++) {
      index = 0;
      Tcor  = 0;
      for (ic=1; ic<=Cmax; ic++) {
        dx = xpix - Cx[ic];
        dy = ypix - Cy[ic];
        if ((int)(dx*dx + dy*dy) <= Raio[ic]*Raio[ic]) {
          index++;
          Tcor = Tcor + Cor[ic];
        }
      }

      if (index > 0)
        color = (int)(Tcor/index);
      else
        color = 0;
      pDC->SetPixelV(xpix,ypix,(color * 16));
    }
  }
}

void DrawJulias(CDC *pDC)
{
  double xmin, xmax, ymin, ymax, fact=1.0;
  double ypy, x, y, x0, y0, xp, yp, const_scr=1.0;
  double deltax, deltay, pmin, qmin, ya, xkp1, ykp1, r;
  register int npix=1024, npiy=768, kcolor;
  register int k, np, nq, npy, ipen;
  char *endptr;

  pmin = -0.74356;
  qmin = 0.11135;
  xmin = -2.0;
  xmax = 2.0;
  ymin = -2.0;
```

```
ymax = 2.0;
kcolor = 255;
if(fact>=1.0 || fact <=0.0)
  fact = 1.0;
else {
  npix = (int)(npix*fact);
  npiy = (int)(npiy*fact);
}
ypy = (double)npiy - 0.5;
deltax = (xmax-xmin)/(npix-1);
deltay = (ymax-ymin)/(npiy-1);

for (np=0; np<=npix-1; np++) {
  x0 = xmin + (double)np*deltax;
  for (nq=0; nq<=npiy-1; nq++) {
    y0 = ymin + (double)nq*deltay;
    x = x0;
    y = y0;
    k  = 0;

    do {
      xkp1 = (x+y)*(x-y) + pmin;
      ya = x*y;
      ykp1 = ya + ya + qmin;
      r = xkp1*xkp1 + ykp1*ykp1;
      k++;
      if (r >= kcolor) {
        ipen = k;
        xp = const_scr*(double)np;
        yp = (double)nq;
        pDC->SetPixelV(xp,yp,ipen);
      }
      if (k == kcolor) {
        ipen = RGB(0, 0, 255);
        xp = const_scr*(double)np;
        yp = (double)nq;
        pDC->SetPixelV(xp,yp,ipen);
      }
      x = xkp1;
      y = ykp1;
    } while (r <= kcolor && k<=kcolor);
  }
}
```

```
}

double MandelSetPoten(double cx, double cy, int maxiter)
{
  double x, y, x2, y2, temp, potential;
  int iter;

  x = cx;
  x2 = x*x;
  y = cy;
  y2 = y*y;
  iter = 0;

  do {
    temp = x2 - y2 + cx;
    y = 2.0*x*y + cy;
    x = temp;
    x2 = x*x;
    y2 = y*y;
    iter++;
  } while ((iter<maxiter) && ((x2+y2)<10000.0));
  if (iter<maxiter)
    potential = 0.5*log(x2+y2)/powl(2.0,iter);
  else
    potential = 0.0;
  return (potential);
}

void DrawMandelbrot(CDC *pDC)
{
  int nx, ny, iy, ix, ipen, maxiter = 16000, iflag=0, iset = 1;
  complex<double> c;
  double xmin=-2.25, ymin=-1.25, xmax=0.75, ymax=1.25;
  cx, cy, potent;
  double diff=0.6482801, test1, test2;

  if ((maxiter>=16000) || (maxiter<=0))
    maxiter = 16000;
  nx = 640;
  ny = 480;
  ymin = -1.125;
  ymax = 1.125;
```

```
for (iy=0;iy<=ny-1;iy++) {
  cy = ymin + iy*(ymax-ymin)/(ny-1);
  for (ix=0;ix<=nx-1;ix++) {
    cx = xmin + ix*(xmax-xmin)/(nx-1);
    c.real(cx);
    c.imag(cy);
    test1 = 2.0;
    if ((cx >= -7.55e-1) && (cx <= 4.0e-1)) {
      if ((cy >= -6.6e-1) && (cy <= 6.6e-1))
        test1 = abs(1.0 - sqrt(1.0-4.0*c));
    }
    test2 = 2.0;
    if ((cx >= -1.275e0) && (cx <= -7.45e-1)) {
      if ((cy >= -2.55e-1) && (cy <= 2.55e-1))
        test2 = abs(4.0*(c+1.0));
    }
    if (test1<=1.0) {
      potent = 0;
      iflag = 1;
      if (iset != 0)
        ipen = 126;
      else
        ipen = 32;
    }
    else if (test2<=1.0) {
      potent = 0;
      iflag = 1;
      if (iset != 0)
        ipen = 104;
      else
        ipen = 32;
    }
    else {
      potent = MandelSetPoten(cx,cy,maxiter);
      iflag = 0;
    }
    if ((potent == 0.0) && (iflag==0))
      ipen = 32;
    else if ((potent !=0) && (iflag==0))
      ipen = (int)(33.0 + 15.0*(potent-33.0)/diff);

    pDC->SetPixelV(ix,iy,ipen);
```

```
    }
  }
}

void CFractalsView::OnDraw(CDC* pDC)
{
  CFractalsDoc* pDoc = GetDocument();

  ASSERT_VALID(pDoc);
  pDC = GetDC();
  switch (pDoc->GetCurrentFractal()) {
    case 0:
      break;
    case 1:
      DrawKamTorus(pDC);
      pDoc->SetCurrentFractal(0);
      break;
    case 2:
      DrawDuff(pDC);
      pDoc->SetCurrentFractal(0);
      break;
    case 3:
      DrawAbstract(pDC);
      pDoc->SetCurrentFractal(0);
      break;
    case 4:
      DrawJulias(pDC);
      pDoc->SetCurrentFractal(0);
      break;
    case 5:
      DrawMandelbrot(pDC);
      pDoc->SetCurrentFractal(0);
      break;
  }
}
```

ANNOTATIONS

Clearly, quite a bit of processing happens when we are drawing the fractals, although the processing will vary from fractal to fractal. Much of the code in the various fractal routines is somewhat duplicative; however, making each of the

functions more-or-less stand-alone makes it easier for you to peel the functions out and use them in another way.

The **include** declarations at the top of the file are pretty straightforward. In addition to the standard MFC **include** statements, we need to include the C math library and the C standard library, as well as the Standard Template Library's definition of the **complex** type. (You will see more about the **complex** type later in this chapter, when we discuss the Mandelbrot-plotting function.) As always, we're also using the **std** namespace, to simplify programming, because we are using the Standard Template Library in places.

```
#include "stdafx.h"
#include "Fractals.h"
#include <cstdlib>
#include <cmath>
#include <complex>
#include "FractalsDoc.h"
#include "FractalsView.h"

using namespace std;
```

CONSIDERING THE DUFFINGS OSCILLATOR

The first major drawing function in the program draws the *Duff fractal* (also known as the *Duffings oscillator*). The Duff fractal traces a series of circles through three simulated dimensions, creating an eventual result that looks similar to an inverted cone. Drawing the Duff fractal in Visual C++ is a difficult task unless you use Microsoft's DirectDraw technology, because the CDC class's **Ellipse( )** method does not allow you to specify a transparent background when you draw the ellipse. So, instead of concentric rings, which is how the Duff fractal should display, the program displays a series of rings drawn over one another, looking a little odd. DirectDraw is, however, well beyond the context of this book; and drawing the circles using other operating systems such as DOS does not result in this overlap.

Three functions control the drawing of the Duffings Oscillator: one function to determine the x-coordinate; one to determine the y-coordinate; and one to determine the value **t**, in radians, which the oscillator uses to determine the y-coordinate (and subsequently the x-coordinate). The functions are as follows:

```
x(n+1) = x(n) + (y(n) / (2 * pi))
y(n+1) = y(n) + (-(x(n)3) + x(n) - 0.25*y(n) + a*cos(t)) / (2 * pi)
t = 0.01*(k1 % 628);
```

The value **t** is in the range between 0 and 2 * pi, and generally increments in fractions of 0.01, although you can change the step size to vary the way in which the figure oscillates.

When you run the Fractals program, choose the Duff fractal, and view the resulting figure, it will look similar to Figure 12-5.

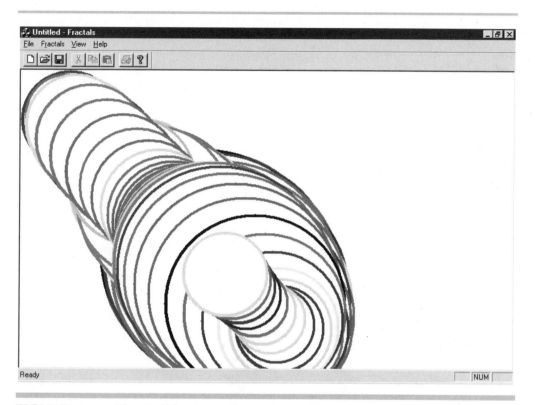

FIGURE 12-5.   The Duff fractal as drawn by the Fractals program

There are actually two routines that draw the Duff fractal. This is essentially because **Ellipse( )** uses the current pen and the current brush to draw its figures on the screen. Because of the way device contexts in Windows manage pens and brushes, it is necessary for the object to go out of scope to avoid errors in pen and brush management. So, the **DuffDraw( )** routine actually draws several (seven) ellipses, then returns to the **DrawDuff( )** routine to determine the next starting point for drawing the ellipses. The **DuffDraw( )** routine accepts three parameters: the device context, and the x and y positions around which the ellipses will be drawn. **DuffDraw( )** also declares some local variables, most notably **i1** and **j1**, which maintain current circle-plotting information, and **c**, which contains a derived offset for drawing the circles. Finally, the function declares some **CPen** objects to manage the drawing colors. Here is **DuffDraw( )**:

```
void DuffDraw (CDC *pDC, double x, double y)
{
    double i1, j1, c;
    int i;
    DWORD Color;
    CPen* pOldPen;
    CPen DrawPen;
    // CBrush* pOldBrush;
    // CBrush DrawBrush;
```

It's worth noting the stubs for the **CBrush** object declarations. Although the
program does not use them as constructed, you could just as easily draw filled
circles rather than hollow circles. The output in such a case, however, will look
significantly different. As discussed above, the optimal goal is to draw transparent
circles, a feature not supported by the MFC GDI drawing features.

```
    Color = RGB(rand() % 255, rand() % 255, rand() % 255);
    DrawPen.CreatePen(PS_SOLID, 4, Color);
    pOldPen = pDC->SelectObject(&DrawPen);
    // DrawBrush.CreateSolidBrush(Color);
    // pOldBrush = pDC->SelectObject(&DrawBrush);
```

After declaring the objects, the program creates a random RGB color value and
then creates a pen with width 4 (pixels) having the random color assigned to the
Color variable. The program code then selects the pen into the current device
context, as required by MFC. If you were using brushes to draw filled circles, you
could also select the brush into the device context at this time, as the stubs show.

Next, the program code declares the drawing points for the circles themselves,
assigning those values to the **i1** and **j1** variables. It is necessary to do this because
the Duff fractal only describes values in a limited range. For **x**, the values are
between about –2 and 2; for **y**, the values are between about –1 and 1:

```
    i1 = 150.0*x + 320.0;
    j1 = -176.0*y + 240.0;
```

The fixed values in the equations offset onto the screen; if you are using a display
larger than 640 x 480, you will likely want to increase these offset values—and the
multipliers—to achieve a more meaningful spread over your computer's screen.

Now that we know the points on screen corresponding, in general, to the points
described by the fractal equation, we can go ahead and draw the circles onto the screen:

```
    for (i = 1;i < 8;i++) {
      c = 0.09*i;
      pDC->Ellipse((int)(i1+c),(int)(i1-c), (int)(j1+c),
          (int)(j1-c));
    }
```

The loop simply draws seven ellipses, all the same color, across a range of points. You can see this drawing when you run the program, because the application will actually seem to cycle, drawing seven circles and then returning to the calling function, deriving another pair of starting points and cycling again.

```
    pOldPen = pDC->SelectObject(pOldPen);
//      pOldBrush = pDC->SelectObject(pOldBrush);
    return;
}
```

When it finishes drawing the circles, the program simply cleans up after itself—returning the pen color to what it was before the program entered the function, and doing the same with the brush, if you so choose.

After the function finishes, it returns to the calling function—in this case, the **DrawDuff( )** function, which performs the mathematical calculations for deriving the Duff fractal and calls the drawing routine for the fractal. The **DrawDuff( )** function is called from the **CFractalsView::OnDraw( )** function, which invokes it if the user selected the Duff option from the Fractals menu. The function accepts a pointer to the current device context, and defines a bunch of local variables. As with all the other fractal functions you will see in this chapter, all these different variables are used by the functions within the program to compute each point described by the function. Here is **DrawDuff( )**:

```
void DrawDuff(CDC *pDC)
{
  int k1;
  double a, cl, t, x, y, x1, y1, pi=3.141592653589793, twopi;

  x = 1.0;     // initial value must be between -2.0 and 2.0
  y = 0.0;     // initial value must be between -1.0 and 1.0
  t = 0.0;     // initial value must be between 0 and 6.25
  a = 0.3;     // initial value must be between 0 and 1
  twopi = 2.0*pi;
```

As you will see throughout, many of the variables are defined individually, rather than in-line. We did this so that you can more easily "play" with the values yourself and see the various results. In the case of the Duff fractal, the four values noted in the code can be varied to change the results of plotting the fractal. You can also change the value of **k1**, which will affect the way the fractal is drawn. The **twopi** variable, of course, is simply the mathematical pi multiplied by 2. After setting the initial values, the program enters the loop that specifies the number of iterations of the computation. Note that you can set this value much higher, and the program will oscillate through an extended series; 500 is just a good "getting started" number. Here is the **for** loop:

```
  for (int loop = 0; loop < 500; loop++) {
    k1++;
```

```
x1 = x + y/twopi;
y1 = y + (-(x*x*x) + x - 0.25*y + a*cos(t))/twopi;
```

The fractal changes the way it displays information so rapidly because of the interlocking nature of the x and y variables in the equations. As you can see, each time through the loop the function computes **x1** (the new **x** value) as a function of the old **x** and old **y** values. It then goes on to compute **y1** (the new **y** value) as a function of the old **x** and old **y** values, and the result of the cosine of **t** multiplied by the constant **a** defined at the beginning of the loop. The lack of a straight relationship between the x and y values is crucial for the creation of fractals; as you move on to some of the more complex fractals in the remainder of this chapter, you will find that the Duff equation is actually relatively simple.

After computing the new values for **x1** and **y1**, the program code effectively increments **t** by a fractional value:

```
t = 0.01*(k1 % 628);
x = x1;
y = y1;
DuffDraw(pDC, x, y);
}
}
```

(Although, if the loop exceeds 628, **t** will actually cycle between 0.01 and 6.28, an approximation of **2 * pi**.) You might also set the iterator to increase by 0.02 every time, using an assignment in the form **t = 0.02*(k1 % 314)**. The code then sets **x** and **y** to their new values and invokes the drawing routine **DuffDraw( )**. The result of all this looping is the graphic in the previous Figure 12-5.

The Duffings oscillator, though an interesting figure—and valuable to consider here as a starting point—is comparatively simple in the way it is generated. More interesting figures are produced when one draws at the pixel level and generates a more complex series of points. The last three fractals that we consider in this chapter will actually go as far as to plot each point in the display area—even if nothing appears at that point. First, though, we'll look at the Kam Torus fractal, which does not go quite so far.

THE KAM TORUS FRACTAL

The Kam Torus fractal draws a series of *tori*. A torus is a surface having Genus 1, and therefore possessing a single "hole." The usual torus in 3-D space is shaped like a donut, but the concept of the torus is extremely useful in higher dimensional space as well. The usual 3-D "ring" torus is known in older literature as an *Anchor Ring*. The Kam Torus graphic is created by superimposing a series of points within a certain locus of points (often called an *orbit* in fractal literature) generated by a set

of equations, with a variable incremented each time through the drawing routine. The three fractions that govern the drawing are as follows:

```
x(0) = y(0) = orbit / 3
x(n+1) = x(n)*cos(a) + (x(n)²-y(n))*sin(a)
y(n+1) = x(n)*sin(a) - (x(n)²-y(n))*cos(a)
```

After each trip through the loop, the **orbit** value is incremented by some fixed constant (a *step size*). The parameters used by the function include the size of the angle **a** (expressed in radians), the step size for incrementing the **orbit** value, the ending value for the **orbit** value, and a points-per-orbit value that controls the number of points drawn each time through the loop. You can also create a three-dimensional variant of the fractal figure by treating the **orbit** value as the z-coordinate for each drawing. With both the 2D and the 3D variants, you can adjust the value that controls the maximum number of iterations, to control the number of orbits plotted and, therefore, the complexity of the figure. In the Fractals program, the number of orbits plotted is controlled by the values that the program sets when it starts to draw the figure.

In each invocation of the Fractals program, the figures drawn by the **DrawKamTorus( )** routine will vary, because the program code uses randomizing functions to generate the equation's start point. In fact, in any two invocations, the figure may look as different as the two illustrated in Figure 12-6.

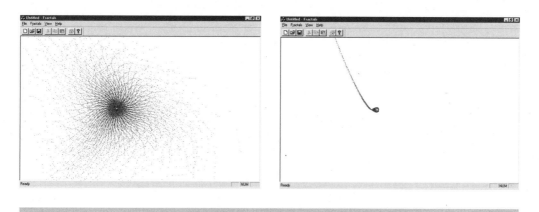

FIGURE 12-6.   Two different iterations of the Kam Torus fractal

Like the **DrawDuff( )** routine, the **DrawKamTorus( )** routine accepts as its only parameter a pointer to the device context. **DrawKamTorus( )** then defines a series of **int** and **double** values for use in computing the point to draw on the screen. After

defining the variables, the routine sets some values that you may change if you are plotting on a screen larger than 640 x 480. Here is **DrawKamTorus( )**:

```
void DrawKamTorus(CDC *pDC)
{
  int a, c, nx, ny;
  time_t t;
  double an, can, san, can1, san1, ax, ay;
  double x, xa, x1, x2, x3, y, y1, y2, y3, rand1, rand2;
  nx = 320;
  ny = 240;
  ax = 400.0;
  ay = ax;
  c = 1;
```

The program code next seeds the random-number generator using the **srand( )** function, and generates a series of random values that are used as the basis for the fractal's creation. After creating the random values, the code also computes two cosines and two sines of those values—one multiplied by just less than 0, and one multiplied by just more than 0. Here is that code:

```
srand((unsigned) time(&t));
rand1 = rand() % 20000;
rand2 = rand() % 20000;
rand1 = 5.0e-5*rand1;
rand2 = 5.0e-5*rand2;
an = 10.0*(rand1-rand2);
can = 0.99*cos(an);
san = 0.99*sin(an);
can1 = 1.01*cos(an);
san1 = 1.01*sin(an);
```

Finally, as shown next, the program code assigns initial values to the **x3** and **y3** variables, then enters the main **do** loop that does all the drawing of the fractal. The program will exit the **do** loop when either the **x2** or **y2** value exceeds the permitted range.

```
x3 = 0.01;
y3 = 0.01;
do {
  xa = x3*x3 - y3;
  x2 = x3*can1 + xa*san1;
  y2 = x3*san1 - xa*can1;
  x3 = x2;
  y3 = y2;
```

```
x = x2;
y = y2;
a = 0;
```

After entering the **do** loop, the program code generates some initial start values for the series of plots. The Kam Torus fractal actually plots a series of plots. The inside loop, which you will see in just a moment, plots a series of points not exceeding 100 points. The outside loop, which starts at the **do** in the code fragment just above, will plot until the **x2** or **y2** value exceeds the limit on values.

In any event, within the loop, the **xa**, **x2**, and **y2** values are computed based on the current **x3** and **y3** values, as well as by using some of the random information generated at the beginning of the function. The program code then enters a second, interior **do** loop, which actually generates and plots points:

```
do {
    xa = x*x - y;
    x1 = x*can + xa*san;
    y1 = x*san - xa*can;
```

Inside the interior loop, the program code gets down to the business of computing the current point to plot. The **xa** value is calculated based on the current **x** and **y** values and is then used, together with the cosine and sine values computed at the time of entry to the function, and the current **x** value, to generate the **x1** and **y1** values.

The program code then sets **x** and **y** equal to **x1** and **y1**, increments the internal counter variable (which makes sure that no more than 100 points are plotted each time through the internal loop), and then paints a pixel on the screen:

```
    x = x1;
    y = y1;
    a++;
    pDC->SetPixelV((int)(ax*x+nx) -1, (int)(ay*y+ny) + 1, c);
}   while ((fabs(x1)<=2.0e3) && (fabs(y1)<=2.0e3) && a <=100);
```

The color of the pixel is specified by the variable **c**, which is a random color variable that changes each time through the outer loop. Note that, in addition to exiting any time **a** exceeds 100, the program will also exit whenever the absolute value of **x1** or **y1** exceeds 2,000:

```
    c = rand() % 32767;
} while ((fabs(x2) <= 2.0e3) && (fabs(y2) <= 2.0e3));
return;
}
```

Back in the exterior loop, the program sets a new color value for the color in which to draw the next series of pixels. Then it checks and makes sure that neither **x2** nor **y2** has exceeded the 2,000 limit. If either has, the program exits the loop and exits the function. If **x2** and **y2** haven't exceeded 2,000, the program loops again, computing a new start point and drawing another 100 points based on it.

THE ABSTRACT FRACTAL

The next fractal we will examine—the Abstract fractal—is the first one to use the common method of drawing fractals: setting the color for every point within the drawable range. As you'll see later with both the Julia and the Mandelbrot fractal, using this method allows us to generate exceptionally complex figures. In addition, you'll observe in the Abstract fractal that this method allows us to generate seemingly random figures without recognizable form. Although the Abstract fractal (Figure 12-7) is interesting, it doesn't exactly seem to "make sense."

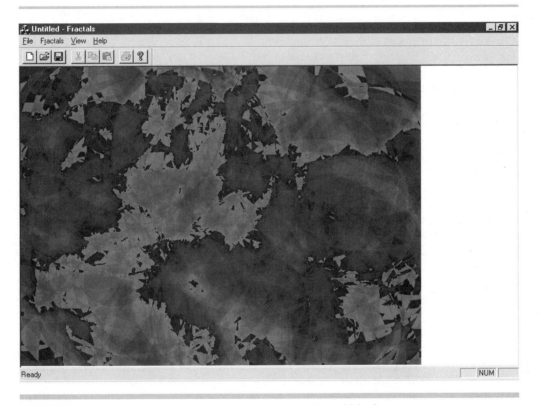

FIGURE 12-7.   The Abstract fractal draws in reds and blacks

The Abstract fractal doesn't particularly work from any of the recorded fractal-generating functions, but simply applies fractal theory to a drawing series. It uses a random-number generator to create double values—a slightly more complex process than creating random integers. To create these random double values, it uses a custom procedure called **abs_random( )**. This function accepts no parameters and returns a single double value to the calling function.

Within the function, the program declares four local variables, one to maintain random integer values, and one to maintain the generated double values:

```
double abs_random(void)
{
  int random_integer, temp_integer;
  double random_double, temp_double;
```

The program code then generates two random integers—one in the range between 0 and **RAND_MAX**, and one in the range between 0 and 32767.

```
  random_integer = rand();
  random_double = (double)random_integer / RAND_MAX;
  temp_integer = rand() % 32767;
  temp_double = (double)temp_integer / 1000000000L;
  random_double += temp_double;
  return(random_double);
}
```

The program uses each of the generated integer values to generate a double value, resulting in a value somewhere between 0 and 1. It returns the random value as its result.

The **DrawAbstract( )** function then accepts as its sole parameter a pointer to the device context (like the other fractal functions), and declares some local variables that it then uses to perform its processing:

```
void DrawAbstract(CDC *pDC)
{
  int color, npix, npiy, iopt = 1;
  float Tcor;
  int xpix, ypix, Cmax, ic, index, dx, dy, Rmax;

  npix = 640;
  npiy = 480;
  Cmax = (rand() % 2000) + 500;
  Rmax = (rand() % 320) + 1;
  int Raio[Cmax], Cx[Cmax], Cy[Cmax];
  float Cor[Cmax];
```

As with the other fractal programs, this one is set to work within a 640 x 480 environment. If yours is larger, you can increase the **npix** and **npiy** values. Additionally, the program generates a random number between 500 and 2,500 to define the number of shapes in the fractal, and a random number between 1 and 320 to specify the maximum possible radius/width of the shape.

The program code then enters the outside **for** loop, which counts from 1 to the maximum number of shapes generated earlier, as indicated by the **Cmax** variable. It then specifies a random **x** value for that shape in the **Cx** array, a random **y** value in the **Cy** array, and a random size value in the **Raio** array. Here is that code:

```
for (ic = 1; ic < Cmax; ic++) {
   Cx[ic] = (int)(npix*abs_random());
   Cy[ic] = (int)(npiy*abs_random());
   Raio[ic] = (int)(Rmax*abs_random());
```

Next, the **if** statement checks to see what color values to use—either black and gray from the 12-color palette, or all 256 colors from the 256-color palette. The default (as set above) is for the 256-color palette.

```
   if (iopt == 0)
      Cor[ic]  = (float) (16.0*abs_random() + 15.0);
   else
      Cor[ic] = (float) (256.0*abs_random());
}
```

After initializing the arrays that it will use to draw the information onto the screen, the program begins to iterate through all the pixels on the screen. The outside **for** loop iterates through **x** values, and the inside loop iterates through the possible **y** values. The program then enters a third **for** loop, which iterates through the arrays defined previously:

```
for (xpix=0; xpix < (npix-1); xpix++) {
   for (ypix=0; ypix < (npiy-1); ypix++) {
      index = 0;
      Tcor  = 0;
      for (ic=1; ic < Cmax; ic++) {
```

Inside the third loop, two values, **dx** and **dy**, are generated based on the current value of the first and second loops, and the random values within the **Cx** and **Cy** arrays at the current point. The program then compares those two values against the random radius value:

```
         dx = xpix - Cx[ic];
         dy = ypix - Cy[ic];
         if ((int)(dx*dx + dy*dy) <= Raio[ic]*Raio[ic]) {
```

If the generated result is less than the radius squared, the program increments the **Tcor** and **index** variables—**index** by 1, and **Tcor** by the corresponding color value in the **Cor** array:

```
      index++;
        Tcor = Tcor + Cor[ic];
      }
    }
```

If **index** is greater than 0 when the loop exists (as it almost always will be), the program code sets the color for the current pixel to the total color value (**Tcor**) divided by the index, yielding an average color value. The program then paints that point with the color value:

```
    if (index > 0)
      color = (int)(Tcor/index);
    else
      color = 0;
    pDC->SetPixelV(xpix, ypix,(color * 16));
    }
  }
}
```

The Abstract fractal function uses interesting relationships of random numbers and predefined tests to return fractal-like output; however, it is not a completely pure fractal because of the role randomness plays in the output's creation. Random seed values are crucial for fractal creation—but they should generally be constrained to seed values, rather than being an intrinsic part of each step of the computation.

THE JULIA SET FRACTAL

You saw the usefulness of random seed values when you looked at the Kam Torus fractal. Two of the most well-known fractals, however—the Mandelbrot set and the Julia set—do not use random values at all. In fact, these sets draw their results based on known start values. (Although you could feasibly cycle through a sequence of random start values to see the effect on the sets.) You can see the output of the Julia fractal function in the Fractals program in Figure 12-8.

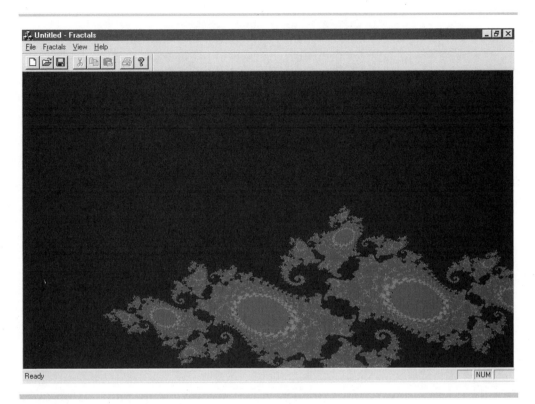

FIGURE 12-8. The Julia set draws complex fractals

As mentioned, Julia sets were named for mathematician Gaston Julia. They can be generated by a simple change in the iteration process described later in this chapter for the Mandelbrot set. To describe a Julia set, you must start with a specified value for **C**, a complex number with both real and imaginary parts. *Complex numbers* are numbers of the form **a + (b * i)**, where **i** represents the square root of –1 (an imaginary number). For the Julia set, the initial value of **Z** corresponds to that complex number. For **Z**, the real component corresponds to the x-coordinate, and the imaginary component corresponds to i (the square root of –1) multiplied by the y-coordinate. To draw the fractal, you then repeat the mathematical function **Z(n+1) = Z(n)^2 + C**, for each value of **Z** in the series described by **(0..n)**.

There is a Julia set corresponding to every point on the complex plane—meaning there are an infinite number of Julia sets. But the most visually interesting sets tend to be found for the **C** values where the M-set (that is, the computed Mandelbrot point set related to the Julia set) image is busiest. Go too far inside the range of values, and the corresponding Julia set is a circle. If you go too far outside the range, the Julia set breaks up into scattered points.

Let's take a look at the **DrawJulias( )** function, which draws Julia set fractals. Like the other fractal functions, it takes in only a pointer to the device context as its sole parameter, and then proceeds to define a number of variables that it will use internally to generate the image itself. Here is the **DrawJulias( )** function:

```
void DrawJulias(CDC *pDC)
{
  double xmin, xmax, ymin, ymax, fact=1.0;
  double ypy, x, y, x0, y0, xp, yp, const_scr=1.0;
  double deltax, deltay, pmin, qmin, ya, xkp1, ykp1, r;
  int npix=640, npiy=480, kcolor;
  int k, np, nq, npy, ipen;
```

Note that the function uses more variables than the others that you have seen so far; most of the variables' uses will become clear as you explore farther in the function. Some of these, however, should look familiar—the **npix** and **npiy** functions, most notably, define the outside boundaries of where to draw, and may be adjusted on your system.

```
  pmin = -0.74356;
  qmin = 0.11135;
  xmin = -2.0;
  xmax = 2.0;
  ymin = -2.0;
  ymax = 2.0;
  kcolor = 255;
```

As shown just above, each of these variables may be set to other values; you can play with the values within the source code, or create a dialog box that lets users set their own values at run time (you can also take them as command-line parameters, on a DOS or UNIX system). The **fact** variable, as shown next, also lets you specify what fraction of the total screen space to use. The default of 1.0 specifies the entire space, but you can make it any value between 0.0 and 1.0.

```
  if(fact>=1.0 || fact <=0.0)
    fact = 1.0;
  else {
    npix = (int)(npix*fact);
    npiy = (int)(npiy*fact);
  }
  ypy = (double)npiy - 0.5;
  deltax = (xmax-xmin)/(npix-1);
  deltay = (ymax-ymin)/(npiy-1);
```

The **deltax** and **deltay** values correspond to the difference between the maximum and minimum x and y values, divided by the screen size, as set in the last two assignments above. Then the program, like the code for the abstract fractal, cycles through each pixel in the drawing area using two **for** loops—one for the x value, and one for the **y** value. The **np** variable will correspond to the current x value, and the **nq** variable will correspond to the current y value. The x0 variable is set each time through the loop, and corresponds to the minimum x value plus the current value of the loop, multiplied by the x delta value, as shown here:

```
for (np = 0; np <= npix-1; np++) {
    x0 = xmin + (double) np * deltax;
    for (nq = 0; nq <= npiy-1; nq++) {
```

Inside the interior loop, the **y0** value is computed similarly, using the minimum y value plus the current value of the loop multiplied by the delta value. The program then sets x and y equal to those initial values, and initializes the constant **k** to 0:

```
        y0 = ymin + (double) nq * deltay;
        x = x0;
        y = y0;
        k  = 0;
```

The program then enters the loop, which actually draws the pixels that make up the fractal. Unlike the other two loops, however, the code for this third loop is all contained with a **do** loop, which iterates as long as the **r** and **k** values are less than the **kcolor** value, set to 256 earlier (but which could be smaller):

```
        do {
            xkp1 = (x+y)*(x-y) + pmin;
            ya = x*y;
            ykp1 = ya + ya + qmin;
            r = xkp1*xkp1 + ykp1*ykp1;
```

The program then computes real and imaginary parts of the complex number **z** specified by the Julia set's governing function. The code here uses double values to represent the two parts of the complex number. (We use complex numbers in drawing the Mandelbrot set, and you can choose to implement complex numbers within your own programs however you wish.) The **xkbp1** variable contains the real portion of the number, and the **ykbp1** variable contains the imaginary portion of the number. The function then squares the real and imaginary parts of the number, generating a double result, which is stored in the variable **r**. Then the program increments the **k** value, and checks the variable **r** against the maximum value specified in **kcolor**:

```
            k++;
            if (r >= kcolor) {
```

If **r** is greater than the maximum value, that means the point *escapes towards infinity* on the fractal. Points escaping towards infinity are drawn in the color specified by the **k** value, and are drawn at the point specified by the **np** and **nq** values, as shown in the following code:

```
ipen = k;
xp = const_scr*(double)np;
yp = (double)nq;
pDC->SetPixelV(xp,yp,ipen);
}
```

On the other hand, the Julia set also describes points governed by attraction—points *moving inward toward a center.* Such points will always have a value where **k** equals the max, and we draw them here in blue. (They can be drawn in any color you want, provided it is significantly different from the other color values in the fractal.)

```
if (k == kcolor) {
    ipen = RGB(0, 0, 255);
    xp = const_scr*(double)np;
    yp = (double)nq;
    pDC->SetPixelV(xp,yp,ipen);
}
```

It is important to note that the point may seem to be escaping towards infinity, and yet may also have a **k** value equal to **kcolor**. In such cases, the point will always be drawn as blue, not one of the other colors.

And finally:

```
    x = xkp1;
    y = ykp1;
  } while (r <= kcolor && k<=kcolor);
 }
 }
}
```

The drawing function exits whenever **r** or **k** exceeds **kcolor**, which then results in moving on to the next pixel in the series.

THE MANDELBROT SET FRACTAL

The Julia set is certainly very interesting and represents one of the most well known fractals in mathematics. However, the most recognized fractals in mathematics are probably those defined by the Mandelbrot set. The Mandelbrot set, like the Julia set, uses complex numbers and predefined starting points to draw points described by the fractal's equation. Although there are great number of Mandelbrot variations (just as there are Julia variations), all of them look similar to Figure 12-9.

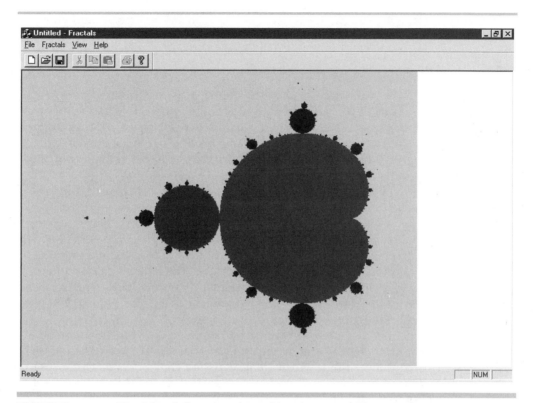

FIGURE 12-9. The Mandelbrot set drawn by the Fractals program

The Mandelbrot set is the classic fractal—it's the only set implemented in many plotting programs, and the source of most of the printed fractal images published in recent years. Despite all of its kudos and recognition, however, the Mandelbrot fractal is simply a graph: the x (horizontal) and y (vertical) coordinate axes represent ranges of two independent quantities. When plotting in 2D, the set uses different colors to symbolize levels of a third quantity that depends on the first two—just as was done with the Julia set. Plotting in 3D, the color quantity would instead represent a z-coordinate value that you would use to plot the fractal through a third dimension.

Just like the Julia set once again, the Mandelbrot's x-axis represents ordinary, real numbers; and the y-axis represents the series of imaginary numbers. So the fractal starts with any point on the complex plane—**C**, a constant. Then the fractal selects another complex number—this time, one that can vary—**Z**, a variable. To plot the fractal, you start with **Z=0** (where the real and imaginary axes cross), and you calculate the value of the fractal expression as follows:

```
Z(n)   = plot
Z(n+1) = Z^2 + C
```

In mathematical terms, you iterate the function $Z(n+1) = Z(n)^2 + C$. For certain values of **C**, the result "levels off" after a while. For all others, it grows without limit.

It turns out that testing whether a point is in the Mandelbrot set yields important information even if that point is found to be outside of the set. Substantial information can be gained by studying the *electrostatic potential* the set creates in the region outside of the set.

To grasp this in physical terms, imagine a metal pipe of very large diameter standing up on end. Standing up in the middle of this pipe is a very thin, stick-like object with the same length as the pipe, and with the unusual property of having a cross-section shaped like the Mandelbrot set. If the stick is given a potential of zero, and the pipe is given a high potential, an electrical field will be created in the region between the stick and the pipe. When the diameter of the pipe is increased to infinity, then a plane cutting horizontally through this system will represent the complex plane with the Mandelbrot set at its center. The infinite region containing the electrical field is the complement of the Mandelbrot set.

Equipotential lines, which are lines connecting points of equal potential, can be drawn in the Mandelbrot-complement region of this horizontal plane. These lines form a series of concentric rings, which are near-perfect circles at great distances from the origin, and are increasingly distorted and twisted closer to the Mandelbrot set region. These equipotential lines, and the *field lines* that cross them at right angles, tell us a lot about the shape and other characteristics of the Mandelbrot set.

A remarkable mathematical property of this system is that the potential of any point in the Mandelbrot-complement set is a simple function of its *escape time*. Escape time is defined as the number of iterations needed for the value of the Mandelbrot function to escape beyond a circle of some (arbitrary) large radius centered at the origin. Since the entire Mandelbrot set lies inside the circle of radius 2, any radius greater than or equal to 2 can be used. The larger the radius, however, the more accurate the approximation of the Mandelbrot complement set.

Put simply, the potential of a point in the Mandelbrot complement set is measured by how quickly the value diverges toward infinity. In the example program, we measure the potential of points within the Mandelbrot set purely as a means of determining the color of each point that we plot in the set. In the figure, then, the drawn colors correspond loosely to the colors of the set as the value diverges towards infinity. The program uses the **MandelSetPoten( )** function to measure the potential of a given point described by the parameters **cx** and **cy**:

```
double MandelSetPoten(double cx, double cy, int maxiter)
{
    double x, y, x2, y2, temp, potential;
```

```
int iter;

x = cx;
x2 = x*x;
y = cy;
y2 = y*y;
iter = 0;
```

When we first enter the **MandelSetPoten( )** function, the program sets the local **x** and **y** variables equal to the passed-in x- and y-coordinates (within the **cx** and **cy**) parameters. The code then generates values for x- and y-squared (represented by **x2** and **y2** in the code), and initializes the **iter** counter variable to 0. The **do** loop will test the code to see if the counter variable **iter** exceeds the cap value passed in within **maxiter**, as part of its exit test.

Within the **do** loop, then, is where we measure the actual potential of the value. We do this by generating new values for **x** and **y** based on their previous values and on incoming values of **cx** and **cy**. We then square **x** and **y** again. Relatively quickly, we can then determine whether the point tends towards infinity or tends towards some finite point. When reaching either conclusion, the program exits the **do** loop and moves on to the corresponding **if** statement. Here's the **do** loop:

```
do {
    temp = x2 - y2 + cx;
    y = 2.0*x*y + cy;
    x = temp;
    x2 = x*x;
    y2 = y*y;
    iter++;
} while ((iter < maxiter) && ((x2 + y2) < 10000.0));
```

Within the **if** statement, the program determines whether the loop was exited because the maximum number of test iterations was reached, or because the value of x-squared plus y-squared exceeds 10,000 (meaning it tends towards infinity). If the value tends towards infinity (**iter < maxiter == TRUE**), then the potential is determined as the natural logarithm of x-squared (represented by **x2**) plus y-squared divided by 2 (represented by **y2**), raised to the number of iterations, as shown here:

```
if (iter < maxiter)
    potential = 0.5 * log(x2 + y2) / powl(2.0,iter);
```

Otherwise, the point tends towards a finite endpoint and is deemed to have no potential, so the code sets the **potential** variable to 0. In any event, the program exits and returns the potential value to the **DrawMandelbrot( )** function:

```
else
    potential = 0.0;
return (potential);
}
```

The **DrawMandelbrot( )** function, basically, has the sole purpose of computing the current value of **x** and **y**, as well as assigning a color value to the pixel that corresponds to its potential value as returned by the **MandelSetPoten( )** function. At its entry, the function defines a set of values to be used subsequently for computing the current **x** and **y** points of the function. **DrawMandelbrot( )** also declares the value **c**, of the templated-type **complex**, defined by the Standard Template Library. Note in the declaration that **c** is of type double.

The **maxiter** flag specifies the maximum number of iterations that the program will go through each time it checks the potential of points within the **MandelSetPoten( )** function. You can vary this iterations value, but the program currently cuts it off at 16,000. Higher values will result in a more-accurate coloring, and lower values a less-accurate coloring of the fractal. The **iset** value instructs the program to draw the different potentials in two different colors; if you set this value to a non-1 value, the program will draw the potentials in the same color. Here is **DrawMandelbrot( )**:

```
void DrawMandelbrot(CDC *pDC)
{
  int nx, ny, iy, ix, ipen, maxiter = 16000, iflag = 0, iset = 1;
  complex<double> c;
  double xmin = -2.25, ymin, xmax = 0.75, ymax;
  double diff = 0.6482801, test1, test2, cx, cy, potent;
```

The **if** statement checks to make sure the value for **maxiter** is within the range the program deems prudent; you can, of course, raise or lower the values in this statement, or open the number of iterations to be input by the user.

```
  if ((maxiter >= 16000) || (maxiter <= 0))
    maxiter = 16000;
```

The next set of statements set some limits on values as appropriate to the environment in which you are drawing. All of the following values are customizable and will control the size, resolution, and repetitiveness of the figure:

```
  nx = 640;
  ny = 480;
  ymin = -1.125;
  ymax = 1.125;
```

Next, the code enters the outer of the two loops it uses to draw the Mandelbrot—this one corresponds to the y-coordinate in the drawing area, and the inner loop corresponds to the x-coordinate in the drawing area. Each time through the outer loop, the program code derives a value for **cy** based on the limits of the values for **y**, and the current value of the counter variable—that is, the line the program is currently on. The program then enters the inner loop, which counts through x-coordinate values in sequence until it reaches the set limits for the screen, drawing a color in each pixel. Following is the code that starts both of the **for** loops and determines the value for **cy**:

```
for (iy = 0; iy <= ny-1; iy++) {
   cy = ymin + iy*(ymax-ymin)/(ny-1);
   for (ix = 0; ix <= nx-1; ix++) {
```

Next, the program code creates the **cx** value. Like the **cy** value, the **cx** value is a function of the difference between the maximum and minimum allowable **x** values, the current value of the loop, and the maximum x-coordinate. The program then assigns the resulting **cx** value (which corresponds to the current x-coordinate) to the real portion of the **c** variable, and assigns the **cy** value (which corresponds to the current y-coordinate) to the imaginary portion of the **c** variable:

```
cx = xmin + ix*(xmax-xmin)/(nx-1);
c.real(cx);
c.imag(cy);
```

The maximum value for **test1** and **test2**, which the program uses to help it determine what color value to attach to the individual pixel, is 1. The code, therefore, sets the default value outside that range, and then checks the values of **cx** and **cy**. If they fall within certain ranges, the code changes the value of the test variables. In the first case, **test1,** the resulting value is the absolute value of 1 minus the square root of the quantity 1 minus 4 multiplied by the complex number **c**:

```
test1 = 2.0;
if ((cx >= -7.55e-1) && (cx <= 4.0e-1)) {
  if ((cy >= -6.6e-1) && (cy <= 6.6e-1))
    test1 = abs(1.0 - sqrt(1.0-4.0*c));
}
```

A similar process is used to set the value of the **test2** variable, although the test is across two different ranges, and the result is the absolute value of the quantity 4 multiplied by the complex number **c,** plus 1:

```
test2 = 2.0;
if ((cx >= -1.275e0) && (cx <= -7.45e-1)) {
  if ((cy >= -2.55e-1) && (cy <= 2.55e-1))
    test2 = abs(4.0*(c+1.0));
}
```

With some values now set for **test1** and **test2**, depending on the current value of **cx** and **cy**, the program code moves on to determining what color to paint the pixel:

```
if (test1 <= 1.0) {
   potent = 0;
   iflag = 1;
   if (iset != 0)
     ipen = 126;
```

```
    else
       ipen = 32;
}
```

In this first set, if the **cx** and **cy** values fell within the prescribed range, the program sets the drawing pen to either 32 or 126, depending on whether the potentials are drawn in different colors. Or:

```
else if (test2 <= 1.0) {
    potent = 0;
    iflag = 1;
    if (iset != 0)
       ipen = 104;
    else
       ipen = 32;
}
```

The second test occurs only when the first **if** statement evaluates to **false**. Again, it sets the drawing pen to either 32 or 104, depending on whether the potentials are drawn in different colors. As in the first test, pixel color determination occurs at this point only if the **cx** and **cy** values fell within the prescribed range. Otherwise, the code falls through to the last **else**, which calls the **MandelSetPoten( )** function to determine the potential value for the pixel:

```
else {
    potent = MandelSetPoten(cx,cy,maxiter);
    iflag = 0;
}
```

After calling the **MandelSetPoten( )** function to get the potential for the pixel, the code falls through into a final test. If the **iflag** variable is equal to 0—which occurs only if the program invoked the **MandelSetPoten( )** function—the program checks the **potent** variable. If it, too, is 0, the program draws with color 32 (black); otherwise, the program generates a color value for the pixel based on the returned potential value. (This color value will fall somewhere between 0 and 32; you may want to adjust it, depending on the number of colors you are displaying and the palette you use.) Following is the code for this final test:

```
if ((potent == 0.0) && (iflag==0))
    ipen = 32;
else if ((potent !=0) && (iflag==0))
    ipen = (int)(33.0 + 15.0*(potent-33.0)/diff);
```

After establishing the color to draw the pixel—by whatever means it uses—the program invokes the **SetPixelV( )** function to actually draw the pixel on screen. It then loops back through again, drawing each pixel on screen in turn:

```
    pDC->SetPixelV(ix,iy,ipen);
}
```

```
  }
}
```

As with all the other fractal functions, you may want to modify the values used by this function just to see the various results. As with the Julia set, there are an infinite number of possible Mandelbrot sets. The Mandelbrot sets, however, tend to return to the same form (the rounded shape shown in Figure 12-9). This is different from the Julia set, which shows a great deal less consistency.

All of the fractal functions discussed in this chapter are called by the **OnDraw( )** method in the **CFractalsView** class. This method is automatically called by the frame window whenever a change occurs to the frame window (such as resizing). **OnDraw( )** is automatically invoked whenever the document calls **UpdateAllViews( )**. In the Fractals program, we simply check the **GetCurrentFractal( )** method to see if we're updating because a user wants to draw something. If so, the **switch** statement processes the request; if not, **OnDraw( )** simply clears the screen. Here is **OnDraw( )**:

```
void CFractalsView::OnDraw(CDC* pDC)
{
  CFractalsDoc* pDoc = GetDocument();

  ASSERT_VALID(pDoc);
  pDC = GetDC();
  switch (pDoc->GetCurrentFractal()) {
    case 0:
      break;
```

The trick, of course, is that each time through the function, the **case** checking invokes one of the fractal drawing routines and then sets the current fractal value to 0—so that the next time through the function, the program won't try to redraw the previously requested fractal.

```
    case 1:
      DrawKamTorus(pDC);
      pDoc->SetCurrentFractal(0);
      break;
    case 2:
      DrawDuff(pDC);
      pDoc->SetCurrentFractal(0);
      break;
    case 3:
      DrawAbstract(pDC);
      pDoc->SetCurrentFractal(0);
      break;
    case 4:
      DrawJulias(pDC);
      pDoc->SetCurrentFractal(0);
```

```
      break;
    case 5:
      DrawMandelbrot(pDC);
      pDoc->SetCurrentFractal(0);
      break;
  }
}
```

As noted previously, you could use a memory device context, as opposed to the already defined device context, to maintain information about the current image on the screen and to redraw that image, providing the user with another option that would actually clear the device context. To perform such processing, you would have to add (into the constructor for the **CFractalsView** class) a call to the **CDC::CreateCompatibleDC( )** function. Whatever variable into which you placed the memory device context would need to keep its scope throughout the class, and could then be used by the component functions and the **OnDraw( )** function without the loss of the image each time the user refreshed the display.

The examples in this chapter provide an excellent introduction to the world of fractals, but they do not, by any means, cover the complete range of possibilities for drawing fractals in your own programs. You can vary the drawing routines shown here. You can also consult complex mathematics (linear algebra or fractal-specific) texts to learn other interesting functions that can be used to create fractals within your own programs. The important characteristics to keep in mind about most fractal-drawing functions is that they will almost all use complex numbers to generate the x- and y-coordinates for the fractals, as well as the colors for each of the pixels within the fractals—colors which the drawing functions, generally, will use to represent the value or scale of the z-coordinate.

An
Object-Oriented
Expression Parser

By Herbert Schildt

g_parser.h   parser2.h
parser1.h

T his chapter creates an *object-oriented expression parser* that can be used to evaluate an algebraic expression, such as (10 – 8) * 3. Expression parsers are quite useful and are applicable to a wide range of applications. They are also one of programming's more elusive entities. For various reasons, the procedures used to create an expression parser are not widely taught or disseminated. Indeed, many otherwise accomplished programmers are mystified by the process of parsing expressions.

In reality, expression parsing is straightforward, and in many ways is easier than several other programming jobs. This is because the task is well defined and works according to the strict rules of algebra. This chapter develops three versions of a class called **parser** that implements what is commonly referred to as a *recursive-descent parser*. The first two are nongeneric versions. The final version uses templates and may be applied to any numeric type.

Parsing Fundamentals

Before explaining parser development, a brief overview of expressions, parsing, and tokenizing is necessary.

Expressions

Since an expression parser evaluates an algebraic expression, it is important to understand the constituent parts of an expression. Although expressions can be made up of all types of information, this chapter deals only with numeric expressions. For our purposes, *numeric expressions* are composed of the following items:

- ◆ Numbers
- ◆ The operators +, –, /, *, ^, %, =
- ◆ Parentheses
- ◆ Variables

Here, the operator ^ indicates exponentiation, as it does in BASIC, and = is the assignment operator, as in C++. These items can be combined in expressions according to the rules of algebra. Here are some examples:

```
10 – 8
(100 – 5) * 14/6
a + b – c
10 ^ 5
a = 10 – b
```

Assume this precedence for each operator:

highest	+ − (unary)
	^
	* / %
	+ −
lowest	=

Operators of equal precedence evaluate from left to right.

In the examples, all variables are single letters (in other words, 26 variables, **A** through **Z,** are available). The variables are not case sensitive (**a** and **A** are treated as the same variable). For the first versions of the parser, all numeric values are elevated to **double**, although you could easily write the routines to handle other types of values. Finally, to keep the logic clear and easy to understand, only a minimal amount of error checking is included.

Parsing Expressions: The Problem

If you have not thought much about the problem of expression parsing, you might assume that not much effort is required. However, to better understand the problem, try to evaluate this simple expression:

10 − 2 * 3

You know that this expression is equal to the value 4. Although you could easily create a program that would compute that *specific* expression, the question is how to create a program that gives the correct answer for any *arbitrary* expression. At first you might think of an algorithm something like this:

```
a = get first operand
while(operands present) {
        op = get operator
        b = get second operand
        a = a op b
}
```

This routine gets the first operand, the operator, and the second operand, and then performs the first operation. It then gets the next operator and operand, performs the next operation, and so on. However, if you attempt to use this simplistic approach, the expression 10 - 2 * 3 will evaluate to 24 (that is, 8 * 3) instead of to 4 because this procedure neglects the precedence of the operators. You cannot just take the operands and operators in order from left to right, because the rules of algebra dictate that multiplication must be done before subtraction, et cetera. Furthermore, the problem only gets worse when you add parentheses, exponentiation, variables, unary operators, and the like.

Although there are a few ways to write a set of routines that evaluate expressions, the recursive-descent parser developed here is the one most easily written by a person. It is also the most commonly used. In the course of this chapter you will see how it got its name. (Some of the other methods used to write parsers employ complex tables that must be generated by another computer program. These are sometimes called *table-driven parsers*.)

Parsing an Expression

There are a number of ways to parse and evaluate an expression. For use with a recursive-descent parser, think of expressions as *recursive data structures*—that is, expressions defined in terms of themselves. If, for the moment, we assume that expressions can use only +, −, *, /, and parentheses, all expressions can be defined with the following rules:

> *expression* -> *term* [+ *term*] [− *term*]
>
> *term* -> *factor* [* *factor*] [/ *factor*]
>
> *factor* -> *variable*, *number*, or (*expression*)

The square brackets designate an optional element, and the -> means produces. In fact, the rules are usually called the *production rules* of an expression. Therefore, for the definition of *term* you could say: "*Term* produces *factor* times *factor*, or *factor* divided by *factor*". Notice that the precedence of the operators is implicit in the way an expression is defined.

The expression

> 10 + 5 * B

has two terms: 10, and 5 * B. The second term contains two factors: 5 and B. These factors consist of one number and one variable.

On the other hand, the expression

> 14 * (7 − C)

has two factors: 14 and (7 − C). The factors consist of one number and one parenthesized expression. The parenthesized expression contains two terms: one number and one variable.

This process forms the basis for a recursive-descent parser, which is a set of mutually recursive functions that work in a chainlike fashion and implement the production rules. At each appropriate step, the parser performs the specified operations in the algebraically correct sequence. To see how the production rules are used to parse an expression, let's work through an example using the following expression:

9 / 3 – (100 + 56)

Here is the sequence that you will follow:

1. Get the first term, 9 / 3.
2. Get each factor and divide the integers. The resulting value is 3.
3. Get the second term, (100 + 56). Because it begins with an opening parenthesis, start recursively analyzing the subexpression.
4. Get each term and add. The resulting value is 156.
5. Return from the recursive evaluation and subtract 156 from 3. The answer is –153.

If you are a little confused at this point, don't feel bad. This is a fairly complex concept that takes some getting used to. There are two basic things to remember about this recursive view of expressions. First, the precedence of the operators is implicit in the way the production rules are defined. Second, this method of parsing and evaluating expressions is very similar to the way humans evaluate mathematical expressions.

Tokenizing an Expression

Most often, and as is the case with this chapter's examples, the expression to be evaluated is represented as a character string. In order to evaluate such an expression, you need to be able to break the string into its components. This operation is fundamental to parsing, but is not actually part of the parser proper. Since all three parsers developed in this chapter use the same function to perform this task, we will examine that function now.

Each component of an expression is called a *token*. For example, the expression

A * B – (W + 10)

contains the tokens A, *, B, –, (, W, +, 10, and). Each token represents an indivisible unit of the expression. In general, you need a function that sequentially returns each token in the expression individually.

The tokenizing function must also be able to skip over spaces and tabs and detect the end of the expression. The function that we will use to do this is called **get_token( )**, which is a member function of each version of the **parser** class.

Besides the token itself, you will also need to know what type of token is being returned. For the parsers developed in this chapter, you need only three types: **VARIABLE**, **NUMBER**, and **OPERATOR**. (**OPERATOR** is used for both operators and parentheses.) These values are defined by the enumeration **typesT**, which is part of the **parser** class.

The **get_token( )** function is shown in the following listing. It obtains the next token from the expression pointed to by **exp_ptr** and puts it into the variable **token**. It puts the type of the token into the member variable **tok_type**. The variables **exp_ptr**, **token**, and **tok_type** are members of the **parser** class. Also shown is the helper function **isdelim( )**.

```
// Obtain the next token.
void parser::get_token()
{
  register char *temp;

  tok_type = UNDEFTOK;
  temp = token;
  *temp = '\0';

  if(!*exp_ptr) return; // at end of expression

  while(isspace(*exp_ptr)) ++exp_ptr; // skip over white space

  if(strchr("+-*/%^=()", *exp_ptr)){
    tok_type = OPERATOR;
    // advance to next char
    *temp++ = *exp_ptr++;
  }
  else if(isalpha(*exp_ptr)) {
    while(!isdelim(*exp_ptr)) *temp++ = *exp_ptr++;
    tok_type = VARIABLE;
  }
  else if(isdigit(*exp_ptr)) {
    while(!isdelim(*exp_ptr)) *temp++ = *exp_ptr++;
    tok_type = NUMBER;
  }

  *temp = '\0';
}
```

```
// Return true if c is a delimiter.
bool parser::isdelim(char c)
{
  if(strchr(" +-/*%^=()", c) || c==9 || c=='\r' || c==0)
    return true;
  return false;
}
```

Look closely at the preceding functions. After the first few initializations, **get_token( )** checks to see if the null terminating the expression string has been found. It does so by checking the character pointed to by **exp_ptr**. Since **exp_ptr** is a pointer to the expression being analyzed, if it points to a null the end of the expression has been reached. If there are still more tokens to retrieve from the expression, **get_token( )** first skips over any leading spaces. Once the spaces have been skipped, **exp_ptr** is pointing to either a number, a variable, an operator, or—if trailing spaces end the expression—a null. If the next character is an operator, it is returned as a string in **token**, and **OPERATOR** is placed in **tok_type**. If the next character is a letter instead, it is assumed to be one of the variables. It is returned as a string in **token**, and **tok_type** is assigned the value **VARIABLE**. If the next character is a digit, the entire number is read and placed in its string form in **token**, and its type is **NUMBER**. Finally, if the next character is none of the preceding, it is assumed that the end of the expression has been reached. In this case, **token** is null, which signals the end of the expression.

The function **isdelim( )** is a helper function that simplifies the task of determining if a character is a *delimiter*, which is a character used to separate one token from another.

As stated earlier, to keep the code in this function clean, a certain amount of error checking has been omitted and some assumptions have been made. For example, any unrecognized character may end an expression. Also, variables may be of any length, but only the first letter is significant. You can add more error checking and other details as your specific application dictates.

To better understand the tokenization process, study what **get_token( )** returns for each token, and type in the following expression:

A + 100 – (B * C) / 2

Token	Token Type
A	VARIABLE
+	OPERATOR
100	NUMBER
–	OPERATOR

Token	Token Type
(	OPERATOR
B	VARIABLE
*	OPERATOR
C	VARIABLE
)	OPERATOR
/	OPERATOR
2	NUMBER
null	null

Remember that **token** always holds a null-terminated string, even if it contains just a single character.

The remainder of this chapter develops three parsers. The first implements a minimal parser that works only with constant values. The second parser adds support for the use of variables. The third example implements the parser as a template class that can be used to parse expressions of any numeric type.

A Simple Expression Parser

This section develops a simple parser that can evaluate expressions consisting solely of constants, operators, and parentheses. This parser does not handle expressions that contain variables. Furthermore, all constants are assumed to be of type **double**. Though quite simple, the purpose of this first parser is to clearly show the key elements of recursive-descent parsing. It is, however, fully functional within its limitations.

Code

Following is the code for the simple parser called **parser1.h**.

parser1.h

```
/* This module contains the recursive descent
   parser that does not use variables.

   Call this file parser1.h
*/

#include <iostream>
#include <cctype>
#include <cstring>
using namespace std;
```

```
class parser {
  enum typesT { UNDEFTOK, OPERATOR, NUMBER};
  enum errorsT { SERROR, PARENS, NOEXP, DIVZERO };

  char *exp_ptr;  // points to the expression
  char token[80]; // holds current token
  typesT tok_type;  // holds token's type

  void eval_exp2(double &result);
  void eval_exp3(double &result);
  void eval_exp4(double &result);
  void eval_exp5(double &result);
  void eval_exp6(double &result);
  void atom(double &result);
  void get_token();
  void serror(errorsT error);
  bool isdelim(char c);
public:
  parser();
  double eval_exp(char *exp);
};

// Constructor
parser::parser()
{
  exp_ptr = 0;
}

// Parser entry point.
double parser::eval_exp(char *exp)
{
  double result;

  exp_ptr = exp;

  get_token();
  if(!*token) {
    serror(NOEXP); // no expression present
    return 0.0;
  }
  eval_exp2(result);
  if(*token) serror(SERROR); // last token must be null
```

```
  return result;
}

// Add or subtract two terms.
void parser::eval_exp2(double &result)
{
  register char op;
  double temp;

  eval_exp3(result);
  while((op = *token) == '+' || op == '-') {
    get_token();
    eval_exp3(temp);
    switch(op) {
      case '-':
        result = result - temp;
        break;
      case '+':
        result = result + temp;
        break;
    }
  }
}

// Multiply or divide two factors.
void parser::eval_exp3(double &result)
{
  register char op;
  double temp;

  eval_exp4(result);
  while((op = *token) == '*' || op == '/' || op == '%') {
    get_token();
    eval_exp4(temp);
    switch(op) {
      case '*':
        result = result * temp;
        break;
      case '/':
        if(!temp) serror(DIVZERO); // division by zero attempted
        else result = result / temp;
        break;
      case '%':
```

```
        result = (int) result % (int) temp;
        break;
    }
  }
}

// Process an exponent.
void parser::eval_exp4(double &result)
{
  double temp, ex;
  register int t;

  eval_exp5(result);
  if(*token== '^') {
    get_token();
    eval_exp4(temp);
    ex = result;
    if(temp==0.0) {
      result = 1.0;
      return;
    }
    for(t=(int)temp-1; t>0; --t) result = result * (double)ex;
  }
}

// Evaluate a unary + or -.
void parser::eval_exp5(double &result)
{
  register char  op;

  op = 0;
  if((tok_type == OPERATOR) && *token=='+' || *token == '-') {
    op = *token;
    get_token();
  }
  eval_exp6(result);
  if(op=='-') result = -result;
}

// Process a parenthesized expression.
void parser::eval_exp6(double &result)
{
  if((*token == '(')) {
```

```
    get_token();
    eval_exp2(result);
    if(*token != ')')
      serror(PARENS);
    get_token();
  }
  else atom(result);
}

// Get the value of a number.
void parser::atom(double &result)
{
  switch(tok_type) {
    case NUMBER:
      result = atof(token);
      get_token();
      return;
    default:
      serror(SERROR);
  }
}

// Display a syntax error.
void parser::serror(errorsT error)
{
  static char *e[]= {
      "Syntax Error",
      "Unbalanced Parentheses",
      "No expression Present",
      "Division by zero"
  };
  cout << e[error] << endl;
}

// Obtain the next token.
void parser::get_token()
{
  register char *temp;

  tok_type = UNDEFTOK;
  temp = token;
  *temp = '\0';
```

```
  if(!*exp_ptr) return; // at end of expression

  while(isspace(*exp_ptr)) ++exp_ptr; // skip over white space

  if(strchr("+-*/%^=()", *exp_ptr)){
    tok_type = OPERATOR;
    // advance to next char
    *temp++ = *exp_ptr++;
  }
/* not used by this parser
  else if(isalpha(*exp_ptr)) {
    while(!isdelim(*exp_ptr)) *temp++ = *exp_ptr++;
    tok_type = VARIABLE;
  }
*/
  else if(isdigit(*exp_ptr)) {
    while(!isdelim(*exp_ptr)) *temp++ = *exp_ptr++;
    tok_type = NUMBER;
  }

  *temp = '\0';
}

// Return true if c is a delimiter.
bool parser::isdelim(char c)
{
  if(strchr(" +-/*%^=()", c) || c==9 || c=='\r' || c==0)
    return true;
  return false;
}
```

Here is a program that demonstrates the parser:

```
#include <iostream>
#include "parser1.h"
using namespace std;

int main()
{
  char expstr[80];

  cout << "Enter a period to stop.\n";
```

```
    parser ob; // instantiate a parser

    for(;;) {
      cout << "Enter expression: ";
      cin.getline(expstr, 79);
      if(*expstr=='.') break;
      cout << "Answer is: " << ob.eval_exp(expstr) << "\n\n";
    }

    return 0;
}
```

Here is a sample run:

```
Enter a period to stop.
Enter expression: 10-2*3
Answer is: 4

Enter expression: (10-2)*3
Answer is: 24

Enter expression: 10/3
Answer is: 3.33333

Enter expression: .
```

ANNOTATIONS

This first parser can handle the following operators: +, −, *, /, and %. In addition, it can handle integer exponentiation (^) and the unary minus. The parser can also deal with parentheses correctly. Let's take a close look at how it works.

All three expression parsers developed in this chapter are built upon the **parser** class. The first expression parser uses the version shown here. Subsequent versions expand upon it.

```
class parser {
  enum typesT { UNDEFTOK, OPERATOR, NUMBER};
  enum errorsT { SERROR, PARENS, NOEXP, DIVZERO };

  char *exp_ptr;  // points to the expression
  char token[80]; // holds current token
  typesT tok_type;  // holds token's type

  void eval_exp2(double &result);
  void eval_exp3(double &result);
```

```
    void eval_exp4(double &result);
    void eval_exp5(double &result);
    void eval_exp6(double &result);
    void atom(double &result);
    void get_token();
    void serror(errorsT error);
    bool isdelim(char c);
public:
    parser();
    double eval_exp(char *exp);
};
```

The **parser** class begins by defining two enumerations. The first is **typesT** and it defines the constants that represent the types of tokens that can be returned by **get_token( )**. Since this version of the parser does not accept variables, **typesT** does not define the token type **VARIABLE**, mentioned earlier; but subsequent versions of the parser will. The enumeration **errorsT** defines constants that represent the types of errors the parser can report.

The **parser** class contains three private member variables. The expression to be evaluated is contained in a null-terminated string pointed to by **exp_ptr**. Thus, the parser evaluates expressions that are contained in standard ASCII strings. For example, the following strings contain expressions that the parser can evaluate:

"10 – 5"

"2 * 3.3 / (3.1416 * 3.3)"

When the parser begins execution, **exp_ptr** must point to the first character in the expression. As the parser executes, it works its way through the string until the null-terminator is encountered.

The **token** and **tok_type** members hold the current token and its type. These are assigned values by calling the **get_token( )** function. As explained, the **token** member contains the current token as a string, and **tok_type** contains a value of the enumeration **typesT**.

The entry point to the parser is through **eval_exp( )**, which must be called with a pointer to the expression to be analyzed. The actual evaluation of an expression takes place in the mutually recursive functions **eval_exp2( )** through **eval_exp6( )**, plus the **atom( )** function, which returns the value of a number. These functions form the recursive-descent parser. They implement an enhanced set of the expression production rules discussed earlier. The comments at the start of each function describe its role in parsing the expression. In subsequent versions of the parser, a function called **eval_exp1( )** will also be added.

The **serror( )** function reports syntax errors. It takes arguments of type **errorsT**. The functions **get_token( )** and **isdelim( )** are used to dissect the expression into its component parts and were described earlier. Notice, however, that the code in

get_token( ) that reads variable names has been commented out. Since this parser cannot handle variables, there is no reason for **get_token( )** to accept them. Attempting to use a variable simply results in a syntax error. The ability to handle variables is added in the next section.

To understand exactly how the parser evaluates an expression, work through the following expression. (Assume that **exp_ptr** points to the start of the expression.)

    10 – 3 * 2

When **eval_exp( )**, the entry point into the parser, is called, it gets the first token. If the token is null, the function prints the message **No Expression Present** and returns. However, in our example, the token contains the number **10**. Since the first token is not null, **eval_exp2( )** is called. As a result, **eval_exp2( )** calls **eval_exp3( )** and **eval_exp3( )** calls **eval_exp4( )**, which in turn calls **eval_exp5( )**. Then **eval_exp5( )** checks whether the token is a unary plus or minus, which in this case, it is not, so **eval_exp6( )** is called. At this point **eval_exp6( )** recursively calls either **eval_exp2( )** (in the case of a parenthesized expression), or **atom( )** to find the value of a number. Since the token is not a left parenthesis, **atom( )** is executed and **result** is assigned the value 10. Next, another token is retrieved, and the functions begin to return up the chain. Since the token is now the operator –, the functions return up to **eval_exp2( )**.

What happens next is very important. Because the token is –, it is saved in **op**. The parser then gets the next token, which is **3**, and the descent down the chain begins again. As before, **atom( )** is entered. The value 3 is returned in **result** and the token * is read. This causes a return back up the chain to **eval_exp3( )**, where the final token 2 is read. At this point, the first arithmetic operation occurs—the multiplication of 2 and 3. The result is returned to **eval_exp2( )** and the subtraction is performed. The subtraction yields the answer 4. Although this process may at first seem complicated, work through some other examples to verify that the method functions correctly every time.

Let's now look at how syntax checking is handled by the parser. In expression parsing, a syntax error is simply a situation in which the input expression does not conform to the strict rules required by the parser. Most of the time, this is caused by human error—usually typing mistakes. For example, the following expressions are not valid for the parsers in this chapter:

    10 ** 8
    (10 – 5) * 9)
    / 8

The first expression contains two operators in a row, the second has unbalanced parentheses, and the last has a division sign at the start of an expression.

As mentioned, syntax checking is handled by the **serror( )** function, which is called when an error is found. The recursive-descent method makes syntax checking easy because each function knows precisely what type of token it should receive at any given point. As syntax checking is implemented, the entire parser is not terminated on syntax error. It simply reports the error and continues on. This can lead to multiple error messages. It is, of course, possible to change this behavior; some suggestions are given at the end of this chapter.

This parser would be suitable for use by a desktop calculator, as is illustrated by the preceding program. Before it could be used in a more sophisticated application, however, it would need the ability to handle variables. That is the subject of the next section.

A Parser That Accepts Variables

All programming languages, scientific calculators, and spreadsheets use variables to store values for later use. Before our parser can be used for such applications, it needs to be expanded to include variables. To accomplish this, you need to add several things to the previous parser. First, of course, are the variables themselves. A function that obtains the value of a variable, and a function that handles the assignment operator, are also needed.

Code

parser2.h

The code for the parser that accepts variables, **parser2.h**, is shown in the following listing.

```
/* This module contains the recursive descent
   parser that recognizes variables.

   Call this file parser2.h
*/

#include <iostream>
#include <cctype>
#include <cstring>
using namespace std;


const int NUMVARS = 26;

class parser {
  enum typesT { UNDEFTOK, OPERATOR, NUMBER, VARIABLE};
  enum errorsT { SERROR, PARENS, NOEXP, DIVZERO };
```

```
  char *exp_ptr;  // points to the expression
  char token[80]; // holds current token
  typesT tok_type;  // holds token's type
  double vars[NUMVARS]; // holds variables's values

  void eval_exp1(double &result);
  void eval_exp2(double &result);
  void eval_exp3(double &result);
  void eval_exp4(double &result);
  void eval_exp5(double &result);
  void eval_exp6(double &result);
  void atom(double &result);
  void get_token();
  void putback();
  void serror(errorsT error);
  double find_var(char *s);
  bool isdelim(char c);
public:
  parser();
  double eval_exp(char *exp);
};

// Constructor
parser::parser()
{
  int i;

  exp_ptr = 0;

  for(i=0; i<NUMVARS; i++) vars[i] = 0.0;
}

// Parser entry point.
double parser::eval_exp(char *exp)
{
  double result;

  exp_ptr = exp;

  get_token();
  if(!*token) {
    serror(NOEXP); // no expression present
```

```
      return 0.0;
  }
  eval_exp1(result);
  if(*token) serror(SERROR); // last token must be null
  return result;
}

// Process an assignment.
void parser::eval_exp1(double &result)
{
  int slot;
  typesT ttok_type;
  char temp_token[80];

  if(tok_type==VARIABLE) {
    // save old token
    strcpy(temp_token, token);
    ttok_type = tok_type;

    // compute the index of the variable
    slot = toupper(*token) - 'A';

    get_token();
    if(*token != '=') {
      putback(); // return current token
      // restore old token - not assignment
      strcpy(token, temp_token);
      tok_type = ttok_type;
    }
    else {
      get_token(); // get next part of exp
      eval_exp2(result);
      vars[slot] = result;
      return;
    }
  }

  eval_exp2(result);
}

// Add or subtract two terms.
void parser::eval_exp2(double &result)
{
```

```
  register char op;
  double temp;

  eval_exp3(result);
  while((op = *token) == '+' || op == '-') {
    get_token();
    eval_exp3(temp);
    switch(op) {
      case '-':
        result = result - temp;
        break;
      case '+':
        result = result + temp;
        break;
    }
  }
}

// Multiply or divide two factors.
void parser::eval_exp3(double &result)
{
  register char op;
  double temp;

  eval_exp4(result);
  while((op = *token) == '*' || op == '/' || op == '%') {
    get_token();
    eval_exp4(temp);
    switch(op) {
      case '*':
        result = result * temp;
        break;
      case '/':
        if(!temp) serror(DIVZERO); // division by zero attempted
        else result = result / temp;
        break;
      case '%':
        result = (int) result % (int) temp;
        break;
    }
  }
}
```

```
// Process an exponent.
void parser::eval_exp4(double &result)
{
  double temp, ex;
  register int t;

  eval_exp5(result);
  if(*token== '^') {
    get_token();
    eval_exp4(temp);
    ex = result;
    if(temp==0.0) {
      result = 1.0;
      return;
    }
    for(t=(int)temp-1; t>0; --t) result = result * (double)ex;
  }
}


// Evaluate a unary + or -.
void parser::eval_exp5(double &result)
{
  register char  op;

  op = 0;
  if((tok_type == OPERATOR) && *token=='+' || *token == '-') {
    op = *token;
    get_token();
  }
  eval_exp6(result);
  if(op=='-') result = -result;
}


// Process a parenthesized expression.
void parser::eval_exp6(double &result)
{
  if((*token == '(')) {
    get_token();
    eval_exp2(result);
    if(*token != ')')
      serror(PARENS);
    get_token();
  }
  else atom(result);
}
```

```cpp
// Get the value of a number or a variable.
void parser::atom(double &result)
{
  switch(tok_type) {
    case VARIABLE:
      result = find_var(token);
      get_token();
      return;
    case NUMBER:
      result = atof(token);
      get_token();
      return;
    default:
      serror(SERROR);
  }
}

// Return a token to the input stream.
void parser::putback()
{
  char *t;

  t = token;
  for(; *t; t++) exp_ptr--;
}

// Display a syntax error.
void parser::serror(errorsT error)
{
  static char *e[]= {
      "Syntax Error",
      "Unbalanced Parentheses",
      "No expression Present",
      "Division by zero"
  };
  cout << e[error] << endl;
}

// Obtain the next token.
void parser::get_token()
{
  register char *temp;
```

```cpp
  tok_type = UNDEFTOK;
  temp = token;
  *temp = '\0';

  if(!*exp_ptr) return; // at end of expression

  while(isspace(*exp_ptr)) ++exp_ptr; // skip over white space

  if(strchr("+-*/%^=()", *exp_ptr)){
    tok_type = OPERATOR;
    // advance to next char
    *temp++ = *exp_ptr++;
  }
  else if(isalpha(*exp_ptr)) {
    while(!isdelim(*exp_ptr)) *temp++ = *exp_ptr++;
    tok_type = VARIABLE;
  }
  else if(isdigit(*exp_ptr)) {
    while(!isdelim(*exp_ptr)) *temp++ = *exp_ptr++;
    tok_type = NUMBER;
  }

  *temp = '\0';
}

// Return true if c is a delimiter.
bool parser::isdelim(char c)
{
  if(strchr(" +-/*%^=()", c) || c==9 || c=='\r' || c==0)
    return true;
  return false;
}

// Return the value of a variable.
double parser::find_var(char *s)
{
  if(!isalpha(*s)){
    serror(SERROR);
    return 0.0;
  }
  return vars[toupper(*token)-'A'];
}
```

To try the enhanced parser, you may use the same **main( )** function that you used for the simple parser. Just be sure to include **parser2.h** rather than **parser1.h**. With the enhanced parser, you can now enter expressions like the following:

A = 10 / 4
A + B
C = A * (F – 21)

Here is a sample run:

```
Enter a period to stop.
Enter expression: A = 10+5
Answer is: 15

Enter expression: B = A / 3
Answer is: 5

Enter expression: C = A * B
Answer is: 75

Enter expression: .
```

ANNOTATIONS

The code for the second parser is largely the same as the first. The only changes are various additions required to support the use of variables.

To begin, the identifier **VARIABLE** is added to the **typesT** enumeration, as shown here:

```
enum typesT { UNDEFTOK, OPERATOR, NUMBER, VARIABLE};
```

This constant is assigned to **tok_type** when a variable is read. Also, the code to handle variable names in **get_token( )** is no longer commented out.

As stated earlier, the letters **A** through **Z** are used for variables. The variables are stored in the **vars** array shown here, which is a member of the **parser** class:

```
double vars[NUMVARS]; // holds variables's values
```

Each variable uses one array location in a 26-element array of **double**s.

The **parser** constructor is modified so that it initializes the array of variables, as shown here:

```
// Constructor
parser::parser()
{
```

```
   int i;

   exp_ptr = 0;

   for(i=0; i<NUMVARS; i++) vars[i] = 0.0;
}
```

The variables are initialized to 0 as a courtesy to the user.

A function is needed to look up the value of a given variable. Because the variables are named **A** through **Z**, they can easily be used to index the array **vars** by subtracting the ASCII value for **A** from the variable name. The member function **find_var( )**, shown here, accomplishes this:

```
// Return the value of a variable.
double parser::find_var(char *s)
{
  if(!isalpha(*s)){
    serror(SERROR);
    return 0.0;
  }
  return vars[toupper(*token)-'A'];
}
```

As this function is written, it will actually accept long variable names, but only the first letter is significant. You can modify this to fit your needs.

The **atom( )** function is enhanced to handle both numbers and variables. The new version is shown here:

```
// Get the value of a number or a variable.
void parser::atom(double &result)
{
  switch(tok_type) {
    case VARIABLE:
      result = find_var(token);
      get_token();
      return;
    case NUMBER:
      result = atof(token);
      get_token();
      return;
    default:
      serror(SERROR);
  }
}
```

Notice that the **case** statement now checks for tokens of type **VARIABLE**. When a variable is encountered, its value is obtained and placed into **result**.

Technically, the foregoing additions are all that is needed for the parser to use variables correctly; however, there is no way for these variables to be given a value. Often this operation is done outside the parser, but you can treat the equal sign as an assignment operator (which is the way it is handled in C++) and make it part of the parser. There are various ways to do this. The method used by the second parser is to add another function, called **eval_exp1( )**, to the **parser** class. This function now begins the recursive-descent chain; therefore **eval_exp1( )**, not **eval_exp2( )**, is called by **eval_exp( )** to begin parsing the expression. Following is the **eval_exp1( )** function:

```
// Process an assignment.
void parser::eval_exp1(double &result)
{
  int slot;
  typesT ttok_type;
  char temp_token[80];

  if(tok_type==VARIABLE) {
    // save old token
    strcpy(temp_token, token);
    ttok_type = tok_type;

    // compute the index of the variable
    slot = toupper(*token) - 'A';

    get_token();
    if(*token != '=') {
      putback(); // return current token
      // restore old token - not assignment
      strcpy(token, temp_token);
      tok_type = ttok_type;
    }
    else {
      get_token(); // get next part of exp
      eval_exp2(result);
      vars[slot] = result;
      return;
    }
  }

  eval_exp2(result);
}
```

As you can see, **eval_exp1( )** needs to look ahead to determine whether an assignment is actually being made. This is because a variable name always precedes an assignment, but a variable name alone does not guarantee that an assignment expression follows. That is, the parser will accept A = 100 as an assignment but is also smart enough to know that A / 10 is not. To accomplish this, **eval_exp1( )** reads the next token from the input stream. If it is not an equal sign, the token is returned to the input stream for later use by calling **putback( )**, shown here:

```
// Return a token to the input stream.
void parser::putback()
{
  char *t;

  t = token;
  for(; *t; t++) exp_ptr--;
}
```

A Generic Parser

The two preceding parsers operated on numeric expressions in which all values were assumed to be of type **double**. While this is fine for applications that use **double** values, it is certainly excessive for applications that use only integer values, for example. Also, by hard-coding the type of values being evaluated, the application of the parser is unnecessarily restricted.

Fortunately, by using a class template, it is an easy task to create a generic version of the parser that can work with any type of data for which algebraic-style expressions are defined. Once this has been done, the parser can be used both with built-in types and with numeric types that you create.

g_parser.h

Code

Here is the generic version of the expression parser. Call this file **g_parser.h**.

```
/* A generic parser.

   Call this file g_parser.h
*/


#include <iostream>
#include <cctype>
#include <cstring>
using namespace std;
```

```
const int NUMVARS = 26;

template <class PType> class parser {
  enum typesT { UNDEFTOK, OPERATOR, NUMBER, VARIABLE };
  enum errorsT { SERROR, PARENS, NOEXP, DIVZERO };

  char *exp_ptr;  // points to the expression
  char token[80]; // holds current token
  typesT tok_type;  // holds token's type
  PType vars[NUMVARS]; // holds variable's values

  void eval_exp1(PType &result);
  void eval_exp2(PType &result);
  void eval_exp3(PType &result);
  void eval_exp4(PType &result);
  void eval_exp5(PType &result);
  void eval_exp6(PType &result);
  void atom(PType &result);
  void get_token(), putback();
  void serror(errorsT error);
  PType find_var(char *s);
  bool isdelim(char c);
public:
  parser();
  PType eval_exp(char *exp);
};

// Constructor
template <class PType> parser<PType>::parser()
{
  int i;

  exp_ptr = 0;

  for(i=0; i<NUMVARS; i++) vars[i] = (PType) 0;
}

// Parser entry point.
template <class PType> PType parser<PType>::eval_exp(char *exp)
{
  PType result;
```

```
  exp_ptr = exp;

  get_token();
  if(!*token) {
    serror(NOEXP); // no expression present
    return (PType) 0;
  }
  eval_exp1(result);
  if(*token) serror(SERROR); // last token must be null
  return result;
}

// Process an assignment.
template <class PType> void parser<PType>::eval_exp1(PType &result)
{
  int slot;
  typesT ttok_type;
  char temp_token[80];

  if(tok_type==VARIABLE) {
    // save old token
    strcpy(temp_token, token);
    ttok_type = tok_type;

    // compute the index of the variable
    slot = toupper(*token) - 'A';

    get_token();
    if(*token != '=') {
      putback(); // return current token
      // restore old token - not assignment
      strcpy(token, temp_token);
      tok_type = ttok_type;
    }
    else {
      get_token(); // get next part of exp
      eval_exp2(result);
      vars[slot] = result;
      return;
    }
  }

  eval_exp2(result);
}
```

```cpp
// Add or subtract two terms.
template <class PType> void parser<PType>::eval_exp2(PType &result)
{
  register char op;
  PType temp;

  eval_exp3(result);
  while((op = *token) == '+' || op == '-') {
    get_token();
    eval_exp3(temp);
    switch(op) {
      case '-':
        result = result - temp;
        break;
      case '+':
        result = result + temp;
        break;
    }
  }
}

// Multiply or divide two factors.
template <class PType> void parser<PType>::eval_exp3(PType &result)
{
  register char op;
  PType temp;

  eval_exp4(result);
  while((op = *token) == '*' || op == '/' || op == '%') {
    get_token();
    eval_exp4(temp);
    switch(op) {
      case '*':
        result = result * temp;
        break;
      case '/':
        if(!temp) serror(DIVZERO); // division by zero attempted
        else result = result / temp;
        break;
      case '%':
        result = (int) result % (int) temp;
        break;
```

```
    }
  }
}

// Process an exponent.
template <class PType> void parser<PType>::eval_exp4(PType &result)
{
  PType temp, ex;
  register int t;

  eval_exp5(result);
  if(*token== '^') {
    get_token();
    eval_exp4(temp);
    ex = result;
    if(temp== (PType) 0) {
      result = (PType) 1;
      return;
    }
    for(t=(int)temp-1; t>0; --t) result = result * ex;
  }
}

// Evaluate a unary + or -.
template <class PType> void parser<PType>::eval_exp5(PType &result)
{
  register char  op;

  op = 0;
  if((tok_type == OPERATOR) && *token=='+' || *token == '-') {
    op = *token;
    get_token();
  }
  eval_exp6(result);
  if(op=='-') result = -result;
}

// Process a parenthesized expression.
template <class PType> void parser<PType>::eval_exp6(PType &result)
{
  if((*token == '(')) {
    get_token();
    eval_exp2(result);
```

```cpp
    if(*token != ')')
      serror(PARENS);
    get_token();
  }
  else atom(result);
}


// Get the value of a number or a variable.
template <class PType> void parser<PType>::atom(PType &result)
{
  switch(tok_type) {
    case VARIABLE:
      result = find_var(token);
      get_token();
      return;
    case NUMBER:
      result = (PType) atof(token);
      get_token();
      return;
    default:
      serror(SERROR);
  }
}


// Return a token to the input stream.
template <class PType> void parser<PType>::putback()
{
  char *t;

  t = token;
  for(; *t; t++) exp_ptr--;
}


// Display a syntax error.
template <class PType> void parser<PType>::serror(errorsT error)
{
  static char *e[]= {
      "Syntax Error",
      "Unbalanced Parentheses",
      "No expression Present",
      "Division by zero"
  };
  cout << e[error] << endl;
```

```
}

// Obtain the next token.
template <class PType> void parser<PType>::get_token()
{
  register char *temp;

  tok_type = UNDEFTOK;
  temp = token;
  *temp = '\0';

  if(!*exp_ptr) return; // at end of expression

  while(isspace(*exp_ptr)) ++exp_ptr; // skip over white space

  if(strchr("+-*/%^=()", *exp_ptr)){
    tok_type = OPERATOR;
    // advance to next char
    *temp++ = *exp_ptr++;
  }
  else if(isalpha(*exp_ptr)) {
    while(!isdelim(*exp_ptr)) *temp++ = *exp_ptr++;
    tok_type = VARIABLE;
  }
  else if(isdigit(*exp_ptr)) {
    while(!isdelim(*exp_ptr)) *temp++ = *exp_ptr++;
    tok_type = NUMBER;
  }

  *temp = '\0';
}

// Return true if c is a delimiter.
template <class PType> bool parser<PType>::isdelim(char c)
{
  if(strchr(" +-/*%^=()", c) || c==9 || c=='\r' || c==0)
    return true;
  return false;
}

// Return the value of a variable.
template <class PType> PType parser<PType>::find_var(char *s)
{
```

```
  if(!isalpha(*s)){
    serror(SERROR);
    return (PType) 0;
  }
  return vars[toupper(*token)-'A'];
}
```

As you can see, the type of data now operated upon by the parser is specified by the generic type **PType**.

The following program demonstrates the generic parser:

```
#include <iostream>
#include "g_parser.h"
using namespace std;

int main()
{
  char expstr[80];

  // Demonstrate floating-point parser.
  parser<double> ob;

  cout << "Floating-point parser.   ";
  cout << "Enter a period to stop\n";
  for(;;) {
    cout << "Enter expression: ";
    cin.getline(expstr, 79);
    if(*expstr=='.') break;
    cout << "Answer is: " << ob.eval_exp(expstr) << "\n\n";
  }
  cout << endl;

  // Demonstrate integer-based parser.
  parser<int> Iob;

  cout << "Integer parser.   ";
  cout << "Enter a period to stop\n";
  for(;;) {
    cout << "Enter expression: ";
    cin.getline(expstr, 79);
```

```
    if(*expstr=='.') break;
    cout << "Answer is: " << Iob.eval_exp(expstr) << "\n\n";
  }

  return 0;
}
```

Here is a sample run:

```
Floating-point parser.  Enter a period to stop
Enter expression: a=10.1
Answer is: 10.1

Enter expression: b=3.2
Answer is: 3.2

Enter expression: a/b
Answer is: 3.15625

Enter expression: .

Integer parser.  Enter a period to stop
Enter expression: a=10
Answer is: 10

Enter expression: b=3
Answer is: 3

Enter expression: a/b
Answer is: 3

Enter expression: .
```

As you can see, the floating-point parser uses floating-point values, and the integer parser uses integer values.

ANNOTATIONS

The generic parser provides the same functionality as **parser2.h**, except the generic version can be used with any type of numeric data. This is accomplished by specifying the type of data operated upon by the parser as generic. Aside from this change, the parser works as explained earlier.

About one thing, however, be careful: The parser still must operate on standard numeric data types. For example, consider this fragment from **atom( )**:

```
case NUMBER:
  result = (PType) atof(token);
  get_token();
  return;
```

Although the data type of a value is **PType**, the **atof( )** function is still used to convert the string contained in **token** into its binary equivalent. This means you cannot instantiate a **g_parser** for objects that cannot be automatically converted from **double**—such as **complex**, for example. Of course, you could enhance the parser to recognize the **complex** type and handle it separately.

Enhancing and Improving the Parser

To keep them easy to understand and easily adaptable, the parsers in this chapter represent minimal, "no-frills" implementations. It is, however, quite easy to improve and enhance the parsers. Here are some ideas.

Since only rudimentary error checking is performed by the parsers, you might want to add detailed error reporting. For example, you could highlight the point in the expression at which an error was detected. This would allow the user to more easily find and correct a syntax error.

As explained in the annotations to the first parser, a syntax error does not terminate the execution of the parser, and multiple syntax-error messages may be issued. This can be an annoyance in some situations, but it can be a blessing in others because multiple errors may be caught. If you wish to stop the parser when an error is encountered, the best way is to implement the **serror( )** function so that it executes some sort of reset. A good way to do this is through the use of C++'s exception-handling mechanism (implemented through **try**, **catch**, and **throw**). Also, depending on the situation, you might use the function pair **setjmp( )** and **longjmp( )**. These two functions allow a program to branch to a *different* function. Therefore, **serror( )** could execute a **longjmp( )** to some safe point in your program outside the parser.

As the parser now stands, it can evaluate only numeric expressions. However, with a few additions, it is possible to enable the parser to evaluate other types of expressions, including strings, spatial coordinates, or complex numbers. For example, to allow the parser to evaluate string objects, you must make the following changes:

1. Use the standard **string** class to represent strings.

2. Define a new token type called **STRING**.

3.   Enhance **get_token( )** so that it recognizes quoted strings.

4.   Add a new case inside **atom( )** that handles **STRING**-type tokens.

After implementing these steps, the parser could handle string expressions like these:

a = "one"

b = "two"

c = a + b

The result in **c** should be the concatenation of **a** and **b**, or **"onetwo"**.

Here is one good application for the parser: Create a simple, pop-up application that accepts an expression entered by the user and then displays the result. This would make an excellent addition to nearly any commercial application. If you are programming for Windows, this would be especially easy to do.

Implementing
Language
Interpreters in C++

By Herbert Schildt

sb_parser.cpp   SBASIC.CPP

Have you ever wanted to create your own computer language? If you're like most programmers, you probably have. Frankly, the idea of being able to create, control, enhance, and modify your own computer language is very appealing. However, few programmers realize how easy and enjoyable it can be. Be assured that the development of a full-featured compiler is a major undertaking; the creation of a language interpreter, on the other hand, is a much simpler task. In this chapter, you will learn the secrets of language interpretation and see a working, practical example.

Interpreters are important for four widely separate reasons. First, interpreters can provide a truly interactive environment. Many applications, such as robotics, benefit from an interactive rather than a compiled environment. Second, because of the nature of language interpreters, they are especially well suited for interactive debugging. Third, interpreters are excellent for "script languages," such as query languages for database managers. And finally, interpreters allow the same program to run on a variety of different platforms. Only the interperter's run-time package must be implemented for each new environment. This is the reason Java was initially designed as an interpreted language.

Although compilers will always be at the front line of programming, interpreters have re-emerged as an important part of the programming environment. It is quite likely that you will need to write some form of interpreter (perhaps for a script language) during your career as a C++ programmer. Fortunately, C++ is an ideal language for creating interpreters.

In order to illustrate how an interpreter is designed, it is necessary to actually interpret some language. Although C++ would seem an obvious choice, it is simply far too large and complicated a language to easily create an interpreter for. The source code for an interpreter for even a small subset of the C++ language would be far too large to fit into a chapter of this book! Instead, we will use a subset of standard BASIC, hereafter referred to as *Small BASIC*, to illustrate interpreter techniques.

BASIC is chosen for three reasons. First, BASIC was designed to be an interpreter, which simplifies the task of implementing an interpreter for it. For example, standard BASIC does not support local variables, recursive functions, blocks, classes, overloading, templates, etc.—all of which increase the complexity of an interpreter. (This is why C++ is a much more difficult language to interpret than is BASIC.) The same principles used to interpret BASIC, however, will also apply to any other language, and you can use the routines developed here as a starting point.

The second reason for selecting BASIC is that a reasonable subset can be implemented with a relatively small amount of code. Finally, BASIC is chosen because most programmers have at least a passing acquaintance with it. If you don't know BASIC, don't worry. The commands used in Small BASIC are trivially easy to understand.

PROGRAMMER'S NOTE   *If you are particularly interested in interpreters, you will find the C interpreter described in* C: The Complete Reference, 3rd Edition, *Herbert Schildt, Osborne/McGraw-Hill, 1994, particularly interesting. If you think you might like to try your hand at a C++ interpreter, the C interpreter described there will be a good starting point.*

The Small BASIC Expression Parser

The single most important part of a language interpreter is the expression parser. As you know, an expression parser is used to transform numeric expressions such as (10 – X) / 23 into a form that the computer can understand and evaluate. Small BASIC adapts the expression parser developed in Chapter 13. (If you have not yet read Chapter 13, do so now. It provides the detailed description of the parser.) Although its fundamental operation is unchanged, the parser used for Small BASIC is sufficiently different that a specialized version is required.

Many of the changes to the parser allow it to handle the syntax of the BASIC language. For example, the parser must be able to recognize the BASIC keywords; it must not treat the = sign as an operator; and it must evaluate relational operators. The **get_token( )** function is substantially altered to handle the expanded demands placed upon it.

Other differences between the parsers in Chapter 13 and the one used here arise from efficiency considerations. For example, since both the interpreter itself and the expression parser read the same source code, it is more efficient for both subsystems to use the same pointer into the program being interpreted. In the parsers developed in Chapter 13, a pointer to the expression being evaluated was passed to the parser. But in the version used here, the pointer to the program being interpreted is global and both the interpreter and the parser use it. There are other smaller differences which are designed to improve the overall speed of the interpreter. Because interpreters are slow by nature, these efficiency enhancements are important.

Since the Small BASIC parser is optimized and integrated with the interpreter, the parser is no longer encapsulated within its own class. Instead, it is implemented using stand-alone functions. The side benefit of this is that both the interpreter and the parser can share some of the same code. For example, both use **get_token( )** and **serror( )**. It must be emphasized that encapsulating the parser (as is done in Chapter 13) would have been possible. Not doing so, however, allows the interpreter code to be streamlined in several instances.

Since the Small BASIC expression parser uses the same techniques described in Chapter 13, you will have no trouble following its operation. However, before examining the code, a few general comments are in order. We will begin by defining precisely what an expression is as it relates to Small BASIC.

Small BASIC Expressions

As they apply to the small BASIC interpreter developed in this chapter, expressions are composed of the following items:

- ◆ Integers
- ◆ The operators + − / * ^ = ( ) < > >= <= <>
- ◆ Variables

In BASIC, the ^ indicates exponentiation. The = is used for both assignments and for equality; relative to BASIC expressions, however, it is an operator only when used in a relational expression. (In standard BASIC, assignment is a statement and not an operation.) Not equal is denoted as < >. These items can be combined in expressions according the rules of algebra. Here are some examples:

7 − 8

(100 − 5) * 14 / 6

a + b − c

10 ^ 5

A < B

The precedence of the operators is as follows:

highest:	( )
	unary + −
	^
	* /
	+ −
lowest	< > <= >= <> =

Operators of equal precedence evaluate from left to right.

Small BASIC makes the following assumptions. All variables are single letters; this means 26 variables, the letters A through Z, are available for use. Although standard BASIC supports more variable names by allowing a number to follow a letter, as in X27, the Small BASIC interpreter developed here does not in the interest of simplicity. The variables are not case sensitive; **a** and **A** will be treated as the same variable. All numbers are integers, although you could easily write the routines to handle other types of values, such as floating-point numbers. Finally, no string variables are supported, although quoted string constants can be used for writing messages to the screen. These assumptions will be built into the parser.

Small BASIC Tokens

In Small BASIC, each token has two formats: external and internal. The external format is the text form that you use when writing a program. For example, "PRINT" is the external form of the PRINT command. Although it is possible for an interpreter to be designed in such a way that each token is used in its external text format, this is seldom (if ever) done because it is horribly inefficient. Instead, the internal format of a token, which is simply an integer, is used. For example, the PRINT command might be represented by a 1; the INPUT command by a 2; and so on. The advantage of the internal representation is that much faster routines can be written using integers rather than strings.

It is the job of **get_token( )** to convert the token from its external format into its internal format. Keep in mind that not all tokens will have different formats. For example, there is no advantage to converting most of the operators, because they are already single characters in their plain-text form.

Code

sb_parser.cpp

Following is the entire expression parser, modified for use in the small BASIC interpreter. You should put this code into its own file. (When added together, the code to the parser and the interpreter make a fairly large file, so two separately compiled files are recommended.) The meaning and use of the external variables will be described shortly, when the interpreter is discussed.

```
/* The Small BASIC expression Parser

   This parser is an adaptation of the parser
   described in Chapter 13.  It is
   designed to support simple language
   interpreters, such as Small BASIC.

   Call this file sb_parser.cpp
*/


#include <iostream>
#include <cctype>
#include <cstdlib>
#include <cstring>
using namespace std;

// The Small Basic token types.
enum typesT { UNDEFTOK, OPERATOR, NUMBER, VARIABLE, COMMAND,
              STRING, QUOTE };
```

```
// The Small Basic command tokens.
enum SBtokensT { UNKNCOM, PRINT, INPUT, IF, THEN, FOR, NEXT, TO,
                 GOTO, GOSUB, RETURN, EOL, FINISHED, END };

/* These are the constants used to call serror() when
   a syntax error occurs.  Add more if you like.
   NOTE: SERROR is a generic error message used when
   nothing else seems appropriate. */
enum errorsT
    { SERROR, PARENS, NOEXP, DIVZERO, EQUAL_EXP,
      NOT_VAR, LAB_TAB_FULL, DUP_LAB, UNDEF_LAB,
      THEN_EXP, TO_EXP, TOO_MNY_FOR, NEXT_WO_FOR,
      TOO_MNY_GOSUB, RET_WO_GOSUB, MISS_QUOTE };

enum double_ops { LE=1, GE, NE };

extern char *prog;  // points into the program
extern char *p_buf; // points to start of program

extern int variables[26]; // variables

extern struct commands {
  char command[20];
  SBtokensT tok;
} table[];

extern char token[80]; // holds string representation of token
extern typesT token_type; // contains type of token
extern SBtokensT tok; // holds the internal representation of token

void eval_exp(int &result);
void eval_exp1(int &result);
void eval_exp2(int &result);
void eval_exp3(int &result);
void eval_exp4(int &result);
void eval_exp5(int &result);
void eval_exp6(int &result);
void atom(int &result);
void putback();
void serror(errorsT error);
typesT get_token();
SBtokensT look_up(char *s);
```

```
bool isdelim(char c);
bool is_sp_tab(char c);
int find_var(char *s);

// Entry point into parser.
void eval_exp(int &result)
{
  get_token();
  if(!*token) {
    serror(NOEXP);
    return;
  }
  eval_exp1(result);
  putback(); // return last token read to input stream
}

// Process relational operators.
void eval_exp1(int &result)
{
  // Relational operators.
  char relops[] = {
    GE, NE, LE, '<', '>', '=', 0
  };

  int temp;
  register char op;

  eval_exp2(result);
  op = *token;
  if(strchr(relops, op)) {
    get_token();
    eval_exp1(temp);
    switch(op) { // perform the relational operation
      case '<':
        result = result < temp;
        break;
      case LE:
        result = result <= temp;
        break;
      case '>':
        result = result > temp;
        break;
      case GE:
```

```
            result = result >= temp;
            break;
        case '=':
            result = result == temp;
            break;
        case NE:
            result = result != temp;
            break;
        }
    }
}

//   Add or subtract two terms.
void eval_exp2(int &result)
{
    register char op;
    int temp;

    eval_exp3(result);
    while((op = *token) == '+' || op == '-') {
        get_token();
        eval_exp3(temp);
        switch(op) {
            case '-' :
                result = result - temp;
                break;
            case '+':
                result = result + temp;
                break;
        }
    }
}

// Multiply or divide two factors.
void eval_exp3(int &result)
{
    register char op;
    int temp;

    eval_exp4(result);
    while((op = *token) == '*' || op == '/') {
        get_token();
        eval_exp4(temp);
```

```
    switch(op) {
      case '*' :
        result = result * temp;
        break;
      case '/':
        if(!temp) serror(DIVZERO); // division by zero attempted
        result = result / temp;
        break;
    }
  }
}

// Process integer exponent.
void eval_exp4(int &result)
{
  int temp, ex;
  register int t;

  eval_exp5(result);
  if(*token== '^') {
    get_token();
    eval_exp4(temp);
    if(!temp) {
      result = 1;
      return;
    }
    ex = result;
    for(t=temp-1; t>0;  t--) result = result * ex;
  }
}

// Is a unary + or -.
void eval_exp5(int &result)
{
  register char op;

  op = 0;
  if((token_type==OPERATOR) &&
     *token=='+' || *token=='-')
  {
    op = *token;
    get_token();
  }
```

```
    eval_exp6(result);
    if(op=='-') result = -result;
}


// Process parenthesized expression.
void eval_exp6(int &result)
{
  if(*token == '(') {
    get_token();
    eval_exp2(result);
    if(*token != ')')
      serror(PARENS);
    get_token();
  }
  else
    atom(result);
}


// Find value of number or variable.
void atom(int &result)
{
  switch(token_type) {
    case VARIABLE:
      result = find_var(token);
      get_token();
      return;
    case NUMBER:
      result = atoi(token);
      get_token();
      return;
    default:
      serror(SERROR);
  }
}


// Find the value of a variable.
int find_var(char *s)
{
  if(!isalpha(*s)){
    serror(NOT_VAR); // not a variable
    return 0;
  }
  return variables[toupper(*token)-'A'];
```

```
}

// Display an error message.
void serror(errorsT error)
{
  char *p, *temp;
  int linecount = 0;
  register int i;

  static char *e[]= {
    "Syntax error",
    "Unbalanced parentheses",
    "No expression present",
    "Division by zero",
    "Equal sign expected",
    "Not a variable",
    "Label table full",
    "Duplicate label",
    "Undefined label",
    "THEN expected",
    "TO expected",
    "Too many nested FOR loops",
    "NEXT without FOR",
    "Too many nested GOSUBs",
    "RETURN without GOSUB",
    "Double qoutes needed"
  };
  cout << e[error];

  p = p_buf;
  while(p != prog) {  // find line number of error
    p++;
    if(*p == '\r') {
      linecount++;
    }
  }
  cout << " in line " << linecount << ".\n";

  temp = p;  // display line with error
  for(i=0; i<20 && p>p_buf && *p!='\n'; i++, p--);
  for(; p<=temp; p++) cout << *p;

  throw(1); // throw an exception
```

```
}

// Get a token.
typesT get_token()
{
  register char *temp;

  token_type = UNDEFTOK;
  tok = UNKNCOM;
  temp = token;

  if(*prog=='\0') { // end of file
    *token = '\0';
    tok = FINISHED;
    return(token_type=OPERATOR);
  }

  while(is_sp_tab(*prog)) ++prog;  // skip over white space

  if(*prog=='\r') { // crlf
    ++prog; ++prog;
    tok = EOL; *token='\r';
    token[1]='\n'; token[2]=0;
    return (token_type = OPERATOR);
  }

  if(strchr("<>", *prog)) { // check for double op
    switch(*prog) {
      case '<':
        if(*(prog+1)=='>') {
          prog++; prog++;
          *temp = NE;
        }
        else if(*(prog+1)=='=') {
          prog++; prog++;
          *temp = LE;
        }
        else {
          prog++;
          *temp = '<';
        }
        temp++;
        *temp = '\0';
```

```
      break;
    case '>':
      if(*(prog+1)=='=') {
        prog++; prog++;
        *temp = GE;
      }
      else {
        prog++;
        *temp = '>';
      }
      temp++;
      *temp = '\0';
      break;
  }
  return(token_type = OPERATOR);
}

if(strchr("+-*^/=;(),", *prog)){ // operator
  *temp = *prog;
  prog++; // advance to next position
  temp++;
  *temp = '\0';
  return (token_type=OPERATOR);
}

if(*prog=='"') { // quoted string
  prog++;
  while(*prog!='"'&& *prog!='\r') *temp++ = *prog++;
  if(*prog=='\r') serror(MISS_QUOTE);
  prog++; *temp = '\0';
  return(token_type=QUOTE);
}

if(isdigit(*prog)) { // number
  while(!isdelim(*prog)) *temp++ = *prog++;
  *temp = '\0';
  return(token_type = NUMBER);
}

if(isalpha(*prog)) { // var or command
  while(!isdelim(*prog)) *temp++ = *prog++;
  token_type = STRING;
}
```

```
  *temp = '\0';

  // see if a string is a command or a variable
  if(token_type==STRING) {
    tok = look_up(token); // convert to internal rep
    if(!tok) token_type = VARIABLE;
    else token_type = COMMAND; // is a command
  }
  return token_type;
}


// Return a token to input stream.
void putback()
{

  char *t;

  t = token;
  for(; *t; t++) prog--;
}


/* Look up a token's internal representation in the
   token table.
*/
SBtokensT look_up(char *s)
{
  register int i;
  char *p;

  // convert to lowercase
  p = s;
  while(*p){
    *p = tolower(*p);
    p++;
  }

  // see if token is in table
  for(i=0; *table[i].command; i++)
    if(!strcmp(table[i].command, s))
      return table[i].tok;
  return UNKNCOM; // unknown command
}
```

```
// Return true if c is a delimiter.
bool isdelim(char c)
{
  if(strchr(" ;,+-<>/*%^=()", c) || c==9 || c=='\r' || c==0)
    return true;
  return false;
}

// Return true if c is space or tab.
bool is_sp_tab(char c)
{
  if(c==' ' || c=='\t') return true;
  else return false;
}
```

ANNOTATIONS

The parser as it is shown can handle the following operators: +, –, *, /, integer exponentiation (^), the relational operators, and the unary minus. The parser also deals with parentheses correctly. Notice that it has six levels as well as the **atom( )** function, which returns the value of a number.

At the core of the Small BASIC parser is the **get_token( )** function. This function is an expanded version of the one shown in Chapter 13. The changes here allow it to tokenize not just expressions, but also other elements of the BASIC language, such as keywords and strings.

In Small BASIC, the program is stored as one long, null-terminated string. The **get_token( )** function progresses through the program a character at a time. The next character to be read is pointed to by a global character pointer. In the version of **get_token( )** shown here, this pointer is called **prog**. The **prog** pointer is global because it must maintain its value between calls to **get_token( )** and allow other functions access to it.

The parser developed in this chapter uses six token types: **OPERATOR**, **VARIABLE**, **NUMBER**, **COMMAND**, **STRING**, and **QUOTE**. **OPERATOR** is used for both operators and parentheses. **VARIABLE** is used when a variable is encountered. **NUMBER** is for numbers. The **COMMAND** type is assigned when a BASIC command is found. **STRING** is a temporary type used inside **get_token( )** until a determination is made about a token. Type **QUOTE** is for quoted strings. The global variable **token_type** holds the token type. The internal representation of the token is placed into the global **tok**.

Look closely at **get_token( )**. Because people like to put spaces into expressions to add clarity, leading spaces are skipped over using the function **is_sp_tab( )** which returns **true** if its argument is a space or tab. Once the spaces have been skipped, **prog** will be pointing to either a number, a variable, a command, a carriage return/linefeed, an operator, a quoted string, or a null if trailing spaces end the program. If a carriage return is next, **tok** is set equal to **EOL**, a carriage return/linefeed sequence is stored in **token**, and **OPERATOR** is put into **token_type**.

Next, the function checks for double operators such as <=. The **get_token( )** function converts double operators into their internal representation. The values **NE**, **GE**, and **LE** are defined by an enumeration outside of **get_token( )**. If the next character is a single operator, it is returned as a string in the global variable **token**, and the type of **OPERATOR** is placed in **token_type**. Otherwise, the function checks for a quoted string. If none is encountered, **get_token( )** checks if the next token is a number, by seeing if the next character is a digit. If, instead, the next character is a letter, then it will be either a variable or a command (such as **PRINT**). The function **look_up( )** compares the token against commands in a table and, if it finds a match, returns the appropriate internal representation of the command. (The **look_up( )** function will be discussed later.) If a match is not found, then the token is assumed to be a variable. Finally, if the token is none of the above, it is assumed that the end of the expression has been reached and **token** is null, signaling the end of the expression.

To better understand how this version of **get_token( )** works, study what the function returns for each token and type for the following expression:

PRINT A + 100 – (B * C) / 2

Token	Token Type
PRINT	COMMAND
A	VARIABLE
+	OPERATOR
100	NUMBER
–	OPERATOR
(	OPERATOR
B	VARIABLE
*	OPERATOR
C	VARIABLE
)	OPERATOR
/	OPERATOR
2	NUMBER

Remember that **token** will always hold a null-terminated string, even if it contains just a single character.

To evaluate an expression, set **prog** to point to the beginning of the string that holds the expression; and call **eval_exp( )** with the variable you want to hold the result. Notice that **eval_exp1( )** is different from the one shown in Chapter 13. As you might recall, **eval_exp1( )** was used in the earlier chapter to handle the assignment operator. In BASIC, however, assignment is a statement, not an operation. Therefore, **eval_exp1( )** is not used for assignment when parsing expressions found in BASIC programs. Instead, it is used to evaluate the relational operators. If you use the interpreter to experiment with other types of languages, then you may need to add a function called **eval_exp0( )**, which would be used to handle assignment as an operator.

One other important difference between the parser classes here and in Chapter 13 is that in Chapter 13, the null terminating the string that held the expression indicated the end of the expression. In this version, the end of the expression is signaled by the end of the line or anything else that is not part of an expression, such as a BASIC command.

You should pay special attention to the **serror( )** function, which is used to report errors. When a syntax error is detected, **serror( )** is called with the identifier of the error that occurred. The function then displays the appropriate error message, the line number in which the error occurred, and part of the line that contains the error. As the comments preceding the **errorsT** enumeration indicate, the "syntax error" message is used when nothing else applies. Otherwise, a specific error is reported. Notice that **serror( )** ends by throwing an exception using a **throw** statement. This exception must be caught by a **catch** statement that takes some reasonable action. For the purposes of the Small BASIC interpreter, the **catch** statement is found in **main( )** and simply stops program execution.

As stated earlier, the Small BASIC interpreter will only recognize the variables **A** through **Z**. Each variable will use one array location in a 26-element array of integers called **variables**. This array is defined in the interpreter code as shown here, with each variable initialized to 0:

```
int variables[26] = { // 26 user variables, A-Z
  0, 0, 0, 0, 0, 0, 0, 0, 0,
  0, 0, 0, 0, 0, 0, 0, 0, 0,
  0, 0, 0, 0, 0, 0, 0, 0
};
```

Because the variable names are the letters **A** through **Z**, they can easily be used to index the array **variables** by subtracting the ASCII value for **A** from the variable name. The function **find_var( )** finds a variable's value. As it is currently written, **find_var( )** will actually accept long variable names, but only the first letter is significant. You can modify it to enforce single-letter variable names if you like.

The Small BASIC Interpreter

Interpreters consist of two pieces: the parser, which evaluates expressions, and the interpreter proper, which actually executes the program. In this section the interpreter module is examined.

SBASIC.CPP

Code

All the code for the Small BASIC interpreter, except those elements found in the expression parser file, is shown in the following listing. You should compile both the interpreter and the parser files and link them together. Call the executable version SBASIC.

```
/* A Small BASIC interpreter

   You can easily expand this interpreter or
   use it as a starting point for developing
   your own computer language.

   Call this file SBASIC.CPP
*/

#include <iostream>
#include <fstream>
#include <cctype>
#include <cstdlib>
#include <cstring>
using namespace std;

const int NUM_LAB = 100;
const int LAB_LEN = 10;
const int FOR_NEST = 25;
const int SUB_NEST = 25;
const int PROG_SIZE = 10000;

// The Small Basic token types.
enum typesT { UNDEFTOK, OPERATOR, NUMBER, VARIABLE, COMMAND,
              STRING, QUOTE };

// The Small Basic command tokens.
enum SBtokensT { UNKNCOM, PRINT, INPUT, IF, THEN, FOR, NEXT, TO,
                 GOTO, GOSUB, RETURN, EOL, FINISHED, END };
```

```
/* These are the constants used to call serror() when
   a syntax error occurs.  Add more if you like.
   NOTE: SERROR is a generic error message used when
   nothing else seems appropriate. */
enum errorsT
      { SERROR, PARENS, NOEXP, DIV_ZERO, EQUAL_EXP,
        NOT_VAR, LAB_TAB_FULL, DUP_LAB, UNDEF_LAB,
        THEN_EXP, TO_EXP, TOO_MNY_FOR, NEXT_WO_FOR,
        TOO_MNY_GOSUB, RET_WO_GOSUB, MISS_QUOTE };

char *prog; // points into the program
char *p_buf; // points to start of program

int variables[26]= { // 26 user variables,  A-Z
  0, 0, 0, 0, 0, 0, 0, 0, 0,
  0, 0, 0, 0, 0, 0, 0, 0, 0,
  0, 0, 0, 0, 0, 0, 0, 0
};

// keyword lookup table
struct commands {
  char command[20]; // string form
  SBtokensT tok; // internal representation
} table[] = { // commands must be entered lowercase
  "print", PRINT, // in this table.
  "input", INPUT,
  "if", IF,
  "then", THEN,
  "goto", GOTO,
  "for", FOR,
  "next", NEXT,
  "to", TO,
  "gosub", GOSUB,
  "return", RETURN,
  "end", END,
  "", END  // mark end of table
};

char token[80];
typesT token_type;
SBtokensT tok;
```

```
// label lookup table
struct label {
  char name[LAB_LEN]; // label
  char *p; // points to label's location in source file
} label_table[NUM_LAB];

// support for FOR loops
struct for_stack {
  int var; // counter variable
  int target; // target value
  char *loc; // place in source code to loop to
} fstack[FOR_NEST]; // stack for FOR/NEXT loop

char *gstack[SUB_NEST]; // stack for gosub

int ftos;  // index to top of FOR stack
int gtos;  // index to top of GOSUB stack

void print();
void scan_labels();
void find_eol();
void exec_goto();
void exec_if();
void exec_for();
void next();
void fpush(struct for_stack i);
void input();
void gosub();
void greturn();
void gpush(char *s);
void label_init();
void assignment();
char *find_label(char *s);
char *gpop();
struct for_stack fpop();
bool load_program(char *p, char *fname);
int get_next_label(char *s);

// prototypes for functions in the parser file
void eval_exp(int &result);
typesT get_token();
void serror(errorsT error), putback();
```

```
int main(int argc, char *argv[])
{
  if(argc!=2) {
    cout << "Usage: sbasic <filename>\n";
    return 1;
  }

  // allocate memory for the program
  try {
    prog = new char [PROG_SIZE];
  } catch(bad_alloc xa) {
    cout << "Allocation Failure\n";
    return 1;
  }

  p_buf = prog;

  // load the program to execute
  if(!load_program(prog, argv[1])) return 1;

  // begin main interpreter try block
  try {
    scan_labels(); // find the labels in the program
    ftos = 0; // initialize the FOR stack index
    gtos = 0; // initialize the GOSUB stack index
    do {
      token_type = get_token();
      // check for assignment statement
      if(token_type==VARIABLE) {
        putback(); // return the var to the input stream
        assignment(); // must be assignment statement
      }
      else // is command
        switch(tok) {
          case PRINT:
            print();
            break;
          case GOTO:
            exec_goto();
            break;
          case IF:
            exec_if();
            break;
```

```
          case FOR:
            exec_for();
            break;
          case NEXT:
            next();
            break;
          case INPUT:
            input();
            break;
          case GOSUB:
            gosub();
            break;
          case RETURN:
            greturn();
             break;
          case END:
            return 0;
        }
    } while (tok != FINISHED);
  } // end of try block

  /* catch throws here.  As implemented, only
     serror() throws an exception.  However,
     when creating your own languages, you can
     throw a variety of different exceptions.
  */
  catch(int) {
    return 1; // fatal error
  }

  return 0;
}

// Load a program.
bool load_program(char *p, char *fname)
{
  ifstream in(fname, ios::in | ios::binary);
  int i=0;

  if(!in) {
    cout << "File not found ";
    cout << "-- be sure to specify .BAS extension.\n";
    return false;
  }
```

```
  i = 0;
  do {
    *p = in.get();
    p++; i++;
  } while(!in.eof() && i<PROG_SIZE);

  // null terminate the program
  if(*(p-2)==0x1a) *(p-2) = '\0'; // discard eof marker
  else *(p-1) = '\0';

  in.close();
  return true;
}

// Find all labels.
void scan_labels()
{
  int addr;
  char *temp;

  label_init(); // zero all labels
  temp = prog;  // save pointer to top of program

  // if the first token in the file is a label
  get_token();
  if(token_type==NUMBER) {
    strcpy(label_table[0].name, token);
    label_table[0].p = prog;
  }

  find_eol();
  do {
    get_token();
    if(token_type==NUMBER) {
      addr = get_next_label(token);
      if(addr == -1 || addr == -2) {
        (addr == -1) ? serror(LAB_TAB_FULL) : serror(DUP_LAB);
      }
      strcpy(label_table[addr].name, token);

      // save current location in program
      label_table[addr].p = prog;
    }
```

```
    // if not on a blank line, find next line
    if(tok!=EOL) find_eol();
  } while(tok!=FINISHED);
  prog = temp; // restore original location
}


// Find the start of the next line.
void find_eol()
{
  while(*prog!='\n'  && *prog!='\0') ++prog;
  if(*prog) prog++;
}


/* Return index of next free position in label array.
   -1 is returned if the array is full.
   -2 is returned when duplicate label is found.
*/
int get_next_label(char *s)
{
  register int i;

  for(i=0; i<NUM_LAB; ++i) {
    if(label_table[i].name[0]==0) return i;
    if(!strcmp(label_table[i].name, s)) return -2;
  }

  return -1;
}


/* Find location of given label.  A null is returned
   if label is not found; otherwise a pointer to the
   position of the label is returned.
*/
char *find_label(char *s)
{
  register int i;

  for(i=0; i<NUM_LAB; ++i)
    if(!strcmp(label_table[i].name, s))
      return label_table[i].p;
  return 0; // error condition
}
```

```cpp
/* Initialize the array that holds the labels.
   By convention, a null label name indicates that
   the array position is unused.
*/
void label_init()
{
  register int i;

  for(i=0; i<NUM_LAB; ++i)
    label_table[i].name[0] = 0;
}

// Assign a variable a value.
void assignment()
{
  int var, value;

  // get the variable name
  get_token();
  if(!isalpha(*token)) {
    serror(NOT_VAR);
    return;
  }

  // convert to index into variable table
  var = toupper(*token)-'A';

  // get the equal sign
  get_token();
  if(*token != '=') {
    serror(EQUAL_EXP);
    return;
  }

  // get the value to assign
  eval_exp(value);

  // assign the value
  variables[var] = value;
}

// Execute a simple version of the BASIC PRINT statement.
void print()
{
```

```
int result;
int len=0, spaces;
char last_delim, str[80];

do {
  get_token(); // get next list item
  if(tok==EOL || tok==FINISHED) break;
  if(token_type==QUOTE) { // is string
    cout << token;
    len += strlen(token);
    get_token();
  }
  else { // is expression
    putback();
    eval_exp(result);
    get_token();
    cout << result;
    itoa(result, str, 10);
    len += strlen(str); // save length
  }
  last_delim = *token;

  // if comma, move to next tab stop
  if(*token == ',') {
    // compute number of spaces to move to next tab
    spaces = 8 - (len % 8);
    len += spaces; // add in the tabbing position
    while(spaces) {
      cout << " ";
      spaces--;
    }
  }
  else if(*token==';') {
    cout << " ";
    len++;
  }
  else if(tok!=EOL && tok!=FINISHED) serror(SERROR);
} while (*token==';' || *token==',');

if(tok==EOL || tok==FINISHED) {
  if(last_delim != ';' && last_delim != ',')
    cout << endl;
}
else serror(SERROR);
```

```
}

// Execute a GOTO statement.
void exec_goto()
{
  char *loc;

  get_token(); // get label to go to

  // find the location of the label
  loc = find_label(token);
  if(loc==NULL)
    serror(UNDEF_LAB); // label not defined

  else prog = loc;  // start program running at that loc
}

// Execute an IF statement.
void exec_if()
{
  int result;

  eval_exp(result); // get value of expression

  if(result) { // is true so process target of IF
    get_token();
    if(tok!=THEN) {
      serror(THEN_EXP);
      return;
    } // else, target statement will be executed
  }
  else find_eol(); // find start of next line
}

// Execute a FOR loop.
void exec_for()
{
  struct for_stack stckvar;
  int value;

  get_token(); // read the control variable
  if(!isalpha(*token)) {
```

```
    serror(NOT_VAR);
    return;
  }
  // save index of control var
  stckvar.var = toupper(*token)-'A';

  get_token(); // read the equal sign
  if(*token != '=') {
    serror(EQUAL_EXP);
    return;
  }

  eval_exp(value); // get initial value

  variables[stckvar.var] = value;

  get_token();
  if(tok!=TO) serror(TO_EXP); // read and discard the TO

  eval_exp(stckvar.target); // get target value

  /* if loop can execute at least once,
     push info on stack */
  if(value >= variables[stckvar.var]) {
    stckvar.loc = prog;
    fpush(stckvar);
  }
  else // otherwise, skip loop code altogether
    while(tok!=NEXT) get_token();
}

// Execute a NEXT statement.
void next()
{
  struct for_stack stckvar;

  stckvar = fpop(); // read the loop info

  variables[stckvar.var]++; // increment control var

  // if done, return
  if(variables[stckvar.var] > stckvar.target) return;
```

```
    fpush(stckvar);  // otherwise, restore the info
    prog = stckvar.loc;  // loop
}


// Push the FOR stack.
void fpush(struct for_stack stckvar)
{
  if(ftos==FOR_NEST)
    serror(TOO_MNY_FOR);

  fstack[ftos] = stckvar;
  ftos++;
}


// Pop the FOR stack.
struct for_stack fpop()
{
  if(ftos==0)
    serror(NEXT_WO_FOR);

  ftos--;
  return(fstack[ftos]);
}


// Execute a simple form of the BASIC INPUT command.
void input()
{
  char var;
  int i;

  get_token(); // see if prompt string is present
  if(token_type==QUOTE) {
    cout << token; // if so, print it and check for comma
    get_token();
    if(*token != ',') serror(SERROR);
    get_token();
  }
  else cout << "? "; // otherwise, prompt with ?
  var = toupper(*token)-'A'; // get the input var

  cin >> i; // read input

  variables[var] = i; // store it
}
```

```
// Execute a GOSUB command.
void gosub()
{
  char *loc;

  get_token();

  // find the label to call
  loc = find_label(token);
  if(loc==NULL)
    serror(UNDEF_LAB); // label not defined
  else {
    gpush(prog); // save place to return to
    prog = loc;  // start program running at that loc
  }
}

// Return from GOSUB.
void greturn()
{
  prog = gpop();
}

// Push GOSUB stack.
void gpush(char *s)
{
  if(gtos==SUB_NEST)
    serror(TOO_MNY_GOSUB);

  gstack[gtos] = s;
  gtos++;
}

// Pop GOSUB stack.
char *gpop()
{
  if(gtos==0)
    serror(RET_WO_GOSUB);

  gtos--;
  return(gstack[gtos]);
}
```

ANNOTATIONS

Since the code for the Small BASIC interpreter is fairly long, we'll examine each section separately.

The Keywords

As stated at the start of this chapter, Small BASIC interprets a small subset of the BASIC language. Here are keywords that it recognizes:

PRINT

INPUT

IF

THEN

FOR

NEXT

TO

GOTO

GOSUB

RETURN

END

The internal representation of these commands—plus **EOL**, for end-of-line, and **FINISHED**, which signals the end of the program—are enumerated as shown here.

```
enum SBtokensT { UNKNCOM, PRINT, INPUT, IF, THEN, FOR, NEXT, TO,
                 GOTO, GOSUB, RETURN, EOL, FINISHED, END };
```

Notice that **SBtokensT** begins with **UNKNCOM**. This value is used by the **look_up( )** function (discussed shortly) to indicate an unknown command.

In order for the external representation of a token to be converted into the internal representation, both the external and internal formats are held in an array of structures called **table**, shown next. Notice that a null string marks the end of the table.

```
// keyword lookup table
struct commands {
  char command[20]; // string form
  SBtokensT tok; // internal representation
```

```
} table[] = { // commands must be entered lowercase
  "print", PRINT, // in this table.
  "input", INPUT,
  "if", IF,
  "then", THEN,
  "goto", GOTO,
  "for", FOR,
  "next", NEXT,
  "to", TO,
  "gosub", GOSUB,
  "return", RETURN,
  "end", END,
  "", END  // mark end of table
};
```

The function **look_up( )**, shown next, uses **table** to return either a token's internal representation or a **UNKNCOM** if no match is found. (This function is part of the parser file, discussed earlier.)

```
/* Look up a token's internal representation in the
   token table.
*/
SBtokensT look_up(char *s)
{
  register int i;
  char *p;

  // convert to lowercase
  p = s;
  while(*p){
    *p = tolower(*p);
    p++;
  }

  // see if token is in table
  for(i=0; *table[i].command; i++)
    if(!strcmp(table[i].command, s))
      return table[i].tok;
  return UNKNCOM; // unknown command
}
```

Loading the Program

No integral editor is included in the Small BASIC interpreter. Instead, you must create a BASIC program using a standard text editor. When Small BASIC begins, the program is read in and then executed by the interpreter. The function that loads the program is called **load_program( )**.

```
// Load a program.
bool load_program(char *p, char *fname)
{
  ifstream in(fname, ios::in | ios::binary);
  int i=0;

  if(!in) {
    cout << "File not found ";
    cout << "-- be sure to specify .BAS extension.\n";
    return false;
  }

  i = 0;
  do {
    *p = in.get();
    p++; i++;
  } while(!in.eof() && i<PROG_SIZE);

  // null terminate the program
  if(*(p-2)==0x1a) *(p-2) = '\0'; // discard eof marker
  else *(p-1) = '\0';

  in.close();
  return true;
}
```

As the comments indicate, this function will discard any trailing **EOF** marker found in the text file. As you may know, some editors append an end-of-file marker; others do not. The **load_program( )** function handles both cases.

The Main Loop

All interpreters are driven by a top-level loop that operates by reading the next token from the program and selecting the appropriate action to process it. The Small

BASIC interpreter is no exception. The main loop for the Small BASIC interpreter looks like this:

```
do {
  token_type = get_token();
  // check for assignment statement
  if(token_type==VARIABLE) {
    putback(); // return the var to the input stream
    assignment(); // must be assignment statement
  }
  else // is command
    switch(tok) {
      case PRINT:
        print();
        break;
      case GOTO:
        exec_goto();
        break;
      case IF:
        exec_if();
        break;
      case FOR:
        exec_for();
        break;
      case NEXT:
        next();
        break;
      case INPUT:
        input();
        break;
      case GOSUB:
        gosub();
        break;
      case RETURN:
        greturn();
        break;
      case END:
        return 0;
    }
} while (tok != FINISHED);
```

First, a token is read from the program. Assuming no syntax errors have been made, if the token is a variable, then an assignment statement is occurring.

Otherwise, the token must be a command, and the appropriate **case** statement is selected based on the value of **tok**. Let's see how each of these commands works.

The Assignment Function

In BASIC, assignment is a statement, not an operation. The general form of a BASIC assignment statement is

var-name = expression

The assignment statement is interpreted using the **assignment( )** function shown here:

```
// Assign a variable a value.
void assignment()
{
  int var, value;

  // get the variable name
  get_token();
  if(!isalpha(*token)) {
    serror(NOT_VAR);
    return;
  }

  // convert to index into variable table
  var = toupper(*token)-'A';

  // get the equal sign
  get_token();
  if(*token != '=') {
    serror(EQUAL_EXP);
    return;
  }

  // get the value to assign
  eval_exp(value);

  // assign the value
  variables[var] = value;
}
```

The first thing **assignment( )** does is to read a token from the program. This will be the variable whose value will be assigned. If it is not a valid variable, an error will be reported. Next, the equal sign is read. Then, **eval_exp( )** is called so that the value to assign to the variable can be computed. Finally, the value is assigned to the variable. The **assignment( )** function is surprisingly simple and uncluttered because the expression parser and the **get_token( )** function do much of the "messy" work.

The PRINT Command

In BASIC, the PRINT command is actually quite powerful and flexible. Although it is beyond the scope of this chapter to create a function that supports all the functionality of the PRINT command, the one developed here embodies PRINT's most important essential features. The general form of the Small BASIC PRINT command is

> PRINT *arg-list*

where *arg-list* is a comma- or semicolon-separated list of expressions or quoted strings. The function **print( )**, shown next, interprets the PRINT command.

```
// Execute a simple version of the BASIC PRINT statement.
void print()
{
  int result;
  int len=0, spaces;
  char last_delim, str[80];

  do {
    get_token(); // get next list item
    if(tok==EOL || tok==FINISHED) break;
    if(token_type==QUOTE) { // is string
      cout << token;
      len += strlen(token);
      get_token();
    }
    else { // is expression
      putback();
      eval_exp(result);
      get_token();
      cout << result;
      itoa(result, str, 10);
      len += strlen(str); // save length
    }
    last_delim = *token;

    // if comma, move to next tab stop
```

```
  if(*token == ',') {
    // compute number of spaces to move to next tab
    spaces = 8 - (len % 8);
    len += spaces; // add in the tabbing position
    while(spaces) {
      cout << " ";
      spaces--;
    }
  }
  else if(*token==';') {
    cout << " ";
    len++;
  }
  else if(tok!=EOL && tok!=FINISHED) serror(SERROR);
} while (*token==';' || *token==',');

if(tok==EOL || tok==FINISHED) {
  if(last_delim != ';' && last_delim != ',')
    cout << endl;
}
else serror(SERROR);
}
```

The PRINT command can be used to print a list of variables and quoted strings on the screen. If one item is separated from the next by a semicolon, then one space is printed between them. If two items are separated by a comma, the second item will be displayed beginning with the next tab position. If the list ends in a comma or semicolon, then no newline is issued. Here are some examples of valid PRINT statements:

PRINT X; Y; "THIS IS A STRING"

PRINT 10 / 4

PRINT

The last example simply prints a newline.

Notice that **print( )** makes use of the **putback( )** function to return a token to the input stream, because **print( )** must look ahead to see whether the next item to be printed is a quoted string or a numeric expression. If it is an expression, then the first term in the expression must be returned to the input stream so that the expression parser can correctly compute the value of the expression.

The INPUT Command

In BASIC, the INPUT command is used to read information from the keyboard into a variable. It has two general forms. The first is

INPUT *var-name*

which displays a question mark and waits for input. The second form is

INPUT *"prompt-string", var-name*

which displays a prompting message and waits for input. The function **input( )**, shown next, implements the INPUT command.

```
// Execute a simple form of the BASIC INPUT command.
void input()
{
  char var;
  int i;

  get_token(); // see if prompt string is present
  if(token_type==QUOTE) {
    cout << token; // if so, print it and check for comma
    get_token();
    if(*token != ',') serror(SERROR);
    get_token();
  }
  else cout << "? "; // otherwise, prompt with ?
  var = toupper(*token)-'A'; // get the input var

  cin >> i; // read input

  variables[var] = i; // store it
}
```

The operation of this function is straightforward and should be clear after you've read the comments.

The GOTO Command

In standard BASIC, the most important form of program control is the lowly GOTO. The object of a GOTO must be a line number, and this traditional approach is preserved in Small BASIC. However, Small BASIC does not require a line number for each line; one is needed only if that line will be the target of a GOTO. The general form of the GOTO is

GOTO *line-number*

The main complexity associated with the GOTO is that both forward and backward jumps must be allowed. Satisfying this constraint efficiently requires that the entire program be scanned prior to execution and the location of each label be placed in a table. Then, each time a GOTO is executed, the location of the target line can be looked up and program control transferred to that point. The table that holds the labels is declared like this:

```
// label lookup table
struct label {
  char name[LAB_LEN]; // label
  char *p; // points to label's location in source file
} label_table[NUM_LAB];
```

The routine that scans the program and puts each label's location in the table is called **scan_labels( )** and is listed here along with several of its support functions:

```
// Find all labels.
void scan_labels()
{
  int addr;
  char *temp;

  label_init(); // zero all labels
  temp = prog;   // save pointer to top of program

  // if the first token in the file is a label
  get_token();
  if(token_type==NUMBER) {
    strcpy(label_table[0].name, token);
    label_table[0].p = prog;
  }

  find_eol();
  do {
    get_token();
    if(token_type==NUMBER) {
      addr = get_next_label(token);
      if(addr == -1 || addr == -2) {
        (addr == -1) ? serror(LAB_TAB_FULL) : serror(DUP_LAB);
```

```
      }
      strcpy(label_table[addr].name, token);

      // save current location in program
      label_table[addr].p = prog;
    }

    // if not on a blank line, find next line
    if(tok!=EOL) find_eol();
  } while(tok!=FINISHED);
  prog = temp; // restore original location
}

// Find the start of the next line.
void find_eol()
{
  while(*prog!='\n'  && *prog!='\0') ++prog;
  if(*prog) prog++;
}

/* Return index of next free position in label array.
   -1 is returned if the array is full.
   -2 is returned when duplicate label is found.
*/
int get_next_label(char *s)
{
  register int i;

  for(i=0; i<NUM_LAB; ++i) {
    if(label_table[i].name[0]==0) return i;
    if(!strcmp(label_table[i].name, s)) return -2;
  }

  return -1;
}

/* Find location of given label.  A null is returned
   if label is not found; otherwise a pointer to the
   position of the label is returned.
*/
char *find_label(char *s)
{
  register int i;
```

```
  for(i=0; i<NUM_LAB; ++i)
    if(!strcmp(label_table[i].name, s))
      return label_table[i].p;
  return 0; // error condition
}


/* Initialize the array that holds the labels.
   By convention, a null label name indicates that
   the array position is unused.
*/
void label_init()
{
  register int i;

  for(i=0; i<NUM_LAB; ++i)
    label_table[i].name[0] = 0;
}
```

Two types of errors are reported by **scan_labels( )**. The first is duplicate labels. In BASIC (and most other languages) no two labels can be the same. Second, a full label table is reported. The table's size is defined by **NUM_LAB**, which you can set to any size you desire.

Once the label table has been built, it is quite easy to execute a GOTO instruction as is shown here in **exec_goto( )**:

```
// Execute a GOTO statement.
void exec_goto()
{
  char *loc;

  get_token(); // get label to go to

  // find the location of the label
  loc = find_label(token);
  if(loc==NULL)
    serror(UNDEF_LAB); // label not defined
  else prog = loc;  // start program running at that loc
}
```

The support function **find_label( )** looks up a label in the label table and returns a pointer to it. If the label is not found, a null—which can never be a valid pointer—is returned. If the address is not null, it is assigned to the global **prog**, causing execution to resume at the location of the label. (Remember, **prog** is a pointer to the place at which the program is currently being executed.) If the label is not found, an undefined label message is issued.

The IF Statement

The Small BASIC interpreter executes a subset of the standard BASIC's IF statement. In Small BASIC, no ELSE is allowed. (However, you will find it easy to add the ELSE once you understand the operation if the IF.) The IF statement takes this general form:

> IF *expression rel-op expression* THEN *statement*

The statement that follows the THEN is executed only if the relational expression is true. The following function, called **exec_if( )**, executes the IF statement:

```
// Execute an IF statement.
void exec_if()
{
  int result;

  eval_exp(result); // get value of expression

  if(result) { // is true so process target of IF
    get_token();
    if(tok!=THEN) {
      serror(THEN_EXP);
      return;
    } // else, target statement will be executed
  }
  else find_eol(); // find start of next line
}
```

The **exec_if( )** function operates as follows. First, the value of the relational expression is computed. If the expression is true, the target of the THEN is executed; otherwise, **find_eol( )** finds the start of the next line. Notice that if the expression is true, the **exec_if( )** simply returns. This causes the main loop to iterate and the next token is read. Since the target of an IF is a statement, returning to the main loop simply causes the target statement to be executed as if it were on its own line. If the expression is false, then the start of the next line is found before execution returns to the main loop.

The FOR Loop

The implementation of the BASIC FOR loop presents a challenging problem that lends itself to a rather elegant solution. The general form of the FOR loop is

> FOR *control-var = initial-value* TO *target-value*
> .
> .
> .
> NEXT

The Small BASIC version of the FOR allows only positively running loops that increment the control variable by 1 at each iteration. The STEP command is not supported.

In BASIC, as in C++, loops may be nested to several levels. The main challenge presented by this is keeping the information associated with each loop straight. (That is, each NEXT must be associated with the proper FOR.) The solution to this problem is to implement the FOR loop using a stack-based mechanism.

At the top of the loop, information about the status of the control variable, the target value, and the location of the top of the loop in the program is pushed onto a stack. Each time the NEXT is encountered, this information is popped, the control variable updated, and its value checked against the target value. If the control value exceeds the target, the loop stops and execution continues with the line following the NEXT statement. Otherwise, the updated information is pushed back onto the stack and execution resumes at the top of the loop.

Implementing a FOR loop in this way works not only for a single loop but also for nested loops, because the innermost NEXT will always be associated with the innermost FOR. (The last information pushed on the stack will be the first information popped.) Once an inner loop terminates, its information is popped from the stack and an outer loop's information, if it exists, comes to the top of the stack. Thus, each NEXT is automatically associated with its corresponding FOR.

To support the FOR loop, a stack must be created that holds the loop information, as shown here.

```
// support for FOR loops
struct for_stack {
  int var; // counter variable
  int target; // target value
  char *loc; // place in source code to loop to
} fstack[FOR_NEST]; // stack for FOR/NEXT loop
```

The value of **FOR_NEST** defines how deeply nested the FOR loops may be (25 is generally more than adequate).

The FOR stack is managed by two stack functions called **fpush( )** and **fpop( )**, which are shown here.

```
// Push the FOR stack.
void fpush(struct for_stack stckvar)
{
  if(ftos==FOR_NEST)
    serror(TOO_MNY_FOR);

  fstack[ftos] = stckvar;
  ftos++;
}


// Pop the FOR stack.
```

```
struct for_stack fpop()
{
  if(ftos==0)
    serror(NEXT_WO_FOR);

  ftos--;
  return(fstack[ftos]);
}
```

Now that the necessary support is in place, the functions that execute the FOR and NEXT statements can be developed as follows:

```
// Execute a FOR loop.
void exec_for()
{
  struct for_stack stckvar;
  int value;

  get_token(); // read the control variable
  if(!isalpha(*token)) {
    serror(NOT_VAR);
    return;
  }
  // save index of control var
  stckvar.var = toupper(*token)-'A';

  get_token(); // read the equal sign
  if(*token != '=') {
    serror(EQUAL_EXP);
    return;
  }

  eval_exp(value); // get initial value

  variables[stckvar.var] = value;

  get_token();
  if(tok!=TO) serror(TO_EXP); // read and discard the TO

  eval_exp(stckvar.target); // get target value

  /* if loop can execute at least once,
     push info on stack */
  if(value >= variables[stckvar.var]) {
    stckvar.loc = prog;
```

```
    fpush(stckvar);
  }
  else // otherwise, skip loop code altogether
    while(tok!=NEXT) get_token();
}


// Execute a NEXT statement.
void next()
{
  struct for_stack stckvar;

  stckvar = fpop(); // read the loop info

  variables[stckvar.var]++; // increment control var

  // if done, return
  if(variables[stckvar.var] > stckvar.target) return;

  fpush(stckvar);  // otherwise, restore the info
  prog = stckvar.loc;  // loop
}
```

You should be able to follow the operation of these routines by reading the comments. As the code stands, it does not prevent a GOTO out of a FOR loop; however, jumping out of a FOR loop will corrupt the FOR stack and should be avoided.

The stack-based solution to the FOR loop problem can be generalized to all loops. Although Small BASIC does not implement any other loop statements, you can apply the same sort of procedure to any type of loop, including the WHILE and DO/WHILE loops. Also, as you will see in the next section, the stack-based solution can be applied to any language element that may be nested, including calling subroutines.

The GOSUB

Although Small BASIC does not support true stand-alone subroutines, it does allow portions of a program to be called and returned from using the GOSUB and RETURN statements. The general form of a GOSUB/RETURN is

GOSUB *line-num*
.
.
.
line-num
subroutine code
RETURN

Calling a subroutine, even the limited subroutines as implemented in BASIC, requires the use of a stack. The reason is similar to that given for the FOR statement: to allow nested subroutine calls. Because it is possible to have one subroutine call another, a stack is necessary to ensure that a RETURN statement is associated with its proper GOSUB. The GOSUB stack is defined as follows:

```
char *gstack[SUB_NEST]; // stack for gosub
```

As you can see, the **gstack** is simply an array of character pointers. It holds the location in the program to return to, once a subroutine has finished.

Here are the function **gosub( )** and its support routines:

```
// Execute a GOSUB command.
void gosub()
{
  char *loc;

  get_token();

  // find the label to call
  loc = find_label(token);
  if(loc==NULL)
    serror(UNDEF_LAB); // label not defined
  else {
    gpush(prog); // save place to return to
    prog = loc;  // start program running at that loc
  }
}


// Return from GOSUB.
void greturn()
{
  prog = gpop();
}


// Push GOSUB stack.
void gpush(char *s)
{
  if(gtos==SUB_NEST)
    serror(TOO_MNY_GOSUB);

  gstack[gtos] = s;
  gtos++;
}
```

```
// Pop GOSUB stack.
char *gpop()
{
  if(gtos==0)
    serror(RET_WO_GOSUB);

  gtos--;
  return(gstack[gtos]);
}
```

The GOSUB command works like this: When a GOSUB is encountered, the current value of **prog** is pushed onto the GOSUB stack. (This is the point in the program to which the subroutine will return once it is finished.) The targeted line number is looked up and its associated address assigned to **prog**. This causes program execution to resume at the start of the subroutine. When a RETURN is encountered, the GOSUB stack is popped and this value is assigned to **prog**, causing execution to continue on the next line after the GOSUB statement. Because the return address is pushed onto the GOSUB stack, subroutines may be nested. In each case, the most recently called subroutine will be the one returned from when its RETURN statement is encountered. (That is, the return address of the most recently called subroutine will be on the top of the **gstack** stack.) This process allows GOSUBs to be nested to any depth.

Using Small BASIC

Here is a sampling of programs that Small BASIC will execute. Notice that both upper- and lowercase are supported for the keywords. You will want to write several of your own programs, too. Also, try writing programs that have syntax errors and observe the way the Small BASIC reports them.

The following program exercises all of the commands supported by Small BASIC. Call this program TEST1.BAS.

```
PRINT "This program demonstrates all commands."
FOR X = 1 TO 100
PRINT X; X/2, X; X*X
NEXT
GOSUB 300
PRINT "hello"
INPUT H
IF H<11 THEN GOTO 200
PRINT 12-4/2
PRINT 100
200 A = 100/2
IF A>10 THEN PRINT "this is ok"
```

```
PRINT A
PRINT A+34
INPUT H
PRINT H
INPUT "this is a test ",y
PRINT H+Y
END
300 PRINT "this is a subroutine"
    RETURN
```

Assuming you called the Small BASIC interpreter SBASIC, you will use the following command line to run TEST1.BAS:

SBASIC TEST1.BAS

Small BASIC will automatically load the program and begin execution.
The next program demonstrates nested subroutines:

```
PRINT "This program demonstrates nested GOSUBs."
INPUT "enter a number: ", I
GOSUB 100

END

100 FOR T = 1 TO I
  X = X + I
  GOSUB 150
NEXT
RETURN

150 PRINT X;
    RETURN
```

This next program illustrates the INPUT command:

```
print "This program computes the volume of a cube."
input "Enter length of first side ", l
input "Enter length of second side ", w
input "Enter length of third side ", d
t = l * w * d
print "Volume is ", t
```

The next program illustrates nested FOR loops:

```
PRINT "This program demonstrates nested FOR loops."
FOR X = 1 TO 100
  FOR Y = 1 TO 10
    PRINT X; Y; X*Y
  NEXT
NEXT
```

The following program exercises all of the relational operators:

```
PRINT "This demonstrates all of the relational operators."
A = 10
B = 20
IF A = B THEN PRINT "A = B"
IF A <> B THEN PRINT "A <> B"
IF A < B THEN PRINT "A < B"
IF A > B THEN PRINT "A > B"
IF A >= B THEN PRINT "A >= B"
IF A <= B THEN PRINT "A <= B"_
```

Enhancing and Expanding the Interpreter

It is quite easy to add commands to the Small BASIC interpreter. Just follow the general format taken by the commands presented in the chapter. To add variable types, you will need to use an array of structures to hold the variables, with one member in the structure indicating the type of the variable and the other member holding the value. To add strings, you will need to establish a string table. You might want to use the C++ **string** class to support strings in Small BASIC. This would allow a one-to-one translation between BASIC string operations and C++ **string** operations.

One other point: As written, the various enumerations and constants used by the interpreter and the parser are simply duplicated in each file. This is appropriate for its presentation in a book. However, as you enhance and expand the interpreter, you will want to move these types of declarations into a header file that is included in all the files comprising the interpreter. This not only makes things easier as your project grows in size, it prevents one file from being out-of-sync with another.

Creating Your Own Computer Language

Enhancing or expanding Small BASIC is a good way to become more familiar with its operation and with the way that language interpreters function, but you are not limited to the BASIC language. You can use the same techniques described in this chapter to write an interpreter for just about any computer language. You can even invent your own language that reflects your own programming style and personality. In fact, the interpreter skeleton used by Small BASIC is a perfect "test bench" for any type of special-language feature that you might want to try.

For example, to add a REPEAT/UNTIL loop to the interpreter, you need to follow these four steps:

1.   Add REPEAT and UNTIL to the **SBtokensT** enumeration.

2.   Add REPEAT and UNTIL to the **commands** table.

3.   Add REPEAT and UNTIL to the main loop **switch** statement.

4.   Define **repeat( )** and **until( )** functions that process the REPEAT and UNTIL commands. (Use the **exec_for( )** and **next( )** as starting points.)

One final thought: The types of statements that you can interpret are bounded only by your imagination. Don't be afraid to experiment.

Exploring the Standard Template Library

By Andrew Gayter

I n this chapter we will explore one of the most important subsystems defined by the C++ language: *The Standard Template Library*, or *STL*. The STL consists of standardized containers, iterators, algorithms, and function objects that together provide a powerful toolbox of generic building blocks on which complete applications can be built.

A major advantage of using the STL to develop programs is that the most common algorithms, data structures, and memory allocations are already provided. Gone are the days of "re-inventing the wheel."

The object-orientated paradigm promotes code reuse through the deployment of existing classes and predefined functionality. The STL is an ideal candidate for applications where code "recycling" is paramount. It can help cut development costs and improve timelines—a major advantage where market pressures demand frequent updates of applications.

The samples contained in this chapter have been designed and implemented to demonstrate how the STL can be applied to some basic and advanced programming tasks. The samples cover topics such as sorting, searching, set operations, and stream I/O. You will also see how to implement a custom container.

PROGRAMMER'S NOTE   *The samples contained within this chapter have been developed using the Microsoft implementation of the STL. Whenever possible, it is important to use the latest version of the Microsoft compiler, because many enhancements and fixes have recently been applied.*

Some of the samples use a **#pragma** *preprocessor directive to disable some of the warnings generated by the Microsoft compiler. If you prefer, the directive can be removed without any detrimental effect.*

Standard Template Library Overview

This chapter assumes that you are at least moderately familiar with the STL and its standardized set of generic containers, algorithms, and functions. Given its size, a detailed description of the STL is far beyond the scope of this chapter. Following is an overview of STL's chief elements and a quick "refresher course" for all developers.

Containers

The STL *containers* are the basic building blocks of the template library. This does not mean, however, that in order to do anything with the STL you have to define your own containers. Far from it. The STL provides a rich set of built-in containers and substantial additional functionality that can be integrated with new or existing C++ applications. Also, in many cases the STL provides highly optimized algorithms that remove the need for writing your own.

For storing data, the STL provides a number of containers that implement many traditional data structures such as arrays and lists. Here are the containers supported by the STL:

STL Container	Description
vector	A dynamic array
deque	A double-ended queue
list	A bi-directional, linear list
map	An associative container allowing unique keys
multimap	An associative container allowing duplicate keys
set	An associative container for storing unique sets
multiset	An associative container for storing nonunique sets
queue	A standard queue
stack	A standard stack
priority_queue	A priority queue

Each container has its particular use, and it is important for the developer to analyze the containers to make sure that the correct choice is made. The most commonly used containers are vectors, lists, deques, and maps.

One of the simplest containers within the STL is the **vector**. It is easily compared with a traditional array. However, it does have quite a few benefits that make it the ideal choice for storing data in a sequence. The vector is dynamic—as elements are added, it grows to accommodate them. The sequences contained by the vector can be sorted, copied, moved, and modified using either STL algorithms or user-supplied algorithms.

The **list** container is one of the most versatile and supports operations such as **splice( )**, **merge( )**, and **unique( )**.

The **deque** container provides a double-ended queue.

Associative containers such as the **map** container are ideal choices when data that has an associated key value is to be stored.

Iterators

Many of the STL *algorithms* can be applied to containers, since iterators provide a consistent interface in which elements can be accessed. *Iterators* are similar to C++ pointers and can be used to iterate over and provide access to contained elements. Iterators are categorized based on the operations they can perform, as follows:

◆ Ouput

◆ Input

◆ Forward

◆ Bi-directional

◆ Random access

For example, a *forward* iterator only provides the ++ operator, whereas the *bi-directional* iterator provides both the ++ and – – operators. *Random access* iterators are the most useful type because they provide a complete set of iteration and comparison operators. The type of iterators supported by the STL containers varies. For example, vectors and deques support random access iterators, but list and map containers support only bi-directional iterators.

Throughout the rest of this chapter we will be using the following generic names to refer to the various iterator types:

Generic Name	Iterator Type
RanIt	Random access iterator
InputIterator	Input iterator
FwdIt	Forward iterator
OutIt	Output iterator
BidIt	Bi-directional iterator

Algorithms

The STL implements around 60 algorithms that can be used on elements. They provide quick and convenient ways in which data can be manipulated, sorted, and searched.

Many of the provided algorithms can perform complex manipulations of data. For example, the partition algorithm can be used to "partition" data into a logical sequence as follows: "Make all the elements that are greater than x appear after all those elements that are less than x."

User-Defined Function Objects

The STL also allows the developer to supply *user-defined function objects*. A function object is useful when iterating over elements within a container. Normal algorithms do not maintain information between consecutive calls (unless static variables are used). A function object, however, can maintain information between consecutive calls by utilizing contained member variables. This is useful when a final result has to be calculated for the whole sequence (e.g., summation).

Though the theory of the STL is interesting, its practical application to common programming tasks is more useful. Many of the following samples can be combined or modified to accommodate your own needs. Don't be surprised, for example, if simply introducing other algorithms or function objects provides functionality that you've just spent weeks developing on your own. STL provides generalized solutions to a wide variety of programming problems.

STL Sorting

A number of sort algorithms are available for use on containers. Three of these—**sort( )**, **partial_sort( )**, and **sort_heap( )**—are illustrated in the sections that follow.

Sort Algorithm	Purpose
sort( )	A general purpose sort
partial_sort( )	Sorts only a portion of a container
sort_heap( )	Sorts a heap

The sort( ) Algorithm

The first sorting algorithm we will examine is **sort( )**. This is a straightforward sort that is quite easy to use. The only restriction is that the container must be one that supports random access iterators (a **vector**, for instance).

Following are the **sort( )** algorithm prototypes:

```
template<class RanIt>
    void sort(RanIt begin, RanIt end);

template<class RanIt, class Pred>
    void sort(RanIt begin, RanIt end, Pred pr);
```

The first version of **sort( )** is quite straightforward; it uses **operator<( )** to sort the elements into ascending order. The second version replaces **operator<(x , y)** with **pr(x,y)**; this allows you to supply your own comparison function.

Code

Here is an example that demonstrates **sort( )** by sorting a vector.

```
/*-------------------------------------------------------------------*/
/*
/*   STL sort( )
/*
/*
/*-------------------------------------------------------------------*
/#include <vector>
#include <iostream>
#include <algorithm>
using namespace std;

void Print(int x)
{
  cout << x << endl;
}

int main()
{
  vector<int> v(5);
  v[0] = 5;
  v[1] = 6;
  v[2] = 3;
  v[3] = 9;
  v[4] = 7;

  sort(v.begin(), v.end() );
  for_each(v.begin(), v.end(), Print);

  return 0;
}
```

Here is the output from this program:

```
3
5
6
7
9
```

ANNOTATIONS

In this example of **sort( )**, a vector of integers is used to store five integer values. The **sort( )** algorithm is used to sort the integers into ascending order. To print the results to **cout**, a user-defined function, **Print( )**, has been defined and used by the **for_each( )** algorithm.

The **for_each( )** algorithm is useful in cases where the container has to be iterated, and operations performed on each element in the container. Here is the prototype for **for_each( )**:

```
template <class InputIterator, class Func>
    Func for_each(InputIterator begin, InputIterator end, Func fn);
```

Here, the function specified by *fn* is applied to all elements in the range determined by *begin* and *end*. The example program could have been easily written without **for_each( )**, but this algorithm often simplifies code.

To use the predicate version of **sort( )**, we simply include a function object or function pointer as the third argument. For example, to sort the vector in reverse order, try the following.

```
sort(v.begin(), v.end(), greater<int>);
```

Here we are using the STL-supplied **greater( )** function object, demonstrating how easy it is to supply other function objects to STL algorithms.

The partial_sort Algorithm

Another sorting algorithm that is quite useful is **partial_sort( )**, which can be used to "partially" sort a sequence. The prototype for **partial_sort( )** is as follows:

```
template<class RanIt>
    void partial_sort(RanIt begin, RanIt middle, RanIt end);
```

Code

The following code demonstrates **partial_sort( )**.

partial_sort.cpp

```
/*------------------------------------------------------------------*/
/*
/*   STL partial_sort( )
/*
/*
/*------------------------------------------------------------------*/
#include <vector>
#include <iostream>
```

```
#include <algorithm>
using namespace std;

void Print(int x)
{
  cout << x << endl;
}

int main()
{
  vector<int> v(10);

  v[0] = 5;
  v[1] = 6;
  v[2] = 3;
  v[3] = 9;
  v[4] = 7;
  v[5] = 0;
  v[6] = 1;
  v[7] = 12;
  v[8] = 2;
  v[9] = 4;

  partial_sort(v.begin(), v.begin()+4, v.end() );
  for_each(v.begin(), v.end(), Print);

  return 0;
}
```

Here is the output from this program:

```
0
1
2
3
9
7
6
12
5
4
```

In this example, the **partial_sort( )** function is used to sort only the first four elements in the vector: 0, 1, 2, 3.

The sort_heap( ) Function

The function **sort_heap( )** can be used to sort an existing container that has been converted to a heap by the use of the **make_heap( )** algorithm. Here is the **sort_heap( )** prototype:

```
template<class RanIt>
  void sort_heap(RanIt begin, RanIt end);
```

A heap is like a binary tree, with the heap's elements representing the tree nodes. The larger element values are found near the root, with smaller element values below. The result of converting a vector to a heap can be seen by printing the contents of the vector to **cout**, after the vector has been converted. For example, let's say we construct an integer vector containing the values 5, 6, 3, 9, 7, 0, 1, 12, 2, and 4, and convert it to a heap. The ordering sequence would become 12, 9, 3, 6, 7, 0, 1, 5, 2, 4.

Code

Here is a program that constructs a heap and then partially sorts it.

sort_heap.cpp

```
/*-------------------------------------------------------------*/
/*
/*  STL sort_heap( )
/*
/*
/*-------------------------------------------------------------*/

#include <vector>
#include <iostream>
#include <algorithm>
using namespace std;

void Print(int x)
{
```

```
    cout << x << endl;
}

nt main()
{
  vector<int> v(10);
  v[0] = 5;
  v[1] = 6;
  v[2] = 3;
  v[3] = 9;
  v[4] = 7;
  v[5] = 0;
  v[6] = 1;
  v[7] = 12;
  v[8] = 2;
  v[9] = 4;

  cout << "contents of vector before make_heap "<< endl;
  for_each(v.begin(), v.end(), Print);
  make_heap(v.begin(), v.end());
  cout << "contents of vector after make_heap" << endl;
  for_each(v.begin(), v.end(), Print);
  sort_heap(v.begin(), v.end());
  cout << "contents of vector after heap_sort" << endl;
  for_each(v.begin(), v.end(), Print);

  return 0;
}
```

ANNOTATIONS

The **make_heap( )** algorithm converts the vector into a heap. Once a sequence has been converted into a heap, the **pop_heap( )** and **push_heap( )** algorithms must be used to add and remove elements.

After the vector has been converted, the **sort_heap( )** algorithm is used to sort it. The sorted heap is then output to **cout**, using **for_each( )** and the user-defined function **Print( )**.

Print( ) has been passed to the **for_each( )** algorithm so that it will be called "for each" element in the vector.

Sorting User-Defined Elements within STL Containers

The sorting and searching operations in the preceding samples are quite simple because they use built-in element types. What if the containers hold user-defined elements? These specific elements may be class objects that could be sorted or searched using any number of criteria.

user_sort1.cpp

Code

The following sample demonstrates how to use the **sort( )** algorithm to sort a container that stores objects of a user-defined type. In this example, a structure called **employee** is defined, which contains various details about workers: name, salary, department, and years of service.

```
/*------------------------------------------------------------*/
/*
/*   STL sort( ) on user defined element types
/*
/*
/*------------------------------------------------------------*/
#include <vector>
#include <string>
#include <iostream>
#include <algorithm>
using namespace std;

struct employee {
   string name;
   int salary;
   string department;
   int years;
};

bool operator==(const employee &x, const employee &y)
{
   return x.name == y.name;
}
```

```cpp
bool operator<(const employee &x, const employee &y)
{
  return x.name < y.name;
}

void printName(const employee &x)
{
  cout << x.name << endl;
}

int main()
{
  vector<employee> v(5);

  v[0].name = "Stan";
  v[0].salary = 20000;
  v[0].department = "admin";
  v[0].years = 1;

  v[1].name = "Beril";
  v[1].salary = 24000;
  v[1].department = "support";
  v[1].years = 1;

  v[2].name = "Tanya";
  v[2].salary = 12000;
  v[2].department = "typing Pool";
  v[2].years = 5;

  v[3].name = "Bill";
  v[3].salary = 100000;
  v[3].department = "director";
  v[3].years = 5;

  v[4].name = "Monica";
  v[4].salary = 50000;
  v[4].department = "typing pool";
  v[4].years = 1;
  sort(v.begin(), v.end());
  for_each(v.begin(), v.end(), printName);
```

```
   return 0;
}
```

Here is the output from this program:

```
Beril
Bill
Monica
Stan
Tanya
```

ANNOTATIONS

First, a structure is defined that holds employee data. In order to place any element into a container, the element must abide by the C++ container requirements. You must supply the equality and less than operators. The operators for **employee** are shown here, and compare the names of the **employees**:

```
bool operator==(const employee &x, const employee &y)
{
   return x.name == y.name;
}

bool operator<(const employee &x, const employee &y)
{
   return x.name < y.name;
}
```

A vector of **employees** is declared, and five employees added. The vector is then sorted using the algorithm **sort( )**. The < operator has been defined to compare the **employees** names, which gives the output:

```
Beril
Bill
Monica
Stan
Tanya
```

User-Defined Sorting Criteria

Let's take a look now at sorting on a criterion other than less than. You can just change the < operator to compare different values other than names, or you can define your own comparison function. The following example shows how to do the latter.

Code

This program demonstrates the **sort( )** algorithm, but employs a user-defined algorithm to perform the sort comparison. In this case, it sorts by salary.

```cpp
/*-------------------------------------------------------------------*/
/*
/*  STL sort( ) on user defined element types and a uses a user
/*  defined sorting algorithm.
/*
/*-------------------------------------------------------------------*/
#include <vector>
#include <string>
#include <iostream>
#include <algorithm>

using namespace std;

struct employee {
  string name;
  int salary;
  string department;
  int years;
};

bool operator==(const employee &x, const employee &y)
{
  return x.name == y.name;
}

bool operator<(const employee &x, const employee &y)
{
  return x.name < y.name;
}

bool BySalary(const employee &x, const employee &y)
{
  if (x.salary < y.salary) return true;
    return false;
}

void printName(const employee &x)
```

```
{
  cout << x.name << endl;
}

int main()
{
  vector<employee> v(5);

  v[0].name = "Stan";
  v[0].salary = 20000;
  v[0].department = "admin";
  v[0].years = 1;

  v[1].name = "Beril";
  v[1].salary = 24000;
  v[1].department = "support";
  v[1].years = 1;

  v[2].name = "Tanya";
  v[2].salary = 12000;
  v[2].department = "typing Pool";
  v[2].years = 5;

  v[3].name = "Bill";
  v[3].salary = 100000;
  v[3].department = "director";
  v[3].years = 5;

  v[4].name = "Monica";
  v[4].salary = 50000;
  v[4].department = "typing pool";
  v[4].years = 1;

  sort(v.begin(), v.end(), BySalary);
  for_each(v.begin(), v.end(), printName);

  return 0;
}
```

Here is the output from this program:

```
Tanya
Stan
```

```
Beril
Monica
Bill
```

ANNOTATIONS

Instead of using the default **sort( )** algorithm that takes only two arguments, in this example we use the predicate version that takes three arguments. The third argument is a function that's used to perform the comparison of the objects being sorted.

To enable the sorting by salary, we pass a user-defined function, **BySalary( )**, as the predicate argument to the **sort( )** algorithm. **BySalary( )** returns a Boolean value that is used by the **sort( )** algorithm to reorder the sequence:

```
bool BySalary(const employee &x, const employee &y)
{
  if (x.salary < y.salary) return true;
    return false;
}
```

The sample illustrates how easy it is to define functions that can be used in conjunction with existing STL algorithms. The ability to do this is a powerful feature of the STL.

Searching STL Containers

Data stored within containers is quite useless unless it can be found simply and easily. The associative containers, such as the map container, use an associated key value for quick retrieval. If containers are being used that form no such associated relationship, they have to be searched in order to obtain specific items.

Various search algorithms have been implemented within the STL to enable complex or simple searches to be performed. Following are some of the search algorithm prototypes:

```
template<class FwdIt1, class FwdIt2>
    FwdIt1 search(FwdIt1 begin1, FwdIt1 end1, FwdIt2 begin2,
              FwdIt2 end2);

template<class FwdIt, class Dist, class T>
    FwdIt1 search_n(FwdIt begin, FwdIt end, Dist n, const T& val);
```

The two algorithms **search( )** and **search_n( )** can be used to search for specified items within a container. The **search( )** algorithm returns a forward iterator, which "points to" the first occurrence of the specified item. The forward iterator can then be used again to search for the next matching item. The **search_n( )** algorithm differs; it requires an extra parameter n, which is used to specify that the search should only consider [0, (*end* − *begin*) − *n*] items.

```
template<class InputIterator, class T>
    InputIterator find(InputIterator begin, InputIterator end,
                    const T& value)
```

```
template<class InputIterator, class T, class Predicate> inline
    InputIterator find_if(InputIterator begin, InputIterator end,
                    Predicate predicate)
```

The **find( )** and **find_if( )** algorithms can be used to return an input iterator at the position of a specified item. An input iterator may then be used to insert a different item into the container at the returned location. The **find_if( )** can be used in conjunction with a conditional algorithm or functor that must return true if the container's item matches a criterion.

It's important for most applications to be able to search containers for specific items. Often the container elements will be in a random order, which means that each element within the container must be examined during a search. However, some of the searching algorithms, including **binary_search( )**, can only operate upon sorted sequences (see the later section on **binary_search( )**).

The find( ) Algorithm

The STL **find( )** algorithm is a simple search algorithm. It searches the container for the first occurrence of the value. Its prototype is as follows:

```
template<class InputIterator, class T>
    InputIterator find(InputIterator begin, InputIterator end,
                    const T& value)
```

The **find( )** algorithm can be used to find an item within a container. It returns an input iterator that can be used to insert an item at the position returned.

find.cpp

Code

The following sample demonstrates how to use the **find( )** algorithm.

```
/*-------------------------------------------------------------------*/
/*                                                                   */
/*   STL find( )                                                     */
/*                                                                   */
/*                                                                   */
/*-------------------------------------------------------------------*/
#include <vector>
#include <iostream>
#include <algorithm>
using namespace std;

int main()
{
  vector<int> v(1000);

  vector<int>::iterator RanIt;
  int i = 0;
  for (i = 0; i < 1000; i++) {
    v[i] = i;
  }
  random_shuffle(v.begin(), v.end());
  RanIt = find(v.begin(), v.end(), 4627 );
  if (RanIt == v.end()) {
    cout << "Item Not found" << endl;
  }
  else
  {
    cout << "Item found" << endl;
  }

  return 0;
}
```

Here is the output from this program:
```
Item Not Found
```

ANNOTATIONS

To make this example more realistic, the vector is initialized with 1,000 elements. The elements are then randomly shuffled, using the algorithm **random_shuffle( )**. This algorithm does exactly what you would expect: It moves the container elements into a randomly ordered sequence. The prototype of **random_shuffle( )** is as follows:

```
template<class RanIt>
  void random_shuffle(RanIt begin, RanIt end);
```

In the **find( )** sample program, the element is not found, because 4627 is not in the sequence. The **find( )** algorithm therefore returns the *end* iterator of a sequence. If the element were in fact found, the value returned would be an iterator "pointing" to the first matching element encountered. For example, if we searched for the value 678, the iterator **RanIt** would be at the position at which 678 was encountered; and by de-referencing the iterator, using ***RanIt**, it would yield the element value 678.

If a sequence contained repeated element values, the iterator returned by the initial **find( )** could be reused to continue the search. For example:

```
RanIt = v.begin();
while(notAllFound) {
  RanIt = find(RanIt, v.end(), value );
  // Do something with RanIt or the contents of
}
```

The binary_search( ) Algorithm

Other searching algorithms exist that can only operate upon sorted sequences. One such algorithm is **binary_search( )**. Using one of the previous samples, we can sort the sequence and then use the **binary_search( )** to find the required element.

Here is the prototype for the binary search algorithm:

```
template<class FwdIt, class T>
  bool binary_search(FwdIt begin, FwdIt end, const T& val);
```

The **binary_search( )** algorithm returns a Boolean result, which indicates success or failure of the search.

Code

binary_search.cpp

The sample demonstrates how to use **random_shuffle( )**, **sort( )**, and **binary_search( )**.

```
/*-----------------------------------------------------------------*/
/*
/*  STL binary_search( )
/*
/*
/*-----------------------------------------------------------------*/
#include <vector>
#include <iostream>
#include <algorithm>
using namespace std;

int main()
{
  vector<int> v(1000);

  int i = 0;
  for (i = 0; i < 1000; i++)
  {
    v[i] = i;
  }

  random_shuffle(v.begin(), v.end());
  sort(v.begin(), v.end());
  if (binary_search(v.begin(), v.end(), 678) == true)
    cout << "Found" << endl;
  else
    cout << "Not found" << endl;

  return 0;
}
```

Here is the output from this program:
```
Found
```

To enable **binary_search( )**, the sequence must be sorted; this is easily achieved by using the **sort( )** algorithm. In the preceding example, the returned Boolean value from the **binary_search( )** is true, because 678 does exist within the sequence.

Using **binary_search( )** to search a sorted sequence is much faster than using a sequential searching algorithm. When a large sequence of data is to be searched, **binary_search( )** will provide superior performance.

Using Function Objects

Function objects are instances of classes that overload the **operator( )**. Function objects can be used in place of function pointers in the STL algorithms, and doing so is often more efficient.

functors.cpp

Code

The following sample demonstrates how to use a function object with the **for_each( )** algorithm.

```
/*---------------------------------------------------------------*/
/*
/*   STL. Using function objects
/*
/*
/*---------------------------------------------------------------*/
#include <vector>
#include <string>
#include <iostream>
#include <algorithm>
using namespace std;

struct employee {
  string name;
  int salary;
  string department;
  int years;
};
```

```
bool operator==(const employee &x, const employee &y)
{
  return x.name == y.name;
}

bool operator<(const employee &x, const employee &y)
{
  return x.name < y.name;
}

template<class _T> class Sum
{
  int total;
public:
  Sum() : total(0) {}
  void operator()(const _T &x) {
    total += x.salary;
  }
  int Total() { return total; }
};

int main()
{
  vector<employee> v(5);
  Sum<employee> s;
  v[0].name = "Stan";
  v[0].salary = 20000;
  v[0].department = "admin";
  v[0].years = 1;

  v[1].name = "Beril";
  v[1].salary = 24000;
  v[1].department = "support";
  v[1].years = 1;

  v[2].name = "Tanya";
  v[2].salary = 12000;
  v[2].department = "typing Pool";
  v[2].years = 5;
```

```
v[3].name = "Bill";
v[3].salary = 100000;
v[3].department = "director";
v[3].years = 5;

v[4].name = "Monica";
v[4].salary = 50000;
v[4].department = "typing pool";
v[4].years = 1;

s = for_each(v.begin(), v.end(), s);
cout << "Sum total of salary " << s.Total() << endl;

return 0;
}
```

Here is the output from this progam:

```
Sum total of salary 206000
```

ANNOTATIONS

The function object template **Sum** is shown here, which adds the salary value of employees to its internal **total** value.

```
template<class _T> class Sum
{
  int total;
public:
  Sum() : total(0) {}
  void operator()(const _T &x) {
    total += x.salary;
  }
  int Total() { return total; }
};
```

A constructor is provided to initialize the **total** member variable. The **for_each( )** algorithm iterates over the contents of the vector; and an instance of **Sum**, **s**, is declared and passed to the **for_each( )** algorithm as its third argument.

The sum **operator( )** is called for each element in the container. Each element's salary value is added to the function object's **total** value. After all the elements have been iterated, the result is assigned to the function object, **s**, and printed to **cout**.

Reading and Writing Containers to Streams

In many cases it is desirable to populate containers from streams. However, the STL containers do not support reading and writing to and from streams directly. To enable the reading and writing of containers to **cin** and **cout**, the STL provides a number of algorithms and iterators that can be used with existing STL containers.

This sample shows how to read and write integers to and from a vector using **cin** and **cout**. The sample uses some of the STL-supplied stream iterators and functors (function objects).

io.cpp

Code

This sample demonstrates reading a series of integers into a vector container.

```
/*---------------------------------------------------------------*/
/*
/*   STL. Reading and writing cin and cout.
/*
/*
/*---------------------------------------------------------------*/
#include <iterator>
#include <vector>
#include <algorithm>
#include <iostream>
using namespace std ;

int main () {

  vector<int> V;

  cout << "Enter a sequence of integers (eof to quit): " ;
  copy(istream_iterator<int>(cin), istream_iterator<int>(),
      back_inserter(V));
  copy(V.begin(),V.end() , ostream_iterator<int>(cout));

  return 0;
}
```

Here is the output from this program:

```
Enter a sequence of integers (eof to quit):

1 2 3 4 5 6 7 \0
```

1 2 3 4 5 6 7

ANNOTATIONS

The **copy( )** algorithm is used in conjunction with the standard iterator type **istream_iterator**, to copy integers into the vector. Spaces between the values in the input stream are interpreted as delimiters, which places each integer into its own vector element. The standard **back_inserter** iterator is used to iterate over the elements during the insertion process.

The algorithm and class prototypes are as follows:

```
template<class InputIterator, class OutIt>
    OutIt copy(InputIterator begin, InputIterator end, OutIt x);
```

The **copy( )** algorithm can be used to copy a sequence of items into a different but compatible container. It only requires that the third parameter be an output iterator that has previously been assigned a position within the new container. This algorithm is useful for copying items from one container to another.

```
template<class Cont> back_insert_iterator<Cont>
    back_inserter(Cont& x);
```

The **back_inserter** template class returns a **back_inserter_iterator**, which can be used to insert items into a container. The container must support the **push_back( )** method.

```
template<class U, class E = char, class T = char_traits<E> > class
istream_iterator :
    public iterator<input_iterator_tag, U, ptrdiff_t> { ...... }
```

An **istream_iterator** is used to extract objects of a specified type from an input stream. It uses a contained object of type **basic_stream** to gain access to the input stream, in this case **cin**.

Reading Container Elements from Files

This next sample takes the previous sample (from "Reading and Writing Containers to Streams") a little further. Instead of using **cin** and **cout** as source and destination streams, a file stream is used.

The functionality to open a file stream, and to read and write its contents is supplied in the header **<fstream>**.

Code

This sample demonstrates how to populate a vector container with strings read from a file.

```
/*----------------------------------------------------------------*/
/*
/*   STL. Reading strings from a file.
/*
/*
/*----------------------------------------------------------------*/
#include <iterator>
#include <vector>
#include <algorithm>
#include <fstream>
#include <string>
#include <iostream>
#pragma warning(disable:4786)
using namespace std;

int main (int argc, char *argv[]) {
  vector<string> V;
  if (argc !=2) {
    cout << "Wrong number of arguments" << endl;
    exit(1);
  }
  std::ifstream from(argv[1]);
  if (!from) {
    cout << "Error opening file" << endl;
    exit(1);
  }
  copy(istream_iterator<string>(from),istream_iterator<string>(),
    back_inserter(V) );

  return 0;
}
```

ANNOTATIONS

This code is actually very similar to the previous stream example, since each string in the file is written to a separate element of the array.

Instead of copying data from the **cin**, the **copy( )** algorithm copies data from the file stream, **from**:

```
copy(istream_iterator<string>(from), istream_iterator<string>(),
    back_inserter(V));
```

Once all the data has been copied into the vector, several types of operations can be performed. For example, searching in memory is far faster than searching on disk.

Notice how the vector is never allocated a size. The dynamic characteristics of the vector allow us to read files that are quite large into memory, because all memory allocation is handled by a default allocator. This can be seen by looking at the template definition of the vector:

```
template<class _Ty, class _A = allocator<_Ty> >
    class vector { ……. };
```

STL allocators implement distinctly run-of-the-mill memory allocations. In fact, whether the allocator template classes are really required is a matter for discussion. However, it may be such that a special kind of memory allocation has to be performed for a specific type of element; for example, a far heap allocation. If this is necessary, then the methods and operations an allocator provides are easily defined for a new allocator template that can handle far heap allocations.

Comparing Strings

Although the **string** class is not strictly a member of the STL, it still satisfies all of the requirements of a container and is often used in conjunction with the other STL elements. For this reason, we've included a simple example that illustrates the use of the **string** class together with a common programming task of comparing strings in a case-insensitive manner. The default string operator **== ( )** compares strings using a case-sensitive comparison.

Code

This sample shows how a function can be written to compare strings using no case. It demonstrates well the kind of operations that can be performed on iterators.

string_compare.cpp

```
/*--------------------------------------------------------------*/
/*
/*   STL. Comparing string using no case comparison.
/*
/*
/*--------------------------------------------------------------*/
#include <string>
```

```cpp
#include <algorithm>
#include <iostream>
#include <cctype>
using namespace std;

int compare_NoCase( const string &s1, const string &s2)
{
  string::const_iterator it1 = s1.begin();
  string::const_iterator it2 = s2.begin();

  while (it1 != s1.end() && it2 != s2.end()) {
    if (toupper(*it1) != toupper(*it2)) {
      return (toupper(*it1) < toupper(*it2)) ? -1 : 1;
    }
    ++it1;
    ++it2;
  }
  return s2.size() - s1.size();
}

int main()
{
  string s1;
  string s2;

  cout << "Input the first string" << endl;
  cin >> s1;
  cout << "Input the second string" << endl;
  cin >> s2;
  if (compare_NoCase( s1, s2) == 0)
    cout << "True: " << s2 << " the same as " << s1 << endl;
  else
    cout << "False: " << s2 << " is not the same as " << s1 << endl;

  return 0;
}
```

Here is the output from this program:
```
Input the first string

Hello World
```

```
Input the second string

HELLO WORLD

True: Hello World is the same as HELLO WORLD
```

ANNOTATIONS

Two string iterators are used to iterate over the two strings. Within the **while** loop, the pre-increment operators of **it1** and **it2** advance the iterators over the characters of the string. The interesting part of this sample is the function that performs the character comparison:

```
if (toupper(*it1) != toupper(*it2)) {
  return (toupper(*it1) < toupper(*it2)) ? -1 : 1;
}
```

The conditional statement compares the two characters that are exposed through the iterators **it1** and **it2**. If

```
*it1 < *it2
```

minus one is returned, which is similar to the C++ function **strcmp( )**.

The **toupper( )** function is part of the Standard C++ function library. It converts the character to uppercase and is declared in **<cctype>**.

If all the characters match, a check is done to make sure that the two strings are the same length:

```
return s2.size() - s1.size();
```

If the return value is 0, then both the strings are the same. If they are of different lengths, then the difference in their lengths is returned.

STL Set algorithms

Some interesting algorithms that are based upon set theory can be used on container data. They are summarized here:

```
template<class InputIterator1, class InputIterator2, class OutIt>
  OutIt set_union(InputIterator1 begin1, InputIterator1 end1,
                  InputIterator2 begin2, InputIterator2 end2, OutIt x);
```

The **set_union( )** algorithm returns the union of two containers and is useful if you want to combine two containers, but you don't want to contain duplicates. For example, if we had two containers containing the elements 1, 2 , 3, 4 and 4, 5, 6, the resulting union would be 1, 2, 3, 4, 5, 6—with no repeat of the element value 4.

```
template<class InputIterator1, class InputIterator2, class OutIt>
    OutIt set_intersection(InputIterator1 begin1, InputIterator1 end1,
            InputIterator2 begin2, InputIterator2 end2, OutIt x);
```

The **set_intersection( )** algorithm returns a container with only elements that appear in both input containers.

```
template<class InputIterator1, class InputIterator2, class OutIt>
    OutIt set_difference(InputIterator1 begin1, InputIterator1 end1,
            InputIterator2 begin2, InputIterator2 end2, OutIt x);
```

The **set_difference( )** algorithm returns a collection of elements that are members of the first input container, but not of the second. For example, two containers with element values 1, 2, 3, 4, 5 and 3, 4, 5 would produce the output 1, 2.

```
template<class InputIterator1, class InputIterator2, class OutIt>
    OutIt set_symmetric_difference(InputIterator1 begin1,
            InputIterator1 end1, InputIterator2 begin2, InputIterator2
            end2, OutIt x);
```

The **set_symmetric_difference( )** algorithm produces a container with elements that are members of either, but not of both, input containers.

Set algorithms do not alter the input sequences that are provided as arguments. Rather, the results are returned in a third container that must be allocated in advance and passed as the third argument to the algorithm.

Finding a Subset of Strings

Using conventional techniques to search for several words would be quite an involved process, but these set theory algorithms allow the tasks to be performed simply, and possibly with higher performance.

Code

This sample uses **set_intersection( )** to establish whether a set of strings contained in one vector are present within another.

et_intersection.cpp

```
/*-------------------------------------------------------------------*/
/*
/*  STL. set_intersection( ).
/*
/*
/*-------------------------------------------------------------------*
/#include <vector>
#include <iostream>
#include <algorithm>
#include <string>
#pragma warning(disable:4786)
using namespace std;

void Print(string x)
{
  cout << x << endl;
}

template<class _T> class Count
{
  int c;
  public:
    Count() : c(0) {}
    void operator()(const _T& x) {
      if (x != "") c += 1;
    }
    int count() { return c; }
};

int main()
{
```

```
  vector<string> first(6);
  vector<string> second(4);
  vector<string> res(4);
  Count<string> cnt;
  first[0] = "this";
  first[1] = "is";
  first[2] = "a";
  first[3] = "set";
  first[4] = "theory";
  first[5] = "test";

  second[0] = "is";
  second[1] = "a";
  second[2] = "set";
  second[3] = "test";

  sort(first.begin(), first.end());
  sort(second.begin(), second.end());

  set_intersection(first.begin(),first.end(),second.begin(),
      second.end(), res.begin() );
  cout << "first" << endl;
  for_each(first.begin(), first.end(), Print);
  cout << "second" << endl;
  for_each(second.begin(), second.end(), Print);
  cout << "Result" << endl;
  for_each(res.begin(), res.end(), Print);
  if (for_each(res.begin(), res.end(), cnt ).count() ==
     second.size())
    cout << "All stings occur in first" << endl;
  else
    cout << "All stings do not occur in first" << endl;

  return 0;
}
```

Here is the output from this program:

```
All strings occur in the first
```

ANNOTATIONS

This example of the **set_intersection( )** algorithm demonstrates its use to find out if one container of strings is present within another.

Two string vectors are created. The string vector **first** is initialized with **"this is a set theory test"**, and **second** is initialized with **"is a set test"**. Each element within the vectors contains separate words. The two string vectors are then sorted into ascending order, using the STL **sort( )** algorithm.

The **first** and **second** begin and end iterators are passed to the **set_intersection( )** algorithm with an instance of a pre-allocated vector of empty strings, **res**, which is passed as a return argument. The **res** argument is used to return the intersection of the **first** and **second** containers. The **first**, **second** and **res** vectors are then streamed to **cout**, using the **for_each( )** algorithm and a user-defined algorithm **Print( )**.

To establish if all the elements in **second** occur within **first,** the elements in **res** have to be counted. The **count( )** function object maintains a **count** property and, when used in conjunction with **for_each( ),** conveniently counts the number of elements. Counting consists of checking each element within the **res** vector for an empty string. If the element contains a valid string, the function object's **count** member variable is incremented by one.

If the number of valid elements contained within **res** is equal to the number of elements in **second,** then all the elements contained within **second** are present within **first**.

It would be a simple task to extend the program to include reading strings from a file stream; the same algorithm could then be used to find a set of strings within the file. This could be put to all sorts of uses. For example, a recruiting agency might have a large number of potential employees that need matching to current vacancies. The file search program could be used to search each employee's records for a matching set of criteria. This would remove all records that *didn't* meet the criteria and thus accelerate the matching of employees to current vacancies.

Serving Prioritized Messages

In modern computing, components and applications may be dispersed throughout a network infrastructure. In many cases, communication is necessary among distributed applications to pass information and for synchronization. Messaging applications are used to pass application data and messages among interoperable applications. In some cases, those messages have to be prioritized according to importance.

The STL provides a convenient container for achieving the prioritization of contained data. The **priority_queue** template class can be used to prioritize data, given a priority criterion. Here is the **priority_queue** template prototype:

```
priority_queue(const value_type *begin, const value_type *end,
    const Pred& pr = Pred(), const allocator_type& al = allocator_type());
```

Code

priority_queue.cpp

This sample demonstrates how to create a message server that sends higher-priority messages first. When messages have equal priority, they leave the queue in the same order they were added.

```cpp
/*--------------------------------------------------------------*/
/*                                                              */
/*   STL priority_queue< >                                      */
/*                                                              */
/*                                                              */
/*--------------------------------------------------------------*/
#include <queue>
#include <functional>
#include <iostream>
using namespace std;

struct Message {
int priority;
  Message() : priority(0) {}
  Message(int p) : priority(p) {}

  void Service() {
    cout << "Message Sent with priority " << priority << endl;
  }
};

bool operator<(const Message &x, const Message &y)
{
  return x.priority < y.priority;
}

bool operator==(const Message &x, const Message &y)
{
  return x.priority == y.priority;
}
```

```
void SendMessage(priority_queue<Message> &q, const Message &m )
{
  q.push(m);
}

void ServeMessages(priority_queue<Message>&q)
{
  while (!q.empty()) {
    Message m = q.top();
    q.pop();
    m.Service();
  }
}

int main()
{
  priority_queue<Message> MessageQueue;
  SendMessage(MessageQueue, Message(5));
  SendMessage(MessageQueue, Message(2));
  SendMessage(MessageQueue, Message(6));
  ServeMessages( MessageQueue );

  return 0;
}
```

Here is the output from this program:

```
Message Sent with priority 6
Message Sent with priority 5
Message Sent with priority 2
```

ANNOTATIONS

A message structure called **Message** is defined and is the element type of the priority queue. The **Message** structure defines two constructors: One is used to assign a default value to the **Message**'s priority-member variable. The second constructor, which overloads the first, is used to assign a user-defined priority level. The two constructors are provided for simplicity, but if preferred you can define only one, which can assign a default value if a value is not specified.

The **Message** structure implements one method called **Service( )**, used by the **ServeMessages( )** function each time an item is removed from the queue.

The comparison operators are provided to enable the **Message** structure to be added to the priority queue. In the code shown just below, the less than operator is defined to return true if the priority of **x** is less than the priority of **y**. The equality operator simply compares the two priorities of **x** and **y** and returns true if they are the same.

```
bool operator<(const Message &x, const Message &y)
{
  return x.priority < y.priority;
}


bool operator==(const Message &x, const Message &y)
{
  return x.priority == y.priority;
}
```

The **main( )** function declares a priority queue of type **Message**. Several messages are created, with different priorities, and added to the priority queue using **SendMessage( ). SendMessage( )** simply pushes the **Message** onto the supplied queue. Here is that code:

```
void SendMessage(priority_queue<Message> &q, const Message &m )
{
  q.push(m);
}
```

When all the messages have been placed onto the priority queue, **ServeMessages( )** is called:

```
void ServeMessages(priority_queue<Message>&q)
{
  while (!q.empty()) {
    Message m = q.top();
    q.pop();
    m.Service();
  }
}
```

ServeMessages( ) first checks that the queue is not empty, and then retrieves a message from the queue using the queue-defined method, **top( )**. Then **pop( )** is used to remove the element from the queue—which is surprising, as one would expect to use **pop( )** to not only remove the element from the queue but return the "popped" element, as well.

Once the element has been retrieved, the **ServeMessages( )** function then calls the message's **Service( )** method—which simply outputs a textual message to **cout**.

If preferred, you can reorganize the priorities so that the lower values have a higher priority. This is done by simply changing the < operator, or by passing a different comparison function or function object to the **priority_queue** class template, as shown here:

```
bool operator<(const Message &x, const Message &y)
{
    return y.priority < x.priority;
}
```

The message server example shown here could be adapted to many different applications. For instance, in a situation where each message is running on a suspended thread, the message server could be used to "wake up" each thread in a prioritized manner. Dependencies could be set up between the stored elements in order to synchronize method execution or data retrieval.

Implementing this kind of functionality without using the STL would be a long and difficult task involving far more lines of code than are seen here.

Binary Tree Container

This final example shows how to create a *binary search tree* that can be used to store elements of any type against a key value. Binary trees provide an excellent data structure for storing elements that need to be searched and accessed quickly.

The implementation of *traversal algorithms* allows the tree to be traversed in a number of ways. For example, the traversal algorithms used in this sample traverse the tree "in order" (**inorder**). This means the items contained by the tree are always retrieved in ascending order. This is useful and saves time because no other data structure or algorithms are necessary—sorting comes for free.

The sample shown here is incomplete and forms a framework to which functionality can be added. It implements the most essential functionality, including **Insert( )**, **Search( )**, and **Remove( )**. It also includes a **Traverse( )** method that traverses the tree **inorder**, using recursion.

Compatibility with STL algorithms is maintained by the implementation of an iterator. The iterator can be used to iterate over the contents of the binary tree **inorder**—that is, items from **begin( )** to **end( )** are in ascending order.

PROGRAMMER'S NOTE *You might find it interesting to compare the binary tree code shown in this chapter with that developed by Art Friedman in Chapter 3. These are two very different variations on the same theme.*

Code

The code demonstrates how to create a container that is based upon a binary tree
binary_tree.cpp data structure.

```cpp
//********************************************************************
//
// Template container class Binary Tree
//
//********************************************************************
#include <iostream>
#include <functional>
#include <iterator>
#include <algorithm>

#pragma warning(disable:4786)
#pragma warning(disable:4550)

using namespace std;


template <class _K, class _Ty, class _Pr = less<_K>,
          class _A = allocator<_Ty> > class BinaryTree
{
    typedef pair<_K, _Ty> value_type;
    _Pr     key_compare;
    typedef _K  key_type;
    typedef _Ty referent_type;
    typedef _A::difference_type difference_type;
    typedef _REFERENCE_X(_Ty, _A) reference;
    typedef _POINTER_X(void, _A) _GenPtr;
    typedef _REFERENCE_X(_Ty, _A) _Vref;
    typedef _REFERENCE_X(_K, _A) _Kref;
    typedef _POINTER_X(_Ty, _A) _Tptr;

    struct _Node;
    typedef _POINTER_X(_Node, _A) _NodePtr;
    typedef _REFERENCE_X(_NodePtr, _A) _NodePref;
    static _Vref _Value( _NodePtr _P ) { return (_Vref)(*_P)._Value(); }
    static _Kref _Key( _NodePtr _P ) { return (_Kref)(*_P)._Key(); }
    static _NodePtr _Z( _NodePtr _P ) { return (*_P).z; }
```

```cpp
    static _NodePtr _Parent( _NodePtr _P) { return (*_P).p; }
    static _NodePtr _Min( _NodePtr _P ) { while (_Left(_P) != _Z(_P))
            _P = _Left(_P); return _P; }
    static _NodePtr _Max( _NodePtr _P ) { while (_Right(_P) != _Z(_P))
            _P = _Right(_P); return _P; }
    static _NodePref _Left(_NodePtr _P) { return (_NodePref)(*_P).l; }
    static _NodePref _Right(_NodePtr _P) { return (_NodePref)(*_P).r; }

    struct _Node {

      value_type item;

      _NodePtr l;
      _NodePtr r;
      _NodePtr z;
      _NodePtr p;

      _Node( key_type k, referent_type v, _NodePtr ll, _NodePtr rr,
                _NodePtr _X, _NodePtr _Y ) {
        item.first = k;
        item.second = v;
        l = ll;
        r = rr;
        p = _X;
        z = _Y;
      }

      key_type &_Key() { return item.first; }
      referent_type &_Value() { return item.second; }

    };

    _NodePtr head;
    _NodePtr z;

public:

    BinaryTree(int max = 10) {
      z = new _Node( 0, 'Z', 0, 0, 0, 0 );
      head = new _Node( 0, 'a', 0, z, z, z );
    }
```

```
~BinaryTree() {
  // Binary tree destructor
  Clear();
  delete z;
  delete head;
}

void Clear(_NodePtr p = 0) {
  // Destroys the contents of the tree.

  if (p == 0) p = _Right( head );
  if (p == z) return;  // Tree empty

  DeleteSubTree( p );

  head->l = head->r = head->p = z;
}

referent_type Search(key_type v)
{
  _NodePtr x = _Right( head );
  z->item.first = v;

  while ( v != x->_Key() )
    x = (key_compare(v, _Key(x))) ? _Left( x ) : _Right( x );
  return _Value(x);
}

void Insert(key_type v, referent_type info)
{
  _NodePtr p;
  _NodePtr x;
  p = head;
  x =  _Right( head );

  while ( x != z ) {
```

```
      p = x;
      x = (key_compare(v, _Key(x))) ? _Left( x ) : _Right( x );
    }
  x = new _Node(v, info, z, z, p, z );
  if (key_compare(v, _Key(p)))
    _Left( p ) = x;
  else
    _Right( p ) = x;
}

void Remove(key_type v)
{
  _NodePtr c, p, x, t;

  if (_Right(head) == z) return; // Tree empty.

  z->item.first = v;
  p = head;
  x = _Right( head );
  while (v != _Key(x) ) {
    p = x;
    x = (key_compare(v, _Key(x))) ? _Left( x ) : _Right( x );
  }

  t = x;

  if (_Right( t ) == z) {
    x = _Left( x );
  }
  else {
    if (_Left(_Right( t )) == z ) {
      x = _Right( x );
      _Left( x ) = _Left( t );
    }
    else
    {
      c = _Right( x );
      while (_Left(_Left( c )) != z) {
        c = _Left( c );
      }
      x = _Left( c );
      _Left( c ) = _Right( x );
```

```
        _Left( x ) = _Left( t );
        _Right( x ) = _Right( t );
      }
    }

    delete t;

    if (key_compare(v, _Key(p)))
      _Left( p ) = x;
    else
      _Right( p ) = x;

    if (x->p)
      x->p = p;
  }

  void Traverse(_NodePtr t = 0)
  {
    // inorder traversal
    // NOTE. This is a recursive function which
    // if used on a large tree may cause stack overflow.
    if (t == 0)
      t = _Right( head );

    if (t != z)
    {
      Traverse(_Left( t ));
      Visit( t );
      Traverse(_Right( t ));
    }
  }

  void Visit(_NodePtr t)
  {
    if (t != 0)
    {
      cout << _Value(t)<< endl;
    }
  }

protected:
```

```
    void DeleteSubTree(_NodePtr p)
  {
    _NodePtr t;
    if (p != z) {
      DeleteSubTree( _Left( p ) );
      t = _Right( p );
      delete p;
      DeleteSubTree( t );
    }
  }

public:

  class iterator;
  friend class iterator;
  class iterator : public _Bidit< _Ty, difference_type> {
  protected:
    _NodePtr _Ptr;

  public:

    iterator() : _Ptr(0) {
    }
    iterator( _NodePtr _P ) : _Ptr(_P) {}

    reference operator*() const {
      return (_Value(_Ptr));
    }

    _Tptr operator->() const {
      return(&**this);
    }

    iterator& operator++() {
      _Inc();
      return (*this);
    }

    iterator &operator++(int) {
      iterator _Tmp = *this;
      ++*this;
      return (_Tmp);
```

```
        }

        iterator& operator--() {
          _Dec();
          return (*this);
        }

          iterator operator--(int) {
          iterator _Tmp = *this;
                --*this;
                return (_Tmp);
        }

          bool operator==(const iterator& _X) const {
          return (_Ptr == _X._Ptr);
        }

          bool operator!=(const iterator& _X) const {
          return (!(*this == _X));
        }

        void _Inc() {

          if (_Right(_Ptr) != _Z(_Ptr))
            _Ptr = _Min(_Right(_Ptr));
                  else {
            _NodePtr _P;
                      while (_Parent(_Ptr) != _Z(_Ptr) &&
                              _Ptr == _Right(_P = _Parent(_Ptr))) {
              _Ptr = _P;
            }
            _Ptr = _P;
          }
        }

        void _Dec() {

          if (_Parent(_Ptr) == _Z(_Ptr))
            _Ptr = _Max(_Right(_Ptr));
          else

            if ( _Parent(_Parent(_Ptr)) == _Ptr)
```

```
            _Ptr = _Right(_Ptr);
          else
            if (_Left(_Ptr) != _Z(_Ptr))
              _Ptr = _Max(_Left(_Ptr));
            else
            {
              _NodePtr _P;
              while ( _Ptr == _Left(_P = _Parent(_Ptr)))
                _Ptr = _P;
              _Ptr = _P;
            }
        }


    };

    iterator begin() {

      if (_Right( head ) == z)
        return iterator( head );

      _NodePtr _P = head;
      return iterator( _Min(_Right( _P ) ) );
    }
    iterator end() {
      _NodePtr _P = head;
      return iterator( _P );
    }
};

void Print( char r )
{
  cout << r << endl;
}

int main()
{

  BinaryTree<char, char> bTree;

  bTree.Insert( 't', 't' );
  bTree.Insert( 'r', 'r' );
```

```
bTree.Insert( 'e', 'e' );
bTree.Insert( 'e', 'e' );


bTree.Traverse(0);


char ans = 1;
while( ans ) {

  cout << "Insert a letter :     1" << endl;
  cout << "Search for a letter : 2" << endl;
  cout << "Delete a letter :     3" << endl;
  cout << "Finish :              4" << endl;

  cin >> ans;

  char c;
  switch( ans ) {

  case '1':
    cout << "Enter a letter to insert" << endl;
    cin >> c;

    bTree.Insert( c, c );
  break;

  case '2':
    cout << "Enter a letter to find" << endl;
    cin >> c;


    if (bTree.Search( c ) != 'Z')
      cout << "Found " << c << endl;
    else
      cout << c << " Not Found" << endl;

  break;

  case '3':
    cout << "Enter a letter to delete" << endl;
    cin >> c;
```

```
        bTree.Remove( c );

      break;

    case '4':
      ans = 0;

    break;

    default:
    break;

    }

    cout << "Tree Contents" << endl;
    for_each(bTree.begin(), bTree.end(), Print );

  }

  return 0;

}
```

ANNOTATIONS

The implementation of this binary tree container differs quite substantially from the one found in Chapter 3. Here it provides the basic functionality, such as insert, remove and search, but it also provides iterator functionality to enable interaction with other STL algorithms and containers.

NODE STRUCTURE

The tree consists of a number of nodes that can be linked together via their left and right branch pointers to form a tree structure. The node structure definition is shown here:

```
// Struct Node. Contains the links and item data.
  struct _Node {

    value_type item;
    NodePtr l; // Left
    NodePtr r; // Right
```

```
NodePtr z; // Terminating node
NodePtr p; // Parent node

Node( key_type k, referent_type v, _NodePtr ll, _NodePtr rr,
     _NodePtr _X, _NodePtr _Y ) {
  item.first = k;
  item.second = v;
  l = ll;
  r = rr;
  p = _X;
  z = _Y;
}

key_type &_Key() { return item.first; }
referent_type &_Value() { return item.second; }

};
```

In the preceding code, a **NodePtr** is defined to be a pointer to a node structure. The macro **_POINTER_X( )**, defined in **<xmemory>** (Microsoft STL-specific), is used to define a node pointer for a standard memory model. The macro **_REFERENCE_X( )**, also defined in **<xmemory>**, is used to create a node reference that can be used to pass node references.

Methods, including **_Min( )**, are declared as being static members and are used throughout the binary tree implementation, and the iterator class for simplifying and reducing the number of lines code.

The **key_type** and **referent_type** and other typedefs are provided to simplify the implementation and improve readability.

Each node contained within the tree holds a node pointer to its parent and the terminating "dummy" node, **z**. The parent node pointer is necessary because the iterator requires access to the parent node.

It may not seem obvious, but there is no difference between using a "dummy" node instead of a NULL value to terminate node branches. Using a dummy node does have one major advantage, however: It provides a convenient way in which to terminate searches, which can be seen in the binary tree's **Search( )** implementation. Every tree implementation must have a root or head, which forms the start of the tree. The **head** node of this binary tree is created when the binary tree is instantiated. The **head** node right, parent, and **z** node pointers are initialized with the binary tree's terminating node, which establishes an empty tree. The following test:

```
If (_Right( head ) == z ) == true
```

can easily be used to ascertain if the tree is indeed empty. This test removes the necessity for maintaining a count or size information.

The terminating node, **z**, is initialized at the same time as the **head** node, but the **z** node has all its node pointers initialized to 0. Each node also contains an STL **pair** structure, which is used to store the item's key and data. The **pair** structure provides two methods to obtain the key and data, which return the pair's **first** and **second** member variables, respectively.

INSERT( )

We will start by examining the **Insert( )** method of the binary tree:

```
void Insert(key_type v, referent_type info)   {
   NodePtr p;
   NodePtr x;
   p = head;
   x =  _Right( head );

   // Locate insertion position
   while ( x != z ) {
     p = x;
     x = (key_compare(v, _Key(x))) ? _Left( x ) : _Right( x );
   }

   // Create a new node and link branch nodes.
   x = new _Node(v, info, z, z, p, z );

   // Insert by connecting parent nodes
   if (key_compare(v, _Key(p)))
     Left( p ) = x;
   else
     Right( p ) = x;
}
```

To insert an item into the tree, the key and data must be specified. The **Insert( )** method first assigns a _**NodePtr**, x; it points to the node to the right of the **head** node. This implies that all the keys of items inserted into the tree must be greater than the **heads** key value. This is indeed true. The **head** is initialized with a key value of 0, which is the smallest value that can be contained within the tree—so all subsequent key values must be greater.

To find the insertion location of a new node, the following rules are applied:

1. If the new item's key value is greater than the key value of the current node, go right.

2. If the new item's key value is less than the key value of the current node, go left.

For example, in the **Insert( )** method of this binary tree, the following code finds the correct node branch in which to insert a new node. The parent node variable is **p,** used to store the position of the new node's parent.

```
while ( x != z ) {
  p = x;
  x = (key_compare(v, _Key(x))) ? _Left( x ) : _Right( x );
}
```

Here **key_compare( )** is an instance of **_Pr,** which may be passed as an argument to the binary tree template and can be any compatible algorithm or functor that compares the key data types. In this example, the default **less< >** template class is used. The **_Key( )** static method is defined by the binary tree class, to extract the key value of a **_NodePtr** parameter. A **while** loop is used to iterate over the linked nodes of the binary tree until **x == z.** When the loop terminates, the variable **p** points to the node that will be the parent of the new node. The parent node's left or right branches will form the link between it and the new node. At this point, the correct left or right branch is not actually known.

Next, the new node is created, and its own left, right, and terminating node branches are initialized to the terminating node, **z.** The new node has its parent node pointer, **p,** assigned to the parent node, which was found in the previous **while** loop. At this point the parent and new nodes are linked together, albeit in the wrong direction (that is, new node's parent pointer to parent). The final piece of code corrects this by assigning the parent's left or right branches to the new node. Again, **key_compare( )** is used to find the correct branch to link.

In the example, the binary tree has the characters **s, t,** and **l** inserted. The **s** gets inserted on the right branch of the **head** node; the **t** gets inserted on the right branch of **s**; and the **l** gets inserted on the left branch of **s**.

SEARCH( )

The next method we are going to look at is **Search( ).** The **Search( )** method of the binary tree is used for finding items that match a specified key value.

```
referent_type Search(key_type v)   {

  NodePtr x = _Right( head );
  z->item.first = v;
  while ( v != x->_Key() )
    x = (key_compare(v, _Key(x))) ? _Left( x ) : _Right( x );
  return _Value(x);
}
```

An interesting feature of **Search( )** is that it assigns the passed key value to the terminating node, **z.** This key assignment creates a terminating condition, because **z** will be encountered at the end of an unsuccessful search. **Key_compare( )** is used to compare key values, and a conditional expression assigns the correct left or right branch node to the variable **x**. The **while** loop compares the passed-in key value and the value contained by **x**. If they match, the loop terminates, and the data contained within **x** is returned because this is the required node. If the search is unsuccessful, the data value contained in **z** is returned.

In the sample, the data 'Z' is contained within the terminating node. This has been done to demonstrate the use of a terminating node in the **Search( )** method.

Let's examine the search process to understand the advantage of using a binary search tree. In the example, the characters **s**, **t**, and **l** are inserted. To find the character **t** only requires a maximum of two key-comparisons. If you were to use an array for storing the same characters, the maximum number of comparisons would be three. In our example, however, the insertion of the characters **s**, **t**, and **l** result in a tree with a depth of 2. Advanced binary search trees, such as *red black trees,* implement functionality to maintain search performance by rotating nodes and branches to limit their depth. In these tree types, although they try to maintain a level of performance, their insertion and deletion routines can be slower than traditionally implemented binary trees.

REMOVE( )

The binary tree **Remove( )** method is responsible for removing items from the tree. It uses a specified key value to locate the item to be deleted, and uses a search routine that is almost identical to that found in the **Search( )** method. Let's examine it piece by piece.

```
// Find the item to delete
   while (v != _Key(x) ) {
     p = x;
     x = (key_compare(v, _Key(x))) ? _Left( x ) : _Right( x );
   }

   t = x;
```

The difference between this **while** loop and the one found in **Search( )** is that the position of the parent is maintained by the **_NodePtr** variable **p**.

The following code finds all the nodes that must be reconnected after the node to be removed is deleted from the binary tree. If this were not done, the deletion of a node would make the tree unusable because all nodes below the deleted node would not be correctly linked.

```
// Find the connected nodes
   if (_Right( t ) == z) {
     x = _Left( x );
   }
   else {
     if (_Left(_Right( t )) == z ) {
```

```
      x = _Right( x );
      Left( x ) = _Left( t );
    }
    else  {
      c = _Right( x );
      while (_Left(_Left( c )) != z) {
        c = _Left( c );
      }
      x = _Left( c );
      Left( c ) = _Right( x );
      Left( x ) = _Left( t );
      Right( x ) = _Right( t );
    }
  }
```

The variable **t** is assigned to the node that was found during the **while** loop. The first condition checks to see if the right branch of **t** is equal to the terminating node, **z**. If it is, then **x** is assigned to the node to the left of **x**.

For example, if the tree contained only the character **t**, the right branch of the **head** would point to the node containing **t**. After the search for the node containing **t**, the parent pointer **p** would point to the **head;** and the variable pointer **t** would point to the node to be deleted. So the first condition in the preceding section of code will be true, because the right branch of the node to be deleted is **z**. The variable **x** is assigned to **z**, and the routine moves to the next section shown here:

```
// Delete the node containing the item
   delete t;

   // Relink tree
   if (key_compare(v, _Key(p)))
     _Left( p ) = x;
   else
     _Right( p ) = x;

   if (x->p)
     x->p = p;
}
```

The node is deleted and the parent is relinked to the "orphaned" nodes below. The **key_compare( )** is used to establish the right or left branch of the parent that should be connected; and the final statement **x->p = p** assigns the relinked node's parent pointer to its new parent.

MANAGING MORE NODES

The discussion in the previous section only explains how to delete a node from the tree when the tree contains only a few nodes. It is slightly more complex when the tree contains many nodes. To show this, we need to examine some of the code once again:

```
// Find the connected nodes
   if (_Right( t ) == z) {
     x = _Left( x );
   }
   else {
     if (_Left(_Right( t )) == z ) {
       x = _Right( x );
       Left( x ) = _Left( t );
     }
     else {
       c = _Right( x );
       while (_Left(_Left( c )) != z) {
         c = _Left( c );
       }
       x = _Left( c );
       Left( c ) = _Right( x );
       Left( x ) = _Left( t );
       Right( x ) = _Right( t );
     }
   }
```

If the left node of the right branch of **t** is equal to **z**, the variable **x** is assigned to the right branch of **x**, and the left branch of **x** is assigned to the left branch of **t**. These statements would be executed if the node on the right branch of the node to be deleted had no further nodes on its left branch and if it had a key value that was greater than the one being deleted.

The next section of code is quite complex; it reflects the case where a node is deleted from a section of the tree that has a number of nodes below it.

```
     else {
       c = _Right( x );
       while (_Left(_Left( c )) != z) {
         c = _Left( c );
       }
       x = _Left( c );
```

```
      Left( c ) = _Right( x );
      Left( x ) = _Left( t );
      Right( x ) = _Right( t );
   }
```

In examining this code, first we'll explain the current positions of the node pointer variables **c**, **x**, and **t**. The **c** is simply a node pointer variable that is used as a temporary variable throughout this section. The other two, **x** and **t,** point to the node to be removed; **t** was assigned to **x** earlier in the **Remove( )** method. For example, if **t** were to be removed from the tree, **x** and **t** would currently be pointing to the node that contained the key value **t**.

The first part of the code assigns **c** to point to the node of the right branch of **x**. The **while** loop is used to find the node that has the least key value, since all nodes to the left have a key value that is less than its parent. When the loop terminates, **c** is pointing to the node *before* the node with the *least* key value. The next assignment assigns **x** to the left node of **c**, which is the node with the least key value. The final three assignments are responsible for relinking nodes around the one to be removed. After the relinking has been done, the node to be deleted can be removed from the tree.

The final section of code of the binary tree **Remove( )** method deletes the node and completes the re-linking of the tree by correctly assigning the parent left or right branches to the re-linked nodes.

```
   delete t;

   // Relink tree
   if (key_compare(v, _Key(p)))
      _Left( p ) = x;
   else
      _Right( p ) = x;

   if (x->p)
      x->p = p;
}
```

The **key_compare( )** determines the correct left or right branch of the parent to assign. Since each node also contains a parent node pointer, the very final assignment allots the node's parent pointer to the parent **p**.

TRAVERSE( )

Before examining the binary tree iterators, we are going to examine the **Traverse( )** method. Several algorithms exist that can "traverse" trees in various orders:

Traverse Method	Recursive Rule
inorder	Visit the left subtree, then visit the root, then visit the right subtree.
postorder	Visit the left subtree, then visit the right subtree, then visit the root.
preorder	Visit the root, then visit the left subtree, then visit the right subtree.
level order	None. Can be translated as reading down from top to bottom and from left to right.

The traversing algorithm implemented for this binary tree is **inorder**, which means that the key values will be found in ascending order. For example, if the values **x, s, m,** and **b** were inserted into the tree, the **Traverse( )** method would encounter the items in the order **b, m, s,** and **x.** Here is the code with the **inorder** traversal:

```
void Traverse(_NodePtr t)  {

    // inorder traversal of the binary tree.
    // NOTE. This is a recursive function which
    // if used on a large tree may cause stack overflow.
    if (t == 0)
       t = _Right( head );

    if (t != z) {
       Traverse(_Left( t ));
       Visit( t );
       Traverse(_Right( t ));
    }
}
```

PROGRAMMER'S NOTE *The note at the start of the routine warns that the **Traverse( )** function is recursive. This is a very important consideration when **Traverse( )** is used on large binary trees. Each time the function is called, it pushes variables onto the program's stack. The larger the number of recursive calls, the more stack space required. Since the stack is of finite size, it is possible to run out. If you are unsure of your tree's size, you might want to substitute the following version of **Traverse( )**, which does not use recursion. It replaces the recursive technique with one that uses a series of labels and a user-defined stack.*

```
void Traverse( _NodePtr t ) {
  y:  while( t != z ) {
         Visit( t );
         stck.push(_Right( t ));
         t = _Left( t );
```

```
        }
    if (stck.empty()) goto x;
      t = stck.top();
      stck.pop();
      goto y;
    x:
}
```

The binary tree **Traverse( )** method checks the passed parameter, and if it is 0 the **_NodePtr t** is assigned to the right node of the head. (Remember, this is the first node in the tree.) The conditional statement checks the current value of **t**; if it is not equal to **z**, then a call to **Traverse( )** is made with the node to the left of **t** passed as an argument. The left subtree of the tree will be traversed until the terminating node **z** is encountered. Once **t == z,** the routine unwinds and the node before **z** is visited. **Visit( )** simply prints the value of the node to **cout**. **Traverse( )** is again called, but this time the right node of the current node is passed as an argument. On reentry to **Traverse( )**, the left subtree of the node will be examined, and so on until the complete tree has been traversed.

CLEAR( )

The binary tree implementation shown here is constructed from nodes that have been dynamically allocated. The **Clear( )** method, defined below, can be called to delete and re-initialize the tree:

```
void Clear(_NodePtr p = 0) {
  // Destroys the contents of the tree.

  if (p == 0) p = _Right( head );
  if (p == z) return;   // Tree empty
  DeleteSubTree( p );
  head->r = z;
}
```

The passed **_NodePtr, p,** is validated, and a simple check is made to determine if the tree contains any nodes. The program then calls the binary tree's protected method **DeleteSubTree( ). DeleteSubTree( )** is a recursive method that is very similar to the **Traverse( )** method. Here is the code:

```
void DeleteSubTree(_NodePtr p) {

  _NodePtr t;
  if (p != z) {
    DeleteSubTree( _Left( p ) );
    t = _Right( p );
    delete p;
```

```
    DeleteSubTree( t );
  }
}
```

Once the nodes below the **head** node have been deleted, the **Clear( )** method re-initializes the right branch of the **head** node to **z**. This is important because a deletion results in the **head**'s right branch "pointing to" uninitialized memory.

The destructor of the binary tree uses **Clear( )** to delete the contents of the tree. It completes the deletion of the tree by deleting both the **head** and **z** nodes. The binary tree destructor is shown here:

```
~BinaryTree() {
  // Binary tree destructor
  Clear();
  delete z;
  delete head;
}
```

ITERATORS

To make the binary tree compatible with other STL algorithms, it is essential that some form of iterator be implemented. In the case of this binary tree container, a nonconstant bi-directional iterator is defined. The iterator class is contained within the binary tree class. Static binary tree functionality allows methods within the iterator implementation to be called. The iterator class is also defined to be a *friend* class of the binary tree. The two methods **begin( )** and **end( )** are defined as methods of the binary tree. Here are their definitions:

```
iterator begin() {
   if (_Right( head ) == z) // Tree empty
     return iterator( head );

   // Returns an iterator which 'points to'
   // the smallest item contained in the tree
   _NodePtr _P = head;
   return iterator( _Min(_Right( _P ) ) );
}

iterator end() {

   // Returns an iterator which 'points to'
   // a terminating iterator.
   _NodePtr _P = head;
   return iterator( _P );
}
};
```

For the purposes of this sample, we will examine only what happens when the **for_each( )** algorithm is used with the binary tree iterators, in the sample's **main( )** routine.

The **begin( )** method checks that the tree contains valid elements. If it does, the method then creates an iterator that contains a node pointer to the node with the *least* key value, which is obtained by using one of the static binary tree members, **_Min( )**. The **end( )** method returns an iterator that contains a node pointer to the **head** of the tree.

```
for_each(bTree.begin(), bTree.end(), Print );
```

The **for_each( )** algorithm, used in the sample to print the contents of the tree, uses the **begin** and **end** iterators of the binary tree. **Print( )** is a user-defined function that prints the values of the nodes. When **for_each( )** is called for the first time, the **begin** and **end** iterators are positioned in the tree so that **begin** is pointing to the node with the least key value, and **end** is pointing to the node **head**. For example, if the characters **s**, **t**, and **l** were added to the tree, the **begin** iterator would be pointing to the node that contains the key **l**, and **end** would be pointing to **head**.

The **for_each( )** algorithm uses the pre-increment operator of the binary tree iterator to obtain the value of the next item in the binary tree. Here is that code:

```
iterator& operator++() {
  _Inc();
  return (*this);
}
```

The **_Inc( )** method is defined by the iterator that increments the position of a contained node pointer, **_Ptr**. The **_Inc( )** method is shown here:

```
void _Inc() {

  // Forward traverse of the binary tree. Moves _Ptr
  // forward by one position each time it is called.
  if (_Right(_Ptr) != _Z(_Ptr))
    _Ptr = _Min(_Right(_Ptr));
  else {
    _NodePtr _P;
    while (_Parent(_Ptr) != _Z(_Ptr) && _Ptr == _Right(_P =
            _Parent(_Ptr))) {
      _Ptr = _P;
    }

    if (_Right(_Ptr) != _P)
```

```
      _Ptr = _P;
  }
}
```

The binary tree iterator class maintains a node pointer member variable, which is used to store a current position within the tree. This node pointer, **_Ptr**, is essential to both **_Inc( )** and its decrementing equivalent **_Dec( )**. When the **begin** and **end** iterators are created, their **_Ptr** is initialized with a node pointer to the least key value or **head**. When **_Inc( )** is called, the iterator used is the one returned from the binary tree **begin( )** method. The beginning of the **_Inc( )** method starts by checking that the **_Ptr** is not at the bottom of a right subtree, by testing the right node of **_Ptr** against **z**. If **_Ptr** isn't at the bottom of a right subtree, it's assigned to the node with the least key value of the current node's left subtree. This is done by using the static function **_Min( )**, defined in **BinaryTree** .

The **while** loop, as shown just below, is used to find the next node in the sequence, by moving up the tree via the node parent pointer. The **_Inc( )** method follows the recursive rule of **inorder** traversal.

```
_NodePtr _P;
  while (_Parent(_Ptr) != _Z(_Ptr) && _Ptr == _Right(_P =
         _Parent(_Ptr))) {
    _Ptr = _P;
  }
```

The first conditional test within the **while** loop is used to check that the parent of **_Ptr** is not the **head** node. The temporary node pointer **_P** is used to maintain the position of the parent and is used in the condition of the **while** loop to find the right node of the current node's parent. The final assignment assigns **_P** to **_Ptr**.

```
  Ptr = _P;
```

Examine the **_Inc( )** method and you can clearly see the inorder recursive rule of "Visit the left subtree, then visit the root, then visit the right subtree." The binary tree container implemented in this sample could be used for many different applications. Implementation of various traversal algorithms could be used to implement a parse tree, for example. However, the use of the inorder traversal algorithms implemented in this sample means that the tree is always sorted. The implementation of the iterator class allows the tree to be traversed in either ascending or descending order and facilitates interaction with a great number of STL algorithms.

C/C++ for CGI Design

By Lars Klander

clock.cpp

post.h (from post.exe)

post.cpp (from post.exe)

I
f you have been developing programs for any length of time, it is almost inevitable that you will, sooner or later, need to write programs that run from the World Wide Web or the Internet. In Chapter 9, you saw techniques for creating client programs that access the Internet. In addition to the client that accesses the Internet, however, the Internet's client-server model requires that there must be a server somewhere that sends information back to the client. While there are different protocols that Internet transmissions use, probably the most commonly used protocols today are the HyperText Transport Protocol (HTTP) and the Transport Control Protocol/Internet Protocol (TCP/IP). These two protocols are necessary for the generation and transmission of Web pages to client browsers—by far the largest use of the Internet, with the possible exception of e-mail.

In this chapter, you will learn about the client-server model used on the Internet. You'll study two programs that use the principles of Internet transmissions to generate new Web pages or Web objects for users to view.

The CGI Architecture

Historically, programmers have created applications that serve up custom Web responses with an architecture known as CGI, which stands for Common Gateway Interface. Such extensions run as simple executables. If the client asks the server to run the program, the server in turn expects to spawn a whole new process and steal the results of the program by reading the data written to the standard output device. In implementation, the standard output is generally redirected to a pipe that looks like a file, as far as the spawned program is concerned.

In most applications, the server then reads the file and holds onto it briefly before sending it off to the client machine. As soon as the spawned program is done and the server's operating system terminates the running process, the server fires off the results to the client. This approach to writing server extensions is pretty easy to understand. Since the program is simply a plain old C/C++ program, the developer can write it using familiar tools and by doing very little work above and beyond writing a command-line utility.

The downside to CGI development is that the server has to do an enormous amount of work to start and manage the spawned process. Spawning a process, after all, causes the operating system to allocate substantial memory, read the executable image from a file, and then get the program running. While the program is running, the operating system has to facilitate communication between the application and the server. Moreover, in most operating systems, throwing data from one process to the next in this kind of architecture is not a lightweight operation. Finally, once the program is done executing, all of the setup work has to be undone. On top of all this, the server has to spawn a copy of the executable for each one of the 50,000 or so users who might be hitting the CGI request all at the same time.

Because of its power and flexibility, however, CGI is still the method of choice for most programmers trying to create Web-based solutions—although many variations on the CGI model have sprung up in recent years. For example, servers based on the Windows NT platform can support CGI applications, but they also support a much more efficient method for implementing extension applications (known as ISAPI, and beyond the scope of this chapter).

It is important to understand that CGI applications can be written in any language. Most CGI developers use either PERL, a language specifically designed for writing CGI programs, or C/C++ to create their CGI programs. However, if you are running Windows NT for your server (or any other Microsoft-compatible operating system), you could write your CGI programs in Visual Basic if you wanted to. Additionally, most database providers have in recent years created tools to help you build servers that spool out files to clients. Many development tools, such as Cold Fusion, also provide a simple means to extend the features that your server offers. Nothing, however, beats C/C++ for power and flexibility.

PROGRAMMER'S NOTE *Most CGI programmers refer to all CGI applications—whether written in PERL, C/C++, or another development language—as "CGI scripts." In general, this chapter will use "CGI script" and "CGI application" interchangeably.*

FTP and HTTP: State vs. Stateless

As you probably know, the Internet supports more than one protocol, including FTP and HTTP. FTP provides a continuous Internet connection until an error occurs or until you break the connection. Because the FTP connection is continuous, it is a *state-maintaining connection*. The HTTP protocol, on the other hand, is *stateless*. Stateless means that a browser and server combine to make a network connection, and both later break the connection. For example, when you connect to a Web site, your browser and the server create a connection that lets the server download the site's HTML (HyperText Markup Language) file to the browser.

After the browser receives the file, the server breaks the connection. As your browser *parses* the HTML file (that is, breaks the file down into its component parts), the browser may encounter HTML references to images, Java applets, or other objects that must then be downloaded from the server. Each time the browser must download a file, it must establish a new connection to the server.

A primary reason for developing some of the new HTML standards (such as Dynamic HTML) is that stateless transmissions are by nature very slow. On one hand, because the server and browser must establish a new connection for each downloaded file (which causes delays in delivering content to users), much of the Web's promise remains unrealized. On the other hand, stateless HTML is much more efficient from the server perspective than the new proposed standards. To illustrate the differences, Figure 16-1 compares server handling of stateless HTML, to the way servers might handle some of the proposed, nonstateless HTML.

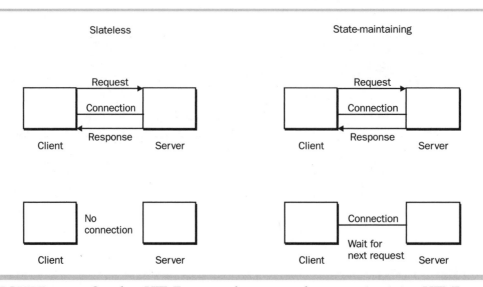

FIGURE 16-1. Stateless HTML versus the proposed, state-maintaining HTML

The Efficiency of Stateless Communications

A single HTTP request and response pair is a *transaction*. HTTP uses a TCP/IP (Transport Control Protocol/Internet Protocol) connection that is maintained only for the single transaction's duration. TCP/IP is the set of protocols that determine the form and transport of communications on the Internet. Neither the client (which usually runs a Web browser) nor the server remembers a connection's last state.

Think about how you browse a Web site, and the HTTP transactions will make sense. As you know, when you click your mouse on a *hypertext* link, or *hyperlink*, your browser moves you to another site. Knowing that you may at any time use a hyperlink to leave a Web site, it is easy for the server to assume you *are* going to leave and thus break the connection first. If you stay, the server simply creates a new connection. When you do leave, the server does not have to do anything else—it has already broken the connection. Releasing connections in this way lets a server respond to other clients, and thereby improves the server's efficiency.

Recently, however, server programmers have experimented with *connection caching*, in which a server does not immediately close a connection after providing a response. By caching the connection, the server can respond quickly when the client "revisits" the site. As Web sites become more complex and offer users more local links, connection caching (for known local links) will improve performance.

PROGRAMMER'S NOTE   *Do not confuse connection caching with the local caching that most browsers perform.*

The Four-Step HTTP Transaction

Before you start to design server-side CGI applications, let's examine the steps taken by the two computers when the client communicates with the server.

Before a client and server can exchange data, they must first establish a connection. Clients and servers on the Internet must also establish connections before they can communicate, using TCP/IP. You also know that clients request data from servers and that servers respond by providing the requested data; these requests and responses are accomplished using HTTP. In addition, you know that servers and clients only maintain their TCP/IP connection for one transaction (HTTP is stateless), and that servers usually close the connection after the transaction is complete.

When you put this information together, you get the four-step HTTP transaction process, described in the following sections.

Step 1: Establish a Connection

Before a client and a server can exchange information, they must first establish a TCP/IP connection—which they will use for the communication underlying the transfer. To distinguish protocols, applications use a unique *port number* for each protocol. Common protocols such as FTP and HTTP have *well-known* port numbers. Developers of client and server programs use the term *well-known* because the ports are commonly used for certain protocols, even though no standards body has specified them as the "correct" ports for those protocols.

The usual port assignment for HTTP is port 80, but HTTP can use other ports—provided the client and the server both agree to use that different port number. Table 16-1 lists the well-known port assignments for commonly used Web and Internet protocol ports.

PROGRAMMER'S NOTE   *TCP/IP treats all ports below 1024 as **privileged ports**, and all well-known port assignments fall under the privileged port category. You should never designate your own port numbers below 1024.*

Step 2: Client Issues a Request

Each HTTP request issued by a client to a Web server begins with a *request method*, followed by an object's URL. To the method and the URL, the client appends the

Protocol	Port Number
File Transfer Protocol	21
Telnet Protocol	23
Simple Mail Transfer Protocol	25
Trivial File Transfer Protocol	69
Gopher Protocol	70
Finger Protocol	79
Hypertext Transfer Protocol	80

TABLE 16-1.   Well-Known Port Assignments on the Internet

HTTP protocol version it uses, followed by a carriage return/line feed (CRLF) character pair. The browser, depending on the request, may follow the CRLF with information the browser encodes in a particular header style. After it completes the preceding information, the browser appends a CRLF to the request. Again depending on the request's nature, the browser may follow the entire request with an entity body (a Multi-Purpose Internet Mail Extensions or MIME-encoded document).

An HTTP *method* is a command the client uses to specify the purpose of its server request. All HTTP methods correspond to a resource (which the client's URL identifies). The client also specifies the HTTP version it is using (such as HTTP 1.0). Together, the method, the URL, and the HTTP protocol version make up the *Request-Line.* The Request-Line is a section within the *Request-Header* field. For example, a client may use the HTTP GET method to request a Web-page graphic from a server.

The client uses a Request-Header field to give the server information about the request itself, and about the client making the request. In a request, the entity body is simply supporting data for the request. To compose the entity body, the client generally uses the name of the data to be transferred by the server. Figure 16-2 shows the process performed by the client and the server when they make a connection and the client sends a request.

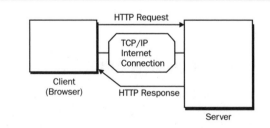

FIGURE 16-2.   Client-server communication on an HTTP request

Step 3: Server Issues a Response

After a Web server receives and interprets a request message, the server responds to the client with an HTTP *response message*. The response message always begins with the HTTP protocol version, followed by a three-digit *status code* and a *reason phrase*. Next, the response message includes a CRLF pair, followed by the particular information requested by the client, which the server encodes in a particular header style. Finally, the server appends a CRLF, optionally following it with an entity body.

The status code is a three-digit number that describes the server's ability to understand and satisfy the client's request. The reason phrase is a short text description of the status code. When combined, the HTTP protocol version, status code, and reason phrase make up the *status line*.

A Response-Header may contain specific information relating to the requested resource, plus whatever MIME declarations the server may require to deliver the response. When a Web server sends a Response-Header to a client, the server usually includes the same information supplied in the client's Request-Header. The entity body (which the server composes in bytes) within the response contains the data the server is transferring to the client. Figure 16-3 depicts the server's response to the client.

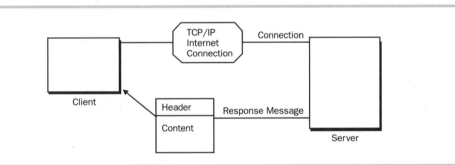

FIGURE 16-3.   The server's response to the client's request

Step 4: Server Terminates the Connection

The server is responsible for terminating a TCP/IP connection with a client after it performs the client's request. However, both the client and the server must manage a connection's unexpected closing. That is, if you click your mouse on your browser's Stop button, the browser must close the connection. Therefore, the surviving computer must recognize the other connected computer's crash. The surviving computer, in turn, will close the connection. In any case, when either one or both parties close a connection, the current transaction always terminates, regardless of the transaction's status. Figure 16-4 shows the complete, four-step HTTP transaction.

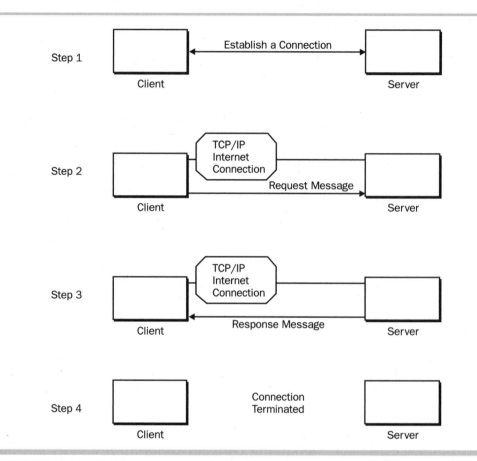

FIGURE 16-4.   The four steps together perform the complete HTPP transaction

A Closer Look at URIs

As you read Web literature, you have doubtless encountered the term *Uniform Resource Identifier (URI)*. Most texts refer to URIs as Web addresses, Uniform Document Identifiers, Uniform Resource Locators (URLs), and Uniform Resource Names (URNs) combined. HTTP defines a URI as a formatted string that uses names, locations, or other characteristics to identify a network resource. In other words, a URI is a simple text string that addresses an object on the Web. Understanding URIs and

URLs is crucial, because the information that the client packs into the URL will often be important for your CGI programs that perform more complete processing.

Inside the URL

To locate a document on the Web, you must know the document's Internet address. A Web document's Internet address is called a Uniform Resource Locator (URL). You can compare the relationship between a URL and a resource, to the relationship between a book and its index. To find information in a book, you look in the book's index. To find a Web resource, you use its address (URL). Web browsers use URLs to locate Web resources.

The basic syntax for a URL is simple. A URL contains two parts, as the following code fragment shows:

```
<scheme>:<scheme-specific-part>
```

The following code fragment shows the full syntax for an HTTP URL:

```
http://<host>:<port>/<path>?<search_part>
```

As you can see, the URL's *<scheme>* portion is *http,* and the *<scheme-specific-part>* identifies a *host,* an optional *port,* an optional *path,* and an optional *search_part.* If you omit the *port* element, the URL will default to the protocol port 80 (the well-known port for HTTP). Do not include the *search_part* within URLs because HTTP does not currently implement this element, though you will often see *search_part* in combination with scripted pages to pass queries. (Search engines, for example, use the *search_part* string within their CGI environments to perform the search that the user requests.)

PROGRAMMER'S NOTE   *URLs are not unique to the Web. In fact, several other protocols use URLs, including FTP, GOPHER, and Telnet. However, all URLs have the same purpose: to identify an object's address on the Internet.*

Relating URLs, Protocols, and File Types

A URL not only provides an address for an Internet object, it also describes the protocol the application must use to access that object. For example, the HTTP URL scheme indicates a Web space (area), while a File Transfer Protocol (FTP) scheme indicates an FTP space. You can think of a space on the Internet as an area reserved for information of a particular type. For example, all Internet FTP documents reside in FTP space.

A URL can also include a *document-resource identifier*. The document-resource identifier specifies the file's format—provided the file's creator has followed the correct naming conventions for the resource. For example, a file with an *html* extension should contain text in the HTML format, and a file with an *au* extension should contain audio.

URL Fragments

As you examine a URL, you may find it easier to identify its exact reference if you break the URL into pieces. To better understand this, consider the following (fake) URL:

```
http://www.osborne.com/books/index.htm
```

In this example, the URL's *<scheme>* specifies the HTTP protocol. The double slashes that follow the colon indicate that the object is an Internet object. After the slashes comes the server's address, which in this case is *www.osborne.com*. Next, the slash separator specifies a directory path, *books*. Finally, the last (rightmost) slash specifies the name (*index*) and, optionally, the document-resource identifier extension that corresponds to the desired object (*htm*).

Breaking a URL into sections is important when you create *relative URLs*, discussed in "Absolute and Relative URLs" later in this chapter.

Looking at URLs and HTML

Explaining HyperText Markup Language (HTML) in detail is beyond this book's scope. For our purposes here, you can view HTML as a language designers use to structure Web documents. Hyperlinks are a significant portion of this structure. When a browser renders a Web document for display, the browser typically highlights the document's hyperlink portions to differentiate them from the normal text. When you create a Web document, HTML lets you control the creation of each hyperlink you add to the document.

You use a special HTML element called an *anchor* to represent a link in a Web document. An HTML anchor is a tag the designer inserts into a Web document to specify a link (a corresponding URL) that the browser should associate with specific text or a graphic image. Designers specify a URL within an anchor element to inform the browser of the linked resource's address.

The following example contains a reference to the *klander.htm* URL, which is up two levels in the directory tree from the current page (as the next section, "Absolute and Relative URLs," explains). The example also references a GIF image file.

```
<A target="main" href="../../klander.htm">
    <img align=bottom src="../../chewie.gif"></a>
```

In other words, the anchor contains the URL of the resource attached to your hypertext or, as in this example, a graphic image.

Absolute and Relative URLs

You already know that a hypertext document is a document that contains hyperlinks. The Web is a maze of hyperlinked documents. When designers create a

Web document, they typically link their document to other documents that they or someone else created; documents may also link to video files, graphics, and other interactive content. Each link requires a URL address to identify the corresponding object. As you have learned, browsers use URLs to locate Web documents. URL addresses come in two types: absolute and relative.

An *absolute URL* specifies an object's complete address and protocol. In other words, if the URL's *<scheme>* (such as *http*) is present, the URL is an absolute URL. The following is an example of an absolute URL:

```
http://www.osborne.com/index.htm
```

A *relative URL*, on the other hand, uses the URL associated with the document currently open in your browser. Using the same *<scheme>*, server address, and directory tree (if present) as the open document, the browser reconstructs the URL by replacing the filename and extension with those of the relative URL.

For example, consider the following absolute URL:

```
http://www.osborne.com/index.htm
```

If a hyperlink within the HTML document specifies a reference to the relative URL AnnotatedArchives/cc++.htm, as shown just below:

```
<A HREF="/AnnotatedArchives/cc++.htm"> C/C++ Annotated Archives Page</A>
```

then the browser will reconstruct the Osborne URL as http://www.osborne.com/ AnnotatedArchives/cc++.htm.

PROGRAMMER'S NOTE   *When you use the single dot (.) in front of the relative URL (for example, .AnnotatedArchives/cc++.htm), it has the same result as entering AnnotatedArchives/cc++.htm.*

CGI's Place in the Web Model

From the user's perspective, the HTTP model is inactive, offering little or no interaction. In short, the user could simply view a Web page's contents without interacting with elements on the page. An *interactive model* was therefore the natural next step in the Web's evolution. Such interactivity was achieved through the use of *interactive forms* created with CGI, including PERL, C/C++, TCL, and other programming languages.

Using HTML entries, a Web designer can create a form that lets users (through their browsers) interact with the server. When users click their mouse on a form's Submit button, the browser sends the form to the server, which in turn runs a program (normally written in PERL or C/C++) that processes the form's entries. Depending on the server program's purpose, the program may generate an HTML-based response that the server sends back to the browser.

Figure 16-5 shows a client-server model that uses CGI. Note how the CGI interface works with information that comes back from the client, performs processing on that information, and then generates result information (which the server sends back to the client). This interaction model is the foundation of all CGI processing (though you may create CGI applications that do not generate HTML results, and so on).

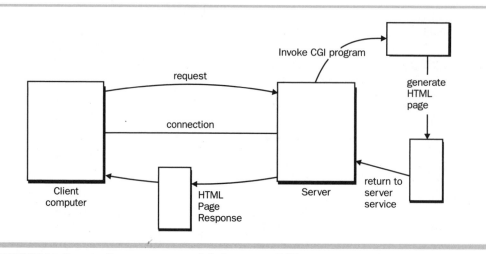

FIGURE 16-5.   A client-server model that uses CGI.

Introducing the Clock Component

Now that you better understand the fundamentals of HTML communications, and you have a vision of how CGI interacts with the model, we can begin working with a simple CGI application that generates a text depiction of the current date and time and sends it back to the client.

> **NOTE**   *It is important to note that this component does not generate a complete HTML page—rather, it generates HTML-style information for inclusion within another page.*

clock.cpp

The Clock Component

The program to implement the clock component is relatively straightforward.

```cpp
#include <iostream>
#include <string>
#include <ctime>
using namespace std;
```

```cpp
// Define Constants
const int Display_Week_Day = 1;
const int Display_Month = 1;
const int Display_Month_Day = 1;
const int Display_Year = 1;
const int Display_Time = 1;
const int Display_Time_Zone = 1;
const char Standard_Time_Zone[4] = "EST";
const char Daylight_Time_Zone[4] = "EDT";

/***************************************************************************/
int main()
{
  char Week_Days[7][10] = { "Sunday", "Monday", "Tuesday",
                            "Wednesday",
                            "Thursday", "Friday", "Saturday" };
  char Months[12][10] =   { "January", "February", "March", "April",
                            "May",
                            "June", "July", "August", "September",
                            "October", "November", "December" };
  char Time_Zone[4];

  tm *ptm;
  time_t *cur_time;

  cout << "Content-type: text/html\n\n";
  // Set up the memory for the time and time time struct.
  cur_time = new time_t;
  ptm = new tm;

  // Get the time, then create the struct with time values.
  time(cur_time);
  ptm = localtime(cur_time);

  // Determine whether it is daylight savings time or not.
  if (ptm->tm_isdst)
    strcpy(Time_Zone,Daylight_Time_Zone);
  else
    strcpy(Time_Zone,Standard_Time_Zone);

  // Display the day of the week if requested.
```

```
if (Display_Week_Day) {
  cout << Week_Days[ptm->tm_wday];
  if (Display_Month)
    cout << ", ";
}

// Display the name of the month if requested.
if (Display_Month)
  cout << Months[ptm->tm_mon] << " ";

// Display the day of the month if requested.
if (Display_Month_Day != 0) {
  if (ptm->tm_mday < 10)
    cout << "0";
  cout << ptm->tm_mday;
  if (Display_Year)
    cout << ", ";
}

// Display the year if requested.
if (Display_Year) {
  cout << ptm->tm_year + 1900;
  if (Display_Time)
    cout << " - ";
  else if (Display_Time_Zone)
    cout << " ";
}

// Display the time if requested.
if (Display_Time) {
  if (ptm->tm_hour < 10)
    cout << "0";
  cout << ptm->tm_hour << ":";
  if (ptm->tm_min < 10)
    cout << "0";
  cout << ptm->tm_min << ":";
  if (ptm->tm_sec < 10)
    cout << "0";
  cout << ptm->tm_sec;
  if (Display_Time_Zone)
    cout << " ";
}
```

```
// Display the time zone if requested.
if (Display_Time_Zone)
  cout << Time_Zone;

return 0;
}
```

ANNOTATIONS

Most of what the **clock.cpp** program does is relatively straightforward. In analyzing the program, let's start with the constant definitions, which are pretty simple.

```
// Define Constants
const int Display_Week_Day = 1;
const int Display_Month = 1;
const int Display_Month_Day = 1;
const int Display_Year = 1;
const int Display_Time = 1;
const int Display_Time_Zone = 1;
const char Standard_Time_Zone[4] = "EST";
const char Daylight_Time_Zone[4] = "EDT";
```

The first six constants use integer values to instruct the program to display all the information in the date—from the day to the time and time zone. For example, if you want to modify the component to not display the day of the week, you can simply change the value of the **Display_Week_Day** constant to 0. The last two constants define the time zone in text; you should modify these values to reflect the location of your server. If you are in California, for example, you'd change the zones to **PST** and **PDT**.

After declaring the constants used for processing, the program enters the **main( )** function to generate the actual output that goes to the client:

```
int main()
{
  char Week_Days[7][10] = { "Sunday", "Monday", "Tuesday",
                            "Wednesday",
                            "Thursday", "Friday", "Saturday" };
  char Months[12][10] =   { "January", "February", "March", "April",
                            "May",
                            "June", "July", "August", "September",
                            "October", "November", "December" };
  char Time_Zone[4];
```

The program code first defines several arrays, which it then uses to generate the string information. The **Week_Days** array is a multidimensional character array corresponding to the seven days of the week. The **Months** array, similarly, corresponds to the 12 months of the year. The **Time_Zone** array maintains the information about the current time zone—either standard or daylight savings time.

Next, the program declares a pair of variables that will maintain time information within the CGI program. The program will use the variables to construct the components of the date and time string:

```
tm *ptm;
time_t *cur_time;
```

The first output to **cout** tells the receiving location (which, in this case, is a client browser) that the information coming to it is text, formatted as HTML:

```
cout << "Content-type: text/html\n\n";
```

In general, when you send CGI information down the pipe to the client, you will always format it as **text/html**. Doing so lets your CGI application send full HTML-style documents to the client, including placing tags on specific components, and so on. (You will see HTML formatting in the next program example.)

As you might expect, after you create the variables needed to store the information, you must initialize those variables—here, you initialize the variables, telling the compiler to set aside the memory for them:

```
// Set up the memory for the time and time structure.
cur_time = new time_t;
ptm = new tm;
```

You have not yet, however, assigned the actual time values to the variables, which the program does next:

```
// Get the time, then create the struct with time values.
time(cur_time);
ptm = localtime(cur_time);
```

The **time** function returns the current time in seconds since midnight (00:00:00) on January 1, 1970—an important value, but not particularly useful unless you want to perform a lot of processing on the value. Luckily, C/C++ provides the **localtime** function to simplify your processing. The **localtime** function converts a time stored as a **time_t** value and stores the result in a structure of type **tm**. The **localtime** function returns a pointer to the structure result (which you, in turn, store within the **ptm** pointer).

The fields of the structure type **tm** store the following values, each of which is an **int**:

tm_sec	Seconds after minute (0–59)
tm_min	Minutes after hour (0–59)
tm_hour	Hours after midnight (0–23)
tm_mday	Day of month (1–31)
tm_mon	Month (0–11; January = 0)

tm_year	Year (current year minus 1900)
tm_wday	Day of week (0–6; Sunday = 0)
tm_yday	Day of year (0–365; January 1 = 0)
tm_isdst	Positive value if Daylight Saving Time (**dst**) is in effect; 0 if **dst** is not in effect; negative value if status of **dst** is unknown. The C++ run-time library assumes United States rules for implementing the calculation of Daylight Saving Time (DST).

You will then use the values that you have placed within the **ptm** pointer to determine the current time information and perform the appropriate processing within the CGI program.

Much of the program code is pretty straightforward—a series of simple **if** statements that display output to the HTML file based on the value of the members within the **ptm** pointer.

```
// Determine whether it is daylight savings time or not.
if (ptm->tm_isdst)
   strcat(Time_Zone,Daylight_Time_Zone);
else
   strcat(Time_Zone,Standard_Time_Zone);
```

The first **if** statement, just above, checks the **tm_isdst** member to determine whether the current time is a Daylight Saving Time reflection. If it is, the program sets the **Time_Zone** variable to Daylight time—otherwise, it sets the **Time_Zone** variable to Standard Time.

Next, the program code checks to determine whether it should display weekday name information. If so, the program sends the value within the **Week_Days** array that the **ptm** structure specifies as the current day to the HTML file:

```
// Display the day of the week if requested.
if (Display_Week_Day) {
   cout << Week_Days[ptm->tm_wday];
   if (Display_Month)
      cout << ", ";
}
```

For example, if the current day is Sunday, the **tm_wday** member will have a value of 0, instructing the program code to send the **Week_Days[0]** member to the client.

After sending the day of the week, the program checks to see if it is printing out the month. If it is, it inserts a comma between the weekday string and the month string. If the constant specifies that the program should display the month, the **if** statement uses another **cout** statement to send the current month (indicated by the **tm_mon** member) to the output.

```
// Display the name of the month if requested.
if (Display_Month)
   cout << Months[ptm->tm_mon] << " ";
```

The next **if** statement performs processing similar to the other statements, but does check to determine whether the value is less than 10. If so, a 0 is inserted before the actual day value—a formatting step to ensure that the date and time string maintains a consistent look. If the day of the month is after the 9th, the program simply outputs the day. Then, it checks to see if the program is going to display the year—if so, it inserts another comma between the day and the year.

```
// Display the day of the month if requested.
if (Display_Month_Day != 0) {
  if (ptm->tm_mday < 10)
    cout << "0";
  cout << ptm->tm_mday;
  if (Display_Year)
    cout << ", ";
}
```

Next, the program displays the year information:

```
// Display the year if requested.
if (Display_Year) {
  cout << ptm->tm_year + 1900;
    if (Display_Time)
      cout << " - ";
    else if (Display_Time_Zone)
      cout << " ";
}
```

It generates the year information by adding the integer value of the year to 1900. If the year is after 1999, the program will still display the year value correctly. As for other statements, the program checks to determine what it will display next, sending in a dash if the time is coming, and a space if only the time zone is coming.

The next section of the code displays the time information:

```
// Display the time if requested.
if (Display_Time) {
  if (ptm->tm_hour < 10)
    cout << "0";
  cout << ptm->tm_hour << ":";
  if (ptm->tm_min < 10)
    cout << "0";
  cout << ptm->tm_min << ":";
  if (ptm->tm_sec < 10)
    cout << "0";
```

```
    cout << ptm->tm_sec;
    if (Display_Time_Zone)
      cout << " ";
  }
```

Just as the code did with the month information, here it appends a leading zero to values under 10, and otherwise simply displays the pure value by itself. Finally, the code checks to see if the time zone is coming next, and if so sends a space to prevent the output from running together.

The program code ends by sending the time zone string to output—resulting in the entire string showing up in the browser:

```
  // Display the time zone if requested.
  if (Display_Time_Zone) {
    cout << Time_Zone;
    return 0;
}
```

All told, this program does not do any significantly different processing than it would if you ran it from the command line—which you can do, and you'll receive the current date output from the file. The trick to running the program from within your Web pages is that it will place the output at exactly the point within the page where you invoke the component. The Web page code, then, embeds the actual text returned by the program. You will see more about this in the next section.

A CGI Script That Uses the HTTP POST Method

Now that you have seen the basics of CGI at work, you should be pretty comfortable with it. Your CGI code's output really is not significantly different from regular text output; the CGI programming simply redirects the output to another location. The second example that you will work with in this chapter takes the basic CGI principles demonstrated in the **clock.cpp** example, and takes them a bit further by generating an entire page and a CGI-style form.

In the example, the program simply displays a basic form that asks for the user's name, e-mail address, and phone number. The user can then click on the Send! button, and the CGI script will process the entry and send back a response.

The program **post.exe** was created within Microsoft's Visual C++ 6.0 using the MFC framework; however, the majority of the program processing occurs within the **post.h** header file and the **post.cpp** file. Those are the files that you will focus on in this discussion. You can find all the program files that make up the application on the companion CD-ROM that accompanies this book.

Code

The following code displays the contents of the two files:

```cpp
// post.h : main header file
// . . . App Wizard generated code

#ifndef __AFXWIN_H__
    #error include 'stdafx.h' before including this file for PCH
#endif

#include "resource.h"          // main symbols

//////////////////////////////////////////////////////////////////////////

// CPostApp:
// See post.cpp for the implementation of this class
//

class CPostDoc;
class CMainFrame;
class CPostView;

class CPostApp : public CWinApp
{
public:
    CPostApp();

    CPostDoc *m_pDoc;
    CMainFrame *m_pFrame;
    CPostView *m_pView;
    CStringArray m_saParams;

    // Overrides
    // ClassWizard generated virtual function overrides

    //{{AFX_VIRTUAL(CPostApp)
public:
    virtual BOOL InitInstance();
    virtual int ExitInstance();
    //}}AFX_VIRTUAL
```

```
   void ParseCmdLine(CString& sIniFile, CString& sContentFile,
      CString& sOutputFile);
   void ParseIniFile(CString sIniFile);
   void CreateResponse(CString sOutputFile, CString sIniFile);

// Implementation

  //{{AFX_MSG(CPostApp)
  //}}AFX_MSG
  DECLARE_MESSAGE_MAP()
};

//
// post.cpp file
// C/C++ Annotated Archives Chapter 16
//
// Simple form processing of the HTTP POST method

#include "stdafx.h"
#include "Post.h"
#include "mainfrm.h"
#include "Postview.h"

#ifdef _DEBUG
  #undef THIS_FILE
  static char BASED_CODE THIS_FILE[] = __FILE__;
#endif

///////////////////////////////////////////////////////////////////////

// CPostApp

BEGIN_MESSAGE_MAP(CPostApp, CWinApp)
  //{{AFX_MSG_MAP(CPostApp)
  //}}AFX_MSG_MAP
  // Standard file based document commands
  ON_COMMAND(ID_FILE_NEW, CWinApp::OnFileNew)
  ON_COMMAND(ID_FILE_OPEN, CWinApp::OnFileOpen)
END_MESSAGE_MAP()

///////////////////////////////////////////////////////////////////////
```

```
// CPostApp construction

CPostApp::CPostApp()
{
  m_pView = NULL;
  m_pFrame = NULL;
}

/////////////////////////////////////////////////////////////////////////

// The one and only CPostApp object

CPostApp theApp;

/////////////////////////////////////////////////////////////////////////

// CPostApp initialization

BOOL CPostApp::InitInstance()
{
  LoadStdProfileSettings();  // Load standard INI file options
(including MRU)

  m_pFrame = new CMainFrame;
  m_pView = new CPostView;
  CCreateContext newContext;
  newContext.m_pNewViewClass = NULL;
  newContext.m_pNewDocTemplate = NULL;
  newContext.m_pLastView = NULL;
  newContext.m_pCurrentFrame = NULL;
  newContext.m_pCurrentDoc = NULL;
  DWORD dwStyle = WS_OVERLAPPED;

  // Make a frame with 0 (no) dimensions since this is background
  // process
  if (!m_pFrame->Create(NULL, NULL, dwStyle, CRect(0,0,0,0),
     NULL, NULL, 0L, &newContext))
    return FALSE;

  m_pMainWnd = m_pFrame;
  // Make a view with 0 (no) dimensions
  m_pView->Create(NULL,NULL,WS_CHILD,CRect(0,0,0,0),m_pFrame,
```

```
      AFX_IDW_PANE_FIRST,&newContext);
  m_pView->OnInitialUpdate();
  if (m_lpCmdLine[0] != '\0') {
    CString sIniFile;
    CString sContentFile;
    CString sOutputFile;
    ParseCmdLine(sIniFile, sContentFile, sOutputFile);
    ParseIniFile(sIniFile.GetBuffer(0));
    CreateResponse(sOutputFile, sIniFile);
   }
  PostQuitMessage(0);
  return TRUE;
}

int CPostApp::ExitInstance()
{
  if (m_pView)                        // Clean up
    delete m_pView;
  if (m_pFrame)
    delete m_pFrame;
  return 0;
}

void CPostApp::ParseCmdLine(CString& sIniFile,
    CString& sContentFile, CString& sOutputFile)
{
  CString sCmdLine = m_lpCmdLine;
  int nCmdPos = 0;
  int nWordPos = 0;

  while (nCmdPos < sCmdLine.GetLength() &&
      (sCmdLine[nCmdPos] == ' ' || sCmdLine[nCmdPos] == '\t'))
    nCmdPos++;

  nWordPos = nCmdPos;

  while (nCmdPos < sCmdLine.GetLength() &&
      sCmdLine[nCmdPos] != ' ' && sCmdLine[nCmdPos] != '\t')
    nCmdPos++;

  sIniFile = sCmdLine.Mid(nWordPos, (nCmdPos - nWordPos));

  while (nCmdPos < sCmdLine.GetLength() &&
```

```
          (sCmdLine[nCmdPos] == ' ' || sCmdLine[nCmdPos] == '\t'))
     nCmdPos++;

  nWordPos = nCmdPos;
  while (nCmdPos < sCmdLine.GetLength() &&
      sCmdLine[nCmdPos] != ' ' && sCmdLine[nCmdPos] != '\t')
     nCmdPos++;

  sContentFile = sCmdLine.Mid(nWordPos, (nCmdPos - nWordPos));
  while (nCmdPos < sCmdLine.GetLength() &&
      (sCmdLine[nCmdPos] == ' ' || sCmdLine[nCmdPos] == '\t'))
     nCmdPos++;

  nWordPos = nCmdPos;
  while (nCmdPos < sCmdLine.GetLength() &&
      sCmdLine[nCmdPos] != ' ' && sCmdLine[nCmdPos] != '\t')
     nCmdPos++;

  sOutputFile = sCmdLine.Mid(nWordPos, (nCmdPos - nWordPos));
}

void CPostApp::ParseIniFile(CString sIniFile)
{
  int nIniPos = 0;
  int nBufLen;
  CString sLine;
  char lpszBuf[2048];

  nBufLen = GetPrivateProfileSection("Form Literal",
      (LPSTR)lpszBuf,2048,sIniFile.GetBuffer(0));

  do {
    sLine = "";
    while (nIniPos < nBufLen &&   lpszBuf[nIniPos] != '\0') {
      sLine += lpszBuf[nIniPos];
      nIniPos++;
    }
    nIniPos++;
    if (sLine != "") {
      m_saParams.Add(sLine);
    }
  } while (sLine != "");
```

```
}

void CPostApp::CreateResponse(CString sOutputFile, CString sIniFile)
{
  int i;
  int nIndex;
  CString sResponse;
  CFile fOutput;
  CFileStatus fStatus;
  CString sUser;
  CString sKey;
  CString sVal;

// Send HTML format
  sResponse = "Content-type: text/html\r\n";
  sResponse += "\r\n";
  sResponse += "<!DOCTYPE HTML PUBLIC \"-//W3O//DTD W3 HTML 3.0//EN\"
    >\r\n";
  sResponse += "<HTML>\r\n";
  sResponse += "<HEAD>\r\n";
  sResponse += "<TITLE>POST Application</TITLE>\r\n";
  sResponse += "</HEAD>\r\n";

  for (i = 0; i < m_saParams.GetSize(); i++) {
    sKey.Empty();
    sVal.Empty();
    if ((nIndex = m_saParams[i].Find('=')) != -1) {
      sKey = m_saParams[i].Left(nIndex);
      sVal = m_saParams[i].Right(m_saParams[i].GetLength() -
    nIndex - 1);
    }
    if (sVal == "") {
      sResponse += "<H1>Please enter all data</H1>\r\n";
      break;
    }
    sUser += "<H3>";
    sUser += sKey;
    sUser += ": ";
    sUser += sVal;
    sUser += "</H3>\r\n";
  }
```

```
    if (i == m_saParams.GetSize()) {
      sResponse += "<H1>Server's Reply:</H1>\r\n";
      sResponse += sUser;
    }
    sResponse += "</BODY>\r\n";
    sResponse += "</HTML>\r\n";
    if (fOutput.Open(sOutputFile.GetBuffer(0),
        CFile::modeCreate | CFile::modeWrite | CFile::typeBinary)) {
      fOutput.Write(sResponse.GetBuffer(0),sResponse.GetLength());
      fOutput.Close();
    }
}
```

ANNOTATIONS

The **post.h** header file starts off with some MFC-specific code, and then includes the resource file attached to the project. The resource file defines the values for some string resources attached to the project, as well as view information (even though the application does not use a view implementation). Let's look at the contents of the header file:

```
// post.h : main header file
// . . . App Wizard generated code

#ifndef __AFXWIN_H__
    #error include 'stdafx.h' before including this file for PCH
#endif

#include "resource.h"        // main symbols
```

The next four declarations declare the instances of the classes used by the application. The **CPostDoc** class contains information about the application's document class, which maintains document data. The **CPostApp** class contains information about the Windows application and is derived from the MFC-defined **CWinApp** class.

```
class CPostDoc;
class CMainFrame;
class CPostView;

class CPostApp : public CWinApp
{
```

The **CPostApp** class includes a default constructor and four member variables, as shown next. Three of the variables are pointers to other classes used by the application. The fourth variable declares a **CStringArray** object, which supports an array of string objects.

```
public:
  CPostApp();

  CPostDoc *m_pDoc;
  CMainFrame *m_pFrame;
  CPostView *m_pView;
  CStringArray m_saParams;
```

After declaring the public variables, the header file defines the functions that the class will use:

```
// Overrides
  // ClassWizard generated virtual function overrides

  //{{AFX_VIRTUAL(CPostApp)
public:
  virtual BOOL InitInstance();
  virtual int ExitInstance();
  //}}AFX_VIRTUAL

  void ParseCmdLine(CString& sIniFile, CString& sContentFile,
      CString& sOutputFile);
  void ParseIniFile(CString sIniFile);
  void CreateResponse(CString sOutputFile, CString sIniFile);
```

The **InitInstance( )** and **ExitInstance( )** functions are Windows-specific extensions that perform initialization and cleanup for each instance of an application. The next three functions are all custom functions used by the application to perform its processing. The **ParseCmdLine( )** function will parse the information within the command line. The **ParseIniFile( )** function parses an INI file that the **ParseCmdLine( )** function creates. And finally, the **CreateResponse( )** function generates the actual HTML code that the program will send back to the user.

The last of the code within the header file declares the Visual C++ message maps, which the framework automatically produces when you create the application. For the Post application, the message maps perform no significant purpose.

```
// Implementation

  //{{AFX_MSG(CPostApp)
  //}}AFX_MSG
```

```
  DECLARE_MESSAGE_MAP()
};
```

The **include** statements at the top of the **post.cpp** file simply include header files for the other classes used by **CPostApp**, as well as the MFC-specific file necessary for the application to execute correctly.

```
#include "stdafx.h"
#include "Post.h"
#include "mainfrm.h"
#include "Postview.h"
```

The **#ifdef** series of statements perform processing on behalf of the Visual C++ integrated debugger. The **THIS_FILE** variable is simply set equal to the name of the **post.cpp** file, returned by the __FILE__ macro.

```
#ifdef _DEBUG
  #undef THIS_FILE
  static char BASED_CODE THIS_FILE[] = __FILE__;
#endif
```

The message map section handles message maps for the standard MFC application. The two message maps defined here are defaults for the MFC framework that Visual C++ uses; they perform no important processing for the post application, simply ensuring that the file includes everything necessary within the framework to perform its processing correctly.

```
BEGIN_MESSAGE_MAP(CPostApp, CWinApp)
  //{{AFX_MSG_MAP(CPostApp)
  //}}AFX_MSG_MAP
  // Standard file based document commands
  ON_COMMAND(ID_FILE_NEW, CWinApp::OnFileNew)
  ON_COMMAND(ID_FILE_OPEN, CWinApp::OnFileOpen)
END_MESSAGE_MAP()
```

The constructor for the **CPostApp** class initializes the pointers to the two support classes to NULL. It does so because the application, in generating its output, does not use either the view or the frame. They are simply stubs in the event you should need them later when expanding the program's functionality.

```
CPostApp::CPostApp()
{
  m_pView = NULL;
  m_pFrame = NULL;
}
```

Every Windows application that uses the MFC framework will initialize a single instance of an object that corresponds to the application, as shown here:

```
CPostApp theApp;
```

In general, the framework will call this instance the **theApp** object, and you will not change the name of this instance.

The **InitInstance( )** function is called each time an instance of the application is created, as the following fragment indicates:

```
BOOL CPostApp::InitInstance()
{
   LoadStdProfileSettings();  // Load standard INI file options
```

In other words, if ten users access the CGI application, the **InitInstance( )** function will be called ten times, once for each instance of the application opened by the users. The **LoadStdProfileSettings( )** function is another Windows-specific API function, which loads information about the files most recently used, the preview structure of the application, and so on.

The next two lines initialize the members defined within the **post.h** header file that correspond to the single instances within the class of the frame window and the view.

```
m_pFrame = new CMainFrame;
m_pView = new CPostView;
```

A **CCreateContext** structure contains pointers to the document, the frame window, the view, and the document template. The program code creates an instance of the structure, called **newContext**, as shown here:

```
CCreateContext newContext;
```

It also contains a pointer to a **CRuntimeClass** that identifies the type of view to create. The run-time class information and the current document pointer are used to create a new view dynamically.

The MFC framework uses the **CCreateContext** structure when it creates the frame windows and views associated with a document. When creating a window, the values in this structure provide information used to connect the components that make up a document and the view of its data. You will only need to use **CCreateContext** if you are overriding parts of the creation process.

Because the Post application does not use many elements of the MFC document-view architecture, the application overrides the members of the **newContext** structure, to include **NULL** pointers to objects that the framework normally uses but the Post application does not.

```
newContext.m_pNewViewClass = NULL;
newContext.m_pNewDocTemplate = NULL;
newContext.m_pLastView = NULL;
newContext.m_pCurrentFrame = NULL;
newContext.m_pCurrentDoc = NULL;
```

The **dwStyle** variable contains the Windows-defined **WS_OVERLAPPED** constant, a system value that specifies the appearance of a created window:

```
DWORD dwStyle = WS_OVERLAPPED;
```

You will use the variable when you create the zero-dimension frame window used by the application.

Next, you create a frame window with no dimensions and with the overlapped style, as well as the changed **newContext** structure:

```
if (!m_pFrame->Create(NULL, NULL, dwStyle, CRect(0,0,0,0),
    NULL, NULL, 0L, &newContext))
  return FALSE;
```

Doing so creates a window that does not have any dimensions—the application does not write to any windows (it is a background application), and so you create a window that does not have width or height.

After creating the no-dimension frame window, the application sets the framework's pointer to the main window, to that no-dimensional window. Next, the application performs processing similar to what it did when creating the no-dimensional frame window to create a no-dimensional view. Then the view is updated based on the set of nonvalues.

```
m_pMainWnd = m_pFrame;
// Make a view with 0 (no) dimensions
m_pView->Create(NULL,NULL,WS_CHILD,CRect(0,0,0,0),m_pFrame,
    AFX_IDW_PANE_FIRST,&newContext);
m_pView->OnInitialUpdate();
```

Next, the code checks to see whether the command line contains any parameters. If it does not, the program will fall through the **if** statement and, as you will see later, exit. If parameters do exist, the program creates three string values which will be passed into the **ParseCmdLine( )** function.

```
if (m_lpCmdLine[0] != '\0') {
  CString sIniFile;
  CString sContentFile;
  CString sOutputFile;
```

After calling the **ParseCmdLine( )** function and creating the INI file, the program code parses the INI file. Finally, it crafts and sends the response to the client within the **CreateResponse( )** function.

```
  ParseCmdLine(sIniFile, sContentFile, sOutputFile);
  ParseIniFile(sIniFile.GetBuffer(0));
  CreateResponse(sOutputFile, sIniFile);
```

After performing its processing, the program will exit and call the **ExitInstance( )** function to clean up the instance. In general, **ExitInstance( )** performs much like a destructor, deleting memory allocations, releasing pointers, and so on.

```
}
PostQuitMessage(0);
return TRUE;
}
```

The **ExitInstance( )** function will clean up the application's allocations in the reverse order of creation. So, it first deletes the allocation for the pointer to the view:

```
int CPostApp::ExitInstance()
{
  if (m_pView)                    // Clean up
     delete m_pView;
```

and then deletes the allocation for the pointer to the frame window:

```
  if (m_pFrame)
     delete m_pFrame;
  return 0;
}
```

As mentioned earlier, the **ParseCmdLine( )** function accepts three incoming string variables, passing out information that corresponds to the parsed command-line contents within the variables:

```
void CPostApp::ParseCmdLine(CString& sIniFile,
    CString& sContentFile, CString& sOutputFile)
{
  CString sCmdLine = m_lpCmdLine;
  int nCmdPos = 0;
  int nWordPos = 0;
```

The function begins by declaring a string that contains the command line's contents. Then it initializes the two integer variables used to process the contents of the command line to 0 (the leftmost position in the command line).

The **while** loop that starts the function counts through the characters in the command line, from the left, until it finds the first letter in the command line that is not a space or a tab. When it finds such a character, it exits the loop and continues processing.

```
  while (nCmdPos < sCmdLine.GetLength() &&
      (sCmdLine[nCmdPos] == ' ' || sCmdLine[nCmdPos] == '\t'))
    nCmdPos++;
```

The program code sets the word-tracking variable to the position of the first letter, then uses a **while** loop to cycle through to the end of the word:

```
  nWordPos = nCmdPos;
  while (nCmdPos < sCmdLine.GetLength() &&
      sCmdLine[nCmdPos] != ' ' && sCmdLine[nCmdPos] != '\t')
    nCmdPos++;
  sIniFile = sCmdLine.Mid(nWordPos, (nCmdPos - nWordPos));
```

When the **while** loop encounters a space, tab, or the end of the command line, it will exit and continue processing.

Then the code repeats the processing it performed earlier, finding the beginning of the next word, and counting through until the end of the next word is encountered. Finally, the program code assigns the second word to the **sContentFile** variable:

```
while (nCmdPos < sCmdLine.GetLength() &&
    (sCmdLine[nCmdPos] == ' ' || sCmdLine[nCmdPos] == '\t'))
  nCmdPos++;

nWordPos = nCmdPos;
while (nCmdPos < sCmdLine.GetLength() &&
    sCmdLine[nCmdPos] != ' ' && sCmdLine[nCmdPos] != '\t')
  nCmdPos++;
sContentFile = sCmdLine.Mid(nWordPos, (nCmdPos - nWordPos));
```

The code within the function performs its looping steps one last time, pulling the third command-line parameter out and placing its value within the **sOutputFile** member variable:

```
while (nCmdPos < sCmdLine.GetLength() &&
    (sCmdLine[nCmdPos] == ' ' || sCmdLine[nCmdPos] == '\t'))
  nCmdPos++;

nWordPos = nCmdPos;
while (nCmdPos < sCmdLine.GetLength() &&
    sCmdLine[nCmdPos] != ' ' && sCmdLine[nCmdPos] != '\t')
  nCmdPos++;

sOutputFile = sCmdLine.Mid(nWordPos, (nCmdPos - nWordPos));
}
```

Recall from earlier in this chapter that the **InitInstance( )** function, after it finishes parsing the command line, calls the **ParseIniFile( )** function, which processes the information in the file named by the **ParseCmdLine( )** function. The function begins by declaring some automatic variables, including a pair of counting integers, a **CString** variable that will contain each line from the INI file in turn, and a **char** array that the program uses when invoking the system function to read from the INI file.

```
void CPostApp::ParseIniFile(CString sIniFile)
{
  int nIniPos = 0;
  int nBufLen;
  CString sLine;
  char lpszBuf[2048];
```

The **GetPrivateProfileSection( )** function is a Windows API function that reads information from an INI file. In this case, the function retrieves everything inside the Form Literal section of the INI file:

```
nBufLen = GetPrivateProfileSection("Form Literal",
         (LPSTR)lpszBuf,2048,sIniFile.GetBuffer(0));
```

The rest of the function then parses the character array retrieved from the INI file. It uses a **do** loop to process the contents.

The **do** loop will iterate each time it pulls a complete line (indicated by a **NULL** character) from within the character array. When it reaches the array's end—that it, when **sLine** contains a **NULL** string—the loop will exit.

```
do {
   sLine = "";
```

The **while** loop increments the position counter until it finds a **NULL** character, indicating the end of the current line. Within the loop, each character that is *not* **NULL** is appended to the **sLine** string. When the loop finds the **NULL** character, it will fall through the loop.

```
while (nIniPos < nBufLen &&   lpszBuf[nIniPos] != '\0') {
   sLine += lpszBuf[nIniPos];
   nIniPos++;
 }
```

The next **if** statement checks to make sure that the line contains a string. If it does, the string is added to the string array that you defined earlier. If there's no string, the **if** statement performs no processing and falls through to the end of the loop.

```
nIniPos++;
if (sLine != "") {
  m_saParams.Add(sLine);
 }
```

The loop's ending condition checks to determine whether there was a string value located. If there was, the loop repeats; otherwise, the loop exits and the function exits.

```
} while (sLine != "");
}
```

As explained earlier in this chapter, the **InitInstance( )** function parses the INI file and then calls the **CreateResponse( )** function. **CreateResponse( )** uses the contents of the **m_saParams** member variable to generate the HTML file that the application sends back to the client.

The **CreateReponse( )** function begins its processing by again declaring a pair of local counter variables. It also creates a single string member (**sResponse**), which will contain the text sent by the program back to the client. Then the function creates

---

a file object, to which the program will write the string when it finishes constructing the string:

```
void CPostApp::CreateResponse(CString sOutputFile, CString sIniFile)
{
  int i;
  int nIndex;
  CString sResponse;
  CFile fOutput;
```

The **fStatus** variable maintains status information about the file object, such as its date and time of creation and so on. The **sKey** value will contain the e-mail address, and the **sVal** member will contain the phone number for the user:

```
  CFileStatus fStatus;
  CString sUser;
  CString sKey;
  CString sVal;
```

The function begins its actual processing by creating the HTML file headers for the file. As you saw previously with the **clock.cpp** program, the program code specifies that the content type of the file is **text/html**, so the browser knows how to interpret the code correctly. It then specifies HTML header information required by the protocol, and specifies the title for the generated HTML page:

```
  // Send HTML format
  sResponse = "Content-type: text/html\r\n";
  sResponse += "\r\n";
  sResponse += "<!DOCTYPE HTML PUBLIC \"-//W3O//DTD W3 HTML 3.0//EN\"
    >\r\n";
  sResponse += "<HTML>\r\n";
  sResponse += "<HEAD>\r\n";
  sResponse += "<TITLE>POST Application</TITLE>\r\n";
  sResponse += "</HEAD>\r\n";
```

The program next starts a loop to process each string within the string array for the application:

```
  for (i = 0; i < m_saParams.GetSize(); i++) {
```

The loop will continue to process until the application finishes retrieving the INI file's contents.

The **Empty( )** function clears the value of a string object without deleting the object itself. The value is cleared because it will contain different entries for each time through the loop.

```
    sKey.Empty();
    sVal.Empty();
```

The next **if** statement checks the value within the current string in the array to ensure that it contains an equals sign—which the INI file will contain for each entry:

```
if ((nIndex = m_saParams[i].Find('=')) != -1) {
    sKey = m_saParams[i].Left(nIndex);
    sVal = m_saParams[i].Right(m_saParams[i].GetLength() -
    nIndex - 1);
}
```

For example, an INI file entry might read:

```
Name = Osborne Reader
```

The program code within the **if** statement pulls the parameter name (**Name**) from the INI file and assigns it to the **sKey** variable, then pulls the value (**Osborne Reader**) from the INI file and assigns it to the **sVal** variable.

The next **if** statement checks to make sure the user has input a value for all the fields. If not, the program sends back a Web page telling the user to enter all the data, rather than the field-specific information:

```
if (sVal == "") {
    sResponse += "<H1>Please enter all data</H1>\r\n";
    break;
}
```

After verifying that the values for each parameter are okay, the information for each parameter is appended to the **sUser** variable:

```
    sUser += "<H3>";
    sUser += sKey;
    sUser += ": ";
    sUser += sVal;
    sUser += "</H3>\r\n";
}
```

(By the way, the program code uses the **<H3>** tag to format the text displayed in the Web page. You could, of course, change this formatting as appropriate in your own applications.)

After processing all the strings within the array, the program code will fall through to the next **if** statement:

```
if (i == m_saParams.GetSize()) {
    sResponse += "<H1>Server's's Reply:</H1>\r\n";
    sResponse += sUser;
}
```

The foregoing **if** statement checks to ensure that the user entered valid values for all parameters. If not, the program code will simply return the "Enter all values" message you saw earlier, rather than displaying any parroted information within the response page. If the user did enter valid values, the program code appends a header to the file, then appends all the information parsed from the INI file.

Finally, the code takes the necessary code to close out the HTML tags created at the beginning of the function, and appends it to the end of the page. The **sResponse** string now contains an entire Web page (albeit a very simple one):

```
sResponse += "</BODY>\r\n";
sResponse += "</HTML>\r\n";
```

The **if** statement tries to create the output file. If successful, it writes the **sResponse** string to the file. If unsuccessful, it simply falls through and exits the program. The user will get an HTTP error when the application exits if it is unable to write the file correctly.

```
if (fOutput.Open(sOutputFile.GetBuffer(0),
    CFile::modeCreate | CFile::modeWrite | CFile::typeBinary)) {
  fOutput.Write(sResponse.GetBuffer(0),sResponse.GetLength());
  fOutput.Close();
  }
}
```

Using CGI Applications

Now that you have performed the majority of the necessary work to make the Post application execute, you must create support on your server to serve up the CGI output to the client. As you know, when a browser retrieves an HTML Web document, it first contacts the server and then requests the document (typically, your browser issues an HTTP GET method to the server). Next, if the document exists, the server responds by providing the HTML document to the browser, and then closes the connection.

When you write a CGI script, the only changes to this process occur on the server side. The browser (client) has no knowledge that the server is invoking a CGI script, and the browser doesn't care how it receives its data back from the server. From your point of view, you only need to be concerned with server I/O when you write CGI scripts. A browser will contact the server program, which will in turn run your CGI script. Your script will then perform the processing necessary to accomplish your desired output.

Normally, your server provides your script's output to the browser via HTML. To accomplish this task, the server program adds the necessary header information to your script's output (if any) and sends the header information along with your script's data back to the browser program that originally invoked the server. The server then closes the browser's connection, and waits for another connection request.

As you may know, servers that run on 32-bit operating systems (such as Windows 95/98 or Windows NT) typically handle requests from multiple users simultaneously. This implies that several users can use your script concurrently, without your having to write special code. In general, most servers will create as many instances of the CGI script/program as necessary to serve the users requesting information from the server.

The Server/CGI Program Relationship

When the server program invokes your CGI script, the server must perform several key operations, which include the following:

◆ Invoking the script and providing the necessary data sent from the browser to your script

◆ Providing the values for environment variables that are accessible by your script

◆ Handling your script's output, including the addition of header information necessary for a browser to successfully interpret the script's data

As you know, HTTP is the protocol Web clients and servers use to communicate. The HTTP header information helps programs communicate efficiently; therefore, you should look closely at the header information provided by a server to a browser. For example, when a server program is ready to send data to a browser, the server program sends a set of headers that describe the status of the data, the data type (the file's content), and so on. The browser, in turn, uses the Content-Type header to prepare to render the data that follows. The server is responsible for providing this meta-information each time it sends data to a browser.

Accessing the CGI Script/Program from the Browser

You cannot execute a CGI script directly from a browser program. To use a CGI script, you need to locate the script on a computer where an HTTP server resides. For you to view the script's intended output using a browser, the server must run your script. In general, you'll use the server's **cgi-bin** directory (or **cgi\bin** or another derivative) as the location for the scripts accessed by the server (they must be compiled and ready to execute).

You must also create a client page that calls the CGI executable. A page that works with the CGI application we're studying would look similar to the following:

```
<!DOCTYPE HTML PUBLIC "-//W3O//DTD W3 HTML 3.0//EN">
<HTML>
<HEAD>
<TITLE>C++ Annotated Archives</TITLE>
<META NAME="AUTHOR" CONTENT="Osborne Reader">
</HEAD>
<BODY>
```

```
<P>
<H1>Example using HTTP POST method</H1>
<HR>
<FORM METHOD="POST" ACTION="/cgi-bin/post.exe">
<H2>Enter your name, e-mail address, and phone number, below:<H2>
<P>
<PRE>
        Name: <INPUT NAME="Name" VALUE="">
     Address: <INPUT NAME="E-Mail" VALUE="">
       Phone: <INPUT NAME="Phone" VALUE="">
</PRE>
<P>
To run this form, click this button:
<INPUT TYPE="submit" VALUE="Send!">
</FORM>
<HR>
</BODY>
</HTML>
```

The key features here are in the form declarations. The first section of the file ends at the **</HEAD>** tag, as shown here:

```
<!DOCTYPE HTML PUBLIC "-//W3O//DTD W3 HTML 3.0//EN">
<HTML>
<HEAD>
<TITLE>C++ Annotated Archives</TITLE>
<META NAME="AUTHOR" CONTENT="Osborne Reader">
</HEAD>
```

The HTML file first states its type, then some title information, and some meta-information that search engines can read. It also initializes the page to display HTML.

```
<BODY>
<P>
<H1>Example using HTTP POST method</H1>
<HR>
<FORM METHOD="POST" ACTION="/cgi-bin/post.exe">
```

The next few statements perform formatting and some basic display. The key statement here, however, is with the **<FORM>** tag. The tag lets the browser know that a form is coming. The **METHOD** attribute tells the form that it will use the HTTP **POST** function to send the data, and the **ACTION** attribute tells the client what program to call on the server to perform the desired task. Note that the client program is within the cgi-bin directory off the server's root directory.

```
<H2>Enter your name, e-mail address, and phone number, below:<H2>
<P>
<PRE>
          Name: <INPUT NAME="Name" VALUE="">
       Address: <INPUT NAME="E-Mail" VALUE="">
         Phone: <INPUT NAME="Phone" VALUE="">
</PRE>
```

The next lines display the actual input form itself. Each of the **INPUT NAME** values will translate to parameter entries within the INI file. The **VALUE** parameter specifies that the default value for each of the entries is a NULL string.

```
<P>
To run this form, click this button:
<INPUT TYPE="submit" VALUE="Send!">
</FORM>
<HR>
</BODY>
</HTML>
```

Finally, the **TYPE="submit"** value tells the form that is should display a button. When the client clicks on the button, the client will then send the information to the server, using the **POST** method—which has the same effect as invoking the server program with a series of command-line parameters.

When you load the HTML file and send the data within its fields, the server will invoke the program, pass in the values you entered, and return an HTML page to you that contains the response you built within the **CreateReponse( )** function.

Index

X

What's On the Companion CD-ROM

The companion CD-ROM that accompanies this book includes all the source code printed within the archives. Each chapter in the book has its own directory, within which all the source code for that chapter is saved. In some cases, source code may be within additional subdirectories in the tree below the chapter directory—typically when the application is a Visual C++ application and includes a project file.

For non-Visual C++ applications contained within multiple source code and header files, the corresponding MAKE (.MAK) file for the application will compile and link the application as detailed within the chapter.

For chapters with simpler source-code sets—such as a series of only .CPP files—no further explanation is included on the CD-ROM. For chapters with more complex sets of programs, the root directory of the chapter contains a **readme.txt** file with additional information about the directories and files that make up the chapter's programs.

If you decide to copy the files from the CD-ROM to your hard drive, be sure to change the "read-only" attribute to off, or some compilers may not let you access the files. If you have any questions or problems regarding the contents of the CD-ROM, please contact Lars Klander at lklander@lvcablemodem.com.